TENTH EDITION

Global Politics

Juliet Kaarbo
UNIVERSITY OF KANSAS

James Lee Ray
VANDERBILT UNIVERSITY

WADSWORTH
CENGAGE Learning™

Australia • Brazil • Japan • Korea • Mexico • Singapore • Spain • United Kingdom • United States

WADSWORTH
CENGAGE Learning

Global Politics, **Tenth Edition**
Juliet Kaarbo
James Lee Ray

Senior Publisher: Suzanne Jeans

Executive Editor: Carolyn Merrill

Development Editor: Thomas Finn

Assistant Editor: Katherine Hayes

Editorial Assistant: Angela Hodge

Associate Media Editor: Caitlin Holroyd

Senior Marketing Manager: Amy Whitaker

Marketing Coordinator: Josh Hendrick

Marketing Communications Manager:
Heather Baxley

Associate Content Project Manager:
Sara Abbott

Art Director: Linda Helcher

Print Buyer: Paula Vang

Senior Rights Acquisition
Account Manager, Text: Katie Huha

Production Service:
S4Carlisle Publishing Services

Senior Photo Editor: Jennifer Meyer Dare

Cover Designer: Blue Bungalow Design

Cover Image: © Photolibrary

Compositor: S4 Carlisle Publishing Services

For product information and technology assistance, contact us at
Cengage Learning Customer & Sales Support, 1-800-354-9706

For permission to use material from this text or product, submit
all requests online at **www.cengage.com/permissions**
Further permissions questions can be emailed to
permissionrequest@cengage.com

Library of Congress Control Number: 2009944039

ISBN-13: 978-0-495-80264-8
ISBN-10: 0-495-80264-6

Wadsworth
20 Channel Center Street
Boston, MA 02210
USA

Cengage Learning is a leading provider of customized learning solutions with office locations around the globe, including Singapore, the United Kingdom, Australia, Mexico, Brazil and Japan. Locate your local office at **international.cengage.com/region**

Cengage Learning products are represented in Canada by Nelson Education, Ltd.

For your course and learning solutions, visit **www.cengage.com**

Purchase any of our products at your local college store or at our preferred online store **www.cengagebrain.com**

Printed in the United States of America
1 2 3 4 5 6 7 14 13 12 11 10

Contents

PART II

Actors in Global Politics: Power and Policy   95

4   The Power of States and the Rise of Transnational Actors   96

5   Inside States: The Making of Foreign Policy   140

PART IV

Interactions of Actors: Economic Relations

12   Regional Economic Integration in the Global Political Economy   431

PART V
Global Challenges   463

13   The Global Environment and Its Inhabitants   464

14 Globalization: Contemporary Dynamics and the Future of World Politics   501

References   537

Index   575

Maps

Preface

Global Politics has long been praised for providing students with the historical and theoretical background to understand the complexities of international relations. Indeed, one of the key strengths of the text continues to be its clear, comprehensive coverage of the historical and theoretical bases of world affairs. It introduces the major theories and paradigms important in the study of international relations, integrates theory into the discussion of many topics, and presents a straightforward history of the international system from its inception to the present. But more than a discussion of what has occurred in the past and why, this Tenth Edition is also a thorough study of the contemporary issues and events influencing modern international relations. These topics include globalization, one of the most important processes affecting relations between states and nonstate actors today, as well as coverage of the developing world, ethnic conflict, regional integration, international norms, the politics of environmental problems, and challenges to state power and sovereignty. In short, Global Politics develops three key themes—the historical, the contemporary and policy-oriented, and the theoretical—and emphasizes the extent to which they complement one another.

The Framework of the Tenth Edition

Global Politics is arranged in five parts: (1) theory and history, (2) states, transnational actors, and foreign policy, (3) security relations, (4) economic relations, and (5) global challenges. This organization highlights the text's hallmark coverage of history and theory, and also spotlights today's most urgent issues and the latest developments in the study of international relations.

Developments in global politics relating to security and economic issues have been incorporated throughout the Tenth Edition. These include the on-going occupation of Iraq, the conflict between Russia and Georgia, ethnic and religious conflicts (such as in Iraq, Darfur, and Georgia), the state of World Trade Organization negotiations in the Doha Round, the Lisbon Treaty in the European Union, nuclear proliferation (including on-going developments in Iran and North Korea), international terrorism (including the attacks in London and Madrid, and the 2008 bombing in

Mumbai), the global economic crisis that began in 2007 and the reactions to it, and the election of Barak Obama as the 44th President and how this might affect U.S. global relations. Several new Policy Choices boxes have been added to the Tenth edition.

The breakdown of content and revisions, chapter-by-chapter, is as follows:

- Chapter 1, "Theories of Global Politics," covers six major perspectives on international relations (realism, liberalism, idealism, neo-Marxism, constructivism, and feminist perspectives) and clearly explains the premise and significance of each theory.

- Chapter 2, "The Historical Setting," covers ancient times to World War II, including the development of nations and states and imperialism, as well as a new Policy Choices, examining whether Britain should have appeased Hitler. A discussion of how the major theoretical perspectives interpret and use history is included in both Chapters 2 and 3.

- Chapter 3, "The Modern Era," provides a fully updated treatment of global politics since World War II, including updated sections on ethnic conflict in the post–Cold War era (the Arab-Israeli conflict, Darfur, tensions in India and Sri Lanka, Sunni-Shia conflict in Iraq, and the Russia-Georgia conflict), nuclear proliferation (Iran and North Korea), the Bush Doctrine and the on-going war against terror, an expanded discussion of failed states (Somalia and Haiti), and coverage of the financial crisis of 2008 and its global economic implications.

- Chapter 4, retitled "The Power of States and the Rise of Transnational Actors," now includes information on both state and nonstate actors, such as the piracy off the coast of Somalia. The chapter features material on state formation and power, plus sections on multinational corporations, nongovernmental organizations, international terrorism, and a new Policy Choices, Should States Support the Activities of NGOs?

- Chapter 5, "Inside States: The Making of Foreign Policy," explores the foreign policy approach: how what goes on inside states explains why states may not act as expected in response to international conditions. The chapter discusses public opinion, political institutions, interest groups, bureaucratic politics, and the psychology of leadership. Coverage includes groupthink in the previous Bush administration and early indications of how Barak Obama will lead.

- Chapter 6, renamed "International Conflict: Explaining Interstate War," discusses the causes of interstate wars at the system level, state and dyadic level, and decision-making level of analysis, and applies these levels to the World War I, World War II, and Cold War cases.

- Chapter 7, "Ethnic Conflict and International Terrorism," focuses first on ethnic conflict globally, including the recent conflict in Georgia and UN involvement in Rwanda, with discussions of the meaning of ethnicity, the prevalence of ethnically based wars, and various causes of and solutions to ethnic conflict. It then covers the definition of terrorism, an expanded analysis of its history and origins, and its impact on the world today, noting recent events in Mumbai and around the Middle East. Finally there's a new Policy Choices box, analyzing the effectiveness of the War on Terror.

- Chapter 8, "Efforts to Avoid Conflict: Alliances, Arms, and Bargaining" focuses on global relations among states, including states' use of alliances, arms, and bargaining to deter and compel other states, with expanded coverage of newer forms of balancing. It also includes updated material on efforts to control conventional and mass destruction weapons, such as the nuclear programs in North Korea and Iran.

- Chapter 9, "Global Security Efforts: International Organizations, Law, and Ethics," continues the discussion with coverage of the international organizations, ethics, norms, and laws that govern state behavior and attempt to avoid, or at least regulate, international conflict. The chapter explores the complex relationship between the United States and the United Nations, as well as the role of international organizations in humanitarian intervention.

- Chapter 10, "Interdependence Among Rich States: International Political Economy in the North," initiates the discussion of economic relations among states with coverage of the basic concepts of macroeconomics. It discusses economic liberalism, mercantilism, and economic systems throughout the world, focusing on international trade and finance, and also examines the impact of multinational corporations on the global economy. New to this edition is coverage of the 2008–2009 financial crisis with its global economic implications, and a new Policy Choices feature, examining whether economic liberalism should be the basis of the world economy.

- Chapter 11, "The Developing States in the International Political Economy," describes the problems that developing countries encounter in the international economic system and provides explanations for the gap in wealth between the North and the South. The chapter includes material on the role of multinational corporations in economic dependency and the role of international organizations in economic development, as well as coverage of Latin America's increasingly leftist orientation and the Doha round of trade negotiations.

- Chapter 12, "Regional Economic Integration in the Global Political Economy", shifts the focus away from state boundaries in the international system and toward the development of regional economies, and includes the Association of Southeast Asian Nations (ASEAN), the Economic Community of West African States (ECOWAS), Mercosur in South America, and updated and expanded coverage of the European

Union (EU). A new section discussing various theoretical perspectives on regional institutions has also been added.

- Chapter 13, "The Global Environment and Its Inhabitants," describes contemporary challenges to the global community. This edition provides updated statistics and developments on food and natural resource shortages, population growth, and global warming, as well as the politics that complicate solutions to global environmental problems.

- Chapter 14, "Globalization: Contemporary Dynamics and the Future of World Politics," is a discussion of economic, political, and cultural globalization. It describes the role of technology in the development of globalization, explores its historical roots, and, with new expanded coverage of views that oppose globalization, asks students to consider the benefits and disadvantages of living in an increasingly interdependent world.

Features of the Tenth Edition

The Tenth Edition includes a number of helpful pedagogical features for students. The "POLICY CHOICES" boxes, which were so well received in previous editions, have been retained and expanded. These boxes analyze crucial contemporary issues in a debate format, with arguments for and against each position that bring the issue to life and help students think critically about the presented material. New topics are "Should Britain have Appeased Hitler?" (Chapter 2); "Should States Support the Activities of NGOs?" (Chapter 4); "Is the War on Terror an Effective Policy for Addressing Terrorism?" (Chapter 7); and "Should Economic Liberalism Be Abandoned as the Basis for the Global Economy?" (Chapter 10). The Tenth Edition also includes a marginal glossary that defines KEY TERMS on the pages of the text where they are first introduced, as well as a brief outline on the opening page of each chapter that previews key content. Each chapter concludes with a bulleted SUMMARY and a list of KEY TERMS with page references. An extensive list of references by chapter is located at the end of the text, and there are both name and subject indexes at the end of the text for ease of reference.

Supplements

Instructor's Resource CD

A **test bank** in Microsoft® Word and ExamView® computerized testing offers a large array of well-crafted multiple-choice and essay questions, along with their answers and page references.

An **Instructor's Manual** includes learning objectives, chapter outlines, discussion questions, suggestions for stimulating class activities and projects, tips on integrating media into your class, simulations, and suggested readings and Web resources.

A variety of **blank maps** of different areas of the world can be printed out or used online to test students' knowledge of important geography.

Companion Website

Students will find open access to learning objectives, tutorial quizzes, chapter glossaries, flashcards, and crossword puzzles, all correlated by chapter. Instructors also have access to the Instructor's Manual.

Wadsworth News Video for 2010 DVD

This collection of three- to six-minute video clips on relevant political issues serves as a great lecture or discussion launcher.

The Rand McNally Atlas of International Politics

This atlas offers maps of the world showing political organization, population statistics, and economic development; maps highlighting energy production and consumption, major world conflicts, migration, and more; and extensive regional coverage. Students will find it useful for understanding world events and to supplement their studies with "Global Politics."

Acknowledgments

For the Tenth Edition, Juliet Kaarbo acknowledges the support of the University of Kansas and, while on a research fellowship at Bilkent University in Ankara, support from the Scientific and Technical Research Council of Turkey. Ryan Beasley provided extensive and valuable feedback and suggestions on many sections of this edition. Jeffrey Lantis, Mariya Omelicheva, Phil Schrodt, and Brent Steele, lent materials, perspectives, and support. Adam Brown and Will Delehenty served as the research assistants for this edition, and their work is very much appreciated.

The following people provided extensive, detailed, and helpful comments on this edition:

David V. Edwards, Professor of Government, Univ. of Texas at Austin
Daniel Masters, Department of Public and International Affairs, University of North Carolina Wilmington
Christopher M. Sprecher, Texas A&M University
John Conybeare, University of Iowa

Juliet Kaarbo
Lawrence, Kansas

PART I

Theoretical Perspectives and Historical Background

CHAPTER 1

Theories of Global Politics

global politics The relations among different actors in the world, the characteristics of those relations, and their consequences.

lobal politics concerns the relations between different actors in the world, the characteristics of those relations, and their consequences. It has to do with the nature of those actors, how they have changed over time, and how their interactions have changed over time. Global politics, also commonly referred to as *international politics, world politics,* or *international relations,* includes questions of international conflict (for example, why do countries and ethnic groups go to war with one another, and what contributes to peaceful relations?), questions of international economics (for example, why and how do states enter into trading agreements with one another, and how is wealth distributed in the world?), and questions that transcend actors but confront them nonetheless (for example, what contributes to global environmental problems, and how is cultural, political, and economic globalization changing world politics?).

The major purpose of this book, *Global Politics,* is to help students understand world politics in the past, present, and future. The process begins in this first chapter with a discussion of theoretical perspectives on the way international relations operate. **Theoretical perspectives** of international politics provide answers to these basic questions: Who are the main actors in international politics? Why do actors do what they do in international politics? What are the underlying factors that govern relationships in global politics? How have international relations changed or stayed the same over the centuries? What accounts for conflict and cooperation in international politics?

theoretical perspectives Alternative interpretations of how international relations work, why actors do what they do, and what underlying factors govern relationships in global politics.

Each of the theoretical perspectives presented in this chapter provides *different* answers to these questions. Each perspective is based on different assumptions about humans, governments, and international politics. Each can provide a different analysis of the same event in international politics, such as the Vietnam War, the signing of the North American Free Trade Agreement, the rise of the World Trade Organization, internal conflict in Sudan, or the U.S.-led invasion of Iraq. The purpose of this chapter is to discuss and compare these alternative takes on international politics. This chapter presents an overview of these theoretical perspectives. Subsequent chapters will illustrate how these perspectives can be used to explain more specific topics of international politics.

Understanding alternative theoretical perspectives is important for understanding world politics for two main reasons. First, everybody already has some theoretical perspective in mind when they consider international relations. Even students new to the subject bring with them sets of assumptions about the world and its actors. When you read about current events or the history of international relations, you are seeing the "facts" through a particular lens. Knowing what lens you are using and what alternative lens may be available will help you better understand how you are interpreting the facts and how facts may be seen in different ways.

Second, understanding alternative theoretical perspectives allows students of international relations to analyze global politics in the future, long after they finish reading this book or taking courses on the subject. When students learn only history and contemporary issues and the particular explanations of historical and contemporary events, their knowledge of global politics is limited in time, because new issues and events are always arising. Students who understand more general theoretical perspectives have the capability of analyzing international relations that have yet to take place. Thus, the theoretical perspectives provide more long-lasting analytical tools.

The most prominent theoretical perspectives for understanding global politics are realism, liberalism, idealism, neo-Marxism, constructivism, and feminist perspectives. Each perspective has a different focus for understanding international relations. It is not the case that one perspective is clearly "right" and the other is clearly "wrong"; all have something to contribute to our understanding of world politics. One perspective, however, may be more appropriate than others for certain parts of international relations or better at explaining certain events. Indeed, the study of global politics is about discovering what the various theoretical perspectives do best.

Realism

realism A theoretical perspective for understanding international relations that emphasizes states as the most important actor in global politics, the anarchical nature of the international system, and the pursuit of power to secure states' interests. Also known as "Realpolitik" or "power politics."

Thucydides Greek historian who wrote about the Peloponnesian Wars between the Greek city-states Athens and Sparta in 431–404 B.C.E. Thucydides' accounts described and explained the relations between these actors in a realist approach.

Morgenthau Considered the father of modern realist thought with his work, *Politics Among Nations*, first published shortly after World War II.

Realism is the first theoretical perspective for understanding international relations that we consider, because it has historically been the dominant lens through which world leaders and scholars alike have understood global politics. Indeed, realism can be traced back to Thucydides' account of the Peloponnesian Wars between the Greek city-states Athens and Sparta in 431–404 B.C.E.[1] **Thucydides,** a historian, described and explained the relations between these actors with realist propositions. Realism was also the dominant way leaders in Europe in the seventeenth through early twentieth centuries understood international relations. It was during this period that the modern international system was created, largely based on realist notions. After World War II, scholars of international relations embraced realism as the dominant perspective for explaining global politics. The chief advocate of the realist theory of international politics was Hans J. **Morgenthau,** considered the father of modern realist thought. His classic text, *Politics Among Nations: The Struggle for Power and Peace,* was first published shortly after World War II and carefully defined the realist theoretical perspective that most scholars would then adopt.[2] Because of this dominant position, in many ways, all of the other theoretical perspectives for understanding global politics are reactions to and criticisms of realism.

The first proposition of realism, also known as Realpolitik, is that states are the most important actors in global politics. **States** are governments that exercise supreme, or sovereign, authority over a defined

states Governments that have legal sovereignty over a defined territory.

sovereignty The legal notion that states are the ultimate authority over their territory and no other actor in the international system has the right to interfere in states' internal affairs.

territory. **Sovereignty** means that states are legally the ultimate authority over their territory and no other actor in the international system has the legal right to interfere in states' internal affairs. States are the countries such as France, Indonesia, Nicaragua, Senegal, Turkey, Ukraine, and the United States, on world maps. For realists, it is these states, and not their leaders, their citizens, business corporations, or international organizations, that are the key actors and determine what happens in the world. States can, if they choose, control all other actors, according to realism. Realism is state-centric because of the central and predominant position that states play in this perspective.

The second proposition of realism answers the question, why do states act the way they do in international politics? States, according to realism, pursue their interests, defined as power. State interests, rather than their values or ideological preferences, are the reason behind every state act. And it is the maximization of power that is in a state's interest. Thus, everything a state does can be explained by its desire to maintain, safeguard, or increase its power in relation to other states.[3]

Iraq's invasion of Kuwait in August 1990, for example, was a power move, according to the realist perspective. It had nothing to do with its leader, Saddam Hussein or his personality. It had nothing to do with the authoritarian nature of the Iraqi political system or any anti-Western beliefs held by some in the Middle East. For realists, it was simply a chance for Iraq to maximize its power against Kuwait and the other key states in the region. For realists, the invasion of Kuwait was in Iraq's interest, and it would have happened regardless of the leader, political system, or beliefs in Iraq. Similarly, the reaction of the United States and its decision to lead a military effort to oust Iraq from Kuwait was also about interests and the maximization of power. The U.S. interests and power in the region were threatened by the Iraqi invasion, and so the reason behind the U.S.-led Desert Storm operation had nothing to do with the humanitarian interests to save the Kuwaiti people or pure economic interests to safeguard a supply of cheap oil; it had to do with maintaining its power in the region. With this focus on power as the primary goal of states, realist ideas are also known as the *power politics perspective*.

Why is the maximization of power in a state's interest? The answer to this question is based on the definition of the primary actor, the state. Because states exercise sovereign authority over a defined territory, and no other actor in the international system has a higher authority over states, there is no world government to look after individual states' interests. According to realism, the defining feature of global politics is that the international system exists as an **anarchy**.[4] Anarchy does not mean chaos or confusion, but simply the lack of an overarching political authority or world government. Without a central government, international politics is akin to the philosopher Thomas Hobbes' "state of nature" or "state of war" in which individuals must fend for themselves and life is "nasty, brutish, and short."[5] For realists, anarchy is what makes international politics so very different from domestic politics, which occurs

anarchy According to realism, a defining feature of the international system wherein there is no overarching political authority or world government; different from "chaos" or "disorder."

inside countries. Within political systems, individuals can live peacefully knowing that there is a government to provide them protection in the form of national defense and internal police and to provide laws that deter or punish those who seek to harm their individual interests. States in the international system enjoy no such luxury. Without an international world authority, they must look out for their own interests. The way they do this, according to realism, is by securing and maintaining their power. Maintaining power is a rational response to the anarchic international system.

Because each state must follow a self-help strategy to protect its own interests, states are naturally competitive with each other, eyeing one another with necessary suspicion. Conflict, then, is an inevitable outcome, and for realists, conflict and the use of force is the central concern in international politics. War is a means by which states compete for power, and, relatedly, the key components of power are military in nature, because ultimately it is the goal of every state to survive and to protect its territorial integrity (if not its citizens as well) in a conflict-ridden world. Typically such "protection" translates into military forces. In a dangerous world, states seek greater security by building up their military forces, by making military alliances, and, if necessary, by the prudent use of military force.

After military intervention in Iraq in 2003, U.S. troops often came under attack. The realist perspective sees such conflict and the use of military force as an inevitable part of global politics.
(Scott Nelson/Getty Images)

For realism, the pursuit of power and political interests is separate from economic spheres, moral spheres, and any other sphere of human activity. Moreover, power considerations must come first. Action taken in the name of economic wealth must be evaluated according to how it contributes to or detracts from the national interests. Realists, for example, sometimes worry that their state's economic ties with other states, in the form of trade agreements and investment deals, unnecessarily constrain their state and make them dependent on and at the mercy of others' interests. Even if an economic agreement will make more money for the state, realists would caution against it if it detracted from the state's independence or contributed to the power of a potential enemy. Realists also caution against applying moral principles to state actions. They frown on human rights policies that do not further the power of a state and may even threaten its power.

One of the advantages of the realist theory is that it can serve as an explanation for global politics across the many centuries of state interaction. Indeed, the focus in realism is on continuity. Because all states, no matter when, no matter where, are all motivated by the same drive to protect their interests by maximizing their power, realism sees great continuity in international relations. Despite all the changes in world politics throughout time, realists say that states are basically doing the same thing as they did all along: seeking power. And realists point out that because of this, conflict remains a dominant feature of the international landscape today.

Criticisms of Realism

Realism has dominated twentieth-century thinking about global politics so much that most other contemporary theoretical perspectives can be considered reactions to and criticisms of realism. Not all of these alternative theories criticize each proposition of realism. Rather, they focus on particular points of realism and offer divergent ways of thinking about international relations. The most prominent alternatives to realism today are liberalism, idealism, neo-Marxism, constructivism, and feminist perspectives. Their reactions to realist propositions are summarized in Table 1.1.

Liberalism

liberalism A theoretical perspective emphasizing interdependence between states and substate actors as the key characteristic of the international system.

Next to realism, **liberalism** is the most accepted alternative theoretical perspective for understanding global politics. In this context, *liberalism* and *liberal* are not to be confused with the terms as they are used to mean left-of-center in domestic politics in the United States. Rather, liberalism has a special meaning when applied to an understanding of international politics. Whereas realism stresses great continuity in international relations across the centuries, contemporary liberalism sees great changes.

TABLE 1.1

Realism and Its Critics

Main Realist Propositions	Main Criticisms*				
	Liberalism	*Idealism*	*Neo-Marxism*	*Constructivism*	*Feminist Perspectives*
Sovereign states are most important actors	Transnational and substate actors are increasingly important		Economic divisions are more important than political/ state divisions		Women are important actors left out by a focus on male-led states
States pursue their interests defined as power	Power is no longer primarily military in nature; economics is important	States are motivated by morality and values		Power, like all other concepts, is subjectively constructed	Military power and individual state interests are masculine ways of thinking
States maximize power to protect themselves in an anarchic world; conflict is inevitable	Interdependence means states' interests are intertwined and cooperation is likely	States cooperate to further values, such as peace	Economic conflict between social classes and between the core and periphery is inevitable	Cooperation and conflict depend on states' social understandings	Security is multidimensional and achieved through cooperation
There is great continuity in global politics across time	The post–World War II world is very different		Historical processes such as the development of capitalism and imperialism continue to affect global politics		

* As noted in the text, not all of the alternative theories criticize each proposition of realism. Rather, they focus on particular points of realism, offering divergent ways of thinking about international relations.

interdependence The condition in which states and their fortunes are connected to each other.

In particular, states and societies became so interdependent by the second half of the twentieth century that, according to liberalism, the way they relate to each other changed in fundamental ways. **Interdependence** means that states and their fortunes are connected to each other. What happens inside one state can have significant effects on what happens inside another state, and the relations between two states can greatly affect the relations between other states. While the fortunes of states may have always been connected, or interdependent, liberalism proposes that a particular kind of interdependence came to characterize the international

complex interdependence The dominant feature of global politics according to liberalism. Complex interdependence has three specific components: multiple channels, multiple issues, and the decline in use of and effectiveness of military force.

transnational actors Global actors, such as nongovernmental organizations, multinational corporations, intergovernmental organizations, and private organizations, that operate across borders and share the world stage with states.

multinational corporations Large companies doing business globally, which may have plants and factories in more than one state, pay taxes in more than one state, or have investments in more than one state.

nongovernmental organizations Transnational, private organizations that have members and activities across state borders.

intergovernmental organizations Actors whose members are states, such as the United Nations, the Organization of American States, and the North Atlantic Treaty Organization.

substate actors Actors within a state that interact with others outside the state, such as local businesses that import goods from abroad and provincial governments that establish trade missions in other countries.

system, beginning after World War II and in place by the 1970s. According to liberalism, **complex interdependence** became the dominant feature of global politics.[6] Complex interdependence has three specific components: multiple channels, multiple issues, and the decline in the use of and effectiveness of military force.

First, complex interdependence means that there are multiple channels among a variety of actors in international politics. Because realism sees states as the only significant actors, international politics is really confined to state-to-state relations. Although liberalism does not deny that these interstate connections remain important, it proposes that states are not the only important actors in global politics. There are a variety of nonstate actors that liberalism sees as sharing the world stage with states. **Transnational actors** operate across state borders and include **multinational corporations** (MNCs), which are large companies doing business globally. These organizations may have plants or factories in more than one state, pay taxes in more than one state, or have investments in more than one state. McDonald's, Colgate-Palmolive, General Foods, and General Motors are MNCs. **Nongovernmental organizations** (NGOs) are another type of transnational actor. NGOs are private, international organizations that act across borders and have members in different states, such as the Catholic Church, Greenpeace, the Red Cross, and Amnesty International. In addition, **intergovernmental organizations** (IGOs) are actors whose members are states—for example, the United Nations, the European Union, the Organization of American States, and the North Atlantic Treaty Organization—and can become fairly independent from the states that govern them. Liberalism views IGOs, NGOs, and MNCs as important international connections across state boundaries.

In addition, relations between **substate actors** also make up the multiple channels in a complex interdependent world. Substate actors may be businesses that are not multinational, because they essentially operate within a single border but may buy imported goods from abroad to make their products. Substate actors also include provincial governments that establish trade missions in other countries. California, Texas, and New York are "provinces" in the United States that have extensive relations and diplomatic representation with other parts of the world. Substate actors may also include individuals who travel abroad or have friendships with individuals in other countries. With the growing activity of substate and transnational actors, liberalism sees a complex web of connections across the globe. Focusing only on state-to-state relations, as realism does, misses an important part of world politics, according to liberalism. Furthermore, states are not the only actors to have interests that drive their actions. Nonstate actors have their own goals and interests that sometimes diverge from those of the state.

The second component of complex interdependence is that there are multiple issues, not just military security, that are of interest to the variety of global actors. Economic, ideological, religious, and cultural issues are part of the global agenda. Furthermore, security issues do not dominate the agenda, as realism assumes. Even issues that realism sees as purely domestic, or internal to the state, can become tangled up in international politics. Environmental regulations, for example, may be adopted by a government to safeguard the health of its citizens, but they can also have an effect on the state's trading partners, if imports to the country must meet the regulations as well. In this way, domestic policy can automatically become foreign policy because of the connections between issues, the multiple channels operating in the world, and the interdependence among actors. Realism's division of issues as either foreign or domestic, argues liberalism, is out-of-date and artificial.

Finally, complex interdependence means that military force is not as effective or frequently used as it was in the past. Many of the issues that are of concern to states and nonstate actors do not lend themselves to military solutions. It is difficult to solve global environmental problems, for example, through military interventions or the detonation of a nuclear bomb. These actions simply make the problem worse. It also does not make sense for a state to conquer a trading partner through military force to address a trade imbalance, because this would destroy the very economic market to which the state and its businesses want to export goods. Complex interdependence means that states are constrained in their use of military power, because the use of this power only harms the multiple interests of states and other actors.

These three components of complex interdependence—multiple channels, multiple issues, and the ineffectiveness of military force for some issues—lead liberalism to expect much more cooperation in global politics than does realism. This is the key point of disagreement between the two perspectives. While liberals do not deny that conflict occurs, they argue that cooperation is the norm and realism exaggerates the importance of and frequency of conflict. Liberals point out that states trade peacefully; they sign nonaggression pacts; they share military responsibilities; some have very small militaries or even no military at all (such as Costa Rica); and some military rivalries that have endured for centuries (such as France and Germany) have now transformed into military and economic partnerships. At best, realism does not account for the considerable cooperation that occurs in international relations; at worst, this cooperation violates realist expectations.

Why do states cooperate if the world is so dangerous and anarchic? According to liberalism, states cooperate, because it is in their interests to do so. Because the world is so interdependent, states realize that hostile actions are likely to harm their interests as much as those of any potential rival. Also, liberalism points out that the multiple channels that connect nonstate actors constrain states. Even if leaders of states recognize security threats and want to employ conflictual means, they often face resistance from the public or powerful interest groups, such as MNCs, that benefit more from cooperation. Of course, it is easier for the public and interest groups to constrain leaders in political systems that are democratic and provide avenues of influence. In democracies, where opposition is legal and allowed, and citizens can hold their leaders accountable for their actions through competitive elections, the multiple channels across societies are more likely to constrain leaders from conflict. Thus, liberalism expects the effects of complex interdependence to be more significant in a more democratic world.

The spread of democracy is just one factor that liberalism cites to account for the rise of complex interdependence in the twentieth century. With the end of World War II, the fascist regimes of Italy, Germany, and Japan were transformed into democracies. The end of World War II also brought on the beginnings of decolonization when the European empires gave up their territorial possessions around the globe. In some cases, such as India, these newly independent countries became democratic for the first time. Other factors are also important in the rise of interdependence. The invention of nuclear weapons meant that force, or at least all-out war, was less of an option for the major powers. For the first time in history, using the ultimate weapon in one's military arsenal meant risking significant damage to all humanity.

Also after World War II, wealth began to be distributed around the world to more economies as well, instead of being concentrated in Europe. The United States became the largest economy in the world and spread its wealth through aid packages (such as the Marshall Plan to war-torn Western Europe after World War II) and through a military presence around the globe during the Cold War competition with the Soviet Union. Multinational corporations also spread out across the globe. In the 1970s, oil-producing states begin cooperating with each other to make money off the oil-needy economies of Japan, Western Europe, and the United States. And by the 1980s, newly rich economies sprang up in Asia: in South Korea, Taiwan, Singapore, and Indonesia. This new distribution of wealth meant that more countries and their economies were tied together more than ever before.

Finally, liberalism points to the technological developments that allowed for increased global communication and transportation. With phones, television, jet planes, faxes, the Internet, and satellites, the world community has become increasingly capable of being in touch and informed on a global scale. The "shrinking" of the world has meant that there are more significant connections, which are encouraging cooperation between states. While these factors—such as democratization, the globalization of the world economy, and technological innovation—occurred over the course of the second half of the twentieth century, there has been noticeable development in these areas in the past twenty years. With the end of the Cold War rivalry between the United States and the Soviet Union (and the collapse of the Soviet Union), democratization, economic globalization, and global communications have reached an unprecedented stage. Liberals say that this makes complex interdependence even more critical for understanding current and future world politics.

The last major difference between realism and liberalism concerns the role of international organizations. Not only are international organizations increasingly present in global politics, serving as a potential challenge to states as the dominant actor, but liberalism sees states as actively promoting the rise of international organizations, particularly intergovernmental organizations in which states are members. International institutions such as the United Nations and the World Trade Organization facilitate cooperation, which liberals see as in the interests of states. International institutions provide an arena for communication and diplomatic bargaining and an alternative to conflictual means. International institutions also help states establish agreements and international law that can provide incentives for cooperation and organized collective responses for punishing states that do not cooperate. Furthermore, international institutions can actually change a state's interests by developing new norms of international behavior, such as the respect for human rights, and by developing mechanisms for areas of cooperation, such as in economic integration.[7] Realism, however, sees these institutions as a threat to state sovereignty and state interests that have little impact on state behavior.[8]

Contemporary liberalism, as a theoretical perspective for understanding global politics, has its roots in many strands of liberal philosophies. Writers of eighteenth-century enlightenment and rationalism, such as the French philosopher Montesquieu and the German philosopher Immanuel Kant, argued that individuals, and states as well, are not inherently evil and can learn to live peacefully if good social institutions are created around them.[9] Contemporary liberalism incorporates these ideas in its focus on international institutions and law as positive and desired ways to foster cooperation. Nineteenth-century liberalism, also known as **classical liberalism,** stressed the importance of the individual and democratic political systems. Philosophers such as John Stuart Mill argued that individuals were capable of satisfying their own interests, and the role of the state should merely be to help provide stability and peace for the realization of individual interests.[10] Contemporary liberalism incorporates these ideas in its focus on how individuals in a democracy can articulate alternative interests to those of the state and on how democratic constraints can produce cooperation. Finally, contemporary liberalism is consistent with early-twentieth-century liberal writings, such as those by U.S. President Woodrow Wilson, who argued that war was partly a product of nondemocratic countries and that war could be prevented through international organizations. Wilson argued that U.S. participation in World War I was about "making the world safe for democracy" by destroying authoritarian governments and empires in Europe. He designed the League of Nations, an international organization whose goal was to make war extremely unlikely. Wilson's ideas are even more closely associated with idealism and will be discussed in more detail later in this chapter.

With these philosophical roots, contemporary liberalism offers a fairly comprehensive alternative perspective on the fundamental features of

classical liberalism
The nineteenth-century philosophy that stressed the importance of the individual and democratic political systems.

global politics. Liberalism's chief disagreements with realism concern the predominance of states, the expectation for cooperation versus conflict, the role of international institutions, and the focus on change versus continuity in international politics.

Idealism

idealism A theoretical perspective, in contrast to realism, that focuses on the importance of morality and values in international relations.

Idealism is not as comprehensive as liberalism in its criticism of realism. Rather, idealism focuses on one key point: the absence of morality in realism. Morals and values, not state interests, should and do shape individual and state behavior, according to idealism. Idealism's focus on what states "should" do makes it different from other theoretical perspectives. By prescribing how states should behave, idealism is a more normative, or prescriptive, theory.

Idealism sees realism's emphasis on power politics as blind to the underlying values that states try to promote and worries that the realist perspective makes the use of military force an acceptable means without consideration of the ends for which it is used. For most idealists, war must be a last resort, because it takes away human life, a value idealism sees as universally held by all.

Idealism shares many features with liberalism and grows out of some of the same philosophical foundations, including the writings of Immanuel Kant. According to idealism, humans are basically good, and it is social institutions that drive them to immoral acts. Perfecting social institutions is not only possible but is the key to promoting cooperation and peace in the global society. Thus, like liberalism, idealism sees a role for international organizations in world politics. For liberals, states participate in intergovernmental organizations and desire cooperation, because it serves their *interests* or the interests of nonstate actors that constrain states. For idealists, cooperation is desirable, because it promotes a *value*—peace—and avoids something morally questionable—war. These were the values that motivated idealists such as Woodrow Wilson to design the League of Nations during the time period between World War I and World War II. The League was meant to promote the values of peace and democracy, but it failed to prevent the Second World War. After World War II, idealist values surfaced in a new international security organization, the United Nations. The charter signed by members of the United Nations obliges states to pursue peaceful means for resolving conflicts. Efforts by the United States, under President George W. Bush, to democratize the Middle East were consistent with idealism in that democracy was a political ideology and value to be promoted.[11]

Applying values to international politics is not easy, and idealism does not offer specific guidelines for how to do so. Although most idealists agree that human rights, for example, is an especially important value to uphold, there is considerable disagreement over which human rights are the most important and whether they should be considered universal.

ISSUE: The advanced industrialized economic states are challenged when they try to balance the economic advantages of trade with China against security and human rights concerns. Realism, idealism, and liberalism offer alternative policy prescriptions on this question.

Option #1: The advanced economic states should limit their economic ties with China.

Arguments: (a) Realists are concerned that trade with China strengthens a potential threat to other states' security. Economic exchanges on technology can be used for military purposes, and China can use its economic gain to fund its growing military. Furthermore, Chinese threats to Taiwan and its transfer of nuclear technology to Iran and Pakistan should not be rewarded with economic ties. (b) Idealists argue that China should be punished with economic isolation because of its violation of individual political and religious rights, its use of child labor, and its suppression of self-rule in Tibet. The advanced economic states should hold economic exchanges as a reward to China if it conforms to these values.

Counterarguments: (a) China is not a great threat. Although it has a large military, it is not sophisticated technologically and does not come close to matching the capabilities of the United States, the main power with a significant presence in Asia. Furthermore, internal divisions will keep China more focused at home and away from hostile adventures. (b) The application of Western values to China is cultural imperialism and is an intrusion of sovereignty. The advanced economic states would themselves see such intrusions into their own internal politics as unacceptable.

Option #2: The advanced economic states should pursue more economic ties with China.

Arguments: (a) Liberals argue that economic cooperation and interdependence will restrain China from threatening behavior since it is in China's interest to prosper economically, and military threats would harm those interests. (b) Liberals also argue that political liberalization will follow economic liberalization and that more contact with other democracies will eventually undermine the authoritarian government in China, thus addressing human rights concerns. (c) Liberals argue that given the importance of economics today and the profits that can be made from the Chinese market, it is not in the interests of the advanced economic states to sacrifice wealth for security or moral values.

Counterarguments: (a) Increased economic cooperation with China in the past has not diminished its threatening behavior, and democratic structures are not in place to allow those who oppose conflictual policy to influence Chinese decision makers. (b) Human rights violations have continued despite increased economic cooperation with China in the past. (c) Economic trade with China is not that profitable (the United States, for example, has a trade deficit with China), and there are other sources of economic wealth that do not compromise security and values.

These issues lead to a number of questions: Should one society impose its morals on another, or are values culturally relative? Should societies that value women's rights, equal rights between ethnic groups, economic equality, freedom from torture, freedom from the death penalty, or democratic political rights apply those values to others who do not? Disagreement also occurs over when to use military force in the name of other values. Idealism does not mean pacifism, and many idealists would argue that full force should be used in situations that have moral imperatives, such as the prevention of genocide. Yet because idealists also believe that one should weigh the moral end with the immoral consequences of killing, the actual balance of values in a particular situation can spark considerable debate. Idealists, however, would say that debating which values are important and how to apply values to international politics is far better than ignoring values by stressing interests, as realism and liberalism do. The Policy Choices box demonstrates some of the key differences among realism, liberalism, and idealism on the question of trade with China.

Neo-Marxism

Neo-Marxism A theoretical perspective that focuses on the international system of capitalism, exploitation, and the global competition among economic classes.

Neo-Marxism disagrees most fundamentally with the realist state-centric assumption. Whereas realism focuses on the international system of anarchy and state competition for power, the neo-Marxist perspective focuses on the international system of capitalism, the competition among economic classes, and the relationship of politics and society to capitalist production.[12]

For this perspective, economics is the primary explanation for world politics. In this way, it is Marxist in its orientation. But whereas Marx concentrated on class conflict within countries, neo-Marxists concentrate on global class conflict.

core Countries where the most advanced economic activities take place and wealth is concentrated.

Many neo-Marxists take a historical view of global politics, tracing the development of the world economic system. According to this perspective, the world economy has always been divided into a **core** (the "haves"), in which the most advanced economic activities take place and wealth is concentrated, and a **periphery** (the "have nots"), in which the less advanced economic activities occur and wealth is scarce. Over time, particular country economies may move from core to periphery or vice versa, but what is constant across history is that the globe is split into this core-periphery international division of labor and the economic conflict that is inherent in this divide. "As a consequence, the core receives the most favorable proportion of the system's economic surplus through its exploitation of the periphery, which, in turn, is compelled to specialize in the supply of less well rewarded raw materials and labor."[13] Since the development of **capitalism** (a "mode of production . . . dominated by those who operate on the primacy of endless accumulation"),[14] a significant change in the world system, the core has primarily consisted of

periphery Countries where the less advanced economic activities occur and wealth is scarce.

capitalism The dominant mode of economic production today, in which the means of production are privately owned and goods and services are distributed in a free market for profit.

the industrialized economies of Europe and eventually North America and parts of East Asia, and the periphery has consisted of the economies based on the extraction of raw materials in Africa, Latin America, parts of Southeast Asia, and the Middle East.

This particular division of labor did not develop arbitrarily, but instead was a product of the historical expansion of the European powers that in the sixteenth century began colonizing the rest of the world. Colonization involved changing the conquered territories' economies to suit the needs of the European powers. In most parts of Latin America and Africa, for example, agricultural economies designed to feed the population for centuries were destroyed and replaced by luxury crops (largely goods exported for Europeans) such as bananas and sugar cane or raw materials such as gold. This **imperialism** changed the nature of the world economic system to the advantage of the European powers, and the conflict between the core and the periphery involved economic and political domination to ensure continued economic gain on the part of the core.[15] **Dependency theory,** one variation of neo-Marxism, argues that even after the colonized areas became independent, the core continued to exploit the periphery through neo-imperialism—not outright occupation of the areas but indirect domination through military interventions, control of international organizations, biased trading practices, and collusion with corrupted elites who governed the periphery.[16] Some neo-Marxists focus on the hegeomony of social and economic classes and the states and international organizations they control to maintin their positions of power. Neo-Marxists are highly critical of multinational corporations who they accuse of using the powers and policies of states to support conditions that are profitable for them—conditions such as wage controls and little financial or environmental regulation.

The implications of and debates surrounding neo-Marxism will be discussed in more detail in Chapter 11. At this point, however, it is important to recognize the alternative vision of global politics that it presents compared to other theoretical perspectives. Its focus on economics contrasts greatly with the realist focus on military power. Compared to liberalism, which also recognizes the importance of economic relations, neo-Marxism stresses the historical circumstances that created the capitalist division of labor. Moreover, whereas liberalism sees interdependence as fostering cooperation among states and other nonstate actors, the neo-Marxist perspective sees a particular kind of interdependence—dependence of the periphery on the core—as fostering conflict among global economic classes. Modern neo-Marxists also focus on forms of exploitation, not just on the basis of class, but also on the basis of race, gender, ethnicity, sexual orientation and other social/economic/cultural constructs. Although neo-Marxism can be used as an explanatory framework—to explain international politics—it also (like idealism) has a normative side in that it seeks economic equality, justice, legitimacy, and the emancipation of the global working class.

imperialism The domination of a population and territory by another state. The European imperial powers established colonies throughout the world from the sixteenth to the early twentieth century.

dependency theory A theoretical perspective arguing that after the colonized areas became independent, the core continued to exploit the periphery through neo-imperialism—not outright occupation of areas but through indirect domination.

Constructivism

constructivism
Theoretical perspective that proposes that the physical world is much less important than the social world and that important aspects of global politics are socially "constructed" through systems of norms, beliefs, and discourse.

Constructivism represents yet another challenge to realism. To better understand constructivism, we need to look at its basic roots, which (as the name implies) involve "construction." Although we typically think of construction as involving physical things, like buildings or cars, constructivists consider how the social world is built. There are many different kinds of constructivists, but they all tend to support the idea that the physical world is much less important than the social world and that important parts of the physical world are actually built of, or "constructed" by, the social world.[17]

Consider a thief. What exactly is a "thief"? You might readily answer that a thief is a person who steals things. But then you are left with the question of what it means to "steal" things. Again, you might answer that it means taking things that do not belong to you. But, then, what does "belong to" mean? Surely, a constructivist might argue, we know that different societies around the world define things like stealing and possessions differently. Some societies do not even operate on the basis of private property, and thus, the notion of stealing is largely absent. This same sort of thinking applies to actions as well. Murder, for example, is understood very differently depending on how each society defines it. The physical acts may be remarkably similar, but killing a prisoner, a political dissident, an unplanned baby, or a trespasser can all be constructed as very different. We can see, then, that a "thief" or a "murder" are best thought of not as real things, but rather as ideas that are constructed from the rules of a society or a particular social context. Two people might witness a person take something away from another person or end the life of another person, but the physical act could have entirely different meanings to each of the observers. We might even say that thieves and murders do not exist, except insofar as a particular society defines them (constructs them) into existence. The physical world, it would seem, is far less important than how the social world constructs that physical world.

But how does this apply to international relations, and how does constructivism represent a challenge to realism? If realism is purportedly based on what is "real," then constructivism confronts realism by questioning "reality." Realists (and Liberals) tend to objectify the world by asserting that there is a single, knowable, true world that is separate from one's social context. Constructivists counter that there is no certain, permanent, factual reality, and even if there were, physical truths matter less than social constructions. Thus, constructivism questions some of the basic claims of realism.

Take the concept of a "state." Recall that states are the central actors according to a realist perspective, and it is the pursuit of state power that drives international relations. Indeed, realists contend that all states are the same in that they are actors pursuing their objective self-interests. But what is a "state"? A realist would answer that it is a government that exercises sovereign authority over a defined territory. But, then, what is a "government," and what is "sovereign authority"? Certainly the notion of government varies from society to society, as do conceptions of both sovereignty and authority. Moreover, a constructivist might ask what these "objective interests" are that realists espouse; these things are not "facts" in the sense that they truly exist somewhere. Rather, they are constructed from various understandings associated with different societies and cultures. Thus, it becomes important to understand how a state or a society conceives of itself and its interests, rather than simply asserting that all states are the same. Furthermore, constructivists want to know what the shared understanding of state and sovereignty is in the international society as this is what provides meaning for state actions. Constructivists are more interested in understanding shared subjective meanings than the objective.

Constructivists apply the same logic to the concept of anarchy, which is central to realism. Realists look at anarchy as the most important characteristic of the international system, because each state must then fend for itself rather than appeal to some higher authority. But can we really say that anarchy is a universal truth, viewed and responded to in the same fashion by all the world across all time? Alexander Wendt, one of the best-known constructivists, tackles this very issue in an article titled "Anarchy Is What States Make of It: The Social Construction of Power Politics."[18] In this article, he suggests that identities and interests of states are not independent of, and are constructed by, their interactions—much as thieves and murders are not independent of, and are constructed by, the social context. Thus, when realists take as a starting point the self-interested nature of states, and only then consider how they will interact with one another, they are presupposing something. They are, in effect, treating interests as given, and then trying to determine how states will interact. They might say that *because* states are self-interested, they will use force to maximize power when they interact in an anarchical system. But a constructivist would say that interests are not given and that a state will have different interests depending on its interactions. Indeed, the notion of anarchy itself is not a universal but rather is constructed based on the social context. The social context in this instance is the actual interactions of states (an international society). Thus, anarchy (like thieves and murders) will be defined differently depending on how states interact. Anarchy is just what states make of it.

Constructivists argue that states' constructions of the international systems influence global politics more than do any objective conditions. One important type of social construction, **international norms,** can have powerful effects on how states act and understand international relations.[19] Constructivists point out that what is right, wrong, or appropriate, and even what is in a state's interest is the product of the collective social context of global politics. Norms against the slave trade, norms against the use of war for offensive purposes, and norms condoning the

international norms Socially agreed-upon standards and expectations about appropriate behaviors of states and other international actors.

interference in internal affairs for human rights have, according to constructivists, been socially constructed and reinforced by states' behavior and now act as serious constraints on what states perceive as acceptable behavior.

Feminist Perspectives

feminist constructivism
Perspective that rejects the idea of a universal truth, instead arguing that gender and the way gender is defined colors different understandings in world politics.

Much of the feminist perspective in international politics is consistent with the constructivist perspective. Feminist constructivism examines the hidden assumptions about gender in the understanding and practice of global politics. Indeed, **feminist constructivism** rejects the idea that there is a universal truth, instead arguing that gender and the way gender is defined colors different understandings of world politics. Feminists argue, for example, that international relations theorizing is largely based on masculine assumptions and reasoning.[20]

Specifically, the principles of realism and its vocabulary are rather masculine in perspective. Realism's preoccupation with conflict, domination, and war, for example, reflects a more masculine way of thinking about human and state relations. Thus, far from accepting a dog-eat-dog conception of autonomous states vying for supremacy as if it were a "real" property of the international system, feminists argue that this is merely a masculine construction of global politics.

Furthermore, realism's definition of power as control contrasts with feminine definitions of power as the ability to act in concert or action taken in connection with others. Feminists argue that this conception of power is practiced by weaker states but that realism, with its focus on major powers, largely ignores these aspects of international relations. Feminists also define security, a central concept in realism, differently: "Many IR [international relations] feminists define security broadly in multidimensional and multilevel terms—as the diminution of all forms of violence, including physical, structural, and ecological. . . . Most of these definitions start with the individual or community rather than the state or the international system."[21] Like idealism, feminism also criticizes realism for its amoral stance. Moral issues, particularly human rights issues, are an important part of a broad definition of security but are marginalized in the realist perspective.

Feminism might appear to be more comfortable with liberalism and its focus on cooperation and idealism with its attention to morality, but many feminists reject the liberal philosophy of individual interests, as opposed to community interests, that underlie both of these alternative perspectives. In sum, many feminists argue that a deconstruction of the dominant perspectives of international relations will reveal that women have been "systematically omitted in the quest to represent elite male experience and images of reality, as reality per se. . . . The result is a Tradition and a discipline, and indeed a whole International Relations community, that has rendered women invisible."[22] Consequently, feminists argue, the study of international relations, especially the dominant realist perspective, is masculine in its perspective and thus is only a partial description of international politics.

Another part of the feminist perspective concerns the impact that men and women have on international politics and the impact that international politics has on men and women. It may not be surprising that our perspectives on international relations are masculine biased, because males hold most of the important leadership positions. Politics in general, and perhaps especially international politics, has always been male dominated. According to the World Bank, only about 18 percent of the world's parliamentarians are female.[23] A perusal of the names of the foreign ministers and defense ministers in all the states of the world shows that only a few are female; also, only a very small minority of ambassadors to the United Nations are female.

What effect does this underrepresentation of women in leadership positions have on global politics? The answer to this question depends on how differences between men and women are explained. **Essential feminism** argues that women are inherently different from men in ways that make their contributions to politics differ greatly. According to this argument, men and women have essential biological differences that lead them to think and behave differently in ways that might affect international relations. In most countries, for example, a gender gap exists in public opinion: men tend to be more supportive of war and conflictual means for addressing their countries' problems than are women. If more women were leaders, the argument continues, "a truly matriarchal world, then, would be less prone to conflict and more conciliatory and cooperative than the one we inhabit now."[24]

Most feminist scholars in international relations do not subscribe to the view that gender differences are biologically determined.[25] Rather, they see gender roles as socially constructed or created and reinforced by the social environment. This view recognizes the differences between men and women and the alternative ways of thinking and behaving that arise from the feminine standpoint but rejects any biological determinism and inherent superiority of women. **Liberal feminism** also rejects biological determinism, but rather than focusing on the unique contributions that women can make, it stresses the similarities between men and women and the entitlement for women to the same rights and responsibilities that men enjoy. From this point of view, women can contribute in the same ways as do men with equal capability (e.g., as women leaders, soldiers, and suicide bombers) although political, economic, and social structures, in addition to gender stereotypes, often block their entry into such positions. Liberal feminists point to the women who have held leadership positions, such as India's Indira Gandhi, Israel's Golda Meir, and Great Britain's Margaret Thatcher, who were as conflictual as men in their foreign policies. More generally, a comparison of female and male leaders reveals that "both female and male leaders rely on . . . the use

essential feminism
The idea that women are inherently different from men in ways that make their contributions to politics differ greatly.

liberal feminism
Perspective that stresses the similarities between men and women and the entitlement for women to the same rights and responsibilities that men have.

of force. . . . Furthermore, both female and male leaders' average use of violence is equal. According to this evidence, female leaders are not more peaceful than their male counterparts."[26] Other feminists would counter that women leaders must conform to socially constructed male roles in order to get into the positions usually reserved for men.

While women are not well represented in the public sphere of global politics, feminists point out that their contribution in the private sphere is no less important, even though it has often been ignored by both politicians and scholars. Women in their public and private work contribute greatly to the international economy. Diplomatic wives support their ambassador husbands through rearing their children and hosting parties. Women make up a good percentage of regular armed forces, even though they are often restricted to noncombat roles. In many revolutionary movements, women participate in the full range of armed conflict.[27]

Women, however, tend not to benefit as greatly from their roles in global politics, and a significant part of the feminist perspective is demonstrating the impact that global politics has on women. For example, "feminists tend to focus on the consequences of what happens during wars rather than on their causes. . . . They draw on evidence to emphasize the negative impact of contemporary military conflicts on civilian populations. . . . As mothers, family providers, and care-givers, women are particularly penalized by economic sanctions associated with military conflict."[28] Discrimination against women, in part because they make up half the human race, is arguably the single most profound human rights issue in the world today. Worldwide, women typically earn less than men either because they are in lower-paying jobs or earn less for the same job. Most of the work women do is unpaid, particularly in developing countries.[29] "The differences in the work patterns of men and women, and the 'invisibility' of unpaid work not included in national accounts, lead to lower entitlements to women than to men. This inequity in turn perpetuates gender gaps in capabilities."[30]

Liberia's President Ellen Johnson-Sirleaf, Africa's first elected woman leader, is a rare exception to the male-dominated world of international diplomacy.

(Shaun Curry/AFP/Getty Images)

In sum, the feminist perspective serves as another alternative lens through which to view international relations. In asking "Where are the women?" it seeks to uncover the gendered nature of global politics and our understanding of global politics.[31]

SUMMARY

- Theoretical perspectives provide answers to these basic questions: Who are the main actors in international politics? Why do actors do what they do in international politics? What are the underlying factors that govern relationships in global politics? How have international relations changed or stayed the same over the centuries? What accounts for conflict and cooperation in international politics? These issues are important to understand because they make explicit underlying assumptions, present alternative explanations of the same events or "facts," and provide a basis for understanding global politics in the future.

- Realism has been the dominant theoretical perspective. It sees states as the most important actors in global politics. States pursue their interests by maximizing their power, primarily military power, because of the anarchical nature of the international system. As a result, conflict is an inherent part of international politics. Realism sees great continuity in international relations across time periods.

- Liberalism argues that changes in the international system have made nonstate actors—both transnational and substate actors—more important in global politics. The multiple connections across states and substate actors, particularly in democracies, serve to constrain states from engaging in conflicts that might harm their economic interests. Liberalism argues that complex interdependence in the international system means that states engage in and benefit from cooperation, including cooperation in international organizations.

- Idealism proposes that states should and do follow their values in global politics. Foreign policy and international organizations should be constructed to address moral issues of peace and human rights.

- The neo-Marxist perspective focuses on the historical development of the international capitalist economic system, which is divided into a richer core and a poorer periphery. This division of labor has its roots in the imperial adventures of the European powers that, beginning in the sixteenth century, colonized most of the rest of the world. Neo-Marxists argue that the exploitative economic relationships established during colonization continue today.

- Constructivism proposes that the physical world is much less important than the socially constructed world. Constructivists criticize realism for the assumption that there are universal truths. Key realist concepts, such as the "state" and "anarchy," are, for constructivists, more subjective and depend on the context. How such concepts are understood is much more important than is an objective definition of them.

- Feminist perspectives on international politics include arguments that the other major theoretical perspectives, particularly realism, contain masculine assumptions and hence offer only partial understanding of global politics. The feminist perspective also includes assessment of the gender-biased ways in which women and men participate in and are affected by global politics.

KEY TERMS

global politics 3
theoretical perspectives 3
realism 4
Thucydides 4
Morgenthau 4
states 5
sovereignty 5
anarchy 5
liberalism 7
interdependence 8
complex interdependence 9
transnational actors 9
multinational corporations 9
nongovernmental
  organizations 9
intergovernmental
  organizations 9

substate actors 9
classical liberalism 12
idealism 13
Neo-Marxism 15
core 15
periphery 15
capitalism 15
imperialism 16
dependency theory 16
constructivism 17
international norms 18
feminist constructivism 19
essential feminism 20
liberal feminism 20

CHAPTER 2

The Historical Setting

It is important to understand history in order to understand global politics. Recognizing that things happening today have similarly happened in the past and will likely happen in the future, gives us insight into *why* such things happen. Every generation tends to believe that they are living in a special time. And they are right—but they are not so special that they cannot learn something from the past. It is true that the dramatic transformation of global politics since the 1990s—including the end of the Cold War, September 11, 2001, and the global reactions to terrorism—produced events and trends that were unexpected even for professional observers. But it is also true that in some ways, history does repeat itself. Thus, understanding the history of international relations can likely give us some insights about what to expect in the future.

Global Politics in Ancient Times

Relations between different groups of people did not become "global" until technology allowed for those who lived in one part of the world to reach those who lived in other parts of the world. It was not until the early fifteenth century, when advances in math and engineering made it possible to design ocean-worthy vessels with the capability to sail across far distances, that relations become truly international. The history of these international relations, albeit on a smaller scale, is nevertheless important, because it gives an idea of how historical relationships differ from and resemble international politics today.[1]

Greek city-states
Formed between the first and sixth centuries B.C.E., a group of towns or a small city governed by a variety of types of political systems including small oligarchies of the rich, military dictatorships, and limited democracy. Examples include Athens, Corinth, Sparta, and Thebes.

In the eastern Mediterranean in the first to sixth centuries B.C.E., political life was organized within and between small city-states (see Map 2.1). The ancient **Greek city-states,** such as Athens, Corinth, Sparta, and Thebes, consisted of a group of towns or a small city and were governed by a variety of types of political systems, including small oligarchies of the rich, military dictatorships, and limited democracies. The Greek city-state system of international relations is considered a precursor to the modern state system, because the city-states related to each other in much the same fashion that countries relate to each other today. From Thucydides' account of the Peloponnesian War between Sparta and Athens, we know that the city-states waged war against each other, formed alliances, bargained over peace treaties, and established trading relationships.[2] More important, the city-states were independent of each other, and there was no overarching authority that governed their relationships. Although the Greeks did not articulate a legal concept of sovereignty, they operated as if the city-states were sovereign: They had ultimate authority over their territory, and no higher authority interfered in their internal affairs.

empires   Large political units in which the ultimate power rested in the hands of the emperor or the imperial central power. Examples include the Roman Empire, the African kingdoms, the Arab empire, the Mayans, the Aztecs, and the Incas.

The Greek system of international politics was unusual. For most of history, the world has been organized under larger political units or **empires,** and the relations between political units did not adhere to the principle of sovereignty. Some of the great empires include the Persian empire (circa 600–100 B.C.E) the Roman Empire (circa 44 B.C.E–410 C.E.),

Map 2.1   Ancient Greek City-States
(© Cengage Learning)

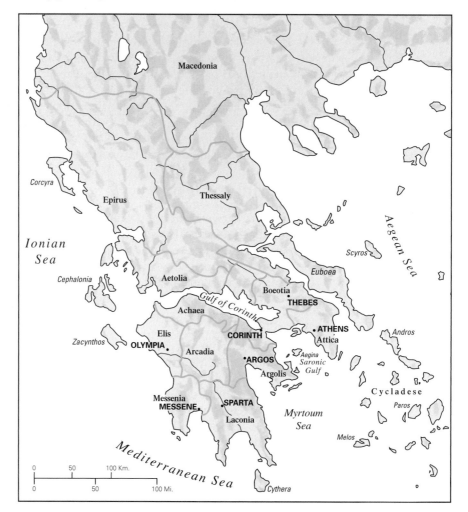

the African kingdoms (600–1200 C.E.), the Arab empire (630–1258 C.E.), the Chinese dynasties (circa 1000–1700 C.E.), and the Latin American empires such as the Mayans (circa 300–900 C.E.), the Aztecs (circa 1325–1520 C.E.), and the Incas (circa 1200 C.E.). Within an empire, ultimate power rested in the hands of the emperor or the imperial central power. Regions *within* the empire may have traded with one another or waged war against each other, but these relationships were sanctioned and governed by the central authority. The central authority also had the right to interfere in the internal affairs of the regions. Regions were not independent. There often was not much activity happening *between* empires, given the lack of technology to travel far distances for most of this historical period. When empires did interact with each other, however, there was also no notion of sovereign rights. Empires interfered in the affairs of others, and victorious empires absorbed vanquished ones, because there was no conception that empires had any right to continue to exist as an independent political unit.

This was true in medieval Europe after the fall of the Roman Empire. No political authority as strong as the former empire came to replace it. Europe was instead governed by small feudal units, principalities, dukedoms, and monarchies and was at one time only loosely linked under Charlemagne's Holy Roman Empire of the ninth century. Yet the Catholic Church served as a religious authority that precluded the total independence of the feudal barons and the monarchs. During this time, the Catholic Church acted as an imperial central power in the area known as Christendom. Within this area, people were governed by both their local lords or kings and their local bishops representing the interests of the Catholic Church in Rome. Christian doctrine underlay the concepts of rights, justice, and other political norms, and even kings were theoretically and often in practice subordinate to the pope. When, in the fifteenth century, Spain and Portugal disagreed over their "discovered" territories in the Western Hemisphere, for example, it was the pope who settled the matter.[3] Questions of war were also a religious matter. The Crusades against non-Christians, for example, were organized by the papal authority, and wars within Christendom had to be justified according to Christian doctrine: "A crusade was an enterprise of all Christendom and had to be proclaimed by the pope, preached and organized by the clergy as well as by lay rulers. It was not a matter for unilateral decision by a lay ruler for his own advantage."[4]

The Emergence of the Modern State and the Contemporary International System

It was when monarchs begin to centralize their power, taking it away from the local feudal rulers, and when philosophers and commercial elites alike began questioning the authority of the Catholic Church, that international relations in Europe began to transform. The first to break from the governance of the Catholic Church were the city-states of northern Italy. The Italian Renaissance of the fifteenth and sixteenth centuries reintroduced to Europe the classic Greek and Roman concepts of justice, rights, and law, and the Italian city-states of the Renaissance period, such as Venice, Florence, and Milan, established themselves independent from papal authority, governing their own internal affairs and conducting their external affairs without interference from a higher authority. The system of relations looked very different from medieval times: These city-states hired mercenaries to wage wars against one another and other foreign powers; they established a permanent diplomatic corps as a communication system; and they viewed war as a legitimate means to secure interests that did not have to be justified according to religious principles. As such, the Italian city-state system of Renaissance Italy was in part a return to the Greek city-state system of independent small states.

In the rest of Europe, the Protestant Reformation that challenged Catholic authority set the stage for conflict as the Catholic Hapsburgs tried to reunify a fracturing Europe. The Hapsburgs were defeated in the Thirty Years' War (1618–1648), a devastating conflict that set the stage for the birth of the modern state and the contemporary international system. Thus, modern European states arose from the destruction of the Thirty Years' War, in which about two-thirds of the total population had disappeared and five-sixths of the villages in the empire had been destroyed.[5] These horrors made it obvious that the Christian community of medieval Europe was fragile indeed and was in need of replacement. The replacement that came out of the **Peace of Westphalia** was the sovereign state. The Peace of Westphalia, signed in 1648, is widely recognized as the dividing line between a medieval Europe dominated by small, localized political units under the comprehensive authority of the Holy Roman Empire and/or the pope and a modern Europe where states became recognized as sovereign. The Holy Roman Empire and the pope continued to exist, but their political power had been all but destroyed.

Peace of Westphalia
Treaty signed in 1648 that is widely recognized as the dividing line between medieval European political institutions and a modern Europe where states became recognized as sovereign.

The concept of sovereignty, in the post-Westphalian period, extended beyond the dimensions described by Jean Bodin, the French legal scholar credited with making the first systematic presentation of the concept in his *Six Books on the State,* published in 1586. Bodin's work was a defense of the divine right of the French king to rule in an absolute manner, but Bodin's concept of sovereignty did not imply a right to rule arbitrarily or above the law. Nor did it originally imply that a state fell under no superior obligations in its relations with other states.[6] But because of the urge to avoid catastrophes such as the Thirty Years' War, the concept of sovereignty came to imply that the state had an absolute power over its subjects and an absolute right to be free from interference by other states in the exercise of that power.[7]

The Peace of Westphalia did not immediately transform Europe from a large collection of small, local entities under one universal authority into a small number of parallel sovereign states. But the idea of states as impenetrable units did develop relatively quickly after 1648. Shortly before 1648, scholars of international law considered it perfectly appropriate for one state to intervene in the affairs of another in order to protect citizens from oppression. But some fifty years later, legal scholars, writing with the benefit of the experience of the Thirty Years' War and the Peace of Westphalia, concluded that such interference by one state in the affairs of another was a violation of sovereignty.[8] Thus, by the beginning of the eighteenth century, sovereign states—a notion only previously seen in isolated, small areas of the world—became the dominant legal principle governing relations among the major powers in Europe. This new Westphalian system was not only a product of religious developments; economic and technological changes also worked to reinforce the sovereign state.

If the divisions in Christendom in the fourteenth and fifteenth centuries had not been accompanied by changes in economic forces and in military technology, the Thirty Years' War and the Peace of Westphalia might have established impenetrable sovereign units that were nevertheless similar in size to the numerous small units that went into that war. Economic changes, however, powerfully reinforced the strength of central political authorities in what were soon to become recognizably modern states. Feudal authorities tended to restrict trade and commerce, making it almost impossible to conduct economic transactions across longer distances, or indeed anywhere outside the jurisdiction of typically quite small feudal political units. As merchants and entrepreneurs who wanted to conduct economic transactions became wealthier and more influential, they increasingly came to value political systems and leaders who could exert their authority over larger areas and enforce commitments to similar entities elsewhere.[9] Dramatic changes in military technology reinforced evolutionary developments in economic forces. Around 1200 C.E., stone castles represented the ultimate in military defense, and they were scattered all over western Europe.

Military technology came to exert a strong force against this state of affairs. "The sudden maturation in 1450 A.D. of the cannon, after a long infancy, as the destroyer of castles made a further and large change in the art of war in favor of the centralized state . . . and in favor of the monarch over the feudal barons."[10] The appearance of gunpowder on the battlefields accelerated the process of eliminating smaller political units in favor of larger units, such as states. Between 1400 and 1600, large numbers of the smaller entities lost their independence; the Thirty Years' War brought this process to a climax. After the Peace of Westphalia, fortified cities and castles increasingly gave way to fortresses lining the borders of states, at least partly because the cities and castles could no longer defend themselves against attackers equipped with the new military technology.

But how did the increasingly powerful monarchs at the head of territorial states acquire the ability to use this new military technology effectively? Changes in warfare favored larger and more expensive armies, which necessitated more taxation.[11] Sovereign states proved themselves more capable than city-states or city-leagues of providing this increased taxing power and rational government.[12] So the evolution and increasing importance of both economic transactions over large areas and innovations in military technology combined to allow territorial, sovereign states to prevail, first in Europe and eventually over the entire globe.

Eighteenth-Century European Relations

Following the Peace of Westphalia, the large important European states, such as Britain, France, the Netherlands, Austria, and the newly emerging Russia and Prussia, were ruled by centralized monarchies, and wars between the states were usually conflicts between royal dynasties.

balance of power A principle that implies it is dangerous for all states to allow any other state to become too powerful.

Typically, one royal family would object to an increase in the power of another royal family. These conflicts and the resulting wars would typically be resolved on the **balance-of-power** principle. This principle implied that it was dangerous for all states to allow any one state to become too powerful. Just what was too powerful was in constant dispute, of course, but in practice, the balance-of-power principle usually served to preserve the existing distribution of power among the great powers. Any change in the status quo that worked to the detriment of a given great power made that state (or royal family) feel entitled to some compensation.[13]

The eighteenth century saw a series of balance-of-power wars, with the British and French being the major protagonists. The wars between kings were fought by soldiers of various nationalities employed for the purpose, and the diplomats who negotiated the peace settlements were virtually indifferent to nationalistic divisions.[14] This cosmopolitanism applied throughout the diplomatic corps of European states. Denmark used German diplomats, Russia employed Englishmen and Frenchmen, and Spain recruited diplomatic talent from Italy and Holland. Indeed, cosmopolitanism extended to heads of states. Britain had a German king, and the Spanish king was a grandson of Louis XIV of France.

Napoleon, pictured at the height of his power in 1812, revolutionized international politics by his heavy reliance on conscription to create armies infused with the spirit of nationalism.

(Jacques-Louis David, *Napoleon in His Study,* Samuel H. Kress Collection, © 1994 Board of Trustees, National Gallery of Art, Washington)

The Impact of the French Revolution

The new, modern, sovereign state, brought into existence at the end of the seventeenth century, and the balance-of-power system operating on the European continent would soon face a challenge that would transform the nature of the state, as well as the nature of international relations. This challenge came in the form of nationalism and expressed itself in the eighteenth century in the French Revolution.

The original aims of the revolution were liberty, equality, and brotherhood for the French people. The aims implied the end of aristocratic rule in France, but more importantly, they implied that the state belonged to the people. Kings could no longer say, *L'état, c'est moi* (I am the state). The acts of the government came to be viewed as acts of the citizenry, and the revolutionary French constitution of 1793 was ratified by a large popular majority. As popular will linked itself with the actions of its political representatives, tremendous support for the government arose. As a consequence, the government came to be regarded as the head of a national society of French people; not, as in the case of the old monarchy, the ruler of a mere geographical expression.[15] Thus, in the context of the French Revolution, **nationalism,** or the identification of a people to a social community that is often linguistically, ethnically, or religiously based, meant that the government of France, the state, was legitimate not because of religious authority, or the family dynasty of a monarch, but because it represented the nation of the French people.

nationalism The identification of a people to a social community that is often based on shared language, ethnicity, and/or religion.

If the French Revolution had been self-contained, its impact on international politics might have been less dramatic. But the revolution became expansionist. The French became convinced that their ideals were too good and too important to be confined in application to one state, and with Napoleon's leadership they set out to spread those ideas throughout Europe. To do this, Napoleon used the *levée en masse,* or conscription. Soldiers were no longer mercenaries, but patriots who fought in defense of or for the glory of the state. Eventually, the other states of Europe found they could not resist or defeat an army of patriots without copying its methods and its nationalism. France's enemies became nationalistic in self-defense. Even so, it took the combined forces of Napoleon's enemies almost two decades to finally defeat him at Waterloo in 1815.

Nineteenth-Century European Relations

Following the disruptive Napoleonic wars, the victors sought to reestablish order in Europe. The leaders of the great powers met at the **Congress of Vienna** and signed agreements that they hoped would restore stability. The agreements solidified the notion of state sovereignty. States agreed to preserve territorial boundaries to prevent future disputes, create buffer states (such as the Netherlands and Belgium) as small allies, and return to the balance-of-power principle that had operated in the eighteenth century. Fearing a French-like revolution in their own countries, the monarchs were also anxious to quell the flames of nationalism and democracy, and thus monarchies were restored and reinforced across Europe, even in France.[16]

Congress of Vienna A meeting between the leaders of the great powers, following Napoleon's defeat in 1815, which resulted in agreements designed to restore stability and solidify the notion of sovereignty.

The goal of restoring stability among the great powers was successful, and the international political system of the nineteenth century was relatively peaceful, compared to previous centuries. During this period, known as the **Concert of Europe,** there was no conflict in which all five major powers—Austria, Britain, France, Prussia, and Russia— were involved at the same time. Wars between the states occurred, such as the Crimean War in 1854 and the Franco-Prussian War of 1870, but one or more of the major powers stayed neutral in each of these conflicts. One source of continuity during the Concert of Europe was

Concert of Europe The nineteenth century period of relative peace, with no major conflict between the primary powers.

the consistently important role played by Great Britain. If Britain was not always clearly the most powerful state, it was never very far from being so. Britain's power and security rested first on its navy, which dominated the seas the world over and made any attack across the English Channel unlikely to succeed. The second solid basis for Britain's nineteenth-century security was its manufacturing ability.[17] The Industrial Revolution, the use of energy to drive machinery, began in Britain with the invention of the steam engine in 1769 and quickly fueled Britain's economic growth. Britain rapidly became the economic hegemon, the most powerful economy.

During the late nineteenth and early twentieth centuries, Britain's predominance facilitated a new era of international trade. Indeed, the second half of the nineteenth century saw the development of a truly international economy. Previously,

> throughout the first half of the nineteenth century, almost all economic activity was conducted either at the local level or (in those few countries such as Great Britain and France that had succeeded in abolishing internal impediments to economic exchange) on a national wide scale. Where international trade did exist, it was largely confined to distinct commercial regions defined by physical proximity.[18]

Thanks to the British promise that its currency was as good as gold, known as the *gold standard*, currency relations were fairly stable during this time, allowing countries to engage in considerable amounts of international trade.[19] As a result, the major economies were highly integrated, depending on trade with one another to a degree that would not be seen again until late in the twentieth century.

The Age of Imperialism

At roughly the same time that Europe came to be dominated by states, Europe began to dominate the world, setting the stage for the emergence of sovereign states around the globe. The Europeans first sent explorers to stake claims. After the explorers, and sometimes with them, came traders and colonizers, who began exploiting the economic and human resources of conquered areas. *Imperialism* refers to the domination of a population and territory by another state, and the European imperial powers established colonies throughout the world from the sixteenth to the early twentieth centuries. The fact that post-Westphalian Europe was divided into independent states rather than united in an empire was probably crucial to its global pursuits. There can be no doubt that China in the early Middle Ages was a more advanced society than Western Europe economically, technologically, and scientifically.[20] But empires, such as those in Asia, were overcentralized, rigid, and relatively unproductive in economic terms. As a result, in this view, East Asia came to be dominated by Europe.

The first wave of imperialism occurred in the sixteenth and seventeenth centuries when the British, Dutch, French, Portuguese, and Spanish established colonies in the Western Hemisphere. Most of these colonies would gain their independence in the last part of the eighteenth century and the early part of the nineteenth century. This included the war of independence by the American colonies, aided by the French, against the British. The Europeans then turned their attention to the rest of the world, and in a second wave of imperialism in the late nineteenth and early twentieth centuries, the major powers began intensely competing for colonies in Asia, Africa, and the Middle East. Indeed, although the European powers did not directly engage in all-out war with each other back on the continent during the Concert of Europe, they nevertheless competed with each other in colonization outside Europe, and colonial possessions became part of their calculations of the balance of power among them.

Britain's industrial and naval capability allowed it to establish the largest empire and prompted British imperialists of the time to boast that "the sun never sets on the British empire." Eventually, other growing powers would join in and acquire their own imperial possessions, as Japan did in East Asia, Russia in Central Asia, the United States in the Pacific and Caribbean, and Germany and Italy in the Middle East and Africa. (For the pattern of colonization, see Map 3.2 on page 62.) The result was a carving up of the world, and only a few areas, such as Iran, Siam, and Ethiopia, remained independent. Even in areas that had gained their independence from colonial powers, such as Latin America, the larger states dominated their affairs. In the early part of the twentieth century, the United States effectively controlled many countries in the Caribbean and Central America.[21]

In the areas that were still colonies, imperial powers mined natural resources such as gold, grew luxury crops including sugar, and acquired slaves, incorporating these geographic areas into the modern world system. As a result, Europe became increasingly advanced in economic terms, and the peripheral areas lagged far behind, becoming more and more dominated by Europe economically as well as politically.[22] The Europeans saw themselves as spreading "civilization" throughout the world. If they benefited more from the emergence of the modern world system, this was, from their viewpoint, only natural, because they had started down the road to economic development earlier than other countries, the very regions they were now "assisting" in the effort to catch up. This process included instances of brutal exploitation, including the development of the slave trade. Still, in the view of some, such as British economist Joan Robinson,[23] the misery of being exploited by capitalists was nothing compared to the misery of not being exploited at all. Incorporation into the Euro-centered international economic system created lots of problems, but people who remained isolated from that system did not live in a pristine paradise either.

In addition to the human and economic consequences of the imperial age, colonization was the means by which the European model of international politics based on sovereign states was exported. Moreover, when the colonies eventually became independent,

> non-European states were admitted as members of the [international] society . . . provided that they adopted its rules. . . . The great powers also insisted that all governments should observe certain European economic standards and commercial practices, particularly where they affected foreigners. Non-European candidates were judged not merely by how they conducted their external relations, but also by how they governed themselves. Communities that were culturally non-European had to learn these laws and practices and adjust to them, often at some cost to their own societies. The insistence on western values . . . played an important part in the integrating process which established the European-dominated global international society.[24]

Thus, by the end of the nineteenth century, European politics was becoming global politics.

The Twentieth-Century World Wars

In retrospect, it is easy to see that the beginning of the twentieth century brought several developments that would be detrimental to the Concert of Europe. Probably the most important was the increasing power of three states. To the west, the United States was already superior to Britain in economic productivity and would soon surpass Britain in military strength as well. In the east, Japan was proving to be a major power in wars against China and Russia, making it very difficult for Britain to maintain its customary domination of the seas in that area. In Europe, Germany began to challenge Britain's ability to preserve a balance of power on the European continent.

In addition, while the monarchs did their best to stave off the forces of nationalism, their efforts ultimately failed. Although none of the conflicts was great enough to seriously disrupt the system set up at the end of the Napoleonic era, wars of national liberation became commonplace. The Greeks fought for liberation from the Turks. The Poles rose up against the Russians. The Hungarians and the Italians rebelled against the Austrians. And so it went until Serbian nationalistic aspirations led to the First World War and thus helped to destroy the European system established a hundred years earlier by the major powers at the Congress of Vienna in 1815.

The Breakdown of the Nineteenth-Century Alliance System

For some time, the British were unconcerned about the rise of Germany. Otto von Bismarck, chancellor of the German Empire from 1871 to 1890, had long followed a policy of keeping the German navy small, and as long as Germany maintained that policy, it did not seem threatening. In fact, at the beginning of the century, the British, because of colonial rivalries, tended to regard the French with more suspicion than they did the Germans. The suspicion was sufficiently strong that for a while, the British were inclined to come to an understanding with Germany and perhaps even to become aligned in some way with the **Triple Alliance** of Germany, Austria-Hungary, and Italy.[25] But this inclination was wiped out by a combination of French conciliation and German belligerence. The French agreed to give the British a free hand in Sudan and Egypt in return for the British giving the French a free hand in Morocco. Meanwhile, the Germans made it obvious that they intended to build a navy to challenge Britain's control of the seas. The result of these developments was the Entente Cordiale between Britain and France in 1904 and, with the addition of Russia, **Triple Entente.** The entente was faced with the Triple Alliance of Germany, Austria-Hungary, and Italy. With this development, the very fluid alliance system that had operated during the Concert of Europe, with Britain playing the key role as balancer, came to an end. In its place, Europe became divided into two rigid camps. (See Map 2.2 for the alliances.)

After a number of international crises over the next decade, war was ultimately sparked on June 28, 1914, when a Serbian nationalist, apparently hoping for the liberation of fellow Slavs under Austrian rule, assassinated Archduke Franz Ferdinand, heir to the throne of Austria-Hungary. Austrian leaders had long been concerned about separatist movements in their empire, and they were determined to strike back at Serbia, a nation that, in the Austrian view, sympathized with and supported these movements. Austria's determination was heightened when Germany, on July 5, assured it of support if conflict with Serbia brought Austria into conflict with Russia. Austria delivered an ultimatum to Serbia on July 23, to which Serbia made a very conciliatory reply. Even so, on July 28, Austria declared war on Serbia. By August 6, 1914, France, Great Britain, and Russia were at war with Germany and Austria-Hungary. The Allies were later joined by Japan, Italy, and the United States, while Bulgaria and Turkey fought on the side of the Germans and the Austrians.

Triple Alliance The alliance between Germany, Austria-Hungary, and Italy established in the early twentieth century.

Triple Entente The alliance between Britain, France, and Russia established in the early twentieth century.

The First World War

Before the outbreak of the war, there was great optimism in Europe. After all, the nineteenth century had brought enormous benefits:

> There were dramatic advances in material living standards, health and education, and also in the sciences and the arts. It was an age of industrial and technical revolution, and of great strides in man's mastery of the environment. The middle class acquired an increasing say in most of the communities of

Map 2.2   Choosing Sides in the First World War

During the First World War, the Central Powers of Germany, Austria-Hungary, and Bulgaria faced the opposition not only of the Triple Entente (Great Britain, France, and Russia) but also of their several allies, including the United States.

(© Cengage Learning)

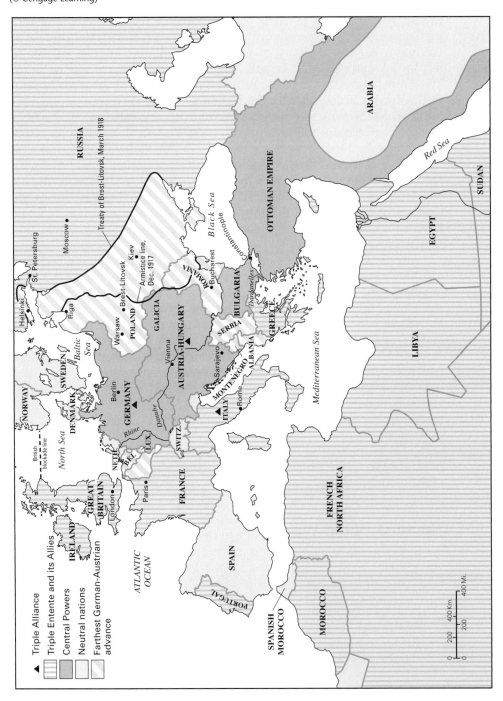

Europe, with a new industrial working class crowding on its heels. The whole world seemed to become Europeanized. It became difficult not to believe in progress.[26]

World War I shattered much of this optimism. The war would leave more than 15 million dead, and many of those who survived would long remember the horrors of trench warfare and mustard gas. This result came about despite the expectation of leaders in 1914 that either war would not occur or that it would be a short one.[27] Four years later, the Europeans looked around to see the devastating effects such miscalculations could bring.

One of the most important outcomes of the First World War on international politics was the weakening of Europe. The European states had been in unquestioned command of the global political system until 1914. By 1917, one important European state, Russia, was on the verge of dropping out of the war, and the rest were locked in a seemingly endless stalemate. It took a non-European state, the United States, which did not join the war until 1917, to break the deadlock. By then, the Austro-Hungarian Empire had been destroyed and Germany, Britain, and France severely damaged.

The Russian Revolution of 1917, in which the Bolshevik Communist Party (led by Vladimir Lenin) came to power, was in no small part another effect of the war. It might have occurred in any case, but the war revealed inefficiencies of the Czarist regime and subjected the Russian people to such hardships that they became less tolerant of the government's inadequacies.[28] Alone among the major combatants, the United States emerged more powerful than it had been at the beginning of the war. It was, in fact, already the most powerful state in the world according to many tangible indicators. The First World War significantly enlarged the role of the United States in the global political system.

Another important impact of the war was in the realm of political ideas. The war had been fought, according to U.S. President Woodrow Wilson, to make the world safe for democracy. It had been won, as no one could fail to notice, by the more democratic states (the United States, Great Britain, and France), while the nondemocratic states (Germany, Austria-Hungary, the Ottoman Empire, and Russia) had fallen to pieces. The war served to enshrine the intertwined (but not synonymous) values of democracy and **national self-determination**—the right of a community that identifies itself as a nation to form a state to govern itself. These twin ideas delegitimized empires. Applying the principle of national self-determination, Wilson led the effort to break up the Austro-Hungarian and Ottoman empires, creating new states such as Poland, Turkey, and Czechoslovakia. In the Middle East, former colonial possessions were placed under international control and would gain their independence after World War II.

Finally, any discussion of the effects of the First World War would be incomplete without emphasizing how it created conditions conducive to

national self-determination
The principle that a community that identifies itself as a nation has the right to form a state to govern itself.

the next world war. In addition to the lasting hatreds it created (or reinforced), the First World War had several important effects on the international economic system that shaped the process leading to the Second World War. The United States emerged, by a considerable margin, as the most important economic unit in the world, and Great Britain, France, and Germany became dependent on it. Furthermore, the war (and perhaps the provisions of the peace treaty) devastated the German economy in a manner that paved the way for the appearance, and later the success, of Adolf Hitler.

Postwar Settlements and the Interwar Years

In the months immediately following World War I, U.S. President Wilson was anxious to move beyond the days of balance-of-power and sphere-of-influence politics, which he saw as dangerous principles that had led Europe to near total collapse. The major instrument through which such principles would be replaced was an international organization, to be called the *League of Nations*. As the president of the strongest victor in the war, Wilson provided the major impetus behind the creation of such an organization, but there was widespread agreement on the need for such a body. Many European leaders were of the opinion that the war came about largely by default, because the forces of negotiation and peaceful settlement marshalled against it suddenly collapsed.[29] In short, they believed that the war had occurred, because the leaders had had no time or place to talk things over when the crisis began. The League of Nations would provide the opportunity for a cooling-off period and a forum for negotiations to avoid the next war.

There were also, however, important areas of disagreement about the League among the victorious powers. One area was the disposition of Germany's colonies. Wilson wanted to make these colonies the common property of the League and have them administered by small nations. Britain wanted to annex the colonies outright. A compromise was accomplished whereby the British dominions obtained the territories they desired under a loose mandate from the League. This agreement, in effect, was based on old sphere-of-influence ideas, thus revealing Wilson's idealism to still be at odds with European conceptions of international relations.

The French were even less idealistically inclined than the British. In an important sense, France had been the real loser in the war. It had lost 10 percent of its active male population, the highest proportion of any of the major participants. Also, the largest and most dreadful battles had been fought on French soil. The additional deliberate German destruction meant that fully a third of France was devastated. Almost 300,000 homes had been destroyed and some 3 million acres of land made unfit for cultivation.[30] Finally, France's war debts were staggering.

French leaders were absolutely desperate to assure their people that they would never have to battle the Germans again. Their major concern was that Germany be kept under control, and they were not willing to rely on Wilson's ideals without a solid base of concrete force behind them. France proposed the establishment of an international peace force to keep the Germans in check and wanted to take all of Germany's land west of the Rhine, an area containing some 5 million people, and create one or two republics that would be under French control. The United States, however, rejected both of these proposals.

Another, eventually crucial, disagreement between Wilson and Britain and France concerned the matter of reparations. Before the peace conference, Wilson had promised Germany that it would suffer no punitive damages. Germany had signed the armistice on condition that the Allies would ask for payment only for damages to civilians and their property. But the British and the French wanted to make Germany pay the whole cost of the war. This intent was understandable: the British and the French had suffered much more from the war than the Americans had. Realizing this, and despite his reservations, Wilson agreed to expand the definition of civilian damages, increasing reparations by about 100 percent.

At the eleventh hour on the eleventh day of the eleventh month of 1918, the armistice that ended the First World War went into effect. Three days earlier, a new German republic, known as the Weimar Republic, was proclaimed. It could not have been born at a less propitious time. Within a matter of seven months, the new government was faced with the responsibility of signing the **Treaty of Versailles,** the treaty to officially end the First World War. The publication of the treaty in Germany in May 1919 caused an outcry throughout the country. Mass meetings were organized, the provisional president of the republic called the terms "unrealizable and unbearable," and the German delegate to Versailles called the treaty "intolerable for any nation."[31]

Treaty of Versailles
Agreement, signed in 1919, that officially ended the First World War and established the terms for Germany's punishment.

The treaty took land away from the German people. Seven million people were no longer living under German sovereignty, and Germany was virtually disarmed. Article 231 of the treaty held Germany responsible for the war. But the provision of the treaty that had perhaps the most lasting impact concerned reparations. The exact amount was not stipulated in the treaty, but the Germans were to make a preliminary payment of $5 billion between 1919 and 1921. That gave some indication of what was to come. Then in April 1921, the Allies presented Germany with a total reparations bill of $33 billion. By that time, the German mark had begun to fall in value. It was normally valued at 4 to the U.S. dollar, but by the end of 1921 it had fallen to a value of 75 to the dollar. That was the beginning of the most spectacular inflationary spiral in the history of the industrialized Western world. In 1922, the value of the German mark fell to 400 to the U.S. dollar, and by the beginning of 1923, it took 7,000 marks to buy a dollar's worth of goods. When the French occupied the Ruhr Valley, the value of the mark dropped to 18,000 to the dollar. By July, it was 160,000 to the dollar; by August, 1 million to the dollar; by November, 4 billion. From then on, the value of the mark compared to the dollar had to be calculated in the trillions. It took a wheelbarrow full of money to buy a loaf of bread, assuming either was to be found.

This was the scene in Germany as Adolf Hitler made his first marked impression on the body politic, when he staged a ludicrously premature attempt to begin his ascent to power in Germany. He was arrested, tried, convicted, and sentenced to five years in prison on April 1, 1924.[32] Undiscouraged, he spent his time in prison dictating a book, *Mein Kampf*, that described in some detail his plans for the establishment of a thousand-year Reich, or empire, in Germany.

In time, Germany recovered from its economic problems, due in large part to a flow of U.S. capital used to pay reparations and renew Germany's productive capacities. Unemployment dropped, wages rose, and neither Hitler nor his Nazi Party was prominent. But the importance of the U.S. economy to German prosperity was soon to become forcefully apparent. In fact, Great Britain and France as well as Germany had become heavily dependent on the United States economically. In the 1920s, U.S. investors and Wall Street banks poured money into Germany, which used much of it to pay reparations to Great Britain and France, which in turn used that money to pay their First World War debts to the United States.

Then the stock market crash of 1929 happened, and the supply of money in the circular flow from Wall Street and other sources in the United States suddenly stopped. The Germans could no longer pay their reparations, which meant that Great Britain and France could not pay their war debts. The only possible alternatives for the Germans, the British, and the French were to default on their debts or increase their exports to the United States in order to accumulate dollars to pay the debts. President Herbert Hoover and the Congress moved to eliminate the second possibility (and to ensure the first) by putting the Smoot-Hawley Act into effect in June 1930, raising U.S. tariff rates to their highest point in history. "Over a thousand economists had pleaded with the president not to sign the bill, pointing out that higher rates would hamper foreign exports, block collection of the war

In the early 1920s, inflation in Germany was so severe that people, such as this German woman, used their paper money for fuel in their stoves and fireplaces.
(© Bettmann/Corbis)

debts, invite foreign retaliation, and embitter foreign relations. The predictions proved true."[33] At least as important as the domestic impact was the international effect of the increased tariffs. "The atrocious Smoot-Hawley tariff of 1930 . . . more than any other act of policy, spread the Depression to Europe."[34]

Great Depression A consequence of the 1929 stock market crash. The U.S. economic depression spread to other areas of the world, especially postwar Europe.

The effect of the **Great Depression** on German electoral politics was immediate and dramatic. In 1928, before the crash, the Nazis had received 810,000 votes and elected twelve of their members to the Reichstag, the German parliament. In the September 1930 elections, after millions of people had been thrown out of work and thousands of small businesses had failed, Hitler's party won almost 6.5 million votes and 107 seats in the Reichstag, thus becoming the second-largest party in the legislature. The Communist Party in Germany also gained as a result of the Depression. Although its gains were not as spectacular (from 3.2 million votes in 1928 to 4.6 million in 1930), its rise undoubtedly smoothed the way for Hitler's rise to power. By 1932, the Nazi Party was the largest political party in the country. In January 1933, Hitler was named chancellor. On March 27, 1933, the German legislature passed what was called the Enabling Act, which served as the formal basis for the establishment of Hitler's dictatorship. He never received a majority of the votes, but a single party rarely does in a multiparty system of the type Germany had at the time. The Nazis used terror and intimidation; there can be no quarrel about that, but they also attracted millions of uncoerced voters.

The economic policies of Hitler, based on large-scale borrowing for public expenditures that were principally civilian in the early years, worked well and quickly. "The result," as one well-known economist has pointed out, "was a far more effective attack on unemployment than in any other industrial country. By 1935, German unemployment was minimal."[35] So Hitler came to power in part because many Germans hoped (correctly, as it turned out) that he could help them with their economic problems. He also appealed to Germans of all classes because of his denunciation of the Versailles treaty, his condemnation of Jews, and because he was an alternative to the Communists.

Challenges to the Status Quo

Scholars of international politics view the 1930s as notable for the successful challenges to the international status quo mounted by Japan, Italy, and Germany. Let us take a look at the assertive policies that each of these dissatisfied major powers adopted.

The first challenge to the status quo was made by Japan when it invaded Manchuria in 1931. Japan was a rapidly growing power in the decades before 1931, taking advantage of the First World War to acquire several German colonial outposts and to extend its economic and political privileges in China. Perhaps even more important, Japan dramatically increased exports to the Asian markets that were cut off from their traditional European suppliers by the war. By the end of the war, Japanese strength had become so apparent that it was accorded great power status at the Paris Peace Conference.

Overall, the early 1920s were good years for Japan economically and politically. But in 1927, Japan began to have domestic economic problems that were soon exacerbated by the onset of the Depression. The reaction of all the industrialized states to the Depression was to erect high tariff walls to protect jobs. Japan, particularly dependent on international trade, was hit hard. At a time when Japan was feeling the pressure of the high tariff barriers around the world, China began an effort to counter Russian and Japanese influence in Manchuria, which China considered its territory. Japanese interests were quite extensive; Manchuria accounted for some 40 percent of Japan's foreign trade and investment at the time.[36] In reaction to the increased flow of Chinese people into the area, as well as anti-Japanese propaganda and incidents, the Japanese army took matters into its own hands. In 1931, manufacturing an incident involving the dynamiting of a Japanese-controlled railroad track, the army moved to clear Manchuria of Chinese troops and establish complete control.

The League of Nations urged China and Japan to restore normal relations, and took great pains to avoid taking sides on the issue. Eventually, almost a year and a half after the Japanese invasion, the League called for an autonomous Manchuria under the control of China, as well as safeguards for Japanese interests there. When the report was adopted, the Japanese delegation walked out and announced that Japan was resigning from the League. The incident set an unfortunate precedent for the League, and the United States did not help the situation. Speeches were made and warnings given, but it was obvious to the Japanese, especially because the United States had never joined the League, that American resistance to Japan's actions would go no further. Obviously, words alone did not convince the Japanese to withdraw from Manchuria.

The next challenge to the League of Nations came from Italy. In 1922, Benito Mussolini came to power. He benefited almost immediately from the general worldwide economic advance, and by 1929, he could claim that he had put an end to inflation and reduced unemployment. However, Italy, like Japan, suffered during the Great Depression. The underlying immobility and rigidity of the Italian economy under fascism was to prove a matter of first-rate importance for the rest of the world. The international depression deprived fascism of its only real claim to material success, and Mussolini's regime was politically weak.[37]

In 1935, Mussolini attacked Ethiopia, and the League of Nations responded initially with surprising forcefulness. Italy was officially branded the aggressor, and the League voted to institute an embargo of arms, ammunition, and implements of war against Italy. But this embargo was never effectively enforced, partly because the United States refused to cooperate with the League. Britain and France, the most important states within the League, were apparently motivated by the fear that strong action against

Italy might drive Mussolini into the arms of Hitler. They still hoped at this point that Italy might be an ally against Germany if the need arose. So Britain allowed all the Italian military forces and equipment to pass unchallenged through the Suez Canal. By June 1936, Mussolini proclaimed Ethiopia an Italian province. In December 1937, Italy followed Japan in resigning from the League of Nations, and Mussolini continued his aggressive policies by annexing Albania in the spring of 1939.

If Mussolini killed the League in Ethiopia, Hitler buried it, along with the Versailles peace treaty. First, he violated the disarmament provisions of the Versailles treaty. Then, in March 1936, he occupied the Rhineland, which according to the peace settlement, was supposed to be a demilitarized zone. At this early stage, Germany's military strength was quite modest, and it is clear that Hitler would have had to back down in the face of any substantial resistance. But he met virtually no resistance at all. The German troops simply marched in behind blaring bands; there was no battle order whatsoever.[38]

Munich Agreement
Negotiated settlement in 1938 in which Great Britain and France agreed to cede to the ethnically German Sudetenland to Hitler's Germany.

In 1938, Hitler officially incorporated Austria into the Third Reich. Later that year, he began to demand a solution to the problem involving the people of German ethnic background who lived in a part of Czechoslovakia known as the Sudetenland. At a meeting in southern Germany in September, the British and the French gave in to Hitler's demands, under threat of military action. In the **Munich Agreement,** Czechoslovakia was forced to cede to Germany 11,000 square miles of territory containing all the fortifications in the Czech defense line. The loss of territory left the country helpless. By April 1939, Hitler had absorbed the rest of the Czechoslovakian state into his empire. Yet Hitler was still not satisfied. There was one more territorial change that he considered necessary. On September 1, 1939, Germany attacked Poland in an effort to bring about that change. Britain and France responded this time, having pledged to protect Poland from the same fate as Czechoslovakia. The Second World War was under way. The Policy Choices box summarizes the debate over how to respond to Hitler's demands in 1938.

The Second World War

The Second World War was the most lethal international conflict in the history of the world, and it set the stage for international politics for the rest of the twentieth century. One of the crucial turning points in the process that led to the war involved a contest between Germany and the Western democracies of Britain and France for an alliance with the Soviet Union.

From the beginning, the Western powers seemed to have a better chance than the Germans of obtaining the Soviets' signature on a treaty. Ideologically, the British and French democracies were hardly compatible with the Soviet Union, but neither were they as unremittingly hostile as Nazi Germany. And the Soviet Union had an old score to settle with

ISSUE: What would you have done, if you were in British Prime Minister Chamberlain's position in 1938, with Hitler making demands about bringing ethnic Germans together into the greater German state? Germany claimed that German ethnic minorities were being abused and repressed in the Sudetenland of Czechoslovakia, thus giving an air of legitimacy to his demands. In hindsight, it is easy to see that Hitler was actually bent on dominating all of Europe, and Chamberlain has forever been saddled with the negative term "appeasement." Appeasement has come to mean the failed policy of giving in to the demands of those who will stop at nothing. But at the time, the situation was complex, information was often scarce and unreliable, and the prospect of facing another major conflict in Europe less than twenty years after "The Great War" (World War I) was far from appealing. Did Chamberlain show weakness, only to encourage further demands from Hitler, or were his actions a reasonable choice given the reality of the time?

Option #1: Britain should have stood firm against increasing German demands.

Arguments: (a) Hitler had written Mein Kampf by the mid-1920s, revealing the magnitude of his racism and the scope of his malevolent ambitions. This should have revealed his deeper intentions. Against such an actor, stiff resolve rather than negotiation is required. (b) Regardless of Hitler's intentions, Britain could clearly see a rising power emerging in Germany. In order to remain strong, Britain should have balanced against that power no matter what the specific motivations of Germany or its leaders. (c) Britain was in a position of leadership in the international system. Its sacrifice of parts of Czechoslovakia to Germany only weakened the resolve of other powers at the time.

Counterarguments: (a) Governments are extremely complex. One could not predict that Hitler's attitudes would determine the overall course of events, anymore than knowing President G. W. Bush's attitudes could have predicted the 2003 war in Iraq. (b) Britain was in no military position to confront Germany; agreeing to German demands on Czechoslovakia bought time for Britain and France to better prepare militarily. (c) Great Britain could not have prevented the events of World War II alone, and the other major powers—such as the U.S. and Russia—could not or would not have supported a British confrontation of the Nazi regime in 1938.

Option #2: Britain should have tried to secure a peaceful resolution, at virtually any cost.

Arguments: (a) War is an extremely bloody and horrible thing—killing soldiers and civilians alike. Statesmen should take *extraordinary* steps to prevent something so catastrophic, even if it means giving in on important demands. (b) Hindsight is 20/20. The magnitude of the eventual outcome should not blind us about the quality of the decisions that Britain made at the time. People and governments should not be so easily judged by those who already know the outcomes. (c) Czechoslovakia was not the first, nor will it likely be the last, country to be sacrificed to satisfy the interests of greater powers. Such sacrifices have at times prevented an even larger war from occurring.

(continued)

Counterarguments: (a) "Peace at any price" means the strong can do what they want and the weak will suffer what they must. War is horrible, but peace without adequate protections of the powerless is not a better option. "Peace" should not have meant selling out the Czechoslovakian government. (b) The eventual war should have been predictable, given the information that was available at the time. Weariness of warfare, lack of military preparedness, and insufficient allies drove Britain's decision making, simply delaying the inevitable conflict. (c) Winston Churchill, who would follow Chamberlain as Prime Minister of Great Britain, clearly saw the shortcomings of appeasing Hitler, stating that ". . . a disaster of the first magnitude has befallen Great Britain. . . ." Even if Hitler's intentions were not fully clear, prominent politicians, such as Churchill, saw the Munich agreement as a sham.

the Germans. The terms of the treaty reflected Lenin's desperation to get out of the war. When the Soviets dropped out of the First World War, their departure was formalized by the Treaty of Brest-Litovsk, which they signed with the Germans. Russia gave up 32 percent of its population, or 56 million people. The territory Russia lost contained 73 percent of its iron ore, 89 percent of its coal, and 33 percent of its railway mileage. In addition, Russia agreed to pay Germany an indemnity of 6 billion marks. Thus, in the 1930s, the Soviets felt that some revision of boundaries and

Germany's Hitler (here represented by German Foreign Minister von Ribbentrop, far left) and the Soviet Union's Stalin (middle) signed a nonagression pact in 1939. Also present was the Soviet Commissar for Foreign Affairs Molotov (far right).

(AP Photo/AP Images)

spheres of influence was desirable. Hitler did not seem likely to allow such revisions; perhaps with the help of the Western powers, the Soviets could bring them about.

Despite the advantages the British and the French had, the Germans won the contest. In August 1939, the **Nazi-Soviet Pact,** in which the Soviet Union and Germany agreed to divide up Poland, was announced. What brought the two dictatorships together? In retrospect, Hitler's motives were quite obvious. Given his actions during the war, one may surmise that he never gave up his idea of acquiring *lebensraum* (living space) in the east. And he knew that his planned attack on Poland might involve him in a war with Britain and France, especially if the two could count on a Soviet ally. Once the Nazi-Soviet Pact was signed, Hitler did not have to worry that his attack on Poland would lead him into a two-front war, and he could hope that without a Soviet ally, Britain and France would refrain from serious opposition to his Polish venture. Even as he signed the pact with the Soviets, Hitler almost certainly knew that he would someday violate it.

The motives of Joseph Stalin, who rose to power after Lenin's death in 1924, are not quite as easily discerned as Hitler's. It is clear that Stalin was reluctant to sign a pact with the Western powers, because he doubted their willingness to abide by it in the event of a German attack on the Soviet Union. He suspected that both Britain and France might be happy to see the Nazis and the Communists engage in prolonged bloodletting. Furthermore, France and Britain were unable to get Poland to agree to allow Soviet troops onto Polish soil if Germany attacked Poland. This heightened Stalin's suspicions that the pact proposed by the West was a ruse designed to bring about war between Germany and the Soviet Union. Finally, Stalin, like Hitler, was worried about a two-front war. Germany's ally, Japan, was much on Stalin's mind as he signed the pact with Hitler.

If Stalin's plan was to stay out of world war, it seemed to work for a while. By agreement, both the Germans and the Soviets moved against Poland, which ceased to exist as an independent entity. According to their treaties with Poland, the British and the French declared war on Germany. Hitler's initial successes in the ensuing months were spectacular. It took him a little over two weeks to defeat Poland. Denmark, Norway, Belgium, the Netherlands, and, most surprising, France fell in quick succession. After one year of fighting, Hitler seemed invincible and well on his way to adding Great Britain to his list of victims. But Great Britain's resistance proved more substantial than Hitler had planned and may have influenced him to make the decision that ultimately led to disaster: He decided to attack the Soviet Union.

To some extent, the decision was a strategic gamble on Hitler's part. His idea was that once he had defeated the Soviet Union, he could turn the full force of his military might against the British, finally accomplishing the victory that so far had eluded him. At bottom, however, Hitler's

Nazi-Soviet Pact An August 1939 agreement between Germany and the Soviet Union in which both countries agreed to remain neutral toward each other, to divide up Poland, and to allow Soviet annexation of the Baltic states.

decision to forsake his attack against the British seems to have been an ideological one. Fifteen years earlier in *Mein Kampf* he had written:

> And so we National Socialists take up where we broke off six hundred years ago. We stop the endless German movement toward the south and west of Europe and turn our gaze toward the lands of the East. . . . When we speak of new territory in Europe today we must think principally of Russia and her border vassal states. Destiny itself seems to wish to point out the way to us here. . . . This colossal empire in the East is ripe for dissolution, and the end of Jewish domination in Russia will also be the end of Russia as a state.[39]

Hitler's attack on the Soviet Union, like Napoleon's on Russia in 1812, was a disaster. The Soviets managed to hold off the German onslaught until the harsh Russian winter became an ally of sorts to the Russian army, disrupting Germany's lines of supply and subjecting German troops to freezing temperatures and weather conditions with which they were not equipped to deal. That alone might have been enough, in the long run, to be Hitler's undoing. But just about the time the German troops began to have trouble in the Soviet Union, one of Germany's allies took the step that ensured the premature dissolution of Hitler's so-called 1,000-Year Reich.

The Germans did not have previous knowledge of Japan's attack on **Pearl Harbor,** nor did they approve of it. Rather, they had hoped that Japan would be menacing enough to keep the United States out of the European war. They did give assurances to the Japanese government that if it became involved in a war with the United States, it would have the support of Germany. But these assurances were apparently calculated only to encourage the Japanese to assume a menacing posture toward the United States, not actually to attack it.

Pearl Harbor   A 1941 Japanese attack that surprised and severely damaged U.S. naval forces, leading to the U.S. entry into World War II.

Japan's motives were largely economic. Japan needed a new source of oil, especially after the United States put an embargo on U.S. oil exports to Japan in August 1941. The most convenient alternative source for the Japanese was the Dutch East Indies (now Indonesia), but to capture these oil fields, the Japanese fleet would first have to neutralize the Philippines, at that time a U.S. colony. The Japanese idea was to deliver a punishing blow to the United States at Pearl Harbor, then resist the U.S. counterattack so vigorously and persistently that the United States would tire of the struggle and allow the Japanese to keep the gains in China, Southeast Asia, and Indonesia that they felt were necessary to sustain their economy. From the Japanese point of view, the United States had expressed unreasonable opposition for years to their economic and political expansion in East Asia.

The Japanese plan did not work. The productive and military power of the United States eventually overwhelmed Japan, especially when the Americans added nuclear weapons to their arsenal. Similarly, the Germans, having already suffered a grievous blow in the Soviet Union, found themselves totally unable to withstand the combined weight of the Russians from the East and the Americans from the West. By the end of 1945, both Japan and Germany were occupied countries. (Italy had fallen in 1943.)

The Impact of the Second World War

Aside from the total defeat of the three challengers to the international status quo, probably the most important impact of the Second World War on the global political system was the subsequent emergence of two **superpowers,** the United States and the Soviet Union. When Germany attacked the Soviet Union in 1941, there was a widespread expectation that Soviet resistance would be short-lived. When these expectations were proved wrong, and the Soviets defeated the Germans, their true strength came to the light.

superpowers   After the Second World War, the two dominant countries in the global political system: the United States and the Soviet Union.

The emergence of a **bipolar** world in which two states had the preponderance of power was especially dramatic in comparison with the fate of Europe. The fall of Europe had begun in the First World War, but this fact was at least partially hidden by the withdrawal of the United States into isolationism and the revolution in the Soviet Union. After the Second World War, the only European state with credible pretensions to great power status was Great Britain. But within two or three years of the war, Great Britain's pretensions were shown to be unwarranted. It was no longer able to fulfill its previous global ambitions and responsibilities: By 1947, India had gained its independence, to be followed by Ceylon (now Sri Lanka) and Burma (now Myanmar), and British withdrawal from Greece and Palestine. Europe, the center of world political power for at least 300 years, gave way to a more global competition for power.

bipolar   When most power in the international system is divided between two states.

Theoretical Perspectives on the History of Global Politics

Each of the theoretical perspectives presented in Chapter 1—realism, liberalism, idealism, neo-Marxism, constructivism, and feminist perspectives—looks at the history of international relations through a different lens and hence focuses on different time periods and the meaning and importance of historical events to our current understanding of global politics. Moreover, each perspective employs history as evidence to support its arguments.

Realism, for example, uses the history of relations among the Greek city-states as portrayed in Thucydides' account of the Peloponnesian War to show that the pursuit of power is a constant feature of international relations. The Peace of Westphalia and the development of sovereign states is the time period that is most important for realism, as the anarchical system it established is what leads states to follow their interests by maximizing their power. Because of the modern state system that developed at this time, the great powers of the eighteenth century engaged in balance-of-power politics. This balancing continued in the nineteenth century, and realists point to the relative peace that was maintained during the Concert of Europe in their argument that balance-of-power politics is not only natural but can produce stability. The age of imperialism is also important for realism, because it extended the European system of sovereign states to the rest of the globe. In the early twentieth century, realists point to the failed experiment with the League of Nations in the interwar years as evidence against idealist notions that value-based institutions can constrain states from pursing their interests. Finally, realism sees the rise of the Cold War following World War II and the astounding shifts in the balance of power as furthering the argument that power and the balance of power are the critical concepts for understanding international relations.

Although liberalism argues that the most important developments in international history occurred in the second half of the twentieth century (the subject of the next chapter), there are some parts of earlier times that are relevant to the liberal perspective. The French and American revolutions, for example, championed the idea of political democracy, which, for liberalism, is important in that it allows substate actors to constrain states from engaging in conflict and push states into entering cooperative agreements. The growth of world trade under the British gold standard and the age of imperialism is also important for liberalism as it laid the seeds for economic interdependence that would mature in the twentieth century. Finally, liberals often point to the history of the 1930s as evidence that economic conflict, in the form of tariffs and other trade barriers, can create the conditions, such as the rise of Hitler in Germany, that lead states to war.

The democratic ideals that spawned the French and American revolutions in the eighteenth century are also important to idealism. The political and social rights articulated in the constitutions and other writings of that period are the historical origins of modern conceptions of human rights. The heyday of the idealist perspective came later, between the wars of the early twentieth century. Blaming balance-of-power politics and the Concert of Europe alliance system for the horrors of World War I, idealists, including Woodrow Wilson, called on states to pursue values such as democratization and national self-determination. Even though realists would blame idealist thinking for World War II, idealists use World War II as a historical example of the need for values to guide states' behavior. Using only interest-based calculations, modern idealists argue, might lead states to ignore the genocidal acts of leaders like Hitler.

The history of international relations is most important for the neo-Marxist perspective, which is more consciously historical in its view of global politics. This perspective argues that it is impossible to understand the nature of the current world economic system without an account of the historical development of the global capitalist system, beginning in the age of imperialism. According to advocates of this approach, this integration into the global economic system dominated by Europe was disastrous for the long-run future of the peripheral areas outside Europe. They became trapped in a role in the international division of labor that was fraught with difficulties. Thus, according to this perspective, the historical events of the sixteenth to early twentieth centuries created the economic and political dependency that continues today in the former colonies.

Constructivism and feminism are not as connected as the other theoretical perspectives to the history of global politics. They do, however, offer alternative interpretations of historical events and developments. Because constructivism is focused on society, important historical turning points involve dramatic changes in the nature of international society. As different actors communicate with one another, they begin to develop different ideas and discourses that construct the nature of international relations. The relative isolation of the Greek city-states, for example, provides for a very different social context than does the relative interdependence associated with the modern era. As each international society constructs both actors and interests, international relations will depend on the exact nature of that society. Indeed, constructivists might argue that historical changes in international relations have really been less about the distribution of power than the distribution of ideas. Take, for example, the idea of a "state." Clearly, territory, armies, wealth, and resources existed prior to the Treaty of Westphalia and the formal development of things called "states." Yet the creation, modification, and reinforcement of the concept of states through time by the society of international actors dramatically changed the course of international relations. States were constructed, and international relations were transformed.

The feminist perspective analyzes any given historical event and development by asking two questions: What role did women play that traditional historians have ignored, and what effect did this have on women? The rise of the modern state and capitalism, for example, had powerful effects on how gender was conceived and on gender relations:

> In the transition from feudalism to early states, smaller household/domestic production predominated and . . . "production and family life" for most people were inseparably entwined. . . . In this context of social production within patriarchal households, wives were subordinated but hardly "dependent"; their work was essential to the survival of the unit and to that extent respected. Gradually, the industrialization process removed labor and resources from the household, and the site of "production" shifted to the factory. The structural and ideological separation of "family," "economy," and "politics" was clearly a gender differentiated process with far-reaching consequences including devaluing "women's work" and shaping gender conceptions to associate women with "homemaker" and men with "worker."[40]

In this way, the rise of the modern state and modern economic relations would affect the way women would be allowed to participate in global politics and how global politics would be understood.

SUMMARY

- In ancient times, international relations operated very differently. For much of the world's history, empires dominated relations between various actors. Within empires, there was an overarching authority: the imperial center. Between empires, there was little notion of independence and noninterference. A notable exception occurred in ancient Greece, where city-states related to each other in much the same way that sovereign states relate to each other today.

- The modern state and the modern international system emerged after the Thirty Years' War with the Peace of Westphalia in 1648. With this agreement, the overarching authority of the pope in Christendom was replaced by the notion of sovereign states, and in the eighteenth century, European states operated on the balance-of-power principle.

- States came to dominate the international system in a process marked in the seventeenth and eighteenth centuries by religious divisions and the evolution of long-distance economic transactions, as well as related technological developments that provided central governments with greater power. The French Revolution introduced nationalistically inspired armies to international politics.

- Nineteenth-century European relations were relatively stable. The period known as the Concert of Europe was absent of total war between the major states, partly due to Britain's rise as the most powerful state and its policy of playing the balancer between other states.

- From the sixteenth to the early twentieth centuries, the major European states and eventually other powers colonized and in other ways dominated much of the rest of the world, making the capitalist economic system as well as the system of sovereign states global.

- The foundation for the modern international system was laid in the First World War, which arose out of a confrontation between Germany and Austria-Hungary, on the one hand, and Russia, France, and Great Britain, on the other. The war served to enshrine democracy and national self-determination as values in international politics. It weakened the major powers of Europe.

- In the interwar period, France was intent on crippling Germany so that it could never rise again. This effort failed, partly because terrible inflation at the beginning of the 1920s, coupled with the Great Depression in the late 1920s and early 1930s, helped create conditions favorable to Adolf Hitler's rise to power. Italy and Japan joined Hitler's Germany in an assault on the international status quo in the late 1930s. This assault was halted only by the Second World War, which weakened Europe further and led to the emergence of the United States and the Soviet Union as twin superpowers.

• Each of the major political perspectives uses different parts of the history of international relations to advance their claims about global politics. Realism concentrates on the development of the sovereign state and the anarchical international system. Realism also points to the balance-of-power principle that seemed to operate among the ancient Greek city-states and the major powers in eighteenth- and nineteenth-century Europe. Liberalism focuses on the historical origins of democracy and economic interdependence, and idealism on the failure of the balance-of-power system and the recognized importance of international institutions designed to further the value of peace. Neo-Marxism focuses on the development of the international capitalist system and its division of labor with a core and a periphery; constructivism, on important historical turning points involving dramatic changes in the nature of international society; and feminism, on the effects of the development of the modern political and economic structures for women and conceptions of gender.

KEY TERMS

Greek city-states   25
empires   25
Peace of Westphalia   28
balance of power   30
nationalism   31
Congress of Vienna   31
Concert of Europe   31
Triple Alliance   35
Triple Entente   35

national self-determination   37
Treaty of Versailles   39
Great Depression   41
Munich Agreement   43
Nazi-Soviet Pact   46
Pearl Harbor   47
superpowers   48
bipolar   48

CHAPTER 3

The Modern Era

International relations in the second half of the twentieth century serves as the immediate backdrop to contemporary global politics, characterized by ethnic and religious conflicts, nuclear proliferation, terrorist threats, and globalization. Understanding the Cold War, decolonization, and changes in the international economy of this period is critical for understanding today's and tomorrow's global landscape. Contemporary history is also illustrative of alternative theoretical perspectives because these focus on different aspects of the modern era and offer contrasting interpretations of its historical development.

The Origins and Early Years of the Cold War

The post–World War II period began with high hopes. Leaders from around the world convened in Bretton Woods, New Hampshire, in 1944 to design international economic organizations that they hoped would rebuild the war-torn economies and avoid another economic depression like the one experienced in the 1930s. The International Monetary Fund and the World Bank were two of the organizations that came out of this initiative. The leaders of fifty-one states also convened in San Francisco in 1945 to create the United Nations. The primary purpose of the United Nations was to help states resolve conflicts of interest peacefully and avoid war. With these new initiatives, there seemed to be great promise that a new global order could be established. In fact, a new order would emerge over the next few years, but it was one that was largely unexpected and unwelcomed. Perhaps it was inevitable that at the climax of a gigantic struggle such as the Second World War, the settlements and agreements arrived at by the victorious coalition would shape the primary conflicts in the years to follow. No matter what these settlements contained, some of the parties would be dissatisfied, and their dissatisfaction would form the basis of future conflicts.

Conflict over Eastern Europe

Perhaps the most heated and important conflict in the months immediately following the war involved Poland and the rest of the Eastern European countries. (Map 3.1 shows how the continent was divided after World War II.) Great Britain, after all, had resorted to war in the first place to ensure the existence of an independent Poland. After the United States entered the war, U.S. President Franklin D. Roosevelt was anxious to protect the interests of the Poles at least partly because of his desire to avoid alienating an important voting bloc in the United States. So both countries began to press the Soviets about the future of Poland well before the Soviets had established their presence in that country. Conflict centered first on which government in exile would be recognized as the official representative of Poland. The British and the Americans favored one group in London, and the Soviets set up another more to their liking.

Map 3.1 Squabbling over Eastern Europe After the Second World War

The roots of the Cold War developed as the Soviets moved into the power vacuum left in Eastern Europe when the Germans retreated at the end of the war.

(© Cengage Learning)

The Soviets had several reasons to be suspicious of the Poles in London. In the years following the First World War, when the Soviets were weak and unable to resist, Poland had taken territory the Soviets considered their own. Mutual suspicions between the Poles in London and the Soviets were solidified by a controversy surrounding the discovery in 1943 by German soldiers of a mass grave for Polish army officers in the Katyn Forest in Russia. The Nazis accused the Soviets of these mass executions, while the Soviets blamed the Nazis. (The Soviets, under Mikhail Gorbachev's influence admitted that Stalin probably ordered the massacre.) The Polish government in exile in London believed the Nazi charges against the Soviets. If there had ever been any chance of compromise between the Poles in London and the Soviets (and it is not clear that there was), this incident certainly undermined it.

Yalta Conference
1945 meeting of Roosevelt, Stalin, and Churchill to discuss the future of Eastern Europe.

The future of Poland and other Eastern European states was one of many topics discussed at a 1945 meeting of Roosevelt, Stalin, and British Prime Minister Winston Churchill at the **Yalta Conference** in the Russian Crimea. One result of this discussion was that Stalin was persuaded to endorse the Declaration on Liberated Countries, which promised free elections and other democratic practices and liberties in Eastern European countries where the Red Army had been victorious over the Nazis.[1] Roosevelt's acceptance of this promise was to provoke controversy in the years following the war, because Stalin, from the U.S. point of view, did not keep his promise. Elections were not held in Poland until 1947, and even then they were not what the Western powers considered the free and unfettered elections that had been promised in the Yalta declaration. The outcome in Poland would soon be seen in the rest of Eastern Europe, as the Soviet Union began to dominate the governments of Czechoslovakia, Hungary, Bulgaria, Romania, Albania, and East Germany.

Critics of Roosevelt charged that the U.S. president must have been incredibly naive to accept Soviet promises with regard to Eastern Europe after the Second World War and that his acceptance paved the way for a Communist takeover in these countries. In support of such critics, it must be said that there is good evidence that Roosevelt was more optimistic during the war about the prospects for U.S.-Soviet postwar cooperation than subsequent events proved was warranted. But it is important not to overlook the basic, if obvious, fact that at the time Roosevelt accepted Stalin's pledge concerning free elections in Eastern Europe, the Soviet Union had troops there, and the United States did not. A refusal by Roosevelt to accept Stalin's word on the matter might have put a serious strain on a coalition that was never entirely solid. Roosevelt was particularly concerned that the Soviets join the United States in the upcoming assault on Japan, which, in the days before an atomic bomb had been successfully exploded, was expected to be very difficult. In retrospect, of course, we know that the United States did not need help against Japan. But Roosevelt did not have the benefit of this hindsight.

In any case, the Soviet satellization of Eastern Europe was an important step toward the Cold War with the United States. But the view that the Cold War was a result of aggressive Soviet actions in Eastern Europe and elsewhere is hotly disputed. Several U.S. writers, for example, argue that Soviet policies in Eastern Europe were essentially defensive and that it was U.S. hostility toward the Soviets that was primarily responsible for the onset of the Cold War.[2] This controversy essentially turns on the question of which country took the actions that precipitated the Cold War conflict. Defenders of the United States point to Bolshevik propaganda against the Western nations from the earliest days of the Russian Revolution, the Soviet Union's control of Eastern Europe (including the Soviet-engineered coup against the democratically elected government in Czechoslovakia in 1948), its refusal to remove its troops from Iran in 1946, its pressure on Turkey for access to ports, and its blockade of the western sectors of Berlin in 1948 as evidence of Soviet hostility. Defenders of the Soviet Union, in contrast, point to the invasion of the Soviet Union by several Western states (including the United States) in an attempt to dismantle the revolutionary government in the years when it was struggling to survive, the U.S. delay in opening the western front against German forces, the U.S. preference for a strong, unified Germany (which the Soviets, as well as the French, saw as a threat), and the establishment in 1949 of the first postwar military alliance in Europe, the **North Atlantic Treaty Organization** (NATO), as evidence of American hostility.

It is difficult to say who started the Cold War (and alternative explanations are discussed in Chapter 6), but it is clear that by 1949, the Allies of the Second World War had divided Europe along an **"iron curtain,"** in British Prime Minister Churchill's words. The Soviet Union would develop its own atomic bomb in 1949 and would form its own military alliance, the **Warsaw Pact,** in Eastern Europe in 1955 in response to West German reunification. Germany itself would remain divided until the end of the Cold War in 1990.

North Atlantic Treaty Organization (NATO) Military alliance established in 1949 among the United States and West European states.

iron curtain Term coined by British Prime Minister Churchill referring to the Cold War division of Europe.

Warsaw Pact Military alliance established in 1955 among the Soviet Union and East European states.

The British Retreat and the U.S. Policy of Containment

The global power of the nineteenth century, Great Britain, was still in control of much of its possessions around the world, and although the British were not defeated in the Second World War, it soon became obvious that they had been severely weakened politically and economically. As a result, they were forced to pull back from areas of the world where they had previously exerted influence or control. In the British retreat from global leadership, power vacuums were created, and none was filled without conflict. In 1947, Britain pulled out of its colony India, sparking conflict between the Hindu majority and the Muslim minority that continues today. In 1948 the British pulled out of Palestine. This area had been the scene of civil strife between Jews and Arabs from the time the British had been given a League of Nations mandate to rule the region after the First World War.

Also about this time, Britain announced to the U.S. government that it could no longer support the government of Greece, then under attack by rebels, some of whom were Communists. President Truman decided to take over British responsibilities there, but the decision concerning Greece was embedded in and overshadowed by a decision of much wider application: the decision to institute the policy of **containment.** Henceforth, Truman announced, "It must be the policy of the United States to support free peoples who are resisting attempted subjugation by armed minorities or by outside pressures."[3] If this did not mark the beginning of the Cold War, it was at least an official pronouncement of it. From this time on, there was no doubt as to which country in the West was going to lead the struggle against the Soviet Union. The United States had decided not to return to the days of "splendid isolation" when it tried to stay out of world politics. Instead, it would head the new alliance and seek to contain the Soviet Union.

The U.S. containment policy was designed to thwart any future expansionist moves by the Soviet Union. In the minds of U.S. policymakers, given Soviet actions in the early years after the Second World War, the nature of the Communist political system, and the nature of the bipolar international system, aggression by the Soviets was inevitable. Containment was about demonstrating U.S. resolve to meet and resist the Soviets. To do so, containment required a U.S. military presence in Europe as well as economic aid to strengthen the economies of allies. The **Marshall Plan** was an aid package to war-torn Europe designed for this purpose. It aimed to prevent Communist parties from coming to power in Western Europe and to bring the economies of Western Europe firmly into the capitalist fold of the world economy dominated by the United States. The Marshall Plan in particular and containment policy in general were born in Europe and first applied to the conflict between the United States and the Soviet Union in the European region. It did not take too long, however, for the policy of containment and the Cold War to become global.

The Cold War in Asia

Eastern Europe was certainly not the only sector of the globe where victory by the Allies in the Second World War would lead to conflict between the United States and the Soviet Union in the Cold War. A broadly similar process took place in China. The Japanese had taken over large areas of that country during the war, pushing the Nationalist, conservative government of Chiang Kai-shek farther into the hinterland. In the meantime, the Communists, under Mao Zedong, took advantage of the Japanese invasion to strengthen their organization. The Japanese tended to concentrate on the cities as they took over Chinese territory, leaving the peasants in the countryside more or less on their own. The

containment U.S. foreign policy strategy instituted after World War II to prevent Soviet expansion.

Marshall Plan Aid package to war-torn Western Europe designed to strengthen the area's economies and prevent Communist parties from coming to power.

Communists moved into this breach, organizing the peasants, carrying out some land reform measures, and generally strengthening this important part of their power base.

When the Japanese evacuated the country, the stage was set for the culmination of the struggle between Mao and Chiang. Despite considerable financial aid and free advice from the United States, Chiang was unable to quash the Communist rebellion, and in 1949, he was forced to flee to the island of Taiwan. The People's Republic of China was proclaimed on October 1 of that year. Although Mao first tried to maintain independence from the Soviet Union, Communist China and the Soviets would sign an alliance treaty in 1950. The United States would assume for many years that Mao was a puppet of the Soviet Union and supported the Taiwan government as the legitimate representative of the Chinese people. Economic and military support for Taiwan would become part of the U.S. containment policy in Asia. Politically, the United States backed Taiwan's bid to control the Chinese seat on the United Nations Security Council, against the wishes of the Soviet Union.

Just as in China, the defeat of the Japanese created conditions conducive to conflict in Korea, which had been formally annexed by Japan in 1910. In the final days of World War II, the Soviet Union and the United States came to an agreement that the Soviets would accept the surrender of the Japanese troops to the north of the thirty-eighth parallel, while the Americans would accept a similar surrender south of that parallel. The agreement was carried out by both sides without serious problems. But problems soon developed. The Americans and the Soviets ruled their zones separately, and by 1948, North Korea and South Korea had become, in effect, two separate states. Border tensions between the two halves were constant; each side threatened to liberate the other, and while the Americans armed the South, the North received military aid from the Soviets.

In June 1950, North Korea invaded South Korea.[4] The motives for this invasion have been the topic of lively speculation. There is widespread agreement that the North Korean government was heavily influenced by the Soviets and therefore, the Soviets must have known about and approved the North Korean invasion plan. But why? At the time, the Americans and West Europeans were fearful that the attack was a diversionary tactic that Stalin adopted to pin down the United States in Asia so that he could move against Western Europe. Later, with the benefit of hindsight and knowledge of the conflict between Communist China and the Soviet Union, some observers surmised that the Korean War was Stalin's scheme to get the United States and the Chinese into a prolonged land war in Asia, thus weakening both. In his memoirs, Nikita Khrushchev insisted that the invasion was the brainchild of North Korean premier Kim Il Sung, who managed to convince Stalin that the South Koreans would greet the northerners as liberators, thus ensuring an easy, quick victory for the North.[5] Stalin also must have been influenced by the announcement of Secretary of State Dean Acheson on January 12,

1950, that Korea was outside the defense perimeter of the United States. Stalin was, finally, justifiably confident that the North Koreans would be able to defeat the South Koreans unless the latter got outside help.

Whatever the motivation, the attack by the North Koreans met with immediate success. With the U.S. and South Korean defenders rapidly reaching desperate straits, the United States, seeing the conflict as the first test of the new containment policy, urged the United Nations to resist the invasion. According to the UN Charter, the international community was supposed to collectively respond to the violation of state borders with a coordinated military response if necessary, and the Korean conflict provided the Security Council, the UN's highest authority, with its first test for the newly created United Nations. The UN's response to get involved was ensured by the great influence of the United States in the organization and by the absence of the Soviet Union from the Security Council. (The Soviets were temporarily boycotting the council to protest its exclusion of Communist China.) Eventually the United States and sixteen other nations sent additional troops to Korea and managed to halt the progress of the North Koreans.

In fact, the success of the UN forces (of which the U.S. contingent was by far the largest)[6] was so substantial and relatively easy that it brought about a change in U.S. policy in the middle of the war. When the intervention began, Acheson had explained that the UN troops were in Korea solely for the purpose of restoring the Republic of Korea to its status prior to the invasion from the North.[7] But as the UN forces moved up the peninsula, the temptation to bring about a more permanent solution to the problem posed by the North Korean government proved decisive. Instead of merely pushing the North Koreans back into their own territory, the UN troops moved to unify all of Korea by force. The U.S. government and General Douglas MacArthur, who commanded the UN forces, strongly believed that the Chinese would not intervene, despite Chinese warnings to the U.S. government that they would not allow UN troops to eliminate the North Korean government next to their border.[8]

But the Chinese did intervene, with immediate and dramatic success. Only after many months of hard fighting were the Chinese forced to halt their advance. As the war dragged on, its unpopularity in the United States grew, and the presidential election of 1952 resulted in the victory of Dwight Eisenhower, who promised to end the conflict. The new president did manage to bring about an armistice, partly by threatening to use nuclear weapons, which ended the fighting in July 1953 but did little or nothing to solve the problems that had fueled the conflict in the first place. Korea remains divided into two states today.

Another consequence of the Korean conflict was the further deterioration of relations between the United States and Communist China. This was due in part to the assumption by policymakers that the Communist bloc of the Soviet Union and Mao's China was monolithic. Although the two states did have ideology in common, the alliance between the Soviets and the Chinese had, in retrospect, several powerful forces working against it. Relations between the Chinese and Russian empires had been unfriendly since the sixteenth century. And the fact that the Chinese have for centuries regarded their country as the Middle Kingdom—that is, at the center of the civilized world and surrounded by "barbarians"— must have made it difficult for them to accept another country's leadership even under the best of conditions.

By 1956, doctrinal disputes between the Soviets and the Chinese began to arise. At the Twentieth Party Congress in 1956, in the same speech in which he denounced Stalin, Khrushchev announced that there was no inevitability of war between the Communist and capitalist worlds. From Khrushchev's viewpoint, this modification of Leninist doctrine was a reasonable compromise in the face of possible worldwide nuclear destruction. To the Chinese, it smacked of inadmissible timidity. In October 1957, Mao Zedong made a speech at an international Communist conference in Moscow in which he emphasized dogma. He talked of the "east wind prevailing over the west wind" and insisted that even if the capitalist imperialists did plunge the world into nuclear war, only they would be banished from the face of the earth; the socialists would survive. About a year later, the Chinese began what appeared to be an attempt to take over the Taiwanese-controlled offshore islands of Quemoy and Matsu. From the Chinese perspective, the Soviets refused to back up these efforts with sufficient vigor. Convinced, perhaps, of the recklessness of their allies, in June 1959, the Soviets renounced an earlier agreement to help the Chinese develop their own atomic weapons.[9] Sino-Soviet relations deteriorated rapidly from that point, and in 1960, Soviet advisers left China, and Soviet aid to China stopped. In 1969, the two Communist states engaged in military conflict in border clashes on the Ussuri River.

Decolonization and Regional Conflict in the Cold War Context

decolonization
Process in which colonies became independent from imperial powers.

The end of World War II also brought about the end of the age of imperialism. Following the war, the process of **decolonization,** in which the imperial powers voluntarily gave up or were forced to give up their colonial possessions, began. Syria, Lebanon, and Palestine, for example, which had been placed under international mandate after World War I, became independent. Britain's retreat from its status as a global power brought independent states on the Indian subcontinent and in Africa. Eventually French and other European colonies in Africa and Asia would gain their independence (see Map 3.2). The result was a dramatic increase in the number of sovereign states in the international system. The number of states almost doubled between 1940 and 1970.

Decolonization was often, although not always, a violent process. Britain's exit from India led to war between the Muslims and Hindus

Map 3.2 Decolonization 1945–1980
(© Cengage Learning)

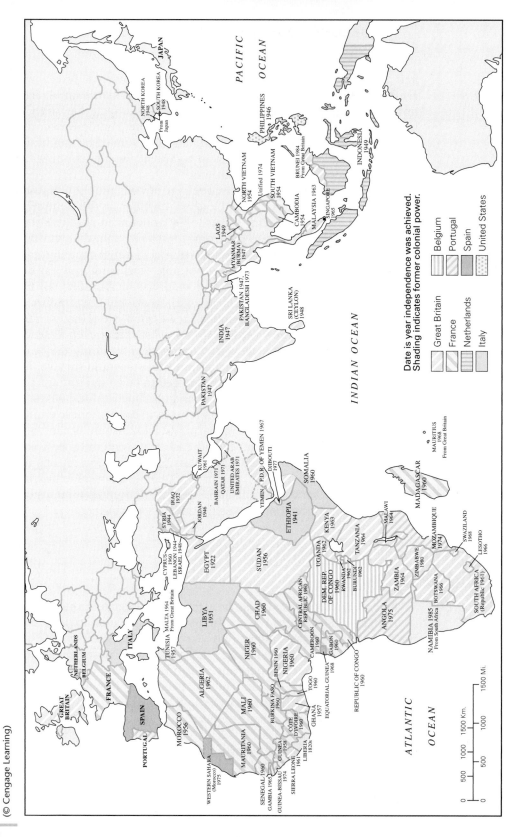

Date is year independence was achieved.
Shading indicates former colonial power.

Great Britain
France
Netherlands
Italy

Belgium
Portugal
Spain
United States

PACIFIC OCEAN

JAPAN

NORTH KOREA 1948
SOUTH KOREA 1948
From Japan

PHILIPPINES 1946

INDONESIA 1949

BRUNEI 1984
From Great Britain

NORTH VIETNAM 1954
Unified 1974
SOUTH VIETNAM 1954
CAMBODIA 1954
MALAYSIA 1963
SINGAPORE 1965
LAOS 1949
MYANMAR (BURMA) 1947

PAKISTAN 1947
BANGLADESH 1973

INDIA 1947

SRI LANKA (CEYLON) 1948

PAKISTAN 1947

INDIAN OCEAN

MAURITIUS 1968
From Great Britain

MADAGASCAR 1960

SOMALIA 1960

KUWAIT 1961
BAHRAIN 1971
QATAR 1971
UNITED ARAB EMIRATES 1971
YEMEN 1967 / P.D.R. OF YEMEN 1967
DJIBOUTI 1977
ETHIOPIA 1941
KENYA 1963
MALAWI 1964

IRAQ 1932
JORDAN 1946
SYRIA 1944
CYPRUS 1960
LEBANON 1944
ISRAEL 1948
EGYPT 1922
SUDAN 1956
UGANDA 1962
TANZANIA 1964
RWANDA 1962
BURUNDI 1962
DEM. REP. OF CONGO 1960
CENTRAL AFRICAN REPUBLIC 1960
ZAMBIA 1964
ZIMBABWE 1980
MOZAMBIQUE 1975
SWAZILAND 1968
LESOTHO 1966

TUNISIA 1957
MALTA 1964
From Great Britain
LIBYA 1951
CHAD 1960
NIGER 1960
NIGERIA 1960
CAMEROON 1960
GABON 1960
ANGOLA 1975
NAMIBIA 1985
From South Africa
BOTSWANA 1966
SOUTH AFRICA (Republic 1961)

GREAT BRITAIN
NETHERLANDS
BELGIUM
FRANCE
ITALY
SPAIN
PORTUGAL

MOROCCO 1956
ALGERIA 1962
MALI 1960
MAURITANIA 1960
WESTERN SAHARA 1975 (Morocco)
SENEGAL 1960
GAMBIA 1965
GUINEA-BISSAU 1974
GUINEA 1958
SIERRA LEONE 1961
LIBERIA 1826
BURKINA FASO 1960
GHANA 1957
CÔTE D'IVOIRE 1960
TOGO 1960
BENIN 1960
EQUATORIAL GUINEA 1968
REPUBLIC OF CONGO 1960

ATLANTIC OCEAN

0   500   1000   1500 Km.
0   500   1000   1500 Mi.

and the establishment of two separate states, India and Pakistan. The French fought a long war in Algeria before that former colony gained its independence and another long conflict in Indochina before an independent Vietnam was established. Many of these conflicts quickly became caught up in the competition between the United States and the Soviet Union. Indeed, the term **Third World** originated during the Cold War and was applied to the states that were not directly part of the United States–Western Europe–Japan alliance (the First World) or the Soviet Union–Eastern Europe alliance (the Second World). The two superpowers, particularly the United States in the early years of the Cold War, would see in the process of decolonization an opportunity to win allies and control strategic areas in the struggle between communism and capitalism. Although many of the new states tried to remain nonaligned, most were eventually aided by either the Soviet Union or the United States. In many of the struggles for independence, one or both of the superpowers became indirectly or directly involved militarily. For the United States, aiding the side in the civil war that was anti-Communist (although not necessarily pro-democratic) was part of the global strategy of containment.

Third World Cold War term for states that were not directly part of the U.S.-led or Soviet-led alliances.

Vietnam

One example of the application of the containment policy in a Third World conflict was in Southeast Asia, in Vietnam. Before the war, Vietnam had been a French colony. It remained officially so even with the Japanese occupation during World War II. Vietnamese nationalists known as the Vietminh had staged uprisings against the French before the Japanese arrived. The Japanese, after their arrival, cooperated with the French in an attempt to stamp out the Vietminh, but by September 1945, the Vietminh were in effective control of the country and issued a declaration of independence. Their reign was short-lived. After the war, the former French colony was divided at the seventeenth parallel, with the northern part of the country becoming the Chinese zone and the southern part the British zone. The Chinese and the British interpreted their mandates to restore law and order in dramatically different ways. The Chinese recognized the de facto Vietminh regime. The British, anxious to establish the principle that prewar colonies be returned to their rightful owners, set about dismantling the Vietminh regime in the South to transfer control of that area back to the French.

The French experienced problems almost from the moment they reassumed control. For the first few troubled years after the war, the United States opposed the efforts of the French, viewing them as dedicated to reimposing an outdated colonial regime and regarding the Vietminh as fighters for national liberation. As late as 1947, President Truman was so opposed to French policy in Vietnam that he insisted that U.S.-produced propellers be removed from British aircraft sent to French troops there.[10] This attitude was to change quite rapidly without any essential change in the war taking place in Southeast Asia. With the increase in tensions between the Soviets and the Americans and the victory of the Communists in China, the Americans by 1950 had come to see the French as defenders of the non-Communist world and the Vietminh as agents of a worldwide Communist conspiracy. Accordingly, the U.S. government began to support the French military in Vietnam economically.

After his election in 1960, President John Kennedy inherited from the Eisenhower administration a commitment to the government of Ngo Dinh Diem in South Vietnam that already involved the presence of some 1,000 U.S. advisers to the South Vietnamese military. When Kennedy's aides recommended that he send 8,000 military troops to Vietnam, he instead sent 15,000 more advisers, who were supposed to avoid actual combat. They did not seem to help the situation substantially, and Kennedy became increasingly convinced that nothing would unless Diem, the Catholic leader of a predominantly Buddhist Vietnam, was replaced. The U.S. government looked the other way when a coup d'état in South Vietnam resulted not only in Diem's removal from office but also in his death. The removal of Diem did not stabilize the government of South Vietnam. Instead, a series of generals succeeded Diem, and the situation deteriorated further. When Kennedy was assassinated, Lyndon Johnson was faced with a problem in South Vietnam that he ultimately found insoluble.

Johnson delayed any serious increase in U.S. involvement during the election year of 1964. Then, in 1965, he became convinced that some forceful response to the deteriorating situation in South Vietnam was necessary, and he committed large numbers of U.S. combat troops. That was the beginning of the escalation by the United States and counterescalation by North Vietnam that ended in disaster for Johnson. His military advisers would request additional troops, and Johnson would grant only half the number requested, feeling that he was following a wise, middle-of-the-road course and not willing to risk losing the domestic support he needed for his programs at home. The air force would submit an ever-expanding list of targets in the North to be bombed, and Johnson would trim that list at least partially, again feeling that his strategy was a moderate, reasonable one. The problem was that no matter how strongly Johnson resisted the pressures from the military, the escalatory trend continued. Eventually, the army wanted 1 million soldiers and Johnson could barely hold the line at 550,000. The reaction from the North Vietnamese was always the same: no movement toward the bargaining table, which the Americans were trying to bring about, and counterescalation through infiltration of more men and supplies into the South. Finally, in March 1968, following months of domestic unrest in the United States and precipitously falling ratings in the public opinion polls, President Johnson announced that he would not seek re-election.

Richard Nixon, who won the presidency in the 1968 election, inherited peace negotiations begun under Johnson and pledged to end U.S.

military involvement in Southeast Asia. Nixon did manage to get a peace settlement, but only after incursions into Laos and Cambodia, a bombing campaign against North Vietnam unprecedented in its scope and intensity, and the deaths of thousands more Americans and Asians. Saigon, the South Vietnamese capital, was taken by Communist forces in 1975, a little more than a year after the settlement was signed.

The Arab–Israeli Conflict

After the Second World War, both the Palestinians and the Israelis claimed the land of Palestine, which had previously been controlled by Turkey and then Britain, as their national right.[11] In the first Arab-Israeli war of 1948, Israel captured all the land that the United Nations had declared would be divided into two—a Palestinian state and a Jewish state (see Map 3.3). The conflict between Jews and Arabs in the Middle East thus began before the Cold War and would continue after the Cold War ended. But this regional conflict, like many others, could not escape the superpower rivalry, and this already complex dispute would be caught up in the dynamics of the Cold War almost immediately after Israel declared its statehood in 1948.

The United States, concerned about containing Soviet influence in the Middle East, saw in the new state a potential strategic ally and was the first state to recognize Israel in 1948. Egypt, the strongest Arab state, was the self-proclaimed leader of the Arab world and coordinated the resistance against Israel. Gamal Abdel Nasser became Egypt's leader in 1954 and looked to both the United States and the Soviet Union for assistance. But when Egypt formed a military alliance with Saudi Arabia, Syria, and Yemen and recognized Communist China in 1956, the United States responded by withdrawing an offer to fund the building of the Aswan Dam there. Nasser, in turn, took control of the Suez Canal away from the British, sparking the **Suez crisis.** Britain, France, and Israel then coordinated an invasion of the Egyptian Sinai, confident of U.S. support. In one of the oddest moments of the Cold War, the United States sided with the Soviet Union and condemned the British, French, and Israeli invasion. After threats from both superpowers, Britain, France, and Israel withdrew. The United States went against its allies in the Suez case because of its anticolonialism policy, its desire to remain on good terms with the oil-rich Arab states, and, equally important, its fear that going against Egypt would drive Nasser into the Soviet orbit. Despite U.S. support of Egypt for this reason, Egypt would turn to the Soviets after the Suez crisis.

"The fear that a pro-Communist Syria would also threaten the adjacent pro-Western regimes of Jordan, Lebanon, and Turkey, prompted Washington to step up military assistance to those states, while American arms supplies flowed into Israel to counter the ominous buildup of Russian weaponry in Egypt."[12]

Suez crisis Cold War confrontation between Egypt, which nationalized the Suez Canal, and Britain, France, and Israel.

Map 3.3   Conflict in the Middle East

The control of territory has been at the center of much of the Arab-Israeli conflict.
Israel's borders have significantly changed from the original UN partition (see inset),
through the Six-Day War, to today.

(© Cengage Learning)

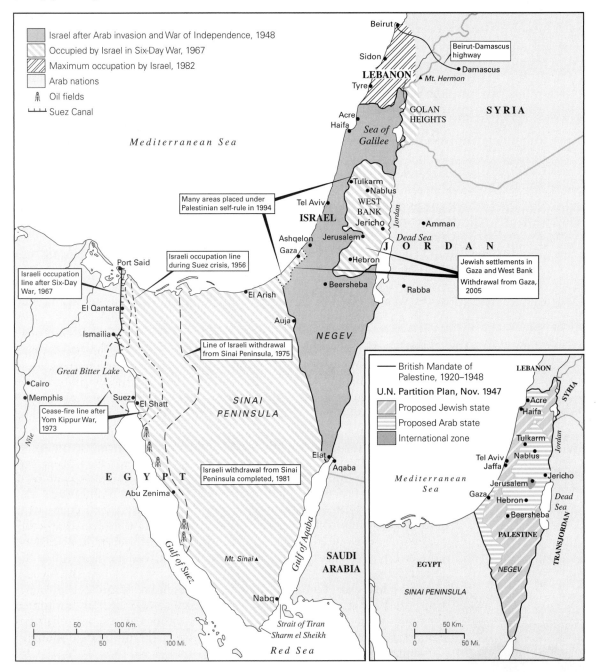

From then on, Middle East tensions would become even more dangerous, always risking the possibility of superpower intervention. In 1958, the United States invaded Lebanon to support an anti-Communist government. In 1967, armed with Soviet weaponry, Nasser threatened Israel, and Israel preempted the attack. The **Six-Day War** has had long-lasting impact as Israel emerged with control over the Egyptian Sinai and Gaza Strip, the Syrian Golan Heights, and the Jordanian West Bank, including Jerusalem. Although they had armed opposing sides, the superpowers communicated to each other in the Six-Day War that they would not get further involved. This commitment would be tested again in the 1973 Yom Kippur War when Egypt and Syria launched a surprise attack against Israel. Again, both superpowers armed their sides, the Soviets threatened to involve its own forces, and the United States put its forces on nuclear alert. Eventually, however, the superpowers backed a United Nations cease-fire and the introduction of UN peacekeeping troops in buffer zones. In 1978, with the signing of the U.S.-brokered Camp David Accords, some of the territorial conflict was addressed. Egypt and Israel agreed to a peace treaty in which Israel would return the Sinai Peninsula to Egypt in exchange for Egyptian recognition of the state of Israel. Most Arab states opposed the Egyptian-Israeli agreement and the other territorial conflicts between Israel and its neighbors, and the issue of statehood for Palestinians remained unresolved through the end of the Cold War.

Six-Day War 1967 conflict in which Israel occupied territories previously controlled by surrounding Arab states.

Other Superpower Involvement in the Third World

Vietnam was not the only Third World country in which the United States was deeply involved. In the early 1950s, the Central Intelligence Agency supported a coup d'état in Guatemala and in Iran. In the 1960s, the United States aided an attempt to overthrow the Cuban government in the Bay of Pigs invasion and intervened with over 20,000 armed personnel in the Dominican Republic. The pattern of intervention in these countries was largely the same: The United States saw nationalists or Communists as a threat to allied governments and feared that not doing something to support their allies would lead to an expansion of the Soviet sphere of influence and a perception of American weakness on the part of the Soviets that would encourage further Communist expansion. Short of invasion or coups, the United States would support friendly governments around the globe militarily and economically in an effort to contain Soviet influence. States such as Israel, South Africa, Pakistan, Iran, and Nicaragua became America's client states, and were supported allies in the Cold War struggle.

Although the Soviet Union did not militarily involve itself in the Third World to the extent that the United States did (however, it did use force against its own "allies" in Hungary in 1956 and Czechoslovakia in 1968), it did become involved in the race for patron states, particularly by the late 1960s and early 1970s. Soviet support to Egypt, Cuba, Somalia, and India would ensure that in each region of the world, conflicts that may have begun even before the Cold War became part of the superpower competition. Even if the roots of most these conflicts lay in the process of decolonization or regional rivalries and not in the Cold War, the money and arms that supported the sides certainly intensified and probably prolonged these conflicts. These **proxy wars,** in which the United States and the Soviet Union supported opposing sides, became part of the landscape of the Cold War. Because one or both of the superpowers were usually involved in these regional conflicts, the United Nations failed to operate as its architects had hoped. Collective security could not be achieved because each superpower had the opportunity to prevent UN action. Instead, the United Nations turned to peacekeeping operations in which military personnel were introduced into a region after a cease-fire had been negotiated.

proxy wars Conflicts in which the United States and the Soviet Union supported opposing opposite sides.

Changes in East-West Competition

Despite superpower involvement in proxy wars and regional competition, the Cold War remained "cold"—there was never any direct military confrontation between the two main belligerents. The Cold War did, however, undergo some dramatic transformations during its course. In particular, technological developments rendered the competition for military power, so important to more traditional wars, a stalemate. By the late 1960s, **nuclear parity** had been achieved. Because the Soviet Union and the United States had roughly equal capacity to destroy each other, the consequences of actual conflict reached doomsday proportions. This, and the proximity to war that the superpowers approached during the Cuban missile crisis, sparked reconsideration of the rivalry and a significant relaxation of tensions in the 1970s, only to be renewed again in the 1980s and up until the final days of the Cold War.

nuclear parity A balance of nuclear capabilities.

Two Cuban Crises

The Kennedy administration's 1,000 days were marked by several dramatic events in international affairs. One was the invasion of Cuba at the Bay of Pigs in 1961. The plan for this invasion originated in the Eisenhower administration shortly after Fidel Castro assumed power. The invasion was carried out by a small number of Cuban exiles who were financed, organized, and led into combat by agents of the Central Intelligence Agency (CIA).[13] It was assumed that the invasion would spur massive numbers of Cubans who were opposed to Castro to active rebellion. It did not, because there was poor coordination between the invading forces and the Cuban anti-Castro underground, and almost certainly because there was less opposition to Castro than the CIA had supposed. The total failure of the invasion was ensured when President Kennedy decided not to approve overt and substantial support for the effort by the U.S. Air Force.

The Bay of Pigs fiasco, along with the construction of a wall between East and West Berlin by the government of East Germany, set the stage

Cuban missile crisis 1962 superpower confrontation over Soviet attempt to place nuclear weapons in Cuba.

for the **Cuban missile crisis** in 1962. The Soviets had hoped to slip missiles into Cuba secretly in order to prevent another attempt by the United States to overthrow their Communist ally.[14] The United States discovered the missiles as they were being built and put a naval blockade into effect to prevent the Soviet Union from delivering more missiles. Kennedy might well have firmly resisted this Soviet move in any case, but his opposition was stiffened by the fear that having denied air support to the Bay of Pigs invaders and having failed to take effective action against the construction of the Berlin Wall, he could not acquiesce in the secret shipment of missiles to Cuba without leading Khrushchev to believe that the United States would not actively resist other bold moves on the part of the Soviets.

In the end, the Soviets backed down, turning around ships headed for Cuba with additional missiles and agreeing to remove those already in Cuba. Although neither the American people at the time nor any others outside high government circles in the United States and the Soviet Union were aware of this secret arrangement, "it appears . . . that the withdrawal of [American] Jupiter missiles from Turkey in the spring of 1963 was indeed part of a private deal that led to the withdrawal of the Soviet missiles from Cuba in November, 1962."[15] Khrushchev put the best possible light on the affair, arguing that his primary aim was the defense of Cuba and that because in return for the removal of the missiles, he had obtained a promise from the United States not to attack the island, his aim was accomplished. "The Cuban missile crisis has assumed genuinely mythic significance. . . . [It] represents the closest point that the world has come to nuclear war."[16]

Détente

The Cuban missile crisis produced a desire on the part of the United States and the Soviet Union to "peacefully coexist" and take steps to avoid nuclear war. In 1963, the "hot-line agreement" established direct communications between the White House and the Kremlin. By the end of the 1960s, both sides had reached the conclusion that serious arms control negotiations were in their interests.

These negotiations, known as the Strategic Arms Limitation Talks (SALT), produced an agreement to limit the number of intercontinental ballistic missiles that each side could have and was signed during President Nixon's trip to the Soviet Union in 1972. This was the high point of **détente,** or relaxation of tensions, with the Soviet Union.

détente Period of relaxed tensions between the United States and the Soviet Union during the Cold War.

At the same time, Nixon was pursuing détente with China.

Nixon journeyed over twenty thousand miles in February 1972 to become the first American president in history to set foot on Chinese soil. After several days of intensive negotiations, . . . the two governments issued a joint communiqué in the city of Shanghai. . . . This declaration candidly recorded the differences that continued to separate the United States and China. . . . On a positive note, both governments agreed to foreswear the pursuit of "hegemony" in East Asia as well as to oppose any other nation's efforts to that end (an unmistakable warning to Moscow).[17]

The Shanghai communiqué also established economic and cultural ties between China and the United States.

Rapprochement with China was particularly dramatic and significant because formal diplomatic communication between China and the United States had been almost nonexistent for more than two decades.

What brought about the sudden improvement in relations between Nixon, known for his rigid, vigorous anticommunism, and the leaders of China and the Soviet Union? Certainly, the most important factors contributing to the improvement in relations both between the United States and the Soviet Union and between the United States and China included the continuing conflict between the two Communist states themselves and their rising military-industrial might. As Henry Kissinger, Nixon's chief foreign policy adviser, observed in his memoirs, "China's cautious overtures to us were caused by the rapid and relentless Soviet military buildup in the Far East. . . . That China and the United States would seek rapprochement in the early 1970s was inherent in the world environment."[18] The conflict between the Soviet Union and China led both countries to fear isolation from each other and from the United States. This made both amenable to any move by the United States to improve relations. In turn, the United States could not view the rising power of these two great Communist states with equanimity, especially if there were to be continued antagonism with them.

The Rebirth of the Cold War

Détente between the United States and the Soviet Union was short-lived. The latter half of the 1970s was marked by what some observers referred to as a rebirth of the Cold War, although relations between Western Europe and the Soviet Union continued to improve on many fronts. Some architects of foreign policy in the United States were undoubtedly put into a belligerent mood by the fall of Saigon to the Communists in 1975. This mood was not improved when in the same year, Angola achieved independence from Portugal in an armed struggle joined by Soviet-supported Cuban troops.

Still, Jimmy Carter came into the presidency in 1976 vowing to cut defense expenditures. He left that post in 1980 in the wake of a campaign based on the promise of significant *increases* in the defense budget, as well as condemnations of his Republican predecessors for allowing previous budgets to shrink to dangerously low levels. Obviously, something had happened to change Carter's view of relations between the United States and the Soviet Union rather drastically. The election of 1980 resulted in a victory for Ronald Reagan, who was even more enthusiastic than Carter about strengthening the country's defenses. Many U.S. voters apparently were more concerned about the Soviet threat and less concerned about escalating defense budgets than they had been not too many years before.[19]

Perhaps the increasing distance in time from the painful experience of Vietnam made Americans more inclined to flex their military muscle. Events in Iran also had an important impact on American perceptions about the U.S. role in the world. First, in January 1979 the shah of Iran, whom the CIA had played a crucial role in restoring to power in 1953, was deposed, to be replaced by a revolutionary government headed by the Ayatollah Ruhollah Khomeini. The shah had been one of the more reliable allies of the United States in a strategically important area of the world for almost two decades. His fall contributed to an impression that the United States was losing its grip on the drift of world affairs. That impression was reinforced when another long-time ally, Anastasio Somoza, was overthrown in Nicaragua in July 1979 by a coalition of forces that contained some undeniably anti-American elements. Finally, U.S. feelings of impotence were heightened dramatically when Iranian students took ninety people hostage in the U.S. embassy in Tehran in November 1979, and the U.S. government could not secure their release for 444 days.

One can argue persuasively that none of these problems was created by military weakness on the part of the United States, and one can claim even more convincingly that significant increases in nuclear capabilities were irrelevant to their solution. But when the Soviet Union invaded Afghanistan in December 1979, proponents of such arguments were quite noticeably rare. President Carter announced that the invasion had been an important educational experience for him with regard to his attitude about the Soviets. He retaliated by imposing an embargo on grain shipments to the Soviet Union and boycotting the 1980 Olympics in Moscow. He also declared that the invasion of Afghanistan had created the most dangerous threat to peace since the Second World War.

In retrospect, that invasion can be seen as the beginning of a period of tense relations between the United States and the Soviet Union. Antagonism between the Americans and the Soviets was fueled by actions on the part of both superpowers that may well have been defensive from their respective points of view but looked aggressive to their counterparts. From the Soviet vantage point, the operation in Afghanistan was meant to protect socialism in that country and perhaps stem the tide of Islamic fundamentalism so visible in Iran and so threatening to continued control of Islamic elements in the Soviet Union. In 1983, when the Soviets shot down a Korean airliner (en route from New York to Seoul) filled with civilian passengers as it flew over Soviet territory, the Soviets claimed that they were protecting themselves from a provocative spy mission. Americans viewed the act as barbaric. In the atmosphere created by that incident, the United States began to deploy new intermediate-range missiles in Europe in 1983, and the Soviets broke off arms talks with the Americans.

From the Soviet point of view, President Reagan was unpredictable and often aggressive in the early years of his administration. He referred to the Soviet Union as the "evil empire." He significantly increased the U.S.

defense budget, even in the face of massive budget deficits. He ordered an invasion of the tiny Caribbean island of Grenada in 1983. He waged covert war against the Sandinista government in Nicaragua. Perhaps of greatest concern to the Soviets, he insisted on pushing ahead with the development of the Strategic Defense Initiative (SDI), or Star Wars as it came to be called, designed to prevent nuclear war by providing the technological means to knock incoming missiles out of the air before they hit their targets.

Changes in the International Economy and the Rise of Interdependence

The end of U.S. involvement in Vietnam and U.S. détente with the Soviet Union and China occurred at the same time that changes in the international economy were becoming evident (see Chapter 10). Until the 1970s, the United States had occupied an obviously dominant position in the international economic system. By 1971, however, Western Europe and Japan competed with the United States on much more equal terms economically. Problems in the U.S. economy, stemming in part from the Vietnam War, reinforced the trend away from U.S. dominance. When President Nixon announced in 1971 that the United States would no longer automatically convert dollars into gold, the whole international economic system set up after the Second World War was suddenly deprived of one of its key supports. By 1973, the U.S. dollar was basically allowed to "float" against other currencies of the world, and the "fixed" exchange rate system that had been established at the Bretton Woods conference was essentially abandoned. In principle, this meant that each country could now attempt to exercise control over the value of its currency, and thereby influence its imports, exports, and the likelihood of attracting foreign money for investment. In practice, however, this has proved difficult, and countries often find their currencies rising or falling depending on a wide variety of international factors over which they have little control.

Organization of Petroleum Exporting Countries (OPEC) Organization of developing countries whose economies rely on oil export revenues.

The early 1970s was also an economically volatile period due to activities undertaken by the **Organization of Petroleum Exporting Countries (OPEC)**. In 1973, OPEC successfully quadrupled the price of oil, causing a significant economic transformation that shook the foundations of global economics once again. Suddenly huge sums of money were passing from the economically wealthy regions of the world to previously economically poor regions of the world. With this change in the distribution of wealth came changes in international trade and finance. Moreover, because oil is not just a product but a vitally important element of both economic and military security, there was a dramatic shift in terms of thinking about international security. The Cold War had clearly demarcated the United States and the Soviet Union as the principal actors on the world stage, each vying for some advantage over the other. But as rising petroleum prices squeezed the industrial capacities of the superpowers, attention was shifted away from bipolarity and toward a greater appreciation of economic interdependence. Indeed, both of these shocks to the system—the abandonment of the fixed exchange rate system and the rise of OPEC—highlighted the interdependence of the economies of the richer countries. It became obvious that political and economic decisions in one industrialized society could have dramatic consequences for all the others.

The rise of economic interdependence by the 1970s was in part due to the increase in international trade to unprecedented levels. The trading regime that the United States and its allies had established after World War II worked to bring down political barriers to trade and expand the exchange of goods across borders. Related to this development were the multinational corporations, which did business in more than one country (see Chapter 4). By the 1970s, these corporations were large in number and size and connecting the economies of many states together in complex ways. Despite the economic turmoil of the 1970s, the increase in trade and multinational business seemed to be benefiting the wealthier states. This was not true for the developing world, at least those without oil. Although there had been great hopes after decolonization that these new states would follow the path of economic development of the United States, Europe, and Japan, this did not happen for most (see Chapter 11). Indeed, by the 1970s, it was clear that the gap between the wealth in the developed world and the wealth in the developing world was growing. And in addition to severe poverty, many states were facing serious internal and external security threats, complicated by the superpower competition. At the time, the developing world, encouraged by the success of OPEC, banded together in the United Nations to call for fairer economic relations. Indeed, the developing world was able to use the United Nations to promote economic and social development issues at the same time the Security Council was largely ineffective because of the Cold War. By the end of the 1970s, however, the economic situation in the developing countries had worsened, and political tensions among them hampered efforts at collective attempts to renegotiate economic relationships with the wealthier states.

In addition to a recognition that the world was more economically interdependent, the 1970s brought a recognition of the environmental interdependence of the world (see Chapter 13). In 1972, the United Nations held its first conference on the environment in Stockholm, Sweden. This was an important meeting in that it raised the awareness of environmental problems, such as air and water pollution, although significant international efforts at solving environmental challenges did not take place after the end of the Cold War.

The End of the Cold War

It is instructive to remember how grim international politics looked by the middle of the 1980s and how much change occurred in the ensuing decade. By the end of 1988, the United States and the Soviet Union had

Intermediate-Range Nuclear Forces (INF) Treaty   1988 agreement between the United States and the Soviet Union to dismantle a whole category of nuclear weapons.

agreed for the first time to dismantle a whole category of nuclear weapons, in an agreement formalized in the **Intermediate-Range Nuclear Forces (INF) Treaty.** That was widely expected to be a first step toward a strategic arms reduction treaty (START) that would call for significant reductions in strategic weapons by both superpowers (see Chapter 8). Toward the end of his term in office, President Reagan had several cordial summit meetings with his Soviet counterpart. The eight-year war between Iran and Iraq finally ended in 1988. The Soviets pulled their troops out of Afghanistan. The Cubans pulled their troops out of Angola. The Sandinistas in Nicaragua lost an election and allowed a peaceful transfer of power to their opponents.

There is little doubt that the most dramatic political events in the late 1980s and the first half of 1990s took place in the Communist world. A decade of reforms in China culminated in massive prodemocracy demonstrations in Beijing in the spring of 1989. Those demonstrations were firmly repressed, and many of the leaders of the prodemocracy movement were jailed or executed. But as a result of reforms instituted in the late 1970s and early 1980s in the wake of the crackdown at Tiananmen Square, China's economic output and exports grew faster than either India's or the Soviet Union's and even more rapidly than those of the well-known economic superstars in its neighborhood: Taiwan, South Korea, Singapore, and Hong Kong (see Chapters 10 and 11).

The young man standing in front of Chinese tanks on Tiananmen Square became symbolic of popular resistance to the Chinese regime during demonstrations there in June of 1989.

(© Bettmann/Corbis)

Gorbachev Soviet leader who initiated political, economic, and foreign policy reforms, leading to the end of the Soviet Union and the Cold War.

perestroika Russian term referring to Gorbachev's restructuring of the economy.

glasnost Term referring to Gorbachev's political reforms for greater openness.

The story in the rest of the Communist world (when it was Communist and afterward) was virtually the mirror image of that in China. In Eastern Europe, and especially in the Soviet Union, dramatic strides toward political liberalization and democracy coincided with equally dramatic economic deterioration. Mikhail **Gorbachev** came to power in 1985 and put into effect his policies of ***perestroika*** and ***glasnost***—the former referring to market-oriented economic reforms, the latter to political

A demonstrator pounds away the Berlin Wall as East Berlin border guards look on from above the Brandeburg Gate. The destruction of the Berlin Wall symbolized the end of the Cold War.

(REUTERS/David Brauchli/Landov)

reforms in the direction of greater openness and democratization. The political reforms certainly did decrease autocratic controls, but the economic reforms never achieved anything like the Chinese successes.

Gorbachev instituted an equally profound revolution in foreign policy, especially in Soviet relations with its erstwhile satellites in Eastern Europe. "In 1989," according to one historian, "while the nations of Western Europe celebrated the bicentenary of the French Revolution, the nations of Eastern Europe reenacted it."[20] In that year, a long process of liberalization in Poland culminated in open parliamentary elections, and other states were soon to follow Poland's lead. As the *Los Angeles Times* observed in the wake of the 1989 revolution in Eastern Europe, "It took 10 years in Poland, 10 months in Hungary, 10 weeks in East Germany, and 10 days in Czechoslovakia."[21] By the end of the year, the regime of Nicolae Ceauşescu in Romania had also been overthrown. By 1991, even the long-isolated regime in Albania was liberalizing in various ways. In October 1990, East and West Germany were unified in one Federal Republic of Germany, and in 1991, the Warsaw Pact was officially disbanded. The Cold War was over (see Map 3.4).

Map 3.4   Europe (1991) After the Disintegration of the Soviet Union
(© Cengage Learning)

The consequences of the end of the U.S.-Soviet rivalry became quite evident when Iraq attacked Kuwait in August 1990. The attack led the United States to lead a coalition of states against Iraq and eventually evict it from Kuwait. What made the operation historic was the cooperation of the United States and the Soviet Union in the framework of the UN Security Council. Throughout its history, the United Nations had been largely ineffective at responding to aggression because in almost every instance, the United States or the Soviet Union supported opposite sides in the conflict and thus one of the superpowers would veto UN action against its ally. After months of negotiations among Security Council members, the Soviet Union agreed to support the operation against Iraq, with which it previously had a close relationship. To those who were part of the coalition, it seemed that the United Nations was finally working the way it was designed, prompting U.S. President George H. W. Bush to declare that a **new world order** had emerged.

new world order Term used by U.S. President George H. W. Bush to describe the new political structure of the world at the end of the Cold War.

Political reform in the Soviet Union came to a screeching halt in August 1991, when a group of high-level conservative Communists in the party, the army, and the KGB (the Soviet intelligence and security agency) deposed Gorbachev and began to restore the old system. But Boris Yeltsin, a reformist leader who had withdrawn from the Communist Party and established legitimacy by winning a free election for the presidency of the Russian Republic, took the lead in resisting the coup attempt, which collapsed under the combined pressures of popular resistance and its leaders' incompetence and indecision. By the end of 1991, not only was the Communist Party of the Soviet Union deprived of its power; the Soviet Union itself dissolved, to be replaced by its constituents, fifteen formerly Soviet Socialist republics, such as Russia, Ukraine, and Tajikistan.

Political reforms in the Soviet Union and Eastern Europe seemed to have a kind of demonstration effect, encouraging emulation around the world. Throughout the 1980s, military dictatorships were replaced by more democratic regimes in Latin America.[22] In Asia outside the People's Republic of China, a trend toward democracy in the 1980s and early 1990s was visible in Taiwan, South Korea, the Philippines, Nepal, Mongolia, and Bangladesh. In 1991, one informed observer in Africa declared that "after decades of unspeakable repression at the hands of authoritarian regimes, Africans stand at the threshold of a new epoch. Across the continent, millions are demanding freely elected legislators, an independent judiciary and an accountable executive."[23] The Middle East has not been fruitful ground for democratic reforms, but even there, Turkey and Pakistan moved in a democratic direction in the 1980s, King Hussein of Jordan instituted a series of liberalizing reforms, the newly unified Yemen showed some signs of moving in a pluralist direction, and Algeria's socialist regime moved toward multiparty elections (which were, however, postponed indefinitely in 1991).

Overall, from the early 1970s to 2006, the number of democratic states in the world increased from about forty to almost ninety, with more than fifty additional states moving in a democratic direction. In 1973, about half of the people in the world lived in states with regimes that could be classified as "free" or "partly free." By 2009, that proportion had increased to a little over three-quarters.[24]

Figure 3.1 shows the trend toward democratization since 1950. "In the 1980s and 1990s, the world made dramatic progress in opening up political systems and expanding political freedoms. Some 81 countries took significant steps toward democracy. . . ."[25] Nevertheless, this trend toward democratization may be tenuous and reversing. Many states "that took steps towards democracy after 1980 have since returned to more authoritarian rule: either military, as in Pakistan since 1999, or pseudo-democratic, as in Zimbabwe in recent years. Many others have stalled between democracy and authoritarianism, with limited political freedoms and closed or dysfunctional politics."[26] Recent anti-democratic trends can be seen in countries worldwide, including Nigeria, Russia, Thailand, Venezuela, Bangladesh, the Philippines, and Kenya.[27] In the Middle East, non-democratic regimes are well-entrenched and "steps toward democracy in the Arab world . . . are slowing, blocked by legal maneuvers and official changes of heart."[28] Many partly democratic states, including Russia and many other former Soviet republics, are increasingly seeing Western efforts at promoting democracy as interference in their internal affairs.[29] Efforts to promote democratization are discussed in Chapters 6 and 7.

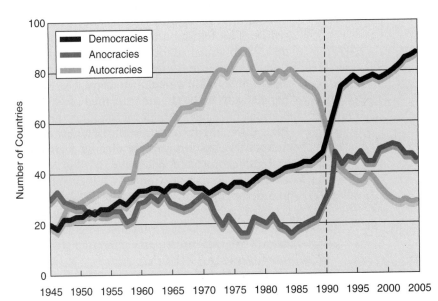

Figure 3.1 Global Regimes by Type, 1950–2006

Anocracies are countries with governments in the mixed or transitional zone between autocracy and democracy.

Source: Reprinted with permission from Amy Pate, "Trends in Democratization: A Focus on Instability in Anocracies," in PEACE & CONFLICT 2008 by J. Joseph Hewitt, Jonathan Wilkenfeld, and Ted Robert Gurr, Boulder: Paradigm Publishers 2008. (p. 27)

Center for Int'l. Dev. & Conflict Mgmt

The Post–Cold War World: Challenges to Sovereignty

The optimism from the political, economic, and security developments in the late 1980s and early 1990s quickly sobered in the face of ethnic conflict, nuclear and terrorist threats, and the disintegration of states by the beginning of the twenty-first century. The world economy is also struggling with the effects of rapid globalization. Many of these issues and the national and international responses to them have led some to question the future of the sovereign state as the distinction between domestic politics and international politics increasingly blurs. Indeed, some have suggested that global politics may be entering a "post-Westphalian phase" in which sovereign states are not the primary way the international system is organized. The outcome of this potential reorganization, however, is quite uncertain.

Ethno-Religious Conflict and Failed States

The bloody, seemingly endless dissolution of Yugoslavia and the murderous war among the Serbians, the Croats, the Muslims, and Kosovars did much to diminish post–Cold War euphoria. For years, the international community, whether in the form of the United Nations, NATO, or the European Union, seemed impotent and sometimes incompetent in the face of interminable warfare between and within the republics in the former Yugoslavia. Civil war first erupted in 1991, when Croatia and Slovenia declared their independence. The international community eventually recognized them as sovereign states, and the old Yugoslavia was dead. War then turned to Bosnia, where, during the course of more than three years, more than 200,000 people would lose their lives, and brutal violations of human rights occurred. The conflict eventually erupted in Kosovo and Macedonia. In the Kosovo conflict, NATO resorted to force in the spring and summer of 1999 with a bombing campaign of Serbia. Although the wars in most of Yugoslavia ended in negotiated agreements, the future stability of the area remains uncertain, particularly when the peacekeeping forces leave.

What made the ethnic strife in the former Yugoslavia especially disheartening was that such conflict was not isolated to the Balkans. Ethnic and religious groups—groups that perceive themselves to be culturally distinct—in South Africa, Burundi, India, Egypt, Mexico, and Azerbaijan also were emersed in brutal conflict. In Rwanda in 1994, political and ethnic violence between the Hutu and Tutsi groups resulted in more than 800,000 deaths. In a three-month period, more than 5,000 people a day were massacred, leaving one-tenth of the people in the country dead. Ethnic strife played a key role not only in the dismantling of Yugoslavia but also in the breakup of the Soviet Union. Although ethnic conflicts did increase in number and intensity after the end of the Cold War, this is part of a longer-term trend since the 1950s of rising ethnic violence.

This trend has recently shown signs of changing, as the high number of ongoing conflicts may have peaked in the 1990s.[30]

Still, ethnic and religious conflict inside countries and across their borders remains a feature of the contemporary global political landscape. Tensions between Hindus and the Muslim minority in India remain high, with periodic associated violent events. In Sri Lanka, the twenty-six year civil war between the Tamil minority fighting for autonomy and the Sri Lankan government escalated in violence as government authorities claimed a military victory over the rebels. In 2008, Russia launched a full-scale invasion of Georgia in support of ethnic separatists in the enclaves of South Ossetia and Abkhazia. In China, tensions between the Turkic-speaking Muslim Uighurs and Han Chinese (the dominant ethnic group in China) erupted in violence in 2009. In the Middle East, the Israeli-Palestinian conflict continues. The end of the Cold War helped establish limited Palestinian control over the Gaza territory and parts of the West Bank, but the final status of key territories remains unresolved and violence between Palestinians and Israel persists. In Iraq, fighting between Sunni and Shia Muslims added to conflict already present between the U.S. military, the insurgents fighting against their presence, and foreign groups joining them. By 2006, Iraq was on the brink of full-scale civil war, despite the presence of U.S. troops.[31]

In Darfur, a region in western Sudan, the conflict between rebel groups, drawn from some of the region's non-Arab ethnic groups, and government-backed militias (known as the "Janjaweed"), composed from several small Arab nomadic tribes, has brought devastating results. Since the current conflict began in 2003, the Janjaweed have attacked the civilian population living in Darfur, and an estimated 300,000 people have been killed, thousands have been raped, and 2.5 million refugees have fled their homes. The United States has called the killings an act of genocide, and the International Criminal Court has issued arrest warrants, charging Sudan's president and rebel leaders with war crimes. Despite the signing of a peace agreements, and the presence of an African Union-United Nations peacekeeping force, the situation remains dire today.[32] The Sudanese government had objected to the peacekeeping mission, citing concerns for state sovereignty.

The ethnic and religious conflict occurring in the post–Cold War era is particularly destructive and intractable for many reasons. First, it is occurring in some of the poorest regions in the world, in states with little legitimacy, and in states with no stable framework on which to build. Most disturbing, many of these conflicts are not simply political fights to win control of the state, but fights where the only acceptable outcome to all sides is to rid the area of the others' presence, one way or the other. Hence, there is not even any pretense of following traditional rules of war, such as those pertaining to the distinction between civilians and military personnel. In many of these conflicts, the fighting is not carried out by traditional military forces, but by undisciplined, highly autonomous groups of fighters, making negotiations difficult, if not impossible. Causes and potential solutions to ethnic conflict in global politics will be discussed in more detail in Chapter 7.

Internal conflict between ethnic and religious groups is one of the most important causes of failed states, but it is not the only one.[33] States need a viable political framework to function effectively. There have been a number of failed states or states on the verge of failing, such as Somalia and Haiti, where no governing power is clearly in charge. This type of instability in the post–Cold War period usually occurs in states experiencing ethno-religious conflict, in states where the superpowers have pulled out their support and left a power vacuum, and in states that are so economically devastated that stability is impossible. In such cases, food shortages, refugee crises, or significant human rights violations may ensue. **Failed states** may also arise after military interventions. In both Afghanistan and Iraq, following U.S.-led interventions and regime change, there have been significant challenges to establishing legitimate political authority and internal security. Failed, or failing, states are problems for the international community.[34] "Although the phenomenon of state failure is not new, it has become much more relevant and worrying than ever before. In less interconnected eras, state weakness could be isolated and kept distant. Failure had fewer implications for peace and security. Now, these states pose dangers not only to themselves and their neighbors but also to peoples around the globe. Preventing states from failing and resuscitating those that do fail are thus strategic and moral imperatives."[35] There are economic consequences as well. The recent piracy in the Indian Ocean is directly connected to the failed state of Somalia.

The challenge for the international community, if it gets involved is separating the internal factions, constructing a legitimate political framework, and carrying out this work in a way that gives some chance to the newly constructed state. The United Nations, at its creation in 1945, rejected this kind of mission, indicating that internal wars in sovereign states were out of its jurisdiction. In many instances, that is exactly what the UN and member states such as the United States have recently attempted to do. There has developed in the international community more concern for the internal conditions of states, particularly human rights conditions, and more action has been taken to address these conditions (see Chapter 9). Examples include NATO's intervention in Kosovo, the arrest of political and military leaders for war crimes committed in the former Yugoslavia, Rwanda, and Liberia, and U.S. interventions and state-building policies in Haiti, Somalia, Afghanistan, and Iraq. There is also a growing consensus that military operations alone are doomed to fail without accompanying diplomacy, reconstruction and economic development. According to one analyst, "we are all nation builders now."[36] Such interventions in the domestic affairs of states, however, are inconsistent with the Westphalian conception of state sovereignty and may suggest a dramatic change in global politics.

failed states Unstable countries with no clear functioning government.

Security Threats

The celebration of several successful arms reduction agreements between the United States and the Soviet Union (and later Russia) after the Cold War was accompanied by concerns over new security threats. **Nuclear proliferation,** or the spread of nuclear weapons into the hands of more actors, became an important issue on the global agenda in the 1990s. India and Pakistan, rivals in South Asia, both joined the "nuclear club" when they conducted nuclear tests in 1998. North Korea became a nuclear power when it tested a nuclear bomb in 2006, despite years of diplomacy and sanctions to prevent it. Concerns about Iraq's potential to develop and deploy nuclear weapons led to the creation of UN inspections of Iraq's military facilities, and Iraq's resistance to those inspections led to U.S. attacks in the late 1990s and eventually a U.S.-led intervention into Iraq in 2003. The Policy Choices box summarizes the significant international debate over the intervention. Iran has also been part of the nuclear proliferation debate. Although Iran insists its nuclear activities are only for peaceful, energy purposes, other countries remain unconvinced.

nuclear proliferation
Spread of nuclear weapons into the hands of more actors.

In addition to concerns about nuclear weapons, fears of the spread of biological and chemical weapons have surfaced. Although most states have signed treaties that ban the use of such weapons, several states have not signed the treaties and some that have signed nevertheless maintain stockpiles of them. Chemical and biological weapons are relatively attractive to poorer, developing countries because they are cheap to produce and fairly easy to hide, making the proliferation of them very difficult to track. This concern has been heightened recently now that more states have ballistic missile capability, allowing them to hit targets with conventional or unconventional (chemical and biological) bombs. The potential threat from suspected Iraqi stockpiles of chemical and biological weapons was another stated reason for the U.S.-led intervention in 2003.

The proliferation of nuclear and other weapons of mass destruction (discussed in more detail in Chapter 8) has implications for state sovereignty. The first, a more practical question, concerns how states go about preventing proliferation. As the situations in Iraq, Iran, and North Korea demonstrate, states resist interference in their sovereignty. The second question is more fundamental. Given the development of such destructive capability, is sovereignty more important than the international interest in preventing the development and possible use of such weapons?

Terrorist threats also highlight the potential change away from state-centered conceptions of global security. Targeting civilians for political purposes by non-state actors is not a new phenomenon. Yet, the number of terrorist attacks has increased in the twenty-first century. Contemporary terrorist groups, such as Al Qaeda, are quite transnational, with membership and coordinated attacks in a number of countries. The attacks of September 11, 2001, on the World Trade Center and the Pentagon in the

ISSUE: In late 2002 and early 2003, the international community, particularly the UN Security Council, was faced with the question of how to deal with Iraq and its possible weapons of mass destruction programs. The following arguments divided the international community *at the time* and continue to surface in the debate over whether the United States should have initiated military intervention as it did in March 2003. Since the invasion, additional questions regarding the integrity of the intelligence on pre-war Iraq and the effectiveness of post-war planning and occupation have entered the debate over the intervention in Iraq.

Option #1: Regime change should occur through the use of military force.

Arguments: (a) Iraq and its leader, Saddam Hussein, represented a grave security threat to its neighbors and the rest of the world. Iraq resisted disarming itself of the capabilities to build weapons of mass destruction, and its past actions demonstrated its willingness to commit aggressive acts. (b) Iraq was a "rogue" state that had been or was likely to support terrorist networks like Al Qaeda. Changing the regime in Iraq would have helped dismantle the support network for such groups and addressed the post-September 11 global terrorist threat. (c) It was important for the control of Iraqi oil to be in the hands of a cooperative regime, given the importance of this economic asset to the world economy.

Counterarguments: (a) Military intervention was not the only solution to the Iraqi security threat and should have been used only as a last resort. After several years, UN inspectors had returned to Iraq and were making progress in verification and disarmament. There was no imminent threat to justify intervention at the time. (b) There is no known link between Iraq and groups such as Al Qaeda, which historically have been opposed to secular regimes like Saddam Hussein's Iraq. Moreover, military intervention and "occupation" of Iraq would itself likely spark more terrorism. (c) Using military force to acquire needed resources is imperialistic and lacks legitimacy.

Option #2: Military force should not be used.

Arguments: (a) Military intervention in Iraq, particularly with the aim of changing the political leadership and government, represented a violation of the UN Charter and the principle of state sovereignty, the bedrock of international law. (b) Given the ethnic and political tensions within Iraq and between Iraq and its neighbors (Saudi Arabia, Turkey, Iran, Kuwait, and Jordan), military intervention would destabilize an already unstable region, spreading insecurity throughout the region. (c) The human consequences of war (civilian casualties, refugees, economic strife, civil wars that might be sparked) outweighed the potential threat in this case.

Counterarguments: (a) State sovereignty should not be used as a cloak to keep a brutal dictator in power, a leader who himself violated international law and the UN Charter. (b) The Iraqi regime was a central feature of regional insecurity, having attacked Iran in 1980 and Kuwait in 1990. (c) Repressive regimes that maintain power will, if unchecked, create greater suffering and hardship. Declining infrastructure, squandered resources, and persecution of various sectors of society are more devastating on a human level over the long term.

United States heightened attention to this transnational issue and helped to produce a broad coalition of actors dedicated to countering such non-state actor threats. This effort was termed the "global war on terror" by U.S. policymakers, and "has already surpassed the amount of time that the United States fought World War II. And by any measure, it has . . . had a seismic effect on the United States and the entire world."[37] Counterterrorism is a difficult goal, as the terrorist attacks in Madrid in 2004, in London in 2005, and in Mumbai in 2008 demonstrate. And despite all the state power put toward his capture, Osama bin Laden is suspected to still operate part of the Al Qaeda network somewhere along the border between Afghanistan and Pakistan.[38]

How the world copes with contemporary security issues, such as terrorism and proliferation, is affected by the distribution of power in the international system, the policies pursued by great powers, and the reaction to them. In the twenty-first century, the United States sits at a position of economic and military predominance. On almost every dimension of state power (discussed in Chapter 4), the United States dwarfs other actors in world politics. Indeed one analyst refers to the post-Cold War era as the United States' "unipolar moment" and another labels the United States an "überpower."[39]

This position arguably led the United States to pursue unilateral policies, particularly under the leadership of George W. Bush. As the first U.S. president in the new millennium, "Bush had set in motion a revolution in American foreign policy. It was not a revolution in America's goals abroad, but rather in how to achieve them. In his first thirty months in office, he discarded or redefined many of the key principles governing the way the United States should act overseas. He relied on unilateral exercise

Suicide bombers targeted London buses and the subway system, killing over 50 people and injuring more than 700 in July 2005.
(© Peter Macdiarmid/epa/Corbis)

Bush Doctrine Set
of policies proposed by
U.S. President George
W. Bush emphasizing
unilateralism,
preemption, and military
strength.

of American power rather than on international law and institutions to get his way. He championed a proactive doctrine of preemption and de-emphasized the reactive strategies of deterrence and containment."[40] The **Bush Doctrine** encapsulated this change in U.S. foreign policy, proposing that unilateral and preemptive action may be necessary and that U.S. military predominance is critical in the post-September 11 era.[41] Members of the Bush administration also advocated that democratization of the Middle East was feasible and was the best strategy to secure U.S. interests in the region and in fight against terrorism. These views were used by U.S. policymakers to justify intervention in Iraq in 2003.

Much of the rest of the world disagreed with the Bush Doctrine and its application in Iraq. Moreover, many were alienated by what they saw as arrogance in the United States' treatment of others. With the Bush administration's division of the world into those that were with the United States and those that were against it and with the criticism and ostracism of long-time allies when they disagreed with the U.S. approach, the image of the United States suffered.[42] The failure to democratize and stabilize Iraq and charges of prisoners' rights abuses in prisons in Iraq, Afghanistan, and Guantanamo Bay further depleted goodwill toward the United States. Indeed, very few people in the rest of the world viewed the United States favorably by 2006. In a survey of people in fifteen countries, the Pew Global Attitudes Project found that "America's global image has again slipped and support for the war on terrorism has declined even among close U.S. allies like Japan. The war in Iraq is a continuing drag on opinions of the United States, not only in predominantly Muslim countries but in Europe and Asia as well. And despite growing concern over Iran's nuclear ambitions, the U.S. presence in Iraq is cited at least as often as Iran—and in many countries much more often—as a danger to world peace."[43] According to the survey, only in Great Britain did a majority (56 percent) of people express a favorable opinion of the United States. In some predominantly Muslim countries, such as Jordan and Turkey, fewer than 20 percent of the respondents held favorable opinions of the United States.[44] The disenchantment with the United States and its policies is arguably greater and more intense in the Muslim world (see Map 3.5). "As is the case with many great powers, the United States has a problem of being unpopular abroad. But in the Muslim world, the issue is different and far deeper. The United States is not simply seen as being mean-spirited or unfair. . . . [I]n the wake of the Iraq War especially, nearly 90 percent of the inhabitants of Muslim countries view America as the primary security threat to their country."[45]

While anti-Americanism in the Muslim world may serve the interests of certain religiously fundamental groups, it is more than that: "The ferment within the Muslim world must be viewed . . . through a geopolitical rather than theological perspective. . . . Hostility toward the United States, while pervasive in some Muslim countries, originates from specific political grievances—such as Iranian nationalist resentment over

Map 3.5   Modern Islam, 2005

Source: McKay et al., *A History of World Societies*, 7th ed. (Boston, MA: Houghton Mifflin, 2007), p. 1046. Data from *CIA World Factbook*, 2005. Reprinted by permission of Bedford/St. Martin's.

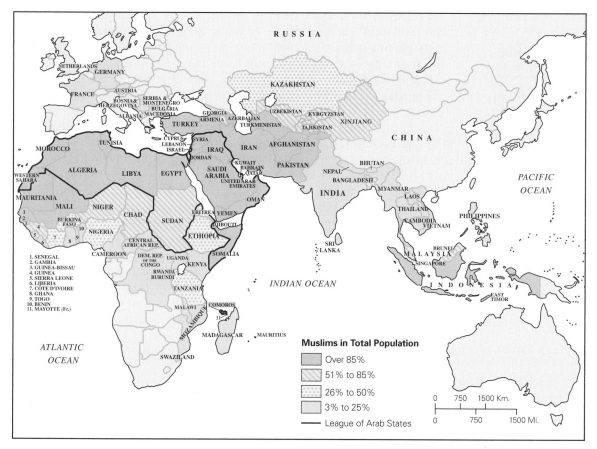

the U.S. backing of the Shah, Arab animus stimulated by U.S. support for Israel or Pakistani feelings that the United States has been partial to India—than from a generalized religious bias."[46]

As the situation in Iraq deteriorated from 2003 to 2007, the strategies associated with the Bush Doctrine and the Bush administration—strategies such as preemption, democratization and regime change, and unilateralism—came under severe criticism, including in the United States. Outside the United States, U.S. policies ". . . angered even America's closest allies, many of whom came to see their role not as America's partner but as a brake on the improvident exercise of its power. It weakened their support for American actions. And it undermined their willingness to cooperate in dealing with those challenges that were common to all."[47] The Policy Choices box summarizes the controversy surrounding the Bush Doctrine.

Although most world opinion welcomed the election of President Obama, (and he was awarded the Nobel Peace Prize in 2009 for his efforts to strengthen international cooperation) it is too early to tell if this will have a lasting effect on support for the United States and U.S. policies. Furthermore, many blame the United States for the recent financial crisis and economic problems in their own countries.[48]

Globalization

globalization
Economic, political, and cultural integration across state borders.

States are also struggling with issues related to economic **globalization**. Although interdependence increased dramatically by the early 1970s, the integration of economies at the beginning of the twenty-first century is more geographically widespread (more parts of the world are connected) and is deeper (more connections across economies have developed). Trade, production, and investment are now truly multinational. "Consider the Microsoft Xbox—a high-technology game console containing cutting-edge technology. Manufacturing is outsourced to a Taiwanese company. The Intel processors are sourced from any of 11 production sites, including China, Costa Rica, Malaysia and the Philippines. Graphics processors are manufactured by a U.S. company at a plant in . . . China. The hard drive is assembled in China from components produced in Indonesia. Final assembly has recently been moved from Mexico to China. The Xbox is a microcosm of what is happening under globalization."[49] Even this edition of this textbook was revised in Turkey, copy-edited in India, and published in the United States.

The end result of further globalization is the development of one world market, uncomplicated by state boundaries. Efforts toward creating single markets across states have recently been made in various regions of the world, including South America with Mercosur, North America with the North American Free Trade Agreement, southern Africa with the Southern African Development Community, and Asia with the Asian Pacific Economic Community. In Western Europe, the move toward a single economy began over fifty years ago, but only recently did the European Union reach its highest level of integration with its single currency, the euro.

World Trade Organization
Intergovernmental organization dealing with the rules of trade between states

States are certainly struggling with their responses to increased globalization. While the economic advantages associated with greater interdependence are attractive to many states, the costs are worrisome as well. Some political leaders in the United States, for example, were concerned that the creation of the **World Trade Organization** (WTO) would establish an authority that could infringe on state sovereignty if states violated global free trade principles. Furthermore, free trade often clashes with other issues, such as security, human rights, labor standards, and environmental regulations, and recent protests at WTO meetings demonstrate some of the intense backlash against globalization. The poor economies of the South—containing the less economically developed countries—also fear that globalization simply means an Americanization of the world economy, with all profit returning to the multinational corporations in the North—consisting of the richer, industrialized economies.

ISSUE: The Bush Doctrine, articulated by the U.S. president in speeches and developed in official policy documents in 2002, represented a significant break with both past U.S. foreign policy practices as well as with some general international laws and principles. The justification for such a change was largely rooted in the fight against terrorism, itself a response to the attacks of September 11, 2001. Key aspects that generated the most controversy are the Bush Doctrine's emphasis on military preemptive strikes and its focus on unilateral action.

Option #1: Unilateral and preemptive actions are necessary approaches to contemporary security threats.

Arguments: (a) Terrorism represents a new kind of threat that limits the effectiveness of traditional deterrence. Thus, states must be allowed to act preemptively and unilaterally if necessary to attack and destroy terrorist organizations before they strike. (b) With the spread of weapons of mass destruction in the hands of rogue states and terrorist organizations, states no longer have the luxury of watching tanks and troops amass on their borders to make a determination that a military threat is imminent. States must act preemptively to prevent future threats. (c) When capability is distributed, responsibility is distributed. When capability is concentrated in the hands of one state, such as the United States, that state bears disproportionate responsibility for ensuring global stability. The United Nations is not always capable and willing to effectively respond to threats.

Counterarguments: (a) Terrorist threats are better met with cooperative action to track down and treat individual terrorists as criminals. Multilateral coalitions that isolate or confront states that harbor terrorist groups are more effective than is unilateral preemptive action. (b) Though the costs of waiting to fight only truly defensive wars may at times be high, the chaos of allowing all actors in the international system to take military action based on speculative or distant threats would be far worse. If all states followed the logic of the Bush Doctrine, there would be unrestrained interventions in the pursuit of narrow national interests. (c) The U.S. capability to act alone does not mean that it should. The United States does not have the exclusive right and responsibility for determining when action is required. As signatories of the United Nations charter, states have agreed that the Security Council shall determine the existence of threats to peace and the measures to take to restore security.

Option #2: Unilateral and preemptive actions are dangerous to world peace.

Arguments: (a) The Bush Doctrine undermines international law based on the protection of state sovereignty. Although international law is evolving to allow for the violation of state sovereignty, it is only doing so in the extreme cases of genocide and large-scale humanitarian crises, and then only multilateral forces are seen as legitimate. Weakening international law and norms is not in the interest of the United States or the international community. (b) Unilateral action generates animosity, even from traditional allies. Aggressive intentions of others are difficult to judge, and without clear signs of an imminent threat, preemptive action will be seen as illegitimate. (c) Unilateral military actions are not effective against threats

(continued)

of weapons of mass destruction. Multilateral efforts to track and control the prolif-eration of weapons of mass destruction are more effective than are military attacks on "rogue" states.

Counterarguments: (a) International law allows for action taken in self-defense and should evolve to account for the nature of new threats. International laws designed to regulate state-to-state interactions are simply inadequate for dealing with such nonstate actors. States should not be constrained by the UN Charter, which was written in a very different period of world politics. (b) Although states should work to influence how their actions are judged by others, they should not be constrained by them. Policies that promote a state's national interests and protect it from threats are inherently legitimate. (c) The use of force is an effective way to deal with states that refuse to comply with international rules and represent a danger to others.

Increased interdependence also means that economic crises, such as the financial crises that hit Russia and Asia in the 1990s, quickly spread through the international economy to affect many other states. This was also true for the economic downturn that more recently started in the financial sector in United States. This economic crisis, which some have compared to the Great Depression of the 1930s, left few countries untouched and may have profound implications for globalization. The richest economies, all affected by the crisis, responded with state inter-vention into the economy (with, for example, more regulation and finan-cial assistance to failing banks and companies) and economic liberal philosophies that underlie globalization came under heavy criticism.[50] According to one analyst, this means that ". . . the politics as well as the finance of globalization has now been profoundly altered" and that "even before the financial meltdown, advocates for globalization . . . had become deeply worried, as globalization has become a concept with overwhelm-ingly negative connotations."[51] Globalization is not necessarily doomed by this crisis, however. Although states are tempted to turn inward and pursue national economic interests and sacrifice global economic coop-eration, the international community might use this as an opportunity to further globalization by, for example, cooperating to stabilize the global monetary system.[52] The international community's responses to the recent economic crisis are discussed in Chapters 10, 11, 12, and 14.

What is clear from the recent crisis is that globalization has trans-formed the balance of economic power in the international system (Chapter 4 details different conceptions and indicators of power). Although the United States still has the world's largest economy and the dollar is sought in times of uncertainty, ". . . Washington today is in no position to dictate to the rest of the world, as it did after World War II, the contours of a new global financial architecture."[53] According to many, the twenty-first century will turn into an "Asian century," with the emergence of China and India as important economic and geopolitical powers.[54] One analyst argues, "This tectonic shift will pose a challenge to the U.S.-dominated global institutions that have been in place since the 1940s."[55] Global political institutions, another form of globalization, may have to significantly change to reflect the new power balance if they are to continue.

Political globalization can be seen in the increased importance of international organizations, such as the United Nations, and nongovernmental organizations, such as human rights advocates, that act across borders and provide services there were in the past reserved for sovereign states (see Chapters 4, 9, and 14). Cultural globalization refers to the notion that people around the world are conforming in their habits (such as watching the same television shows and eating the same food) and their attitudes (such as beliefs about democracy and human rights). While there is considerable debate about the novelty of contemporary globalization, there is certainly strong opposition and countertrends occurring in global politics and there are indications that the global economic downturn may be slowing down all forms of globalization. Chapter 14 discusses economic, cultural, and political globalization and the impact that current trends may have on the sovereign state system.

Theoretical Perspectives on Global Politics in the Modern Era

Each of the theoretical perspectives presented in Chapter 1—realism, liberalism, idealism, neo-Marxism, constructivism, and feminist perspectives—reflects on the history of global politics in the twentieth century by focusing on different time periods and events and by using alternative interpretations of history as evidence to support the perspective's arguments.[56]

For realism, the Cold War was completely understandable, if not predictable. Given the international condition of anarchy, realists assume that the two most powerful states will come into conflict and attempt to balance each other through military buildup, alliance formation, and spheres of influence. Thus, the behavior of the United States and the Soviet Union during the Cold War was perfectly natural. The advent of nuclear weapons, according to realists, transformed what might have been a traditional conflict resulting in a conventional war into an indirect or "cold" war, but the underlying power dynamics and competition remained the same as they were in ancient Greece and eighteenth- and nineteenth-century Europe. Détente made sense to realists such as Richard Nixon and Henry Kissinger, because the tripolar balance of power between the United States, the Soviet Union, and China was roughly equal, and stability could be maintained among the great powers in the twentieth century as it had been during the Concert of Europe. Detente did not mean that competition would cease, however, and thus the superpower interventions in regional conflicts that persisted into the 1970s and 1980s were inevitable as part of the power struggle. Once the distribution of power in the international system changed, as it did with the end of the Cold War, realists expected the dynamics of global politics to change as well, but they did not expect an end to conflict, as many had hoped. Indeed, recurring conflicts of interests in the post–Cold War period between, for example, the United States and China and security threats coming from regional powers that seek nuclear weapons are inevitable given that states continue to maximize their power, as realists expect.

Whereas realism sees continuity across the history of international relations in the twentieth century, liberalism sees great change. As discussed in Chapter 1, developments after World War II, such as the spread of democracy, decolonization, nuclear weapons, the integration of the world economy, and technological developments that facilitated contact between actors in global politics, contributed to the rise of complex interdependence. As a result, global politics become the product of more non-state actors, particularly with the increase in multinational corporations and nongovernmental organizations interested in economic and other nonsecurity issues. These actors with multiple interests and the linkages that developed among them served to constrain states from conflict and encourage cooperation. For liberalism, détente and the trade agreements it included were recognition that the basis for power had shifted to economic sources and that states were interdependent and had more to gain from cooperation. Interdependence further eroded the dominance of security conflicts by facilitating political liberalization in the Soviet Union and economic liberalization in China. In the post Cold–War world, liberals point to the powerful forces of globalization and democratization that are changing international politics and challenging the state-centric system.

In contrast to realism, idealism looks at the Cold War not in terms of a conflict of interests but a conflict of values. On the one side, the conflict was about capitalist and individualist values; on the other side, it was about Communist and social values. Idealists argue that it is difficult to understand the vehemence that characterized the conflict without accounting for this clash of ideology and values. Realists would counter that the ideological rhetoric of the Cold War was simply window dressing— that at its heart, the conflict was a power struggle. Idealists also see that values played a role in the end of the Cold War, starting with agreements signed during détente. In 1975, thirty-three European and North American states signed the Final Act of the European Security Conference in Helsinki, Finland. The Helsinki agreement included a provision on human rights and political freedom. While the Soviet Union and East European states routinely violated many of the rights they had agreed to protect, the agreement nevertheless established a norm of behavior, and the discrepancy between the rhetoric of the agreement and the behavior of the governments spawned the growth of many dissident groups across the Soviet bloc in the 1970s and 1980s. Many of these groups, pursuing the values of human rights that are important to idealism, would play a significant role in transforming their countries and ending the Cold War. For idealists, the application of values in global politics is particularly important in the types of conflicts in the post–Cold War period. Ethnic conflict and a variety of war crimes, idealists argue, provide moral imperatives for the global community to respond. Values dividing cultures and religions are also key to current global debates, according to idealists.

For the neo-Marxist perspective, the international economy of the twentieth century has its roots in earlier times. What is particularly salient about the modern era, however, is the continued division of labor into the core, in the North, and periphery, in the South, even after decolonization. Many former colonies remain tied to the economies of the imperialist powers in many respects. The difficulties that these states have experienced in economic development are, according to this perspective, due to the structure of the international economy. In the post–Cold War era, neo-Marxists point to the different effects that globalization is having on core and periphery economies.[57]

Constructivism and feminism provide alternative interpretations of historical events in the modern era. Constructivists, for example, argue that a state's action during the Cold War had less to do with the "real" situation of a bipolar system and more to do with the state's understandings of their interactions and their identities in world politics. Along these lines, constructivists argue that the Cuban missile crisis was a "crisis" only because of how the "Cuban problem" and the "Soviet threat" were constructed by U.S. policymakers. The missiles themselves, after all, were not more of a threat based in Cuba than they were based in the Soviet Union; they could hit the United States from either location. Thus, according to constructivists, the threat from the missiles was not real but constructed. This, they argue, helps explain why U.S. foreign policy toward Cuba remains largely hostile and unchanged despite the disappearance of the "Soviet threat." U.S. foreign policy has more to do with the construction of the "Cuban problem," which continues unchanged.[58] In contemporary global politics, constructivism emphasizes the importance of socially constructed norms and institutions that constrain the highly powerful United States. For constructivists, "the debate in the [UN] Security Council over war with Iraq highlighted this complex interplay between institutional norms and processes, the politics of international legitimacy and the power of the United States. Washington commanded the material resources to oust Saddam Hussein from power, but without Security Council endorsement it has struggled to shake off an aura of illegitimacy and illegality, seriously undermining [the U.S.] . . . occupation and reconstruction."[59]

For feminism, the military conflict of the Cold War that dominated the second half of the twentieth century was masculine in character, and the preoccupation with power and the superpower rivalry masked or ignored more feminine issues and agendas. The Cold War did, however, depend on women, affect women, and affect conceptions of gender:

> A lot of women and men in Poland, Chile, South Africa, and
> France never served in their governments' militaries; yet between

1945 and 1989 their lives were also militarized. The militarization which sustained Cold War relationships between people for forty years required armed forces with huge appetites for recruits; it also depended on ideas about manliness and womanliness that touched people who never went through basic training.[60]

Feminists are now asking what the end of the Cold War means for women. As men and women who fought in the proxy wars that have now ended return to civil society, a renegotiation of gender roles must occur. As the Soviet systems were dismantled across Eastern Europe, the number of women representatives in parliament has declined.[61] As ethnic conflict has spread, local and international women's groups have fought to get rape, a form of violence that has occurred in many of the recent ethnic conflicts, classified as a violation of human rights.[62] As globalization pressures lead some to embrace economic and political integration, some women protest that economics is being pursued at the expense of health, environmental, and safety concerns and that the new global economic structures, such as the World Trade Organization, are even more patriarchal than are state governments.

SUMMARY

- Despite high hopes for peace and stability after the Second World War, disagreements between the Soviet Union and the United States over the future of Eastern Europe formed an important basis for the beginning of the Cold War. By 1949, the United States had formed a military alliance, the North Atlantic Treaty Organization, to protect Western Europe from Communist encroachment and began developing a global policy of containment.

- The Cold War quickly spread to Asia as the Communists won the civil war in China in 1949. When North Korea invaded South Korea in 1950, the United States led a UN military mission against North Korea.

- Decolonization following World War II would dramatically increase the number of sovereign states by 1970. These states, called the Third World during the Cold War, rarely escaped the superpower rivalry as internal conflict within them became proxy wars and as they became client states in the competition for allies around the globe.

- By the 1960s, the Soviet Union and China became vigorous enemies. Not coincidentally, relations between the Soviet Union and the United States improved when the Soviet dispute with China became even more serious at the beginning of the 1970s. The United States pursued more peaceful relations with both the Soviet Union and China in a period known as détente. But détente between the United States and the Soviet Union did not survive the Soviet invasion of Afghanistan in 1979, and the Cold War was reborn.

● The world economic system underwent dramatic changes by the 1970s as the dominance of the United States declined with the rise of strong economies in Western Europe and Japan. The 1970s also revealed the dependence of these economies in the North on the states in the South, particularly with the development of OPEC.

● The dramatic end of the Cold War in the late 1980s and early 1990s, the cooperation between the United States and the Soviet Union in the war against Iraq in 1991, and the disintegration of the Soviet Union signaled significant changes in world politics. A period of euphoria following the end to many conflicts and a wave of democratization was replaced by concerns over ethnic violence, failed states, nuclear proliferation, and the challenges of globalization and economic crises. U.S. policies based on unilateralism, preemption, and regime change, as well as continued violence in Iraq, generated much criticism and resentment in most of the rest of the world.

● Each of the major political perspectives uses different parts of the history of international relations in the second half of the twentieth century to advance their claims about global politics. Realism concentrates on the Cold War rivalry, liberalism on the rise of economic interdependence, and idealism on the value conflicts and growing concern over human rights. The world economic system perspective focuses on the continued division of the international capitalist system into a core and a periphery, constructivism on how the Cold War rivalry was socially constructed, and feminism on the masculine nature of the Cold War and the effects that the Cold War and its end have had on women.

KEY TERMS

Yalta Conference   56
North Atlantic Treaty
 Organization   57
iron curtain   57
Warsaw Pact   57
containment   58
Marshall Plan   58
decolonization   61
Third World   63
Suez crisis   65
Six-Day War   67
proxy wars   68
nuclear parity   68
Cuban missile crisis   69

détente   69
Organization of Petroleum
 Exporting Countries (OPEC)   72
Intermediate-Range Nuclear
 Forces (INF) Treaty   74
Gorbachev   75
perestroika   75
glasnost   75
new world order   77
failed states   81
nuclear proliferation   82
Bush Doctrine   85
globalization   87
World Trade Organization   87

PART II

Actors in Global Politics: Power and Policy

The Power of States and the Rise of Transnational Actors

For at least three hundred years, sovereign states have been the most important political organizations in the global system. Their preeminence has not gone unchallenged, and there are good reasons to believe that these particular organizations may not allow humankind to deal with problems that have become more serious in the twenty-first century. Even so, states are still a very important kind of political entity and are likely to remain significant. An understanding of global politics necessarily involves a grasp of the essential characteristics of states, including states' power to influence other states. States, however, are not the only international actors on the global stage. Organizations that transcend state boundaries include nongovernmental organizations, multinational business corporations, and terrorist groups. There is indication that the number and significance of these organizations are rising and that they represent a challenge to the power of states, if not to the state system itself.

Nations and States

nation A community of people sharing a common identity, often based on shared history and culture.

The terms *nation* and *state* are commonly treated as interchangeable in discussions of international relations. The name of the subfield itself, inter*nation*al relations, is an example of this practice. Even though the term includes "nation," the subfield actually focuses on states most of the time. Strictly speaking, *nation* and *state* are not exactly interchangeable terms, and the distinction between them shows signs of becoming particularly important in the future. A **nation** is "a named human population sharing an historical territory, common myths and historical memories, a mass, public culture, a common economy and common legal rights and duties for all members."[1] It is a psychological concept because it concerns humans' attachments to the group with which they identify. The basis of national identity is often shared ethnicity, language, or religion. A state, in contrast, is a political organization or a government that exercises supreme authority over a defined territory.[2]

multinational states States that contain more than one nation.

multistate nations Nations that cross the boundaries of several states.

stateless nations Nations that cross many state boundaries but are not really represented in any state.

One of the major sources of tension in global politics today is that nation boundaries are not contiguous with state boundaries. There are several states that contain more than one nation; they are **multinational states.** The state of Great Britain, for example, contains the English, Irish, Scottish, and Welsh nations. Most states in Africa contain many, many ethnic groups, some of which identify themselves as nations. Furthermore, there are many nations that cross the boundaries of several states; they are **multistate nations.** The nation of Korea, for example, crosses the states of North Korea and South Korea. Some nations that cross many state boundaries are really not represented in any state; they are **stateless nations.** The Kurdish nation, for example, is a minority in Iraq, Iran, and Turkey. In rare cases, nation boundaries roughly match state boundaries in true nation-states. Most of those who identify themselves as part of the

Japanese nation, for example, live inside the state of Japan, and most of those living inside the state of Japan share a Japanese national identity.

Chapter 7 will discuss the sources of national identity and the consequences that national identity has for states and global politics. While nations are a growing force of transformation and change in the international system, they have not replaced states as the dominant way the system is organized. States remain the main actor on the global stage.

The Power of States

power   The ability of an actor to influence others. State power is largely influenced by state capabilities, but it is a multidimensional concept.

If states have traditionally been considered the most important kind of political organization in the global system, the **power** of states has been treated as the most important concept in the study of world politics. Power, as discussed in Chapter 1, is the central concept in the realist theoretical perspective. States, according to realism, pursue their interests, defined as power. Everything a state does can be explained by its desire to maintain, safeguard, or increase its power in relation to other states.

But what *is* power? Although it is central to the study of world politics,[3] the concept has been defined in a confusing variety of ways. Perhaps the two most important types of definitions of power distinguish between what a state *possesses* and what a state is able *to do*. One important definition is provided by Hans Morgenthau in his classic text, *Politics Among Nations*: "When we speak of power, we mean man's control over the minds and actions of other men."[4] This has to do with influence. But it is quite clear that many analysts also think of power as being embodied in resources that a state possesses, such as the size of its population, its geographical size, or the size of its gross national product (GDP; see discussion that follows).[5] Not surprisingly, the theoretical perspectives introduced in Chapter 1 differ on which components of state power are most important.

The Paradox of Unrealized Power

Most of the confusion about power arises from the complex relationship between a state's control over resources (what it possesses), on the one hand, and its ability to affect the behavior of others or to control outcomes in international disputes, conflicts, and wars (what it can do), on the other. Some confusion might be avoided if we (1) reserved the word *power* to refer to the resources or capabilities that give a state the potential to control outcomes and (2) referred to the actual ability of states to control outcomes as *influence*. But the confusion surrounding the concept of power in the analysis of international politics cannot be resolved with a couple of simple definitional distinctions. If State A is more powerful than State B in the sense that it possesses more resources, then we expect State A also to prevail in conflicts, at least most of the time. Exceptions to that rule are surprising, regardless of whether we define power as control over resources *and* control over outcomes or whether we reserve the term *influence* for the latter type of control. But exceptions do exist. For example, the United States, with its vast nuclear arsenal and much larger military force, took on North Vietnam in a conflict over the fate of South Vietnam, and North Vietnam won. The Soviet Union invaded Afghanistan in 1979 and pulled its troops out in 1989, leaving behind a chaotic situation that persists to this day. In short, although the Soviets did not exactly lose the war in Afghanistan, the government the Soviets were protecting did not last long after their departure. It seems fair to conclude that the tremendous advantage in resources that the Soviets had over Afghanistan did not make it easy for them to prevail. They fought for ten years and left behind a shaky government that ultimately fell to Islamic groups that they (the Soviets) had been determined to keep out of power.

paradox of unrealized power A situation in which a state that possesses greater military capabilities loses in conflicts to apparently much weaker actors.

A common response to this kind of **paradox of unrealized power** (in which far more powerful states lose in conflicts with apparently much weaker states) is that the ostensibly more powerful states somehow failed to translate their powerful resources into actual power. The United States did not win the Vietnam War, according to this type of explanation, because it did not want to win badly enough, or at least not as much as the North Vietnamese did. Similarly, the former Soviet Union got bogged down in Afghanistan for so long and with such uncertain results, because it did not devote sufficient effort to the task. "He had the cards but played them poorly" is the theme of such explanations.[6] Explanations of this type are dangerous, because they are difficult to disprove. You might devise an argument, for example, that in asymmetric conflicts, the actor with the bigger army will always win. A critic could point out that although the United States had a much bigger army than North Vietnam, it lost the war against that country. You could save your argument by saying that the state with the bigger army will always win unless it does not really want to, and that is what happened in Vietnam. But you could then try to save your argument with that tactic in every imaginable case. In doing so, you would really be admitting that bigger armies are not really that important, that it is indeed the will to win that is critical.

When we try to predict when power, or capabilities, will translate into influence, it is best to realize that there are various types of power, including the will to win, that factor into a state's ability to influence others. In addition to the military power and resolve, power comes from economic resources, values, control of the agenda, ideas, and cooperative abilities. Thus, states with great capabilities do not necessarily always have influence.

Military Capabilities

The best strategy for dealing with the paradox of unrealized power begins with the realization that such upsets in asymmetric conflicts between states, especially if they escalate to war, are unusual.[7] The

Roman historian Tacitus, as well as Comte de Bussy, Frederick the Great, Napoleon, and Voltaire (among others), have all been credited with aphorisms to the effect that "God is always on the side of the larger battalions." In other words, when two states engage in conflict, the leaders and generals of both may pray for success, but usually the state with the greater military force has a better chance of having its prayers answered, thus allegedly revealing God's preferences in such matters. It is for this reason that realism typically focuses on military capabilities as the primary ingredient in a state's power.

If, for example, we look at the thirty wars between two states that occurred between 1816 and 1965, we find that the state with the larger armed force won all but nine of those conflicts.[8] A review of interstate wars involving major powers over the past 500 years shows that major powers usually win wars they fight against minor powers and, further, that in more recent centuries, major powers have become involved more often in wars with minor power opponents only. Not surprisingly, the percentage of victories that major powers achieved in those more recent wars has increased.[9] "Most interstate wars [are] won by the stronger nation or coalition. . . . Examples of conflicts in which militarily inferior nations emerged as victors . . . are exceptional rather than typical cases."[10]

Still, the theory based on God's bias in favor of large battalions is much less than perfect, as is demonstrated by the examples of the United States versus North Vietnam and the Soviet Union versus Afghanistan. And, as noted previously, nine states with smaller military forces have won wars between 1816 and 1965. According to one recent study, "Major power states have failed to attain their primary political objective in 39 percent of the military interventions they have initiated since World War II."[11] Furthermore, asymmetric conflicts that are fought between states and guerilla forces or militarized insurgencies, instead of just between states, are not always won by the most powerful. Unlike conventional warfare in which massive numbers of forces attempt to overwhelm the other side with weight and firepower, guerilla fighting (also called **asymmetrical warfare**) involves ambush tactics to wear down the other side, rather than defeat it or capture and hold territory.[12] Insurgent groups have had their successes: "Indeed, they have succeeded against Britain (in Palestine), France (in Algeria), the United States (in Vietnam) and Israel (in Lebanon) in spite of clear battlefield inferiority."[13]

asymmetrical warfare
Unconventional fighting between unequal belligerents that often involves ambush or guerilla tactics to destroy the more powerful side's will to fight, rather than to militarily conquer it.

It is possible to modify the explanation that relies on military capability only slightly, allowing it to deal with the paradox of unrealized power in many cases. If the state with the larger battalions does not win, it can be argued, the state with the smaller battalions must have received help from powerful friends. Thus, the larger battalions do win, in a sense, even if they are not all directly engaged in the conflict. In the case of Vietnam, for example, both Russia and China gave material as well as moral support to the regime in North Vietnam. Some in the United States called for bombing North Vietnam back into the Stone Age or turning it into a parking lot (somewhat contradictory suggestions), and if the contest had been clearly confined to the United States and North Vietnam, there is not much doubt that the United States had the capability to do both. U.S. policymakers rejected those suggestions, and even more moderate ones, at least partly because the moral support offered to the North Vietnamese regime by the Soviets and the Chinese (propaganda in radio broadcasts, speeches in the United Nations, and so on) led them to fear Soviet or Chinese retaliation if they moved too vigorously against North Vietnam. Having accepted that limitation, the United States then found that the material support supplied to North Vietnam by powerful friends (especially the Soviets) made it very difficult to win the war, even if that support was not great enough for North Vietnam to match the United States in military capability.

Similarly, in the Afghan case, there is considerable evidence that the Central Intelligence Agency (CIA) cooperated with Egypt, Saudi Arabia, Pakistan, and China in efforts to funnel military equipment to the Afghan rebels. In fact, the United States devoted billions of dollars to supporting the rebels during the decade-long war.[14] Accordingly, the idea that God is always on the side of the larger battalions unless the smaller battalions get help from powerful friends apparently holds true in the case of the Soviet Union versus the rebels in Afghanistan.

This idea also receives interesting support from the results of the Persian Gulf War in 1991. Before that war began, some people expressed fears that the United States might get bogged down in another Vietnam type of situation in the Middle East. There were good reasons for such fears. The location of the conflict—far away from the United States and right next to (as well as inside) Iraq—created difficulties for the United States. But crucial differences between the challenge the United States faced in Vietnam and that posed by Iraq made it very unlikely that the United States would get into difficulties resembling those that developed in its war against North Vietnam. North Vietnam relied on guerrilla warfare in its own territory; by simply staying in the field for years, its troops outlasted the invaders. Iraq attempted to use conventional means to hold territory where its troops were unwelcome. The most fundamental difference, certainly from the point of view of the theoretical ideas discussed here, was that while North Vietnam had powerful allies, Iraq had none. On the contrary, while China abstained on the key votes regarding the resolutions committing the United Nations to the removal of Iraqi forces from Kuwait, every other major power in the world supported those resolutions and the military effort against Iraq. Since Iraq received no support from powerful friends in 1991, and the United States was not only much more powerful but also received help from its powerful friends, it was understandable that Iraq would be defeated, and quite easily. The same occurred in the 2003 conflict as the more powerful United States, with the help of some allies, easily defeated the Iraqi state, which again did not receive any outside assistance. As the war in Iraq continued, however, it became more like the Vietnamese conflict in the sense that U.S.-led military forces face armed insurgent groups engaging in nonconventional guerrilla fighting.

Overall, powerful friends may be an important part of winning international conflict. Indeed, an analysis of all interstate wars in the years from 1816 to 1992 shows that the initiators of those wars were more likely to win if their targets did not get help from third parties, although this was less true after 1945.[15] An explanation based entirely on a comparison between the military capabilities of the two main belligerents, as well as those of their friends, may not completely account for the outcome of the conflicts in Iraq, what happened in Afghanistan, or the difficulty the United States experienced in Vietnam. One must somehow decide whether the help supplied by powerful friends to the smaller battalions is sufficient, given the difference in power resources available to the contestants, to account for the outcome of the conflict. Was the help that North Vietnam received from the Soviets and the Chinese, for example, sufficient to offset entirely the tremendous superiority in power resources available to the United States over Vietnam? Most believe it was not. How about the help supplied by powerful friends to the Afghan rebels? Again, very few would argue that this was the single deciding factor. Was the superiority of the battalions sent into battle by the United States and its allies sufficient to explain the collapse of the Iraqi army in 1991 and 2003 (which was, after all, rather substantial)? Ultimately,

Guerrilla soldiers load a missile launcher in the mountains of Afghanistan during their ten-year fight (1979–1989) against the Soviet Union.

(Robert Nickelberg/Liason/ Getty Images)

if the analysis of power suggested here is to be entirely convincing, the resources of the larger battalions as well as those of the smaller battalions and their powerful friends will have to be measured. As we will soon see, the measurement of military power is not always as straightforward as it seems.

Even if we take into account help from powerful friends, some international conflicts have surprising winners. The winning side in some conflicts appears to have a lot less power on its side, as indicated by military resources. This suggests that in addition to help from third parties, other factors are important in assessing states' power and predicting the outcomes of international conflict.

The Impact of Resolve

What other factors, then, should we consider in cases such as the Soviet Union's war in Afghanistan or the U.S. war in Vietnam? One possible candidate that we have already mentioned several times is the will to win, or resolve. Indeed, it may not be unusual for a weak state to win since it might enter into a conflict with a stronger state only if it has significant resolve. Although the will to win is often difficult to demonstrate, particularly before a conflict takes place, it is tempting to pursue this idea regarding the impact of resolve on conflict outcomes because it is so plausible.[16] In many asymmetric conflicts in the twentieth century, for example, desires of nationalism and self-determination fueled many wars of national liberation that pitted guerrilla insurgents against conventional state militaries.

In the case of the war between the United States and North Vietnam, many other factors played a role in determining the outcome. Yet it surely seems logically and intuitively obvious that the Vietnamese did have a greater will to win and that this is one important reason they did win. Although the United States did make a determined effort, devoting billions of dollars, tens of thousands of lives, and eight long years to the cause, it still seems clear that North Vietnam's resolve was greater. The stakes of the conflict were much greater for North Vietnam. The United States became involved in the war in defense of relatively abstract principles or distant goals involving the *domino theory* (the idea that if one state became Communist, neighboring states would "fall like dominoes" and become Communist themselves), the importance of upholding commitments, and making the world safer for capitalism. (We will avoid here the controversy regarding which of these factors was most important.) From the North Vietnamese viewpoint, the purpose of the war was immediate, clear, and important: to rid their land of foreign invaders and to unify the country—in short, to liberate it. The United States did have a much larger military force than North Vietnam. But it also had a large number of other foreign policy issues competing for resources, attention, and effort, such as the confrontation with the Soviet Union, the defense of Western Europe, the protection of Israel, and preservation of the stalemate in Korea. For North Vietnam, the war against the regime in the South and its U.S. supporters was close to being its only foreign policy concern, certainly the only really pressing matter to which it devoted substantial resources and persistent attention.

In sum, the North Vietnamese will to win was greater than that of the United States, which had to devote its capabilities to the pursuit of other goals as well. And one need not rely entirely on logical or intuitive arguments to establish this point. The greater North Vietnamese will to win was reflected, for example, in the fact that the maximum number of U.S. troops in Vietnam at the peak of the war was less than 0.25 percent of the U.S. population.[17] North Vietnam mobilized a much larger proportion of its smaller population; the number of North Vietnamese soldiers killed (about 500,000, or 2.5 percent of the population) was probably equal to the number of Americans deployed. The Vietnamese, then, showed a considerably greater willingness to suffer.[18]

Similar arguments can be made regarding the Soviets in Afghanistan. Some estimates indicate that 1 million Afghani soldiers lost their lives in that war out of a population of some 15 million. Soviet casualties numbered about 55,000 (up to 1988) out of a much larger population of 280 million people.[19] Like the United States, the Soviet Union, while it was fighting its war in Afghanistan, had a whole range of other issues with which it was concerned. The rebels in Afghanistan, in contrast, were determinedly single-minded in their goal of ousting the Soviets from their country. Almost certainly, the rebels had a greater will to win the conflict in their own country than did the Soviet army.

Then, too, it seems likely that the Iraqi soldiers who attempted during the 1991 Persian Gulf War to hold their positions in Kuwait against the U.S.-led coalition were devoted to their task with nothing remotely resembling the zeal with which Vietnamese soldiers fought against the American forces during the Vietnam War. The Vietnamese soldiers were fighting for the liberation and unification of their nation. The Iraqi soldiers were fighting to hold on to territory just recently annexed by means of an invasion. Perhaps that is one reason, in addition to the much bigger battalions it faced, that the Iraqi army was expelled from Kuwait with relative ease. In the current conflict in Iraq, however, insurgent groups may have more resolve to expel the U.S. military than the United States has to pursue the difficult goal of stabilizing and democratizing Iraq.

As we have seen earlier, concrete military resources have an important impact on the outcomes of international wars. But even for interstate wars, the balance of resolve may be more closely related to the outcomes than is the balance of power. That is, states with a greater will to win, or resolve, are more likely to win than states that enjoy an advantage only in terms of concrete military resources, such as larger defense budgets.

Economic Capabilities

Extensive military capabilities may indeed reflect a state's economic resources. Realists recognize that economic resources are obviously needed to fund a sizable and good military and to buy a vast number of technologically sophisticated weapons. That capacity indicates the ability of a state to produce both an abundance of military hardware should a long war recur and weapons based on advanced technology, such as missiles, computers, and (perhaps) laser beams of sufficient quality and in sufficient quantity to deter, or perhaps even fight, a nuclear war. Economic power may be so important to military power that we should think about economic sources as the main determinant of a state's power and its potential to have influence.[20] Yet in the cases that demonstrate the paradox of unrealized power, such as the U.S. conflict with Vietnam and the Soviet conflict with Afghanistan, the victor was both militarily and economically weaker than its counterpart. And in both of these cases, one can argue that it was the economic costs on the more powerful state that forced a reconsideration of policies.

Beyond the ability to fund a war effort, many argue that economic muscle is even more important than military might in contemporary global politics. As discussed in Chapter 1, liberalism proposes that military force is not a very effective means to influence many nonmilitary issues, such as trade and environmental problems, that have become increasingly important to states in an era of increased interdependence. Furthermore, even if the issue is military in nature, using military force can harm a state's economic interests. For these reasons, liberals argue that economic power is the most important form of state power. With a strong economy, a state can have influence by threatening to hurt others economically through, for example, trade sanctions or withholding investments, even if it does not have great military capabilities.

Neo-Marxists also place a premium on economic power. The division of labor in the global capitalist system creates a core of the haves and a periphery of the have-nots. For many neo-Marxist interpretations of world politics, military power is the means to ensure economic power. In other words, economic wealth is not viewed as the way to purchase military might, as a realist might see it, but rather, military might is used to perpetuate economic wealth. Thus, dependency theorists argue that the control of the world's largest armies and the control of international security organizations help the core keep the periphery at an economic disadvantage.

The Power of Agenda, Ideas, and Values

Many would argue that the focus on military and economic capabilities as the primary sources of states' power misses the more subtle ways people and states influence each other. Especially in today's world where capabilities are fairly diffused across a great number of states, using threats or promises based on military and economic assets, so-called hard power, can often backfire. What may be more effective is

a soft or indirect way to exercise power. A country may achieve its preferred outcomes in world politics because other countries want to emulate it or have agreed to a system that produces such effects. In this sense, it is just as important to set the agenda and structure situations in world politics as it is to get others to change in particular situations. This—that is, getting others to want what you want—might be called co-optive or **soft power** behavior. Soft power can rest on such resources as the attraction of one's ideas or on the ability to set the political agenda in a way that shapes the preferences others express. . . . [P]olitical leaders and philosophers have long understood the power that comes from setting the agenda and determining the framework of a debate. The ability to establish preferences tends to be associated with intangible power resources such as culture, ideology, and institutions.[21]

Joseph S. Nye argues that the United States has soft power in the form of cultural power—people around the world watch Hollywood films, listen to U.S. rock music, and want to wear Levi jeans—and in the form of agenda-setting power—the United States was able to set up

soft power Influence based on the attraction of one's ideas or on the ability to set the political agenda in a way that shapes the preferences of others.

Russian billboards in St. Petersburg show the spread of Western products to the former Communist country. Many see the attraction of Western goods and values as a form of soft power in global politics.
(Bonnie Kamin/PhotoEdit, Inc.)

international institutions, such as the International Monetary Fund and the United Nations, after the Second World War and continues to dominate these global forums.[22] In a sense, this was a recognition "that global rule through coercion was unsustainable, and that it was preferable to establish global institutions that could further American interests and spread American values."[23]

Idealists might agree that cultural power is important, but they would focus on the values, not the materialistic goods, associated with a culture. Cultural values that others respect give states moral authority. The power of moral authority, for idealism, also comes from consistently applying cultural values to global politics. Soft power and the appeal of cultural values are associated with the "battle for hearts and minds" that many see as especially important in contemporary struggles. Democratizing and stabilizing Iraq, for example, may have less to do with the military force used by the United States to capture insurgents and more with winning the acceptance and support of the people.[24] Constructivists argue that power, like any other concept, depends on its social construction. Constructivism sees power as much more than physical capabilities. In this view, power is not something possessed by actors, like states, but rather is a characteristic of ideas and discourse—that is, how actors and their relationships are defined. Constructivists do not ask, "Which state is more powerful?" but rather, "What are the underlying norms and standards of legitimacy that allowed this state to be represented as powerful?"[25] In a sense, then, power resides in the ability to determine ideas or the ability to set the rules and norms by which actors are constructed. As ideas will undoubtedly exist in advance of any specific conflict of interests between states, the proper focus for international relations lies not in the physical capabilities and conflicts of interests of actors but in the representation of those entities. Power, for constructivists, is about representing and classifying states as "civilized," "rogue," "European," "unstable," "Western," and "democratic," as these terms generate expectations and structure relationships between actors.[26] The power of actors in the international system, in other words, is not determined by military resources but is constructed from the context of existing international practices.

Feminists also question the traditional focus on capabilities as the roots of power. More fundamentally, as discussed in Chapter 1, realism's definition of power as control contrasts with feminine definitions of power as the ability to act in concert or action taken in connection with others:

> Power as domination has always been associated with masculinity since the exercise of power has generally been a masculine activity; rarely have women exercised legitimised power in the public domain. . . . Hannah Arendt, frequently cited by feminists writing about power, defines power as the human ability to act in concert, or action which is taken in connection with others who share similar concerns.[27]

Matching Capabilities to the Task

Given the number of ways we can conceptualize a state's powers, we should consider that resources effective against certain targets for some specific purposes are useless in different situations. In other words, the explanation of a failure to realize power potential may not be, "the card player had good cards but played them poorly," but rather, "the card player had a great bridge hand but happened to be playing poker."[28]

In the case of the United States versus North Vietnam, this perspective would help us see that the United States had many military resources that were not relevant to the contest. Its vast nuclear arsenal, for example, did not help in the political struggle to win the hearts and minds of the people in South Vietnam. Its clearly superior ability to wage conventional war was not relevant to the contest with Vietcong guerrillas. Despite important differences in the two struggles, the Soviets may have discovered in Afghanistan that their nuclear weapons and conventional war-fighting capabilities were equally irrelevant there.

In short, when analyzing conflicts between states in international politics, it is sometimes necessary to admit that not all the power resources available to the side with the larger battalions will be effective. No resource, then, not even the tremendous destructive potential of nuclear weapons, gives a state power over everybody with respect to every political issue. Different kinds of resources lead to power over different groups of people with respect to specific types of issues. This point can be summarized with reference to the scope and domain of different power resources. The *scope* refers to the specific issues over which certain resources allow a state (or any holder of those resources) to exert influence. The *domain* refers to the set of people over whom a given resource allows its possessor to exert influence.[29] God may usually be on the side of larger battalions, but sometimes larger battalions lose if the resources they possess are not relevant to the scope (the issues) or the domain (the set of people) involved in a particular conflict.

Still, the traditional focus on power as the ability to exert brute force is not entirely misleading. Occasions when force is actually used or explicitly threatened are numerically quite small, but the importance of brute force in international politics always lurks beneath the surface of more peaceful transactions. A state may get its way (exert power) by promising economic aid, but the promise may well be more effective if the potential recipient knows that it could become the victim of force if it refuses the aid. Also, force is not used or threatened very often in international politics, but the occasions when it is used or threatened are often more important than those much more numerous occasions when nonmilitary power resources come into play. Indeed, a state's very existence can be at stake on those rare occasions when its ability to exert brute force is actually tested. For that reason, makers of foreign policy are usually conscious, to some extent, of the possibility of war and of the relative ability of the larger states in the system to wage war.

Measuring Power

Although there are various sources of a state's power, their effectiveness depends on the task to which they are applied. Military and economic capabilities stand out as significant factors in a state's ability to influence others. So, which states are the most powerful, militarily and economically, in global politics? It depends on how power is measured.

Indicators of Military Power

Many important writers in the history of international politics have argued that geographical factors can have a crucial impact on a state's power.

Important geographical factors include a large land mass, which is easy to invade but hard to control, and island status and mountain ranges, which provide natural protection from invaders. All of these are important indicators of military power. **Geopolitics,** or the relationship between geography and political power, is, however, always changing. Alfred Thayer Mahan, a U.S. naval officer, noted in 1897 the coincidence between the rise of Great Britain to preeminence in the world and the development of its navy, and he argued that naval capabilities were the key to national power. Sir Halford Mackinder, a British geographer, responded that Mahan had let Britain's temporary predominance lead him to overemphasize the importance of sea power. Actually, according to Mackinder, history reveals a constant battle between sea power and land power, and whereas technological developments favored naval power in the nineteenth century, the advent of railroads and the internal combustion engine meant that land power would assume the dominant position in the twentieth century.[30]

An appreciation of the importance of land power led Mackinder to analyze the globe as a kind of chessboard on which the game of international politics is played. Three-fourths of that chessboard, Mackinder noted, is water. Three contiguous continents—Asia, Europe, and Africa—constitute two-thirds of the available land. Mackinder referred to this land mass as the World Island. The other one-third of the land on the globe is made up of the smaller islands of North America, South America, and Australia. The key to dominating this chessboard, according to Mackinder, was the heartland, roughly the middle of the World Island occupied by the former Soviet Union and Eastern Europe. Mackinder thought the World Island contained such a large proportion of the world's resources that whoever controlled it would, in effect, occupy an impenetrable fortress from which to rule the world. Nicholas Spykman, a U.S. scholar of international politics writing in the early 1940s, criticized

geopolitics The relationship between geography and political power.

Mackinder's ideas and modified the major thrust of geopolitical thinking. He argued that Mackinder was right to emphasize that the balance of power in the World Island was crucial to the security of the "offshore" states. But Spykman also believed that Mackinder had overemphasized the importance of Eastern Europe and the heartland. The key to controlling the World Island, Spykman asserted, is the rimland—the area around the outside of the heartland (roughly, Western Europe, the Middle East, and southern and eastern Asia). Spykman summarized his view with the slogan, "Who controls the rimland rules Eurasia; who rules Eurasia controls the destinies of the world."[31]

Geography and geopolitical ideas may well have served as important bases for assessing the power of nations in the past. But is it not true that contemporary technological developments have made geopolitical thinking obsolete? Surely air power and ballistic missiles with nuclear weapons have made the distinctions and relationships among the heartland, the rimland, and the World Island meaningless. Or perhaps not. It is possible that the new relationship between the United States and the republics of the former Soviet Union, especially Russia, will reduce the significance (as well as the size) of their vast nuclear arsenals in world politics. Furthermore, both traditional geopolitical issues and conventional military means could replace the significance of nuclear technology in the international politics of the Cold War era. If it is not true that future wars will be fought with large arsenals of nuclear weapons and will last only a few minutes, but instead may be more prolonged contests between mostly conventional military forces, then geopolitical ideas may be of renewed importance.[32]

One indicator of military capability that has always been important, and will continue to be so, is a large population. No state with a very small population can be extremely powerful militarily. This correlation does not mean that there is a perfect relationship between military power and the size of a state's population. India, for example, is the second most populous state (next to China) and Indonesia the fourth most populous state (next to the United States), but neither India nor Indonesia is generally considered among the world's greatest military powers.[33] Even so, one of the most obvious criteria for distinguishing powerful from weaker nations is population size. And India and Indonesia may yet succeed in the future in taking advantage of their large populations as a source of influence in the international system.

Other crucial determinants of a state's military power are the size and quality of its military establishment. The nation with the largest army, navy, and air force, though, is not necessarily the world's most powerful state. China, capitalizing on its large population, has the largest number of military personnel[34] and, while certainly a major military power, is not considered the most threatening. This may be because the total supply of available people is becoming progressively less important as military technology becomes more sophisticated and capable of greater destructive power. An army equipped with tactical nuclear weapons will probably be more than a match for a much larger force that is not so equipped. In a sense, war has become more automated, and the importance of sheer numbers of bodies in the military has diminished accordingly.

Measuring the technological capacity and quality of states, however, is difficult. We may recognize that the number of nuclear warheads is important, but by this indicator, Russia is more powerful than the United States, followed by France. One way to indicate both the size and quality of a state's military is to compare military spending (see Chapter 8). By this indicator, the United States clearly emerges as the most powerful, but the next biggest military spenders—China, France, the United Kingdom, Russia, and Germany—are not necessarily more technologically advanced (in the case of China and Russia) or are not considered major military powers for other reasons (in the case of Germany) when compared to states that spend much less on their military.

Indicators of Economic Power

There are also many indicators of economic power. It is safe to say that since the death of Napoleon, the most powerful nation on earth has been the nation with the greatest industrial capacity. Great Britain dominated the world throughout most of the nineteenth century, not only because it had the world's largest navy, but also because it had industrialized earlier and faster than any other country on earth. The rise of U.S. industrial might and U.S. status as the most powerful state in the world in the twentieth century is not coincidental. The two world wars have accentuated the role of industrial capacity in determining a state's power, and the introduction of nuclear weapons into modern military arsenals has continued the trend. Developing and maintaining delivery systems and a large number of nuclear weapons are technologically and economically demanding tasks for any state. A large and sophisticated industrial plant is necessary if a state is to marshal a sufficient quality and quantity of technological abilities and generate enough wealth to bear the cost of nuclear weapons and modern delivery systems.

Economic bases of power also include natural resources. Modern wars and modern economies require large amounts of oil, coal, iron, and other raw materials. If a state has these within its boundaries, its power is enhanced. But this factor alone does not determine a state's power. Both Great Britain and Japan are islands lacking in large supplies of most natural resources, but they both became great military and economic powers. The fact that the United States has, and the former Soviet Union had, great supplies of natural resources within their boundaries gave them an advantage and may be an important reason that both emerged during the Cold War era as the most powerful states in the international system. Furthermore, in an age of interdependence, those that are less dependent

Map 4.1 Countries' GDP around the world

Source: McKay et al., *A History of World Societies*, 7th ed. (Boston, MA: Houghton Mifflin, 2007), p. 1092. Data from *CIA World Factbook*, 2005. Reprinted by permission of Bedford/ St. Martin's.

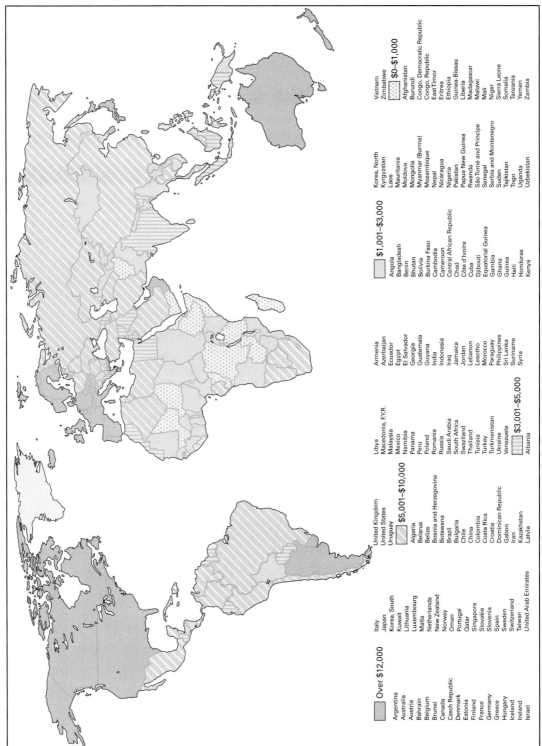

Over $12,000

Argentina
Australia
Austria
Bahrain
Belgium
Canada
Czech Republic
Denmark
Estonia
Finland
France
Germany
Greece
Hungary
Iceland
Ireland
Israel
Italy
Japan
Korea, South
Kuwait
Lithuania
Luxembourg
Malta
Netherlands
New Zealand
Norway
Oman
Portugal
Qatar
Singapore
Slovakia
Slovenia
Spain
Sweden
Switzerland
Taiwan
United Arab Emirates
United Kingdom
United States
Uruguay

$5,001–$10,000

Algeria
Belarus
Belize
Bosnia and Herzegovina
Botswana
Brazil
Bulgaria
Chile
China
Colombia
Costa Rica
Croatia
Dominican Republic
Gabon
Iran
Kazakhstan
Latvia

Libya
Macedonia, FYR.
Malaysia
Mexico
Namibia
Panama
Peru
Poland
Romania
Russia
Saudi Arabia
South Africa
Swaziland
Thailand
Tunisia
Turkey
Turkmenistan
Ukraine
Venezuela

$3,001–$5,000

Albania
Armenia
Azerbaijan
Egypt
El Salvador
Georgia
Guatemala
Guyana
India
Indonesia
Iraq
Jamaica
Jordan
Lebanon
Lesotho
Morocco
Paraguay
Philippines
Sri Lanka
Suriname
Syria

$1,001–$3,000

Angola
Bangladesh
Benin
Bhutan
Bolivia
Burkina Faso
Cambodia
Cameroon
Central African Republic
Chad
Côte d'Ivoire
Cuba
Djibouti
Equatorial Guinea
Gambia
Ghana
Guinea
Haiti
Honduras
Kenya

Korea, North
Kyrgyzstan
Laos
Mauritania
Moldova
Mongolia
Myanmar (Burma)
Mozambique
Nepal
Nicaragua
Nigeria
Pakistan
Papua New Guinea
Rwanda
São Tomé and Principe
Senegal
Serbia and Montenegro
Sudan
Tajikistan
Togo
Uganda
Uzbekistan

Vietnam
Zimbabwe

$0–$1,000

Afghanistan
Burundi
Congo, Democratic Republic
Congo, Republic
East Timor
Eritrea
Ethiopia
Guinea-Bissau
Liberia
Madagascar
Malawi
Mali
Niger
Sierra Leone
Somalia
Tanzania
Yemen
Zambia

on others for natural resources, such as oil, are less constrained in their attempts to influence others. But the history of the past hundred years indicates that access to large quantities of natural resources is sufficient for a state to be powerful; possession is not necessary.

Gross domestic product The value of goods and services produced within a state in a given year.

Industrial capacity and natural resources can contribute to a state's **gross domestic product (GDP)**, a measure of the value of all goods and services produced by the people living in a country and often used as another indicator of economic power.[35] According to this measure, the United States is by far the most powerful, followed by Japan, China, and Germany. Many would argue that GDP overestimates China's economic power, given that China's large population means that its wealth must be distributed over many people. **GDP per capita** takes into account how strong an economy is relative to its size. By this indicator, the four most powerful states are Luxembourg, Qatar, Norway, and Switzerland. The United States drops to seventh place and China to ninety-eighth.[36] Others would argue that both of these measures overestimate the economic power of the United States given that it has a high national debt. Focusing on only this feature of an economy, countries such as Afghanistan and Iran are among the most powerful economic powers in the world because they have the lowest debt.

GDP per capita The value of GDP divided by the population of the state.

Human resources, not just natural resources, may also contribute to a state's economic success. How skilled and educated a state's population is surely matters in its economic production. One measure of education, the literacy rate, puts Georgia as the most powerful country in the world, followed by Estonia and Cuba. Others would argue that an economy is only as healthy as its people are. One measure of the health conditions in a country is the infant mortality rate. Using this indicator, Iceland, Norway, Sweden, Singapore, Finland, Slovenia, and the Czech Republic are the healthiest countries. Using life expectancy at birth, Japan comes out on top, followed by Iceland and Switzerland.[37]

A Simple Index of Power

No index of power can take into account all the factors that allow a state to exercise influence in the international system. But even a simple index based on a few of the important, tangible elements that make a state powerful can reveal key characteristics about the structure of that system. The point is illustrated here by presenting an index based on three concrete factors discussed earlier. The index, shown in Table 4.1, measures a state's power in terms of demographic, industrial, and military dimensions. A state's total population is the indicator that reflects the demographic component of power. Three indicators of industrial capacity are included: (1) urban population, (2) steel and iron production, and (3) energy consumption. Finally, the number of military personnel supported by a state and the size of its military expenditures are the indicators of the military dimension of power. The index score is derived by

TABLE 4.1

Distribution of Power Among Major Powers, 1900–2001

Year	Index Scores by Rank					
	1	2	3	4	5	6
1900	US (19)	GB (18)	GE (13)	RU (11)	FR (7)	AH (4)
1913	US (22)	GE (14)	RU (12)	GB (11)	FR (7)	AH (4)
1925	US (25)	SU (10)	GB (10)	GE (8)	FR (6)	—
1938	US (17)	SU (16)	GE (15)	GB (8)	JA (6)	FR (5)
1950	US (28)	SU (18)	CH (12)	GB (6)	FR (3)	—
1965	US (20)	SU (16)	CH (11)	JA (4)	GE* (4)	GB (4)
1980	SU (17)	US (13)	CH (12)	JA (5)	GE* (3)	—
1995	US (14)	CH (13)	RU (6)	JA (5)	GE (3)	—
2001	US (15)	CH (13)	RU (5)	JA (5)	GE (3)	—

Numbers in parentheses are index scores

AH = Austria-Hungary

CH = China

FR = France

GB = Great Britain

GE = Germany (* Indicates score for West Germany)

JA = Japan

RU = Russia

SU = Soviet Union

US = United States

Source: Figures reflect the Composite Index of National Capability reported in the National Military Capabilities dataset, version 3.02 compiled by the Correlates of War project at the University of Michigan. For descriptions of this project, see J. David Singer, Stuart Bremer, and John Stuckey, "Capability Distribution, Uncertainty, and Major Power War, 1820–1965." in Bruce Russett (ed) *Peace, War, and Numbers,* (Beverly Hills: Sage, 1972) 19–48 and J. David Singer, "Reconstructing the Correlates of War Dataset on Material Capabilities of States, 1816–1985" *International Interactions,* 14 (1987): 115–32.

taking the sum of all six capability components for a given year, converting each state's component to a share of the international system, and then averaging across the six components.

The index is applied to the major powers in the international system since 1900 at key time periods. At the beginning of the twentieth century, according to a fairly firm consensus among scholars of diplomatic history, the following states were the key major powers: Austria-Hungary, France, Great Britain, Germany, Russia, and the United States. Austria-Hungary's status as a great power was permanently destroyed by 1918; Russia and Germany, having also lost status in the First World War, nevertheless regained it by the 1930s. Japan's great power status is also apparent prior to World War II. The Second World War eliminated the Axis powers (Germany, Italy, and Japan) from major power status, and significantly diminished the relative power of Great Britain and France. China first appears on the list of major powers in 1950. At what point Germany and Japan again deserved to be counted as major powers is debatable. In order to trace their ascent to that status during the contemporary era, Japan and Germany are included in Table 4.1 starting in 1965. Japan and Germany replace France and then Great Britain on the list of great powers by the latter part of the twentieth century.

This index of power has obvious limitations (as do the results of its application in Table 4.1). It focuses on military power and ignores the geopolitical factors discussed earlier. It does not take into account who is trying to influence whom to do what, and so may well distort the relative power of different states in specific situations. This limitation is especially relevant, because the index does not take into account alliance ties or any intangible elements of power, such as soft power, skill, will, or purpose—indicators that are much more difficult to quantify. Moreover, the index presented here gives equal weight to each indicator for the whole period under discussion. This is an admittedly arbitrary decision whose main virtue is simplicity, a virtue not to be taken lightly in the context of a preliminary discussion of operational measures of power such as this one. For purposes more ambitious than this discussion, a more complex or refined measure might be justified.

Still, the index quite clearly portrays important changes in the structure of the international system from 1900 to 2001. Notice, for example, the increase in the power of Germany before the First World War. Germany surpassed Great Britain, and by 1913, it had become the most powerful country in Europe. Germany's unseating of the longtime greatest power in Europe (Great Britain) and rapid rise to the top of the power structure on that continent might well have been one of the unsettling elements that caused the system to collapse in 1914. Notice, too, the extent to which the United States benefited, in terms of its power advantage over the other major powers, as a result of the First World War. The substantial increase in the power of Germany before the Second World War is reminiscent of that before the First World War. U.S. supremacy in the international system is reflected quite clearly in the figures for the years immediately following the Second World War, and the emerging power of China in later years is also quite apparent. Finally, the data reflect Japan's appearance as a major actor on the world stage by the 1980s.

Did the Soviet Union really become the most powerful state in the world by 1980, continuing in that position right up to the point of its disintegration? Did China really become almost as powerful as the United States by 2001, as the data for Table 4.1 indicate? There are several good reasons to doubt these implications of the index, because it is biased against the United States in several respects in addition to those already mentioned. Total population, military expenditures, and steel production may all be given too much weight. The index also probably does not give sufficient weight to the productive capacity of the economies of the major powers.

Although the estimation of contemporary Chinese power does reflect the opinion held by many that China is the next likely challenger to the United States,[38] others believe that the components used in this index to assess Chinese power overestimate the importance of China's large population and ignore many factors that are critical to comparing these two states. In economic terms, for example,

> Upon close examination, China's record loses some of its luster. China's economic performance since 1979, for example, is actually less impressive than that of its East Asian neighbors, such as Japan, South Korea, and Taiwan, during comparable periods of growth. Its banking system . . . is saddled with nonperforming loans and is probably the most fragile in Asia. . . . The often breathless conventional wisdom on China's economic reform overlooks major flaws that render many predictions about China's trajectory misleading, if not downright hazardous."[39]

In terms of military power, Chinese military spending and capacity have to be assessed in the context of its technological sophistication. While China will certainly develop many important technologies that are key to military power in the information age, many analysts see that technology will favor the United States for many decades.[40]

In sum, no index of power will capture all the subtle aspects and dimensions of the concept of power as it is used in the study of international politics, although the scores in Table 4.1 are crude indicators that can serve as an important baseline for many efforts to measure power.

Transnational Actors: A Challenge to States' Power?

To assess a state's power in global politics, we should not just consider its capabilities vis-à-vis other states. While states have been the primary focus of attention in the study of international relations, and in this book so far, there are actors of a different kind in global politics, with which states vie for influence. These include intergovernmental organizations, such as NATO and the United Nations, that are composed of states as their members. (Specific international organizations are discussed in several other chapters.) But international actors also include groups or organizations that are quite separate from states, referred to variously as transnational, nongovernmental, or multinational actors. Their distinguishing feature is that although they are involved in activities that include people and objects in different states, they are not formally associated with the governments of states. **Transnational relations** specifically refers to "regular interactions across national boundaries when at least one actor is a nonstate agent or does not operate on behalf of a national government or an intergovernmental organization."[41] Transnational actors are defined by what they are not (they are not states and states are not their members, as they are in international organizations) and by what they do (they operate across borders).

Transnational actors include both business and nonprofit actors that operate across borders. Both types have increased in number quite rapidly in recent decades. There are, for example, more than 78,000 multinational corporations (MNCs).[42] The existence of many small, poor, and badly integrated states in the global political system makes many of these MNCs look relatively strong and effective by comparison. Additionally, there are many nongovernmental organizations (NGOs) that are largely issue focused. The organizations that are reflected in Table 4.2, compiled

transnational relations Interactions across state boundaries when at least one actor is a nonstate actor or an intergovernmental organization.

Somali pirates hijacking a Ukrainian cargo ship in 2008.
(HO/Reuters/Corbis)

TABLE 4.2	
The Growth of International NGOs, 1909–2007	
Year	Number
1909	176
1954	997
1962	1,324
1970	1,993
1981	4,263
1992	4,696
2000	5,936
2005	7,306
2007	7,517

Source: Figures for 2007 are taken from Union of International Associations, *Yearbook of International Organizations: Guide to Global and Civil Society Networks*, Edition 44 2007/2008, *Vol. 2: Geographic Volume International Organization Participation: Country Directory of Secretariats and Membership* (Munich, Germany: KG Saur, 2007), 1719. Figures for previous years are taken from previous editions of this same source. Reproduced with permission of the publisher.

by the *Yearbook of International Organizations*, must have aims that are ". . . genuinely international in character, with the intention to cover operations in at least three countries," must contain members from at least three countries, and must have a constitution giving members the right periodically to elect a governing body and officers.[43] They include such diverse organizations as the International League of Antiquarian Booksellers, the International Basketball Federation, the International Federation of Red Cross and Red Crescent Societies, Save the Children, and the Rainforest Alliance. More rapid and inexpensive communications and transportation have allowed them to organize more effectively and thus to have a bigger impact on the international system. Recently, transnational piracy has garnered world attention. Pirates become transnational actors when they cross into international waters and target foreign ships. In 2008, there were over 100 pirate attacks off the coast of Somalia alone.[44]

The growth of transnational linkages is consistent with the liberal theoretical perspective of international relations (discussed in Chapter 1), which expects increasing cross-national networks to foster more peaceful relations.[45] But nonstate actors that operate across borders and challenge states and their authority may instead choose violence against civilians as their method. "There is no reason to assume that transnational relations regularly promote good causes. Transnational terrorism poses a serious threat to internal stability in many countries, while some scholars have identified Islamic fundamentalism—another transnational social movement—as a major source of future inter-state conflicts."[46]

Transnational actors began to draw the concerted attention of scholars of international politics in the early 1970s, with the onset of détente between the United States and the former Soviet Union, which helped to decrease the pressing importance of national security problems. Détente, in turn, increased the salience of economic issues and other problems outside the area of national security, which nongovernmental actors could address on a more equal footing with states. The 1970s also witnessed some dramatic terrorist attacks, increasingly occurring across borders. By this time, scholars and policymakers alike realized that international actors without formal, organized military forces would play an increasingly important role in international politics. Although the rebirth of the Cold War toward the end of the 1970s and early 1980s refocused attention on national security problems and reduced the attention being given to nongovernmental transnational organizations, the stage seemed set by the end of the twentieth century for transnational organizations to play a correspondingly larger role on the global political stage and for students of global politics to pay more attention to these types of actors. Indeed, "the end of the Cold War should not be underestimated in its impact on international relations theorizing. The failure of traditional international relations theory to at least recognize some underlying trends, pushed many scholars away from structuralist theories such as realism . . . to a renewed appreciation of . . . transnational relations."[47]

This chapter now discusses three types of transnational actors: MNCs, NGOs, and terrorist groups. None of these is necessarily new to the international scene. Yet they are arguably different from their historical counterparts, undoubtedly more significant to world politics, and related to other trends in contemporary world politics, such as the spread of capitalism, the growing importance of international norms, and globalization. It can also be argued that MNCs, NGOs, and international terrorists challenge, as well as operate independently of and even reinforce, the sovereign state system.

Multinational Corporations

Probably the most important type of nonstate actor to emerge in the past two or three decades is the multinational corporation. But corporations that do business in more than one state are not new. As early as the fifteenth century, the Fugger family engaged in financial and trade activities on a multinational basis in several parts of Europe.[48] Many companies, among them Singer, Hertz, Unilever, and Nestlé, have been active in several countries since the early part of the twentieth century.[49] The Krupp organization in Germany sold arms to countries in remote areas of the world before the twentieth century.[50]

Today's MNCs differ from those in the past in three basic ways. First, in the past, companies that did business in several countries were head-quartered in one state, and all or most of their production was centered there. This has changed. International commerce is no longer just inter-national trade, but at least a third of world trade occurs within firms.[51] Today, if a company wants to sell its products in another country, it may set up a subsidiary for manufacturing there, and indeed, sales of foreign affiliates have recently exceeded world total exports. Furthermore, from 1970 to 2006, the total value of **foreign direct investment (FDI)**—the pur-chase or subsidy of a corporation in one country by a corporation head-quartered in another country—rose from $12 billion to $1.2 trillion.[52]

Second, there are many of these companies, and those involved on an international scale have dramatically increased the number of their for-eign subsidiaries. A combination of opportunities presented by improved and inexpensive communication and transportation, the threat of being closed out of new markets, and a desire to take advantage of cheap labor in some developing countries has led to a rapid increase in MNC activ-ity. There are an estimated 78,000 MNCs, with 780,000 foreign affiliates worldwide.[53] The 100 largest MNCs dominate the world economy, con-trolling more than half of all global foreign assets and sales.[54]

The third reason that multinational corporations have become so visible is that they have been spectacularly successful. One of the more dramatic ways to demonstrate the degree of their success is to compare

foreign direct investment (FDI)
The purchase or subsidy of a corporation by a corporation headquartered in another country.

Multinational corporations treat the entire world as their marketplace. McDonald's and Wal-Mart are pictured here, in China.

(© vario images GmbH & Co.KG/Alamy)

economic activities (such as salaries and income) for corporations with the gross domestic products of states. As Table 4.3 shows, many of the largest economic units in the world are corporations, not states. By these measures ExxonMobil is economically larger than Pakistan and New Zealand, and Wal-Mart is larger than Cuba and Uruguay.

TABLE 4.3

The Largest Economic Units: States and MNCs, 2000 (in billions of dollars)

Rank	Name of TNC/economy	Value added*
1	United States	$9,810
2	Japan	4,765
3	Germany	1,866
4	United Kingdom	1,427
5	France	1,294
6	China	1,080
7	Italy	1,074
8	Canada	701
9	Brazil	595
10	Mexico	575
11	Spain	561
12	Korea, Republic of	457
13	India	457
14	Australia	388
15	Netherlands	370
16	Taiwan Province of China	309
17	Argentina	285
18	Russian Federation	251
19	Switzerland	239
20	Sweden	229
21	Belgium	229
22	Turkey	200
23	Austria	189
24	Saudi Arabia	173

(continued)

TABLE 4.3 *(cont.)*

Rank	Name of TNC/economy	Value added*
25	Denmark	163
26	Hong Kong, China	163
27	Norway	162
28	Poland	158
29	Indonesia	153
30	South Africa	126
31	Thailand	122
32	Finland	121
33	Venezuela	120
34	Greece	113
35	Israel	110
36	Portugal	106
37	Iran, Islamic Republic of	105
38	Egypt	99
39	Ireland	95
40	Singapore	92
41	Malaysia	90
42	Colombia	81
43	Philippines	75
44	Chile	71
45	**ExxonMobil**	**63**
46	Pakistan	62
47	**General Motors**	**56**
48	Peru	53
49	Algeria	53
50	New Zealand	51
51	Czech Republic	51
52	United Arab Emirates	48
53	Bangladesh	47
54	Hungary	46
55	**Ford Motor**	**44**

TABLE 4.3   *(cont.)*

Rank	Name of TNC/economy	Value added*
56	**DaimlerChrysler**	**42**
57	Nigeria	41
58	**General Electric**	**39**
59	**Toyota Motor**	**38**
60	Kuwait	38
61	Romania	37
62	**Royal Dutch/Shell**	**36**
63	Morocco	33
64	Ukraine	32
65	**Siemens**	**32**
66	Viet Nam	31
67	Libyan Arab Jamahiriya	31
68	**BP**	**30**
69	**Wal-Mart Stores**	**30**
70	**IBM**	**27**
71	**Volkswagen**	**24**
72	Cuba	24
73	**Hitachi**	**24**
74	**TotalFinaElf**	**23**
75	**Verizon Communications**	**23**
76	**Matsushita Electric Industrial**	**22**
77	**Mitsui & Company**	**20**
78	**E. On**	**20**
79	Oman	20
80	**Sony**	**20**
81	**Mitsubishi**	**20**
82	Uruguay	20
83	Dominican Republic	20
84	Tunisia	19
85	**Philip Morris**	**19**
86	Slovakia	19

(continued)

Rank	Name of TNC/economy	Value added*
87	Croatia	19
88	Guatemala	19
89	Luxembourg	19
90	**SBC Communications**	**19**
91	**Itochu**	**18**
92	Kazakhstan	18
93	Slovenia	18
94	**Honda Motor**	**18**
95	**Eni**	**18**
96	**Nissan Motor**	**18**
97	**Toshiba**	**17**
98	Syrian Arab Republic	17
99	**Glaxosmithkline**	**17**
100	**BT**	**17**

TABLE 4.3 (*cont.*)

*GDP for countries and value added for TNCs. Value added is defined as the sum of salaries, pre-tax profits, and depreciation and amortization.

Source: United Nations Conference on Trade and Development, "Are Transnationals Bigger than Countries" (press release), http://r0.unctad.org/en/press/pr0247en.htm. Used by permission. "How large were the largest TNCs in the world economy in 2000?" from United Nations Conference on Trade and Development (2002). World Investment Report 2002: Transnational Corporations and Export Competitiveness (New York and Geneva: United Nations), p. 90.

In rising to new importance and visibility, MNCs became controversial partly because most of them were American. In the 1970s, seven of the ten largest corporations in the world were American. By 1994, though, out of the ten corporations in the world with the largest annual revenues, only three were American.[55] About half of the largest MNCs in Table 4.3 are primarily American based. Multinational corporations in countries other than the United States are becoming increasingly important, but it is also clear that the United States is still by many measures preeminent in competition among global corporations. The United States is still the primary source of foreign investment in other countries, but EU foreign investment has been growing.[56] In 2007, the U.S. foreign direct investment going abroad amounted to approximately $333 billion; the next most important investors were the United Kingdom with $229 billion and France with $224 billion.[57]

Even if MNCs are largely based in the United States, the relationship between MNCs and the state is a debated question. Are MNCs a tool and a source of power for states, as the neo-Marxism asserts? (See Chapter 1.) Or are MNCs a challenge to states' power because of their transnational ties? Some see MNCs as no longer having any loyalty to the countries that serve as their home bases. They are so intent, according to this view, on serving and taking advantage of the global marketplace that national boundaries, and the political entities they define, are viewed primarily as inefficient nuisances. This attitude is summed up in an article by Robert Reich, former U.S. secretary of labor. According to Reich, corporations have lost their national identity. He points to such corporations as International Business Machines (IBM), in which 40 percent of the employees are non-Americans, and Du Pont, which currently employs 180 Japanese research and development scientists in Yokohama, Japan. Reich's conclusion is that "American-owned corporation[s] . . . have no special relationship with Americans."[58] Although this is not exactly tantamount to an accusation of treason, it certainly does suggest that the lack of national loyalty in MNCs makes their motives, and their activities, highly suspect from the point of view of states.

But it is also possible to counter suggestions that MNCs based in the United States have become so cosmopolitan and so tied to foreign economies that they are no longer really "American." Investors from the United States invest less than 10 percent of the U.S. gross national product (similar to its GDP) in countries outside the United States, not much different than what was invested in 1900.[59] Even with NAFTA, which lessened restrictions on MNCs doing business in Canada and Mexico, fears that U.S. investors would dominate the other states' economies were not realized. "Canadians invested at a more rapid pace in the United States than U.S. firms invested in Canada, and although foreign investment in Mexico soared—from $33 billion in 1993 to $210 billion in 2005—the percentage coming from the United States declined by ten percent."[60] Some American MNCs do earn most of their profits overseas, but they are exceptions to a very different rule. In short, it is possible to mount a plausible argument that "the power of the home country over the multinational [corporation] has not diminished; if anything, it has continued to increase. Corporations have not become national, multinational, or transnational; they remain wedded to their home governments for both political and economic reasons."[61]

Indeed, one analysis of MNCs in the United States, Japan, and Germany found that they remain quite distinct from one another, with "a tendency for MNCs based in those countries to maintain an overwhelming share of the R&D [research and development] spending at home."[62] This same study, addressing the concern that MNCs have so loosened their ties to their home bases that they can no longer be controlled by national governments, concluded that "power, as distinct from legitimate authority, may indeed be shifting within those societies, but it is not obviously shifting away from them and into the boardrooms of supranational business entities."[63] In short, "durable national institutions and distinctive ideological traditions still seem to shape crucial corporate decisions[;] . . . markets in this sense are not replacing political leadership."[64]

The controversy over MNC activities in the world economy and their impact on development of poorer states will be discussed in Chapters 10 and 11. At this time, it is important to note the potential power that MNCs have in global politics. For example, "multinational corporations can use their control over capital to shape the foreign policies of developing states, as well as global economic policies."[65] As discussed earlier in this chapter, many theoretical perspectives see economic power as critical to states' power. For realism, economics is important to power politics because wealth can buy military capabilities to further states' interests. For liberalism, transnational economic power creates interdependence that constrains states. From the perspective of world economic system analysis, economic power structures divide states into a core and a periphery in the international economy. If economic power is important, as these perspectives argue, then MNC control of wealth, outside the influence of the state, is an important shift in the global power structure.

Nongovernmental Organizations

In addition to MNCs, which work on the basis of increasing their profit, there are a number of organizations globally that attempt to influence policies, help people, or connect people across borders:

> A striking upsurge is underway around the globe in organized voluntary activity and the creation of private, nonprofit or nongovernmental organizations. . . . People are forming associations, foundations and similar institutions to deliver human services, promote grass-roots economic development, prevent environmental degradation, protect civil rights and pursue a thousand other objectives formerly unattended or left to the state. The scope and scale of this phenomenon are immense . . . [and] may prove to be as significant . . . as the rise of the nation-state.[66]

Many of these organizations are transnational in scope and are increasingly important players in global politics.[67] "Although there may be no universal agreement on what NGOs are exactly, there is widespread agreement that their numbers, influence, and reach are at unprecedented levels."[68] Early in its history, for example, the United Nations accredited only about forty-one groups as consultative groups to cooperate formally with the UN Economic and Social Council (ECOSOC). Today, more than 3,000 such groups have been recognized by the United Nations.[69]

There is a growing recognition that nongovernmental organizations (NGOs) can have significant effects on state policies and global politics through the creation of international norms, although their degree of influence varies across issues and is greater when they enter the international debate at the initial agenda-setting point of the process,[70] even in security issues.[71] In 1997, a coalition of more than 350 NGOs, including the Vietnam Veterans of America Foundation, Human Rights Watch, and Physicians for Human Rights, and the coalition's leader, Jody Williams, was awarded the Nobel Peace Prize for their efforts in bringing about the Anti-Personnel Landmines Treaty (discussed in Chapter 8). The coalition brought about an amazingly quick and successful negotiation and ratification process.

> Whether the landmine convention is a harbinger of things to come is an interesting question. A similar process was used for the adoption of the Statute of the International Criminal Court. . . . Here again, like-minded countries moved forward with the support of international and nongovernmental organizations without the active support of the United States. The same can be said for the Convention on the Rights of the Child and the various treaties that emerged from the UN Conference on the Environment and Development (1992).[72]

Indeed, NGOs have become particularly active in the area of environmental politics.[73] As discussed in Chapter 13, NGOs such as Greenpeace have become very active, and NGO participation in the Rio Summit and the Convention on Climate Change was unprecedented.

humanitarian relief Assistance to relieve suffering of individuals experiencing hardship.

NGOs have been particularly important in the area of **humanitarian relief** and human rights, and their activities in this area have deep historical roots.[74] One of the oldest NGOs, the **Red Cross/Red Crescent,** was started by a Swiss citizen, Henry Dunant, after witnessing the Battle of Solferino (1859) in northern Italy and the 9,000 wounded who were left unattended on the battlefield. After returning to Geneva, Dunant wrote a book about his experience, concluding [it] with a question: "Would it not be possible, in time of peace and quiet, to form relief societies for the purpose of having care given to the wounded in wartime by zealous, devoted and thoroughly qualified volunteers?" It was this question that led to the founding of the Red Cross. He also asked the military authorities of various countries whether they could formulate "some international principle, sanctioned by a convention and inviolate in character, which, once agreed upon and ratified, might constitute the basis for societies for the relief of the wounded in the different European countries?" This second question was the basis for the Geneva Conventions.[75]

Red Cross/Red Crescent NGO established in 1859 that has as its main objective providing humanitarian assistance and protection to victims of armed conflict.

The International Committee of the Red Cross/Red Crescent continues to provide humanitarian relief today. Other groups, such as Médecins Sans Frontières (Doctors without Borders), established in 1971, coordinate and supply humanitarian relief and health services in times of conflict and natural disasters. This NGO was awarded the Nobel Peace Prize in 1999 for its global efforts. Groups such as CARE and Save the Children also try to alleviate human suffering caused by conflict and poverty.

Beyond humanitarian relief organizations, NGOs have been an important part of the history and development of norms on human rights (see Chapter 9).[76] In the nineteenth century, transnational antislavery groups put pressure on governments to ban the slave trade. Human rights groups were also key in establishing the UN Charter on Human Rights at the time the United Nations was established. One of the more intriguing human rights NGOs to appear in the past twenty-five years is **Amnesty International.** This organization dedicates itself to the release of political prisoners all over the world, as well as securing humane treatment for political prisoners whom it cannot get released. The organization works for the release of such prisoners "provided that [they have] not used or advocated violence."[77]

Amnesty International
NGO dedicated to improvement of human rights, particularly for political prisoners.

Amnesty International's drive to curb human rights violations began in 1961. A London lawyer, Peter Benenson, noticed a newspaper story about Portuguese students who had been imprisoned for taking part in a peaceful demonstration. Benenson organized some friends and acquaintances to agitate for the release of these students. It was presumed to be a temporary campaign, but by the end of the year, the need for a continuing organization had become evident. In 1962, the movement adopted the name Amnesty International, and in 1963, an international secretariat was set up in London. The group today claims a membership of more than 2.2 million members in over 150 countries and was awarded the Nobel Peace Prize in 1977.

> Amnesty International . . . has been using its Urgent Action Network on PeaceNet to mobilize its members to pressure government officials to release political prisoners. It may come as no surprise that dictators and tyrants don't appreciate their actions being made public through this democratic tool.[78]

Supporters of Amnesty International argue that there is little doubt of the need for this organization. Governments now have many sophisticated methods for apprehending political dissidents and abusing them while they are in custody. Miniaturized electronic surveillance equipment to gather information and computerized systems to process information make it difficult for dissidents to escape the clutches of repressive governments. Injections, tranquilizers, cattle prods, electroshock, sleep deprivation, noise bombardment, psychosurgery, and sensory deprivation chambers are among the instruments available to governments bent on torture and behavior modification.

NGOs also perform a variety of functions in international and state governance. They often carry out policy research, monitor state commitments to various international agreements, participate in international negotiations, provide information to international and domestic constituencies about state and business activities and positions, and facilitate ratification.[79] NGOs also function outside traditional governing structures:

NGOs are increasingly taking up functions that were once performed by states. Feeding, public health, development, and education functions have been largely abdicated to NGOs in many regions where states are weak or collapsing, such as sub-Saharan Africa. In Nigeria, public education has generally disappeared under the military regime. The only education taking place in the country is provided by faith-based NGOs such as the Jesuit Mission Bureau.[80]

In addition, NGOs today deliver more official development assistance than does the entire UN system (excluding the World Bank and the International Monetary Fund), and states often use them as intermediaries in foreign aid. Donor governments often see NGOs as more accountable and more efficient than developing states.[81]

NGOs have also had their share of criticism:

One recent study on NGOs and peacebuilding in Bosnia criticized the use of advertising (from signboards to T-shirts) by NGOs to promote their reconstruction programs to potential donors. Such advertising, the study noted, had the effect of denigrating local rebuilding efforts and raising questions about where NGOs were actually putting their money. In Sudan and Somalia, NGOs have subsidized warring factions by making direct and indirect payments to gain access to areas needing assistance. In other conflict settings such as Ethiopia and Rwanda, NGO-constructed roads and camps for civilian assistance have instead been used by combatants.[82]

Another criticism of NGOs concerns their fairly undemocratic nature.[83] Although these organizations often profess to speak for the powerless and voiceless, they themselves are often unaccountable to any constituency and can be closed in their internal decision making. It is also difficult for governments, international institutions, and corporations that want to include NGOs and NGO input to know which NGOs are reputable and which out of the many they should consult. Including all relevant NGOs in policymaking would be a quite cumbersome process.[84]

Nevertheless, the argument can be made that the global political system needs to have organizations that operate outside or possibly above the state framework to put pressure on states to, for example, protect the environment. Similar arguments can be made for analogous organizations, such as Amnesty International, regarding human rights issues. For these and other reasons, probably a growing number of observers of the global political system feel that "the relative power of states will continue to decline. . . . Both in numbers and in impact, nonstate actors have never before approached their current strength. And a still larger role likely lies ahead."[85]

The growing number and importance of nongovernmental organizations is a bit unexpected from the traditional, realist view of global politics. But although realist accounts of international politics typically do not consider transnational organizations because of the importance of states as the central actor in realism (or see them as puppets of states),[86] realism's focus on anarchy as the key characteristic of global politics allows for such nonstate actors to exist since there is no overarching authority to control them. When state and nonstate interests collide, realism would expect power to be the final arbiter, just as it is between states. Thus, from a power-politics perspective,

> when there are conflicts between the state . . . and transnationals, outcomes will depend upon power. . . . For transnational actors, one critical issue is whether or not they must secure legally recognized territorial access, a . . . prerogative possessed by all states, even the smallest and least developed. In some areas, such as raw materials exploitation and civil aviation, access is essential. In others, such as international broadcasting, it is irrelevant. If territorial access is important for transnationals, then states will have bargaining leverage; if it is not, the position of central decision-makers, even in very powerful countries, will be weak.[87]

Other theoretical perspectives stress different forms of power that NGOs can use vis-à-vis states. Constructivism suggests that the use of socially constructed norms has been important for NGO influence.[88] "Nongovernmental organizations have deployed normative resources to compel targeted states to alter their policies through a strategy of shaming."[89] Shaming involves bringing to bear moral pressure to force states to live up to their international obligations or stated values.[90] One study, for example, found that

> States do care about their international reputation and image as "normal" members of the international community. . . . Very few norm-violating governments are prepared to live with the image of a pariah for a long period of time. The Moroccan king, for example, almost completely changed his rhetoric when faced with increasing external criticism . . . [regarding human rights abuses under his leadership]. His self-image as a benign patriarch who cares about his people was shattered by the domestic and international networks. In response, he indicated his desire to belong to the community of civilized . . . nations.[91]

This study concludes that the pressures from nongovernmental organizations were important in improving human rights conditions in Morocco, as well as in Indonesia, the Philippines, Kenya, South Africa, Chile, Guatemala, and Communist Eastern Europe.[92]

NGOs, however, may not be in competition with states or a challenge to the state system. From a liberal, institutionalist perspective, NGOs are important, and not necessarily a threat, to states.

States have incorporated NGOs because their participation enhances the ability, both in technocratic and political terms, of states to regulate through the treaty process. . . . NGO participation provides policy advice, helps monitor commitments and delegations, minimizes ratification risk, and facilitates signaling between governments and constituents."[93]

From an NGO perspective, states are not competitors either. Indeed, many NGOs rely on states for funding and other means of support.[94]

Other theoretical perspectives would also recognize, and welcome, the role of NGOs alongside the state system. Idealism, for example, would find it natural and valuable that some NGOs are stressing values such as humanitarian relief and human rights, particularly when states do not attend to these issues. For feminist perspectives, NGOs have been particularly important, outside the male-dominated state system as they are, for advocating issues such as women's suffrage and women's rights as human rights and putting them on the international agenda.[95] The debate over the relationship between states and NGOs is summarized in the Policy Choices box.

International Terrorism and Terrorist Groups

international terrorist groups Terrorist groups with membership, support, targets, activities, or aims that cross state borders.

Terrorist groups are the third type of transnational actor that we consider in this chapter. Like MNCs and NGOs, today's **international terrorist groups** are related to other trends in international relations, such as globalization, and they represent a potential challenge to states. Also like MNCs and NGOs, contemporary terrorist groups are not new to global politics, although they are arguably different from, more numerous than, and more significant than their historical counterparts. Finally, like these other actors, terrorist groups can be transnational. Although many terrorists operate solely within a single state's borders (such as Timothy McVeigh and associates and their bombing of a federal building in Oklahoma City in 1995), other terrorists act in a transnational fashion, across state boundaries. Operating in many parts of the world, they include the Basque separatist group ETA in Spain and France, the Jaish-e-Mohammed group with activities in Pakistan and India, and Al Qaeda with members reportedly worldwide.

Terrorist incidents are transnational when the actions or targets involve more than one country.[96] The kidnapping and killing of Israeli athletes by members of al-Fatah's Black September terrorist group at the Munich Olympics in 1972 was "the first major contemporary terrorist incident that was truly international in scope."[97] There have since been many more. In 1982, the Lebanese Armed Revolutionary Faction claimed

POLICY CHOICES
Should States Support the Activities of NGOs?

ISSUE: Nongovernmental actors (NGOs) have rapidly been growing in number and increasingly play an important role in international relations. NGOs perform a wide variety of functions, ranging from bringing citizens with common interests together, to coordinating business activities, to advocating for the rights and welfare of disadvantaged citizens, to offering critical humanitarian assistance to disaster victims. But what is their impact on the state-based system? How should states relate to these nongovernmental actors?

Option #1: States should act to support NGOs, as they perform vital functions around the globe.

Arguments: (a) NGOs step in when governments fail to do so. Thousands of people daily would suffer or die without their assistance. (b) NGOs, as neutral actors, can gain access to populations that states, with the baggage of their own self interests and histories, simply cannot. (c) NGOs are a valuable way for people to come together who have common interests and needs. They break down the artificial barriers of sovereign states and foster greater global interdependence.

Counterarguments: (a) NGOs are not simply value-free "do-gooders." They have missions, accept money from donors (often states), and have agendas that may be at odds with various people or governments. (b) NGOs, when they step in where governments have failed to, are actually discouraging governments from owning their responsibilities to their citizens. In the long run, this may allow states to fail and still remain in power. (c) NGOs lack coordination with each other, and this can often make problems worse rather than better. One hundred NGOs trying to help disaster victims might be worse than allowing the state where the disaster happened take charge.

Option #2: States should seek to limit the influence and activities of NGOs.

Arguments: (a) NGOs lack accountability. Their actions, though often admirable, are not always in line with the interests of the people they are assisting. (b) NGOs can save lives, but they can also seek religious converts, push their values, and otherwise leave lasting footprints on people's lives. (c) If states do not limit non-state actors' power, the long-standing, effective, and stable international system based on sovereignty is threatened.

Counterarguments: (a) NGOs represent the power of the people instead of the power of governments. States that seek and support democracy and democratic principles should certainly support NGOs and the activities of citizens working together to address problems and communicate about important issues. (b) NGOs save lives. They may not be perfect actors in all cases, but the good they do far outweighs the possible drawbacks. (c) States continue to hold the lion's share of power in the world, with their national militaries and ability to regulate economies. NGOs are in no way a threat to states.

responsibility for shooting U.S. Lieutenant Colonel Charles Robert Ray in Paris. In 1981, twenty people were injured when a bomb exploded at a U.S. Air Force base in West Germany; the German Red Army Faction claimed responsibility. In 1985, Palestinian gunmen hijacked the *Achille Lauro*, an Italian cruise ship, off the coast of Egypt, killing one American on board. Also in 1985, Abu Nidal's Revolutionary Army Fatah claimed responsibility for attacks on the Rome and Vienna airports. In 1988, a Japanese group, the Organization of Jihad Brigades, claimed responsibility for a car bomb explosion outside a USO club in Italy.[98] "Given the perpetrators' citizenship and the multiple nationalities of the victims, the four simultaneous hijackings on September 11, 2001, were transnational terrorist acts" as well.[99] More recently,

> the 3/11 [train bombings in Madrid, Spain] are transnational because they involved Moroccan terrorists on Spanish soil and killed or maimed victims from a number of countries. The kidnappings of foreign workers in Iraq in 2004 are transnational terrorist events intended to pressure foreign governments to pull out their troops, workers, and diplomats. These acts are also meant to keep other governments from assisting the U.S.-backed fledgling Iraqi government. Clearly, terrorist incidents whose ramifications transcend the venue country are transnational.[100]

Terrorist groups are transnational actors in other ways. "An act can be transnational owing to the foreign ties of its perpetrators, the nature of its institutional or human victims, the target of its demands, or the execution of its logistics."[101] Even groups that operate primarily within a country may receive money from international sources. The Irish Republican Army, for example, was partly funded by Irish Northern Aid, an assistance group established in the United States. Terrorist organizations also share information, weapons, and training facilities, and they create networks and alliances across borders. In 1986, the Red Army Faction of West Germany and Action Direct of France issued a communiqué declaring their intention to attack the North American Treaty Organization (NATO) jointly. This was followed by several attacks—the killing of a French arms sales official and a West German defense businessman and the killing of two Americans in a bombing of a U.S. air base in Frankfurt—for which the groups claimed joint responsibility.[102] An international conference of terrorist groups, all aligned against U.S. forces in Europe, took place in Germany in 1986, with reports of 500 people attending.[103]

Terrorist groups can also be multinational corporations, with businesses in various countries to support their operations. The PLO, or Palestine Liberation Organization (itself a political organization with several terrorist groups historically associated with it) owned farms and shops in Sudan, Somalia, Uganda, Guinea, Tanzania, Mozambique, and Zimbabwe and invested profits in stocks and bonds in Europe and the United States.[104] Osama bin Laden's Al Qaeda group is reportedly involved in banking, agricultural, transportation, and investment companies.[105] Indeed, "it is striking how closely transnational terror groups like Al Qaeda and the Tamil Tigers [of Sri Lanka] have come to resemble large multinational corporations."[106]

The international community has only recently put international terrorism on the global agenda:

> The evolution of terrorism as a major international policy issue . . . occurred only in the last quarter century. Before that, it was generally viewed as ancillary to some other problem. For example, Middle East terrorism was generally viewed as a subset of the Arab-Israeli problem. . . . The perception of a terrorist threat distinct from an insurgent threat emerged in the late 1960s from the worldwide student antiwar protest movement in reaction to the Vietnam War. It spawned such terrorist organizations as the Baader-Meinhof Group in Germany, the Italian Red Brigades, and the Japanese Red Army."[107]

While various efforts to combat terrorism took place in the 1970s, 1980s, and 1990s, the attacks on the United States on September 11, 2001, placed international terrorism front and center on the global agenda.

Terrorism's Challenge to the State System

The history, origins, and definitions of terrorism will be discussed in detail in Chapter 7. At this time, it is important to note that along with multinational corporations and nongovernmental organizations, terrorist groups represent another significant actor outside the authority of states. If contemporary terrorism represents a challenge to the state sovereignty system:

> The use of terrorism implies an attempt to de-legitimise the concept of sovereignty, and even the structure of the state system itself. . . . The gradual transition at the end of the twentieth century away from direct state sponsorship of terrorism, and towards more amorphous groups . . . is a potentially serious development. Obviously, states are far from helpless, but in an increasingly globalised international environment, the traditional state-centric means of responding to such a threat will not work and may even be counterproductive.[108]

Terrorism in the contemporary global context challenges many theoretical perspectives for understanding international politics. Realism, with its focus on states as the primary actors, has particular difficulty accounting for the power of terrorist groups and the policies designed to deal with them:

> For realists . . . transnational terrorism creates a formidable dilemma. If a state is the victim of private actors such as

terrorists, it will try to eliminate these groups by depriving them of sanctuaries and punishing the states that harbor them. The national interest of the attacked state will therefore require either armed interventions against governments supporting terrorists or a course of prudence and discreet pressure on other governments to bring these terrorists to justice. Either option requires a questioning of sovereignty—the holy concept of realist theories.[109]

When states do face terrorist actors, their overwhelming military power, also a key concept of realism, may not translate into victory, because the terrorists may engage in asymmetrical warfare (as discussed earlier in this chapter), which is often a challenge for states to resist. Osama bin Laden, for example, has spoken about "the asymmetric virtues of guerilla warfare. Indeed, the al Qaeda leader has often cited the victory he claims was achieved with this tactic against American forces in Mogadishu, Somalia, during October 1993—when eighteen U.S. Army Rangers and Delta Force commandos were killed in fighting with Somali militiamen and, according to bin Laden, al Qaeda fighters too. . . . For bin Laden, the withdrawal of American military forces that followed is proof that terrorism and guerilla warfare defeat more powerful opponents."[110] Nonstate actors also rely on other forms of power. In the "battle for hearts and minds," for example, groups like al Qaeda, Hezbollah, and Hamas win support and recruit members by providing public services.

> Indeed, in most Islamic countries, radical groups of fundamentalists have developed a social and cultural infrastructure to build an Islamic civil society and fill a vacuum that their countries' governments have neglected. For example during the 1990s in Egypt, Jordan, the West Bank and Gaza, Afghanistan, and Pakistan, radical movements provided health care, education, and welfare for those nations' poor.[111]

Terrorism may indeed be a reaction to weaknesses in the sovereign state system, brought on by other global processes and transnational actors:

> Rather than religious nationalists, transnational activists like bin Laden are guerrilla anti-globalists. Bin Laden and his vicious acts have a credibility in some quarters of the world because of the uncertainties of this moment of global history. Both violence and religion historically have appeared when authority is in question, since they are both ways of challenging and replacing authority.[112]

Globalization is undoubtedly connected with contemporary terrorism.[113] Technology, as one engine of globalization, has been a tool that terrorist groups have used to their advantage. And the backlash against globalization has advantaged terrorists, as it is "fueled by a resistance to unjust' economic globalization and to a Western culture deemed threatening to local religions and culture."[114] Globalization and its backlash will be discussed in more detail in Chapter 14.

For some, then, terrorism represents a new age of global politics, a more transnational, globalized age. Others disagree:

> Even the most prominent international terrorist threat of today, from radical Islamist political organizations, are in reality strongly rooted in the politics of individual sovereign political states. Islamist groups involved in terrorism in Egypt, Israel/Palestine, and Algeria, for example, are far more interested in creating revolutionary Islamic regimes in their own countries than in some utopian desire to submerge them into a larger Islamic political entity.[115]

Yet even if the state system is largely intact, the current wave of terrorism has certainly changed some relationships in that system:

> While we have obviously not seen the last of inter-state war, war between organised states will no longer be the main driving force that it has been in the last 400 years or so. . . . We have already seen evidence of a remarkable shift: States are entering coalitions not to fight a traditional "war" or to deter such a war fought by other states or coalitions. They are aligning in surprising ways to fight the major non-state threat that has successfully targeted the leading state power: the United States. There is a new relationship evolving between formal rivals like Russia and the United States, and China and the United States, and the guiding principle around which they align is not military power but the stability and integrity of the state system itself.[116]

One observer sums up these points nicely, proposing that "the classical realist universe of Hans Morgenthau . . . may therefore still be very much alive in a world of states, but it has increasingly hazy contours and offers only difficult choices when it faces the threat of terrorism."[117]

Transnational actors have proliferated in number and grown in significance because of the changing nature of power and the changes in world politics discussed in previous and subsequent chapters. The end of the Cold War (see Chapter 3), the increase in the number of democratic political systems and their possible implications for state-to-state relations (see Chapters 3 and 6), the changing nature and significance of international law and international norms of democracy and human rights (see Chapter 9), and the rise of global environmental issues on the international agenda (see Chapter 13) all contribute to, and also stem from, contemporary transnational politics.[118] Globalization (see Chapter 14) is also inextricably linked to these trends.

It seems increasingly reasonable to argue that states need to give way to some extent to these nongovernmental political entities. Even the larger and more important states, which dominate an anarchic and politically decentralized global political system, seem ill equipped today to deal with a growing variety of problems such as global environmental issues. Indeed,

> the activities of these organizations are increasingly imping-ing upon functions which previously were jealously guarded by states. Not only have health, education, welfare, and develop-ment functions been carried out by nonstate actors, but MNCs and NGOs are now also active in law enforcement and police training, economic and environmental policy making, land use, and even arms control. [119]

This development represents a potential challenge to the historical and legal sovereign system of states. According to one analyst of these non-state entities, "National governments are sharing powers . . . with busi-nesses, with international organizations, and with . . . nongovernmental organizations (NGOs). The steady concentration of power in the hands of states that began in 1648 with the Peace of Westphalia is over, at least for a while."[120] Thus, transnational actors lead many to question the future of the state as the dominant actor in world politics. Others see a change in the international system that accommodates both state- centered and nonstate-centered political relations.[121] Some, for example, argue that a world civil society is growing alongside the state that not only seeks to influence state behavior but involves actors who have political signifi-cance in their own right relating to each other outside of state-to-state relations.[122] Others have suggested that the world has bifurcated into a state-centric world, in which states interact much as they have historically, and a multicentric world, in which transnational actors and international organizations dominate, and that these two worlds operate simultaneously, sometimes independently and sometimes influencing one another.[123]

SUMMARY

- *Nation* is a psychological concept, referring to a group of people who identify with each other based on a common language, ethnicity, or re-ligion. *State* is a political concept, referring to a government that exer-cises authority over a territory. State boundaries are rarely contiguous with national boundaries.

- Power is a confusing concept, because it often refers to capabilities (what states possess), as well as influence (what states can do). Because occasionally states that seem powerful in terms of capabilities fail to have influence, it is important to separate these issues and deal with the paradox of unrealized power.

- There are a variety of sources of a state's power. Military capabilities, primarily the size of armed forces, are a fairly good predictor of influence in international conflict, especially if the capabilities of allies are considered. However, less tangible factors, such as the will to win, seem to be important in many cases of conflict, including conflicts between states and nonstate actors engaging in asymmetrical warfare.

- Economic power, especially given changes in the international system, is another source of state power. Alternative conceptions of power include soft power, based on what others want to emulate and the control of the agenda, and moral authority. Others argue that power should be thought of in terms of ideas that make influence possible and in terms of the ability to cooperate. It is important to think of power according to the type of task for which capabilities are employed.

- Both economic and military capabilities can be measured in a variety of ways. Different measures often point to different power rankings. An index of power seeks to include multiple measures and can show the relative change in states' power over time.

- Transnational relations that involve multinational corporations, nongovernmental organizations, and terrorist groups may represent the wave of the future. Certainly these types of transnational actors are having a significant impact on global politics. The global political system today faces numerous problems that a state-dominated system may find impossible to resolve. Transnational organizations have become increasingly visible in recent decades and may pose a challenge to states' power.

- MNCs have proliferated in the past twenty or thirty years and have been very successful. MNCs are controversial, because they have been dominated by American firms, and they are seen as potential challenges to states because of their size and their transnational interests.

- NGOs have proliferated over the past few decades and now perform a variety of functions in international and state governance. Their impact in human rights, development assistance, humanitarian relief, security issues, and environmental politics is significant. In many ways, the rise of NGO activity represents a challenge to the state system and the perspectives that place states as the central actors in international politics. In other ways, though, NGOs appear complementary to states and offer avenues for addressing issues that cross state boundaries.

- Many terrorist groups operate transnationally and have international targets. International terrorism is not new but has recently been placed at the top of the international agenda. As nonstate actors, terrorist groups are another challenge to the power of states, the concept of state sovereignty, and the ways we think about global politics.

KEY TERMS

nation 97
multinational states 97
multistate nations 97
stateless nations 97
power 98
paradox of unrealized power 99
asymmetrical warfare 100
soft power 106
geopolitics 109
gross domestic product 113

GDP per capita 113
transnational relations 117
foreign direct investment
 (FDI) 120
humanitarian relief 127
Red Cross/Red Crescent 127
Amnesty International 128
international terrorist
 groups 131

CHAPTER 5

Inside States: The Making of Foreign Policy

unitary actors
Assumption that states are monolithic, with no divisions or opinion differences within government or the larger society.

foreign policy approach The approach to understanding international politics that focuses on how domestic actors seek to influence states' actions and the ways in which foreign policy is made.

In most discussions of global politics (including the previous chapters in this book), people speak of states as the actors in international politics. News agencies, for example, report that "Brazil agreed to trade terms today," or "Indonesia refused to attend a meeting" or "Moscow decided to send troops." In such reports, states or their capitals, are treated as if they are **unitary actors**—monolithic, speaking with one voice, and with no divisions or differences of opinions within the government or the larger society.

This assumption that states are unitary actors is consistent with most theoretical perspectives for understanding global politics. In particular, realism sees sovereign states as having control over the people in its territory and therefore able to quell any divisions. In addition, realism believes that because security is the primary issue facing states, reasonable people will put aside any differences they may have and act with one voice for the sake of national interests. While other theoretical perspectives, such as liberalism and neo-Marxism, do not assume states are unitary (liberalism sees multiple channels existing across states, and neo-Marxism sees economic classes existing across states), they generally do not examine what goes on inside states and how this affects states' foreign policies. Only liberalism's claim that democratic governments are more constrained than nondemocratic governments takes seriously how the politics within states affects the politics between states.

Many who study international relations, however, believe that in order to understand what goes on between states, it is necessary to understand what goes on within them. This is the **foreign policy approach.** "Foreign policy consists of those discrete official actions of the authoritative decisionmaker of a nation's government, or their agents, which are intended by the decisionmakers to influence the behavior of international actors external to their own policy."[1] The foreign policy approach to understanding global politics argues that attention to what goes on inside states can give us a better explanation for why states might not be acting as expected in response to international conditions. France during the Cold War, for example, attempted to defy the constraints of the bipolar Cold War, even opting out of the military structure of the North Atlantic Treaty Organization (NATO).[2] Libyan leader Muammar Qaddafi does not take the limited power of his small state as a given but instead attempts to "exploit the seams" of the international system by crafting a maverick foreign policy.[3] Britain today faces many of the same economic constraints as other European Union (EU) members, but instead has chosen not to join the single currency.[4] Attention to domestic actors and politics, many argue, can help explain why some states challenge international constraints. Part of the explanation may be that they are not in fact unitary. The disagreements that occur within states and how those are resolved are considered domestic sources of foreign policy. Domestic sources of foreign policy include what the public is like, the type of political system, and how decisions get made—particularly the effects of bureaucracies and the characteristics of leaders on the process of making foreign policy.

The theoretical perspectives of realism and liberalism also often assume that states, or their leaders who represent states, are **rational actors.**

rational actors The idea that individuals make decisions through a process that includes clarification of goals, weighing of alternatives and consequences, and selection of optimal course of action.

> The rational model, as usually conceived, maintains that an individual decisionmaker reaches a decision via a clearly defined intellectual process: He or she clarifies and ranks values and goals; then weighs all (or at least the leading) alternative courses of action (policies); the likely consequences (costs/benefits) of each; and ultimately chooses the optimal course(s) of action with regard to the ends pursued.[5]

Because most of the theoretical perspectives discussed in Chapter 1 focus on the constraints of the international system (realism focuses on the anarchical nature of the system and the distribution of power in the system, liberalism on the degree of interdependence, and neo-marxism on the structure of wealth in the international capitalist system), states are assumed to respond rationally to these constraints. While domestic actors may rationally respond to internal constraints, they may also misperceive or ignore both internal and external constraints. The **psychological approach** to foreign policy focuses on leaders' beliefs and images of other countries, their personalities and policymaking styles, and how individuals and groups process information and make choices that may be less than perfect.

psychological approach Focuses on leaders' beliefs, personalities, and styles, and how individuals and groups process information and make decisions.

Public Opinion

public opinion The attitudes that people have regarding their state's goals and policies.

One domestic source of foreign policy is the people themselves. What a state does in international politics may be driven by what the people, rather than just the leaders, think the state should do. **Public opinion** concerns the attitudes people of a state have on a particular foreign policy. The public may be divided over what the state should do, or there may be a consensus. In either event, the public may push state leaders to act in ways that are not necessarily in the optimal interests of the state. When there is a division in public opinion or when leaders' preferences are at odds with public opinion, the state is clearly not unitary. How these differences are negotiated, then, becomes important for understanding state behavior in global politics. For the public to be considered a source of a state's foreign policy, three conditions must be satisfied: (1) The public must have knowledge of foreign policy; (2) public opinion must be stable enough for leaders to judge what the people want; and (3) the public's views must be taken into account by policymakers. According to democratic theory, these conditions must be met for foreign policy to represent "the will of the people." Indeed, we would expect foreign policy to be more affected by public opinion in democracies, compared to authoritarian systems, because democracies have institutionalized means for citizens to influence policy. Even in authoritarian systems, however, the question of the impact of public opinion on foreign policy is not irrelevant.

Does the Public Know or Care about Foreign Policy?

Most people do not know or care very much about international politics. This is true even in democracies such as the United States, where people have access to information on foreign policy issues.[6] Examples abound. "It has been easy to portray the American public as one knowing little about major political issues and not eager to learn more."[7] Surveys show that in 1979, only about 34 percent of Americans knew which two countries were participants in the Strategic Arms Limitation Talks (SALT).[8] The war in Vietnam was one of the most intensely debated foreign policy issues in U.S. history; 58,000 American soldiers lost their lives, and the war generated more domestic unrest than the United States had seen since the Civil War. And yet in 1985, less than two-thirds of the American public knew that the United States had supported South Vietnam against North Vietnam in that war.[9] A study by the National Geographic Society in 1988 reported that many Americans could not find the United States, much less England, Greece, Hungary, or Poland, on a world map and that fully half did not know that France, China, and India have nuclear weapons.[10] Even on economic issues that presumably more directly touch people's lives, Americans are largely ignorant. During the debates of the North American Free Trade Agreement (NAFTA), for example, only 50 percent of Americans had ever heard of the agreement.[11] Ignorance of foreign affairs is not limited to the American public. In France, Germany, and Japan as well as in the United States, only about "20–30 percent of the public indicate serious concern about foreign affairs."[12] In short, it is widely agreed that "the vast majority of citizens hold pictures of the world that are at best sketchy, blurred, and without detail, or at worst so impoverished as to beggar description."[13]

In any society, individuals are most likely to be concerned about problems that affect them directly and over which they feel they have some control. Problems on the scale of international politics often seem to fail on both counts. Wars, economic crises, and coups in one part of the world can have a dramatic impact on the lives of individuals in other parts of the world. The disintegration of the Soviet Union, for example, can lead to reductions in the defense budget and the closing of military bases all over the country. But the connection between events in certain countries and their impact on individuals in other countries is seldom so clear. And even if the effect of international events is great, individuals in the countries affected may not have enough knowledge to be able to see the link between such events and their local impact. Add to this the fact that even when the link is clear, most individuals feel they have no control over the event or its consequences, and it is not hard to see

attentive public The people who attend to and are knowledgeable about foreign policy issues and international politics.

why most people, even in countries whose citizens are on average relatively wealthy and highly educated, do not know or care very much about international politics. The relatively small number of people who do pay attention to and are relatively knowledgeable about foreign policy issues and international politics is sometimes referred to as the **attentive public** and typically consists of no more than 10 percent of the population.[14]

There are reasons to hope that public opinion in most countries of the world is becoming better informed in relation to foreign policies.

> The expansion of analytic skills is . . . worldwide in scope. Not only for citizens in democratic and industrialized societies, but also for Afghan tribesmen and Argentine gauchos, for peasants in India and protesters in Chile, for guerrillas in Peru and students in the Philippines, for blacks in South Africa and Palestinians in Israel, the interdependence of global life and the consequences of collective actions are daily experiences.[15]

One reason for this change is that higher educational levels are increasing almost everywhere. "Enrollments in higher education have been increasing since 1970 in every part of the world. . . . The same has been true since 1960 in primary and secondary education as well, and for both males and females."[16] Another reason has to do with the worldwide spread of television and the Internet. Even in such desperately poor countries as India, over half of the population now has access to television. "Access to television has become sufficiently global in scope that it must be regarded as a change of [fundamental] proportions."[17]

Is Public Opinion Moody or Wise?

Even if the public is interested and informed about foreign policy, they would have great difficulty influencing leaders if public opinion was so unstable that leaders could not confidently discern and predict what the public prefers. The conventional wisdom has been that public opinion on foreign policy is subject to wildly fluctuating moods and cannot be counted on for consistent support of foreign policy commitments.[18] But the available evidence does not consistently support such a negative view of public opinion regarding foreign policy. There certainly are fluctuations in public opinion about foreign policy issues, but they are not unpredictable or irrational shifts.

Opinion shifts in the American public from 1935 to 1985 regarding issues such as isolationism, the Cold War, the Korean War, the United Nations, Vietnam, and détente, for example, were arguably "understandable in terms of changing circumstances and changing information. Moreover, . . . most of them [were] reasonable, or sensible, in that they reflect in a logical fashion the impact of new information."[19] A recent study of Italian public opinion reached a similar conclusion: "The commonly held idea that Italian public opinion is unpredictable and capricious in foreign policy is not supported by the available evidence. Public opinion in Italy does not change more abruptly or more frequently than in the United States, Germany, and France."[20] In a similar vein, the public in the United States seems capable of differentiating between uses of force by the United States for different kinds of purposes in a discriminating way. In general, public opinion responds more favorably to force when it is used to resist aggression than when it is applied to impose internal political change on another state. Improvements in the public approval ratings of presidents "following military action to impose foreign policy restraint [that is, to resist aggression] are nearly 4 percent greater . . . than when internal political change is the principal objective."[21]

In order to respond to foreign policy events and make a judgment, the public may rely on underlying **core values,** which are

core values   The underlying beliefs that the public holds and uses to judge foreign policy.

> underlying beliefs—such as isolationism, anticommunism, non-appeasement, neutrality, and anti-imperialism—that the public holds and uses to judge foreign policy. In Germany and Japan, for example, the public has come to value multilateralism and antimilitarism. In post Cold War Russia and in contemporary India, core values support the maintenance of a "great power" identity.[22]

Core values provide a structure to the public's attitudes on foreign policy and help make sense of information concerning events in global politics.[23]

Does Public Opinion Influence Foreign Policy?

Because only a rather small proportion of the public knows or cares very much about most foreign policy issues, it would be logical to conclude that most people rarely do very much to let their opinions be known or attempt to persuade others to accept their point of view. That logical conclusion is supported by concrete evidence. In the United States, for example, the Vietnam War provoked an unusual amount of interest for a foreign policy issue. Yet a survey of a representative sample of Americans in 1967 found that although most people expressed a concern about the war, most had done nothing to reflect their concern. Only 13 percent reported that they had made any attempt at all to persuade others to change their views on the war. Only 3 percent had bothered to write letters to newspapers or political officials, and only 1 percent had taken part in marches or demonstrations.[24]

Recent issues, however, may have sparked a renewed activism in global politics. Protesters have gathered in large numbers to voice their concerns about globalization at international economic summits. In 2003, world opinion across the globe was against a military intervention in Iraq, and millions of protesters gathered on February 15, particularly in Europe and the United States, to denounce U.S. policy toward Iraq. Despite the numbers, the protesters constituted a very small proportion of the public, and the intervention against Iraq proceeded even with the participation of some European countries in which a large majority opposed the war.[25]

The next logical conclusion would be that public opinion does not have much impact on foreign policy. Logic and some evidence seem to support each other in this regard, but the difficulty in assessing the impact of public opinion should be stressed. Elites that deal with foreign policy issues usually do not feel very constrained by public opinion. Some analysts go so far as to claim that "no major foreign policy decision in the United States has ever been made in response to spontaneous public demand."[26] In many countries, even democratic ones, there are numerous cases in which crucial foreign policy decisions have been taken in the absence of mass public consensus. West Germany's decision to rearm and join NATO in the early 1950s and French decisions to build an independent nuclear force in the 1950s and leave NATO's military institutions in the mid-1960s were made by a small circle of elites without input by the public.[27]

This claim might seem to contradict the experience of many readers who have noticed how closely politicians watch public opinion polls. Even U.S. presidents seem to have reacted to public opinion concerning foreign policy issues rather dramatically in recent times. President Johnson was apparently persuaded not to seek reelection in 1968 by public opposition to his Vietnam War policy. President Carter, faced with rapidly declining popularity as the 1980 election drew near, approved an attempt to rescue the U.S. hostages in Iran, which failed miserably. In 1993, in an apparent response to public concern about increasing immigration, President Clinton continued steps to prevent Haitian refugees from escaping from their homeland into the United States, even though he had condemned his predecessor, George H. W. Bush, for adopting such a policy.[28]

But one can get an exaggerated impression of the impact of public opinion on foreign policy by concentrating on such events. For example, President Franklin Roosevelt, in the years before World War II, was faced with overwhelmingly isolationist attitudes among the general public. Even so, he worked quietly behind the scenes to prepare the United States for war and never swayed from his conviction that the United States would have to resist actively the aggressive policies of Germany and Japan at some point. President Johnson made a concession to public opinion by campaigning as a dove in favor of peace in the election of 1964, but we now know that he planned to escalate the Vietnam War as soon as the election was over. Johnson might have decided not to run for reelection in 1968 because of public opinion against his war policy, but it is less clear that public opinion changed that policy: U.S. involvement in the war continued for five more years. President Carter knew that public opinion polls showed that turning over the Panama Canal to Panama was a tremendously unpopular idea. He negotiated the treaty anyway, apparently figuring that an educational campaign would persuade most of the public (and the U.S. Senate) to support its ratification. He was right. In France, "mass public opinion affects policy only if it reaches top decisionmakers, notably the president. It is often he who decides whether to respond to the public's demands."[29]

Even if the government's policy is in line with public opinion, it is difficult to know who influences whom. Diplomats and other foreign policy officials are fond of saying that "public opinion demanded" a concession or a hardline stand with respect to a foreign policy issue. But does the public influence decisions, or do government officials manipulate public opinion to support their point of view and then announce decisions they had settled on in advance? Probably a majority of scholars believe that elites (people in leadership positions within political, economic, or military organizations) influence the public more than the public influences elites, especially with regard to foreign policy issues. This impression that decision makers tend to treat public opinion as a problem to be dealt with rather than as a guide to policy has been confirmed in recent research based on interviews with officials in the National Security Council and the U.S. State Department. The results of the interviews showed quite clearly that "when public opposition does emerge, the reaction of most officials is . . . not to change the policy in question, but to try to educate' the public, thereby bringing public opinion in line with the policy."[30] Most scholars agree that the George W. Bush administration undertook such an effort to influence the public to support the war in Iraq. As the president and his advisers turned their attention toward Iraq after September 11 and the Afghanistan intervention,

> the administration sought to lead the public using a combination of persuasion and priming—especially in relation to WMD [weapons of mass destruction]. . . . So successful were its efforts that before the war the majority of the public believed Iraq possessed WMD; after the war, roughly a third incorrectly believed that the USA had actually discovered WMD . . . [T]he administration chose a public relations strategy that appears to be a prime example of policy 'oversell' . . . : the exaggeration of threats in order to generate public support and overcome domestic opposition.[31]

The public seems to be particularly vulnerable to follow elites on military issues, at least initially. One of the best-known relationships between public opinion and foreign policy in the United States involves the **rally-round-the-flag effect,** which increases the popularity of leaders whenever they elect to use force with respect to some foreign policy issue.[32] The rally-round-the-flag effect is, however, "far from automatic. . . . One can easily identify international crises . . . in which no significant positive rally took place."[33] One analysis of 102 cases in the United States when the public might have been expected to rally around the president reveals that in fact, the average change in

rally-round-the-flag effect An increase in a leader's popularity following the use of force.

the president's approval rating after those cases was 0 percent.[34] Indeed, President George H. W. Bush could not translate the public's approval of the war against Iraq in 1991 into a victory for him in the presidential election of 1992. And in the United Kingdom, in which only a minority supported their country's participation in the Iraq war, a "rally effect" quickly turned that support into a majority at the onset of the war, but just as quickly melted away, only two months into the conflict.[35]

Indeed, the support for leaders in times of conflict may be short-lived, particularly when there are high troop casualties. According to the **"body-bag syndrome,"**

> the public, at least in Western democratic countries, has lost the willingness and endurance to fight and carry the consequences. . . . Especially in the case of humanitarian crises, the public would first of all put pressure on their governments to do something' . . . but when the risks of military actions in the form of casualties become evident it would recoil at the prospect.[36]

The body-bag syndrome did seem to be operating in the U.S. public's support for missions in Korea, Vietnam, and Iraq. Indeed,

> American public opinion became a key factor in all three wars, and in each one there has been a simple association: as casualties mount, support decreases . . . The only thing remarkable about the current war in Iraq is how precipitously American public support has dropped off. Casualty for casualty, support

body-bag syndrome The negative relationship between high levels of troop casualties and public support for a war.

Tens of thousands of people marched across U.S. Cities in January 2007 to protest the continuing war in Iraq.
(AP Photo/Reed Saxon)

has declined far more quickly than it did during either the Korea or the Vietnam War.[37]

Despite these particular cases, systematic evidence of the body-bag syndrome has not been found.[38] Furthermore, a decline in public support that comes with an increase in casualties does not necessarily mean the casualties caused the decline. Instead, some argue the causality flows in the reverse direction: that as public support of the military mission in general declines, tolerance for casualties decline. If the public continues to see the value of the mission, this argument goes, public approval can sustain a large number of casualties.[39] Political scientist John Mueller has argued that the precipitous decline in support for the war in Iraq came when one of the main justifications for the war—the threat from weapons of mass destruction—was largely discredited.[40]

The most important way that public opinion does influence foreign policy may be through the core values or underlying beliefs that the public holds and uses to judge foreign policy. While these general beliefs do not necessarily guide leaders to choose particular policies, they do set parameters beyond which leaders cannot stray or risk retaliation.[41] Core values may be less vulnerable to elite manipulation as well. In Germany, for example, core values such as multilateralism and antimilitarism and other "collective attitudes and perceptions of average citizens may shape the elite discourse by ruling certain initiatives 'in' or 'out' of political bounds."[42] And core values in Britain that stress an "English identity" that is quite separate and stands above a "European identity" are arguably an important factor behind Britain's reluctance to participate fully in the EU and particularly the common Euro currency.[43]

Manipulation of public opinion by leaders may not be successful in all cases. In the war with Iraq, for example, despite the U.S. government's success at influencing public beliefs regarding the threat of weapons of mass destruction and Iraqi-terrorist connections, public support for the war stayed at a fairly stable 60 percent level. If the administration led the public into war, it was partly "because after September 11, the public was inclined to support a war. This would appear to be consistent with previous research that suggests that the effect of elite leadership on foreign policy is more limited than commonly supposed."[44]

Should the Public Influence Foreign Policy?

"Open covenants openly arrived at with input from the populace" was one of President Woodrow Wilson's principles, adopted in the belief that secret deals between professional diplomats and makers of foreign policy were a part of traditional international politics that led to disasters such as World War I. The developers of democratic theory, such as Thomas Jefferson, certainly believed that foreign policy was not a special area to be controlled by an elite group. Wary of a monarchical style of government that dominated the power politics in Europe, the writers of the U.S.

Constitution divided foreign policy powers between the legislative and executive branches, partly in hopes that this would make policy more representative of the people's preferences.

The trouble with that idea, according to anti-Wilsonians and elite theorists, is that an ignorant public opinion creates more problems. The famous diplomat George F. Kennan wrote,

> I sometimes wonder whether . . . a democracy is . . . similar to one of those prehistoric monsters with a body as long as this room and the brain the size of a pin: he lies there in his comfortable primeval mud and pays little attention to his environment: he is slow to wrath—in fact, you practically have to whack his tail off to make him aware that his interests are being disturbed; but once he grasps this . . . he not only destroys his adversary but largely wrecks his native habitat.[45]

The international debate over intervention in Iraq in the winter of 2003 once again focused attention on the role of public opinion—both world opinion and domestic opinion—in foreign policy choices. The overwhelming antiwar opinion around the globe, seen in numerous and sizable protests, led one writer in *The New York Times* to argue that "there may still be two superpowers on the planet: the United States and world public opinion. In his campaign to disarm Iraq, by war if necessary, President Bush appears to be eyeball to eyeball with a tenacious new adversary: millions of people who flooded the streets of New York and dozens of other world cities to say they are against war based on the evidence at hand."[46] British Prime Minister Tony Blair faced even stronger public criticism at home for his choice to support U.S. plans for going to war against Iraq without a United Nations mandate. Despite the public's opposition, both Blair and Bush proceeded to execute the invasion in March 2003, and both were subsequently reelected. In response to the protests, Bush replied that basing foreign policy on the size of demonstrations would be similar to basing policy on a focus group and that "the role of a leader is to decide policy based upon the security, in this case, the security of the people."[47] The Policy Choices box summarizes some of the general arguments for and against public influence on foreign policy.

Differences in Political Systems

It is probably safe to say that in general, public opinion has a greater impact in democratic states than in autocracies. It would be a mistake, however, to conclude that public opinion can be ignored entirely in autocratic, or nondemocratic, states. Public opinion on the war in Afghanistan, for example, apparently affected Soviet foreign policy with respect to that war (and may ultimately have played a role in bringing down the whole regime). Nevertheless, many propositions about the effects of public opinion on foreign policy concern differences in political systems and what these differences imply for how foreign policy is made. In particular, the proposition that democracies are more peaceful than authoritarian political systems has been the focus of much thought and study.

Are Democracies More Peaceful?

The proposition that democracies should be less war prone than nondemocracies is part of the liberal perspective. According to liberal thought, in democracies, where opposition is legal and allowed and citizens can hold their leaders accountable for their actions through competitive elections, the multiple channels across societies are more likely to constrain leaders from conflict. Furthermore, based on the values of political tolerance, democracies supposedly reinforce preferences for nonviolent resolution of conflict. The idea that democratic republics are peace loving has, in fact, a very long history, going back at least to the philosopher Immanuel Kant in 1795. The proposition that democracies are more peaceful has significant implications for global politics. Democratic states were among the most important and powerful nations in the world in the twentieth century, and the number of democratic states in the world has grown significantly in recent years.

The consensus from scholarly research on the question of whether democratic states are less likely than autocratic states to become involved in international wars is that this is not the case: Democracies are not more peaceful than nondemocracies.[48] "Democratic constraints, for example, did not prevent British involvement in the Falklands War, French military interventions in Africa, India's conflicts with China and Pakistan, and Israel's participation in numerous Middle East conflicts."[49] The United States, one of the world's long-standing democracies, was involved in many military conflicts during the Cold War. This may be due to the lack of influence by the public, as discussed previously. Table 5.1 shows the significance of democracies' involvement in major wars from 1946 to 2000. Recent participation by democratic states in the conflicts in Afghanistan, Iraq, and Lebanon further questions the notion that democracies are inherently peaceful.

Moreover, it may be that there is something about democracies that pushes them toward conflict. U.S. presidents, for example, are more likely to be assertive or forceful in their foreign policies in the wake of a loss of support from their own political party.[50] And there is evidence that states that are in the process of democratization may be more conflict prone than either democracies or authoritarian governments.[51] Yet democracies are not as likely to enter wars just prior to an election, compared to earlier in their election cycle, which may mean that leaders are constrained at times by the electoral process from going to war.[52] Most scholars now agree that democracies are in general just as war prone, or conflict prone, as other states, although they tend not to go to war against each other (as will be discussed in Chapter 6).[53]

ISSUE: Leaders often face political opposition, at home or abroad, among the public when making foreign policy. They have a choice as to whether they listen to that opposition, and even change directions in foreign policy, or remain true to their own preferences and perhaps the advice they are receiving from other government officials.

Option #1: Foreign policy should reflect public opinion.

Arguments: (a) Leaders should be held accountable for their actions. Because foreign policy is taken in the name of the state and directly affects the lives and well-being of the people who live in it, it should reflect the interests and the will of the people, not just the leaders. (b) Successful military operations and political objectives depend on public support; without it, the morale of the military is compromised, and the public will not sustain a long and costly policy. Thus, leaders who ignore public opposition are dooming a policy to failure. (c) Global politics today is about soft power and winning hearts and minds. Maintaining favorable world opinion is in a leader's long-term interests. If a state is viewed by the world as acting unilaterally or aggressively, others are less likely to cooperate with it, and there may be more resistance in the form of political opposition or even terrorism against it and its objectives.

Counterarguments: (a) People elect officials for their skills, leadership, and values and should trust their officials to carry out their mandates in specific cases without interference. (b) The public is fickle and does not have the "stomach" for policies that may be costly and lengthy, although useful and in the national interest. (c) Global politics remains anarchic, and states must look out for their own interests, even if that means "going it alone" and in opposition to world opinion.

Option #2: Foreign policy should be made by leaders.

Arguments: (a) Most citizens seem to know little about particular foreign policy issues. Listening to the "ignorant masses" would lead leaders into poor choices. (b) Public opinion only complicates international negotiations. Diplomats are unable to exercise their talents for compromise if the public is a participant in the negotiating process. When the public looks on, diplomats are subject to political pressures that require them to take extreme positions from which it becomes virtually impossible to retreat as negotiations continue. If the uninformed and moody public is kept out of the process, the wisdom and talents of professional diplomats can be given full play, and the result will be a better foreign policy and decreased probability of violent conflict. (c) Open processes that allow public input compromise the secrecy that is often necessary for the successful execution of policies. Letting the public in on what is happening means letting potential adversaries know as well, which can compromise strategy and credibility.

Counterarguments: (a) While citizens may know little about the specifics of a policy, they do hold fairly strong and stable core values, such as protection of human rights and a commitment to multilateralism, that should serve as a guide to leaders in making foreign policy choices. (b) Experts who have had a largely free hand in

(*continued*)

making foreign policy as long as the modern state system has been in existence have made their share of mistakes. Public input holds negotiations and agreements to reflect the national interest, not just the narrow interests of the leader or those groups that are closest to the leadership. (c) Secrecy often pits policy effectiveness against democratic principles. A democracy can be effective only if individuals have knowledge regarding their government's actions. Moreover, often such secrecy arguments have later turned out to have been camouflage for politicians as much as for the protection of the good of the people.

TABLE 5.1

Democratic Participation in Interstate Wars,* 1946–2000

Conflict	Democratic Belligerent(s)
Palestine (1948–49)	Israel
Kashmir (1948–49)	India
Korea (1950–53)	Australia, Belgium, Canada, France, Netherlands, U.K., U.S.
Sinai (1956)	France, Israel, U.K.
Sino-Indian Border (1962)	India
Kashmir (1965)	India
Vietnam (1965–73)	Australia, U.S.
Six-Day War (1967)	Israel
Israel-Egypt Conflict (1969–70)	Israel
Bangladesh (1971)	India
Yom Kippur (1973)	Israel
Falklands (1982)	U.K.
Israel-Syrian Conflict (1982)	Israel
Gulf War (1991)	Canada, France, Italy, U.K., U.S.
Kargil (1999)	India
Kosovo (1999)	France, Italy, U.S., U.K.

*Note: Interstate wars are defined as those having at least 1,000 combat deaths. This excludes other "minor" interventions by democracies such as U.S. actions in Grenada and Panama in the 1980s.

Source: Adapted from David Leblang and Steve Chan, "Explaining Wars Fought by Established Democracies: Do Institutional Constraints Matter?" *Political Research Quarterly* 56(4) (December 2003): 385–400, p. 392. Copyright © 2003 by Sage Publications. Reprinted by permission of Sage Publications; four Indian conflicts added by authors.

How Do Differences in Political Institutions Affect Foreign Policy?

Although democratic institutions do not necessarily constrain states from going to war, differences in political systems and their institutions do affect foreign policy. Some of the starkest differences can be seen within the family of democracies. The United States, France, Japan, and Germany, for example, differ in terms of the degree to which political institutions are centralized and the degree to which the state dominates public opinion.[54] The United States appears to have the least centralized political institutions; the impact of public opinion there is correspondingly more important. In France, the highly centralized domestic political structure seems to have the greatest dampening impact on the influence of public opinion on foreign policies. In Germany and Japan, the influence of public opinion on foreign policies falls somewhere in between the extremes of the United States and France and is more mediated by political parties.[55]

Part of the differences in these institutions stem from how leaders are elected. In the United States, a presidential system of democracy, both the president and members of Congress are elected by the people and are thus, in theory at least, accountable to the public. Within the executive branch, however, presidents are constitutionally supreme (as President Truman said, "The buck stops here"), and because presidents enjoy a separate electoral mandate from the people, they do not necessarily have to listen to others in their political party or in the legislature. In parliamentary systems, the people do not vote for the leader, the prime minister; rather, they vote for a party or party representatives to the legislature. The leader of the party with the most seats in parliament usually then becomes the prime minister and in many countries holds no special constitutional authority above other cabinet members. Thus, leaders of parliamentary democracies are not directly accountable to the public, but they do share power with the rest of the cabinet and are accountable to their party, which can replace them even without a national election. British Prime Minister Margaret Thatcher, for example, was not voted out of office by the British public in 1990, but she was replaced (by John Major) when she did not get enough votes from her own political party, partly because of her party's disapproval of her policy toward the European Community. Most of the time, however, prime ministers whose party controls a majority of seats in the legislature do not worry about opposition from parliament, because party members tend to vote strictly along party lines and thus all legislation is almost guaranteed approval.

Contrast this to the U.S. presidential system, in which legislators often vote against presidents even if they are from the same party. The division of powers between the legislative and executive branches means that Congress can be quite an influential player in foreign policy. With the requirement that the U.S. Senate must ratify all foreign treaties by a two-thirds majority, Congress has the potential to severely constrain U.S. participation in international agreements. Indeed, the failure of the U.S. Senate to ratify U.S. membership in the League of Nations is seen as a key development on the road to World War II. More recently, the U.S. Senate refused to ratify the Comprehensive Test Ban Treaty (to be discussed in Chapter 8) over the president's objections. Congress does not always exercise its power, however. In security policy particularly, Congress often defers to presidential wishes. Congress is more likely to exert influence over trade, aid, and other budget-related issues, which are often seen as more relevant to congressional district interests. Indeed, "when it comes to trade policy, no other legislative body has as much influence and authority relative to the executive branch as does the U.S. Congress."[56] But even in trade policy, Congress has acceded power to the executive branch. For example, by giving the president **fast-track authority** on key trade legislation,

fast-track authority   An important power that can be used by the U.S. president to speed up the process and decrease Congressional influence on key trade legislation.

> Congress gives itself sixty days, from the time a trade agreement is presented to it, to vote the measure cleanly up or down; no amendments are permitted under fast track. . . . Fast track's achievement was to make clear Congress's determination to overcome the morass of conflicting parochial interests and vote directly and expeditiously on major trade matters.[57]

Without fast-track authority in 1993, NAFTA would not have been ratified in anything like the form that it was negotiated by U.S. Presidents George H. W. Bush and Bill Clinton.

ratification   The final step necessary for a state to approve international agreements.

While most other countries do not face **ratification** constraints as significant as those in the U.S. political system, some other democratic systems must go directly to the public to ratify foreign treaties. In these direct referenda, the public votes to accept or reject a proposed foreign policy. In 1992, for example, the French public and the Danish public voted on the controversial Maastricht Treaty (to be discussed in Chapter 12), which included plans for a common currency for the EU. The French public followed the lead of their president and passed the treaty, but the Danish rejected it. Similarly, in 1994, the people of Sweden, Austria, Finland, and Norway voted on whether to join the EU. The Swedes and the Austrians voted yes, and the Norwegians voted no (as they had previously in 1972), and Norway remains one of the only Western European countries outside the EU. Thus, in political systems with institutions that require or allow for a referendum on a foreign policy, leaders must face the public directly for approval of their foreign policy initiatives.

Parliamentary systems also differ according to how majoritarian or proportional they are. In majoritarian systems, two parties dominate the political system, and one party usually can gain a majority on its own in the parliament, thus controlling the entire cabinet. In Great Britain, for example, either the Conservative Party or the Labour Party dominates the parliament and the cabinet, depending on the election results.

In contrast, in systems with electoral laws that favor more proportional representation, many parties are represented in parliament, and no single party controls a majority of the seats. The result is the formation of a coalition cabinet in which the various ministries (such as prime minister, defense minister, and foreign minister) are divided among two or more parties. Cabinets in Germany, Israel, and the Netherlands, for example, have more than one party, and if the parties disagree over a foreign policy decision, they must negotiate their differences. At times, multiparty cabinets fail to overcome their internal differences and are unable to respond to international decisions. At other times, small "junior" parties can have a significant influence on the direction of a country's foreign policy.[58]

The main effect of political institutions on foreign policy, then, concerns what type of potential constraint a leader faces. In presidential systems, the constraint primarily comes from the public or an opposing legislature. In majoritarian parliamentary systems, constraints are most likely to be felt within the leaders' own party. In proportional parliamentary systems, the prime ministers face potential opposition within their own party and within the cabinet from other political parties. To be sure, leaders can sometimes ignore these various pressures. Sometimes they are held accountable for this and sometimes they are not, but the effect of political institutions is to filter pressure from the public and other organized groups that may oppose the leader's policies.

This difference in the locus of constraint also occurs in nondemocracies. In these states,

> there are often decisionmaking and political constraints, and these are as pervasive as those found in the more established political systems of the advanced industrial [democratic] states. Not only must the . . . leader pay close attention to domestic political opposition . . ., but in many regions there may be a considerable diffusion of power across intensely competitive actors in a highly fragmented setting. Indeed . . . political constraints occur as frequently . . . as they do in modern polities. And if there is anything distinctive about Third World politics, it is the intensity and fluidity of those pressures compared to those of more established political systems.[59]

Indeed, because these states often have authoritarian systems, the leaders lack the legitimacy to rule and often need to take into account opinions of the military (as discussed in the next section), other societal groups, and rival leaders within their own party. The leadership may even be a collective group, such as the Communist Party Politburo was at times during the former Soviet Union, with no single individual who dominates foreign policymaking.

Finally, it is often assumed that because they are not elected, leaders in nondemocracies are not constrained by public opinion. Yet authoritarian leaders, particularly ones with a weak hold on their power, must also take into account societal opinion or risk retribution.

> Although citizens in authoritarian systems cannot vote their leaders out of office, they do have other means of holding leaders accountable, including forming or pledging allegiance to nongovernmental groups who oppose the authoritarian leader, backing a coup and change of government, assassinating a leader, and starting a revolution. Indeed, simply being voted out of office may pale in comparison.[60]

Thus, as in democracies, institutional differences in authoritarian systems—how centralized they are, how much support and legitimacy is behind them, and appointment and accountability patterns—will affect the way that public opinion and domestic opposition in general impact foreign policy.

Interest Groups and Domestic Opposition

Perhaps more important than the influence of public opinion in general is that wielded everywhere by interest groups, in particular as they exert a concentrated effort to have an impact on foreign policy. Interest groups, also known as pressure groups and lobbies, are organized parts of a society that articulate a particular sector's interests and mobilize to pressure and persuade the government. Are their efforts successful? What are generally the most powerful interest groups in a society? How can one tell?

Do Interest Groups Influence Foreign Policy in Democracies?

Certainly there are interest groups in every society that attempt to influence foreign policy, and many of their efforts are visible. Interest groups pay for advertisements in the media, support their lobbying personnel, and contribute to the campaigns of friendly politicians. Other activities of interest groups are less visible. In U.S. politics, lobbyists talk to members of Congress at private lunches, secretly threaten to withdraw financial support from uncooperative senators, offer financial support for subversive CIA activities against unfriendly foreign governments, and so on. The impact they have is difficult to determine.[61] But it is almost as difficult to determine the effectiveness of the more open and visible activities of interest groups. If *influence* means the ability to affect behavior, how does one tell if an interest group is influential? The fact that a group favors a policy that is later adopted is insufficient evidence of the impact of its efforts. The policy might have been adopted anyway. Or the political decision makers may have persuaded the lobbying groups to favor the adopted policy, not vice versa. Finally, some powerful third group, like the media, may have influenced both the lobbying group in question and the political decision makers to favor a given policy. Influence is difficult to trace.

Nevertheless, a variety of interest groups seek to influence foreign policy in a democracy, such as the United States. These groups include religious organizations, which often seek to influence U.S. policy regarding other states' human rights; foreign lobbies, such as the Japan lobby, that represent another country's views and seek to affect foreign relations with that country; and single-issue groups such as nuclear freeze groups or proenvironmental groups that seek to influence policy on a particular issue. There are also many ethnic-based interests groups in the United States, such as the Greek lobby, Transafrica, the Cuban lobby, and the American Israel Political Action Committee (arguably the most successful ethnic interest group). These groups represent U.S. citizens who have ethnic ties with other countries or parts of the world and seek to influence policy toward those countries or regions. It is clear that all types of interest groups are very active and spend many resources trying to influence foreign policy. But it is difficult to detect when they are successful. If, for example, U.S. policy toward Israel is consistent with the American Israel Political Action Committee's position, we do not always know if this is *because* of the interest group's pressure on the government or because U.S. leaders see the policy in the interest of U.S. security or other interests in the region.

Another type of interest group is economic in nature, such as businesses, labor unions, and agricultural groups. These interest groups can have great influence on foreign policy "because they help to generate wealth, and economic welfare has become one of the primary functions of the modern state. Economic groups often have an interest in foreign relations as they seek to promote their foreign business adventures abroad or to protect markets from competitors at home."[62] While these interest groups are certainly influential at times, it is perhaps surprising how often they lose. In the United States, such losses can be attributed partly to the fact that "Congress [gave] up the authority to set individual tariff rates in 1934 when it delegated to the executive the authority to negotiate reciprocal tariff reduction."[63] And historically, the U.S. president is the prime advocate of free trade in the U.S. political process. The group with the greatest interest in opposing increased trade protection consists of all consumers.[64] So in effect, the president represents that group and discourages Congress from engaging in rampant logrolling, in which each member of Congress would trade his or her vote in support of a tariff protecting industries in other congressional districts in return for votes from other members of Congress in favor of interests in his or her district.

Reflecting the growing complexity of global politics, many debates over foreign policies involve several types of interest groups, sometimes working at cross-purposes and sometimes forming coalitions. In the debate within the United States over NAFTA, for example, many powerful interest groups lobbied hard . . . to make ratification of NAFTA extremely unlikely. The AFL-CIO argued that free trade with Mexico would come at the price of lost American jobs; environmental groups such as Friends of the Earth argued that Mexico's lax pollution standards would generate pressure to relax U.S. air quality standards in order to keep manufacturers from relocating to Mexico. Both groups made defeat of . . . [NAFTA] a top lobbying priority for 1991.[65]

On the other side of the issue,

business supporters formed an umbrella organization called the Coalition for Trade Expansion that included more than 500 corporations and lobbyists. Five key business trade associations were represented in this coalition: the Business Roundtable, U.S. Chamber of Commerce, Emergency Committee for American Trade, National Association of Manufacturers, and National Foreign Trade Council.[66]

In the end, the economic agreement, negotiated and supported by two successive presidential administrations, was ratified by Congress (under the fast-track procedure discussed previously).

Even in a comparatively open political system like that of the United States, economic and other interest groups often have a difficult time influencing foreign policy if the leaders are opposed to the interest group's position. In other democracies, such as Great Britain and Germany, interest groups have similar difficulties since most foreign policy is made in the cabinet, which is much less accessible than is the parliament.

Does the Military–Industrial Complex Influence Defense Policy?

One pressure group in a position to exert a significant influence on foreign policy in many countries is the group involved in producing and using a nation's military hardware. The term **military-industrial complex** was introduced into the U.S. political lexicon by President Eisenhower, but the idea that munitions makers successfully plot to bring about large wars so that they can make a profit selling arms goes back much further in the United States and elsewhere. In 1934, some sixteen years after the First World War ended, there was a flurry of interest in the United States in the substantial profits made by weapons manufacturers and banks through sales to the Allies in that war. For months, a Senate committee, headed by Gerald P. Nye of North Dakota, held widely publicized hearings marked by revelations of spectacular profits, and many Americans were convinced by the revelations that they had been maneuvered into the war for the sake of corporate profits.

military-industrial complex Network of defense contractors, the military, and government agencies that may work together to promote military spending and other policies from which they benefit.

Accusations made against the U.S. military-industrial complex during the Vietnam War were not restricted to assertions that it had plotted to bring about the war. Rather, the organization and structure of the U.S. military and its relationship to industries that supply weapons were probed for inherent biases in favor of larger defense budgets. Purchases by the military, for example, are often arranged by generals and retired generals working for weapons manufacturers. Such arrangements are especially cozy from the viewpoint of the military-industrial complex, because the cost of any deals that are made, as well as cost overruns that may occur if the weapons turn out to be more expensive than originally estimated, are passed on to U.S. taxpayers. Taxpayers are unlikely to complain, though, because many of them benefit from a large defense budget, as when large defense contracts are awarded to industries in their districts or when military bases are established near their places of business. Members of Congress in districts blessed with such defense budget largesse are naturally reluctant to trim the budget. In addition, universities that receive large research contracts out of the budget are another part of the complex that pushes for increasingly large defense budgets.[67]

But to say that military-industrial interests play an important role in foreign policy formation is different from saying that they dominate the process.[68] By 1979, the defense budget in the United States was ten times larger than it had been in 1949; but welfare spending in 1979 was twenty-five times that for the year 1949.[69] A significantly larger portion of the budget was spent on social programs even after the Reagan administration made a determined effort to increase the proportion assigned to the Defense Department. And although Reagan's efforts to increase defense budgets were successful, on average the Pentagon's share of the budget was lower as a percentage of the GNP during his years in office than it was during the Kennedy and Johnson years or during the Nixon and Ford years.[70]

The end of the Cold War provided an interesting challenge to the military-industrial complex in the United States, as well as an intriguing opportunity to evaluate its strength and influence. The demise of the Soviet Union denied the U.S. military-industrial complex its primary rationale for large defense budgets. The strongest version of the theory stressing the impact of the military-industrial complex would suggest that the Soviet Union's disappearance should make no substantial difference in the ability of those interests to generate continuing large increases in defense budgets. But the data on defense budgets shown in Figure 5.1 provide a mixed picture. Initially at least, the end of the Cold War (roughly around 1989) appears to have had a definite impact on military expenditures in the United States (this is true whether we focus on American defense budgets in terms of constant dollars as in Figure 5.1 or as a proportion of the federal budget). This decline in defense spending produced a temporary **peace dividend**—a freeing up of money to be spent on other government programs or returned to taxpayers—and is

peace dividend   A freeing up of government revenue to be spent on other programs or returned to taxpayers rather than spending it on the military.

consistent with a systematic analysis of military spending in the United States during the Cold War, which reported that "the greatest influence on change in U.S. military spending was change in Soviet military spending."[71] Yet after almost a decade of declining defense budgets, U.S. defense spending increased, even before the attacks of September 11, 2001. Whether this was in response to new threats, such as nuclear proliferation and failing states, that warrant defense comparable to defense required for facing the Soviet Union, or whether this is a sign that the military-industrial complex was able to influence military spending for its own advantage is unclear. It is certainly true that even quite liberal members of the U.S. Congress, who were traditionally more skeptical of defense expenditures during the Cold War, objected to the shutting down of military bases in *their* districts. In addition, debates over military base closings have revealed that many in Congress are interested in preserving defense expenditures to preserve jobs, even if the expenditures are not necessary for national security.[72]

The record high levels of U.S. defense spending since the attacks of September 11, 2001, are certainly related to the "global war on terror" and the wars in Afghanistan and Iraq. While these security threats seem to be the primary rationale behind defense budgets, the purchase of some high-cost items have been linked to the influence of defense contractors.[73] Particularly controversial has been the awarding of defense contracts by the military in Iraq to certain firms.

Halliburton, a construction and oil company once led by former Vice President Dick Cheney, for example, received roughly six billion dollars in new contracts, most of which were

Figure 5.1   U.S. Defense Budget, 1985–2010
Figures for 2009 and 2010 are estimates. Figures do not include supplementary defense appropriations which, for expenses related to the conficts in Afghanistan and Iraq, have been substantial, totaling more than $800 billion from 2002 to 2008.

Source: Office of Management and Budget. 2009. *Historical Tables Budget of the U.S. Government Fiscal Year 2010*, http://www.whitehouse.gov/omb/budget/fy2010/assets/hist.pdf (Accessed 28 May 2009.)

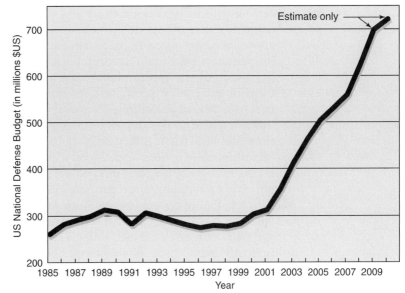

provided on a noncompetitive basis. . . . [In addition] Halliburton admitted numerous overcharges in connection with its reconstruction work in Iraq. This has prompted criticism about the dysfunctional relationships between the DoD [Department of Defense] and contractors.[74]

What Is the Role of Military and Political Opposition Groups in Nondemocracies?

Authoritarian systems, particularly those in larger countries that play the role of regional powers, also have military-industrial establishments that exert influence on the foreign policies of their respective countries. The military in Russia has been humiliated by many developments in recent years. There is some danger that elements in the military, and their supporters, will produce a leader in the coming years bent on restoring the glory of Russia's Cold War years (not to mention some of the budget it shared with the industrial establishment). The military in China also seems intent on increasing its strength and, consequently, Chinese influence in the world. In developing countries, the military-industrial complex loses most of its industrial flavor because these nations are less industrialized and because their armies, navies, and air forces are not supplied by domestic firms. Rather, they get most of their weapons and equipment from one or more of the major powers (Brazil, though, and recently South Africa are two of the world's more important exporters of military weaponry). This dependency on imports weakens the symbiotic ties between the military and industrial elements in most developing countries.

It obviously does not, however, weaken the influence of the military on the foreign policies of less developed or newly industrializing countries. States that fit into these categories differ greatly, and making generalizations about them is dangerous. But the prevalence of military influence and military governments in much of the developing world, at least until the recent global wave of democratization, has been clear. Even in the newly democratic governments in some developing countries, the military has often seemed to be in charge, exerting a controlling influence behind the government (in Guatemala and the Philippines, for example). And the military actively has resisted or subverted democratizing impulses in places such as Peru and Nigeria. The military establishments of a great number of developing countries have a crucial impact not only on foreign policy but on all policy.

Developing countries are often vulnerable to military and political opposition groups because of the weak domestic structures that are characteristic of many of these states, as discussed earlier. The divisions that typically exist, such as economic class divisions and ethnic divisions, are the bases for political opposition to the government and, often, its foreign policy.

What Effects Does Political Opposition Have on Foreign Policy?

Authoritarian governments are often able to resist the influence attempts by political opposition groups, just as democratic governments are often able to resist interest groups. Even if these groups do not influence a particular policy, however, political opposition can still potentially affect foreign policy.

For example, one hypothesis that has a long history among theorists of international relations points to a possible relationship between the amount of internal unrest in a country and the amount of foreign conflict in which it becomes involved. The idea is that societies with a lot of internal opposition, such as riots, strikes, and coups, are those in which the tenure of the ruling elite is likely to be insecure. Leaders in democratic systems facing falling approval ratings are in a similar situation. This insecurity may tempt the elite to distract the attention of restless and dissatisfied citizens by initiating quarrels, perhaps even wars, with other countries. The elite hopes this ploy will take the people's minds off their domestic grievances and focus their antagonism against foreign enemies. It is also a way to build internal cohesion and national legitimacy for the leader. This is often referred to as the **diversionary theory** of war, because leaders attempt to divert the attention away from internal conflict by initiating foreign conflict. It is also called the "scapegoat hypothesis," because leaders may be seeking to find an external actor to blame for their problems at home. Recently, this idea has been termed the "wag-the-dog effect," after the title of a Hollywood film in which the U.S. president created a fictitious war to divert attention away from a sex scandal.

diversionary theory The idea that political leaders attempt to divert attention away from internal conflict by initiating foreign conflict. Also referred to as the scapegoat hypothesis and the wag-the-dog effect.

A real-world example comes from the Persian Gulf War and Saddam Hussein's reasons for invading Kuwait in 1990. There are indications that this decision was a product of economic desperation. Iraq's long war with Iran had left it $70 billion in debt,[75] with a half-million Iraqi soldiers dead in a war that had lasted from 1980 to 1988.[76] In retrospect, some analysts are convinced that "the invasion [was] a desperate attempt to shore up [Hussein's] regime in the face of the dire economic straits created by the Iran-Iraq war."[77]

Researchers who have looked for a general relationship between domestic problems and the use of force have failed to provide convincing evidence for the diversionary theory.[78] It seems that the use of force as a diversionary tactic depends on the type of political system, the strength of the potential target, the nature of the domestic unrest, and the popularity of the regime among core supporters.[79]

Additional evidence suggests that democracies too might try to divert public attention away from internal weakness. Researchers have found that democracies are likely to use force abroad during election years, especially those that occur at times of economic stagnation.[80] Other evidence indicates that U.S. presidents are aware of the rally-round-the-flag effect (the increase in the president's popularity whenever he elects to use force) and initiate forceful policies in order to reap domestic political benefits. U.S. presidents may be particularly likely to use force in response to foreign policy crises if, for example, the economy or their own popularity is declining.[81]

In general, political opposition—in the form of public opinion or organized interests—means that foreign policy may be shaped by factors internal to states as well as external constraints. Indeed, leaders who negotiate international agreements must often simultaneously bargain with opposition back home and with other leaders from other countries or international organizations. This dual pressure on leaders, known as **two-level games,** can mean that foreign policy is forged only when it meets the concerns of both the domestic and the international audiences.[82] In the negotiations over NAFTA, for example, Presidents George H. W. Bush and William Clinton had to consider demands from their international counterparts from Canada and Mexico, as well as demands from the myriad domestic interests that supported and opposed the treaty.

two-level games Dual pressure on leaders whereby international agreements can be forged only when they meet the concerns of both domestic and international audiences.

> Would the North American Free Trade Agreement have been possible without the successful manipulation of the two-level bargaining game by Bush and Clinton? Probably not. Had the Level I [international] negotiators failed to look over their shoulders and consider how commitments made in the trade talks would be received at Level II, it is unlikely they could have fashioned an agreement with enough domestic support for ratification. . . . It is not an overstatement to say, therefore, that when states engage in negotiations, the hardest bargaining is not between states, but within them.[83]

Foreign Policy Bureaucracies

Another important domestic source of foreign policy is how the foreign affairs bureaucracy makes decisions. Almost every modern state has a large bureaucracy in charge of providing intelligence (gathering and interpreting information), developing proposals, offering advice, implementing policy, and, at times, making foreign policy. Individual leaders cannot possibly consider every alternative solution to a problem. There is an infinite number of such alternative solutions, and searching for information about them is costly. Also, estimating the probability of success and the costs of implementing each alternative solution of which the executive and the organization are already aware is an impossible task. Because of the complexities in dealing with the many issues of international politics, governments organize themselves bureaucratically. This means that separate agencies or departments are typically assigned different areas or jurisdictions of policy for which they are responsible. Separate agencies, for example, are responsible for diplomatic relations with different countries, for trade ties, and for different parts of the military. Within these agencies, there is a hierarchical division of labor, with superiors at the top, close to the leaders; at the bottom are the lower-level bureaucrats, who typically gather information and oversee the day-to-day operations of implementing policy.

Although such jurisdictional and hierarchical organization is a necessary part of dealing with a complex world, it can create problems for foreign policy.[84] The different departments, for example, may come into conflict over interpretations of intelligence and what foreign policy should be adopted. Departments tend to develop their own sense of identity, or organizational mission. This stems from their **organizational role**—their job, after all, is to safeguard certain parts of the state's foreign policy—and from the different types of information and experiences that bureaucrats in separate agencies may have.

An example of how organizational roles affect the policy-making process comes from the Soviet bureaucracy's response to events in Czechoslovakia in 1968. Czechoslovakia, under the leadership of Alexander Dubcek, began reforming the Communist Party in 1968. Within the Soviet Union, there was considerable disagreement over what should be done, and the various departments' positions were consistent with their organization roles. For example, those responsible for domestic affairs worried about the effects on the power of reformists within the Soviet Union. Those in charge of ideological supervision feared the contamination of reform into the intellectual and scientific communities. The Soviet internal police and the Warsaw Pact military command saw reforms in Czechoslovakia as a threat to internal order. Agencies responsible for foreign affairs had a different reading. Those interested in improving relations with the West, especially those pursuing dtente with the United States, or with other socialist states, worried about the negative effects of intervention. In the end, the agencies that saw a threat were able to build support for intervention, and the Soviet Union crushed the reform effort with an invasion in August 1968. But for a considerable amount of time, the disagreement within the Soviet Union (clearly not a unitary actor at this point) stemmed from bureaucratic jurisdictional roles.[85]

The conflict in viewpoints may create inconsistent foreign policy if departments are acting on their own and are not coordinating policy. Lack of coordination across agencies was an important part of the failure of the U.S. government to anticipate the terrorist attacks of September 11, 2001.

> It has been well documented that there was a lack of cooperation when it came to sharing intelligence prior to 9/11. The Joint Inquiry and the 9/11 Commission reports demonstrate that the CIA [Central Intelligence Agency], FBI [Federal Bureau of Investigation], and NSA [National Security Agency] hoarded intelligence and failed to share information or work collaboratively.[86]

organizational role The mission of each bureaucratic agency, which may influence how it views the world and the foreign policies it prefers.

Another example of decentralized, bureaucratic policymaking comes from U.S. anti-proliferation policy in the early 1990s. Concerned that the disintegration of the Soviet Union could mean the spread of nuclear technology and nuclear material, the U.S. Congress passed the Nunn-Lugar Soviet Nuclear Threat Reduction Act in 1991, which provided $400 million to be used to ensure the safety and security of former Soviet weapons, to dismantle those weapons, and to prevent proliferation.

> In a classic example of Washington bureaucratic politics, no senior official in the [George H. W.] Bush administration actively supported Nunn-Lugar, but every agency wanted to be in charge of it. While the bill specified that the Department of Defense [DOD] was to be the executive agent for the program, in a move that spelled disaster for rapid action, DOD ceded control to an inter-agency arms control policy working group with participants from the State Department, the Department of Energy, the National Security Council Staff, the Joint Chiefs of Staff, the Arms Control and Disarmament Agency, and the intelligence community. Within the State Department, at least three different offices vied for leadership responsibility for the program.[87]

With so many agencies involved, each having somewhat different views, the anti-proliferation efforts were incoherent at best.

Bureaucratic conflict may also result in compromises that are not necessarily in the best interests of a state's foreign policy. In other words, bureaucratic agencies that meet to resolve their differences may engage in give and take, and in the end, the compromise is in the middle, reflecting the wishes of no one. Such a compromise is termed a **resultant.** In the proliferation example, "the bureaucracy developed a laundry list" of issues to discuss with Moscow, with each agency simply adding on its concerns, without any overarching sense of purpose or coordination.[88] In the lead-up to the Iraq war, policy officials were divided over how large a force was needed. In the end, "a compromise was worked out. The invasion would be heavier than [Defense Secretary Donald] Rumsfeld wanted but not as heavy as [Secretary of State Colin] Powell thought was necessary."[89]

The hierarchical organization within agencies can create problems as well. Faced with severe limitations in information, time, and resources, bureaucracies display a tendency to rely on **standard operating procedures** (SOPs) developed in the past or on a repertoire of prearranged responses or standard routines. SOPs simplify the crucial problem of coordinating the different parts of the bureaucracy. If it becomes obvious that the SOPs are not appropriate to solving the problem at hand, bureaucracies do not usually search for all possible alternatives. If a situation is novel, lower-level bureaucrats may stick to inappropriate SOPs if new procedures have not been developed by their superiors. If bureaucrats do generate new policies to address new problems, they tend to give the most serious consideration to alternatives involving only incremental changes in SOPs.[90]

resultant
Compromises caused by bureaucratic conflict that are not necessarily in the best interests of a state's foreign policy.

standard operating procedures
Prearranged responses or routines used frequently by bureaucracies.

SOPs in Action: The Cuban Missile Crisis and Responses to the September 11 Attacks

SOPs played an important role in the development of the Cuban missile crisis in 1962. The Soviets sent the missiles to Cuba in utmost secrecy, using various deception devices to mislead any observer. Yet when the missiles arrived in Cuba, no attempt was made to camouflage the sites; even more incredible, the surface-to-air missile (SAM), medium-range ballistic missile (MRBM), and intermediate-range ballistic missile (IRBM) sites constructed in Cuba were built to look exactly like the SAM, MRBM, and IRBM sites in the Soviet Union.[91] Also, the Soviet military personnel arrived in Cuba wearing slacks and sport shirts to hide their identity, but they left the Cuban docks formed in ranks of four and piled into truck convoys. Furthermore, they decorated their barracks with standard military insignia. All of these indications, but especially the construction of the missile sites in Soviet style, made it rather easy for the United States, by way of overhead spy flights, to figure out what was happening.

What accounts for this seemingly irrational behavior? Why the great secrecy and deception, on the one hand and the blatant lack of secrecy, on the other? The most plausible answer involves the bureaucratic tendency to adhere to SOPs. The delivery of the missiles to Cuba and their movement from the docks to the sites were the responsibilities of the GRU (Soviet military intelligence) and the KGB (the Communist Party intelligence organization). Security is their SOP, so the missiles were hidden successfully until they reached their sites. After that,

> It appears that the reason the Soviets failed to camouflage the missiles is that the Soviet standard operating procedures for constructing nuclear missile sites did not include the use of camouflage. All previous installations had been on Soviet territory; the installation crews in Cuba simply overlooked the importance of disguising their activities on foreign soil under the watchful eyes of the Americans.[92]

As for the shirt-and-slack-clad soldiers arriving at the Cuban docks, it is reasonable to guess that delivering them there was also the responsibility of organizations devoted to secrecy. But once they had arrived at their Cuban barracks, they adhered to procedures as if they were still in the Soviet Union.

The U.S. bureaucracies involved in the crisis were not immune to the tendency to adhere to SOPs. The list of options considered by President Kennedy and his advisers was affected greatly by the repertoire of prearranged responses that the military had developed in the event of a crisis calling for an attack on Cuba. For example, one option that the U.S. decision makers considered was a surgical air strike that would eliminate the Soviet missiles already in place. The U.S. Air Force insisted that this kind

Shown here is one of the sites where Soviets placed nuclear missiles in Cuba in 1962. Because the missile sites were constructed according to the same standard operating procedures used to erect sites within the Soviet Union, the U.S. government soon realized that Soviet missiles had been delivered to Cuba.

(Courtesy John F. Kennedy, Presidential Library and Museum, Boston)

of strike would result in extensive collateral damage and probably fairly large numbers of Soviet casualties and would not necessarily knock out all the Soviet missiles, but this argument was based on previous plans. The air force was not caught off guard by this opportunity to attack Cuba. Action against Castro by the United States had been anticipated, and a prearranged response had been carefully worked out. The trouble was that given the context of the missile crisis and the desire for a surgical air strike, the response called for a strike of intolerable dimensions. "The 'air strike' option served up by the Air Force called for extensive bombardment of all storage depots, airports, and the artillery batteries opposite the naval base at Guantanamo Bay, as well as all missile sites."[93] In short, when asked about the feasibility of a surgical air strike, the air force had modified its prearranged response, but only incrementally. It added the missile sites to the list of targets to be bombed and subtracted nothing. To do so, the U.S. joint chiefs of staff insisted, would pose an unacceptable risk.

SOPs also affected the imposition of a quarantine by the United States designed to prevent missile-bearing Soviet ships from getting to Cuba. President Kennedy and his advisers decided on the quarantine, and the U.S. Navy set its SOPs into motion. The complexity of the task should not be underestimated. The quarantine was designed to monitor almost 1 million square miles of ocean. The navy assigned 180 ships to the task. Then, virtually at the last moment, the British ambassador suggested to Kennedy that precious time might be gained if the quarantine were modified. Originally, it was designed to intercept Soviet ships 800 miles from Cuba. If the quarantine procedures could be changed so that the Soviet ships would not be intercepted until they got to within, say, 500 miles of Cuba, this delay would give the Soviets a substantial amount of extra time in which, it was hoped, they could change their minds. Kennedy agreed that this was a good idea and immediately ordered the navy to move the line of interception closer to Cuba. Despite Kennedy's orders, the navy complained loudly: Procedures could not be modified at the last minute in such a major way without some colossal foul-up, which, under the circumstances of the missile crisis, would have repercussions of horrifying dimensions. But Kennedy and his secretary of defense, Robert McNamara, were insistent, and the navy finally gave in.

Or did it? The navy did assure Kennedy that the line of interception had been pulled back, but an examination of the evidence on how the sighting and boarding of the ships was timed "confirms other suspicions. . . . Existing accounts to the contrary, the blockade was *not* moved as the President had ordered."[94] In short, even when confronted with the possibility that much of the world might be devastated by a nuclear holocaust, the navy, according to some evidence, refused to modify its SOPs substantially.

Obviously it is not necessary to go as far back in history as the Cuban missile crisis to find examples of the importance of SOPs, especially during times of crisis. The National Commission on Terrorist Attacks Upon the United States cited many bureaucratic routines in its report on how the United States was less than prepared for the events of September 11, 2001. The report stressed that the problem was not that the government agencies followed SOPs, but that there were no SOPs developed for such an occasion. "Existing protocols on 9/11 were unsuited in every respect for an attack in which hijacked planes were used as weapons. What ensued was a hurried attempt to improvise a defense by civilians who had never handled a hijacked aircraft that attempted to disappear, and by a military unprepared for the transformation of commercial aircraft into weapons of mass destruction."[95] The report also cited failure of imagination: some agencies simply never considered the possibility that multiple airplanes could be simultaneously hijacked and that airplanes could be used in suicide attacks; other agencies assumed that any such attacks would come from planes originating outside the United States, which would give them more time to respond. These failures to question prevailing bureaucratic assumptions prevented what the Commission called an "institutionalization of imagination" in the form of new procedures that could deal with this type of threat.[96]

Characteristics of Leaders and the Psychology of Decision Making

At the top of the bureaucracy sits the leader or leaders who are in charge of making decisions. Ultimately, what states do in global politics rests in the hands of these decision makers. They may be particularly constrained by the distribution of power and economics in the international system, as realism and liberalism argue, and thus have very little choice. What the leadership is like, under severe constraints, may not then have much impact on global politics. Many argue, however, that few decisions in international relations are obvious. Constraints can be misinterpreted by the leaders, leaders are not prisoners of constraints, and indeed sometimes leaders attempt to manipulate constraints to their advantage. In particular, when the situation is ambiguous, uncertain, and complex, the characteristics of leaders can have profound implications for the decisions they make.[97] In international relations, leaders often face such situations. Under these conditions, what leaders believe, how they process information, and their leadership style become important factors. When the authority to make government decisions rests with a group of leaders, the nature of group relations is also important.

Leaders' Beliefs

What leaders believe often serves as the basis on which they make their decisions. Leaders form beliefs about themselves, the world, and the nature of politics in a variety of ways. The **psychoanalytic approach** to beliefs, for example, traces individuals' beliefs back to early childhood experiences. Freud, for example, argued that U.S. President Woodrow Wilson's beliefs in the inherent morality of the League of Nations, which led him to resist compromise and the League of Nations to fail ratification by the U.S. Senate, was rooted in Wilson's troubled relations with his religious father.[98] Others focus on how beliefs develop from the time period individuals experience. Different generations, for example, live through different defining historical moments. It has been argued that the reforms of the Khrushchev period in the 1950s had a lasting effect on Mikhail Gorbachev and his generation, thus paving the way for more dramatic reform efforts in the 1980s. For a whole generation, world leaders were affected by the experiences of World War II. Their anti-fascist, anti-isolationist, and anti-appeasement beliefs reflected their shared understanding of this experience. In the United States, leaders of the Vietnam generation have a very different understanding of world politics based on this shared, formative experience.

More important than the origins of leaders' beliefs is the content of those beliefs. Leaders may differ in their beliefs about, for example, nationalism, conflict, or the role that their country should play in world

psychoanalytic approach An approach to leaders that traces individuals' beliefs back to early childhood experiences.

operational code The beliefs of political leaders about the nature of the political universe and the means for dealing with others in politics.

politics. In particular, leaders' operational code serves as a set of over-arching beliefs that may guide leaders' understanding of world politics. A leader's **operational code** concerns his or her beliefs about the nature of the political universe (Is it conflictual or harmonious? Predictable or random?) and the means for dealing with others in politics (How should risks be managed? Are conflictual or cooperative methods more effective?). Operational codes are a general way of describing leaders' ideologies and orientations to politics.[99]

British Prime Minister Tony Blair's beliefs, for example, illustrate the importance of operational codes. Blair had a choice as to whether Britain would participate in the U.S.-led war in Iraq. Blair was not pressured by the United States, nor was it clear that it was in British interests to participate.[100] Rather, "the dominant reason for Blair's commitment to U.S. policy was his intense and rather moral perspective on international politics."[101] Compared to other leaders, Blair believed that the international environment is susceptible to influence (a belief he shared with George W. Bush at the time) and that Great Britain is a very influential actor in the international system.[102]

Blair also saw the world in terms of absolutes, categorizes people and states into "good" versus "bad," and had a strong desire to control outcomes.[103] Consistent with these core principles,

> Blair's foreign policy, both during the Iraq case and in general, has indeed been based on activist, interventionist principles . . . Blair suggested that the principle of noninterference in the

U.S. President Barack Obama meeting with advisors in the Oval Office.

(Pete Souze/Mai/Landov)

internal affairs of states should not be regarded as an insurmountable constraint . . . [and] argued that dictatorial regimes forfeit their sovereign right of noninterference both on moral grounds of harming their people and practical grounds of threatening others.[104]

Another important type of belief that a leader may hold is an **image** of another country. Images are the set of beliefs or perceptions that leaders have about another country regarding its capabilities, motivations, political system, and culture.[105] A particularly powerful image in global politics is the **enemy image.** If a leader holds an enemy image of another country, he or she sees that country as expansionist, militarily threatening and having an immoral culture and an individualistic political system. Ole Holsti described the enemy image that John Foster Dulles, U.S. secretary of state in the Eisenhower administration, held:

> [Dulles] cited Stalin's *Problems of Leninism*, which he equated with Hitler's *Mein Kampf* as a master plan of goals, strategy, and tactics, as the best contemporary guide to Soviet foreign policy. From a careful reading of that book, he concluded, one could understand both the character of Soviet leaders and the blueprint of Soviet policy. Characteristically, he placed special emphasis on the materialistic and atheistic aspects of the Communist creed, attributes he felt ensured the absolute ruthlessness of Soviet leaders in their quest for world domination.[106]

When leaders of two countries hold enemy images of each other, we call this "mirror images." Just as Dulles held an enemy image of Stalin, no doubt Stalin held similar beliefs about the United States.

A third type of belief that has proved to be important in the study of international politics is **analogies.** Analogies are beliefs that a current situation, event, or leader is very similar to a situation, event, or leader from the past. When leaders use analogies to guide their decisions, they use history, or at least their beliefs about what lessons we should learn from history. The Munich analogy became a popular analogy in international politics after World War II. When Hitler continued his aggressive policies after receiving concessions in the Munich agreement in 1938, many drew the lesson that any concession will only encourage any leaders who have committed previous hostile actions.

U.S. President George H. W. Bush, for example, relied heavily on this historical analogy in order to make his decision about what to do after Iraq had occupied Kuwait in 1990. He based his decision on lessons from the 1938 Munich debacle and on the assumption that Hussein and the attack he had launched on Kuwait were reminiscent of Hitler and his surprise attacks in the 1930s.[107] President Bush and his advisers also relied on analogies involving the Vietnam War in this strategic planning. President Bush demanded of the military that they avoid at all costs

image Set of beliefs or perceptions that leaders have about another country regarding its capabilities, motivations, political system, and culture.

enemy image Belief that another country is inherently threatening and immoral.

analogies Beliefs that a current situation, event, or leader is very similar to something or someone from the past.

another Vietnam.[108] Iraqi leader Saddam Hussein, as it turned out, also used analogies and his beliefs about Vietnam. Influenced by both American reactions to casualties in Vietnam and the U.S. retreat from Lebanon after the loss of fewer than three hundred Marines to a terrorist attack in 1983, Saddam told the U.S. ambassador to Iraq in April 1990 (less than four months before the attack on Kuwait), "Yours is a society which cannot accept 10,000 battle dead."[109] Hussein's confidence that he would be able to inflict 10,000 casualties on American forces was apparently based on analogical thinking relating the Iran-Iraq War to his upcoming battle with the United States. After all, his troops had inflicted 750,000 deaths on Iranian soldiers during the 1980s.[110]

The effects of analogies and other beliefs can be dramatic if they are misinformed. Beliefs necessarily simplify a complex world. There is no escaping such simplifying mechanisms; the world is so complicated and so full of information that everyone must be selective, choosing to concentrate on certain bits of information and ignoring others in their beliefs. Whether Saddam Hussein had expansionist motives comparable to Hitler's may never be known with certainty, but applying the Munich analogy to all leaders who commit an act of aggression will certainly mean that opportunities to avoid war through concessions will be missed at times. Analogies that exaggerate the similarities between the current situation and the past will likely produce poor decisions. "Saddam's failure to distinguish between the coalition forces confronting him and the poorly equipped and ill-trained Iranian army led him to the mistaken belief that Iraq's defensive posture would suffice to inflict unacceptable pain on the enemy when and if the coalition forces attacked his troops occupying Kuwait."[111] The Iraqi army found itself unable to mount effective resistance to the devastating attack by coalition forces.

Information Processing

Beliefs that lead to misjudgment are partly caused by the inability of humans to process all available information. We selectively perceive information, ignoring what can be critical pieces. Franklin Roosevelt had at his disposal information that could have led him to anticipate the Japanese attack on Pearl Harbor in 1941. Stalin was warned repeatedly before June 1941 that the Germans were about to attack the Soviet Union. Truman had lots of information from which he might have concluded that the Chinese *would* intervene in the Korean War if General MacArthur led his troops into North Korea. Blair had every indication that the United Nations would not adopt a resolution endorsing the Iraq war, but was apparently "mystified" and "baffled" when a resolution did not materialize.[112] But all these leaders were the victims of perceptual screens that led them to discount or ignore the evidence concerning possible attack from an enemy.

cognitive consistency theories Psychology theories that suggest humans seek out and attend to information that is consistent with the beliefs that they already hold.

There are particular patterns to human information processing that help us predict what information leaders will selectively perceive and what information they will ignore or distort. In general, humans seek out and attend to information that is consistent with the beliefs that they already hold, especially beliefs that are very important to them. Various **cognitive consistency theories** in psychology offer explanations for why this happens when humans process information. When information is inconsistent with existing beliefs, for example, humans might feel cognitive dissonance and are uncomfortable until the dissonance is reduced. They are then motivated to resolve the inconsistency by denying or discrediting the source of the inconsistent information, searching for other information that supports the preexisting belief, or reinterpreting the inconsistent information so that it is consistent. Only rarely will individuals actually change their preexisting beliefs to fit the new information. Part of John Foster Dulles's enemy image of the Soviet Union in the 1950s was his belief that the Soviet economy was inherently weak, on the verge of collapse. Despite numerous indicators to the contrary, Dulles maintained his consistent belief system. Hitler, too, believing in the inherent inferiority of the American military, eventually refused to hear any reports that included statistics on American industrial and military production.

The way we explain cause and effect also has a way of maintaining our beliefs. Attribution theory suggests that humans tend to explain negative outcomes (such as failing a test) through situational attributions (the light was poor) when they occur to ourselves or people we like. When bad things (such as failing a test) happen to people we do not like, humans tend to offer explanations using dispositional attributions (they are not very smart). Alternatively, when good things (getting an A on a test) happen to "good people" (ourselves or people we like), we use dispositional attributions (I am smart), and when good things (getting an A on a test) happen to "bad" people (people we do not like), we use situational attributions (they must have gotten lucky). These attributions reinforce our beliefs about who is good and who is bad. In international politics, where it is rare to know exactly what caused an event, leaders use attributions to reinforce these group images. The end of the Cold War (a good thing) was attributed by Western leaders to something about them, their political systems, and their values ("we stood firm," "democracy won"), and little credit was given to the other side. In international economics, failing economies in the developing states are often explained in terms of "corrupt leaders" (a dispositional attribution) rather than the international system (a situational attribution).

Processing information in the world of international politics is difficult enough in routine situations. Under crisis conditions, when there is little time to respond and high stakes, leaders—because they are human with limited information-processing abilities that become more strained under stress—are likely to make errors in judgment and decisions.[113]

Leadership Styles

**leadership
style** Leaders' work
habits, how they relate
to those around them,
how they like to receive
information, and how
they make up their
minds.

In addition to what leaders believe and how this affects information processing, how leaders approach policymaking can have an effect on a state's foreign policy. **Leadership style**—the leaders' work habits, how they relate to those around them, how they like to receive information, and how they make up their minds—varies across leaders in particular patterns.[114] Some leaders like to be very much involved in the decision-making process; others delegate authority. Some leaders choose a side of an issue and advocate for that side; others act as consensus builders. Some leaders solicit advice from many information sources; others rely on trusted advisers or themselves. Some leaders focus on the policy under consideration; others are more attuned to the politics around them.

Perhaps the most important distinction for assessing a leader's decision-making style is how open or closed the leader is. Leaders with more open styles want to tailor their behavior to fit the demands of the situation, to ascertain where others stand with regard to a problem and consider how other governments are likely to act before making a decision. To become acceptable to the leader, ideas, attitudes, beliefs, and motives must receive external validation from others. Because situational cues are so important to deciphering appropriate behavior, these more responsive leaders seek to create and maintain extensive information-gathering networks to keep on top of what is happening. They want people around them who represent their various constituencies so that they can keep abreast of the needs and interests of those on whom their support depends.[115]

Leaders who have been classified as having open decision-making styles include former U.S. presidents Carter, George H. W. Bush, and Clinton; former Syrian President Havez al-Assad; former Iranian President Hashemi Rafsanjani; former British Prime Minister John Major; former Japanese Prime Minister Eisaku Sato; and former German Chancellor Helmut Kohl. An early assessment of U.S. President Obama also placed him in the category of leaders with open decision-making styles.[116]

Leaders with more closed styles are crusaders for a cause. They are confident of their own positions and policy preferences and have little use for others' advice. What determines their decisions is how they view the situation through their preexisting belief system, regardless of any opposition or warning from others.

> In effect, the leader selectively uses incoming information to support his predispositions. Such leaders tend to choose advisers who define problems as they do and are generally enthusiastic about the leader's ideas. Libya's Qaddafi and Cuba's Castro are examples of predominant leaders whose orientations appear to predispose them to be relatively insensitive to the variety of information in their external environments.[117]

Other leaders who have been classified as having closed decision-making styles are former U.S. Presidents Reagan and George W. Bush, former German Chancellor Konrad Adenauer, and former British Prime Minister Thatcher. British Prime Minister Blair also dominated the decision-making process. "Indeed, accounts of Blair's policy-making style invariably stress his focus upon fundamental principles over detail, his limited information search, and his lack of receptivity to information which does not accord with his existing beliefs."[118] In the lead-up to the Iraq war, Blair preferred to meet with small groups of advisers who agreed with him and stifled full debate on the issue of British support for the U.S.-led war.[119]

The effect that leaders with closed styles have on foreign policy is direct: What the leader perceives, values, and believes is most likely going to be the decision that is made, despite any domestic or international constraints. The effect that leaders with open styles have on foreign policy is indirect. Because these leaders test the waters and often forge compromises between alternative constituencies, just knowing what the leader is like does not tell us what decision will emerge. Knowing that this water testing and compromise forging is going on, however, tells us to look at the positions of those with whom the leader is consulting.

Group Decision Making

Rarely do individuals make decisions on their own. Usually they are part of a group of other people. Even powerful presidents and dictators who have the authority to make foreign policy usually rely on a small group of advisers. Thus, the interactions of humans at the top levels of government are also important to understand. Research on group decision making suggests that groups are often more than the sum of their parts. In other words, when you put people in a social environment, they act differently and the choices they make as a group are not simply the "average" of what each group member might have chosen individually. Groups, for example, may discourage objections to policies for the sake of group cohesion. Groups are also highly susceptible to a forceful leader who steers the others to accept their position. In this way, groups may be particularly prone to engage in risky behavior or foreign policy that ends in failure.[120]

groupthink Excessive concurrence seeking that can occur in small, highly cohesive groups.

In particular, small, highly cohesive groups may have a tendency to engage in **groupthink,** defined by psychologist Irving Janis as excessive concurrence seeking. Janis examined the history of several key U.S. foreign policy decisions, including cases of "success" such as the Marshall Plan and the Cuban missile crisis, and cases that ended in "fiasco" such as the Bay of Pigs invasion and the escalation of U.S. involvement in Vietnam during the Johnson administration:

> In each of the cases, key decisions were made by a cohesive small group composed of a leader . . . and his closest advisers.

And in each case [that ended in a fiasco], . . . group members were keen to preserve the mood of optimism and presumed agreement that prevailed. This desire to minimize controversy compromised the quality of the discussion; crucial information was ignored or misinterpreted, alternatives to the group's preferred course of action were not considered or not taken seriously, and the groups tended to persist in their original policies even when confronted with feedback that the policies were not working out well or that they were fraught with risk.[121]

More recently, the cohesive group of advisers around George W. Bush has been accused of engaging in groupthink. According to *Washington Post* writer Bob Woodward, during the administration's discussions following the September 11 attacks, Bush's style did not foster discussion, as he "directed his energy at forging on, rarely looking back, scoffing at—even ridiculing—doubt and anything less than 100 percent commitment."[122] And a report by the U.S. Senate Committee on Intelligence concluded that groupthink led senior policymakers not to question their assumption that Iraq had weapons of mass destruction.[123] According to one scholar,

It became more difficult for people in the State Department's Intelligence branch to argue caution about intelligence analyses. This took the critical edge off the debate, creating an atmosphere in which Bush and his advisers began to bolster their arguments about what Saddam Hussein allegedly possessed and what he was building. It may also have created a mild climate of groupthink in which critical thinking is suppressed for fear of upsetting the predominant view.[124]

Current research suggests that Janis's conception of groupthink was in some ways limited.[125] Still, the idea that the social and political relationships and influence attempts that exist in small groups is another factor to be added in an understanding of policymaking has become widely accepted, especially given the number of foreign policy decisions made in a small group setting.

SUMMARY

- The foreign policy approach to understanding global politics challenges the unitary actor and rational actor assumptions. Disagreements within states and how those disagreements are managed can help explain why states at times do not act optimally, given international constraints. The domestic sources of foreign policy include what the public is like, what the political system is like, and how decisions are made—particularly the effects of bureaucracies and the characteristics of leaders on the foreign policymaking process.

- The general public probably has a limited impact on the foreign policies of most states, because individuals do not typically know or care very much about international politics, and because they are vulnerable to manipulation by leaders. Yet there is some indication that citizens are becoming more informed, that changes in public opinion are often in reaction to changing circumstances, and that core values serve as a basis from which citizens derive opinions.

- Despite good arguments for why democracies might be more peaceful than nondemocracies, this simply is not the case. Political institutions, however, do have important effects on foreign policymaking. Leaders in presidential systems, for example, face different types of constraints than do leaders in parliamentary and nondemocratic systems.

- Interest groups seek influence on particular policies but are often ineffective or their influence is difficult to detect as the main source of the policy. The military-industrial complex in the United States has obviously been successful in attempts to capture large portions of the federal budget in the United States. Although the end of the Cold War deprived the military-industrial complex of its primary rationale for ever-larger defense budgets, recent defense budgets have increased to Cold War levels.

- Militaries and other political opposition groups can be influential in nondemocracies, especially when the government is not legitimate or is otherwise weak. This internal opposition may push leaders to engage in risky behavior externally, in the hopes of diverting attention away from troubles at home. This diversionary tactic may also occur in democracies when the leader's approval ratings are in danger.

- Foreign policies are often the product to some extent of political infighting among different parts of the bureaucratic apparatus. Bureaucratic organizations tend to disagree based on their organizational roles, pursue inconsistent and incoherent policies due to lack of organization, and adhere to SOPs that do not fit the situation.

- What leaders believe, the images they hold, and the analogies they use can have a profound effect on the decisions they take in the name of the state. Psychological perceptions are especially important because they tend to resist change. Leaders, as humans, often selectively perceive information and make particular attributions to keep their beliefs cognitively consistent.

- A leader's decision-making style may be open or closed and determine whether alternative viewpoints are considered. Alternative viewpoints may be ignored in group settings as well as due to the desire to preserve good relations among group members.

KEY TERMS

unitary actors   141
foreign policy approach   141
rational actors   142
psychological approach   142
public opinion   142
attentive public   144
core values   145
rally-round-the-flag effect   147
body-bag syndrome   148
fast-track authority   155
ratification   155
military-industrial complex   159
peace dividend   160
diversionary theory   163

two-level games   164
organizational role   165
resultant   166
standard operating
  procedures   166
psychoanalytic approach   170
operational code   171
image   172
enemy image   172
analogies   172
cognitive consistency
  theories   174
leadership style   175
groupthink   176

PART III

Interactions of Actors: Security Relations

CHAPTER 6

International Conflict: Explaining Interstate War

War is a pervasive part of global politics and has been the central topic of study for scholars of international relations. It has been suggested that since 3600 B.C.E., there have been only 292 years without war, and each decade since 1816 has averaged twenty-two wars.[1] It is estimated that more than 150 million people have died from war-related deaths since 3000 B.C.E.[2] As Figure 6.1 graphically indicates, the destruction of war has worsened across time. "Each of the centuries prior to the sixteenth accounted for less than 1 percent of all war deaths. In fact all of them added together accounted for little more than 4 percent of these deaths, while almost 96 percent of war deaths were estimated to occur in the modern period of history, 1500–2000."[3] "Seventy-three percent of all war-related deaths since 3000 B.C.E. have occurred in the twentieth century A.D."[4] Civilian deaths have been a large part of the increase in war deaths. According to the United Nations, "In recent decades, the proportion of civilian casualties in armed conflicts has increased dramatically and is now estimated at more than 90 percent. About half the victims are children." Indeed, the UN estimates that more than 2 million children have died from armed conflict in the last decade.[5]

Most of the wars throughout history have occurred in the past two centuries. "Since the end of World War II, 236 conflicts have been active in 150 locations, including 124 conflicts in 80 locations after 1988."[6] Indeed, "the 1990s will likely win the dubious distinction of being one of the two most war-prone decades [along with the 1970s] since the Congress of Vienna."[7]

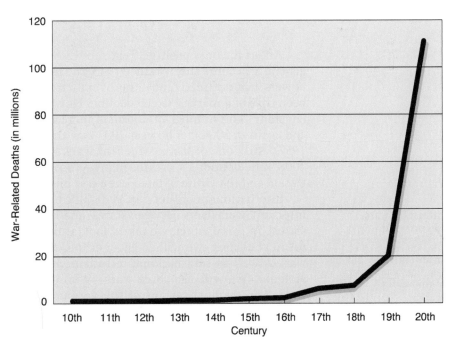

Figure 6.1   War-Related Deaths by Century

Source: Data from William Eckhardt, *Civilizations, Empires and Wars: A Quantitative History of War* (Jefferson, N.C.: McFarland & Company, 1992), p. 125. The numbers from 1500 to 1990 are derived from the definition of war: "any armed conflict, including one or more governments, and causing the deaths of one thousand or more people per year" (p. 125). The numbers for these conflicts were checked against those of other prominent researchers for agreement. Statistics from earlier periods are derived from a series of other authors and aggregation methods again with a high degree of concern for maximizing agreement among sources.

Georgian soldiers march past an apartment building after the area was bombed by Russian jets in August 2008. The conflict between Georgia and Russia involved a full-scale invasion of Georgia in support of ethnic separatists in the enclaves of South Ossetia and Abkhazia.
(Cliff Volpe/Getty Images)

About the only positive trends in warfare to report are that wars have generally become shorter since 1945, the frequency of wars between great powers has declined, and "the overall trend since the early 1990s has been that of a marked, steep decline. However, this decline has not been constant: The number of conflicts increased marginally in 1996, 1999, and again in 2004."[8] The year 2007 saw the fewest number of wars since 1957.[9] Still, one of the most recent wars, between Russia and Georgia in 2008, killed hundreds, created many refugees, and created fiction between Russia and the United States, even if it only lasted a few days.[10]

International conflict can generally be divided into two categories: **interstate wars** (wars between states) and **internal wars** (civil wars within states). In this chapter, we take a look at the causes of interstate wars. In the next chapter, we will consider ethnic conflicts as one type of internal war, as well as transnational terrorism, another source of international violence. We will use three wars—World War I, World War II, and the Cold War—as applications of the various causes of interstate war. We organize our discussion of the complexities of war by classifying causes at different levels of analysis.

interstate wars
International wars or conflicts between states.

internal wars Internal conflict, or civil wars within states.

Explaining Conflict between States: Analyzing Wholes and Parts

Some of the most vigorous and mystifying debates over how best to analyze politics focus on the relationship between entire social systems and their components. Some analysts believe passionately that all valid explanations of political behavior must ultimately deal with individuals. These individualists "insist that no social laws operate independently of human understanding; all explanations can be reduced to the level of the individual and couched in terms of the nature and intentions of these actors."[11] The alternative viewpoint is that explanations of human behavior, and of problems such as war, must focus not on individuals or human nature but on the social structures, or social systems, that emerge as people interact with each other.

The various causes of wars that have been proposed over the centuries have been cast in this debate over the relationship between structures and their components and can be categorized into **levels of analysis**. Level of analysis concerns whether one focuses "upon the parts or upon the whole, upon the components, or upon the system."[12] That is, the level of an analysis is determined by the type of social entity (individual states, for example, or the whole international system) whose behavior or operation the analyst seeks to explain. In other words, levels of analysis have to do with what kinds of questions are posed. One can ask, for example, why some states are more war prone than other states or why individual states are more war prone at some times than at other times. These questions pertain to the national level of analysis. Or one can ask why the international system was less war prone in the nineteenth century than in the twentieth century. Are bipolar international systems more or less war prone than multipolar systems? These questions pertain to the international system level of analysis.

Levels of analysis have to do not only with the types of questions that are asked but also with the answers that are given—in other words, with the type of factors relied on to explain foreign policy decisions or political events. Can war be attributed, for example, to the type of state, certain relationships between states, or the characteristics of the international system? In this way, the level of analysis deals not only with which units one asks questions about but also with which units or social entities should be observed to find out why actors behave as they do.

For example, one school of thought suggests, following the individualist logic, that understanding international war is not difficult: Wars occur because human beings are evil. Our miseries are ineluctably the product of our natures. The root of all evil lies with humans, and thus we are ourselves the root of the specific evil of war.[13] Yet human evil is not a very satisfactory answer for a number of reasons. If people were more

levels of analysis
Concerned with where the focus lies in an explanation: whether it is on components (such as individuals or states) or on systems (such as international structures).

consistently self-centered and lacking in altruism, international wars might occur considerably *less* often than they actually do. In a more evil world, nobody could be found to engage in that brave, self-sacrificing behavior that soldiers characteristically exhibit on the battlefield, usually for very little in terms of personal gain and often at the cost of their lives. War might be at least as much a function of humankind's virtues as of its vices. Even more important from a theoretical viewpoint, humankind's propensity for evil does not vary, at least not much, and only then over eons. Logically, this means that the evil nature of human beings cannot account for variations in international war over time and across space. For example, the international system was relatively peaceful in 1910 but engulfed in war in 1914. What accounts for this difference in the war proneness of the system in those two different years? Surely humankind was not significantly more or less evil in 1910 than in 1914, so the passage of time could not account for the onset of the First World War (or any other war).

Those who have attempted to explain international conflict focus on other explanations. Rather than explaining war in terms of all humans, some theories of war causation point to particular humans: leaders who are charged with making the decision of whether their state goes to war. Others focus on types of states: states with capitalist economies or states with little internal legitimacy, for example. One of the most persistent versions of this idea asserts that dictatorships are bad states. Still others focus on the war proneness of pairs of states. They ask questions such as, Are pairs of democracies less war prone than pairs of nondemocracies? Are certain pairs of states destined to be military rivals? These questions that focus on the characteristics of dyads of states reside at the **dyadic level of analysis.** According to structuralists, the blame for war should be placed not on the internal structure of some states (be they dictatorships or capitalistic) or on relationships between certain types of states, but on the structure of the international system in which all states and dyads must operate. We now turn to the various causes of war between states proposed at the structural, state, dyadic, and decision-making levels of analysis.

dyadic level of analysis
Explanation focusing on characteristics of relationships between two states.

Systemic Explanations of Interstate War

The system, or structural, level of analysis points to characteristics of the international system as the root of war between states. Systemic explanations of war posit that international structures can create consequences that are not intended by any of their constituent actors. In other words, states may go to war because of the nature of the international system, not because they themselves are warlike. International structures as an explanation of war are particularly important in realism and liberalism (see Chapter 1 for the general descriptions of these theories and definitions of their key concepts).

Anarchy

For realism, the primary characteristic of the international system is anarchy. Because the system is anarchic—there is no overarching government—each state must look out for itself or risk losing out in the war of "all against all." In such a system, "it is not only that a state, becoming too fond of peace, may thereby perish; but also that the seeming somnolence of one state may invite a war of aggression that a more aggressive pose by the peace-loving state might have avoided altogether."[14] Because, given the nature of the international system, even peace-loving states need to strike aggressive poses for their own protection, all states are aggressive (or strive to appear so). What results is the **security dilemma**. When one state takes an aggressive action purely for defensive reasons to increase its security, this automatically decreases the security of other states, which then must also undertake aggressive actions for defensive reasons. In such a situation, no state is acting with intentional hostility, but because of the anarchic structure of the international system, one must assume the worst intentions and react accordingly. Under these conditions, wars are bound to break out periodically, and it is the anarchic structure of the international system that is the root cause of those wars. Anarchy, of course, cannot explain why one war occurs while another is averted, since all states face the same anarchic condition, but it does, according to realists, explain the pervasiveness of war generally.[15]

security dilemma
The idea that when one state enhances its power for security, this leads other states to do the same, thereby undermining security for all.

Distribution of Power

In addition to anarchy, realists point to the distribution of power in the international system as another structure-level factor that affects the likelihood of war between states. The distribution of power in the international system can be described in terms of **polarity**—the number of independent power centers, or poles, in the world. If there are several powers that are roughly equal in power, the system is said to be multipolar. If most of the power in the international system is divided between two states, the system is bipolar. If one state holds a preponderance of power, the international system is unipolar, or **hegemonic**. As discussed in Chapter 4, a state's power can be derived from a variety of types of sources and measured in a variety of ways. For realists, however, the determination of power in the international system is largely based on military capabilities.

polarity Number of independent power centers, or poles, in the international system, which can be unipolar, bipolar, or multipolar.

hegemonic Term for unipolar system with one predominantly powerful state.

Although realists agree that the distribution of power is an important factor in the likelihood of war in the international system, they do not agree on which type of system is likely to be most conflictual. For some, multipolar systems, like the one that operated in eighteenth- and nineteenth-century Europe, are the most stable and least likely to produce major power wars. This particular multipolar system is known as the **classical balance-of-power** system. The most basic rule that was

classical balance of power Multipolar system in eighteenth- and nineteenth-century Europe in which states balanced power with fluid alliances.

consciously adhered to by culturally homogeneous European elites dedicated to the preservation of the system was that power ought to be distributed throughout the community of states in such a way that no single state would ever become strong enough to dominate all the rest.[16]

Preserving such a distribution of power meant first that the states supporting the classical balance of power needed to be watching and evaluating one another constantly. Thus, exchanging ambassadors became standard practice. The key type of information on which ambassadors (and spies) concentrated had to do with the power of the other states in the system. Obviously, if the independence of states was to be ensured by preventing any single state in the system from becoming powerful enough to dominate it, each state needed to monitor continually the power of others that threatened to become dominating, as well as the power of those states seeking to counterbalance that threat. States could help themselves by increasing their own power through internal means by, for example, increasing military budgets or the size of their armies, or by augmenting industrial capacity and encouraging population growth. But the most rapid and flexible means of manipulating power within the system of the classical balance of power was the formation of alliances. To maintain the balance of power required flexibility of alliances. Every member of the international system had to be prepared to cooperate with any other member, as circumstances demanded. Ultimately, if one state, or coalition of states, threatened the entire system, a grand alliance involving all the rest could be formed, preserving the equilibrium and the independence of each member state.[17]

Classical balance-of-power theorists also commonly assumed that it was important for one state, the so-called "holder of the balance," to keep a watchful eye on the rest of the system and to step in at the appropriate moment to ally with a weaker coalition about to be crushed by a too-powerful state or coalition. In Europe, Great Britain usually played the role of holder of the balance. Finally, players in this game of classical balance of power typically felt it was important to be moderate in victory; losers of wars, at least on most occasions, would not be humiliated or eliminated. In Europe, "wars . . . were ended by treaties which more often than not, represented a compromise, and in their forms studiously respected the dignity of the defeated party."[18]

Some realists point to this era of classical balance of power in Europe as a notable success and an example of a stable multipolar system. In the period from 1648 to 1792, there were generally no great territorial changes in continental Europe.[19] For a system whose basic purpose was the preservation of the states within it, this period of 144 years with virtually no important changes in boundaries should not pass unnoticed. Perhaps even more important was the absence of system-shattering wars throughout the nineteenth century (after 1815). From the viewpoint of the twentieth century, with its two world wars, the nineteenth century looks almost idyllic, even though there were several rather extensive conflicts, especially in the latter half.[20]

Many argue that the relative peace during the Concert of Europe was due to the balance of power in a multipolar system. Conflict is much more likely in a bipolar system, the argument goes, in which there are only two really important actors. If those two disagree on every important issue, and virtually every other state in the system lines up with one of the two poles, conflict within the international system is bound to be exacerbated. But if there are several important actors in the system, no single issue will be likely to divide the system into two groups of states unremittingly hostile to each other, because some states on one side of one issue will agree with a number of states on the opposing side when another issue arises. Advocates of multipolarity also argue that states must devote considerable attention to one another before they become hostile enough to start a war. In a bipolar system, this is likely to happen. In a multipolar system, no state can devote full energy to concentrating on the dastardly deeds of any other single state, because every state must also worry about several *other* potential enemies.[21]

Others disagree, arguing that a bipolar international system is more stable and a multipolar system more warlike—for example:

> In a world of three or more powers the possibility of making and breaking alliances exists. . . . Flexibility of alignment then makes for rigidity of national strategies: a state's strategy must satisfy its partner lest that partner defect from the alliance. . . . The alliance diplomacy of Europe in the years before the First World War is rich in examples of this. Because the defection or defeat of a major state would have shaken the balance of power, each state was constrained to adjust its strategy, and the deployment of its forces to the aims and fears of its partners.[22]

In short, the multipolar system of the early 1900s may have contributed to the First World War because the major powers were inflexible in defense of their allies. The bipolar system of the Cold War, in contrast, was relatively stable following the Second World War because the superpowers could afford to lose allies (they both "lost" China, for example) without feeling that a war was necessary to prevent such a loss.

The alert reader might have noticed that this point about the superior stability of bipolarity is made with the benefit of a type of levels-of-analysis switch. It is true that if we focus on the relationship among states, the international system before the First World War was multipolar. But if we focus instead on the relationship between *coalitions* of states, then it was bipolar, with two major alliances confronting each other. Thus, the First World War can be attributed to bipolarity or multipolarity, depending on which kind of social entity or actor one chooses to concentrate on.

Consider Table 6.1, which shows two imaginary international systems, with the states assigned power scores similar to those discussed in Chapter 4. In System 1, power is very unevenly distributed. State A possesses 80 percent of the military-industrial capabilities. The occurrence

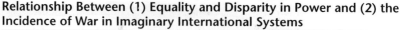

TABLE 6.1

Relationship Between (1) Equality and Disparity in Power and (2) the Incidence of War in Imaginary International Systems

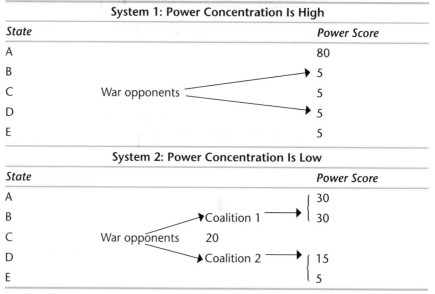

System 1: Power Concentration Is High	
State	*Power Score*
A	80
B	5
C	War opponents	5
D	5
E	5

System 2: Power Concentration Is Low	
State	*Power Score*
A	Coalition 1 → 30
B	30
C	War opponents 20
D	Coalition 2 → 15
E	5

of war in such a system would seem to indicate that power disparity is likely to lead to war. But what if the war breaks out between States B and D, which are evenly matched in power, in spite of the unequal distribution of power in the entire system?

In that situation, we can see that the co-occurrence of high power concentration and war in the *system* presents a misleading picture of the relationship between the distribution of power within the system and the war proneness of *states*. In System 2, in a similar fashion, the co-occurrence of low power concentration and war in the *system* creates the misleading impression that equality between *states* leads to war, when in fact the opponents in the war were two very unequally matched *coalitions* of states.

At issue here is whether balance contributes to peace. If states are unlikely to go to war unless they have a good chance of winning, a balance of power can be dangerous. Others counter that, on the contrary, as long as a balance is maintained, no state will feel confident that it can win a war, and so all states will be reluctant to start one.[23] Both arguments are reasonable, and researchers have attempted to find evidence to support them. One study collected information on the power of all the major powers in the international system from 1820 to 1965 and assessed the extent to which power or military-industrial capability was unequally distributed at five-year intervals.[24] The measure of concentration was used to predict the amount of war experienced by the major powers in the five-year periods following each observation.[25] This study found that, generally, the impact of the distribution of power in the international system on the war proneness of the system is minimal, although this was not true across different time periods. In the nineteenth century but not in the twentieth, greater amounts of war were more likely when power concentration was high; that is, when the distribution of power was unequal.[26]

It is possible that balance worked at preventing major wars in the nineteenth century but not in the twentieth. The leaders of the pre–First World War, European-dominated system shared not only a conscious commitment to the balance of power but also a certain amount of cultural homogeneity. "Europe was an in-group of states which excluded non-European countries. . . . [This] homogeneity was a necessary condition of the balance-of-power system."[27]

But after the First World War, and particularly after the Second World War, the globe came to be dominated by the United States and the Soviet Union, joined eventually by such important non-European states as China and Japan. The elites in these states had distinct worldviews, reinforced (especially in the cases of the United States and the Soviet Union) by opposing ideological principles to which they zealously adhered. Also, in the nineteenth century, there was a relative lack of democratic pressure on foreign policy elites, which (along with the cultural homogeneity) allowed them to pursue flexible balance-of-power policies unencumbered by the necessity to explain them to the people. That democratic pressure, combined with the ideological fervor of the Cold War, robbed (in theory, anyway) the elites in the major powers of the contemporary international system of the ability to arrange and rearrange alliances as necessary to maintain the balance-of-power system. So, in light of all these differences between the twentieth-century system and that of Europe before the First World War, it is not surprising that when the authors of this study analyzed the nineteenth and twentieth centuries *separately*, they found different relationships.

One recent study, however, found support for the notion that power imbalance is related to conflict across time: "Out of all the arguments we look at, the most powerful predictors of war are primarily associated with the concentration of power in the international system."[28] This is a particularly relevant finding for global politics today. By most measures, power in the international system is highly concentrated, with the United States in a preeminent position. Indeed, according to one analyst, the post–Cold War world became America's "unipolar moment."[29] What should we expect in a unipolar system in which a hegemonic state has a preponderance of power?[30] In this situation, too, realists agree that such a distribution of power is an important systemic factor and argue that a high imbalance of power produces stability. States are unlikely to go to war unless they have a good chance of winning, and this opportunity is unlikely to arise unless there is relative equality, that is, a balance of power between the prospective opponents. Unipolar systems lack such a balance and therefore are more stable. This idea is known as

hegemonic stability theory Idea that preeminent power of a hegemon allows it to enforce rules and deters others from initiating conflict.

hegemonic stability theory.[31] A very powerful hegemon in a sense counters the anarchy in the international system in that it can play the role of an overarching authority: It can enforce rules.

Is this the role the United States is playing today? Some argue that despite the relative preponderance of power that the United States holds, the system is not completely unipolar. According to Samuel Huntington,

> There is now only one superpower. But that does not mean that the world is *unipolar*. A unipolar system would have one superpower, no significant major powers, and many minor powers . . . Contemporary international politics . . . is instead a strange hybrid, a *uni-multipolar* system with one superpower and several major powers. The settlement of key international issues requires action by the single superpower but always with some combination of other major states; the single superpower can, however, veto action on key issues by combinations of other states.[32]

While the major powers in today's international system cannot seriously challenge the United States, Huntington argues, they would prefer a multilateral system and resent the unconstrained unilateralism of the United States. Josef Joffe agrees on the point that recent U.S. foreign policies have alienated much of the rest of the world.[33] And although many states see the benefits that come with the United States' preeminent position in the world, there is more tension between the United States and the rest of the world than some variants of hegemonic stability theory would expect.

Even if the United States is in a unipolar position, realists warn that unipolar systems are eventually inherently unstable and dangerous. Hegemons do not last. Either they spread their resources too thin to maintain their hegemonic power, or the capabilities that contribute to power transform, allowing new states to catch up to the hegemon's level. According to **power transition theory**,[34] conflicts are more likely when power transitions are underway. At the core of such shifts are simultaneous increases in productivity linked to industrialization, increased manpower due to demographic growth, and an increase in the capacity of political elites to mobilize natural resources. Sudden changes in national capabilities upset the previous distribution of power. Specifically, major wars are asserted to be most likely when the challenger catches up to the dominant state, impelling a kind of "rear-end" collision.[35]

power transition theory Idea that conflict is likely when rising states challenge weakening hegemons.

Closing in on the hegemon, the challenging state may attack in a bid for power. Seeing a rising challenger, the hegemon may initiate a preemptive war. Thus, while unipolar systems can be quite stable for a long time, they have a built-in dynamic for major war.[36] These ideas certainly hold implications for conflict and cooperation today and in the near future. Power transition theorists point to rising Chinese power and U.S.-Sino relations.

> Should China surpass the United States as the world's most powerful state while having no substantial demands for change

to the international system's organizing principles, power transition theory postulates that catastrophic war likely will be averted. In this case, China will emerge as a "satisfied" preeminent power, much as did the United States when the mantle of international leadership passed from the British. In contrast, should China challenge the United States in the mid twenty-first century, holding deep-seated grievances against the West, its culture, and its imposed international rules and norms, then the probability of war rises dramatically.[37]

Interdependence

While realism focuses on anarchy and the distribution of power as the most important characteristics of the international system, liberalism focuses on how interdependent the system is. How would the degree of complex interdependence affect the likelihood of war? Liberalism argues that multiple channels across states facilitated by international organizations, transnational links among nonstate actors, and the varied non-military issues in which states and other actors have interests means that war becomes more costly and states are constrained from using war as a policy tool.[38] In relationships that are characterized by a high degree of interdependence, the effects of an anarchical system that realists would expect are simply not seen.

> Particularly among industrialized, pluralist countries, the perceived margin of safety has widened: Fears of attack in general have declined, and fears of attacks by one another are virtually nonexistent. . . . Canada's last war plans for fighting the United States were abandoned half a century ago. Britain and Germany no longer feel threatened by each other. Intense relationships of mutual influence exist between these countries, but in most of them force is irrelevant or unimportant as an instrument of policy.[39]

Even in relationships in which force might be contemplated, it is not as effective as it once was, according to liberalism, because of changes in the international system:

> The limited usefulness of conventional force to control socially mobilized populations has been shown by the United States failure in Vietnam as well as by the rapid decline of colonialism in Africa. Furthermore, employing force on one issue against an independent state with which one has a variety of relationships is likely to rupture mutually profitable relations on other issues. In other words, the use of force often has costly effects on nonsecurity goals. And finally, in Western democracies, popular opposition to prolonged military conflicts is very high.[40]

Thus, interdependence, especially when combined with democratic governments, is a system-level factor affecting war, according to liberalism.[41]

Systemic Explanations of Three Wars

Various systemic-level explanations have been advanced to explain the three major conflicts of the twentieth century: World War I, World War II, and the Cold War (for a review of the historical background and major events of these conflicts, refer to Chapters 2 and 3).

The systemic-level explanations of World War I have already been alluded to. Realists point to the distribution of power as a major cause of the war, although they disagree on the nature of that distribution. Those who see the system as multipolar point to the dangers of alliances like those operating in the classic balance-of-power system. The system worked well as long as Britain was dominant, but when Germany's power increased and threatened the multipolar balance, Britain had to abandon its role as balancer and form an alliance with France and then Russia (the Triple Entente) against Germany, Austria-Hungary, and Italy (the Triple Alliance). This rigidity in alliances and "the keen competition between the two camps meant that although any country could commit its associates, no one country on either side could exercise control. If Austria-Hungary marched, Germany had to follow; it could not be left alone in Central Europe. If France marched, Russia had to follow; a defeat by Germany would be a defeat for Russia."[42] Thus, the argument goes, the conflict between Austria-Hungary and Serbia was transformed into a major conflagration by the complex interlocking system of alliances built up by the major powers in this multipolar distribution of power. Others contend that World War I points to the dangers of bipolarity. When the two coalitions formed, they argue, the system ceased to be multipolar. Whether the system was bipolar or multipolar, realists agree that the anarchic nature of the international system and the rise of German power that upset the distribution of power were key system-level factors that contributed to World War I.

The system-level explanation of World War II also features the distribution of power. After World War I, no meaningful balance of power emerged. In particular, World War I had failed to resolve the problem of Germany as a rising power. The postwar settlements had weakened Germany, and without a strong, central power on the continent, a balance could not be maintained. Furthermore, when Germany began to regain its power, there was no check against it. Britain had weakened and could no longer play the balancer role to keep the peace, and the two emerging world powers, the United States and the Soviet Union, withdrew from European international politics for domestic political reasons. Liberals also offer a system-level explanation for World War II, focusing on interdependence. Although the economies of the major powers were fairly integrated by the 1920s, the economic depression that began in the United States with the 1929 stock market crash led many countries to cut their economic ties to each other. Indeed, a series of protectionist policies made the world less interdependent by the mid-1930s. Isolated economies arguably exacerbated the effects of the worldwide depression. Not only did the poor economic conditions in Germany play a key role in Hitler's rise to power, but the lack of connections between countries made war a less costly decision for all. Thus, many countries pursued more interdependence between countries, especially Germany and France, after World War II as a way to bind the fates of countries together, thus changing the nature of the international system in an effort to avoid war.

The Cold War is used in system-level explanations to point out the inevitability of competition in a bipolar world and the stability that a bipolar distribution of power can create. At the end of World War II, the only remaining state with any considerable power was the United States. The British, French, and Germans were exhausted by the two world wars and were clearly not going to be the world powers they once were. The Soviet Union was also devastated by its participation in World War II, but compared to the other European states, it had the size and resources necessary to make a bid for superpower status. By 1949, with the Soviet Union's test of its first atomic weapon, the world had transformed into a bipolar system. The systemic explanation for the onset of the Cold War argues that a high level of hostility was inevitable in such a system. Like two big bullies on the same block, the two superpowers were destined to compete against each other in world politics. The competition for territory, alliances, and allegiances had all the trappings of a war, although the two main belligerents never directly fought each other. This remarkable outcome, often referred to as "the long peace,"[43] has also been attributed to the bipolar nature of the Cold War. The overwhelming power that divided the world into two blocs, the argument goes, combined with the specter of nuclear war, made direct conflict too costly, perhaps even unthinkable. Thus, bipolarity, it is said, explains both the rise of the Cold War and the sustenance of "the long peace."

State- and Dyadic-Level Explanations of Wars

Just as some people may be more accident prone than others, some types of states may be more war prone than others. In other words, certain characteristics of states may make them more likely to become involved in wars. In particular, the nature of a state's economy, the domestic political opposition that a state faces, and the nature of its political system are all featured in prominent state-level explanations of war. When we consider the interaction of the characteristics of two states, we move to the dyadic level for explaining war. Democratic dyads, or pairs of states with democratic governments, seem to be exceptionally capable at avoiding wars.

Type of Economy

The traditional Marxist theory of war argues that states with capitalist economies will be inherently war prone.[44] First, the argument goes, capitalist states often seek to address economic problems that occur at home within their own economy—problems such as overproduction, surplus capital, and unequal distribution of wealth—by engaging in imperialism. Conquering other lands secures new markets, cheap labor, and access to raw materials. Second, while imperialism itself involves military intervention, Marxists expect additional military conflict between capitalist states.

> In a world of many capitalist countries imperialism means economic competition between rival states. Each state strives to gain exclusive control over markets, raw materials, sources of cheap labor, naval bases, and investment opportunities. At some point, these can be gained only at the expense of other capitalist states. Economic conflict eventually leads to military conflict.[45]

Lenin himself argued in his book *Imperialism: The Highest Stage of Capitalism*, written in 1916,[46] that imperialism and eventual military conflict among capitalist states was the inevitable destiny of capitalist states.

There have been many criticisms of this Marxist-Leninist theory of war. One group of arguments focuses on the Marxist assumptions for why capitalist states must engage in imperialism, pointing out, for example, that not all capitalist states were experiencing economic problems at home when they engaged in imperialism and that they often did not secure the benefits of imperialism. Another group of criticisms focuses on the historical record, pointing out that not all capitalist states have engaged in imperialism, that not all conflicts between capitalist states ended in war, that war has been around longer than capitalist economic systems, that wars between capitalist states were not necessarily fought for economic reasons, and that states with socialist or centrally planned economies have often been engaged in conflict, even with each other. To be even-handed, we should entertain the idea that states with centrally planned economies may be more warlike since they are often isolated economically and thus war will not hurt their economy as much as war can dampen profits for capitalist states. Yet this general proposition also fails on historical grounds. States with both types of economies have been involved in major military conflicts.

Even if we accept the criticisms of these theories that capitalist or centrally planned states are inherently more war prone than the other, we are not obliged to reject the idea that economic conditions or forces may indeed provide an explanation for some wars. Conquering others' resources in order to address economic problems may indeed be a major motivation for some states to initiate wars. There is more evidence, however, that good economic conditions may be related to war because that is when states can afford military adventures. War also benefits the economic interests of some groups in a society. Weapons makers, for example, have been accused of advocating high levels of defense spending and even war to turn a profit. Furthermore, the proposition of a military-industrial complex (discussed in Chapter 5) focuses on the relationship among the military, the bureaucracy, and the defense industry as a coalition of economic and political interests that benefit from international conflict. Such coalitions of economic and bureaucratic groups can often logroll their narrow interests to promote over-expansion and empire building, even to the detriment of the country.[47]

Types of Governments and Domestic Opposition

In addition to the systemic-level characteristic of interdependence, liberal explanations of international conflict include the type of political system that states have. Specifically, liberalism expects states with democratic systems to be less war prone than nondemocratic states because of the constraints that are built in to democratic structures and the cultural values of peaceful resolution of conflicts that are related to democratic processes.[48] As discussed in Chapter 5, there is substantial criticism of these reasons behind the liberal expectation of peace-loving democracies, and the evidence supporting this position has been more controversial.

At the heart of the notion that political systems play a role in state choices for war is the presence of domestic opposition. Democracies, liberals argue, are supposedly constrained from choosing war because of an opposition that sees war as violating democratic cultural values or jeopardizing economic benefits that come from peaceful trading relations. Leaders of democratic states can be held accountable through elections if their war policies create significant domestic opposition. Leaders in nondemocratic states can also face opposition to aggressive policies and can sometimes be held accountable by means other than elections, as discussed in Chapter 5 (see the section "What Is the Role of Military and Political Opposition Groups in Nondemocracies?"). Furthermore, states with serious domestic opposition may not be able to mobilize enough of the population and resources to wage war. All of these ideas point to the extent and nature of domestic political opposition as a state-level factor and to the way opposition at home can constrain states from military adventures abroad.[49]

Internal opposition may also push states into going to war. As discussed in Chapter 5 (see the section "What Effects Does Political Opposition Have on Foreign Policy?"), leaders of democracies and nondemocracies may use external conflict to placate domestic opponents or divert attention away from internal conflict. Known as the diversionary, or scapegoat, theory of war,

> it is believed that when states are beset with deteriorating economic conditions, ethnic divisions, increasing political opposition, or civil strife and rebellion, their leaders will seek to end

these internal woes by initiating conflict with an external foe. Presumably, war is undertaken in the belief that it will rally the masses around the globe in the face of a "foreign threat," and that a healthy dose of patriotism is the best medicine for the internal problems facing the government. The external foe, then, becomes a scapegoat. Internal problems are either blamed (unjustly) on the external opponent and victory over the scapegoat is touted as essential to reverse the wretched internal situation, or the war is simply used by the government to divert the attention of citizens from the internal situation.[50]

While there is some evidence that questions a general relationship between the level of internal conflict and the level of external conflict for all states, the diversionary and scapegoat propositions persist and are quite convincing for particular conflicts, including the three great conflicts in the early part of the twentieth century.[51]

Democratic Dyads

democratic peace
Proposition that democratic states will not war against each other.

Although democratic states are just as likely to go to war as nondemocratic states, research suggests that democratic states are less likely to become involved in wars against *each other*. The evidence for the **democratic peace** proposition—that democratic states will not war against each other—is, on the surface at least, convincing and simple. "Even though liberal states have become involved in numerous wars with nonliberal states, constitutionally secure states have yet to engage in war with each other."[52] In other words, these democratic dyads are conflict free. One evaluation of the proposition that democratic states do not fight international wars against each other concludes that "the evidence is conclusive that . . . there is one aspect of the military behavior of democratic states . . . that is clearly distinguished from that of nondemocratic states: . . . democratic states do not fight each other."[53] Perhaps the most profound implication of the democratic peace proposition is that a world full of democratic states would be substantially less prone to war. "The increasing number of liberal states announces the possibility of global peace this side of the grave or world conquest."[54] Other implications of the democratic peace proposition are debated in the Policy Choices box on whether states should intervene in other states to promote democratization.

It is true, of course, that the validity of this proposition is heavily dependent on the definitions of democracy and war that one adopts. It is easy to discredit the idea by adopting very broad definitions; it would be equally easy to make the proposition invulnerable to contrary evidence, but also empirically meaningless, by adopting a definition of *democracy* that is so strict as to eliminate virtually every state that has ever existed. Yet,

> if democracy is defined as a type of political system in which the identities of the leaders of the executive branch and the

ISSUE: Given the findings from research that democratic dyads are not likely to fight each other, many scholars and policymakers have advocated that the promotion of democracy should be a major foreign policy goal of states and is in the interests of the international community at large. At times, advocates argue that intervention in states' affairs, including military intervention, is necessary to bring about democratization and encourage long-term peaceful relations with other democracies. This was, for example, one of the justifications offered for military intervention in Afghanistan in 2001 and in Iraq in 2003.

Option #1: States should actively intervene and support democratization in other states.

Arguments: (a) Scientific evidence and historical experiences suggest that democracies rarely fight each other. A more democratic world would be a more secure, peaceful world. (b) Democratization is a moral imperative as it enhances basic fundamental human rights and political freedom. (c) Military intervention is necessary when autocratic leaders prevent reform and democratic changes.

Counterarguments: (a) It is not yet clear what causes peace between democracies and whether this finding will continue to hold true in the future, with many more democratic states in the world. Furthermore, democratic states are still as conflictual as nondemocratic states. (b) Undemocratic regimes are only one source of human rights violations. Addressing root causes such as poverty will do more to improve people's lives than will regime change. (c) Military intervention itself is a threat to security and often produces long-lasting, destabilizing consequences. Other means, such as economic and political sanctions, can be effective and allow for internal, rather than imposed democratization.

Option #2: Democratization should not be a primary foreign policy goal of states.

Arguments: (a) Countries in transition may be particularly susceptible to internal and external conflict. (b) Imposed democracies usually fail, sometimes leading to more repressive regimes. Indigenous democracy is lasting democracy. (c) Militant democracies bent on enforcing their will around the world may actually risk becoming less free and democratic. Wartime environments often stifle dissent and the exercise of basic political freedoms.

Counterarguments: (a) Transitions, even if difficult and bloody, are ultimately more desirable than organized conflict between well-armed belligerent states, as occurs between nondemocratic dyads. (b) Post-World War II Germany and Japan are examples of how the imposition of democracy can be quite successful, with enough political will and international pressure. (c) Stifling political freedoms is neither necessary nor permanent. Any infringement of liberties caused by military actions abroad will ultimately be corrected.

members of the national legislature are selected in elections involving at least two independent political parties, in which at least half the adult population is eligible to vote, and in which the possibility that the governing party will lose has been established by historical precedent, then . . . none of those [controversial] cases is appropriately categorized as an international war between democratic states.[55]

The absence of wars between democratic states is interesting, but it is not conclusive enough to prove that democratic states are unusually peaceful in their relationships with one another *because* they are democratic. It may be that something else (that is, not the nature of the democratic political system) is contributing to peace. Some critics argue that although democracy may correlate with peace, this is largely because peaceful conditions produce democratic states rather than the other way around.[56] Other critics focus on the number of opportunities that all states have had to fight wars against each other. In recent years, there have been about 190 states in the global political system. This means that there are roughly 17,955 pairs of states in the system (190 times 189 divided by 2). In earlier years, when the number of states was lower (about 50), the number of pairs of states was of course also lower, but it was still quite large. And the number of democratic states has (until quite recently, at least) been relatively small, so that the proportion of pairs made up of democratic states has always been quite small. In short, this means that the fact that democratic states have not fought each other in war may not be as remarkable as it seems at first, because the mathematical probability that they would do so is not very large. The lack of wars between democratic states may in fact be no more remarkable than the absence of wars over the same period between two states whose names both begin with the letter Z. This has been one of the more prominent criticisms of the democratic peace proposition.[57] Given the recent expansion of democratic states, however, for at least the last couple of decades, the statistical chances for two democratic states to get involved in wars with each other have not been trivial.

Others argue that the reason that war between democracies has not occurred may be that modern democratic states are relatively wealthy, that they trade a lot with each other, that they have been unified by common interests created by the threat of a common enemy (the Communist states),[58] or that all democratic states have been under the influence of U.S. hegemony. But European states, for example, have been among the wealthiest and most trade oriented in the world for most of this century, and that did not, before they turned uniformly democratic, prevent them from continually fighting wars against one another. In general, a review of wars in the past century and a half reveals that "of the ten bloodiest interstate wars, every one of them grew out of conflicts between countries that either directly adjoined one another, or were involved actively in trade with one another."[59] In terms of those criteria, Europe should still be a war-prone continent, but for some reason it clearly is not. In addition, some recent research indicates that under certain conditions, international trade can exacerbate, rather than reduce, conflict.[60]

If having a common enemy is a key to peace, why did the opposition of capitalist states, with their many anti-Communist alliances, such as the North Atlantic Treaty Organization (NATO), not prevent wars (and other lower-level military conflicts) among socialist states, such as those between the Soviet Union and Hungary; Czechoslovakia, China, and Afghanistan; China and Vietnam; and Vietnam and Cambodia? Meanwhile, relationships among states on the U.S. side of the Cold War were not always entirely tranquil either. El Salvador fought a war against Honduras in 1969, Turkey and Greece became involved in a war over Cyprus in 1974, and Great Britain fought with Argentina over the Falkland (or Malvinas) Islands in 1982. It is no accident, from the point of view of democratic peace theorists, that all of these wars on the non-Communist side of the Cold War involved at least one undemocratic state, and that clearly common viewpoints on the Cold War were no guarantee of peaceful relationships.[61]

In recent years, there has been an impressive accumulation of evidence supporting the idea that democratic states avoid wars with each other because they are democratic, not because of these other factors.[62] Statistical analyses of data on regime types and the incidence of wars between states, from 1816 to the modern era, suggest that this situation is unlikely to have occurred by chance or to be spurious, that is, brought about by some third factor.[63] In addition, sweeping historical studies of republics, for example, in ancient Greece, among Italian city-states, and among the cantons of historical Switzerland;[64] ethnographic and anthropological studies of territorially based societies;[65] and experiments in social-psychological laboratories[66] all support the democratic peace proposition.

What remains a puzzle is why democracies do not fight each other, especially if they are as war prone as nondemocratic states. To address this puzzle, analysts have primarily focused on two possible theoretical explanations.[67] One is a cultural explanation emphasizing that decision makers in democracies have cultural expectations about how conflicts can be resolved in a peaceful manner, based on compromise instead of violence, which will carry over from their domestic political experiences into international politics, particularly when they are involved in conflicts with other democratic states.[68] A second type of explanation focuses on structural constraints that make it difficult or unlikely for decision makers in democracies to fight wars against each other.[69] This explanation proposes that when democratic governments bargain with each other, they both observe the democratic institutions in their counterparts and infer that opposition to government policies will exist. The constraints that this opposition puts on both governments when two democratic states become involved in a conflict with each other make them much more likely to settle disputes by negotiation rather than through warfare.[70]

These explanations, however, are not without criticism.[71] The cultural explanation, for example, posits that citizens and leaders in democracies are generally more peace loving and deviate from that cultural tendency only when they encounter nondemocracies. Yet it is not clear why they deviate at all from norms and values that are presumably so engrained in their culture. Furthermore,

> while it may be safe to assume that leaders and constituents who share democratic norms will be more tolerant of others who do so also, less certain is whether democratic leaders [and citizens] indeed perceive another country as a democracy or whether they believe that they know how specific leaders of other democratic countries will act, and therefore, whether they can count on these leaders to resolved disputes peacefully. It is an empirical question whether or not leaders of democracies embrace the same values and perceive each other to be ideologically committed to the liberal prohibition against the use of force to settle disputes and on these bases decide not to go to war.[72]

The structural constraint explanation has received the most critical attention. Critics argue that it is based on the assumption that the public does influence foreign policy in democratic systems. As the discussion in Chapter 5 on public opinion demonstrated, it is not at all clear that this is the case, given citizens' lack of knowledge of foreign affairs, the manipulation of public opinion by elites, and the numerous examples of leaders who made foreign policy decisions, including decisions to engage in conflict, without input or against the wishes of the public and who were apparently not held accountable. The structural explanation also assumes that all democracies have structures that give citizens the opportunity to influence foreign policy and that this influence occurs across all democracies, at least in comparison to nondemocracies.[73] Yet, as discussed in Chapter 5, there are important differences, even among democratic states, in the ability of public opinion to have an impact on foreign policy, and public support and opinion can be critical in nondemocracies that suffer from a deficit of legitimacy.

Critical to the notion of the democratic peace, and any other dyadic-level explanation of war, is the interaction of two states. State A must act differently because of the characteristics of state B and vice versa. In the cultural explanation, the pair must see each other as sharing democratic values, as being part of an in-group, so that it can trust it to resolve conflicts in a peaceful manner.[74] In the institutional explanation, because leaders of a democracy have to satisfy the broader public in order to get reelected, they will be more careful about going to war, will put more effort into winning a war, and will more carefully anticipate what effort the other side will put forward.

> Fearing public policy failure, democrats try to avoid contests they do not think they can win. Since two democrats in a dispute both try hard, both can anticipate that, if they go to war,

each will spend lots of resources in a risky situation in which neither is disproportionately advantaged by greater effort. Therefore, democrats are generally inclined to negotiate with one another rather than fight."[75]

This anticipation of what the other side will do is important not only for calculations of war, but also for state decisions regarding alliances, arms buildups, and bargaining strategies, as will be discussed in Chapter 8.

State- and Dyadic-Level Explanations of Three Wars

State-level explanations of World War I have been popular. One such explanation was provided by Lenin himself in 1917. Lenin viewed World War I as the inevitable outcome of capitalist development. As the capitalist states had succeeded by 1914 in carving up much of the world into territories to satisfy their economic needs, they were destined to come into conflict with each other in their competition for more resources, labor, and markets. According to this view, the spat between Austria-Hungary and Serbia served as an excuse to engage in a battle that the major capitalist powers were intent on for more important reasons having to do with the nature of their economic systems. Economic interests of the United States, and key groups within the country, figure prominently in another explanation of World War I. Many charged munitions makers and banks, labeled "merchants of death," with maneuvering the United States into war for profit. World War I is also used as an example of the diversionary and scapegoat propositions. Many of the states involved in the war were experiencing opposition at home: The Austro-Hungarian empire was facing the demands of nationalist groups such as the Serbs; Russia's internal turmoil may have prompted the leaders to go to war rather than admit weakness that might further stimulate opposition to the government; and the controlling groups in Germany may have been looking for ways to put off calls for social reforms. War, then, may have looked like an attractive strategy to weak states facing considerable opposition at home. At the dyadic level, World War I is only one example of democracies (such as the United States and Great Britain) fighting nondemocracies (such as Austria-Hungary and Germany), but not each other.

State-level explanations have also been applied to World War II. Given the worldwide depression and the burdens of war reparations imposed on it in the Treaty of Versailles, Germany was economically devastated. Hitler's scapegoating economic troubles on to internal groups and external enemies helped him secure power and pursue aggressive policies. Another state-level factor points to the nature of the political systems of the actors involved. The two aggressors in the war, Germany and Japan, were fascist dictatorships with little domestic constraint on their decisions. The domestic constraints on the democracies, moreover, may have made them slow to respond. Isolationist opinion in the United States, for example, meant that it was impossible for President Roosevelt to mobilize the country for war until the Japanese attack on Pearl Harbor.

In democratic Britain, the Depression had driven a Labour government out of power in 1931, and it was replaced by a national coalition consisting of the three major parties in Britain: the Labour Party, the Conservative Party, and the Liberal Party. The coalition fell apart when the Labour Party, torn by internal dissension, left the government. The Conservatives effectively ruled the country in the remaining prewar years, and the leaders of the Conservative Party adopted an unwavering policy of appeasement. Neville Chamberlain is most clearly associated with the policy, but it should be remembered that he had great popular support in Britain and it is unlikely that any prime minister who had adopted a much different policy would have lasted very long. Chamberlain became prime minister in 1937. In 1938, Germany's military expenditures were roughly five times larger than Britain's. Chamberlain's deal with Hitler at Munich won for him a tumultuous hero's welcome when he returned to Great Britain. As late as April 1939, both the Labour and the Liberal parties voted against the introduction of conscription, thus reflecting the determination of many Britons to avoid war at any cost.

While World War II looks, in general, like another case of democracies waging war against nondemocracies, it is also an example of some of the debate that scholars have about how to assess the democratic peace proposition. The debate in this case centers on Finland's role in the war. Contrary to the idea that democratic dyads do not go to war against each other, Finland was basically on the side of the Germans; Finnish troops served under German command; German troops served under Finnish command; Finnish citizens were directly recruited into German armed forces; Britain launched an air attack on Finnish territory in 1941; Britain and the United States broke off economic and diplomatic relations with Finland, and Britain, Canada, Australia; and New Zealand declared war on Finland.[76] Nevertheless, consistent with the democratic peace idea, Finland was not a formal ally of Germany; Finland refused to participate in key German offensives in the Soviet Union; the United States never declared war on Finland and never actually fought Finland; and no combat casualties were recorded between Finland and any other democracy.[77] After a careful analysis of the decision-making process on all sides, Elman concludes that "Finland's involvement in World War II is partially consistent with the democratic peace theory" and that the Finnish case suggests that the democratic peace proposition may be less applicable to small states facing severe external threats and to democracies that have highly centralized institutions.[78]

Political systems are also factors in explanations of the rise of the Cold War. Those who point to the Soviet Union's behaviors in Eastern Europe as the origins of Cold War hostilities focus on the nature of a Communist dictatorship: Stalin had little, if any, domestic opposition constraining him, and the isolation of the Soviet economy meant that aggressive policies cost it little in trade. Others who point to behaviors of the United States in Western Europe as the source of Cold War tensions focus on the nature of the U.S. capitalist economy: U.S. economic interests needed to create and dominate a market in Western Europe in which to make profits. Furthermore, in order to address domestic opposition to a U.S. military presence in Europe, U.S. leaders had to exaggerate the Soviet threat and put the struggle in moral terms of good versus evil, which would resonate with the U.S. public. The lineup of mostly (but not all) democratic states in the NATO alliance against the nondemocratic states in the Warsaw Pact is also consistent with the democratic peace proposition.

Decision-Making-Level Explanations of Wars

The cause of international conflict may also be located within states at the decision-making level of analysis. This level focuses on policymaking processes and how characteristics of those processes lead countries down paths that they may not have intended, or at least did not clearly think through according to traditional standards of rational actors and rationality. Recall from Chapter 5 that the foreign policy approach to international politics rejects many of the assumptions of system-level theories, such as realism and liberalism. Specifically, foreign policy analysts believe that treating the state as a unitary actor ignores the divisions that occur within states. These domestic sources of foreign policy may at times propel states to war. Furthermore, the psychological approach believes that how leaders define the situation is key to an understanding of the choices they make. What leaders believe about their domestic and international constraints and what images they hold of other countries can provide clues about their choices for conflict.

Bureaucratic Politics and Standard Procedures

At the decision-making level of analysis, many point to the way in which bureaucracies are organized. As discussed in Chapter 5, governments are divided up into several bureaucratic agencies responsible for gathering information, providing advice, and implementing policies in their jurisdictions. One consequence of this bureaucratic organization is that the numerous agencies tend to see decisions, including decisions about war, differently based on their organizational roles. Bureaucratic units, such as those representing military interests, may search for information and advocate policies that are more aggressive given that their job is to emphasize and protect the country from threats and such threats justify their existence, and budgets. In the decision to begin aerial bombing in Vietnam, the air force was the prime supporter:

> The air force, like no other advocate, was fighting for the credibility of a part of its organizational identity and the preservation

of primary missions by arguing that bombing would "work" in Viet-Nam before it was begun, maintaining that it was effective after it was started, and protesting that it could not produce victory unless it was conducted with more vigor after it appeared to fail.[79]

Another consequence of bureaucratic decision making is that bureaucracies tend to rely on prearranged standard operating procedures. Standard operating procedures are typically functional but may be misapplied in a particular situation and tend to be inflexible once they are put into action:

> The key intervening variable between military plans and the outbreak of war is the inflexible implementation of an existing plan (under conditions where it is no longer optimal). This can increase the likelihood of war by requiring an early mobilization, which generates a momentum of its own and triggers a nearly irreversible action-reaction cycle.[80]

Thus, bureaucracies may identify a particular situation as a threat and initiate a predetermined procedure to deal with threat without stepping back to assess the nature of the threat and whether the previous plans actually are appropriate for the particular situation.

Beliefs and Perceptions

What leaders believe and how they process information is another factor at the decision-making level that can explain why wars occur. Particularly dangerous are beliefs or images that another country is aggressive and evil. Seeing the other as evil or immoral often prevents any compromises that might avert war and may prolong a war until an unconditional surrender is achieved. Furthermore, these enemy images (see Chapter 5) can become a self-fulfilling prophecy when leaders begin treating the other country as an enemy—by responding to its leaders in hostile language, developing a military defense against it, or breaking off diplomatic relations. Upon seeing such actions, the country begins perceiving the other as the enemy, responds in kind, and in the end becomes the enemy they were believed to be.

Also, because strongly held beliefs are very resistant to change, any information that a leader receives that is inconsistent with the enemy image is often ignored, denied, or distorted. The way that information is processed to fit existing beliefs and images means that cooperative gestures may be missed, leading the states further down the path to war.

> Because the process of organizing and simplifying can result in errors in judging information and political events, images can lead to either harmful or beneficial decisions which in confrontational situations can serve to increase or decrease the level of

conflict intensity. Psychologically, once conflict begins to intensify, it is much more likely for an actor to move with the flow of escalation than to stop and back down. As conflict intensifies, it becomes even harder to achieve the accurate communication and shared understandings necessary for deescalation.[81]

(For more on how information is processed to be consistent with preexisting beliefs, in general and in the case of Tony Blair's decision making on the Iraq war, see Chapter 5.)

In this way, enemy images can create misperceptions regarding the likelihood of war.[82] Leaders who have enemy images are likely to exaggerate the likelihood of conflict, because they see the other as inherently aggressive. For example,

> Anthony Eden's estimation of the threat posed by Egypt's nationalization of the Suez Canal in 1956 illustrates the impact of cognitive predispositions on the overestimation of threat. The prime minister's formative experience was Britain's appeasement of Mussolini and Hitler in the 1930s, appeasement that resulted in war. . . . Fifteen years later, when confronted with the Egyptian nationalization of the canal, Eden could only see President Nasir as yet another dictator. He did not consider the critical differences between Nasir in Egypt in 1956, and Mussolini in 1935 and Hitler in Germany in 1938. Rather, he saw what he expected and what he expected to see was a threat of massive proportions.[83]

Leaders may also underestimate the likelihood of war if they have a belief that the other country lacks a will to fight or is too constrained domestically. During the Korean War, U.S. policymakers ignored China's warnings that if UN troops moved north, China would intervene in the war. U.S. President "Truman and [U.S. General] MacArthur were convinced that China neither would nor could intervene in Korea and believed that their frequent pronouncements of America's nonaggressive intentions would reassure the Chinese leader. . . . They simply did not see the intervention coming."[84] Perceptions about the likelihood of winning a war may also influence a leader's decision to pursue war. "Military optimism is especially dangerous when coupled with political and diplomatic pessimism. A country is especially likely to strike if it feels that, although it can win a war immediately, the chances of a favorable diplomatic settlement are slight and the military situation is likely to deteriorate."[85]

Decision-Making-Level Explanations of Three Wars

Explanations of the beginning of World War I have featured the decision-making-level of analysis in addition to the other levels. One explanation emphasizes the importance of bureaucracies and the military technology that was expressed in certain standard operating procedures.[86] Generals of the time were convinced that rapid mobilization of forces would be crucial in determining who would win the next war. Accordingly, in Germany and Russia particularly, but also in Austria-Hungary and France, the armies made elaborate plans to ensure rapid mobilization. After Austria-Hungary attacked Serbia, Russia mobilized. Germany did not respond immediately; Kaiser Wilhelm sent a telegram to his cousin Nicholas, the Russian czar, requesting that he show some sign of good faith that would allow the kaiser to avoid issuing his own mobilization orders. The czar canceled a general mobilization order and substituted an order for partial mobilization. But the Russian military bureaucracy would not respond to a change in its operating procedures for full, rapid mobilization. The generals feared the consequences of trying to convert to partial mobilization once general mobilization had been initiated. Czar Nicholas then became convinced that such a sudden change of plans might throw his military organization into chaos, and he reinstated the original general mobilization order.

When Kaiser Wilhelm realized that Russia was not going to pull back from its general mobilization, he and his advisers decided that they must proceed quickly with their own. But because the German army was aware that France and Russia were allied, and because the German generals assumed that the Russian army would take longer than the French army to mobilize effectively, the German plan called for mobilization and attack against the French first. The French would be quickly defeated, and the Russians could be dealt with in turn. So although the Russians were responding to the threat from Germany's ally, Austria-Hungary, the German war plans called for an attack against France. At the last moment, Kaiser Wilhelm was led to believe (with help from the British) that France might be kept out of the war even if Germany became involved against the Russians. Therefore, Wilhelm decided that to give France a chance to stay out, Germany ought to turn its troops around and attack Russia instead. But the German generals were as reluctant as the Russian generals to change their plans at the last moment. Helmuth von Moltke, the German chief of staff, reportedly broke down in tears at the suggestion that such a thing might be attempted. Historian Barbara Tuchman describes the process that the kaiser wanted to modify in the hour of crisis:

> Once the button was pushed, the whole vast machinery for calling up, equipping, and transporting two million men began turning automatically. Reservists went to their designated depots, were issued uniforms, equipment, and arms, formed into companies and companies into battalions, were joined by cavalry, cyclists, artillery, medical units, cook wagons, blacksmith wagons, even postal wagons, moved according to prepared railway timetables to concentration points near the frontier

where they would be formed into divisions, divisions into corps, and corps into armies ready to advance and fight. . . . From the moment the order was given, everything was to move at fixed times according to a schedule precise down to the number of train axles that would pass over a given bridge within a given time.[87]

The fact that Austria-Hungary and France also had rapid mobilization schedules, an important element in the pressure on Russia and Germany, adds strength to the argument that the state of military technology and the bureaucratic organizations administering it were important causes of the war. With all sides so intent on rapid mobilization, had the assassination of Archduke Franz Ferdinand not taken place, some crisis was bound to lead to war sooner or later.

The reluctance by the Russians and the Germans to alter their prearranged responses in this moment of crisis also corresponds with theories of the making of foreign policy emphasizing factors other than standard operating procedures and prearranged responses. Undoubtedly, under the pressure of the moment, there was a tendency to simplify matters, resulting in a number of misperceptions:

> Before World War I, all of the participants thought that the war would be short. They also seem to have been optimistic about its outcome. . . . Some of the judgments of July 1914 were proven incorrect—for example, the German expectation that Britain would remain neutral and Germany's grander hopes of keeping France and even Russia out of the war. Furthermore the broader assumptions underlying the diplomacy of the period may also have been in error. Most important on the German side was not an image of a particular country as the enemy, but its basic belief that the ensuing events would lead to either "world power or decline."[88]

The tendency to simplify, misperceive, and focus on information consistent with prior beliefs is not unique to policymakers in World War I:

> The list of misperceptions preceding World War II is also impressive. . . . Few people expected the blitzkrieg to bring France down; the power of strategic bombardment was greatly overestimated; the British exaggerated the vulnerability of the German economy, partly because they thought it was stretched taut at the start of the war. Judgments of intentions were even less accurate. The appeasers completely misread Hitler; the anti-appeasers failed to see that he could not be stopped without a war. For his part, Hitler underestimated his adversaries' determination. During the summer of 1939, he doubted whether Britain would fight and, in the spring of 1940, expected her to make peace."[89]

Entrenched beliefs also play an important part in many explanations of how the Cold War between the United States and the Soviet Union began and how hostile relations continued for decades. Specifically, one can point to the perceptions that the superpowers formed about each other in the first few years following World War II. Despite the high hopes for friendly postwar relations that leaders in both countries seemed to have, each began to perceive the other as committing hostile, threatening acts. The United States was appalled at Soviet actions in Eastern Europe and viewed Soviet control over governments in Poland, Hungary, and Czechoslovakia, for example, as contrary to the promises for elections in those countries that Stalin had made at Yalta. Furthermore, Soviet support for a divided and weak Germany, pressure on Turkey for access to its ports, and threats against Iran for oil concessions were increasingly viewed by American policymakers as evidence of hostile, expansionist intentions and of the need to contain the Soviet Union.

The Soviets for their part viewed the aid package to Western Europe, the aid to Greece fighting a Communist insurgency, support for a strong Germany, and Churchill's speech in the United States in 1946 calling for English-speaking peoples to unite and use the atomic bomb that "God has willed" to the United States against the Soviet Union as evidence of Western hostility.[90] Even when "the United States offered to extend aid to the Soviet Union to assist in the reconstruction of its economy after the war, Soviet leaders suspected that the United States was seeking a market to absorb the expected surplus of peacetime production."[91] By the late 1940s, and certainly by the beginning of the Korean War in 1950, both sides had strong enemy images of each other that directed their attention toward information that confirmed their perceptions and away from information that disconfirmed their perceptions. For example, when the Soviet Union ceased its pressure and threats against Iran in 1946, even though the Soviets did not receive the oil concessions they were after, U.S. policymakers did not use this piece of information to alter their emerging view of the Soviets.

The mirror enemy images that Soviet and American leaders held persisted throughout much of the Cold War and led policymakers in both countries to interpret the others' behaviors as consistent with their assumptions. Most U.S. leaders, for example, believed for a long time that all Communist states and movements were part of a monolithic bloc directed from Moscow. Thus, despite the differences between Communist China and the Soviet Union and despite Communist and socialist movements that originated independently, any group or leader with some connection to communism was assumed to be part of the Soviet threat, and numerous U.S. military interventions and supported coups (such as in Iran, Guatemala, the Dominican Republic, Cuba, Grenada, and Vietnam) took place because of suspected, and usually exaggerated, links to Moscow.

Multilevel Explanations of War: Using Caution When Comparing Levels of Analysis

Convincing explanations of war come from the various levels of analysis: the system, the state, dyads, and the decision-making process. Even the same war can be explained by factors at all levels, as with World War I, World War II, and the Cold War. The implication of this point is not that one kind of analysis is better than another but that analyses on different levels can lead to distinctly different conclusions regarding the relationship between the explanatory factors and behaviors or events being analyzed. Those conclusions, though apparently contradictory, may be equally valid. The contradictions are only apparent, and they are a function of the relative independence of the different levels of analysis.

Imagine, for simplicity, that there are only three pairs of states (dyads A, B, and C) in a hypothetical international system we want to investigate. Imagine further that we are interested in the relationship between the extent to which these pairs of states are democratic and the amount of war involving those same pairs of states. Looking first at Pair A and considering three successive time periods (t_0, t_1, and t_2), we find that when Pair A's democracy scores go up, it experiences more war, and when they go down, it becomes involved in less war. In other words, in this imaginary system (and its imaginary nature should be emphasized), we find, contrary to the democratic peace proposition, that war is positively related to democracy: As the pair of states becomes more democratic, it gets involved in more military conflict.

Inferring a causal connection from this covariation would be risky. First, only three time periods have been considered; the degree of democracy within this pair of states and instances of war between them might have gone up and down together that many times just by chance. Also, perhaps some third factor, such as the amount of unrest in the state, has an impact on both democracy and war that causes them to covary. (In principle, it could also be true that war has a positive impact on democracy rather than democracy having a positive impact on war.) But suppose, for the sake of this example, that investigations of all those possibilities reveal that none of them applies. For Pair A, the positive correlation between democracy and war indicates that the former causes the latter.

Suppose further that analyses of Pairs B and C in the same hypothetical system reveal the same pattern between democracy and war. In other words, we find that for each pair of states in the system, the greater its degree of democracy, the more war it experiences. It might then seem logical to conclude that the higher the average level of democracy in the system, the greater the amount of war that will occur. But such a conclusion would constitute a level-of-analysis error. Consider Table 6.2, showing the relationship between the level of democracy and war experience of dyads of states A, B, and C. Notice that as the democracy scores for the three time periods for each pair of states go up, the numbers representing

TABLE 6.2

An Imaginary System-Wide Profile Showing Pairwise- and System-Level Relationships

	t_0	t_1	t_2
Pair A			
Democracy	10	40	20
War	5	10	5
Pair B			
Democracy	15	10	20
War	20	15	40
Pair C			
Democracy	30	15	20
War	40	10	30
Total System			
Democracy	55	65	60
War	65	35	75

the amount of war experienced go up too. Similarly, as the democracy scores go down (for example, for Pair A from t_1 to t_2), so too does the amount of war it experiences. For every pair of states, there is a positive relationship between democracy and war.

Now consider the data pertaining to the entire system, obtained by adding up the numbers on democracy and war for the separate pairs of states. In the international system as a whole, there is a negative relationship between the level of democracy and the amount of war. On the system level of analysis, as the level of democracy in the system increases, the amount of war decreases. And conversely, when democracy at the system level goes down, the amount of war increases.

This system-level negative correlation may or may not reflect a causal connection between democracy and war. The point is that one cannot safely infer that a pattern existing on a lower level of analysis necessarily also exists on a higher level, or vice versa. That is, it would be a logical mistake (a level-of-analysis error) to infer the system-level relationship from the patterns revealed on the lower, dyadic level of analysis. It would also be a mistake to focus on the negative system-level relationship between democracy and war depicted in Table 6.2 and to conclude that the democratic pairs of states (or individual democratic states) are likely to experience less war.

Similarly, if one finds a positive relationship between the number of alliances in the international system and the amount of war that occurs, it would be a mistake to conclude that states with many alliances are more likely to become involved in wars. The system-level correlation might occur because smart states form protective alliances, whereas dumb states avoid alliances and fight the wars. Even though, in such a case, there would be a positive correlation between the number of alliances and the amount of war in the international system, the relationship between alliances and war on the national level of analysis might be negative in every case.

Thus, caution must be exercised when comparing levels of analysis. Levels of analysis primarily provide students of global politics a way to categorize various factors that are involved in the very real problem of war between states. These factors, such as lack of an overarching authority, economic and political relationships, and psychological beliefs about "the enemy," can also be found within the levels of analysis that explain ethnic conflict, to be explored in Chapter 7.

SUMMARY

- War is a pervasive part of global politics. Statistics indicate that the frequency and destruction of war, both interstate and internal war, have increased throughout history. Studies of international politics can focus on a variety of social entities, such as individual leaders, states, groups of states, or the entire international system. Such levels of analysis have to do with what kinds of questions are asked (such as why some states are war prone versus why some systems are war prone) and the answers that are given (such as wars are caused by certain types of states versus wars are caused by individual leaders).

- The system level of analysis points to characteristics of the international structure as the root of war between states. Realism focuses on the anarchy in the international system and the security dilemma it creates and on the distribution of power in the international system. Some argue that multipolar systems such as the classic balance-of-power system in nineteenth-century Europe are the most stable. Others point to the relative stability of the Cold War bipolar system. Hegemonic stability theorists believe that unipolar systems are the most stable, although during times of power transition, major war can erupt. Liberalism looks to the degree of interdependence at the system level, arguing that economic connections between states make war less likely.

- At the state level of analysis, arguments have been made that the type of economic system and economic factors operating in the state can contribute to war. Opposition in political systems may also serve to constrain or push states into war. Although opposition in democracies does not necessarily mean that these types of states are more peaceful, dyads of democracies are typically less likely to experience war. Potential explanations for the dyadic democratic peace have been the focus of much recent research. Some argue that democracies apply their cultural values of peaceful resolution of conflicts to other democracies and others that the structural features of democracies constrain states when they both are democracies.

● Decision-making processes, such as bureaucratic procedures, can factor into decisions for war. Decision making by leaders is also susceptible to biases in beliefs and perceptions, biases that favor war.

● Convincing explanations of war come from all levels of analysis: the system, the state, dyadic, and the decision-making process. Even the same war can be explained by factors at all levels, as with World War I, World War II, and the Cold War.

KEY TERMS

interstate wars   184
internal wars   184
levels of analysis   185
dyadic level of analysis   186
security dilemma   187
polarity   187

hegemonic   187
classical balance of power   187
hegemonic stability theory   192
power transition theory   192
democratic peace   198

CHAPTER 7

Ethnic Conflict and International Terrorism

Although scholars of global politics have generally focused on understanding wars between states (see Chapter 6), there is renewed interest in internal wars. This is partly because of their pervasiveness: "In every year since the end of World War II, the number of ongoing internal armed conflicts has exceeded the number of interstate conflicts. . . . The number of interstate conflicts has remained fairly stable."[1]

Scholars of global politics are also interested in civil wars, because they are rarely isolated: A foreign actor actively aids one side or the other or directly intervenes in the war, or the internal war has international consequences. From 1989 to 2005, one or more sides in twenty-four civil wars received military support from outside governments.[2] Most recently, internal conflict in Georgia led to foreign intervention by Russia. Generally,

> most intrastate conflicts do not remain confined within the borders of a single country. Nominally internal conflicts typically exhibit transnational (i.e., cross-border) characteristics, such as the outflow of refugees, the illicit international trade in natural resources and weapons, and the transit across international borders of rebel and government forces.[3]

The most recent internal conflicts are of global concern, particularly since the events of September 11, 2001.[4] Internal conflicts can generate terrorism, another source of violence in global politics. Terrorism can certainly remain inside borders during a civil war, but can also become transnational, as discussed in Chapter 4. Internal conflicts can also weaken states so that their territory becomes a refuge for international terrorist activities.

In this chapter, we take a look at two types of conflict important in contemporary world politics: ethnic conflict and terrorism. To assess these sources of violence, we examine definitions of ethnicity and terrorism, their history, the role of religion, the origins of these types of violence, and the difficulties the international community has in dealing with ethnic conflicts and international terrorist groups.

Ethnic Conflict in Global Politics

As with interstate war, a variety of factors contribute to ethnic conflicts, a type of international and civil war that has become particularly pervasive, severe, and consequential since the end of the Cold War. Ethnic strife threatens the integrity and even the existence of a set of countries that spans the globe. Ethnic conflicts certainly appeared to be involved in the process that led to the dissolution of the Soviet Union. French separatists in Quebec, some fear, could set off a chain reaction that might lead to the dissolution of Canada. The largest democratic state in the world, India, is besieged by conflict focusing on ethnic grievances and China experienced its worse incidence of ethnic violence in decades when ethnic Han clashed with ethnic Uighurs in the western part of the country in the summer of 2009.

Probably the ethnic conflict grabbing the biggest, ugliest headlines in the post–Cold War era occurred in the former Yugoslavia (see Chapter 3), but the conflict in Rwanda involved genocide of unimaginable proportions. In his book, *We Wish to Inform You That Tomorrow We Will Be Killed with Our Families*, Philip Gourevitch wrote:

> Decimation means the killing of every tenth person in a population, and in the spring and early summer of 1994 a program of massacres decimated the Republic of Rwanda. Although the killing was low-tech—performed largely by machete—it was carried out at dazzling speed: of an original population of about seven and a half million, at least eight hundred thousand people were killed in just a hundred days. Rwandans often speak of a million deaths, and they may be right. The dead of Rwanda accumulated at nearly three times the rate of Jewish dead during the Holocaust. It was the most efficient mass killing since the atomic bombings of Hiroshima and Nagasaki.[5]

The Rwandan conflict was between the Hutus and the Tutsis:

> In November of 1992, the Hutu Power ideologue Leon Mugesera delivered a famous speech, calling on Hutus to send the Tutsis back to Ethiopia by way of the Nyabarongo River, a tributary of the Nile that winds through Rwanda. He did not need to elaborate. In April of 1994, the river was choked with dead Tutsis, and tens of thousands of bodies washed up on the shores of Lake Victoria.[6]

Unfortunately, internal conflict in Africa did not stop with Rwanda. As the twenty-first century began, ethnic conflicts in Liberia and Congo, for example, continued to take lives, create refugee crises, destroy economies, and spread weapons. In Sudan, after a twenty-year war between the Muslim-dominated government in the North and the Christian population in the South in which more than a million people were killed, conflict erupted in the western region of Darfur. The Sudanese government responded to insurgent militia groups by backing other militias. According to one observer,

> Because the insurgents were mostly blacks, the government tapped the Darfuri Arab tribes for militiamen, telling them that the *abid* (slaves) were about to take over. The strategy worked wonderfully. Soon the Darfuri Arab militias, known as the *janjaweed* (which can be loosely translated as "the evil horsemen") were looting, burning, raping, and killing entire black villages.[7]

Sudanese refugees in West Darfur in 2004.
(Nic Bothma/Corbis)

The violence in Darfur has been astonishing. More than 30,000 are estimated to have been killed and 2.5 million have been displaced (either within Sudan or across the border into Chad).

Although the study of interstate war is often separate from the study of ethnic conflict, there are a number of similarities in the factors that are relevant to both types of conflict. The causes of both interstate and ethnic wars, for example, can be traced to political and economic relationships, lack of an overarching authority, legitimacy needs of leaders, a history of rivalry, and psychological images and identities. Moreover, in the case of both interstate and ethnic conflict, it seems that more than one of these various factors are operating in a particular war and the multiple factors that are involved often relate to each other in a complex, and reinforcing, fashion.

What Is Ethnicity?

ethnic group People who perceive themselves as distinct in terms of language, origins, physical appearance, or region of residence.

An obvious prerequisite to a useful discussion of ethnicity and ethnic conflict in international politics is a clear definition of the term **ethnic group**. With ethnic conflict so prominent in the news on a daily basis, it might seem that everyone must have a clear idea what *ethnic* means. Appearances are deceiving. For example, in the early 1990s, the former Yugoslavia was the site of probably the most publicized "ethnic" conflict in the world. And yet it can be argued that ethnicity had nothing to do with it. "Yugoslavia's ethnic war is waged among three communities [the Muslims, the Croatians, and the Serbians] possessing no distinct physical characteristics or separate anthropological or racial origins. . . . The notion of an exclusive, and exclusionary ethnic existence for each of the Yugoslav peoples is an invention."[8]

Similarly, historically in Rwanda,

> Hutus and Tutsis spoke the same language, followed the same religion, intermarried, and lived intermingled, without territorial distinctions, on the same hills, sharing the same social and political culture in small chiefdoms. The chiefs were called Mwamis, and some of them were Hutus, some Tutsis; Hutus and Tutsis fought together in the Mwamis' armies; through marriage and clientage, Hutus could become hereditary Tutsis, and Tutsis could become hereditary Hutus. Because of all this mixing, ethnographers and historians have lately come to agree that Hutus and Tutsis cannot properly be called distinct ethnic groups. Still, the names Hutu and Tutsi stuck . . . and . . . the source of the distinction is undisputed: Hutus were cultivators and Tutsis were herdsmen. This was the original inequality: cattle are a more valuable asset than produce, and although some Hutus owned cows while some Tutsis tilled the soil, the word Tutsi became synonymous with a political and economic elite.[9]

When Belgium ruled the Rwandan territory as a colony, the Belgians decided that the Tutsi were a superior "race" and issued ethnic identity cards to separate the groups.

> Whatever Hutu and Tutsi identity may have stood for in the pre-colonial state no longer mattered; the Belgians had made ethnicity the defining feature of Rwandan existence. . . . With every schoolchild reared in the doctrine of racial superiority and inferiority, the idea of a collective national identity was steadily laid to waste.[10]

Although it is often assumed that for an ethnic group to qualify as such, it must have some distinguishing physical or "racial" characteristic, this is clearly not the case. Consistent with the constructivist perspective, ethnic groups can be considered socially constructed or "imagined communities."[11] This recognition, however, can lead to a definitional strategy suggesting that if any group subjectively defines itself as an ethnic group, it qualifies as one. While the subjective nature of ethnic identity is important, one can identify many subjectively defined ethnic groups on objective criteria. A recent comprehensive review of ethnic minorities, for example, defines communal groups (that is, ethnic groups) as "people who share a distinctive and enduring collective identity based on a belief of common descent and on shared experiences and cultural traits."[12] This project uses five relatively specific cultural traits to identify ethnic groups: (1) language or dialect, (2) social customs, (3) religious

Map 7.1 Sunni and Shia Distribution

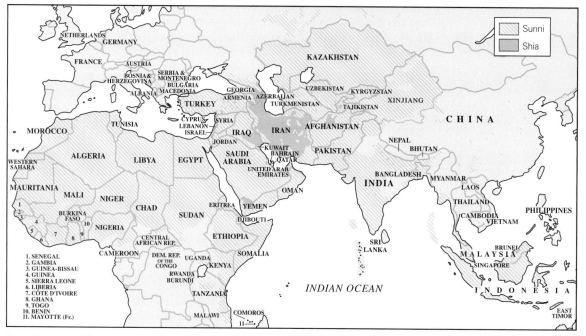

Source: Courtesy of the University Libraries, The University of Texas at Austin.

beliefs, (4) physical appearance, and (5) region of residence.[13] For the purpose of this discussion, we will define an ethnic group as one that perceives itself to be culturally distinct in terms of its language, customs, religious beliefs, physical appearance, or region of residence.

These bases of distinction tend to go together. Indeed, only about 10 percent of minorities in the developing world are distinct in terms of only one of these cultural characteristics.[14] Most ethnic groups that perceive themselves as such not only have different languages but also have at least one other distinctive cultural trait having to do with their customs, religious beliefs, physical appearance, or the place where they live. As we have seen, it can be argued that the civil war in the former Yugoslavia did not constitute ethnic conflict, because the Croats, the Muslims in Bosnia, and the Serbs are not "racially" distinct. But because these groups are distinct in terms of their religious beliefs and their region of residence, they are distinct ethnic groups by our definition, and they can be said to have engaged in ethnic conflict.

Similarly, the conflict between Sunni and Shia Muslims in the Middle East qualifies as ethnic conflict, according to our definition. The difference between Sunnis and Shias lies in a historical disagreement over the succession to the Prophet Muhammad for the spiritual leadership of

Muslims. Thus, although both groups are similar in many ways—both groups have members who are Arabs and speak Arabic (although both groups contain non-Arabs as well, particularly Farsi-speaking Iranians who make up the majority of Shias), and all are Muslim—their **sectarian** (intra-religious) differences separate them into distinctive and enduring communal groups. Although Sunnis and Shias live throughout the Middle East, they also tend to reside in separate regions that have either a Sunni or Shia majority (see Map 7.1).

sectarian Pertaining to intra-religious divisions.

The Scope of Ethnic Conflict in the Contemporary Global System

Because defining an ethnic group is difficult, there are widely disparate estimates of how many such groups there are in the world. One source asserts there are 862 ethnic groups globally.[15] A geographer has identified 5,000 nations, or distinct communities, in the contemporary world that could claim to be national peoples.[16] Using the definition and criteria discussed in the previous section and focusing on disadvantaged groups and groups that have organized to promote their collective interests, one group of researchers, led by Ted Robert Gurr has identified 275 such groups.[17]

Not only are there many ethnic groups in the world; it is safe to conclude that the politics, domestic and international, of virtually every state in the world is affected in important ways by the activities of these ethnic groups. Gurr declares that about three-fourths of the 161 largest countries in the world have at least one politicized minority.[18] There are very few states in the world that are ethnically homogeneous (see the discussion of nations versus states in Chapter 4). Moreover, "Wherever one looks in the world there seems to be an unresolved ethnic conflict underway."[19] Indeed, "since the end of the Cold War, a wave of ethnic conflict has swept across parts of Eastern Europe, the former Soviet Union, and Africa. Localities, states, and sometimes whole regions have been engulfed in convulsive fits of ethnic insecurity, violence, and genocide."[20] The human and political costs of ethnic conflict have already reached substantial proportions and threaten to get worse. There were some eighty guerrilla and civil wars fought by rebelling ethnic groups from 1945 to 1980, such as the Karen and Kachin in Burma, the Nagas and the Tripuras in India, the Eritreans in Ethiopia, the Palestinians in Israel, the Kurds in Iraq, and the Basques in Spain.[21] Because of this ethnic conflict, there have been "rights denied, immiseration, exodus of refugees, mass murder, democracy subverted, development deferred . . . and regional wars."[22] The list of ethnic problems in the world seems nearly endless:

> The war in Bosnia-Herzegovina has received the most attention in the West because of the intense coverage it has received from the Western media, but equally if not more horrific conflicts are

underway in Afghanistan, Angola, Armenia, Azerbaijan, Burma, Georgia, India, Indonesia, Liberia, Sri Lanka, Sudan, and Tajikistan. Other trouble spots abound—Bangladesh, Belgium, Bhutan, Burundi, Estonia, Ethiopia, Guatemala, Iraq, Latvia, Lebanon, Mali, Moldova, Niger, Northern Ireland, Pakistan, the Philippines, Romania, Rwanda, South Africa, Spain, and Turkey, for example.[23]

Some of the ethnic conflict is confined within the borders of a single state, but most are not and thus they become international in scope.[24] This is in part because quite often, ethnic groups are spread over the boundaries of states. More than two-thirds of ethnic groups in the developing world have ethnic compatriots in two or more adjacent countries.[25] Such situations can create pressures to extend the political power of the homeland to include the ethnic compatriots currently outside the boundaries of the country in which they live. Annexation of another state, or part of it, based on ethnic ties, is known as **irredentism.**

irredentism Annexation of an area that includes ethnic compatriots residing in another state.

> Irredentist movements usually lay claim to the territory of an entity—almost invariably an independent state— in which their in-group is concentrated, perhaps even forming some local majorities. The original term *terra irredenta* means territory to be redeemed. . . . The territory to be regained sometimes is regarded as a part of a cultural setting (or historic state) or an integral part of one homeland.[26]

Even without irredentist pressures, ethnic conflict can become international when ethnicity combines with nationalism and ethnic groups seek self-determination and work toward creating a new state in the international system. (See Chapter 2 for a historical discussion and definitions of nationalism and national self-determination.) According to one definition of nationalism, it is present when "individual members give their primary loyalty to their own ethnic or national community" and "these ethnic or national communities desire their own independent state."[27] Ethnic conflicts also become internationalized because other members of the international community have economic, security, or political interests affected by the conflict or become involved for humanitarian purposes. That ethnic minorities are often subjected to discrimination and that current state boundaries seldom coincide with the physical distribution of ethnic groups has made ethnic conflict a virtual epidemic.

Ethnic conflict is not new, as a moment's reflection on the legendary battle between David and Goliath or the Roman custom of throwing Christians to the lions will reveal. In more recent times, Turkish groups in the Ottoman Empire are suspected of murdering about 1.5 million Armenians, mostly during the First World War.[28] The Nazis in Germany killed 6 million Jews and perhaps as many as 14 million people of other ethnic groups, such as Slavs, Serbs, Czechs, Poles, and Ukrainians.[29]

Figure 7.1   Trends in Armed Conflicts for Self-Determination, 1956–2006

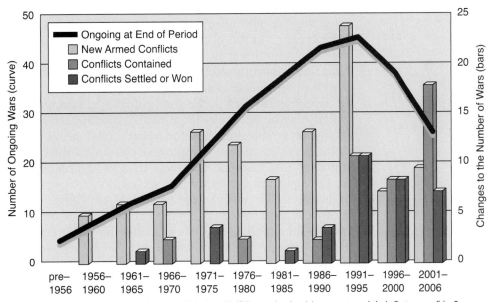

Source: Reprinted with permission from David Quinn, "Self-Determination Movements and their Outcomes," in *Peace and Conflict 2008* by J. Joseph Hewitt, Jonathan Wilkenfeld, and Ted Robert Gurr Boulder, CO: Paradigm Publishers, 2008, p. 35.

There were mass murders of members of ethnic groups in East Bengal in 1971, in Kampuchea in 1977, and in Uganda in 1978.

It is true that violence focused on or fostered by ethnic conflict did increase in the early 1990s, but "the eruption of ethnic warfare that seized observers' attention in the early 1990s was actually a culmination of a long-term general trend of increasing communal-based protest and rebellion that began in the 1950s and peaked immediately after the end of the Cold War. The breakup of the USSR and Yugoslavia provided opportunities for new ethnonational claims and the eruption of a dozen new ethnic wars between 1988 and 1992. In the global south, more than two dozen ethnic wars began or restarted in roughly the same period, between 1988 and 1994."[30] The good news is that ethnic conflict may have peaked in the mid-1990s. Figure 7.1 shows that the number of ongoing conflicts reached a height in the early 1990s and declined thereafter. There is also

> evidence that more ethnonational wars have been settled or contained through international engagement and negotiations since the early 1990s than in any decade of the Cold War. Examples include the settlement and deescalation of ethnonational rebellions by the Miskitos and other coastal peoples in Nicaragua (1990), the Gagauz in Moldova (1995), the Moros in the Philippines (. . . 1996), and the Chakmas in Bangladesh (. . . 1997)."[31]

Gurr, however, warns that "the ebb in new ethnopolitical conflicts since the early 1990s and the expanding repertoire of strategies for managing them do not mean that communal violence is about to disappear as a challenge to global or regional order. Ethnic rioting in Indonesia, communal and civil war in Eastern Congo, and ethnic cleansing in Kosovo illustrate the ever-present possibility that ethnic conflicts can recur and morph in unexpected and deadly ways."[32]

Keeping in mind that ethnic conflict has occurred for centuries and that it may be on a decline, it is still appropriate to ask why there was an apparent explosion of ethnic passions and ethnic conflict and violence in the years immediately following the end of the Cold War. It might be admitted first that the academic field of international politics (as well as, perhaps, the contemporary global political system) is ill equipped to deal with, or to explain persuasively, this outburst of ethnic passion, because it has a history of ignoring ethnic groups and their relationship to international politics. As one specialist in ethnic conflict observes, "The post-war world has been dominated by the ideological battle between Western liberalism and Soviet style Marxism," and "neither of these systems of belief have shown much concern for ethnicity."[33] "Liberals" in the classic Western tradition have tended to see the emphasis on collective rights by emotional ethnic groups as a dangerous threat to the individual human rights that they hold dear. Marxist scholars have tended to view ethnic groups and their ethnically based political passions as annoying diversions on the road to communism. Religious differences, an increasingly important part of many ethnic conflicts, have also been ignored by scholars of international relations.[34] "Paradigms like realism [and] liberalism . . . placed their emphasis on military and economic factors as well as rational calculations, all of which left little room for religion."[35] In short, as the prominent analyst of ethnicity Walker Connor argued several decades ago, international politics as an academic field has had a regrettable tendency to treat ethnicity as an "ephemeral nuisance."[36]

The Role of the International System and Economic Modernization in Ethnic Conflict

There are many competing expectations on the role of the international system and economic forces in ethnic conflict. During the Cold War, for example, it was commonly hypothesized that the structure of the international environment, a bipolar system, fueled ethnic conflict. Although bipolarity presumably prohibited conflict between the major powers, it encouraged it among its clients.[37] In other words, during the Cold War, it often appeared that antagonism between the superpowers made ethnic conflicts worse. In Angola, for example, the United States and other Western powers tended to support the Ovimbundu people in the southern part of the country against the Soviet-supported Mbundu-led coalition that controlled the government. The result was a civil war that dragged on for years. Because of situations like this, during the Cold War the competition between the superpowers.

> to complete a network of international alliances in such a way as to maximize the number and wealth of allies and trading partners, tremendously enriched and inflated ethnic movements, particularly in the Third World. The injection of external resources into domestic ethnic conflicts resulted in larger, better organized, and more violent ethnic movements. The consequences . . . were a lengthening and escalating of conflict, often resulting in civil wars, and a decreased likelihood of negotiated settlements.[38]

But the end of the Cold War has hardly seemed to be a cure-all for the world's epidemic of ethnic strife. On the contrary, it and the end of communism obviously brought to the surface a host of violent conflicts in Eastern Europe and the former Soviet Union. And the end of global competition between the superpowers has not brought to an end many conflicts that previously seemed to be primarily a function of that competition. We can now see that even without superpower encouragement, ethnic conflict in Angola, Sudan, Afghanistan, Burundi, Burma, Iraq, Turkey, and other places continues.

In many ways, current ethnic conflicts are simply the latest expressions of the principle of national self-determination that was legitimized as a political value and international norm by Woodrow Wilson after World War I when empires began to be dismantled, and colonies became independent. The application of the self-determination principle continued with post–World War II decolonization. Current conflicts are the logical next step.

> The same principles which fashioned out of European colonialism many Third World independent states, became the platform upon which challenges to those state boundaries were mounted. Nationalism against colonialism became sub-nationalism against the new states. This confrontation between nationalism and ethnic subnationalism was a predictable outcome clearly implied in anti-colonialist argumentation.[39]

The debate over whether the Cold War encouraged or dampened ethnic passions and conflict is reminiscent of an even more fundamental issue regarding the relationship between economic modernization and ethnicity. Traditional Western scholarship has viewed ethnicity as a phenomenon destined to be overcome by broader, stronger modernizing forces. "Twentieth century approaches to the study of ethnicity in politics can be traced to the writings of Marx and Durkheim, both of whom evaluated ethnic identities as part of a larger set of phenomena subject to transformation by the forces of economic modernization."[40] For Marx, as we have noted, attachment to ethnic groups was an annoying obstacle that

modernization theory The idea that economic modernization assimilates peoples and that identity to the country replaces ethnic and religious attachments.

would surely and ultimately give way to more powerful forces, moving the nations of the world to socialism. For the sociologist Emile Durkheim, and then a whole generation of scholars associated with **modernization theory,** nation-building efforts were destined to erode old-fashioned loyalties to smaller, outdated, even quaint ethnic groups. Similar to the liberal expectation that increased interdependence would ameliorate interstate conflict,

> a major assumption of western social science in the post-war decades was that ethnic conflict would disappear as nations modernize and minority groups were assimilated. Industrialization would lead to increased contact and community between different groups. Urbanization would take place. Gradually this would result in . . . acculturation, which would result in a transfer of loyalty from the ethnic group to the nation-state.[41]

Modernization theorists also assumed that religion, as a basis of ethnic identity, would be replaced with secularism.[42] In other words, states were to become melting pots in which anachronistic divisions between ethnic and religious groups would dissolve and everyone would adopt the more modern attitude of loyalty to one's country.

History has not been kind to this theory and there has emerged something of a consensus that rather than ameliorating ethnic conflict, economic modernizing forces actually increase its likelihood. "Although many scholars endorsed . . . [the] melting pot modernization approach, the weight of . . . evidence eventually overwhelmed these theoretical arguments."[43] Now it is more commonly argued that modernizing and centralizing governments provoke a backlash from ethnic groups that fear losing their identity in the move toward a more integrated state or that economic modernization increases contact between ethnic groups that increasingly perceive themselves in competition with each other. Walker Connor, for example, argues that "economic modernization does not undermine ethnic divisions but invigorates them by bringing together previously isolated ethnic groups that suddenly find themselves competing for the same economic niches."[44] Modern life also represents a threat to religious traditions, leading many groups to fight to preserve them.[45] Others believe that economic processes in the most recent decades, with their emphasis on computers, decentralization, and flexibility, also encourage ethnic passions. In the computer information age, economic producers are able to offer ever more specialized, personalized products for ever more narrowly defined consumer groups in grocery stores, hobby shops, automobile dealer showrooms, and bookstores. These processes may be driving people apart rather than assimilating them in a "melting pot."[46]

Other Causes of Ethnic Conflict

It is tempting to see ethnic conflict as inevitable, as an expression of deep animosities between groups that are destined to fight. Indeed, one of the first theories about the proliferation of violent ethnic conflict was the *ancient hatred* explanation, which was mainly the creation of journalists covering the various wars in Europe, Africa, and Asia. The core idea was that the ethnic groups locked in murderous combat had a long history of conflictual intergroup relations. Historically, the periods of relative peace in intergroup relations arose when strong central authority managed to keep tenuous intergroup harmony through the use of rewards and sanctions. Whenever central authority weakened, though, interethnic relations became marked by hostility and violence. From this it follows that under communist rule in countries like Yugoslavia, ethnic relations were kept in check by strong authoritarian elites like Tito; however, when the center itself became weak and crumbled in the early 1990s, the relations between the constituent ethnic groups—Serbs, Croats, Slovenes, Kosovars, Macedonians, Bosnian Muslims, Montenegrins— naturally regressed back to violence.[47]

One problem with this explanation is that it does not account for why some ethnic groups live peacefully with each other, while others do not. It also ignores the fact that in many situations, such as in the former Yugoslavia, relations between groups were not simply held in check by powerful authorities but at times were quite harmonious and positive. In Yugoslavia, "the rivalries in question had been dormant for decades. In the early 1980s, intermarriage rates among Serbs, Croats, and Bosnian Muslims were high in ethnically mixed areas . . . [and] ethnic hostility was low. Conflict among these groups was kept alive primarily in ethnic stereotypes falling far short of hatred."[48] In Darfur, Sudan, intermarriage between "Blacks" and "Arabs" was also quite common until violence erupted in 2003. The ancient hatreds perspective also leaves out the political, economic, and social conditions and goals of many ethnic groups in conflict. In Darfur,

> when the *janjaweed* were organized into coordinated military units and assigned to camps they shared with the regular army, it is not possible to characterize what was happening as spontaneous violence. Ethnic tensions in Darfur were and still are real, and recurring droughts have made them worse. But they themselves were not sufficient to unleash the violence we have seen. They were the raw material, not the cause.[49]

Ethnic groups may engage in conflict in situations of a collapsed state or a power vacuum not because of enduring hatreds, but because of uncertainty and a fear of discrimination if they do not control the state. In this way, ethnic groups fight for the same reason that realists argue states fight. In situations of anarchy, in which there is no overarching government, groups face a security dilemma and must protect themselves. Because groups in anarchical situations are not likely to possess strong military capabilities,

> their military strength becomes largely a function of their 'groupness' or 'cohesion.' But because all sides . . . stress their groupness and cohesion, each appears threatening to the other. Under these conditions, the only way to assess the intentions of other groups is to use history. But prevailing political conditions may lead to nationalist interpretations of history. The result . . . is a 'worst case analysis' whereby every group thinks the other is the enemy.[50]

Even without complete anarchy, weak and unstable states often give rise to insurgencies and civil wars.[51] The political vacuum and struggle for power that arose after the U.S.-led invasion of Iraq may have sparked such conditions, leading to high levels of sectarian conflict unprecedented in modern Iraqi history.[52] One criticism of this anarchy explanation is that ethnic conflicts are not isolated to failed states, but mostly occur where governments continue to have some control, where the condition of anarchy is not present. Furthermore, this perspective "stresses material factors and parsimony, at the expense of a vast array of other motivations—religious, ideological, and emotional—that fuel domestic conflict."[53]

Material factors are nevertheless important. Of the 275 communal groups identified by Gurr's Minorities at Risk project, about 65 percent are the victims of economic discrimination, and about 73 percent were the targets of political discrimination in 1994–1995.[54] The **theory of relative deprivation** expects groups that perceive themselves as relatively worse off to mobilize:

theory of relative deprivation The idea that groups that perceive themselves as relatively worse off than others will mobilize and take action.

> The theory of relative deprivation is useful for explaining the rise of ethnic political mobilization not only among economically backward groups but also among relatively prosperous ethnic groups, such as the Sikhs in India, the Tamils in Sri Lanka, and the Tutsis in Central Africa. When such groups perceive a threat to their privileged position, or if they become victims of state discrimination, they too may take to political action. After all, as the theory suggests, it is the realization by a group that it is receiving less than it deserves and that others are receiving more that motivates the group to take political action. Applying this concept to ethnic conflict . . . , it is easy to understand why perceived disadvantage or discrimination (real or imaginary) by a group regarding its status (sociocultural, economic, political) is an underlying cause for political action.[55]

Theories such as relative deprivation that focus on the economic and political grievances of groups do not directly explain why it is that ethnicity is such an important base for group identity and comparisons to other groups. Many argue that "socioeconomic factors may form the basis of discontent but that only discontent based on ethnocultural identity can lead to ethnonationalism and secessionist sentiments."[56] Some see ethnic identities as the basic, or primordial, identity that is salient for people.

Psychologically, ethnicity can be an easy category for people to simplify the world. Social psychologists argue that categorization is a natural way that people function in an information-rich, complex world, and **social identity theory** suggests that categorizing people into groups helps promote an individual's self-esteem. Categorization includes a division of peoples into "us" (in-groups) and "them" (out-groups). Once such categorization occurs, people tend to process information that reinforces group boundaries and develop an in-group bias, or **ethnocentrism,** seeing their own group in a favorable light and the out-group in an unfavorable light. Research suggests that "the mere perception of belonging to two distinct groups . . . is sufficient to trigger intergroup discrimination favoring the in-group. In other words, the mere awareness of the presence of an out-group is sufficient to provoke intergroup competitive or discriminatory responses on the part of the in-group."[57] People, for example, tend to see the in-group as more heterogeneous than it often is and the out-group as more homogeneous ("*they* are all alike") than it often is. Furthermore, people will remember more about the in-group, discount information that is inconsistent with their stereotype of the out-group, explain away any success achieved by the out-group, and make decisions that reward the in-group and penalize the out-group, often without recognizing that they are doing so.[58] In extreme situations, the need for social identity and the way stereotypes are maintained through errors and biases in information processing may produce a dehumanized view of out-group members. Once dehumanization occurs, killing members of the out-group is not that uncomfortable, because they are seen as less than human. Dehumanizing other ethnic groups is similar to leaders seeing other countries with an enemy image, with similar effects of increasing the likelihood of conflict.

Political leaders often recognize the power that group identity can play in mobilizing the masses to commit violent behavior. The **instrumentalist approach** to ethnicity and ethnic conflict focuses on the role that elites play in highlighting, or even creating, ethnic identities for political ends:

> From this perspective, ethnic identity, one among several alternative bases of identity, gains social and political significance when ethnic entrepreneurs, either for offensive or defense purposes or in response to threats or opportunities for themselves and/or their groups, invoke and manipulate selected ethnic symbols to create political movements in which collective ends are sought. At such moments, ethnicity can be a device as much as a focus for group mobilization by its leadership through the select use of ethnic symbols.[59]

social identity theory Theory suggesting that group membership promotes self-esteem and creates favorable in-group biases.

ethnocentrism Belief that one's ethnic group is superior to others.

instrumentalist approach Explanation of ethnic conflict focusing on leaders' use or creation of ethnic divisions for political ends.

Leaders within states may use ethnic identities for the same reasons that leaders of states may go to war: to divert attention and enhance their legitimacy. In Sudan, for example, "Darfur represents the latest example in which Khartoum [the government] has used its policy of Arabization in an effort to bolster or restore its hegemony."[60]

Leaders are successful at manipulating ethnic identity for instrumental ends when there is a history of group antagonism, and there are severe economic problems.[61]

> In the Balkans, there is no doubt that leaders of the former Yugoslavia, particularly Serbian head, Slobodan Milosevic, helped cause the fighting by inflaming ethnic nationalism. . . . Milosevic (and others) stirred up ethnic conflict in order to realize their personal interest of remaining in power. . . . Recognizing that he could not hold on to power in a multiethnic Yugoslavia . . . , Milosevic deliberately fostered a racist nationalism that resulted in the replacement of most of Yugoslavia with a state that had a clear Serbian majority.[62]

The Belgians, as the colonial power in Rwanda, also used ethnicity for political means. By cultivating separate Hutu and Tutsi identities, they

Soldiers in the Kosovo Liberation Army (KLA) in March 1999, during the conflict between Kosovars and Serbs in Yugoslavia.
(David Brauchli/AP Photo/AP Images)

POLICY CHOICES
Dealing with Ethnic Grievances

ISSUE: There are many ethnic groups in the world who wish to have states of their own, but this would involve the dismemberment of currently existing states. Whether the international community should, or effectively can, address the intensity and scope of ethnic conflicts raises many issues and concerns.

Option #1: The international community should treat all of these problems as matters of domestic concern only.

Arguments: (a) International institutions, such as the United Nations, and global powers, such as the United States, should conserve their resources to deal with the truly international problems. (b) The international community will avoid having to choose which internal disputes to deal with and which to disregard. (c) The international community will avoid the risks of making situations worse by intervening.

Counterarguments: (a) Ethnic problems may invite unilateral interventions from single states in the various regions, creating international problems that might have been easier to deal with at an earlier stage. (b) Because most ethnic conflicts are increasingly domestic rather than international, international institutions such as the United Nations risk becoming irrelevant to the globe's most serious conflicts. (c) Hundreds of thousands of people may suffer oppression at the hands of governments that are insensitive to the needs or aspirations of minority ethnic groups.

Option #2: The international community should energetically defend the principle of national self-determination, which suggests that all peoples deserve to have their own states if they so desire.

Arguments: (a) An active policy of self-determination would allow the United Nations to become a major player in attempts to resolve the most serious violent conflicts in the global system today. (b) Hundreds of thousands of people could be rescued from insensitive, perhaps even racist, oppression. (c) Interventions on behalf of oppressed peoples might undermine autocratic governments, leading to their replacement by democratic governments.

Counterarguments: (a) Operations on behalf of oppressed minorities could become too expensive, perhaps bankrupting the United Nations. (b) Activism of this sort by the international community might encourage additional minorities to aspire to establish their own states, increasing instability on a global scale. (c) Schisms and disagreements about which minorities are truly oppressed and deserving of external support may weaken the ability of the United Nations to deal with truly international problems.

focused any potential conflict between these groups, diverting attention away from the fact that they were ruling over both.

As with the causes of interstate war, the causes of ethnic conflict seem individually insufficient to explain all ethnic violence.

> People do feel strongly about their ethnicity, but very few convinced nationalists actually go as far as to exterminate their neighbors. Maniacal leaders clearly play an important role in civil wars, but simply saying so does not explain why some end up as powerful demagogues while others simply rant in obscurity. Economic grievances and security dilemmas can also push groups toward violence, but such explanations predict far more conflict than actually occurs in the world.[63]

Thus, as in wars between states, all levels of analysis—the structural condition of the state, the strategies of leaders, and the beliefs of the masses—all contribute to an understanding of why ethnic conflict occurs. Some even argue that conditions at all levels must be present to spark ethnic war:

> It is the interaction between these factors—all of them necessary conditions for ethnic war—which causes ethnic violence to begin and escalate. There can be no violence without hostile feelings, and hostile feelings are unlikely to be widespread unless groups have a history of conflict, conflicting symbolic interests, and negative stereotypes of each other. . . . Even in these conditions, violence can only be sustained if the war effort is organized by extremist leaders who gain or hold power by outflanking more moderate rivals. Unless all of these factors operate to a sufficient degree, any ethnic violence which occurs is likely to be brief and on a relatively small scale.[64]

Resolving Ethnic Conflicts

Given the long-term trend of increasing violence and the global implications of these conflicts, the international community is wrestling with ways to address this problem (see the Policy Choices box on ethnic grievances). An attempt to anticipate the future of ethnic conflicts throughout the world needs to take into account, unfortunately, the extent to which ethnic conflicts in Europe have been "resolved" in roughly the Yugoslavian fashion: with "ethnic cleansing," forced migrations, and displaced peoples. "Europe's nationality problem was solved by wars and population transfers over the span of centuries."[65] Peace settlements after the First World War redrew boundaries in such a way as to decrease the percentage of ethnic peoples without a state or self-government from about 26 percent in 1910 to about 7 percent in 1930. As a result of the Second World War, 20 million people settled in new homelands. Often they were relocated with little attention to their own interests or wishes.

For example, "3 million Germans [were] forced to abandon lands their families had occupied for centuries, banished with nothing but tattered clothes and bandaged feet into a harsh winter. The expulsion of Sudeten Germans from their villages in Czechoslovakia still resonates . . . as one of World War II's most contentious incidents."[66] As a result of such episodes of brutality and relocation, the share of Europe's total population belonging to ethnic minorities without autonomy or self-government was reduced to about 3 percent.[67]

The implications of this history of relationships among ethnic groups in Europe for much of Asia, the Middle East, and Africa are sobering, if not downright depressing. Nationalism as an ideological movement emerged in Europe as a result of the French Revolution in the late eighteenth century. It took nearly two centuries of massive relocations and wars for the peoples of Europe to sort themselves out and redraw boundaries in such a way that the distributions of ethnic groups and national boundaries were made largely congruent. And even so, the United Kingdom has yet to resolve the situation in Northern Ireland; Spain faces continuing conflict with the Basques and Catalans; and France still has problems with the Bretons and the Corsicans. Must Africa, Asia, and the Middle East go through these relocations and wars to establish a match between the physical distribution of peoples and legitimate national boundaries? Or to put this partially rhetorical question in more specific but equally gloomy terms, are "Arab-Israeli Wars," complete with refugees and relocations, destined to be duplicated throughout the rest of the Middle East, in Africa, and in Asia?

Anyone who wishes for a more peaceful and stable global political system in the twenty-first century must hope that this is not the case. Even centuries of wars and relocations in Europe have not resolved all the ethnic problems there, and Stalin's forced relocations of millions in the Soviet Union certainly did not resolve all of those ethnic conflicts. It is, in fact, nearly futile to hope that peaceful relationships among the ethnic groups of the world can be established by relocating people and redrawing national boundaries. Africa, for example, is faced with probably the greatest number of ethnic conflicts of all the continents. These problems are often traced to Africa's colonial heritage. "Africa . . . is a continent of a thousand ethnic and linguistic groups squeezed into some 50-odd states, many of them with borders determined by colonial powers in the last century with little regard to traditional ethnic boundaries."[68]

Consider Map 7.2 showing the geographical distribution of ethnic groups in Africa. The colonial powers did undoubtedly draw national boundaries in Africa that arbitrarily cut across or combined disparate ethnic groups. However, the number and distribution of ethnic groups in Africa is such that even had they attempted to be more sensitive in that regard, they would have found it nearly impossible to satisfy all the national aspirations of the various ethnic groups. There are too many of them, and they are not organized in neat, state-size geographical packages.

Map 7.2 Ethnic Groups of Africa

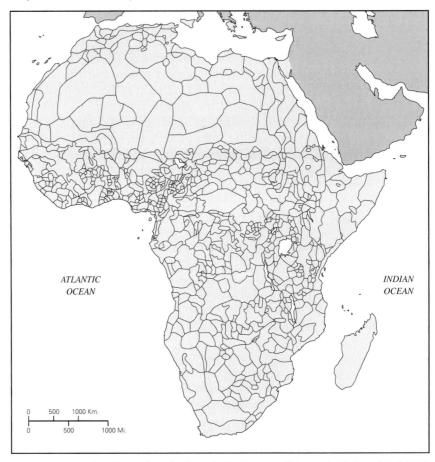

ATLANTIC
OCEAN

INDIAN
OCEAN

Source: Systematic Political Geography, 4th ed., Martin Ira Glassner and Harm J. de Blij. Copyright © 1989 by John Wiley & Sons, Inc. Reproduced with permission of John Wiley & Sons, Inc.

Obviously there are many areas in Africa where ethnic groups are intermingled in the same territory. Ethnic peace will never come to Africa (or anywhere else in the world) if it depends on every ethnic group's satisfying its aspirations to national autonomy and self-determination. In short, no amount of national boundary redrawing is going to resolve all, or even most, of the ethnic conflicts in the world.[69] Such redrawing of boundaries historically creates as many problems as it resolves. The former Soviet Republic of Georgia, for example, broke away from Russia, to be confronted itself by a rebellion by ethnic enclaves in South Ossetia and Abkhazia.[70]

The Eritreans successfully established independence from Ethiopia, but "the Eritrean nationalists themselves are an amalgam of Muslims and

Christians who, if they gain autonomy, are likely to fracture along . . . ethnic lines."[71] In the former Yugoslavia, the Macedonians became independent from Serbia, only to face irredentist pressures from the 20 percent of its population that is Albanian, not to mention its even smaller Serbian population. There may be no end in sight to this kind of process. As Kosovo, formerly part of Serbia and Yugoslavia, declared its independence in 2008 and was recognized as sovereign by the United States and much of Europe, "some of the world's most powerful countries are fearful the move will encourage separatist movements elsewhere to intensify their often bloody struggles and give hope to nascent independence groups that have not yet begun to fight."[72]

It is incumbent on those of us who live in the major industrialized countries, secure in our national identities within states with a long history of democracy and stability, not to be condescending toward ethnic groups with frustrated desires for national autonomy and self-determination. It is too easy for us to say (or feel), "Why can't those people (in Rwanda, Lebanon, Georgia, Burundi, India, or Northern Ireland) just give up their delusions of national grandeur and learn to live together?" Even so, the conclusion of Ted Gurr, the author of one of the more comprehensive surveys of ethnic conflicts in the world, seems reasonable. He observes that a strategy of reconstructing the state system so that state boundaries correspond more closely to the social and cultural boundaries among ethnic communities would "create as many problems as it resolved." According to Gurr,

> A more constructive and open-ended answer is to pursue the . . . coexistence of ethnic groups and plural states. . . . [Ethnic] groups should have the protected rights to individual and collective existence and to cultural self-expression without fear of political repression. The counterpart of such rights is the obligation not to impose their own cultural standards or political agenda on other peoples."[73]

Indeed, Gurr attributes the decline in ethnic conflict in the second half of the 1990s to a "regime of managed ethnic heterogeneity." This regime includes a recognition of the rights of minority peoples and the right of ethnic groups to have some degree of autonomy within states, democratization that institutionalizes these rights, and an increasingly accepted "principle that [maintains] disputes between communal groups and states are best settled by negotiation and mutual accommodation."[74] Democratic governance is one logical solution to the ethnic conflict. "Minorities in the . . . democracies . . . have two distinctive traits. Their grievances usually are expressed in protest, rarely in rebellion, and the most common response by government . . . is to accommodate their interests rather than forcibly subordinate or incorporate them."[75] In states where governmental power is exercised autocratically, struggles for control of the government are likely to be more desperate and violent.

In general, democratic "societies bleed off conflict in divergent directions, preventing that fatal congruence of cleavages and oppositions that leads to intense struggles over societal powers and consequent extreme violence."[76]

But it is difficult to impossible to initiate democratic reforms in a country already torn by ethnic conflict. In fact, many analysts are convinced that transitions to democracy are likely to increase ethnic strife and other sources of internal conflict, even if relatively entrenched, stable democracy may ultimately prove to be an important solution to it. Carment and James provide systematic evidence that "high political constraint [by which they mean democratic controls on the use of political power] reduces threat perception and belligerent behavior" by states involved in conflict over ethnic issues.[77] But they believe that this finding must be taken with a grain of salt, arguing that politicians in democratic countries might use ethnic grievances and strife for their own purposes in ways that could increase conflict.

The challenges of democratization in a country with ethnic and religious divisions were evident after the 2003 military intervention of Iraq. Although Arabs constitute a majority (80 percent) of the population, there is a large Kurdish minority that has long fought for national self-determination. Iraq is also divided along sectarian lines—with roughly 60 percent Shia and 35 percent Sunni Muslims. Larry Diamond, an expert on democratization and senior adviser to the Coalitional Provisional Authority in Baghdad in 2004, spelled out the tasks facing the United States and a new post-Saddam Iraqi government:

> The political challenges in Iraq from around 9 April 2003—when Saddam's regime fell in Baghdad and a U.S.-led postwar administration began to assert itself—resembled many of the other recent post–conflict-reconstruction or nation-building efforts. Once the Ba'athists [Saddam Hussein's ruling political party] were ousted from power, the vacuum of political authority had somehow to be filled, and order on the streets had to be reestablished. The state as an institution had to be restructured and revived. Basic services had to be restored, infrastructure repaired, and jobs created. Fighting between disparate ethnic, regional, and religious groups—many of them with well-armed militias—had to be prevented or preempted. The political culture of fear, distrust, brutal dominance, and blind submission had to be transformed. Political parties and civil society organizations working to represent citizen interests, rebuild communities, and educate for democracy had to be assisted, trained, and protected. A plan needed to be developed to produce a broadly representative and legitimate new government, and to write a new constitution for the future political order. And sooner or later, democratic elections would need to be held.[78]

These tasks proved to be quite difficult. Although sovereignty was officially transferred from U.S. authorities to an appointed interim government, voters approved a new constitution, and elections were held, criminal and sectarian violence escalated. Shias and Sunnis attacked each others' mosques and religious gatherings and each group targeted spiritual leaders from the other. And Sunnis have been suspicious of the political process, which they see as dominated by the majority Shias. By mid-2006, most observers agreed that Iraq had descended into civil war.[79]

As the Iraqi experience illustrates, state-building and democratization involves many difficult issues, including the timing of the first elections.

> Ill-timed and ill-prepared elections do not produce democracy, or even political stability, after conflict. Instead they may only enhance the power of actors who mobilize coercion, fear, and prejudice, thereby reviving autocracy and even precipitating large-scale violent strife. In Angola in 1992, in Bosnia in 1996, and in Liberia in 1997, rushed elections set back the prospects for democracy and, in Angola and Liberia, paved the way for renewed civil war.[80]

The United States is not the only international actor to engage in state-building and face the challenges of democratization in countries divided by ethnic conflict. The United Nations, as will be discussed in more detail in Chapter 9, recently involved itself in efforts to deal with ethnic conflicts in Yugoslavia, Somalia, Cyprus, Lebanon, Kashmir, India, and Rwanda. Efforts by the international community to deal with ethnic strife in Rwanda were particularly controversial, with some analysts arguing that those efforts actually provided a base of operations for those who committed genocide, thus prolonging the conflict for years.[81] According to one observer, "The pre-cold war, cold war, and post–cold war record on intervening militarily to promote the more ambitious goals of political and economic development yields a cautionary lesson—don't."[82]

Despite the difficulties of democratization and resolution to ethnic conflict, the international community remains interested in these tasks (see the Policy Choices box in Chapter 6 for more on the pros and cons of democratization). Ethnic conflicts can present moral imperatives—such as the prevention of genocide—and can affect the political, security, and economic interests of other states. As already mentioned, ethnic conflicts frequently become internationalized and can easily spark interstate conflicts. Ethnic conflict can also produce terrorist groups and these groups can become significant transnational actors. The terrorist attacks in Mumbai India in 2008, rooted in the conflict between Pakistan and India over Kashmir, are an example of the interrelationship between group conflict, terrorism, and interstate conflict. International terrorism, along with ethnic conflict, is another significant source of violence in contemporary global politics.

International Terrorism

As discussed in Chapter 4, international terrorist groups are significant nonstate actors in contemporary international politics and in some ways represent a challenge to the sovereign state system. Although international terrorism is not new, its contemporary features include a strong connection to religion, a worldwide presence that uses globalization in a sophisticated way, and an increase in the number of deaths of targeted civilians. After the attacks in the United States on September 11, 2001, transnational terrorism and states' attempts to fight terrorism have become a central aspect of global politics.

Defining Terrorism

terrorism Acts of intimidation against civilians committed by nonstate actors for political motives.

Any useful discussion of terrorist groups or terrorism must first deal with the question, "What is **terrorism**?" As is the case with most questions on this subject, the answers are both numerous and controversial.[83] The standard summary of this controversy asserts that "one person's terrorist is another person's freedom fighter," because terrorism is a highly charged political term used by most people to refer to political violence (or any other political tactic) of which they disapprove:

> In their conflict with the Palestinians, for example, the Israelis claim the moral high ground by pointing to the means their opponents employ, notably suicide bombings. . . . The Palestinians, in contrast, focus on ends. Israel, they argue, is intent on continuing its occupation of the West Bank and the Gaza Strip. Opposing this occupation is legitimate, in their eyes, and the huge disparities in strength leave them no alternative to terrorism.[84]

The term *terrorism* often comes with a moral judgment. One definition is that "terrorism is the deliberate, systematic murder, maiming, and menacing of the innocent to inspire fear in order to gain political ends. . . . Terrorism . . . is intrinsically evil, necessarily evil, and wholly evil."[85] The problem is then defining what are "evil" political ends and what ends justify certain means. Because there is usually considerable disagreement on what is moral, defining terrorism in moral terms becomes problematic. The French Resistance and the Polish Underground were labeled terrorists by Germany in World War II, but others would certainly disagree, believing that resisting Nazi occupation was a moral cause. This is not to say that terrorist acts should not be held to moral and legal standards, but that it becomes problematic if morality is part of the very definition of terrorism.

Because of the moral judgment connected to the label *terrorism*, defining groups as terrorists has become a tool that political actors use to undermine the legitimacy of their enemies:

> The political nature of determining under what circumstances
> a violent international political act should be considered terror-
> ism is illustrated by [the] U.S. State Department's official list
> of states supporting terrorism. . . . With no objective criteria for
> deciding when countries should be placed on or removed from
> the list, inclusion is a purely political decision.[86]

For example, Syria remained on the list for years even though the State
Department testified it had no evidence of Syrian support for terrorism.[87]
Since September 11, the tool to define enemies as terrorists has become
even more powerful. China, for example, "has launched its own 'war on
terror.' Beijing now labels as terrorists those fighting for an independent
state in the northwestern province of Xinjiang."[88] China uses, as do many
other states, the term *terrorist* partly in an attempt to avoid condemnation from the international community of its activities against internal
groups. The term terrorism, then, is unfortunately related to the judgment
of the morality of the actor's objective and the political consequences of
being labeled a terrorist.

Less judgmentally, Thomas Schelling points out that the diction-
ary defines the term as "the use of terror, violence, and intimidation to
achieve an end."[89] A CIA-sponsored study has defined international terror
as "the threat or use of violence for political purposes when (1) such action
is intended to influence the attitude and behavior of a target group wider
than its immediate victim;, and (2) its ramifications transcend national
boundaries."[90] The main problem with these definitions is that they are far
too broad. They would include under the same rubric an incredibly diverse
array of phenomena. According to these definitions, terrorism includes
more than the hijacking of airplanes or the random machine-gunning of
people in airports. The bombing of civilian populations in cities by both
sides in the Second World War, the invasion of Germany by Allied troops,
the nuclear bombing of Hiroshima and Nagasaki, the arrest and torture
of political prisoners, and the execution of criminals (or imprisonment
of criminals, for that matter) would all qualify as terrorism according to
these definitions. A more useful definition might stipulate that terrorism
is "the use of violence for political purposes by nongovernmental actors."
This definition, however, is still broad, because it would include attacks
on states by revolutionaries or guerrillas, such as the French Resistance
or the Polish Underground in the Second World War, and many feel that
guerrilla fighters who restrict their targets to the military forces of the
government they are trying to overthrow should not be labeled terrorists.
Indeed, "a condemnation of terrorism is not a denunciation of revolutionaries or guerillas. It is only a reiteration of the limits of violence that
a civilized society is willing to permit. It does not in any sense preclude
the right to revolution, which is a recognized and protected right under
international law."[91]

noncombatant targets Targets, such as civilians and certain military personnel that are not engaged in military combat.

A more tenable distinction, perhaps, is offered by those who argue that "in terrorism, the perpetrators *deliberately* choose **noncombatant targets** and relatively indiscriminate means."[92] It is probably easier to discriminate between combatants and noncombatants than between those who are innocent and those who are not. Even that distinction, though, is not free of ambiguities. President Reagan denounced as terrorism the 1983 attack that killed 241 U.S. Marines in Beirut. He had argued previously that "freedom fighters" act against military targets, while "terrorists" attack innocent civilians. Can soldiers be classified as noncombatants? Reagan's answer to that question with respect to the bombing of the marines' barracks in Lebanon was that the Marines were noncombatants. He argued that those troops were on a peacekeeping mission and that they were asleep when they were attacked. Furthermore, if terrorism is restricted only to noncombatants, would the September 11, 2001, bombing of the U.S. Pentagon, the headquarters of the U.S. military, qualify as a terrorist act? As is obvious in these cases, the question of whether soldiers can be classified as noncombatants is likely to spark considerable debate even among those determined to conduct a relatively dispassionate analysis of terrorism.[93]

Another problem with defining terrorism as violence against noncombatants is how to classify political assassinations. Politically motivated murders of leaders of states are frequently considered acts of terrorism. The U.S. State Department's list of "Significant Terrorist Incidents, 1961–2003," for example, includes the assassination of Indian Prime Minister Indira Gandhi in 1984 and the attempted assassination of former U.S. President George Bush in 1993. Most of the popular historical examples of terrorists are assassins as well. Yet, just as with military personnel, it is difficult to view state officials as innocent civilians in political conflicts.

Title 22 of the U.S. Legal Code (Section 2656[d]) defines *terrorism* as "premeditated, politically motivated violence perpetrated against non-combatant targets by subnational groups or clandestine agents. . . . The term international terrorism' means terrorism involving citizens or the territory of more than one country."[94] This definition is reasonably specific and avoids many or even most of the problems posed by the definitions discussed previously. The only possibly questionable phrase is "clandestine agents," which opens the door to the idea that states can commit terrorism through such agents.

States and their agents, clandestine or not, certainly commit violence for political purposes against noncombatant targets and this violence inspires "terror." Furthermore, the violence perpetrated by governments is a problem incomparably greater in scope and intensity than terrorism.[95] But most who offer analytical definitions of terrorism believe that if any definition is going to be sufficiently precise to be useful, such violence is not terrorism. An act of unjustifiable violence by a government should certainly be called an atrocity but not terrorism. Of course, it is true that states can sponsor terrorism and terrorist agents and that this is a significant problem, as will be discussed shortly. Still, there can be a distinction made between states sponsoring terrorism and states themselves engaging in political violence against noncombatants.

Another aspect missing in these definitions is the drama associated with terrorism and the fear it is meant to inspire. The murdering of a man in his wheelchair during the *Achille Lauro* cruise ship hostage crisis was certainly designed to instill terror. The visual image of airplanes crashing into the twin towers of the World Trade Center seemed to be crafted to shock an audience accustomed to Hollywood films. "Terrorist strategy is basically psychological in nature. The first step is to create mass terror, not mass destruction. . . . The second step is to manipulate political disaffection created by this psychological reaction either to intimidate governing authorities into acceding to specified political demands, or else to get rid of the government entirely."[96] Indeed, "terrorists choose their targets to appear to be random, so everyone feels at risk—when getting on a plane, entering a federal building, or strolling a market square. Businesspeople, military personnel, tourists, and everyday citizens . . . are generally the targets of terrorist attacks."[97]

As we can see, there are numerous ways to define terrorism. Yet there seems to be a consensus in the academic community on key ingredients to classifying acts as terroristic: "the underlying political motive [as opposed to a purely criminal or personal motive], the general atmosphere of intimidation, and the targeting of those outside of the decision-making process."[98] Terrorist groups are nonstate actors that commit such acts.

The History of Terrorism

It is easy to get the impression that terrorism is a quite recent phenomenon, almost entirely dependent on, and so to a great extent a result of, modern communications media, especially television. One analysis of three groups of religious terrorists that existed centuries ago—the Thugs (Hindu), the Assassins (Islamic), and the Zealots (Jewish)—makes it clear that terrorist activity on a significant scale has occurred at least since the days of the Roman Empire. Clearly, terrorism is not a phenomenon produced solely by excessive attention from modern media. The Assassins, for example, "did not need mass media to reach interested audiences, because their prominent victims were murdered in venerated sites and royal courts, usually on holy days when many witnesses were present." In general, the idea that "terrorist operations require modern technology to be significant" is a "misconception."[99]

Other historical examples of international terrorist groups include Narodnaya Volya ("The People's Will"), operating in Russia in the late 1800s and early 1900s, and the Internal Macedonian Revolutionary Organization (IMRO), formed in the 1890s. "For several years, the IMRO waged guerilla warfare, sometimes employing terrorist tactics, against the Turkish rulers of their region. . . . Other nations both assisted and interfered in the struggle. Bombings and kidnappings, as well as the murder of civilians and officials were frequent."[100]

In the modern age of terrorism, one analyst has identified four waves.[101] The first wave, beginning at the end of the nineteenth century, was characterized by anarchism as a motive and assassination as a method, including the assassination of the Austrian archduke in Sarajevo in 1914 that sparked World War I. The second wave was primarily a reaction to decolonization after World Wars I and II and involved groups fighting for national self-determination. The third wave came in response to criticism of the United States in Vietnam and Israel in the Middle East. This wave was more transnational in character, and airline hijacking was the most popular method used. Presumably the fourth wave, beginning with the Iranian revolution in 1979 and growing significantly in the post–Cold War era, involves religion more directly as a motive, or at least as a rhetorical and recruitment tool.[102]

Hezbollah Political and military Shia Islamic group in southern Lebanon.

International terrorism in the 1980s was largely connected to Israel's invasion of Lebanon and U.S. support for Israel and its involvement in the Lebanese civil war. "The most militant of [the Lebanese] Shiite organizations was **Hezbollah,** whose guerrilla arms inaugurated the tactic of massive truck or vehicle bombs. . . . The American embassy in Lebanon was bombed twice . . . [and] the American embassy in Kuwait was also bombed."[103] A Hezbollah suicide bomber was responsible for the attack on the U.S. Marine barracks in Beirut in 1983.

Furthermore, the 1980s saw an increased involvement of states supporting or "sponsoring" terrorism.[104] There were reports, for example, that Libya maintained camps within its borders capable of training 5,000 men at a time.[105] Several terrorist training camps were located in Syria in the 1980s.[106] And Iran was suspected of sponsoring several Islamic groups, including the Lebanese Hezbollah.[107] State sponsorship of terrorism in the 1980s was also connected to the Cold War rivalry between the United States and the Soviet Union. In 1984, one report claimed that "an ever-increasing flow of arms and ammunition, manufactured in the Soviet Union, Czechoslovakia, and East Germany, have been shipped to the PLO via East Germany and Hungary."[108] In addition, the United States has funneled millions of dollars in support of such "nongovernmental perpetrators of violence for political purposes" as the rebels in Afghanistan and the contras in Central America.

One disturbing result of state-supported terrorism is that terrorists acquire access to increasingly sophisticated military technology. Even in the 1970s, terrorists were arrested in Rome, Paris, and Kenya with anti-aircraft missiles and portable rocket launchers.[109] When the Israelis attacked the PLO camps in Lebanon in 1982, they found that the Soviets had supplied that organization with rocket launchers and radar-guided anti-aircraft cannon.[110] The ultimate fear along these lines is that some state at some time would supply weapons of mass destruction to a terrorist group. The Aum Shinrikyo group in Japan used poisonous sarin gas in an attack on the Tokyo subway system in March 1995, and the bombing of New York's World Trade Center in 1993 was intended to involve cyanide gas.[111] Most worrisome is evidence that al Qaeda has a long history of trying to develop chemical, biological, and nuclear capabilities.[112] Most analysts agree, however, that most terrorist groups do not yet have the financial or technical capabilities to acquire, assemble, and deliver these weapons of mass destruction.[113]

The decline of state sponsorship of terrorism in the 1990s was associated with a decline in terrorist attacks. In 1992, according to a U.S. State Department report (using its own definition of terrorism), "the number of international terrorist incidents dropped sharply [36 percent] . . . falling to its lowest level in 17 years." State Department officials claimed that this decline was attributable to "the disappearance of the Communist governments in Eastern Europe and the Soviet Union that provided support and safe haven for terrorist groups."[114] Certainly, the decline in leftist terrorists in the post–Cold War period is partly attributed to the decline of the Soviet empire. Domestic antiterrorism policies by some countries (such as Spain, France, and Germany) and some collective efforts by the European Union and NATO involving coordination and information sharing are also part of the explanation.[115]

Figure 7.2 shows the number of international terrorist attacks occurring each year since 1968, as compiled in the RAND-MIPT Terrorism Knowledge Database. According to this source, the lowest annual total in the last thirty years was 106 incidents in 2000, down from a high of 434 incidents in 1985. The number of incidents generally declined from 1988 to 2003. Since the beginning of this century, the number of terrorist incidents has increased. The number of fatalities, shown in Figure 7.3, associated with these terrorist events also varies across the years. Before 2001, the deadliest year in this record was 1988, with 702 casualties. Even when the number of incidents was on the decline, the number of deaths generally increased, suggesting that terrorist tactics have become more lethal.[116] The embassy bombings in Kenya and Tanzania, for example, killed 247 and injured 5,500, and the 1993 bombing of the World Trade Center in the United States killed six and injured about 1,000. "The attacks of September 11 fit a pattern but also marked a dramatic escalation of violence," killing more than 3,000 people.[117] In addition, the percentage of international attacks against U.S. targets increased from about 25 percent in the mid-1980s to about 47 percent in 2000.[118]

The higher number of deaths seems to have been caused by more attacks on large numbers of civilians, which may be related to the new types of terrorist groups that have emerged (to be discussed later in this chapter). "Although it is tempting to attribute the increased casualties . . . to better technology available to terrorists, incidents have not really relied on new technologies. Old fashioned bombs were used at the World Trade

Figure 7.2 **Number of International Terrorist Incidents, 1968–2005**

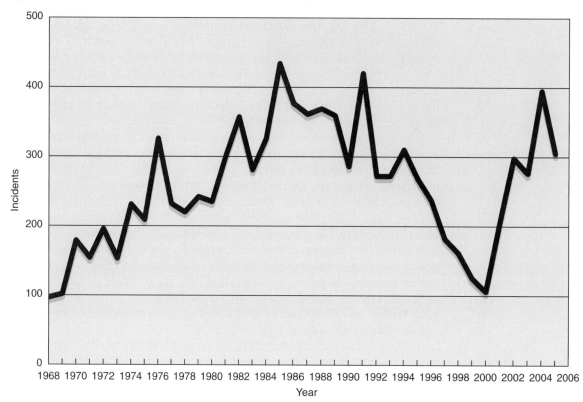

Source: Data from MIPT Terrorism Knowledge Data Base. http://www.tkb.org, accessed October 13, 2006. Data include only international incidents "in which terrorists go abroad to strike the targets, select domestic targets associated with a foreign state, or create an international incident by attacking airline passengers, personnel, or equipment."

Center, . . . Nairobi, and elsewhere. The difference today is that these bombs are often planned to explode where and when maximum carnage would result."[119] The use of cutter knives and "old-fashioned" hijacking of commercial airlines on September 11, 2001, clearly demonstrates that attacks can be quite lethal without sophisticated technology.

The most lethal attacks have been associated with Osama bin Laden and relate to U.S. policy in the Middle East and the **al Qaeda** network:

al Qaeda An international network of terrorist cells, created by Osama bin Laden.

Many sources of the terrorism of the 1990s can be traced to specific events associated with the Persian Gulf war and the Soviet invasion of Afghanistan in December 1979. The post-war sanctions against Iraq and the military enforcement of the no-fly zones in Iraq . . . perpetuated that conflict and mobilized anti-American sentiment. . . . Islamic militants from around the world gained experience fighting the Soviet Union in Afghanistan. . . . After the Soviet withdrawal from Afghanistan in 1989,

Figure 7.3   Number of International Terrorist Fatalities, 1968–2005

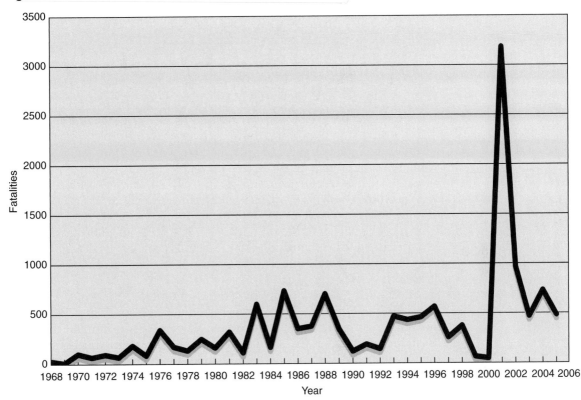

Source: Data from MIPT Terrorism Knowledge Data Base. http://www.tkb.org, accessed October 13, 2006. Data include only international incidents "in which terrorists go abroad to strike the targets, select domestic targets associated with a foreign state, or create an international incident by attacking airline passengers, personnel, or equipment."

the establishment of training camps in Afghanistan by Saudi-born terrorist Osama bin Laden and his al Qaeda organization provided an ongoing arena for the socialization of Islamic radicals from across the world.[120]

Osama bin Laden, son of a wealthy man who owned a construction company and had ties to the royal ruling family in Saudi Arabia, was part of the resistance against the Soviet Union in Afghanistan. Indeed, *al Qaeda* means "the base" and refers to the tracking station that bin Laden established in Pakistan to document the Arabs who went through his guesthouse and training camps on the way to fight in the Afghan resistance. The Muslim opposition to the Soviet Union in Afghanistan was directly encouraged and funded by the United States. The war against the "atheist power" proved attractive; between 1982 and 1992, over 35,000 people from forty Islamic countries joined in the fight.[121] After the Soviet Union withdrew from Afghanistan, bin Laden returned to Saudi Arabia but was restricted in his movements for his criticism of the Saudi government, particularly for allowing the Americans to come into Saudi Arabia after the Iraqi invasion of Kuwait. When he fled Saudi Arabia and was not allowed to return, Sudan accepted him, and there he set up training camps and established ties with groups in Libya, Palestine, Somalia, Bosnia, and the Philippines.[122]

Taliban Fundamentalist Islamic group that supported al Qaeda and ruled most of Afghanistan from 1996 to 2001.

Under pressure from the United States, Sudan expelled him in 1996, at which time bin Laden returned to Afghanistan, soon to be ruled by the **Taliban,** an Islamic government led by teachers and students from seminaries for the training of the Islamic clergy. The Taliban were backed by neighboring Pakistan and, initially, by Saudi Arabia. Bin Laden set up a number of terrorist camps in Afghanistan and significantly influenced the Taliban leadership.[123] During this time period, he has been linked to the attacks on the Khobar towers in 1996 in Saudi Arabia, the embassy bombings in Africa in 1998, and foiled attacks in Jordan and the United States at turn-of-the-century celebrations in 1999. In 1998, he joined forces with groups in Egypt, Pakistan, and Bangladesh to issue a "Declaration of the World Islamic Front for Jihad against the Jews and the Crusaders." Among other things, the declaration criticized the U.S. "occupation" of Saudi Arabia and issued a *fatwa*, or ruling, stating, "To kill Americans and their allies, both civil and military, is an individual duty of every Muslim . . . until their armies, shattered and broken-winged, depart from all the lands of Islam, incapable of threatening any Muslim."[124] Despite the intent of the signatories that the *fatwa* should apply to all of the Islamic faith, the statement to most Muslims was a "grotesque travesty of the nature of Islam and even of its doctrine of jihad ["holy war"]. . . . At no point do the basic texts of Islam enjoin terrorism and murder. At no point do they even consider the random slaughter of uninvolved bystanders."[125]

The attacks of September 11, 2001, seemed, however, to be gruesomely prophesied by the declaration and previous activities of al Qaeda and took the history of terrorism, some say world politics, into a new era. Since then, additional attacks, assumed to be connected with al Qaeda in some form, have occurred in a tourist area of Bali, Indonesia (in 2002), in Casablanca, Morocco (in 2003), and in Riyadh, Saudi Arabia (also in 2003).[126] More recently, in March of 2004, terrorists, assumed to be Spanish-based Moroccans connected to al Qaeda, attacked a Madrid commuter train, killing 191 and injuring more than 1,400 people. In July 2005, fifty-two people died in an attack on buses and subway trains in London. The London bombings were carried out by British-born Muslims, and it is unclear how much al Qaeda played a role in the training of the attackers and the planning of the attacks.[127] al Qaeda is also suspected of involvement in a plot to blow up as many as ten transatlantic planes in August 2006, and groups related to al Qaeda are accused of recent attacks in Lebanon, Algeria, Pakistan, Yemen, and Iran. To many, the attacks in London and Madrid served as further proof that global politics had entered a new phase of terror. Europe, for example, seems to be a new locus of Islamic extremist activity, with both long-time residents and new immigrants joining the now-global, decentralized network associated with al Qaeda.[128]

Still, in the light of the actual amount of suffering and death from international terrorism, it might be argued that it is an over-publicized phenomenon: "[I]t is worth remembering that the total number of people killed since 9/11 by al Qaeda or al Qaeda like operatives outside of Afghanistan and Iraq is not much higher than the number who drown in bathtubs in the United States in a single year."[129] The total number of deaths caused by international terrorist incidents from 1968 to 2005, according to the RAND-MIPT Terrorism Knowledge Base, is 9,858.[130] That is a tragically large number, although not in comparison with the numbers killed by international wars, civil wars, government-sponsored policies of oppression, and so on.

In the end, perhaps, what is most worrisome about international terrorism in the contemporary era is its potential for wreaking massive havoc and suffering with nuclear weapons, biological and chemical weapons, or information warfare techniques that could result in massive dislocations in banking records, airline traffic, and communication networks. "Chances are that of 100 attempts at terrorist superviolence, 99 would fail. But the single successful one could claim many more victims, do more material damage, and unleash far greater panic than anything the world has yet experienced."[131]

The Origins of Terrorism

It is a mistake to believe that terrorism is mindless violence, without purpose other than a release for pent-up frustration:

> The ultimate goals of all international terrorism are political.
> This distinguishes it from nonpolitical violence by criminal elements or the emotionally disturbed. Most terrorist goals involve a sense of grievance, real or imagined, which the perpetrators seek to overcome either by forcing political authorities to accede to their demands or by forcing them from power entirely.[132]

Furthermore, terrorist strategies often obtain their goals. According to one study, " . . . terrorism has been so successful that between 1980 and 2003, half of all suicide terrorist campaigns were closely followed by substantial concessions by the target governments. Hijacking planes, blowing up buses, and kidnapping individuals may seem irrational and incoherent to outside observers, but these tactics can be surprisingly effective in achieving a terrorist group's political aims."[133]

Terrorism can have several tactical aims for resistance groups. For some of the Palestinian groups, these aims include publicizing the groups' cause, "provoking Israel to adopt repressive measures against innocent, uncommitted Arabs in the hope that such measures will lead the latter to join or support the resistance, . . . provoking Israel to retaliate severely against Arab states and thereby undermine diplomatic efforts to achieve peace, . . . [and] dissuading moderate Arab regimes from making concessions to Israel."[134] Like the Palestinians, several groups are ethnic minorities seeking national self-determination:

> Faced with the overwhelming odds in favor of the well-established and well-armed state, many of the peoples seeking to exercise their right to self-determination have been increasingly willing to use less conventional methods and means of waging war. Lacking large popular support from the indigenous population, facing a state whose trained army and weaponry make conventional resistance a mockery, such groups are increasingly willing to use . . . terrorism . . . to achieve their right.[135]

From the late 1960s until the late 1980s, transnational terrorism was primarily motivated by nationalism, separatism, Marxist ideology, racism, nihilism, and economic equality.[136] Some argue that the current wave of modern terrorist activity is distinct because of its religious character. "Older groups like the PLO or the IRA are generally constrained by nationalists or irredentist goals—a Palestinian state, a united Ireland—that are negotiable. . . . What motivates their violence is the desire to obtain a particular political result. Old terrorists are looking to bargain, new terrorists want only to express their wrath and cripple their enemy."[137] Indeed, over the last two and a half decades, groups for which religion provides the dominant objective and who engage in terrorist acts have become more prevalent.[138] Possibly due to a worldwide growth of religious fundamentalism, some analysts view these more religious-based groups as more dangerous "than earlier terrorist groups that wanted to win over the people and, in so doing, did not want to leave massive casualties. During . . . earlier decades, precision attacks were directed at well-defined targets of the establishment."[139] And suicide attacks, possibly motivated by religious notions of martyrdom, have become more prevalent.

> The year 2000 witnessed 37 attacks—a record number. It also signaled the beginning of an upward trend in the number of suicide missions that would span most of the first decade of this century. Thus, between 2000 and 2007, the number of attacks rose steadily each year, from 54 in 2001 to 71 in 2002, 81 in 2003, 104 in 2004, 348 in 2005, 353 in 2006, and 535 in 2007 . . .[140]

Others disagree, arguing that the current type of violence is not particularly new[141] and not particularly related to religion. Islam, for example, strictly prohibits the targeting of innocent civilians, and Islamic "theology cannot explain suicide as a method of terrorism. Here again, the perpetrators and their supporters may twist religion to suit their ends, and to brush aside the basic Islamic doctrine prohibiting suicide."[142] Furthermore, suicide bombing is not a new terrorist tactic. Historically, other groups, such as some Palestinian Islamic and Lebanese Christian groups in the 1950s and 1960s and the Japanese in World War II, used tactics that involved the necessary death of the attacker.[143] And one non-religious group, the Tamil Tigers in Sri Lanka, is "the world leader in suicide terrorism."[144]

Furthermore, "while there is some truth to the notion that Islamism is the leading doctrinal ideology among terrorists today, . . . the political dynamics of the Islamist terrorist groups are overwhelmingly nationalist and ethnic in scope."[145] The origins of al Qaeda terrorism, for example, are decidedly political. Members of al Qaeda, particularly those with roots in Egypt, were first fighting quite authoritarian and repressive regimes, backed by the United States:

> For most of the militants now engaged in al Qaeda, opposition to authority at home, whether peaceful or violent, was ineffective. Local regimes countered dissent with severe repression. As a result, radical frustrations apparently were transferred to the United States as a symbol of both oppression and arrogance. . . . One cannot understand Al Qaeda without understanding the domestic politics of Egypt and Saudi Arabia, or now much of the Muslim world.[146]

Specifically, U.S. support of successive Egyptian governments (after 1979, Egypt became the second largest recipient, following Israel, of U.S. foreign aid) angered groups that had been fighting repression for decades. One of these groups, the al-Gama'a al-Islamiyya, had been active since the 1970s in attempting to overthrow the government, and it began working outside Egypt in the 1990s. Its spiritual leader, the cleric Umar Abd al-Rahman, along with other members of the group, were convicted in the 1993 World Trade Center bombing. Another group, the Egyptian Islamic Jihad, joined forces with Osama bin Laden in 1998, and this alliance "can be interpreted as an outcome of the group's inability to continue its terrorist activities within Egypt."[147]

In contrast to Egypt, in which Islamic dissidents were responding to a secular state, dissidents like bin Laden in Saudi Arabia emerged in a country with a government that supports a strict, fundamentalist version of religious doctrine. Yet Saudi Arabia's relationship with the United States—its alliance with the United States in the Gulf War against Iraq and its continued logistical support of the U.S. presence in the Middle East—angered many Saudis, including groups such as the Saudi Hezbollah. Attacks on U.S. military personnel in Riyadh, Saudi Arabia, in 1995, and on the Khobar towers in 1996 reflected this anger.

Al Qaeda's political motives behind the September 11 attack are presumably related to these objections to U.S. policy:

> The reasoning behind the September 11 attacks was expressed primarily in a statement from bin Laden broadcast in Qatar on October 7. . . . The statement referred specifically to 80 years

of humiliation of Islam. It thus apparently dated the period of humiliation to 1921, the dissolution of the Ottoman Empire, and the establishment of Britain's Palestine Mandate that provided for a Jewish homeland. Specific references to Palestine and Iraq were made, as well as more vague allegations that countries that believe in Islam had been turned against bin Laden by the United States. Bin Laden cited United States retaliation against Afghanistan in 1998 as another grievance.[148]

Today, al Qaeda continues to criticize U.S. policies around the world, including the intervention and occupation of Iraq. "Thousands of Arab volunteers, many of them inspired by bin Laden's words, went to Iraq in the run-up to the U.S. invasion. Some joined the fledgling network created by the longtime bin Laden associate Abu Musab al-Zarqawi, who had fled Afghanistan and come to Iraq sometime in 2002 to begin preparations against the invasion."[149] al Qaeda in Iraq's strategy to force the United States to leave involved sparking sectarian violence between Sunnis and Shi'ites. How new the mix of religion and politics is in the motivations behind current terrorism is unclear. It is certainly the case that:

> Osama bin Laden is no more representative of Islam than Timothy McVeigh is of Christianity, or Japan's Shoko Asahara is of Buddhism. Still, one cannot deny that the ideals and ideas of these vicious activists are permeated with religion. The authority of religion has given bin Laden's cadres what they believe is the moral standing to employ violence in their assault on the very symbol of global economic power. It has also provided the metaphor of cosmic war, an image of spiritual struggle that every religion has within its repository of symbols: the fight between good and bad, truth and evil.[150]

What does seem to be new about contemporary terrorist acts is that they are supported by well-organized and global networks.[151] The coordinated attacks against two U.S. embassies, in Kenya and Tanzania, in 1998 were one of the first signs that a new, transnational, well-organized network of groups was operating. Subsequently, in the trials of suspects in these attacks, the degree of organization, sophistication, and scope of al Qaeda was revealed:

> United States government officials estimate that bin Laden's organization . . . has thousands of operatives who are active, or suspected to be active, in dozens of countries. . . . Many groups, such as the Egyptian Islamic Jihad and the Algerian Armed Islamic Group, are closely affiliated with al Qaeda. . . . The al Qaeda organization, and others like it, have branches that handle finance, documents, public relations, and intelligence. They run businesses. They conduct surveillance of enemy targets. They cultivate journalists to ensure favorable coverage in the

Photographers run past a burning hotel which was one of the targets in a coordinated terrorist attack in Mumbai, India in November 2008. More than 175 people were killed and over 300 wounded in these attacks.
(Arko Datta/Reuters/Corbis)

press. They have sophisticated web sites for both fund raising and recruiting.[152]

After September 11, 2001, al Qaeda has become even more transnational, and more decentralized. With the invasion of Afghanistan and the destruction of the Taliban government, al Qaeda relied more on "associated groups to advance their territorial aims, as well as support al-Qaeda's universal jihad. To this end, its organizers, trainers, financiers and human couriers have dispersed and are moving around the world to provide support to these groups."[153] "The result is that today there are many al Qaedas rather than the single al Qaeda of the past."[154] What is unclear is the degree to which Al Qaeda leaders such as bin Laden direct these other groups and their activities and provide them with training and resources, or simply inspire them. What is certain, however, is that the transnational character of today's international terrorist networks is undoubtedly aided by globalization[155] (see Chapter 14) and makes the design of policies to prevent terrorism more difficult.

Dealing with Terrorism

Most analysts of terrorism agree that it is impossible to completely prevent terrorist attacks. Yet intelligence does work at times. A series of "millennium plots," including a plan to bomb the Los Angeles airport, were foiled in December 1999 and British authorities averted an attempt to blow up transatlantic flights in August 2006.[156] Overall, however, prevention is extremely difficult, and some antiterrorism measures can in fact be counterproductive. Using data on terrorist acts from 1968 to 1988, one study evaluated the impact of various antiterrorist policies. The study concluded that:

> the most effective policies were the installation of metal detectors in January 1973 and the fortification of U.S. embassies in 1976 and thereafter. Although metal detectors decreased skyjackings, they had the unintended effect of *increasing* other types of hostage missions and assassinations. . . . No long-run decrease in terrorism could be attributed to the raid [by the United States on Libya in 1986]. Finally, the Reagan antiterrorism laws did not inhibit terrorism directed against U.S. interests.[157]

The U.S. raid on Libya in retaliation against terrorist activities believed to be sponsored by Libya is one approach to terrorism: relying on conventional military attacks launched against the states that support it. This attack caused a transatlantic maelstrom of controversy. Most Americans approved the action, whereas most Europeans did not. Only the British government cooperated with the attack. The controversy regarding the U.S. attack focused first on its effectiveness and second on its morality. Even officials in the Reagan administration acknowledged initially that the raid on Libya might cause an increase in terrorism in the short run. They also argued, however, that it would decrease terrorism in the long run. Ethical military operations, according to just war principles (see Chapter 9), require discrimination, that is, immunity for noncombatants. Unfortunately, U.S. bombs in Libya killed civilians. The just war doctrine also stipulates that military action must be proportional, doing more good than harm. One critic addressed the idea of using conventional military attacks as a response to terrorist activities even before President Reagan's retaliation against Muammar Qaddafi's Libya. He said that such attacks would "substitute the greater evil of full-scale war, with all its attendant death and devastation and dangers of escalation, for the lesser evil of terrorism."[158]

As mentioned, one study indicates that there was no long-term effect and "the American bombing of Tripoli apparently led Libya to seek revenge by organizing the midair bombing of Pan Am Flight 103 over Lockerbie, Scotland, in December 1988."[159] Yet the suspects for this bombing were eventually indicted, with one convicted, and Libyan sponsorship of terrorist groups does seem to have decreased. How much Libya's change in policies can be attributed to fear of another military attack, however, is debatable, as many analysts believe that these changes were motivated more by Libya's desire to end sanctions and improve its economy.[160]

The raid against Libya is not the only example of military attacks against states accused of sponsoring terrorists. More recently, the United States attacked a pharmaceutical company in 1998 in Sudan, believing there was a connection between the company and Osama bin Laden, who was suspected in the bombing of U.S. embassies in Kenya and Tanzania. At the same time, the United States launched attacks in Afghanistan against suspected al Qaeda training camps. The decision to attack Sudan and Afghanistan was controversial. "In particular, critics disputed the link between the pharmaceuticals plant, chemical precursors, and bin Laden. The retaliatory attacks may have been a signal of American resolve, but they inflicted no serious damage on Al Qaeda's capabilities."[161]

After the September 11, 2001 attacks, the United States, backed by a large coalition of states, again pursued military options as one way of dealing with terrorism. Within weeks, the war against the Taliban government in Afghanistan was launched and eventually succeeded in dismantling the state that had given sanctuary to al Qaeda leaders. But even after the fall of the Taliban, it was unclear if the military campaign caused any significant, long-term damage to the al Qaeda network.[162] In addition to the military strikes, the United States and other countries froze economic assets believed to be linked to al Qaeda, arrested numerous suspected al Qaeda associates, attempted to heighten security, and increased monitoring of suspected individuals. Of course, one justification offered for the military intervention in Iraq in 2003 was the Iraqi regime's suspected links with al Qaeda, although this justification is criticized for being based on faulty and exaggerated intelligence (for a summary of the debate prior to intervention, see the Policy Choices box in Chapter 3).

Many fear that military attacks, such as those on Afghanistan in 1998 and 2001, against terrorist groups can be counterproductive:

> If the terrorists are militarily destroyed, the legitimacy of their cause may still exist and even become stronger, depending on how the operation is perceived. Dramatic cruise missile attacks, for example, play into the mindsets of developing countries (and even of some U.S. allies) affirming the belief that the U.S. is too powerful, takes too many unilateral actions and has too much sway in the world. The ironic result is an overall increase in political sympathy for the terrorists or their cause.[163]

Along this line of thinking, many argue that it is U.S. foreign policy in Afghanistan *after* the defeat of the Taliban and in Iraq *after* the war against Saddam Hussein's regime that is most critical to its antiterrorist goals.[164] If Afghanistan, for example, falls from the international agenda and reverts back into economic despair and civil war, it once again may provide sanctuary for terrorists, and it will serve as an example to those who oppose U.S. policies. Similarly, with regard to Iraq, many argue that the civilian casualties, the rise in sectarian and criminal violence, and the abuse of both prisoners and civilians by the U.S. military are counterproductive if the campaign against terrorist groups involves a "battle for hearts and minds."[165] The treatment of terrorist suspects at the U.S. base in Guantánamo Bay (discussed in Chapter 9) may have also failed in this regard.

Relatedly, another approach to dealing with terrorism is to address the grievances of the terrorists. Many of the most spectacular terrorist incidents, especially those involving Americans and Israelis, have been carried out by Palestinians or groups sympathetic to Palestinians. Providing Palestinians with more support might deprive at least some terrorist organizations of an important source of volunteers for their plans and projects. This was presumably one motive behind the signing of the Oslo Peace Agreement in 1993, but the process of implementing this agreement was accompanied by, and perhaps even provoked, several terrorist incidents in the decade that followed. Beyond addressing specific grievances in the Middle East, a broader strategy may be appropriate. According to one observer,

> much more needs to be done to create a peaceful and stable world order; the major powers must not only cooperate in the fight against terrorism but also deal with its root causes. . . . We are locked in a struggle for ideas and beliefs that demands greater attention be paid to such issues as poverty. . . . A robust global economy is a condition sine qua non in the battle against

Members of Jaysh al-Ummah take part in a training at their base in the Gaza Strip. Jaysh al-Ummah, or the Army of the Nation, is a Palestinian Islamist group modelled on the ideology of Osama bin Laden's al Qaeda.
(Mohammed Salem/Reuters/Landov)

terrorism. By destroying a root cause of frustration—namely grinding poverty—a healthy economy denies terrorists a fresh source of recruits.[166]

Although the idea that terrorism is rooted in poverty is plausible and possible, research fails to find a strong relationship between poor economic conditions and terrorist activity.[167]

What seems to be more important is the nature of the state. Weak states that are divided by ethnic and religious conflict, for example, may see more violence by terrorism.[168] Indeed, addressing the problem of failed and weak states in the international system may also be key to addressing international terrorism. As discussed in Chapter 3 and earlier in this chapter, states' lack of sufficient control over their territory stems from a number of causes, including ethnic conflict. When states fail and political vacuums arise, violence can escalate and create insecurity, poverty, and refugees. Not only are these conditions ripe for terrorist groups to form and recruit members; these countries are attractive to existing terrorist groups. Terrorist groups that can operate outside the structure of state authority can engage in various organizational activities free from interference. Thus, many weak states in the international system, such as Somalia, Sudan, and Afghanistan, might not necessarily actively sponsor terrorism, but become hosts to various terrorist groups. The difficulty of establishing political authority in Iraq after the U.S.-led military intervention has also encouraged international terrorists, including al Qaeda, to establish bases in Iraq and participate in the sectarian violence and attacks against the U.S. military.[169]

Border areas or "brown areas," which are often difficult for states to control, also become attractive locations for terrorist groups. According to one terrorist analyst, "the triborder region of South America [at the intersection of Argentina, Brazil, and Paraguay] has become the world's new Libya, a place where terrorists with widely disparate ideologies—Marxist Colombian rebels, American white supremacists, Hamas, Hezbollah, and others—meet to swap tradecraft."[170] The Lebanese border with Israel has also sparked terrorist activities and conflict. While Israel and others accuse Syria and Iran of directly sponsoring the Lebanese Hezbollah, Israel accuses Lebanon of being too weak to control its southern territory, allowing Hezbollah to operate there. Israel's military attack on Lebanon in July 2006 was its response to this situation, but some charged that this action would prove counterproductive.

Many argue that if terrorism has become an international problem, states cannot deal with terrorist threats unilaterally. The coalition, however shaky, formed against al Qaeda and Afghanistan after September 11 is an example of international cooperation, a fairly new way of dealing with terrorism. Historically, terrorism was seen as an internal issue and elicited little international, coordinated response. "Those attitudes began to change in the 1980s when a number of spectacular

POLICY CHOICES

Is the War on Terror an Effective Policy for Addressing Terrorism?

ISSUE: Although "terrorism" has been around for many centuries, the modern era–with its mass communications technology, increasingly available weapons, and particular political challenges–represents a new global challenge. After the attacks of September 11, U.S. President George W. Bush announced a "War on Terror," which involved extensive resources, covert and overt military operations, and new alliances. Many countries have been reluctant to fully embrace this policy due to doubts about its costs and effectiveness. Since 9/11, however, there have been no terrorist attacks on U.S. soil, and many attribute this to the success of the "War on Terrorism." However, terrorism continues in other parts of the world, and huge expenditures of national wealth are being devoted to efforts to prevent and eliminate terrorism. Is the War on Terrorism an important policy for protecting innocent civilians from those willing to use extreme violence to advance their cause, or is it a misguided use of resources that will ultimately fail to achieve any significant results?

Option #1: The war on terrorism is important for the safety and security of citizens around the world, and thus should be continued.

Arguments: (a) Allowing terrorism to go unchecked would send the message that violating the law and killing innocent people is legitimate, provided you feel strongly enough about your particular cause. Terrorists might feel oppressed but that does not mean we should abandon the rule of law. (b) Sustaining a "war on terror" is not just a catch phrase, but the natural consequence of the erosion of state power. As nonstate actors have more access to technology and increasingly influence world events, controlling or preventing terrorism will become even more crucial. (c) Civilians have a special status in international law, and for good reason. Protecting innocent people is one of the most important responsibilities states assume.

Counterarguments: (a) The best predictors of terrorism are when people feel they have serious grievances and yet have no legitimate political means to address them. Preventing terrorism requires political efforts to shift countries toward more democratic systems, something rarely accomplished through warlike actions. Military approaches to terrorism generate sympathy and recruit more terrorists. (b) Terrorists are forced to use radical and violent tactics, because they lack the massive resources of states; they frequently pursue causes that focus on oppressed people. (c) A terrorist could argue that there are no "innocent people." Citizens who pay taxes and do not resist corrupt and oppressive governments are essentially supporting the system. Defining some people as noncombatants and "off limits" for violence is the same as supporting the status quo and letting the powerful decide right from wrong.

Option #2: The war on terrorism should not be continued, as it lacks a clear policy definition and costs billions of dollars.

Arguments: (a) Terrorism is a *tactic* used by people who feel oppressed. It is not a *thing,* like "drugs," that can be controlled or eliminated. (b) The daily physical threat from terrorism is vanishingly small compared to other daily threats, like starvation, disease, and grinding poverty. The money spent fighting terrorism could more effectively be spent addressing these real and pressing problems facing millions. (c) States get to decide who is and is not a terrorist, but states

(continued)

have perpetrated much more horrific acts than any nonstate terrorist organization. Many anti-terrorist policies are simply another way for states to legitimize their own power and justify their periodic abuses.

Counterarguments: (a) Many crimes cannot be eliminated, but that does not mean we should abandon efforts to try to control or limit their effects. Terrorism, like many domestic crimes, must be deterred and perpetrators must be punished to prevent others from engaging in the same behavior. (b) Terrorism represents not only a physical threat, but a moral one. We must focus the international community on preventing the kind of violence that treats innocent people as legitimate targets. (c) Claiming that states are worse abusers of power than terrorists does not offer a clear alternative to a war on terror. Many states have abused their power, but that does not justify terrorism.

attacks captured the world's attention, and it became apparent that without political cooperation, all countries would be at risk. By mid-1995, there were eleven major treaties and conventions against various kinds of terrorist acts."[171]

The United Nations is a forum for international cooperation against terrorism. Following the 1988 bombing of Pan Am Flight 103 over Lockerbie, Scotland, the Security Council passed a resolution demanding, among other things, an end to Libyan sponsorship of terrorism and Libyan acceptance of responsibility for the Pan Am attack. Later, in 1992, the Security Council imposed an arms and civil aviation embargo on Libya and followed up in 1993 by freezing some Libyan assets and placing an embargo on oil technology on Libya.[172] The Taliban government's refusal to surrender bin Laden after the attacks on the U.S. embassies in Africa in 1998 led to UN sanctions as well.

Despite instances of international cooperation, these efforts may not work, and coalitions can be quite fragile:

> Terrorism's history shows that organizations can be decimated, and . . . can be made less significant but terrorists also can invent new ways to carry out their activities. Previous international efforts were difficult to sustain and similar problems are emerging now. Members do not agree on how to apply the term, and the decision not to use it for groups in Kashmir, Lebanon, and Israel demonstrates that the interests of states simply do not sufficiently coincide, and that some will encourage groups others abhor.[173]

The Policy Choices box summarizes the debate over recent anti-terrorism efforts.

SUMMARY

- Ethnic conflict, attracting major headlines and contributing to the death toll from war in the post–Cold War era, can occur between groups of people who share a collective identity based on a belief of common descent and shared experiences and cultural traits. There are many ethnic groups in the world in conflict over group rights and self-determination. These conflicts typically affect relations between states.

● Ethnic conflict is not a new phenomenon but did increase from the early 1950s to the early 1990s. During the Cold War, ethnic conflicts often became part of the East-West rivalry, but the end of the Cold War did not bring about an end to ethnic conflict. The end of the Cold War contributed to ethnic conflicts in Eastern Europe and the former Soviet Union.

● Many factors contribute to ethnic conflict, including competition over economic resources and economic modernization, historical animosities, anarchical situations in collapsed states, ethnocentric beliefs, and leaders' manipulations of identities for political gain.

● The resolution of ethnic conflict may be as complex as the causes. Democratization can help, but democratization in places with a history of ethnic conflict is difficult to achieve. Redrawing boundaries and recognizing the right of self-determination for all ethnic groups is not feasible in most situations and would not necessarily prevent the continuation of conflict.

● Terrorism might most usefully be defined as the use of violence by nonstate actors for political purposes, typically against noncombatants. Terrorist groups are not new, but they do have new potential to wreak havoc in the international system with weapons of mass destruction. The rise of state-sponsored terrorism in the 1980s and the activity of groups associated with al Qaeda in the late 1990s and early twenty-first century represent the most recent waves of terrorism, which are causing a higher number of deaths. The attacks on the United States on September 11, 2001, brought about a new phase of terrorism and state responses to global networks of terrorists.

● Terrorist groups have a variety of political motives, including national self-determination. Recently, religious-related objectives have become more central to terrorist groups.

● Prevention of terrorism is difficult. Anti-terrorism techniques include retaliatory and preemptive military interventions. Many see military solutions as counterproductive and instead urge the international community to address the grievances and root causes of terrorist groups.

KEY TERMS

ethnic group   218
Sectarian   221
Irredentism   222
modernization theory   226
theory of relative
  deprivation   228
Ethnocentrism   229

instrumentalist approach   229
social identity theory   229
Terrorism   238
noncombatant targets   240
Hezbollah   242
al Qaeda   244
Taliban   246

CHAPTER 8

Efforts to Avoid Conflict: Alliances, Arms, and Bargaining

Given the pervasiveness of interstate conflict, states devote significant attention to preparing for war, trying to prevent attacks from others, and negotiating their differences. This chapter discusses alliances—why they form, their size, who joins with whom, and how they relate to the likelihood of war. The chapter also discusses the acquisition of conventional weapons and **weapons of mass destruction,** their dangers, and how states try to control military buildup and arms races through arms control agreements. States join alliances and arm themselves for both security and other motivations. The post-Cold War era has seen significant efforts to address the nature of old alliances such as the North Atlantic Treaty Organization (NATO) and threats from conventional, nuclear, biological, and chemical weapons.

As we will see in this chapter, states often form alliances and acquire arms in order to prevent others from doing something that they would otherwise do (**deterrence**) or to force others to do something that they would not otherwise do (**compellence**). Alliances often try to achieve extended deterrence by signaling to others that a stronger state's military arsenal will be used to protect their junior alliance partners. In the Cold War, the United States hoped its nuclear arsenal would deter a Soviet attack against its allies around the world. Alliances and arms races may also involve a compellence strategy. In the 1991 Gulf War, for example, the United Nations created a coalition to compel Iraq to leave Kuwait.

Deterrence and compellence involve communicating goals and commitment to other actors through bargaining and negotiation. How states bargain and negotiate alliances and arms agreements is also a topic in this chapter. The strategies that diplomats adopt stem from their efforts to deter or compel, but they also come from the relationship between current and future conflicts and from pressures from domestic constituents. These strategies can have significant effects on the resolution of international conflict in global politics.

weapons of mass destruction (WMD) Nuclear, chemical, and biological weapons.

deterrence Preventing another actor from doing something they would otherwise do.

compellence Forcing another actor to do something they would not otherwise do.

Alliances

alliances Formal associations in which states pledge to militarily protect each other in specified circumstances.

Alliances, or international coalitions, seem to be an inevitable result of interaction among sovereign political units. **Alliances** are "formal associations of states for the use (or nonuse) of military force, in specified circumstances, against states outside their own membership."[1] "Wherever in recorded history a system of multiple sovereignty has existed, some of the sovereign units involved in conflicts with others have entered into alliances."[2] Alliances were part of interstate relations in ancient India and China, in Greece during the era of city-states, and in Renaissance Italy. They have been a constant feature of the political landscape since the rise of the modern state in the mid-seventeenth century.

Why are these coalitions such a prominent part of international relations? The most common answer given by policymakers is that they are a necessary defense against aggression. Often, or perhaps most of the time, defense is the actual motive for the formation of alliances. But some alliances are formed for more aggressive purposes. The pact between Nazi Germany and the Soviet Union in 1939, which resulted in the immediate dismemberment of Poland, is probably the most prominent twentieth-century example of an alliance that was formed precisely for the purpose of carrying out aggression as opposed to deterring it.

Whether for defensive or offensive purposes, alliances are usually formed to give members an advantage in interstate conflicts. But under what conditions states are most likely to form alliances, who will ally with whom, what kinds of alliances are most effective and cohesive, and what effects alliances have on the stability of the international system are issues about which there is still substantial disagreement.

Balancing

The most traditional set of answers is supplied by the balance-of-power ideas of realism discussed in Chapter 6. According to this theory, countries form alliances when any state in their midst becomes so powerful that it threatens to establish hegemony, or domination of the system. Through the mechanism of fluid alliances, the balance is preserved, and if war is not avoided, at least the powerful, aggressive state is denied victory. Most balance-of-power theorists would argue that alliances so used are beneficial, indeed necessary, for the stability of the international system.

balancing Joining an alliance against states or coalitions whose superior resources could pose a threat.

States engaging in **balancing** behaviors "join alliances to protect themselves from states or coalitions whose superior resources could pose a threat. States choose to balance for two main reasons. First, they place their survival at risk if they fail to curb a potential hegemon before it becomes too strong. . . . Second, joining the weaker side increases the new member's influence within the alliance, because the weaker side has greater need for assistance."[3] What do states actually balance against? Stephen Walt argues that while traditionally realists have focused on capabilities or *power*, it is more accurate to say that states balance against *threats*. "Although power is an important part of the equation, it is not the only one. It is more accurate to say that states tend to ally with or against the foreign power that poses the greatest threat. For example, states may balance by allying with other strong states if a weaker power is more dangerous for other reasons. Thus, the coalitions that defeated Germany in World War I and World War II were vastly superior in total resources, but they came together when it became clear that the aggressive aims of the Wilhelmines [German leaders prior to World War I] and Nazis posed the greater danger."[4] Walt believes that balancing against threat, not power, is what drove many states into the U.S. alliance system during the Cold War.[5] Although the power of another state is certainly important (states rarely ally against a state with little capabilities), a state's geographical proximity, perceived aggressive intentions, and the offensive nature of a state's power are other factors that states consider when they assess threats.[6]

Because of balancing, one common pattern of alliance formation can be summarized in the statement, "The enemy of my enemy is my friend." Republican France, for example, allied with Czarist Russia in 1894, because they had a common enemy, Germany. Republican France allied with the Communist Soviet Union in 1935 for the same reason. Two of the clearest examples of the principle "the enemy of my enemy is my friend" in post–Second World War international politics arose from the conflict between Pakistan and India. The two newly independent nations fought over Kashmir in 1947. In the ensuing decade, they developed sharply contrasting political systems. India was democratic, while Pakistan was ruled by a military dictatorship. The dictatorship, though, was staunchly anti-Communist and aligned itself with the Western world in not one but two alliances: the Central Treaty Organization (CENTO) and the Southeast Asia Treaty Organization (SEATO). Despite membership in these two strongly anti-Communist alliances, Pakistan soon found itself with a strong Communist ally. Pakistan's enemy, India, became involved in a border dispute with China, which erupted into a war in 1962. China thus emerged as the enemy of Pakistan's enemy, and by the mid-1960s, Pakistan had membership in two Western military alliances and simultaneously maintained friendship with the People's Republic of China.

This conflict produced more coalitions of strange bedfellows. While Pakistan developed into a military dictatorship strongly allied with the forces of Western democracy, democratic India remained resolutely neutral in the Cold War conflict. But in 1971, as the civil war between West and East Pakistan became more serious and India decided it must intervene, Indian Prime Minister Indira Gandhi (still a democratic leader at the time) abandoned India's long-standing policy of nonalignment and signed a treaty of friendship with the Soviet Union. Why? Because by that time, the Soviet Union was an enemy of India's enemy, China.

Balancing in the more contemporary system may take on new forms. These new forms of balancing employ nonmilitary instruments of power. For example, "soft balancing" involves the use of diplomacy, international institutions, and international law to constrain and delegitimize the actions of a hegemonic United States. "Economic prebalancing" occupies a middle ground between soft balancing and hard balancing. States that pursue economic prebalancing are trying to avoid the risks of engaging in a premature arms buildup aimed at the United States by concentrating first on closing the economic and technological gap between them and the United States."[7] Another new form of balancing is termed "leash-slipping." "States engaging in leash-slipping do not fear being attacked by the hegemon. Rather, they build up their military capabilities to maximize their ability to conduct an independent foreign policy." Europe's attempts to create a common security policy and an integrated military are one current example of "leash-slipping."[8]

Bandwagoning

States may join alliances for reasons other than balancing. **Bandwagoning** is a strategy that involves joining an alliance *with* the stronger power, rather than joining an alliance to balance *against* the stronger power (or threat). States engage in bandwagoning to share in the benefits of an alliance. "Simply put, balancing is driven by the desire to avoid losses; bandwagoning by the opportunity for gain. The presence of a significant threat, while required for effective balancing, is unnecessary for states to bandwagon."[9] Bandwagoning can take several forms. "Jackal bandwagoning" involves several states joining forces to overcome a predominant power, like jackals attacking a lion, in order to share in the spoils of the attack. "Wave of the future bandwagoning" occurs when states perceive that one state will likely prevail in the future. "During the Cold War era, for example, many less-developed countries viewed communism in this way. Consequently, they did not have to be coerced or bribed to join the Sino-Soviet bloc; they did so voluntarily."[10] "Piling-on bandwagoning" comes at the end of a conflict when states on the losing side opportunistically switch their allegiance in order to be on the winning side. At the end of World War II, for example, several states switched from the Axis to the Allied side, because the Allied side was winning. In addition, the Allied powers had announced that states that did not declare war against the Axis coalition by March 1, 1945, would be excluded from membership in the to-be-formed United Nations. "More recently, the overwhelming superior coalition arrayed against Iraq in the 1991 Gulf War exemplifies piling-on bandwagoning behavior."[11] Certain states may be more likely to bandwagon than others. Weaker states, for example, might be more likely to bandwagon than balance.[12]

The Size of Alliances

While bandwagoning reasons for joining alliances would lead us to expect quite large coalitions, others would argue that alliances among large numbers of states, particularly large numbers of major powers, are not in the interests of states and are difficult to maintain. In particular, coalition theory expects that in certain situations, including international relations, "participants create coalitions just as large as they believe will ensure winning and no larger."[13] This is known as the *size principle*; in effect, it predicts that the pattern of alliances in the international system will result from two contradictory intentions held by states: (1) to join a winning coalition and (2) to win as much as possible for themselves. Obviously, the first aim will lead each state to prefer larger alliances, because they can ensure victory. The second leads each state to prefer smaller alliances because they can provide the biggest share of whatever there is to win. The result of such contradictory aims will be alliances that are just as large as they must be to win but no larger, so that alliances will be **minimum winning coalitions.**

Historically, minimum winning coalitions have been quite rare. There are several reasons that coalitions in world politics are often much larger than minimum winning ones. For example, states are unlikely to want to take the risks involved in forming minimum winning coalitions; once the coalition is formed, it may well have to defeat an opposing coalition in a war. Also, any attempt to form a minimum winning coalition may be foiled by the difficulty of measuring power (see Chapter 4). What was thought to be just enough to win may turn out to be insufficient. Even if that problem does not occur, a minimum winning coalition may have to fight long and hard to win the war, whereas a much larger coalition might win easily. Furthermore, despite some complications in recent alliances, a systematic review of the historical record shows that larger international alliances do not show any tendency to break up faster than small alliances do.[14]

It is true, though, that once large alliances are formed, there is difficulty in maintaining them because of the competing interests of states, particularly the interests of the major powers involved. The most spectacular dissolution of a grand coalition took place after the Second World War. During the war, the United States, the Soviet Union, and Great Britain (with some help from France) constituted what was fairly close to a minimum winning coalition. But after the war, with Italy defeated and Japan and Germany nearly prostrate, the Big Three became a grand coalition. Controversy continues among U.S. historians about the origins of the Cold War (see Chapter 3). According to coalition theorists, the Cold War occurred as a more or less inevitable result of the breakup of the grand coalition. The fact that the only state in the world strong enough to threaten the United States was the Soviet Union, and vice versa, also played a role. "Having defeated the Axis, the winners had nothing to win from unless they split up and tried to win from each other."[15]

Actual cases of post–Cold War coalitions also demonstrate the difficulty of maintaining large alliances. On the one hand, the multistate coalition against Iraq, formed after Iraq's invasion of Kuwait in 1990, largely held together for quite a long time after the war. More than a decade later, UN economic sanctions were basically still in place, and the United States still maintained no-fly zones over northern and southern Iraq. Without some support from the coalition, this would have been difficult. On the other hand, the grand Gulf coalition certainly showed the cracks that the size principle would predict, even before the 2003 intervention in Iraq. Substantial opposition to the sanctions increased in the Middle East and from Russia and France. When the United States tried to reconstitute this "grand alliance" in 2002 and 2003, it met considerable resistance from other major powers, including Russia and France. The United States proceeded with some other states, dubbed the "coalition of the willing," but this was a much smaller alliance compared to that in the 1991 Gulf War.

In the wake of the terrorist attacks of September 11, 2001, the coalition against al Qaeda and Afghanistan was quite large, thus violating the minimum winning principle. Yet it too demonstrates the difficulty of maintaining a large alliance. Concerns from Pakistan about the ethnic makeup of the post-Taliban Afghani government, for example, had to be balanced against the preferences of the internal Afghani opposition groups involved in the military campaign against al Qaeda. The debate over the intervention in Iraq in 2003 also brought into question the long-term viability of a large alliance against terrorist groups.

Other Factors in Alliance Formation and Maintenance

Beyond power, threats, gains, and size calculations, states may choose alliance partners for other reasons, and these factors challenge the more traditional, balance-of-power assumptions in the realist theoretical perspective. In particular, "views of international relations that are based exclusively on considerations of security and issues of war and peace may miss a major motivation that states may have in joining alliances and in their foreign policy more generally. If multiple goals can be shown to underlie the formation of alliances, we must question a fundamental premise of realism."[16] States may choose partners, for example, that share a common ideology, common economic and political systems, or similar cultural characteristics. Once alliances are formed, these affinities, institutional arrangements, and norms of alliance behavior may constrain alliance members.[17] States may also join alliances to counter domestic, rather than external, threats, such as poor economic conditions.[18] These factors, various forms of liberalism argue, are important in alliance behavior as well as traditional security concerns.[19]

Recent evidence on the tendency for states to ally with other similar states is mixed,[20] but even if states do ally out of ideological solidarity, it does not necessarily mean the alliance will be long-lasting. Indeed, Walt argues that "certain types of ideology cause conflict and dissension rather than solidarity and alignment. In particular, when the ideology calls for the members to form a centralized movement obeying a single authoritative leadership, the likelihood of conflict among the members is increased."[21] In the Soviet-led alliance during the Cold War, for example, ideological differences between the Soviet Union and some of its alliance partners, particularly Hungary, Czechoslovakia, and China at various times, contributed to alliance problems and even intra-alliance military conflict.

burden sharing How costs of alliance are distributed among member states.

Regardless of ideology, maintaining a cohesive alliance can be complicated by disputes over **burden sharing,** or the costs of the alliance. The burden-sharing debate has been particularly important in the NATO alliance. "Meeting the Soviet threat through coordinated action was the *raison d'être* of the North Atlantic Treaty Organization, . . . but the distribution of the costs of achieving that objective was a persistent source of contention. The allies consistently failed to meet the goal, emphasized by the United States, of bearing the same defense burden."[22] The burden-sharing debate may have arisen from the very nature of the alliance. Providing a collective deterrent to the Soviet threat was in the interests of all; it was a collective good. But as economist Mancur Olson has pointed out, collective goods often lead to uneven contributions by those who benefit from them. In alliances like NATO, he argued, there is a "tendency for the larger' members—those that place a higher absolute value on the public good—to bear a disproportionate share of the burden."[23] Thus, for many years, the United States incurred most of the costs for maintaining the alliance. (The characteristics of collective goods will be discussed further in Chapter 10 in the context of international trade and monetary relations and in Chapter 13 in the context of environmental challenges.)

Alliances and War

At least equal in interest to the question of which nations will ally are questions concerning the effects of alliances on incidences of international war. Alliances have usually been intended to help a state avoid war or to help it win a war already in progress. Whether alliances serve the first purpose well is a matter of some dispute in research on international relations.[24] It may be true that a state threatened with aggression can deter the potential aggressor by acquiring one or more formal allies. But these alliances also may convince the potential aggressor that it is the victim of a strategy of encirclement, which can lead to several undesirable reactions. For example, the aggressor target of the alliances may seek its own alliance partners. Before the initial alliance was formed, the potential aggressor may have had trouble finding such partners, because the important states in the area were not aware of the lines of cleavage in the system. But an alliance or two could conceivably polarize the situation to the point where the potential aggressor will find it easy to form a counteralliance. Also, alliances can clarify the situation in such a way as to allow a potential aggressor to calculate just how much help will be needed to launch a successful war.[25] At worst, the polarized situation can result in the very thing that the original alliance was designed to avoid: an enemy attack. The attack might be carried out either because the original alliance made the enemy afraid or because the enemy's confidence was bolstered by the alliance it created in response to the original coalition.

This analysis is all highly speculative, of course, and it seems fairly clear that in the past, such speculation was influenced heavily by the role that alliances played in the previous big war.

After the Franco-Prussian War of 1870, in which France lost badly partly due to its lack of allies, "statesmen grew more fearful of isolation, and they made greater efforts than in the pre-1870 era to establish and maintain alliances in peacetime."[26] As a result, the rate at which the European great powers formed alliances in the period from 1875 to 1910 was significantly higher than the rate from 1814 to 1874.[27] By 1914, the European state system was virtually honeycombed with formal alliances. These alliances in retrospect seem to have been an important part of the problem that led to a major conflagration because of an intrinsically unimportant spat between Austria and Serbia. Alliance ties drew Germany into the conflict. After Russia became involved, alliances then entangled France and Britain. Thus, alliances came out of the First World War with a rather tarnished reputation. "In the late 1930s . . . policymakers and strategists who had lived through the trench warfare stalemates of 1914–18 believed that conquest was difficult and slow. Consequently they thought that they could safely stand aside at the outset of a conflict, waiting to intervene only if and when the initial belligerents showed signs of having exhausted themselves."[28] So policymakers deliberately avoided commitments to enter into wars immediately in the form of alliance treaties. Again, in retrospect, the avoidance of alliance bonds seemed disastrous. If effective alliances with the targets he attacked before his move against Poland had been formed against Hitler, he might not have begun the Second World War.

Right or wrong, alliances came out of the Second World War with their reputation for deterring aggression restored, at least in the eyes of U.S. policymakers. The United States, in the years following the war, formed the most extensive set of formal alliances in the history of the world: the Rio Pact in Latin America; CENTO in the Middle East; SEATO in Asia; and a treaty between Australia, New Zealand, and the United States (ANZUS) in the South Pacific to implement the U.S. policy of containment. Several bilateral pacts were also concluded, such as the U.S.-Japan Security Treaty, first signed in 1951, which pledged the United States to defend Japan in exchange for the use of Japan's military bases. The keystone of the U.S. system of alliances was NATO, centered on Western Europe. Having already signed an alliance with Communist China, the Soviets soon organized the Warsaw Pact to counterbalance NATO (and in response to the rearming of West Germany in 1955), thus solidifying the bipolarity of the international system (see Chapter 3 for further discussion and definitions of NATO and Warsaw Pact). This proliferation of alliances after the Second World War was inspired, like the rapid rate of alliance formation after the quick Prussian victory over France in 1870, by perceptions regarding the scope and pace of warfare. "Just as the Prussian [victory] over . . . France encouraged statesmen to scramble to line up allies in advance of the next war, the tremendous destructiveness of the Second World War encouraged states that had formerly sought safety in neutrality . . . to lobby for admission to NATO in an attempt to avoid becoming a battlefield in a future war."[29]

The structure of the alliance network that emerged after the Second World War changed considerably over the next few decades and was transformed quite dramatically in 1991. The Sino-Soviet alliance ceased to exist in 1961. For several complicated reasons involving Middle Eastern politics at the time, the United States never did join CENTO, and that organization died. SEATO was disbanded in 1975 after the Communist victories in Vietnam, Laos, and Cambodia. In the confrontation between the United States and the Soviet Union, NATO and the Warsaw Pact were by far the most important alliances for each of the superpowers.

Alliances after the Cold War

When the Warsaw Pact was disbanded in 1991, its demise naturally called into question the continuing necessity and purpose of its major rival, NATO, because there was no apparent power or threat to balance against. Defenders of NATO today insist that it deserves credit for preserving peace in Europe since 1945 and that it would be a mistake to disband it even though the Warsaw Pact is dead. And in fact, fairly soon after the end of the Cold War, NATO's most enthusiastic supporters argued that it was crucial to expand its membership to take in several Central and Eastern European states—not so much as a defense against a possible Russian attack but rather to solidify these new democracies. According to one proponent of NATO's inclusion of new states in East-Central Europe, "An expansion of NATO today . . . must have as its primary purpose the internal transformations of new member states."[30] Thus, domestic factors were an important argument for extending the alliance.

The hope that bringing East-Central European countries into NATO might help solidify their newly democratic regimes seems based in part on the experience of Germany. Making West Germany a member of NATO in the 1950s does seem in retrospect to have solidified its transition from Nazism to democracy. Although there is some evidence that membership in such an alliance will consolidate a nation's democracy,[31] it seems clear that alignment with the United States, for example, is certainly no guarantee of stable democracy. During the 1960s, even though most countries in the region were members of the Rio Pact, "sixteen military coups took place in the Latin American countries."[32]

Some worry about the credibility of an expanded NATO. Will the United States and the rest of NATO respond as promised to attacks on their new allies in East-Central Europe? Even more to the point, will potential attackers believe that NATO would defend its newest members? There is certainly room for doubt. "After seeing how reluctant George [H. W.] Bush and Bill Clinton were to send American troops to Bosnia, . . . it is easy not to visualize a future American president sending American soldiers to central Europe to sort things out there."[33] Although a recent study suggests that alliance commitments are fulfilled in most cases, they are still violated 25 percent of the time.[34]

In 1999, three Central European states—the Czech Republic, Hungary, and Poland—formally joined the NATO alliance, increasing the number of member countries to nineteen. Very soon after they assumed formal membership in NATO, the Czech Republic, Hungary, and Poland faced their first opportunity to be active participants when NATO began its attacks on Yugoslavia due to its treatment of ethnic Albanians in its province of Kosovo.

Instead of being a security liability, the new members were
an asset to the Alliance despite the inadequacy of their armed
forces. Expansion improved NATO's ability to conduct a bombing
campaign . . . and to deploy peacekeeping troops in the Balkans
because, absent expansion, the Czech Republic and Hungary
would likely have lent far less support. . . . Hungary's provision of
military bases, transportation routes, and other forms of logistical
support was strategically significant.[35]

In 2004, seven more countries joined the alliance (Bulgaria, Estonia,
Latvia, Lithuania, Romania, Slovakia, and Slovenia) and in 2009, Albania
and Croatia became members, bringing the total number of states in the
alliance to twenty-eight (see Map 8.1). Other East European countries,
including Macedonia and Bosnia-Herzegovnia, are considered applicant
states. NATO has stated that Georgia and Ukraine will eventually be
in NATO, but there is division within the alliance over this particular
expansion and opposition from Russia.

NATO expansion has occurred over Russian objections. Indeed, one
observer of the alliance notes: Whatever the merits of NATO enlargement—
and they are many—the eastward expansion of the alliance has unquestionably come at the expense of its relationship with Russia."[36] In 2002, the
NATO-Russia Council was established to provide Russia an input in NATO
discussions about a variety of issues, including crisis management, missile
defense, and counterterrorism, but Russia has no say over NATO expansion
and the prospect of Georgia's membership is complicated by the Russian
support for independence for Georgia's breakaway regions.[37] Russia objects
to any further expansion of NATO at its borders and according to one analyst,
"One need not be an apologist for the regime in Moscow or its behavior, or
sympathetic to Russia's national interests, to empathize with its resentment
of this revolutionary overturning of the balance of power [in the region]."[38]

In addition to NATO's new members, the post–Cold War world has
brought new roles to the alliance. During the wars in the former Yugoslavia,
NATO modified its constitution to engage in "out-of-area" operations.
NATO's mission in the Balkans was clearly beyond the defense of an ally
from an outside threat. To many observers, "the NATO intervention in
Kosovo in the spring of 1999 exemplified the challenges of an old alliance that has to adjust to a new world, where enemies and threats are
no longer quite as clearly defined. . . . The Alliance was able to maintain
an impressive degree of cohesion in a situation in which such cohesion
was in no way guaranteed at the outset."[39] NATO has also responded
to threat from a nonstate actor. After the September 11 terrorist attacks
on the United States, NATO, for the first time in the alliance's history,
activated a clause in its charter by which members regard an attack on
one member as an attack on all.[40] Many NATO members took part in the
U.S.-led intervention in Afghanistan, and NATO, operating under United
Nations mandate, officially took over command of the military mission
to provide security to the post-Taliban regime, in 2003.[41]

Map 8.1 The New NATO

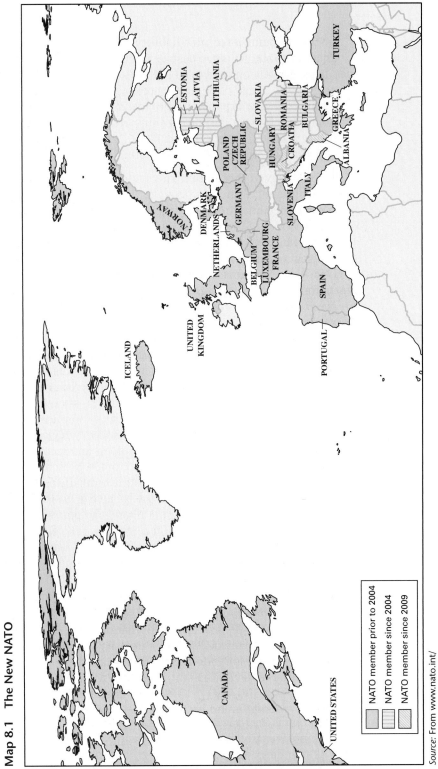

NATO member prior to 2004
NATO member since 2004
NATO member since 2009

Source: From www.nato.int/

Indeed, with little fanfare—and even less notice—the North Atlantic Treaty Organization has gone global, . . . seeking to bring stability to other parts of the world. In the process, it is extending both its geographic reach and the range of its operations. In recent years, it has played peacekeeper in Afghanistan, trained security forces in Iraq, and given logistical support to the African Union's mission in Darfur. It assisted the tsunami relief effort in Indonesia and ferried supplies to victims of Hurricane Katrina in the United States and to those of a massive earthquake in Pakistan.[42]

While some see this role expansion as growth in the alliance, others worry that NATO has an "identity crisis" and is overstretching itself.[43] Moreover, the division within NATO over the U.S.-led intervention in Iraq, may have long-lasting negative effects on the alliance. "While no one in Europe is predicting the death of NATO..., the damage is evident in the renewed willingness of Germany and France to consider a military policy separate from . . . [the Atlantic alliance]. But the larger obstacle may be the widespread perception across the Continent that a political Rubicon has been crossed, and that divisions will not be bridged easily, or soon."[44] Indeed, on the sixtieth anniversary of the establishment of NATO in 2009, the alliance was riddled with disagreements over contributions to the Afghanistan mission, potential membership of Georgia and Ukraine, and relations with Russia.[45]

Arms and Arms Control

In addition to joining alliances, states deal with the potential threat of war by building a military, by acquiring weapons.[46] This may be for offensive purposes in preparation for war, but the acquisition of arms may also be for defensive purposes—to protect territory and citizens and to deter others from attack. States may also acquire weapons for domestic political reasons.[47] As discussed in Chapter 5, military-industrial complexes have long been accused of influencing armament decisions for their own profit. Indeed,

> arms expenditures would seem to be perfect candidates for government decisions arrived at through bureaucratic and incremental processes. They are long-term, noncrisis, budgetary decisions that ordinarily involve a large number of interested domestic actors . . . legislators, political officials in the executive branch, civilian defense officials, military officers in various rival services, manufacturers of weapons and their subcontractors, citizen groups, and so on.[48]

For all of these reasons involving external security and internal politics, the world spends massive amounts of money on arms. Although world military expenditures declined at the end of and following the Cold War, from 1987 to 1998, they have been on the rise since 1999. In 2008, over $14 billion went toward military spending, equal to 2.4 percent of the world's GDP or $216 per person. The current level of military expenditures is higher than the peak of military spending during the Cold War, in 1987–1988. The recent rise is primarily due to the high levels of U.S. military spending, for the "war on terror" generally and for operations in Afghanistan and Iraq specifically, although almost all regions of the world have seen an increase in military spending since 1999.[49]

The United States is by far the biggest spender, accounting for more than 40 percent of the world's total military expenditures. Table 8.1 lists the fifteen top spending states in 2008.

TABLE 8.1

The Ten Top Military Spenders, 2008

Rank	Country	Spending (billions)
1	United States	$607
2	China	84.9*
3	France	65.7
4	United Kingdom	65.3
5	Russia	58.6*
6	Germany	46.8
7	Japan	46.3
8	Italy	40.6
9	Saudi Arabia	38.2
10	India	30.0
11	South Korea	22.6
12	Brazil	15.3
13	Canada	15.2
14	Australia	15.1
15	Spain	14.6

Note: "The Spending figures are in current US dollars." (Perlo-Freeman et al, 2009: 11).
*Estimated spending figures. Data for South Korea, Brazil, Canada, Australia, and Spain are 2007 spending figures.

Sources: 2008 figures are from Sam Perlo-Freeman, Catalina Perdomo, Petter Stålenheim, and Elisabeth Sköns, "Military Expenditure," in *SIPRI Yearbook 2009 Armaments, Disarmament and International Security Summary.* 2009: pp. 10, 11. http://www.sipri.org/yearbook/2009/files/SIPRIYB09summary.pdf Accessed 9 June 2009. 2007 Figures are from Petter Stålenheim, Catalina Perdomo, and Elisabeth Sköns, "Military Expenditure," in *SIPRI Yearbook 2008 Armaments, Disarmament and International Security Summary.* 2008: pp. 10–11. http://yearbook2008.sipri.org/files/SIPRIYB08summary.pdf Accessed 21 May 2009.

arms control Efforts to limit or ban weapons in states' military arsenals.

Often states simultaneously engage in arms buildup and **arms control** efforts. They agree to arms control treaties in order to control the damage of war should it occur or to lessen the likelihood of war. Arms control may simply be arms limitations agreements; putting, for example, a ceiling on the number of a certain type of weapons that states can have. Arms control agreements may also involve disarmament agreements, requiring states to give up a certain class or type of weapons. The buildup and control of arms are important ways that states respond to and deal with international conflict.

Conventional Weapons

arms transfers Sales or gifts of military weapons.

Most of the money that states spend on arms goes for conventional weapons. Conventional weapons are also traded on the world market or given as part of a military assistance program by one state to another. **Arms transfers** of major conventional weapons (measured in value) declined in the early post–Cold War years, held steady in the late 1990s, and declined again in 2001. The United States is the largest weapons supplier, accounting for almost one-third of global arms transfers over the last five years. Together with the United States, Russia, Germany, France, and the United Kingdom supplied the world with 78 percent of the arms transfers from 2004 to 2008.[50] As Table 8.2 indicates, many arms transfers of major conventional weapons go to the developing world—Asia in particular. The top five recipients of major conventional weapons transfers from 2004 to 2008 were China, India, Greece, Turkey, and South Korea.[51]

small arms Typically inexpensive light weapons that an individual can carry.

A growing area of concern regarding conventional weapons is the proliferation of light weapons, or **small arms**, such as pistols, rifles, machine

---

TABLE 8.2

Transfers of Major Conventions Weapons to the Leading Recipients by Region, 2004–2008

Recipients by regions	Share of world arms transfers
Asia	37%
Europe	24%
Middle East	18%
Americas	11%
Africa	7%

Source: Bromley, Mark, Paul Holtom, Pieter D. Wezeman, and Siemon T. Wezeman, Stockholm International Peace Research Institute, "SIPRI Arms Transfers Data, 2008," SIPRI Fact Sheet, April 2009, Figure 1. The trend in transfers of major conventional weapons, 1999-2008. Reproduced with permission.

guns, and shoulder-fired antitank and antiaircraft missiles. Relatively cheap to obtain and easy to transport and hide, light weapons have become extremely significant in many post–Cold War civil conflicts:

> The centrality of light weapons in contemporary warfare is especially evident in the conflicts in Liberia and Somalia. In Liberia, rival bands of guerillas—armed, for the most part, with AK-47 assault rifles—have been fighting among themselves for control of the country, bringing commerce to a standstill and driving an estimated 2.3 million people from their homes and villages. In Somalia, lightly armed militias have been similarly engaged, ravaging the major cities, paralyzing rural agriculture, and at one point pushing millions to the brink of starvation. In both countries, UN-sponsored peacekeeping missions have proved unable to stop the fighting or disarm the major factions.[52]

Small arms in Iraq, particularly "improvised explosive devices" (IEDs) have been a significant cause of injury and death to foreign troops, Iraqi military, and Iraqi civilians. IEDs are small versions of antipersonnel land mines, another type of conventional weapon drawing international attention. Land mines, which cost as little as $3 to $15, "...continue to claim human victims, both during and after conflict, many of them civilians. The Landmine Monitor, the monitoring arm of the International Campaign to Ban Landmines (ICBL), a worldwide network of more than 1,400 NGOs, reported deaths and injuries from landmines and ERW (explosive remnants of war) in 58 countries and seven other territories in 2005–2006. . . ."[53]

What role do arms transfers play in international conflict? The impact of arms transfers to areas of conflict is complex. "While suppliers have different reasons for supplying weapons, the arms suppliers cannot control whether arms deliveries will stabilize or destabilize a particular relationship. Sometimes the weapons help to end a war; in other situations the acquisition of new weapons increases insecurity and could thereby reduce the likelihood of a peaceful solution."[54] Most research on this question supports the view that arms transfers generally increase the likelihood of conflict, although other factors are important as well.[55] For example, one study found that arms transfers from major powers make states more likely to initiate military disputes and to be targets as well.[56] Arms transfers are most worrisome when they are received by parties to ongoing conflicts, such as the Indian-Pakistani conflict, and when they contribute to arms races.

Arms Races and International Conflict

arms race Competitive increase in armaments by two states or coalitions of states.

When rival states engage in significant military buildups, arms races become a concern. An **arms race** is "a progressive, competitive peacetime increase in armaments by two states or coalitions of states resulting from conflicting purposes and mutual fears."[57] Arms races are an example of the security dilemma (discussed in Chapter 6), as one state's decision to arm may simply be for defensive reasons but may be interpreted by another state as an offensive threat. When each state responds to increase its security, the overall result is a less secure situation for all. Many believe that arms races will spiral out of control and contribute to war, and there is evidence to support this claim One study, for example, reports that states involved in serious disputes and an arms race at the same time are substantially more likely to end up in a war against each other than are states involved in disputes when no arms race is underway.[58]

This evidence does not necessarily justify the conclusion that arms races are dangerous. Perhaps states conducting arms races are less likely to get involved in serious disputes in the first place. If that were the case, if one compared states in arms races with states not in arms races (rather than comparing states in serious disputes and simultaneously in arms races with other states in serious disputes but not in arms races), the rapidly arming states would be seen as less likely to become involved in war. Admittedly, it is certainly possible that arms races increase tensions and thus cause wars that otherwise would not have occurred. But it is perhaps equally plausible that states become involved in arms races, because they accurately perceive their disputes with other states as being sufficiently serious to lead to war and that the subsequent wars are more the result of those existing disputes than the result of the arms accumulations themselves. In short, it is clear that "arms races have been a preliminary to war. . . . The major wars of our century—World Wars I and II—have each been preceded by arms races. But just as clearly, many wars have not been preceded by such mutual arms buildups, and many arms races never end in war."[59] While there is comparatively less research on the role of arms races in internal conflicts, recent evidence suggests a similar pattern: The acquisition of arms by warring sides in an internal conflict is associated with, but is not necessary for, an escalation of violence.[60]

Conventional Arms Control

Conventional Armed Forces in Europe Treaty agreement creating military balance of conventional weapons between NATO and the Warsaw Pact at the end of the Cold War.

Nevertheless, states have often entered into arms control agreements to limit damage from conventional weapons or lessen the chances of war from arms races. Indeed, in the early 1920s, at the Washington Naval Conferences, the United States, Japan, France, and Italy agreed to limit the weight of their naval fleets. More recently, the **Conventional Armed Forces in Europe Treaty** (known as the CFE treaty) was a direct response to the end of the Cold War in Europe.

> Signed in 1990 and fully implemented by 1995, the CFE treaty created a military balance between NATO and the Warsaw Pact by reducing to equal levels each group's military holdings in five categories of conventional weapons: tanks, armored combat vehicles, artillery, helicopters, and aircraft. . . . Another measure of the success of the CFE treaty is the fact that it was used as

a model by the Dayton accords for the regional arms control settlement in the former Yugoslavia.[61]

For the most part, however, the control of conventional arms and the limitation of arms buildup through arms transfer have not been a high priority:

> Despite the correlation between high levels of arms imports and chronic instability, control of the conventional arms traffic has been a relatively minor international concern until fairly recently. For most of the Cold War period, arms sales were considered an essential glue to alliance systems and a useful tool in gaining influence in the Third World. Following the Iraqi invasion of Kuwait, however, the world community became much more concerned about conventional arms trafficking. The fact that Saddam Hussein had been able to accumulate a massive military arsenal . . . from external sources led many world leaders to regret their earlier failure to control the arms trade.[62]

One recent effort to monitor the arms trade is the establishment of a voluntary "register" of arms imports and exports so the international community can monitor buildups. This information may be important in directing attention to certain regions, but it does not prevent the buildups. Furthermore, while arms sales have declined in recent years, transfers to some particularly unstable regions remain at very high levels. States do cooperate to impose **international arms embargoes** on some high-conflict regions. In 2008, seven countries and five rebel groups were under mandatory UN Security Council embargoes.[63] Countries under recent UN mandatory embargoes include Iraq, Somalia, and North Korea.

international arms embargoes Agreements to cease arms transfers to threatening or unstable states.

Given the types of post–Cold War conflicts and the proliferation and destructive capabilities of small arms, there have been efforts to monitor and control arms trafficking of this type. Controlling light weapons—what has been called "microdisarmament"—has only recently come on the agenda of the international community and will be difficult given the lack of information on the small arms trade and the black market nature of much of this trade.[64] In the late 1990s, the United Nations established the Panel of Governmental Experts on Small Arms to investigate the problem and potential solutions, and in 2001, the United Nations held its first large conference on the subject, the UN Conference on the Illicit Trade in Small Arms and Light Weapons in All Its Aspects. State and nonstate actors attending the conference agreed, among other measures, to coordinate efforts to track trade in small arms and light weapons, crack down on illicit trade in these weapons, and engage in effective disarmament where possible.

Anti-Personnel Landmines Treaty Agreement to ban production and export of land mines designed to harm or kill people.

Those interested in controlling small arms have tried to build on the success of the **Anti-Personnel Landmines Treaty,** drafted in 1997. Also known as the Ottawa Treaty, this agreement bans production and export of land mines designed to be exploded by the presence, proximity, or contact of a person and that will incapacitate, injure, or kill one or more persons.

> Since the signing of the Ottawa treaty, a remarkably large number of states have moved to add their signatures and ratifications. Within a year, 130 countries had signed it, and the number swelled to 156 by early 2009. But perhaps more significant is that countries quickly expedited the ratification process to approve the treaty. . . . The landmine ban is widely considered the most quickly negotiated and ratified international convention ever.[65]

Still, in 2009, many countries, including China, Israel, Pakistan, Russia, and the United States, had not signed the treaty.

Nuclear Weapons: Thinking the Unthinkable

The nuclear era introduced new concerns about the acquisition of arms. During most of the Cold War era, the United States and the Soviet Union possessed about 95 percent of the world's nuclear warheads. As a result, each superpower had enough firepower to obliterate the other's citizens several times over. Were there *any* good reasons for the Americans and the Soviets to keep stockpiling fantastically destructive weapons for decades, or did the process continue for as long as it did because both sides succumbed to madness, the greed of their respective military-industrial complexes, or incredibly foolish pride?

Because millions of people would have died in almost any nuclear war, it might seem logical to conclude that such a conflict was always unthinkable and virtually certain not to occur. But the nuclear confrontation between the United States and the Soviet Union would have been much less serious and intractable than it was for decades if the probability of nuclear war were virtually zero. In fact, under certain conditions, it might have been rational for one or both sides to initiate a nuclear war, even if we optimistically assume that nuclear weapons have a sobering effect on both sides, leading them to think more conservatively about using them. To the extent that one side believes the other is actually preparing to launch an attack, it may be rational to strike first. Confronted with such a situation, leaders on both sides might reason as follows: Our side, of course, would not dream of committing such a horrifying and repugnant act as launching a first strike. We are too honorable and humanitarian to do such a thing. But I am not so sure about the Soviets [Americans]. Being Communists [capitalists], they are inherently imperialistic. And they know that if they strike first, they will win. Worse, they know that we know that they will win if they strike first. Because they know that we know that they will win if they strike first, they might well conclude that we will strike first, if only to avoid catastrophe. Considering this, they are sure to attack. Thus, we must launch a nuclear attack.

Fortunately, the nuclear confrontation between the United States and the Soviet Union changed so that this logic, based on the ability of a first strike to eliminate all of the enemy's weapons and thereby allow the initiator to escape retaliation, was no longer valid. In fact, a first strike that deprived the other side of any significant ability to retaliate became highly unlikely, at least by the late 1960s. In other words, the leaders of the former Soviet Union and the United States were usually quite confident that if they were the victim of a first strike, their **second-strike capability** would enable them to deliver a devastating counterattack. Second-strike capability was the basis of the nuclear doctrine **Mutual Assured Destruction (MAD)** that came to dominate superpower strategic thinking by the 1970s. The MAD doctrine argued that stability could be maintained between the nuclear powers because they were both vulnerable to each other's second-strike capability. Neither side would attack, because they knew that the other could absorb an initial attack and still render unacceptable damage in a second strike.

But the Cold War nuclear confrontation was often quite tense, because technological developments always posed a danger that a nuclear war might become winnable. As early as 1960, Henry Kissinger pointed out that "every country lives with the nightmare that even if it puts forth its best efforts its survival may be jeopardized by a technological breakthrough on the part of its opponent."[66] And such nightmares were magnified during the Cold War by the fact that each side was making determined efforts to achieve such breakthroughs, whether by developing more accurate intercontinental ballistic missiles (ICBMs), or submarine-launched ballistic missiles (SLBMs), or ballistic missile defense systems like President Ronald Reagan's **Strategic Defense Initiative (SDI)**, a research program to build a space-based system to defend the nation against strategic ballistic missiles.

Innovations of that type were inspired in part because successful deterrence required more than simply second-strike capability. A deterrence strategy was effective *only if* the leaders of the other side could not even imagine that a first strike might be successful. To be more precise, during the Cold War, the leaders of the United States and the Soviet Union had to contend continuously with the possibility that deterrence might break down and a nuclear war might break out if the decision makers on either side became convinced that the other side *imagined* that its enemies *believed* that a first strike might be successful. As long as these reciprocal fears of surprise attack[67] existed, there was always the possibility that a nuclear war might occur—not only because of an accident or insanity but also because one side or the other (or most dangerously, both sides) would find itself in a position where nuclear war seemed, by some calculations, a logical option.

second-strike capability The ability of a state to deliver a devastating counterattack after being attacked by nuclear weapons.

Mutual Assured Destruction (MAD) Strategic doctrine based on the idea that war between the superpowers was deterred when they both were vulnerable to each other's second-strike capability.

Strategic Defense Initiative (SDI) Program to use a space-based technology to strike down incoming missiles.

The Nuclear Arms Race and the Prisoner's Dilemma

prisoner's dilemma
Scenario in which actors following individually rational strategies produce the least-desired outcome.

game theory
Mathematical approach for predicting outcomes of actors' interactions in various scenarios.

The nuclear arms race during the Cold War can also be seen as a rational response to uncertainty. From 1945 until 1993, the United States deployed about 70,000 nuclear warheads, and the Soviet Union made about 55,000. Both states continued to add to their arsenals, partly because of a situation that is known in game theory as the **prisoner's dilemma.**

Game theory is an approach to the study of global politics that focuses on situations that two or more actors find themselves in and the choices that these situations lead actors to make. Game theory is based on mathematics and is also referred to as formal models.[68] Formal models depict actors, such as states, in various situations (games), and assume that they make rational choices, given their individual preferences and the incentives (the rules of the game) (see Chapter 5 for a discussion of rational actors). Game theory predicts the likely outcomes, the solutions to the game, that result from actors' interacting in various scenarios, such as the prisoner's dilemma.

The prisoner's dilemma game gets its name from a story designed to illustrate the underlying dilemma. The structure of such a game is presented in Figure 8.1. In the prisoner's dilemma story, two bank robbery suspects are detained by the prosecutor and placed in separate rooms. The prosecutor tells each of them individually that she has enough evidence to convict them on a minor weapon possession charge, which carries a penalty of five years in jail. She also tells each of them that if he will confess to his and his partner's crime, then the prosecutor will reduce the charges leveled against him (by taking off five years of jail time). The only way the prosecutor can convict either of the suspects for the serious

Figure 8.1 The Prisoner's Dilemma
The game theory matrix shows the payoff to each prisoner for confessing or not confessing a crime to the prosecutor.

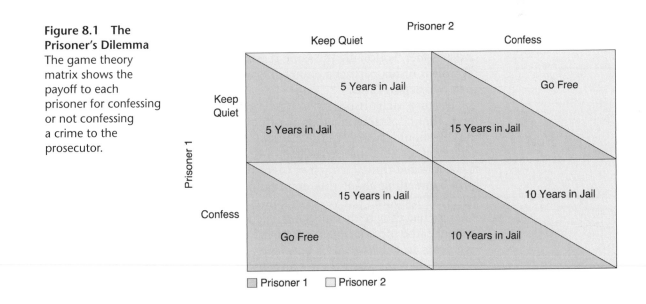

bank robbery charge (which carries a fifteen-year jail sentence), however, is for one of them to confess to their involvement in the robbery. In this scenario, each suspect must decide whether to keep quiet or confess. The cells in Figure 8.1 represent the results (termed "payoffs" in game theory) for each prisoner based on each prisoner's choice of whether to confess or keep quiet. Which is the rational strategy from their individual points of view? Social scientists have debated the definition of rationality at some length, but in the context of games like this, game theorists point out a couple of important ways in which self-interested calculations lead both of the suspects to confess.

Prisoner 1 wonders to himself what would be best for him to do if his partner keeps quiet. If prisoner 1 also keeps quiet (illustrated in the top left box of Figure 8.1), then he will get five years in jail from the weapon possession charge. If he chooses to confess while his partner keeps quiet (illustrated in the bottom left box of Figure 8.1), then he will be charged only with weapon possession (a five-year jail term) but will also be rewarded for supplying evidence for prosecution (with a five-year sentence reduction), resulting in no jail time at all. Clearly, the choice favors confessing (and going free) over keeping quiet (and getting five years of jail time).

But what if prisoner 1's partner decides to confess to his crime instead of keeping quiet? In that case, prisoner 1 will certainly be charged with the serious bank robbery (fifteen years of jail time). He can either keep quiet himself and receive no reduction in his sentence (top right of Figure 8.1), or he can also choose to confess and at least get five years knocked off his sentence (resulting in ten years of jail time; bottom right of Figure 8.1). Again, clearly the choice favors confessing (ten years of jail time) over keeping quiet (fifteen years of jail time). So no matter whether prisoner 1's partner chooses to keep quiet or to confess, prisoner 1 will do less jail time by confessing. To be sure of receiving the shorter jail sentence, prisoner 1 should confess. Of course, the same logic holds for the second prisoner. Following the same reasoning, prisoner 2 will conclude that regardless of his partner's choice, he will do less jail time by confessing than by keeping quiet.

Because each prisoner is rational (in this case, each wants to spend the least amount of time in jail as possible), each will come to the conclusion that he should confess to the crime. Game theorists call this the "dominant strategy" because regardless of the behavior of the other prisoner, it is the rational thing for each of them to do individually. What is particularly compelling about this dominant strategy is that it results in both prisoners spending ten years in jail (the bottom right box of Figure 8.1), whereas had they both kept quiet, each would receive only a five-year jail sentence (the top left box of Figure 8.1). Although they both would prefer five years in jail instead of ten years, they receive the longer sentence, because they followed their individually rational strategy. Individually rational behavior resulted in an outcome that neither individual would prefer. This is why the prisoners have a dilemma: Being rational by trying to get the least amount of jail time as possible actually results in more jail time. By thinking of this scenario in terms of the underlying structure of choices and payoffs, which demonstrates how each individual actor's outcome is dependent on the moves made by the other player, game theory provides some insight into why irrational consequences can result from rational behavior.

The logic of the Prisoner's Dilemma helps to make sense of the nuclear arms race between the United States and the Soviet Union. The United States had to consider the various outcomes that depended on Soviet actions. From the U.S. perspective, the prospect of nuclear superiority (if the Soviets did not engage in the buildup) was tempting, like confessing when your partner in crime remains silent (see again Figure 8.1). And the prospect of nuclear vulnerability (if the Soviets built up their nuclear arsenal but the United States did not) was to be avoided at all costs, like keeping quiet while your partner in crime confessed. Given these options, the United States and Soviet Union chose to build up their nuclear arsenals rather than restraining their buildup (and perhaps spending their money on other things).

Under those conditions, it is not so surprising that the United States and the Soviet Union had very large defense budgets and accumulated weapons at a very rapid rate for four decades after the Second World War. From the point of view of the decision makers on both sides, they were only protecting their countries. But from the point of view of many outside observers, the arms race between the United States and the Soviet Union was dangerous. It would ultimately, many felt, lead to the nuclear holocaust that both sides were ostensibly trying to avoid. Even as recently as 1979, Hans Morgenthau, father of the modern realist perspective, declared that "the world is moving ineluctably toward a third world war a—strategic nuclear war. I do not believe that anything can be done to prevent it."[69]

The arms race between the Soviet Union and the United States was clearly dangerous, not to mention incredibly wasteful in purely economic terms. But it did come to an end without nuclear disaster. This is not a historically unprecedented outcome for arms races, as we have seen. It was, however, the potentially most dangerous arms race in the history of the world. Although their stockpiles of such weapons are much reduced today, the United States and Russia still deploy around 2000 strategic warheads each.[70] Fortunately, "Russia has signed reciprocal agreements with the United States, the United Kingdom and China stating that they will not target their missiles at each other while they are on normal alert status."[71]

Although it is certainly fortunate that the two vast arsenals of the Cold War superpowers are no longer deployed in a tightly organized fashion, ready to initiate what would surely have been the most lethal war in history, the disintegration of the Soviet Union created new dangers.

"The collapse of the Soviet Union left Soviet strategic forces scattered across the newly independent states. Missile and bomber bases were distributed across Russia, Ukraine, Belarus, and Kazakhstan."[72] The good news is that Belarus, Kazakhstan, and Ukraine handed over to Russia all of their nuclear warheads.[73] The bad news is that continued reform in Russia toward democracy is not assured. It is not at all inconceivable that ultranationalist, Communist, or fascist leaders could take over in Russia and return control of massive nuclear power to intensely antagonistic hands. It is also frighteningly possible that the painful and bloody disintegration of Yugoslavia might be duplicated in the former Soviet Union.

The Threat of Proliferation of Weapons of Mass Destruction

Even if Russia and the other republics of the former Soviet Union develop into peace-loving states, the world will not be safe from the threat of nuclear weapons. Nations other than the United States and Russia possess these weapons of mass destruction, although the United States is the only state that has ever used an atomic bomb (as it did twice in Japan in 1945). Great Britain, France, and China have each had nuclear weapons for decades now. The nuclear arsenals of these states are small compared to the United States and Russia. Great Britain has about 160 strategic nuclear warheads, France has 300, and China has approximately 186.[74]

India first exploded a nuclear device in 1974, and in 1998, both India and Pakistan "declared" themselves nuclear powers with a series of underground tests. It is estimated that India has about seventy nuclear weapons and Pakistan has sixty.[75] In 2006, North Korea tested its first nuclear weapon. Outsiders believe that North Korea has enough nuclear material to make at least eight nuclear bombs. Israel has not declared itself a nuclear power, but it is assumed that it has about eighty nuclear weapons.[76] South Africa once had nuclear weapons but has subsequently destroyed them, and Libya claimed that it had come close to building a nuclear bomb before it abandoned its unconventional weapons program and agreed to international weapons inspectors in 2003.[77]

The international community was also concerned about Iraq's nuclear ambitions after the Persian Gulf War in 1991. "[E]ven though Iraq signed the NPT [Nuclear Nonproliferation Treaty] it managed to mount a massive covert program to acquire nuclear and other weapons of mass destruction.... The Iraqi program involved more than 10,000 qualified technical people who remain[ed] in place as a competent cadre."[78] Suspicions that Iraq had continued to develop its nuclear programs led to the return of UN inspection teams in 2002 and were one justification for the U.S-led intervention in Iraq in 2003, although no evidence of nuclear weapons was found post-invasion. Many states possess the technology and material to build nuclear weapons, including Australia, Canada, Germany, Japan, and Ukraine.

The nuclearization of South Asia is of particular concern. In May 1998, India conducted underground testing of several nuclear devices. Within three weeks, Pakistan responded with its own underground nuclear tests, despite intense international pressures. "Given the history of conflict between the two states, most members of the international community viewed the introduction of nuclear weapons into South Asia with alarm. Fueled by religious animosity and disagreements over their border, India and Pakistan had fought three major wars since the British partitioned colonial India into India, East Pakistan, and West Pakistan in 1947. Outbreaks of violence and crises between India and Pakistan had become more frequent in the 1990s"[79] and have continued in recent years. Some analysts attribute this to the increased suspicions over each others' nuclear aims and others argue that India and Pakistan are particularly likely to use their nuclear weapons against each other.[80] Indeed, "soon after the 1998 tests, Pakistani military planners developed more belligerent strategies against India. Dusting off an old plan, in the winter of 1999, Pakistani infantry units . . . snuck into Indian-held Kashmir. The incursion sparked the 1999 Kargil War, in which over 1,000 soldiers were killed on both sides before Pakistani forces reluctantly withdrew. According to U.S. and Indian intelligence, before the fighting ended, the Pakistani military had started to ready its nuclear capable missiles for potential use."[81] Yet, despite ongoing tensions over Kashmir, India and Pakistan, as nuclear powers, have not directly engaged in large-scale conventional war or nuclear conflict.[82] And in 2005, the United States signed a historic nuclear cooperation agreement with India. In the agreement, the United States pledges to assist India's civilian energy program and cooperate with India on energy and satellite testing. In exchange, India agreed to international inspections of its civilian nuclear program, strengthen the security of its nuclear arsenal, and continue to not test nuclear weapons.[83]

North Korean proliferation has been an area of concern for quite some time. When North Korean leaders threatened to build nuclear weapons in the early 1990s, the United States, fearing an arms race in East Asia, responded with its own threats of economic sanctions and considered an attack on North Korean facilities. North Korea responded by deploying many more troops on the border with South Korea, and for several weeks in 1994, a replay of the 1950s Korean War was considered a real possibility. After negotiations, North Korea agreed to freeze and ultimately dismantle its nuclear program in exchange for U.S. funds to construct nuclear power generators that would not yield plutonium. North Korea revealed in 2002 that it did not dismantle its nuclear materials production program. Multiparty talks failed to definitively address the threat of North Korean nuclear proliferation, and North Korea became a nuclear power when it tested a nuclear bomb in 2006. Attention then shifted to dismantling or preventing further development of North Korea's nuclear program. Again, in 2007, North Korea agreed to eventually cease its program but this agreement faltered on North Korean rejection of the terms for verification. In 2009, North Korea test-fired another ballistic missile, declared that it was restarting its atomic weapons program and would begin enriching uranium (in addition to its plutonium program) and conducted a second nuclear test. The United Nations responded with tougher sanctions on North Korea, and the United States announced it would intercept North Korean ships suspected of carrying nuclear material.[84]

Why would North Korea develop nuclear weapons? "The North Koreans have presented a rationale for developing...such a weapon.... They point out that the United States, which has more nuclear weapons than any other country, has labeled North Korea a member of the "axis of evil," thereby making the country a possible target of pre-emptive attack."[85] Others, however, see North Korea's actions stemming more from the regime's strategy of keeping North Korea isolated in order to remain in control of its people and from the economic rewards that it believes it can get from the international community in exchange for promises to give up its nuclear program.[86]

Nuclear Nonproliferation Treaty (NPT) agreement in effect since the 1970s to prevent further nuclear proliferation and promote nuclear disarmament.

Iran is another state receiving attention on the topic of nuclear proliferation. "The issue of Iran's nuclear ambition is complicated. On [the] one hand, Tehran is a signatory to the NPT **[Nuclear Nonproliferation Treaty]** and since the mid-1970s has called for making the entire Middle East a nuclear-free zone. On the other hand, Western powers . . . have suspected that Iran has been secretly developing nuclear capability since the mid-1980s . . . Iranian leaders categorically deny these accusations and assert that their nuclear program is only for peaceful purpose," which is allowable under the NPT.[87] Weapons inspectors from the International Atomic Energy Agency (IAEA) have made accusations that Iran's nuclear energy programs violate some aspects of the Nonproliferation Treaty and that Iran had secretly worked on the potential development of a nuclear bomb, but this agency has not found solid evidence that Iran is developing nuclear weapons.[88] In 2007, a U.S. intelligence report concluded that Iran did not have a weapons program at that time, but that Iranian intentions were unclear. Other reports claim that Iran now has enough enriched uranium to build an atomic bomb.[89] The United Nations Security Council has threatened Iran with sanctions if it does not discontinue enriching uranium, but Iran has not complied.

The Iranian issue is further complicated by decades of poor relations between Iran and the United States, U.S. accusations that Iran sponsors terrorist groups in Iraq and Lebanon, and Iranian suspicions that the United States is determined to militarily dismantle the Iranian regime no matter what Iran does.

Beyond the Iranian and North Korean cases, it is clear that more states might acquire nuclear weapons, and perhaps the threat that these new owners of nuclear weapons will actually use them may be greater than that which existed during the Cold War. International attention to nuclear proliferation has rapidly increased since the end of the Cold War. Today, not only are states' desires for nuclear weapons a concern, but many worry about nuclear capabilities acquired by nonstate actors, such as terrorist groups. According to Graham Allison, founding dean of Harvard's John F. Kennedy School of Government and former assistant secretary of defense for policy and plans, "Given the number of actors with serious intent, the accessibility of weapons or nuclear materials from which elementary weapons could be constructed, and the almost limitless ways in which terrorists could smuggle a weapon through American borders,... a nuclear terrorist attack on America in the decade ahead is more likely than not."[90] Most recently, the international community became concerned that, given the internal conflict in Pakistan, that country's nuclear arsenal is inadequately secured.[91]

Could the spread of nuclear weapons be good news? Could nuclear deterrence provide stability as some argue it did during the "long peace" between the United States and the Soviet Union during the Cold War? It has been argued for some time now that nuclear proliferation in the Middle East has the potential to bring stability to that volatile region.[92] And one analyst argues that nuclear deterrence in South Asia is working, despite the tensions between India and Pakistan.[93] Others have asserted in more general terms that "proliferation may serve the global desire for peace"[94] and that "the spread of nuclear weapons is something that we have worried too much about and tried too hard to stop . . . the measured spread of nuclear weapons is more to be welcomed than feared."[95] The end of the Cold War evoked an argument to the effect that stability in Europe would be enhanced if Germany acquired nuclear weapons and if Ukraine developed nuclear weapons as a deterrent against Russia.[96] Another proliferation "optimist" argues that "the leaders of medium and small powers alike tend to be extremely cautious with regard to the nuclear weapons they possess . . . the proof being that, to date, in every region where these weapons have been introduced, large-scale interstate warfare has disappeared."[97]

One main objection to optimism about the impact of nuclear proliferation in the developing countries involves the vulnerable nature of nascent nuclear forces. One of the possible virtues of the large nuclear forces in the hands of the Soviet Union and the United States was that they made both states relatively safe from the destabilizing impact of technological breakthroughs.[98] Even without such breakthroughs, emerging nuclear forces in the developing world are vulnerable to preemptive strikes, and so they will tempt such strikes. "Even if both sides prefer not to preempt, each may fear that the other side will; consequently, both may decide to launch at the first (perhaps fake) indication of an attack."[99] In addition, in the case of South Asia, "The decade since the...nuclear tests suggests that a principal risk of nuclear proliferation is not that the leaders of new nuclear states will be irrational or suicidal, or even that organizational and other pathologies will result in suboptimal policy formulation. The danger, rather, is that leaders may weigh their strategic options and reasonably conclude that risky behavior best serves their interests. Nuclear weapons do enable Pakistan, as a conventionally weak, dissatisfied power, to challenge the territorial status quo with less fear of an all-out Indian military response."[100]

In the end, perhaps it is most important to point out that the costs of guessing wrong on this issue are not equal in both directions. If nuclear proliferation is discouraged when actually it is beneficial, the cost is the loss of a boost to stability and a somewhat larger probability of conventional wars. If proliferation is encouraged when it is actually dangerous (even if it makes war a less rational option), then tolerating or encouraging proliferation would be experimentation in the absence of any solid evidence on which to base estimates of the results. The Policy Choices box on nuclear proliferation presents some of the issues surrounding proliferation and preventive efforts.

Nuclear Arms Control

Most states recognize the dangers of nuclear proliferation. Even during the Cold War, the Soviet Union and the United States cooperated in an effort to prevent other states from acquiring nuclear weapons. In the 1960s, they helped draft the Nuclear Nonproliferation Treaty (NPT). The hope that this agreement would restrict the nuclear club to a membership of five (China, France, Great Britain, the Soviet Union, and the United States) was crushed in May 1974 when India exploded its first nuclear device.

In 1995, the NPT was extended, and by 2003, 189 states had signed the treaty, making it "the most widely-adhered-to arms control treaty in history" according to the U.S. Department of State.[101] Although North Korea agreed to freeze and ultimately dismantle its nuclear weapon program under the October 1994 U.S.–North Korean Framework Agreement, it announced in 2002 that it had been continuing to develop its nuclear materials program and withdrew from the NPT. Talks to get North Korea to reenter the treaty were stalled for many years before it tested its first nuclear weapons in 2006.[102] India, Israel, and Pakistan have all refused to sign the treaty. In addition to the extension of the NPT, there have been several more specific, significant successes in the antinuclear proliferation effort in recent years. In the early 1990s, South Africa dismantled its arsenal of six nuclear weapons and signed the NPT in 1991. Belarus, Kazakhstan, and Ukraine have not only transferred to Russia all the strategic and nuclear warheads they inherited as a result of the collapse of the Soviet Union, they have also joined the NPT and opened their nuclear facilities to inspection by the International Atomic Energy Agency (IAEA). Algeria agreed to join the NPT in 1995, and Libya

ISSUE: The number of states with nuclear weapons capabilities has increased in the last decade, and more states may be on the verge of testing and stockpiling nuclear weapons. Intuitively this seems to be problematic and almost certainly a recipe for disaster. However, there is another side to this deceptively complicated problem that emphasizes the stability that such weapons can bring and the difficulties of preventing nuclear proliferation.

Option #1: Nuclear proliferation can provide many benefits to the international system and generally should be embraced.

Arguments: (a) Nuclear weapons create stability between actors, because they make the potential cost of going to war too great for states to seriously contemplate. Nuclear rivalry was a main reason the United States and the Soviet Union did not directly fight during the tense Cold War. (b) States acquire nuclear weapons for security and prestige. States that are secure and enjoy status are less likely to initiate conflict and are more likely to cooperate on many international issues. (c) There are no effective strategies to prevent nuclear proliferation—incentives do not stop states from acquiring them and punishments often push them faster toward proliferation.

Counterarguments: (a) States are not necessarily rational actors who calculate costs and then choose courses of action. Decisions are made by fallible humans, religious zealots, and impassioned policymakers, thereby reducing the supposed "rational" effectiveness of nuclear deterrence. Today's international system is very different from the Cold War period—multiple nuclear rivals, protracted conflicts, and unstable states make it less likely that nuclear deterrence would work. (b) Nuclear security may embolden states to engage in more risky, aggressive behaviors. (c) There have been many nonproliferation successes. Extending the deterrence of existing nuclear states, imposing economic sanctions, establishing international monitoring agencies, and incentive-based negotiations have all worked to convince states to forgo nuclear ambitions.

Option #2: Nuclear proliferation constitutes one of the most serious problems facing humanity, and efforts to prevent it should be foremost on the minds of leaders.

Arguments: (a) More actors in possession of nuclear weapons means a greater likelihood of having such weapons get into the hands of rogue states or unstable leaders. (b) Unstable nuclear regimes increase the chance of accidental nuclear war or the transfer of nuclear weapons into the hands of terrorist groups. (c) Although nuclear weapons have killed far fewer people than conventional weapons, the potential destruction is much greater. A nuclear attack in a large city, enacted by a single decision maker, could kill hundreds of thousands in one stroke.

Counterarguments: (a) Claims that certain countries cannot be trusted with nuclear weapons are rooted in prejudice and misunderstanding. The only country ever to have used a nuclear device in hostility is the United States. (b) The international community can implement safeguards to protect nuclear facilities. It is not in the interests of states to share nuclear technology with nonstate actors. (c) The real weapons of mass killing in humanity's arsenal are small arms and light weapons, which are profitable to sell and readily distributed to unstable countries without hesitation. Arguments by arms exporters for limiting nuclear proliferation are thus hypocritical.

announced in 2003 that it would comply with the treaty. Argentina and Brazil have brought into force a nuclear-free zone in that part of the world through the Treaty of Tlatelolco and have also accepted IAEA inspections. Treaties have also created nuclear-weapon-free zones in Africa, Southeast Asia, and Central Asia. International agreements have been reached that designate Antarctica, outer space, the moon, and the seabed as denuclearized areas.[103]

Comprehensive Test Ban Treaty (CTBT) Proposed agreement to ban nuclear weapons testing.

In addition to the NPT, decades of multilateral negotiations produced the **Comprehensive Test Ban Treaty (CTBT),** banning all testing of nuclear weapons. Today, 148 countries have ratified the treaty. Although the United States originally signed the treaty, the U.S. Senate rejected it in 1999.[104]

> The Senate vote marked at least a temporary setback for international efforts to bring the CTBT into force, since the USA is one of the 44 states which must ratify the treaty in order for it to enter into force. The treaty's prospects were given a boost, however, when the Russian Duma voted overwhelmingly to ratify it on April 21, 2000. . . . In addition, in September [2000] Indian Prime Minister Atal Bihari Vajpayee pledged that his government would not conduct further nuclear testing while it attempted to build a consensus on signing the CTBT.[105]

By 2009, however, the treaty had not entered into force as five of the forty-four necessary states (China, Egypt, Indonesia, Iran, US) had not yet ratified the treaty. Newly-elected President Obama promised to push for U.S. ratification, but strong opposition in Congress persists.[106]

The United States and Russia have also engaged in significant bilateral arms reduction efforts, building on the SALT talks during the détente era of the 1970s (see Chapter 3). In 1991, the Strategic Arms Reduction Treaty (START I) was signed, reducing the number of nuclear warheads and delivery systems in each country. In 1993, START II banned all land-based multiple independently targetable reentry vehicles (MIRVs) and committed both parties to make phased reductions in their strategic nuclear forces. The levels of nuclear warheads agreed to in START II were quickly outdated, however, as the United States and Russia announced plans for unilateral cuts that would take their strategic nuclear forces well below START II levels. In 2002, the countries codified these pledges in the Strategic Offensive Reductions Treaty (SORT), better known as the

Moscow Treaty U.S.–Russian agreement to reduce their stockpiles of nuclear warheads by the year 2012.

Moscow Treaty. According to this agreement, each side will reduce its number of warheads to between 1,700 and 2,200 by the year 2012. Both states were already close to reaching that target by 2009 and agreed to further reductions in the next 7 years to between 1500 and 1700 warheads for each side. The general reduction of the number of nuclear weapons in the post–Cold War era, as depicted in Figure 8.2, is quite a remarkable arms control achievement.

Figure 8.2 Reductions in U.S. and Soviet/Russian Strategic Nuclear Forces

Source: Data compiled from the Stockholm Peace Research Institute's *SIPRI Yearbook 1996*, the *SIPRI Yearbook 2002*, and from the U.S. Department of State Shannon N. Kile, Vitaly Fedchenko, and Hans M. Kristensen, "World Nuclear Forces," in SIPRI Yearbook 2009 Armaments, Disarmament and International Security Summary. p. 16, HYPERLINK "http://www.sipri.org/yearbook/2009/files/SIPRIYB09summary.pdf" http://www.sipri.org/yearbook/2009/files/SIPRIYB09summary.pdf. Accessed 9 June 2009.

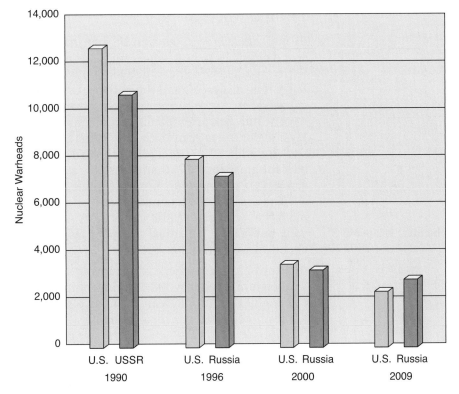

ballistic missile defense (BMD) system Defense system designed to intercept and destroy ballistic missiles.

Talks over nuclear arms reductions between the United States and Russia have been complicated by the U.S. decision (announced in 2001) to withdraw from the 1972 Antiballistic Missile Treaty. Withdrawing from the treaty allows the United States to conduct tests, without any conditions, for a missile defense system. Opposition to the building of a **ballistic missile defense (BMD) system** came from within the United States and from the international community (expressed, for example, by China, Russia, and a number of states in Europe and Asia). "The controversy obstructed efforts to further reduce strategic nuclear arms and gave rise to international concern that the entire framework of nuclear arms control was in danger of breaking down."[107] Opposition to BMDs is based on the concern that they will undermine stability by compromising second-strike capability, the foundation of nuclear deterrence and the ABM treaty. Opponents argue that BMDs do not address the types of threats, such as from terrorists with crude weapons, that states are more likely to face. Supporters counter that BMDs address the real threat from rogue states who are acquiring ballistic missile technology and they can decrease the probability of such an attack by making the probability of success less likely.[108]

Beyond Nuclear

Even if nuclear weapons can be kept under control, the post–Cold War world promises to be a dangerous place because of the rapid spread of ballistic missiles, which can deliver conventional or nuclear weapons over fairly long distances, and the potential diffusion of chemical and biological weapons. Some twenty-five countries, most in the developing world, have acquired or attempted to acquire ballistic missiles. Nine of them are in the Middle East, but India and Pakistan, North and South Korea, Brazil and Argentina, Taiwan, and South Africa either have or have tried to get ballistic missiles.[109] Ballistic missiles are difficult to defend against and can be very accurate with missile-guided technology.

Ballistic missile technology also allows the delivery of chemical and biological weapons. While the horrors of nuclear weapons are relatively well publicized, **chemical weapons** are less familiar. Modern use of chemical weapons dates back to

chemical weapons
Weapons that contain chemical elements, such as chlorine gas and mustard gas.

> April 22, 1915, when German troops entrenched at Ypres, Belgium, opened 6,000 chlorine cylinders, releasing a cloud of deadly gas into the wind blowing toward their French adversaries. Thousands perished in this first large-scale use of chemical warfare. Two years later, Germany introduced another deadly chemical to the battlefield as well: mustard gas. By the war's end, chemical weapons had inflicted 1.3 million casualties, including almost 100,000 deaths.[110]

Chemical weapons were again used in World War II by Italy against Ethiopia and Japan against China.[111] Concern over the proliferation of chemical weapons came to the foreground in the 1980s when Iraq used them against Iran and against Kurds living in Iraq. "The number of countries believed to have chemical weapons programs has grown from about a dozen in 1980 to about 20" near the end of the 1990s.[112] Chemical weapons such as phosgene (a choking agent) or nerve agents (which induce nausea, coma, convulsion, and death) are estimated to be capable, if attached to ballistic missiles, of killing forty to 700 times as many people as missiles equipped with conventional weapons.[113]

biological weapons
Weapons that contain biological agents such as anthrax or plague bacteria.

Biological weapons are even more lethal. Ballistic missiles might be equipped with "bombs," for example, that could spread anthrax, plague bacteria, or the Ebola virus. Germany used anthrax in World War I against its opponents' horses and mules. During World War II, the Soviet Union reportedly used typhus and typhoid fever as a weapon of war, and Japan used plague germs in bombs dropped on China. Many of these diseases can kill within days, vaccines often must be administered before infection to be effective, and antibiotic treatments are of uncertain effectiveness. In short, biological weapons like anthrax delivered by ballistic missiles could be as lethal as at least small nuclear weapons.[114] It is estimated that at least seventeen states possess biological weapons.[115]

Countries such as Iraq, Japan, the former Soviet Union, the United Kingdom, and the United States have developed anthrax as an agent of biological warfare.[116]

Why would nations want to acquire chemical or biological weapons? They are much more lethal than conventional weapons; they have nearly the military effectiveness of small nuclear weapons, and they are cheaper and easier to acquire than nuclear weapons—they are "a poor man's nuclear weapon." Furthermore, ballistic technology is not necessary for the use of chemical and biological weapons; "a crude dispersal system may be enough to kill thousands and cripple a major metropolitan area."[117] In 1993, a U.S. federal agency estimated that "a crop duster carrying a mere 100 kilograms of anthrax spores could deliver a fatal dose to up to 3 million residents of the Washington D.C. metropolitan area."[118]

The bombing of the World Trade Center in New York City in 1993 could have been much worse had the chemical weapon been delivered not in a common truck but in some technologically sophisticated ballistic missile. "The bombing of [the] World Trade Center . . . was meant to topple the city's tallest tower onto its twin, amid a cloud of cyanide gas. Had the attack gone as planned [the cyanide container malfunctioned], tens of thousands of Americans would have died."[119] In 1995, Aum Shinrikyo, a Japanese Buddhist sect, attempted to murder tens of thousands of people by placing eleven bags filled with the nerve gas sarin wrapped in newspapers on five subway trains. Twelve people were killed and more than 5,000 hospitalized. In 1990, in the first known chemical weapons attack by a nonstate actor, the Tamil Tigers used chlorine gas against the Sri Lankan military.[120]

These incidents, in the United States, Tokyo, and Sri Lanka suggest "a trend toward nonstate actors becoming proliferation threats."[121] In light of the September 11 terrorist attacks, there is a heightened fear that groups such as al Qaeda have chemical and biological weapons capabilities.

Indeed, suspicions regarding al Qaeda's aims to use chemical weapons against U.S. forces in Saudi Arabia prompted the U.S. to attack a pharmaceutical plant in Sudan in 1998, following the bombings of U.S. embassies in Africa (see Chapter 7). "[S]ince that time incontrovertible information has repeatedly come to light that clearly illuminates al Qaeda's long-standing and concerted efforts to develop a diverse array of chemical, biological, and even nuclear weapons capabilities."[122] Terrorist groups have not, however, yet taken up chemical and biological agents as their weapons of choice. Indeed, fewer than sixty terrorist incidents out of the 8,000 recorded in the RAND-MIPT Terrorism Knowledge Database involved "any indication of terrorists plotting such attacks, attempting to use chemical or biological agents, or intending to steal or fabricate their own nuclear devices."[123]

Although the threat from nonstate actors is worrisome, the more orthodox international threat posed by states armed with chemical or biological weapons is not to be dismissed lightly. The U.S. government has alleged that several states—including China, India, Iran, North Korea, Pakistan, Russia, Sudan, and Syria—are either seeking chemical and biological weapons or have the capacity to develop them. The United States and the United Nations had been particularly concerned about Iraq's chemical and biological weapons potential in the 1990s. "The UN Security Council . . . placed Iraq under an international sanctions regime in order to compel it to comply with the conditions of Resolution 687, which includes the destruction of its CBW and the termination of the CBW-related programmes under international supervision."[124] The UN inspectors returned to Iraq to verify compliance in 2002, but doubts by the United States and other countries about Iraq's claims that it had completely dismantled all such programs was one of the justifications used for the invasion of Iraq in 2003. However, no clear evidence of chemical or biological weapons programs has been discovered in postwar Iraq.

Efforts to Control Ballistic Missile Technology and Chemical and Biological Weapons

Missile Technology Control Regime (MTCR) Voluntary agreement that seeks to control export and production of missile technology capable of carrying weapons of mass destruction.

Given the threat, there have been a number of attempts to deal with these weapons of massive destruction and their delivery systems. In 1987, the **Missile Technology Control Regime (MTCR)** was established, seeking to control the export and production of missile technology capable of carrying weapons of mass destruction. The MTCR is a voluntary agreement, with no enforcement. From 1987 until 2003, the countries that joined the MCTR grew from seven to thirty-three.[125] In 2003, the Proliferation Security Initiative (PSI) was launched to seize components of ballistic missile technology and other technology for the production or delivery of weapons of mass destruction. The more than ninety countries that participate share intelligence and interdict ships suspected of carrying such technology. According to one analyst,

> It is difficult to gauge the ultimate effectiveness of the PSI, but it has been successfully employed about a dozen times already. The initiative's most prominent accomplishment to date occurred in October 2003, when U.S. intelligence established that equipment for enriching uranium (produced in Malaysia using designs provided by the network led by the Pakistani scientist A. Q. Khan) was on its way to Libya via Dubai. The ship involved was the German-flagged BBC China, and following a request by the United States, the owner of the ship diverted it to an Italian port. The Italian government, a PSI participant,

searched the vessel and seized parts for a gas centrifuge. The action was an important step in exposing Khan's illicit nuclear network and in halting Libya's clandestine nuclear program.[126]

Chemical Weapons Convention (CWC) Agreement whereby signature states pledge to destroy their chemical weapons.

In January 1993, a **Chemical Weapons Convention (CWC)**, which aims for the destruction of all chemical weapons, was opened for signing, and by 2009, 188 states were parties to the convention. For some time, the United States was *not* among those countries. However, shortly before the deadline in April 1997, at which time the convention would have gone into effect whether or not the United States had agreed to it, the U.S. Senate agreed to ratification. The four states that have declared their chemical weapons programs—India, South Korea, Russia, and the United States—are in the process of destroying those weapons.

> The effect of the CWC has probably been to reduce the number of parties with chemical weapons and to reduce the likelihood they will be used. . . . Nevertheless, it is not clear which countries still have CW [chemical weapons] programs because the Convention has not been aggressively implemented and there have been no challenge inspections. Several countries that ratified the CWC have probably terminated their CW programs, but it is suspected that some signatories (such as Iran and China) and several countries that have not ratified the Convention (Egypt, Israel, North Korea, and Syria) may still be developing or producing CW.[127]

The CWC builds on a 1925 Geneva Protocol, an agreement that banned the use, but not production, of chemical weapons in warfare in reaction to the horrors caused by chlorine and mustard gas in World War I.

Biological and Toxic Weapons Convention (BTWC) Agreement banning production, stockpiling, and use of biological agents.

There is also a **Biological and Toxic Weapons Convention (BTWC)**, dating from 1972, that bans the production, stockpiling, and use of biological agents, but ensuring compliance with it is difficult. Although, as of 2009, 175 states had become parties to the convention, the BTWC "has two basic weaknesses. First, because of the dual-use nature of microbial pathogens . . . the line between treaty-permitted and prohibited activities is largely a question of intent. . . . Second, the . . . [convention's] lack of formal verification measure has made it toothless and unable to address a series of alleged violations."[128]

It is clear that although the end of the Cold War may have eliminated the threat of a truly massive nuclear war, at least for the time being, it has not delivered the world from the menace posed by nuclear weapons, ballistic missiles, and chemical or biological weapons. For the foreseeable future, a growing list of state and nonstate actors will continue to threaten their enemies with a deadly combination of nuclear, chemical, and biological weapons of mass destruction.

Bargaining and Negotiation

bargaining and negotiation Formal and informal communication between actors.

When states enter into alliances and arms agreements, they do so through **bargaining and negotiation**—informal and formal communication between actors. Bargaining and negotiation are another way that states try to resolve or avoid conflict and form the bulk of state-to-state relations. Indeed, bargaining takes place on an ongoing basis between most states as they seek to cooperate and enter into mutually beneficial arrangements. States bargain over the NPT, the World Trade Organization, and environmental treaties such as the Kyoto protocol. "Within the realm of international relations, diplomatic negotiation is central to the functioning of the system of nation-states that has evolved over time."[129]

Nonstate actors are part of international bargaining as well. "Increasingly, negotiation situations feature actors that are neither sovereign states nor reliant on those states for membership and direction."[130] At times, substate actors negotiate directly with other states. In 2006, for example, California Governor Arnold Schwarzenegger negotiated with British Prime Minister Tony Blair an agreement to collaborate on research to address problems of global warming, thereby bypassing the U.S. national government.[131] Nongovernmental organizations, such as Greenpeace, also bargain with states and other nonstate actors on a variety of topics (see Chapter 13 on the role of NGOs in environmental issues). States also bargain with terrorists, despite many states' official policies not to negotiate with such groups.[132]

Coercive Diplomacy and Bargaining Strategies

International actors sometimes attempt to bargain by engaging in coercive diplomacy and initiate or imply threats to deter or compel other actors.[133] As we have seen in this chapter, deterrence and compellence are critical strategies in global politics and are the foundation of many decisions to pursue alliances and build up arms. Both deterrence and compellence involve demonstrating capabilities, signaling the credibility of a threat, and communicating to other actors the will and terms of the use of this threat. Alliances and arms involve boosting a state or coalition's capabilities—increasing their power in relation to that of their potential adversaries. Credibility and communication are achieved through successful bargaining and negotiation.

Bargaining strategies in deterrence, for example, are designed to convince the other side that the costs of doing something they want to do (such as attacking) outweigh the benefits that they will achieve from this action (such as control of a territory). To do this, negotiators must convince the other side that they will impose these high costs (attacking back) and that this threat is credible (they really will carry it out) and not a bluff. Many argued that the 1950s U.S. nuclear strategy known as massive retaliation, in which the United States threatened to use its nuclear weapons against the Soviet Union for any unwanted behavior, was not credible. The United States certainly had the capability to do this, but would it really launch an all-out nuclear war over, for example, South Korea or West Berlin, risking Soviet retaliation directly against Washington, DC?

This credibility must be successfully communicated to the other side. Successful communication, unfortunately, requires that the other side receive the threat *as it is intended.* If, for example, the target of the threat does not see the costs as great as the actor that is initiating the threat or sees the benefit of actions differently, the message is not successfully communicated. Under the MAD nuclear strategy, the United States estimated that if it could maintain a second-strike capability that ensured, after absorbing an initial strike from the Soviet Union, that it could destroy 20 percent of the Soviet population and infrastructure, this was a credible deterrent threat. The danger is that the Soviet Union may not have seen this as a great cost. In the Second World War, the Soviets were willing to lose 20 million people, a considerable cost, for the benefit of defeating the German threat. Estimating what the other sides' costs and benefits are and how they weigh those is a very difficult part of coercive diplomacy.

Communicating capability often involves taking a hard bargaining line, but this can sometimes lead to unfortunate outcomes. The United States refused for years to back down in its battle with North Vietnam over the fate of South Vietnam and yet failed to achieve its objective despite that prolonged effort. The logic or theory behind a coercive strategy is that "effective . . . bargaining [is] dependent on exploiting the other side's fear of war through the use of credible threats and punishments, that is, on demonstrating a willingness to accept the risk of war to achieve state objectives."[134] This outlook on international politics leads to what might be called a **"bullying" strategy** of bargaining, because it relies heavily on force and threats of force, as opposed to compromises and "carrots," or rewards, for desired behavior. A bullying strategy relies almost exclusively on severe threats and punishments until and unless the bargainer's demands are accepted.

"bullying" strategy Bargaining strategy relying heavily on force and threats of force.

But diplomatic bargaining is not a simple game in which one succeeds by adopting extreme positions or acting tough all of the time. Data on forty international crises that occurred between 1816 and 1980 indicate that a bullying strategy was used only about 35 percent of the time. Almost as often, the participants in those crises instead used a more flexible and conciliatory **"reciprocating" strategy,** in which one side imitates or duplicates the kind of diplomatic moves made by the other party regarding a dispute or crisis. Bargainers who engage in a reciprocating strategy respond to coercive or bullying moves involving force or the threat of force with threatening or violent moves of their own. But unlike "bullies," who rely on threats or force regardless of what the other side does, reciprocating strategists respond in a

"reciprocating" strategy Flexible bargaining strategy in which one side imitates or duplicates the kind of diplomatic moves made by the other actor.

cooperative or conciliatory way to compromising moves and signals from the other side.[135]

Realists would expect that bullying strategies work better than reciprocating strategies, while others who analyze bargaining believe that this is unduly pessimistic. Such strategies are insufficiently sensitive, in this view, to the danger that hardline bargaining can lead to an escalation of coercive moves that will precipitate wars that neither side wants. In the analysis of forty crises mentioned earlier, bullying strategies led to war in almost two-thirds of the crises in which they were used, while reciprocating strategies achieved either a diplomatic victory or a compromise nearly two-thirds of the time. Does this mean that reciprocating strategies are always preferable? That depends partly on the priority that decision makers involved in international negotiations and crisis situations give to avoiding international war. Clearly, avoiding war is not always the highest priority for policymakers. Sometimes, for example, they may consider it even more important in confrontational situations to achieve victory or avoid defeat. And some evidence suggests that states are more likely to gain a victory by adopting a bullying strategy.[136] In any event, "it is clear that many international actors continue to view military force as a primary way of achieving their goals in contemporary international affairs."[137]

In short, although diplomats may take extreme positions that can backfire, sometimes such positions are effective bargaining tools and the decentralized character of the global political system, where every actor must ultimately protect its own interests, often tempts decision makers to adopt coercive bargaining strategies. But just as often, actors will bargain in a more conciliatory or reciprocating fashion, meeting coercive moves with coercive responses and cooperative signals with cooperation. Coercive strategies may help gain diplomatic victories (and avoid humiliating defeats), especially if the actors employing them seek a change in the status quo, but history also suggests that they carry a higher risk of war than do reciprocating strategies. Those more conciliatory strategies have produced substantially more peaceful outcomes in international disputes.

Diplomats and Their "Games"

diplomats Government officials engaged in negotiations and bargaining.

The job of negotiating across state boundaries is performed by **diplomats**, that is, those people officially engaged in negotiations or bargaining. Diplomats are often misunderstood and unappreciated. In the popular conception, the essence of the diplomatic profession is deceit ("An ambassador is an honest man sent to lie abroad for the commonwealth," Sir Henry Wotton observed in 1604), and professional diplomats are almost universally suspected of having lost touch with their home countries and the values of their citizens. They typically spend so much time out of the country that they only naturally become more sympathetic to the concerns of the "foreigners" with whom they live than does the average citizen who rarely leaves the country; that sympathy can easily be mistaken for diminished loyalty. Also, to the average person, diplomats seem to play a lot of silly games when they negotiate. At the truce negotiations during the Korean War, for example, diplomats spent considerable time and energy discussing the relative height of flags placed on the negotiating table. At the Paris peace talks aimed at ending the Vietnam War, diplomats wrangled for weeks (while soldiers and civilians died) over the shape of the bargaining table. Why do diplomats engage in such seemingly senseless behavior?

An important part of the answer involves a fundamental attitude that diplomats, as well as national leaders, seem to have concerning bargaining and negotiating with their counterparts. Although this concern is not made explicit in every case, diplomats involved in international bargaining are almost always less concerned about the issue immediately at hand than about the impact of the settlement on resolving future issues. Let us consider first the implicit bargaining that goes on between states (and their leaders) over crucial issues of peace and war.

It is highly probable, for example, that in 1939, Britain and France chose to take a hard line against Germany when it invaded Poland not because the leaders in those countries were primarily concerned about Poland but rather because they were worried about how the settlement between Poland and Germany would affect the resolution of future European territorial issues. Because they had already backed down in the

Diplomats from South Korea and North Korea engage in negotiations over the dismantling of North Korea's nuclear weapons program.

(Segye Lee-Won, Lorea Poll/AP Photo/AP Images)

face of several of Hitler's aggressive actions (for example, against Austria and Czechoslovakia), the British and the French felt that they could not allow Hitler to resolve his conflict with Poland with such ease that he would conclude that any future conflict could be settled just as easily and victoriously. Similarly, although Kennedy and his advisers were quite concerned about the missiles the Soviets had placed in Cuba in 1962, the missiles themselves were not their greatest concern. Rather, their main worry was that if they allowed the Soviets to get away with sneaking missiles into Cuba, it would be impossible to predict the Soviets' next scheme, and the ability of the United States to deter such schemes would be called into serious question.[138] At the time of the Vietnam War, Vietnam was not that valuable to the United States either economically or strategically. But U.S. policymakers at the time made clear, with their talk of Munich and the domino theory, that they were very concerned about how an unsatisfactory outcome of the Vietnam War might affect future conflicts. Subversives all over the world, it was believed, might be so encouraged by a North Vietnamese victory that similar wars of national liberation would break out in several other parts of the world.

Nations and their diplomatic representatives are especially concerned about the impact that settling current problems will have on future issues because precedents and the status quo have an almost sacred place in international relations. Diplomats engaged in bargaining are often concerned that a concession on the current issue will imply that concessions on similar or related issues in the future will be expected and will be very difficult to refuse. In short, because the status quo is so important, and because the settlement of an issue can establish a precedent for the settlement of future issues (that is, alter the status quo), diplomats are anxious to avoid giving the impression that they make concessions easily. The shape of the bargaining table may not itself be important, but concessions quickly granted on that issue may create expectations of quick concessions on other issues that will be difficult to overcome.

Some bargaining strategies may also seem puzzling. If, for example, a diplomat creates the impression that he or she is a little crazy for being so stubborn about the shape of the bargaining table, that may not be all bad. As one well-known scholar of bargaining in international politics points out, "If a man knocks at a door and says that he will stab himself on the porch unless given $10, he is more likely to get the $10 if his eyes are bloodshot."[139] In other words, the man is more likely to get the money if he somehow conveys the impression that he is actually crazy enough (because his eyes are bloodshot) to stab himself if refused. Similarly, if a diplomat can convey the impression that he or she is really a tough nut to crack even on such a seemingly minor issue as the shape of the bargaining table, that reputation may stand him or her in good stead during negotiations over the more important issues.

The silly games that diplomats seem to play are also a function of the symbolic value that the process holds and what it reflects about the underlying issues and definition of the conflict. The shape of the table, in other words, can say something about the shape of the conflict. If the table is round, all participants are seen as equal players with equal interests. If it is in the shape of a rectangle, the participants who get to sit at the "head" of the table are in some way already privileged and may see their interests prevail because of the way that the procedures are arranged.

Bargaining and negotiation is also often affected by who is not at the table: each side's constituents back home. Diplomats must return to their domestic political constituents (discussed more extensively in Chapter 5) at the end of negotiations and persuade them that the international agreement for which they bargained is legitimate. Because of this, negotiators are often looking over their shoulders to see how various positions and agreements are being received at home. In fact, they are often simultaneously bargaining with the other actors across from them at the negotiating table and with their domestic constituents to find an agreement that is acceptable to both. This dynamic has been termed *two-level games* (also discussed and defined in Chapter 5) and has been described as follows:

> Each national political leader appears at both game boards. Across the international table sit his foreign counterparts, and at his elbows sit diplomats and other international advisors. Around the domestic table behind him sit party and parliamentary figures, spokesmen for domestic agencies, representatives of key interest groups, and the leader's own political advisors. The unusual complexity of this two-level game is that moves that are rational for a player at one board (such as raising energy prices, conceding territory, or limiting auto imports) may be impolitic for that same player on the other board. . . . Any key player at the international table who is dissatisfied with the outcome may upset the game board; and conversely, any leader who fails to satisfy his fellow players at the domestic table risks being evicted from his seat.[140]

The constant balancing act that two-level games require in international negotiations means that agreements may be difficult to reach and the process may appear a bit convoluted. At times, however, negotiators successfully overcome these challenges and diplomats resolve international disputes.

SUMMARY

- In order to deal with the threat of conflict, states enter into alliances, build up their military arsenals, enter into arms control agreements, and otherwise bargain and negotiate differences with other actors in global politics.

- Coalitions of states emerge with regularity whenever and wherever independent sets of political entities interact. Alliances have often played a vital role in international politics. States may join alliances for a variety of reasons, including balancing against another power or perceived threat or bandwagoning together with a stronger power in order to share in the benefits of an alliance. Alliances may also form based on common ideological, economic, or political affinities. While history suggests that grand coalitions occur more often than one might expect, large coalitions can experience significant difficulty in maintaining the alliance relationships.

- Whether alliances serve the purpose of deterring aggression and creating peace is a question on which analysts seem to differ. History shows that when alliances seem to contribute to war, they will be avoided in the postwar era; when leaders think that a recent war could have been averted by an alliance, allies will be pursued in the postwar period.

- NATO is an alliance born in the Cold War but living on today and expanding with new members in central and eastern Europe. Considerable debate has arisen over the continuation, membership, and role of the alliance, with particular concern about Russian reaction.

- States build up their arsenals for offensive and defensive purposes, as well as for domestic political reasons. World military expenditures are currently on the increase, with the United States as the top spender. States produce and transfer a variety of conventional weapons. Arms transfers are currently declining but remain at high levels in some regions. The proliferation of small arms and land mines has been of high concern in many of the current conflicts. A variety of agreements to control conventional arms have been concluded, including the Moscow Treaty and the Anti-Personnel Landmines Treaty.

- The Cold War confrontation between the United States and the Soviet Union was the most dangerous and pervasive but still peaceful international rivalry in world history. Throughout the Cold War, both sides continued to stockpile nuclear weapons well beyond the point at which each had enough firepower to kill the other's citizens several times over. These stockpiles of weapons may have protected both sides from the threat of a disarming first strike, which might have deprived them of their ability to retaliate. This incredibly dangerous and expensive arms race ended without the global catastrophe that many argued it would ultimately bring. That is not an unprecedented outcome. Most arms races have not ended in international war.

- The end of the Cold War has not liberated the world entirely from the dangers of nuclear weapons and other weapons of mass destruction. Some argue that nuclear proliferation can stabilize tense relationships, just as they did in the Cold War. Nuclear proliferation may have made intentional wars less likely, but may also increase the probability of accidents and unintentional escalation to nuclear conflict. The Nuclear

Nonproliferation Treaty is an important agreement in the effort to control nuclear proliferation. Many countries are acquiring ballistic missiles and attempting to stockpile biological and chemical weapons. Some progress in dealing with these weapons has been made through the CWC and the BTWC.

● Diplomats are often tempted to engage in coercive bargaining and negotiation strategies in order to deter or compel their adversaries. However, coercive diplomacy requires successful communication of capability, commitment, and credibility, which may be difficult to achieve. Coercive bargaining strategies quite clearly carry a greater risk of international war, which can sometimes be avoided with more conciliatory reciprocating bargaining strategies. Diplomats' strategies can also be affected by domestic politics that constrain the moves they can make at the negotiating table.

KEY TERMS

weapons of mass
 destruction (WMD)   260
deterrence   260
compellence   260
alliances   260
balancing   261
bandwagoning   263
minimum winning
 coalitions   263
burden sharing   265
arms control   273
arms transfers   273
small arms   273
arms race   274
Conventional Armed
 Forces in Europe Treaty   275
international arms
 embargoes   276
Anti-Personnel Landmines
 Treaty   276
second-strike capability   278
Mutual Assured Destruction
 (MAD)   278
Strategic Defense
 Initiative (SDI)   278

prisoner's dilemma   279
game theory   279
Nuclear Nonproliferation
 Treaty (NPT)   284
Comprehensive Test
 Ban Treaty (CTBT)   288
Moscow Treaty   288
ballistic missile
 defense (BMD) system   289
chemical weapons   290
biological weapons   290
Missile Technology
 Control Regime
 (MTCR)   292
Chemical Weapons
 Convention (CWC)   293
Biological and Toxic
 Weapons Convention
 (BTWC)   293
bargaining and
 negotiation   294
"bullying" strategy   295
"reciprocating"
 strategy   295
diplomats   296

CHAPTER 9

Global Security Efforts: International Organizations, Law, and Ethics

I n addition to efforts by states to negotiate, build alliances, and engage in arms control, there are more global or collective attempts to address international conflict and security issues. International organizations such as the United Nations have been formed to coordinate efforts to maintain peace, and international law attempts to establish the rights of state and nonstate actors in global politics. Ideas about what is right and wrong (international ethics) and what is expected (international norms) also serve to govern state behavior and to avoid, or at least regulate, international conflict.

International Organizations and Collective Security

I nternational organizations, with permanent structures, membership, and procedures, are one way states have tried to institutionalize diplomacy and collective efforts for peace. The theory of liberalism (see Chapter 1) stresses the importance of international institutions in global politics as arenas for communication, diplomatic bargaining, and an alternative to conflict.[1]

Early Attempts to Organize for International Security

The first serious attempt to establish continuing international institutions to deal with threats to peace was made in the aftermath of the Napoleonic Wars at the beginning of the nineteenth century. The Congress of Vienna (1815), a meeting attended only by the major powers, dealt with several unsettled political problems; states agreed to periodic consultations that became known as the Concert of Europe. This agreement led to a series of international meetings in the next decade that were unprecedented, because they occurred during times of peace. But the grand coalition that served as the basis for the concert was prone to disunity. Although the concert did successfully establish the precedent of peacetime consultations, after the first decade of its existence it met only in the aftermath of wars to arrange settlements.

International peace conferences at The Hague in 1899 and 1907 were meant to deal more directly with the threat of war by decreasing armament levels. They failed. Still, they began an important trend toward a democracy of sorts in international diplomacy, because for the first time at such conferences, small states were invited and thus given a voice. Only twenty-six states attended the 1899 conference, but forty-four sent delegations to the 1907 meeting. The latter meeting might be considered the precedent for the establishment of institutions such as the General Assemblies of the League of Nations and the United Nations.

Collective Security: Principles and Prerequisites

The next Hague conference was scheduled for 1915. It was not held, for obvious reasons, but the process leading to the outbreak of the First

World War convinced many leaders that a permanent international organization was needed. In retrospect, many political leaders and scholars concluded that the First World War had occurred because the decision makers involved had lost control of a situation that none of them wanted to see culminate in a war. If, according to this reasoning, there had been a chance to talk things out, a cooling-off period, none of the conflicts that created the crisis would have proved insoluble. When designing the first major collective attempt at governance through an international institution, the League of Nations, they drew on the concept of **collective security,** which can be defined briefly as the idea that "aggressive and unlawful use of force by any nation against any nation will be met by the combined force of all other nations."[2] Collective security arrangements attempt to safeguard the collective interest of all states against the narrow self-interest of one state that might profit from aggression by inhibiting war through the threat of collective action.

collective security   Idea that aggressive use of force by any state will be met by combined force of all other states.

There are several logical and theoretical requirements for a successful collective security system.[3] For example, if any state that uses force aggressively is to be opposed by the combined force of all other nations, there must be some universally agreed definition of aggression. Otherwise, it will be impossible for the world community to agree when the time has come to impose sanctions. There must also be an international institution that can make authoritative decisions about disputes and designate aggressors. As well, there must be an institution or authoritative process for allocating the costs of resisting aggression. The states of the world must be so committed to peace and so loyal to the world community that they will be willing to forsake their own short-range interests by imposing sanctions against states that are involved in disputes of no immediate concern to them. Also, if the collective security ideal is to be upheld, the members of a collective security organization must be willing to give up the right to fight to change the status quo and to fight against any state *not* willing to give up that right. Alliances are, strictly speaking, logically incompatible with the collective security ideal. That ideal implies a willingness by all states to oppose *any* state committing aggression, whereas alliances involve precommitments to avoid military action against certain states. Finally, if collective security is to preserve peace, there should be a diffusion of power in the international system so that one or two very powerful states cannot withstand the threat of force by the world community.

Just listing some of the logical requirements for a successful collective security system reveals why the League of Nations and the United Nations experienced difficulty maintaining such a system. There is no universally accepted definition of *aggression.* International lawyers have been trying to devise one for more than fifty years. Although the UN General Assembly adopted resolutions in 1969 and 1974 including such a definition,[4] agreement on this definition or, one suspects, on any other is virtually impossible to maintain when the time comes to apply it to concrete cases. In short, "it is sometimes difficult in a crisis to determine who is the troublemaker and who is the victim."[5]

In addition, while political leaders are quite willing to make verbal commitments to the cause of world peace, their actions sometimes reveal that peace is lower on their list of priorities. Leaders are more firmly committed to national security, justice, democracy, national self-determination, or their own credibility. Commitment to the status quo is much less than universal, and several states are unwilling to give up the right to fight to change it. In fact, it might even be argued that aggression is not always a bad thing. "There are good reasons," one analyst argues, "to applaud the 1979 Vietnamese invasion of Cambodia, since it drove the murderous Pol Pot from power."[6] Alliances, and the precommitments they involve, are widespread in the existing international system. Furthermore, even long-standing international friendships not formalized by alliances could cause problems for a collective security system.[7]

The League of Nations

The League of Nations was the first real experiment in collective security and experienced difficulties in applying collective security principles. During the First World War, private societies advocating the establishment of the League sprang up in Britain, France, Italy, and the United States. U.S. President Woodrow Wilson included the creation of such an organization as one of his famous "Fourteen Points" for postwar peace outlined in an address to the U.S. Congress. The South African leader Jan Smuts published a pamphlet calling for the creation of the League, and it proved to be influential, perhaps because of good timing (It was published

A cartoon from the time of the League of Nations recognized the significance, and the irony, of the absence of the United States from the organization.

(Punch Magazine, 10 December 1919)

THE GAP IN THE BRIDGE.

in the month between Wilson's arrival in Europe and the beginning of the peace conference).

The structure of the League was much like that outlined in Smuts' publication. Its three major organs were an assembly, a council, and a secretariat. The assembly consisted of delegations from all the member states, and its main duties involved the election of new members to the organization, debate and discussion of political and economic questions of international interest, and preparation of the annual budget. The council was dominated by the great powers, but it also contained nonpermanent members whose identity and number varied throughout the history of the League. Its most important duty was the resolution of international disputes, and to that end it had the power to advise the member states to institute sanctions against any state committing aggression. The secretariat was an international civil service that handled administrative details for the League and compiled information relevant to the various problems and issues with which the League was confronted.

Under Article 10 of the League's covenant, members pledged "to respect and preserve against external aggression the territorial integrity and existing political independence of all Members of the League."[8] Despite this pledge, member states did not internalize the ideal of collective security:

> Members reestablished alliance systems and refused to take the necessary institutional actions to check aggression. The League was unable to reverse Japan's takeover of Manchuria; the Italian invasion of Abyssinia; the German remilitarization of the Rhineland and subsequent takeover of the Sudetenland; or the intervention by Italy, Germany, and the Soviet Union in the Spanish civil war. The gradual buildup of war machines proceeded apace, and the collapse of the fledgling collective-security system was complete with the German invasion of Poland in 1939. The League broke down and the international community headed down the road to World War II, although the formal dissolution of the League did not occur until 1946.[9]

Although the covenant provided for potentially effective economic and military sanctions against aggressors, it allowed each member to decide whether aggression had been committed and, if so, if sanctions would be applied. These loopholes were not in the covenant as a result of oversight. The founders of the League insisted on them, and it seems unlikely that the absence of loopholes would have made any real difference to the behavior of the League's members. Even if the covenant's articles had mandated sanctions, it is unlikely that many states would have been inclined to apply them.

Much the same kind of argument can be made about the most notorious flaw in the structure of the League: the absence of the United States. This absence was brought about by President Wilson's unwillingness to consult and compromise with the U.S. Senate when the covenant was being drafted, by a bitter personal feud between Wilson and Senator Henry Cabot Lodge, and by widespread isolationist sentiment among a significant number of Americans. After the demise of the League and the ensuing world war, a powerful belief developed that the refusal of the United States to join the League was a crucial cause of its failure. If the United States had not shunned its duty, according to this argument, the League might have been powerful enough to withstand the aggressive policies of Japan, Italy, and Germany.

This thesis can be questioned. The desire of the United States in 1931 to avoid provoking Japan after it invaded Manchuria differed very little from Britain's desire to avoid undue provocation of Italy after it invaded Ethiopia in 1935. It is by no means certain whether membership in the League really would have induced the United States to adopt policies other than those it actually pursued in the Manchurian and Ethiopian crises.[10] In other words, it does not seem likely that mere formal membership in the League would have changed U.S. foreign policy very much. Given that the major threats to the League occurred when the United States was in the throes of the Great Depression, it seems more likely that if the United States had been a member, it might have withdrawn from the League rather than energetically pursuing its obligations under the covenant. Nevertheless, the absence of the United States may have done much to generally damage the legitimacy and credibility of the League. With the United States present in the League, aggressive states might not have taken the action they did, and other states, such as Britain, might have reacted differently to provocations.

The League will always be most famous for its failures, but it was not completely ineffective. It set precedents, in the establishment of the secretariat and in the way the entire organization was structured, that provided valuable lessons for those who later established the United Nations. The League is well remembered for the disputes it did *not* settle, but it did play a role in resolving some conflicts, such as the one between Greece and Bulgaria in 1925.

The United Nations

True or not, the idea that the failure of the United States to enter the League was a terrible mistake that played a significant role in bringing about the Second World War became widely accepted in the United States. The best evidence is the energetic manner in which the U.S. government strove for the creation of the League's successor, the United Nations. By October 1943, the governments of the United States, Great Britain, the Soviet Union, and China had declared their firm intention to create an international security organization after the war. The intention was reaffirmed at several wartime meetings of the Allied coalition, and the final charter was hammered out at a meeting in San Francisco in the spring of 1945.

UN Charter Document that delineates purpose, rules, and institutions of the United Nations.

Security Council UN institution responsible for international peace and security. It is composed of five permanent members with veto power and ten nonpermanent members.

General Assembly Institution in which all member states are equally represented.

Secretariat UN administrative-bureaucratic institution, headed by the secretary-general.

International Court of Justice (World Court) UN-associated tribunal for settlement of disputes between states.

The **UN Charter** was completed in June, and by July, the U.S. Senate had approved it by a vote of eighty-nine to two. The contrast with the U.S. reaction to the League some twenty-five years earlier could hardly have been starker. The distinction was made even sharper by the choice of New York City as the home of the new United Nations.

The structure of the United Nations shares many features with that of the League (see Figure 9.1). The **Security Council,** according to the charter, has the primary responsibility for international peace and security. The five permanent members—China, France, Great Britain, Russia, and the United States—have the power of veto in the Security Council. Ten nonpermanent members also serve on the Security Council and vote on resolutions, but they cannot veto. The **General Assembly** is composed of delegations from all the member states, which by 2006, numbered 192 (see Figure 9.2), and has three principal duties. It determines the budget of the organization and (along with the Security Council) selects the secretary-general, who is the administrative leader of the United Nations, the members of the International Court of Justice, and new members of the United Nations. The General Assembly also debates any topic within the scope of the charter. Finally, the **Secretariat,** headed by the secretary-general (currently Ban Ki-moon), serves as an international civil service charged with administering the organization. The secretary-general makes an annual report to the General Assembly and has the right to speak to it at any time, as well as to propose resolutions to the committees of the General Assembly. The secretary-general also has the authority to bring to the attention of the Security Council any matter that in his or her opinion threatens the maintenance of international peace and security.

The **International Court of Justice (World Court),** composed of fifteen judges elected by the General Assembly and the Security Council, has the two-fold function of serving as a tribunal for the final settlement of disputes submitted to it by the parties and acting in an advisory capacity to the General Assembly, the Security Council, and other organs on questions of a legal nature that might be referred to it.[11] Decisions made by the court are binding, but no state can be brought before the court without its consent. "Some states have accepted the compulsory jurisdiction of the Court in advance under the Optional Clause of the Statute (Article 36), but because of a myriad of reservations and amendments, the general rule is that only those states that are willing to have their controversies adjudicated by the Court will be parties to cases before it."[12]

The United Nations was designed to protect, not challenge, states and state sovereignty. In fact, the United Nations legitimizes sovereignty in that states (not people, nations, regions, or other international actors) are members. In addition, the UN Charter was set up to protect state boundaries. Part of Article 2 of the UN Charter reads, "All members shall refrain in their international relations from the threat or use of force against the territorial integrity or political independence of any state." Chapter VII of

Figure 9.1 Organization of the United Nations

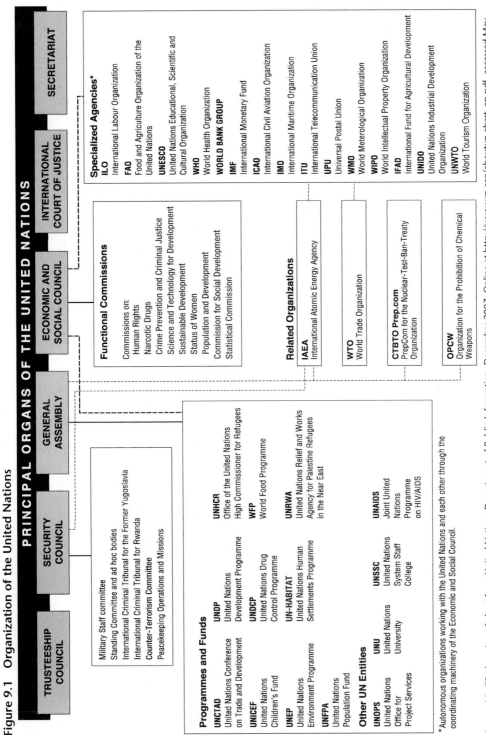

Source: Modified version of chart from United Nations Department of Public Information, December 2007. Online at http://www.un.org/aboutun.chart_en.pdf, accessed May 11, 2009. Copyright © 2007, United Nations. Reproduced with permission.

Figure 9.2 Membership in the United Nations, 1945–2006

Source: Based on Robert E. Riggs and Jack C. Plano, *The United Nations International Organization and World Politics,* 2nd ed. (Belmont, Calif.: Wadsworth, 1994), p. 46. Data for 1993 and 2006 supplied by the authors.

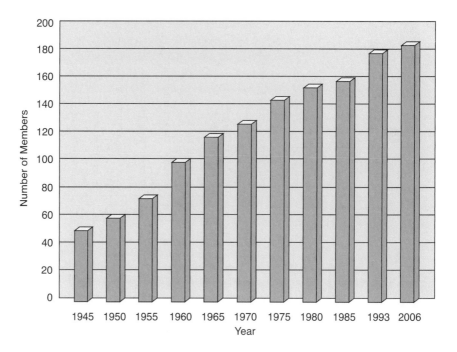

the charter spells out the principle of collective security by stating that the Security Council "may take such action by air, sea, or land forces as may be necessary to maintain or restore international peace and security. Such action may include demonstrations, blockade, and other operations by air, sea, or land forces of Members of the United Nations." Also in Chapter VII, Article 43 of the UN Charter specifies how the member nations are to go about creating a military force for the organization: "All Members of the United Nations . . . undertake to make available to the Security Council, on its call and in accordance with a special agreement or agreements, armed forces, assistance, and facilities, including rights of passage, necessary for the purpose of maintaining international peace and security."

This arrangement, though, is not as airtight as it might appear. First, the military forces, which according to the charter are to be provided to the Security Council, have never materialized. Second, because every permanent member of the Security Council has the right to veto proposals before the council, it is virtually impossible to implement sanctions against one of the major powers. Indeed, the United Nations is a modified form of collective security, because the veto power of the five permanent Security Council members means that collective action could never occur against one of these states. In effect, not all UN members stand equal risk of punishment for violating another state's borders.

The veto power, combined with the Cold War rivalry between the United States and the Soviet Union, has meant that the United Nations has not worked to ensure collective security for most of its history.

During the Cold War, intervention of one state by another divided the two superpowers, and one or the other would veto Security Council action against its ally. During the first two decades of the existence of the United Nations, the United States never used its veto in the Security Council, whereas the Soviet Union vetoed proposals brought to that body 103 times. From 1966 to 1975, the United States used its veto power twelve times, and the Soviet Union vetoed eleven propositions. Between 1976 and 1985, the United States vetoed proposals brought before the Security Council thirty-seven times, while the Soviets vetoed only seven measures. And from 1986 to 1990, the United States exercised its veto power twenty-three times, while the Soviet Union never vetoed a single measure. For most of the post–World War II period, the United States and the former Soviet Union were so powerful that they could not be intimidated by any implicit or explicit threats made by the United Nations in the name of collective security. When the Soviets invaded Hungary in 1956, Czechoslovakia in 1968, and Afghanistan in 1979, and when the United States invaded the Dominican Republic in 1965, Grenada in 1983, and Panama in 1989, the United Nations could do little to deter the invasions, even if it had been able to come to some kind of nearly universal agreement on the culpability of either superpower.

In fact, Chapter VII of the UN Charter has been invoked only twice. The first time was in 1950, when North Korea invaded South Korea. Although the Soviet Union surely wanted to veto any action against North Korea, it was boycotting Security Council meetings (in protest of the seating of the Republic of China, or Taiwan, as the permanent representative of China instead of the People's Republic of China). The UN coordinated collective action proceeded against the North. The Soviet Union learned its lesson and never missed a Security Council meeting again, exercising its veto (as did the United States) to protect its friends. It was not until the end of the Cold War that the five permanent members could agree on a Chapter VII resolution, this time condemning and coordinating action against Iraq for its invasion of Kuwait in 1990.

In one important way, the structure of the United Nations is better suited to the maintenance of collective security than was the League's. The UN Charter

> incorporates more elaborate and ambitious provisions for sanctions. Instead of requiring states to impose economic penalties if and when they unilaterally recognize the existence of aggression, and permitting them the exercise of voluntary participation in military sanctions, the Charter brings all enforcement activity under the aegis of the Security Council, conferring on that body the authority to identify the aggressor, to order members to engage in nonmilitary coercion, and itself to put into action the military forces presumably to be placed at its permanent disposal by members of the organization.[13]

Yet attempts by the United Nations to identify aggressors or targets of collective action have proved difficult. The International Court of Justice can hear only those cases willingly brought to it by both sides of the dispute. The Security Council, as noted, has been hamstrung by the veto any permanent member can impose. The General Assembly is large and unwieldy and, unlike the Security Council, does not have the authority to oblige states to carry out sanctions.

Peacekeeping as an Alternative to Collective Security

Exclusive concentration on UN difficulties in establishing a collective security system as envisioned by the writers of its charter might lead to an overly pessimistic conclusion regarding the organization's contribution to peace. The United Nations has at least partially filled the void created by the failure of its efforts to institute collective security with a technique known as **peacekeeping.** Although the UN Charter says nothing about peacekeeping, the technique was used repeatedly to deal with conflicts during the Cold War era that might otherwise have led to dangerous confrontations between the superpowers.

peacekeeping Troop deployment intended to halt armed conflict or prevent its recurrence in conflict areas.

The origins of peacekeeping can be traced to the earliest days of the United Nations from 1946 to 1949, when it sent small numbers of military personnel to monitor cease-fires and engage in fact-finding missions in the Balkans, Palestine, Indonesia, India, and Pakistan.[14] But the first major example of a peacekeeping force was created in response to a crisis in the Middle East. When Egyptian leader Gamal Abdel Nasser nationalized the Suez Canal in 1956, Great Britain, France, and Israel (each for its own reasons) joined in an attack on Egypt. Much to the surprise of those three states, the United States *and* the Soviet Union demanded that the attack be terminated immediately. Collective action against the attackers was impossible, because France and Great Britain would veto any Chapter VII resolution in the Security Council. The two superpowers also cooperated in getting the General Assembly to pass resolutions calling for an end to the hostilities. To implement the resolutions (and to avoid the introduction of military forces from one or both of the superpowers), the General Assembly created the UN Emergency Force (UNEF). Made up of military forces from ten to twenty-four states at different times in its existence, none of which came from the five permanent members of the Security Council, it was stationed on the Egyptian-Israeli border until 1967. The importance of its contribution to peace in the area may be suggested by the fact that shortly after it was removed, war between Israel and Egypt ensued.[15]

Since 1956, the United Nations has used peacekeeping forces in a number of hot spots around the world. The primary goal of a peacekeeping operation (also called "blue helmets," for the color of the helmets and berets that peacekeeping soldiers wear) is to halt armed conflict or prevent its recurrence. It achieves this goal by acting as a physical barrier, a "thin blue line," between hostile parties and monitoring their military movements. Peacekeeping forces have been normally composed of troops from small or nonaligned states. . . . Lightly armed, these neutral troops were symbolically deployed between belligerents who had agreed to stop fighting; they rarely used force and then only in self-defense and as a last resort. Rather than being based on any military prowess, the influence of UN peacekeepers in this period resulted from the cooperation of belligerents mixed with the moral weight of the international community.[16]

A secondary purpose of peacekeeping is to create a stable environment for negotiations.[17] The United Nations sent a force to Lebanon in 1958, making it easier for the United States to withdraw the Marines it had sent into that country to support the pro-Western Lebanese regime of the time.

In 1960, the United Nations became rather deeply involved in the civil war that broke out in the Congo after Belgian colonial rule had ended. In this case, UN troops became directly involved in the fighting (as they had not in the conflict between Egypt and Israel), and the undertaking became so controversial that the Soviet Union and France refused to pay their share of the expenses for this particular peacekeeping effort. Despite that setback and the financial and political crisis it created for the United Nations, peacekeeping missions have been organized quite often since the UN involvement in the Congo. UN troops were sent to Yemen in 1963, to Cyprus in 1964, and again to the Middle East in the wake of the Yom Kippur War in 1973 and after the invasion of Lebanon by Israel in 1978.[18]

UN peacekeeping forces, shown here in 2001, have been in Lebanon since 1958.

(Courtney Kealy/Getty Images)

After the creation of the United Nations Interim Force in Lebanon (UNIFIL), a decade passed before the United Nations mounted another peacekeeping mission.[19] By 1987, there were only five UN peacekeeping missions in the world, staffed by fewer than 10,000 troops at a cost of $250 million a year. Even as late as 1992, there were only 11,500 UN peacekeepers in the world. Then an explosion of UN activity began. By 1994, some 80,000 UN troops were involved in eighteen peacekeeping missions around the world at a cost of more than $3.3 billion.[20] Overall, since the UN's inception, "Well over 750,000 military and civilian police personnel and thousands of other civilians from 111 countries have served in UN peacekeeping operations."[21]

Although peacekeeping missions are not an attempt to resolve conflicts (and some missions have been in place for almost sixty years), most UN efforts in this area have been successful at creating buffers and maintaining cease-fires. Indeed, one systematic study of more than 350 cases of post–World War II peacekeeping concluded that "peacekeeping works, particularly after the Cold War when most of the attempts to keep peace after civil wars have been made. The presence of international personnel is not a silver bullet, of course, it does not guarantee lasting peace in every case, but it does tend to make peace more likely to last, and to last longer."[22] Peacekeeping is a rather tentative and piecemeal approach compared to the grander sweep of collective security. But it may be an especially important function for the United Nations to carry out in the contemporary era, when most conflicts are internal wars.

And, until recently, the United Nations has not been equipped to implement collective security. Its reaction to the Iraqi annexation of Kuwait in August 1990 suggested that it may be possible for the organization to move beyond peacekeeping and institute a working collective security system. That is essentially what President George H. W. Bush meant when he responded to that crisis by asserting that out of these troubled times, a "new world order can emerge."[23] A working collective security system might come into being, because it now may be possible for the major powers to cooperate in the establishment of such a system, in which an aggressive move, such as Iraq's against Kuwait, will be met by the determined resistance of the world community, working through the institutions of the United Nations.

It is also possible that Iraq's attack on Kuwait created an ideal situation for the concept of collective security that is not likely to be repeated. "The term 'war' still conjures up an image of massed armies clashing on the battlefield. But this kind of war is now largely a thing of the past. The vast majority of violent disputes today (and quite likely of tomorrow) are . . . civil wars."[24] The situation in Iraq in 2003 was not a case for collective security; the debate in the United Nations was over intervention to force compliance with UN resolutions, not about collectively defending the sovereignty of an invaded country. If it is true that international war is now largely a thing of the past, that is a milestone in human events that should not go unnoticed. But if more "old-fashioned" wars of the kind precipitated by Iraq's attack on Kuwait should arise, it is fair to wonder how effective the reaction of the United Nations will be. Collective security is likely to be ineffective so long as the aggressor is a permanent member of the Security Council, a client state of a permanent member, or a country able to amass eight votes from the Security Council's fifteen members.

Peacemaking in Ethnic Conflicts and Failed States

peacemaking Attempt to force or negotiate settlement between warring factions, often in an internal conflict.

When the United Nations intervenes in civil wars, such as those in the former Yugoslavia and Somalia, it often engages in **peacemaking** rather than peacekeeping, because in these places there is no peace to be kept, and in the case of failed states, no stable political authority to confront or defend. The founders of the United Nations certainly did not intend for the organization to be used in internal conflicts, just as they did not envision peacekeeping between states. In Article 2 of Chapter I, the charter reads, "Nothing contained in the present Charter shall authorize the United Nations to intervene in matters which are essentially within the domestic jurisdiction of any state or shall require the Members to submit to such matters to settlement under the present Charter." In spite of this, UN peacemaking operations in the 1990s "were qualitatively and quantitatively different from UN operations that were backed by states during the Cold War. They indicated that the consent of the parties cannot be assumed; the military effectiveness required from and the dangers faced by UN military forces go far beyond the parameters of traditional lightly armed peacekeepers."[25] The question of how well the United Nations is suited to the task of peacemaking as opposed to peacekeeping has been asked numerous times during the increase in UN activity in the post–Cold War era.[26]

After the UN presence in the conflict in Somalia in the early 1990s, for example, a British journalist noted that U.S. and UN intervention in Somalia had flooded the market with arms and put the war on hold, but that when the Americans pulled out, "the politics of Somalia reverted to the *status quo ante*, except that the rich and powerful had become richer and better armed."[27] He also predicted that succumbing to the temptation to send international help to the refugees from the slaughter-filled civil war between the Hutus and the Tutsis in Rwanda would have similarly baneful effects. "Free supplies do not stay free for long. . . . There are already reports of Hutu militias regrouping. They will establish new patterns of leadership, fear, and loyalty. Relief camps motivated by political exile inevitably are umbrellas for revanchism."[28]

This turned out to be an accurate prediction. Some two years later, *The New York Times* published the following account:

> From the start, the Rwandan camps in Zaire have been controlled by the same forces that carried out the genocide in Rwanda and that swear to continue it. . . . The camps, under the flag of the United Nations, became bases for a vicious guerrilla war against Rwanda and local populations in Zaire. . . . Yet for more than two years, the international community has turned a blind eye and poured $1 million a day into supporting them.[29]

Additional reports suggested that the problem of the camps was solved only when the aid workers had fled and Tutsi fighters were able to preempt the arrival of more peacekeepers. "The Tutsis were afraid that once Westerners arrived, they would impose a cease-fire and freeze the situation with the Hutu militia in control once again of the seething camps. They were afraid of a repeat of 1994: Save the children, save the murderers, save the embers of civil war, prolong forever the exile and suffering of the refugees."[30]

In short, at least according to this interpretation, the role of the United Nations in the tragedy that unfolded in Rwanda from 1994 to 1996 and the efforts of the international community were insufficient to prevent a terrible holocaust. The efforts to respond to the refugees created by the civil war ultimately succeeded mostly in substantially prolonging a painful, brutal status quo based on camps that could not have survived (probably) without the intervention of UN and other international agencies; the problem was not resolved until the UN and other relief workers were removed from the situation, after which a rather quick solution was achieved.

The United Nations was also severely criticized when it found itself attempting to protect "safe havens" while war waged on in the former Yugoslavia in the early to mid-1990s. Despite the presence of almost 50,000 peacekeepers, the UN mission was unable to protect the safe havens or prevent ethnic cleansing. "The idea of 'safe areas' brought derision because the least safe places in the Balkans were under UN control. The ultimate ignominy arrived in summer 1995 when two of these enclaves in eastern Bosnia were overrun by Bosnian Serbs whose tactics included mass executions of Muslims. Shortly before this, Serbs had chained UN blue helmets to strategic targets and thereby prevented NATO air raids."[31]

These challenges to UN peacekeeping missions in the 1990s created a temporary mood of caution in the United Nations and the Security Council as the end of the twentieth century neared.[32] The number of UN peacekeeping operations and peacekeepers in the world was reduced and the annual peacekeeping budget of the United Nations fell as well. In addition, unpaid bills for peacekeeping operations piled up. Finally, there was a growing feeling that internal problems within countries might be better dealt with by multinational forces from the region within which a given country falls.[33] Thus, in response to chaos in Albania in early 1997, Italian troops led a peacekeeping force of sorts into that country. The North Atlantic Treaty Organization (NATO) has performed UN-like peacekeeping missions in Bosnia and Kosovo. And in Africa, Nigerian troops led a peacekeeping force sent to Liberia in 1990 by the Economic Community of West African States.[34]

This scaling back of UN peacekeeping operations, however, was temporary. It seems clear that the United Nations feels that it cannot overlook continuing threats to international security, however challenging they may be. Table 9.1 lists the peacekeeping missions in operation in 2009. New missions established in recent years in Darfur Sudan, Haiti, and the Democratic Republic of Congo suggest that the United Nations continues to be involved in difficult internal conflicts. In Kosovo, the UN mission that was established in 1999 after NATO military intervention served to coordinate efforts by the European Union, the Organization on Security and Cooperation in Europe, and several UN agencies to establish civil administration for basic services and political stability.

TABLE 9.1

UN Peacekeeping Operations in 2009 (Year Established)

Africa

1. **MINURSO** United Nations Mission for the Referendum in Western Sahara (1991)
2. **MONUC** United Nations Organization Mission in the Democratic Republic of the Congo (1999)
3. **UNMIL** United Nations Mission in Liberia (2003)
4. **UNOCI** United Nations Operation in Cote d'Ivoire (2004)
5. **UNMIS** United Nations Mission in the Sudan (2005)
6. **UNAMID African Union/United Nations Hybrid Operation in Darfur (2007)**
7. **MINURCAT** United Nations Mission in the Central African Republic and Chad (2007)

Americas

8. **MINUSTAH** United Nations Stabilization Mission in Haiti (2004)

Asia

9. **UNMOGIP** United Nations Military Observer Group in India and Pakistan (1949)
10. **UNMIT** United Nations Integrated Mission in Timor-Leste (2006)

Europe

11. **UNOMIG** United Nations Observer Mission in Georgia (1993)
12. **UNMIK** United Nations Interim Administration Mission in Kosovo (1999)
13. **UNFICYP** United Nations Peacekeeping Force in Cyprus (1964)

Middle East

14. **UNIFIL** United Nations Interim Force in Lebanon (1978)
15. **UNDOF** United Nations Disengagement Observer Force—Golan Heights (1974)
16. **UNTSO** United Nations Truce Supervision Organization—Middle East (1948)

Source: United Nations, United Nations Peacekeeping, Background Note, 31 May 2009, http://www .un.org/Depts/dpko/dpko/bnote.htm, accessed June 18, 2009. Copyright © 2009, United Nations. Reproduced with permission.

Similarly, after the violence that marked East Timor's independence from Indonesia, the UN mission

> was exceedingly ambitious and wide-ranging. It was empowered to exercise all legislative and executive powers and judicial authority; establish an effective civil administration; assist in the development of civil and social services; provide security and maintain law and order; ensure the coordination and delivery of humanitarian assistance, rehabilitation, and development assistance; promote sustainable development; and build the foundation for a stable liberal democracy. To carry out this mandate, authorization was given for a military component of up to 8,950 troops and 200 observers and a civilian police component of up to 1,640 personnel.[35]

state-building Efforts to create stable, legitimate political authority and institutions in post-conflict situations.

These new missions suggest another way UN peacekeeping is changing. Not only is peace to be kept, and sometimes made, but the United Nations is engaged in **state-building** by trying to provide the conditions, training, and mandate for the creation of a stable, democratic political authority. Whether the organization can have long-term success in these efforts remains to be seen.

Other Ways the United Nations Attempts to Promote Peace

Besides responding to aggression, issuing blue helmets to keep ceasefires, and rebuilding war-torn societies, the United Nations engages in a number of activities designed to promote peace through prevention. An important, original goal of the United Nations was to create norms against violence. By signing the charter, states agree to settle disputes by peaceful means. The charter codifies a belief, fairly new to the international community in the twentieth century when the League of Nations and the United Nations were created, that the use of force except in the case of self-defense is unacceptable. Obviously, this norm is not powerful enough to prevent war entirely, but it does seem to affect how states justify war and may work to inhibit war in some circumstances (the role of norms in global politics will be discussed more generally later in this chapter).

The United Nations also seeks to provide a forum for debate as an alternative to fighting. In the United Nations, states can publicly air their points of view and privately negotiate their differences. The United Nations also intervenes diplomatically to avert the outbreak of war by sending inquiries (fact-finding missions) and by mediation (making suggestions about possible solutions and acting as an intermediary between sides) and arbitration (rendering a judgment that all sides agree in advance to accept) of disputes between states. It also attempts to pressure states by instituting diplomatic and economic sanctions. For example,

> UN-imposed sanctions against South Africa reflected the judgment that racial discrimination (apartheid) was considered a threat to peace. Limited economic sanctions, an embargo on arms sales to South Africa, embargoes against South African athletic teams, and selective divestment were all part of a visible campaign to isolate South Africa. These acts exerted pressure whose impact is difficult to quantify, although observers usually assert that they have played an important role [in the dismantling of the apartheid government].[36]

positive peace Resolution of underlying causes of conflict.

In addition, the United Nations seeks to create **positive peace**, which means not just the absence of war, but the resolution of the underlying conditions from which conflict emerges. In this way, it promotes economic and social development and humanitarian affairs. According to the United Nations, although most people associate the United Nations with the issues of peace and security, the vast majority of its resources are devoted to economic development, social development and sustainable development. . . . Guiding the United Nations work is the conviction that lasting international peace and security are possible only if the economic and social well-being of people everywhere is assured.[37]

Economic and Social Council (ECOSOC) UN institutions for economic and social programs on such issues as development, employment, health, and education.

The **Economic and Social Council (ECOSOC)** handles the economic and social programs of the United Nations, serving as a clearinghouse and central administrative body for its associated functional organizations, such as the International Labor Organization (ILO), the International Monetary Fund (IMF), and the World Health Organization (WHO). The United Nations also regularly holds conferences on the environment, population, women, economic development, refugees, and children in an effort to address some of the underlying causes of international conflict, instability, and insecurity. Attention to these issues that are not traditionally considered security matters is important according to both liberal and feminist theories, as discussed in Chapter 1.

The Future of the United Nations

In addition to the criticisms of UN activities in Somalia, Yugoslavia, and Rwanda in the mid-1990s, questions about the future of the United Nations continue to be raised. A critical concern is the funding for the United Nations. As Secretary-General Javier Perez de Cuellar noted at the end of the Cold War, "It is a great irony that the UN is on the brink of insolvency at the very time the world community has entrusted the organization with new and unprecedented responsibilities."[38] By 1992, 80 percent of the UN members had not paid their dues. The United States has been one of the largest UN debtors. Beginning in the 1980s, the United States has at times withheld payment from various UN programs to protest some of the organization's activities. Specifically, under pressure from domestic interest groups, successive administrations barred the use of U.S. funds to international organizations involved in family planning and population control, charging that abortion was being promoted through these activities. In addition, members of the U.S. Congress perceive a disparity between what the United States contributes to the UN budget and the influence of those states within the organization that contribute so much less. Because dues are based on the size of a nation's economy, the United States has annually paid about 25 percent of the UN budget. By the early 1990s, it was paying over 30 percent of the organization's peacekeeping bills. Even more irksome, perhaps, from the point of view of U.S. lawmakers, the eight largest contributors to the United Nations provide 73 percent of the budget but have only 4 percent of the votes in the General Assembly. And the remaining 177 countries in the assembly, which can dominate the proceedings with their votes, contribute only 27 percent of the budget (see Figure 9.3). Yet those countries that contribute only a small portion determine the budget's size and allocation. In the words of Senator Jesse Helms, chairman of the U.S. Senate Foreign Relations Committee, who was highly critical of the United Nations, its annual budget is "voted on by the General Assembly, where the United States has no veto, and where every nation whether democratic or dictatorial, no matter how much or how little it contributes to the United Nations has an equal vote."[39]

In response to this situation, "Under an act of Congress in 1996, the United States stopped paying its 31 percent assessment for peacekeeping operations, unilaterally lowering it to 25 percent and falling steadily deeper into debt. The Clinton administration also made a deal with Congress to cut regular budget payments from 25 percent to 22."[40] Japan, the second-largest contributor, has also threatened to cut its UN payments.[41] The United Nations remains in financial crisis today. Although the United States paid much of its past dues to the United Nations in 2001, it still owed $394 million in 2008.[42] The UN's financial crisis demonstrates how vulnerable international organizations like the United Nations are to states and their domestic politics. The United Nations depends on states to voluntarily contribute funds and other resources, such as peacekeeping troops.

UN supporters point out that as profligate as the United Nations may be in its financial dealings, analyzed in context, it is arguably a bargain. The budget for the Secretariat, for example, is only for a fraction of budgets for major cities, such as New York. Peacekeeping is expensive, but miniscule compared to the U.S. defense budget. According to the United Nations, "A study by the U.S. Government Accountability Office estimated that it would cost the United States approximately twice as much as the UN to conduct a peacekeeping operation similar to the UN Stabilization Mission in Haiti (MINUSTAH). . . ."[43] The peacekeeping budget in 2000 amounted to 30 cents per person in the world.

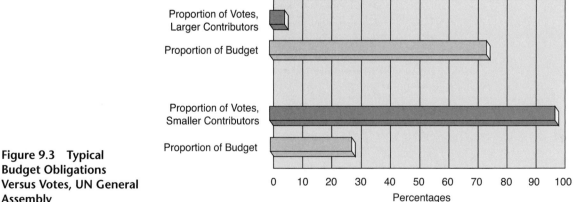

Figure 9.3 Typical Budget Obligations Versus Votes, UN General Assembly

Another criticism of the United Nations that may shape its future concerns its structure and representation. It can, for example, plausibly be argued that the United Nations is too dominated by rich and powerful countries like the United States and that this undermines its legitimacy.[44] Observed from the point of view of poorer countries, the United Nations is under the control primarily of the rich, industrialized countries of the West. Many feel that the representation in the Security Council is anachronistic. The five states that have a veto were selected on the basis of the results of the Second World War. Not only does this leave out major regional powers in the developing world (such as Brazil, India, Nigeria, and Egypt), but it also leaves out states that are clearly economic heavyweights (such as Japan and Germany) and states that contribute heavily to UN peacekeeping operations (such as Canada).[45] In response to this concern, an Independent Working Group convened at the request of the UN secretary-general concluded that "the Security Council [should] be expanded from its present membership of 15 to a total of approximately 23 Members, of whom not more than five would be new Permanent Members."[46] These five new permanent members would probably include Japan, Germany, and representatives from geographic regions such as Asia, Africa, and Latin America, but

> in spite of unequivocal rhetorical support from Washington and
> the fact that many other governments have declared themselves
> in favor of changing the composition of the Security Council,
> each major structural reform opens another Pandora's box:
> Which developing countries should be added? Why should they
> be the most powerful or populous? After a civil war, should a
> splintered state retain its seat? . . . Should there be three perma-
> nent European members? What about the European Union (EU)?
> Which countries should wield vetoes?[47]

It has also been recommended that the scope of the veto be restricted, if such an expansion takes place, so that it would be applicable only to peacekeeping and enforcement measures.

The United Nations has also recently faced the challenge of seeming irrelevant to the world's largest military power, the United States. Although most Security Council members favored continued inspections for weapons of mass destruction in Iraq, the UN was unable to prevent or limit the U.S. intervention in that country in 2003, demonstrating the organization's weakness. According to one view,

> President Bush's doctrine of unilateral preemption, if main-
> tained, challenged the 1945 commitment to collective security
> in the UN Charter. By acting without the UN authorization, or
> early UN ratification after the fact, when no imminent threat
> to U.S. national security seemed to exist, the Bush administra-
> tion circumvented the bedrock principles on which the United

Nations was founded. Other major powers on the Security
Council noted the grave precedent set by U.S. action and sought
ways to constrain Washington's unilateral foreign policy.[48]

Despite the fallout between the United Nations and the United States
over Iraq, the organization and the Bush administration continued to
work together on issues of global importance, including nuclear programs
in Iran and North Korea and the conflict between Hezbollah and Israel in
Lebanon in 2006. Even in Iraq, the United Nations has played some role,
such as assisting in the first elections, although the insecure situation
severely restricted UN activities, particularly after the attack on the UN
building in Iraq in August 2003.

Despite its problems and its current budgetary crisis, it is likely
that the United Nations will continue to be a significant global actor.
It is a vast organization that performs a number of roles in international politics, beyond issues of security and peace. UN agencies such
as the World Health Organization (WHO) and the International Labour
Organization (ILO) are quite active in AIDS policy and workers' rights,
respectively. And the majority of its members from less developed countries (LDCs) find it convenient for a variety of reasons. Many of them
cannot afford to establish embassies throughout the world. The United
Nations provides a place where they can meet and talk with official
representatives of states to which they cannot afford to send ambassadors. This kind of contact is valued, especially at a time when leaders of developing countries generally believe, despite the wide variety
of political and economic structures their countries exhibit, that they
have many important concerns in common. Also, the United Nations
provides a forum and a platform that is probably irreplaceable for most
developing nations. If an official from Zaire makes a speech in Zaire,
for example, it is likely to go unnoticed in most of the rest of the world.
But if Zaire's delegate to the United Nations or a visiting dignitary
from Zaire delivers a speech in the General Assembly, there is at least
a reasonable chance that it will be picked up in *The New York Times*
or *Le Monde*. Finally, the structure of the United Nations allows such
nations not only to maintain contacts with one another but also to use
those contacts to build a coalition that can exert some political clout
in the General Assembly as well as in other UN agencies. And if that
coalition creates an imbalance between majority votes in the United
Nations and actual political power in the international system, this
inequality may not be so bad. In virtually every other forum and arena
of interaction in the global system, LDCs suffer a disadvantage in terms
of their political and economic power in relationship to the industrialized world. Perhaps the United Nations can serve the useful purpose of
partially redressing that imbalance. For all these reasons, it seems fairly
certain that the United Nations will continue to be supported by most
of its members.

The continued existence of the United Nations is in the interest not only of LDCs and the United States but also of the entire global political system. It is possible that debates in the General Assembly and the Security Council serve to exacerbate rather than mollify conflict. It is also possible that in the long run, the United Nations will not be able to enforce fully the ideals of collective security, despite the success of the world community, using UN institutions to a limited extent, in terminating the Iraqi occupation of Kuwait. But at least a couple of lessons gleaned from the historical record of the last century indicate that deemphasizing the United Nations might be a serious mistake. The crisis that culminated in the First World War might conceivably have been resolved if some institutionalized forum for negotiations among the great powers, such as that provided by the Council of the League of Nations or the Security Council of the United Nations, had existed. And certainly one cause of the Second World War was the failure of the major powers to support the League of Nations. Both of these assertions are, to be sure, debatable. Even the most vigorous dissenter must agree, though, that they are not entirely implausible. If there is a reasonable chance that an organization such as the United Nations may help the world avoid catastrophes of the magnitude of the world wars, is it not prudent to preserve the organization? Many in the world seem to think so. The United Nations enjoys support and legitimacy across the globe.[49] In the international debate over intervention in Iraq in 2003, for example, much of the public in many countries expressed their preference that intervention should occur only under a mandate of the United Nations. This is consistent with U.S. public opinion on the United Nations, which generally supports multilateral initiatives over unilateral ones.[50]

At a time when both positive forces such as improved communications and transportation and worldwide problems such as famine, terrorism, nuclear proliferation, and pollution are making it increasingly necessary for the world community to function as a whole, it would surely be a mistake to destroy virtually the only existing symbolic and institutional basis for the community, as flawed as it admittedly is. On a more practical level, intergovernmental organizations such as the IMF and WHO are expanding the scope of their activities and influence. The same can be said for international nongovernmental organizations such as multinational corporations and professional societies. What other organization is better suited to the progressively more important task of monitoring and coordinating the activities of these international and transnational organizations? The United Nations is not likely to evolve into a world government. It might, though, facilitate the coordination of the world community's efforts to deal with problems that cannot be dealt with effectively by states going their separate ways, especially if the major powers agree that the organization ought to be used for such purposes, as they increasingly seemed inclined to do in the post–Cold War era.

International Law

international law Rules governing relations between states, primarily based on treaties, custom, and general legal principles.

In addition to international organizations, states create **international law** as a way to influence behavior, avoid conflict, and maintain peace and cooperation. As described by Hersch Lauterpacht, perhaps one of greatest international law scholars, "The mission of international law is to lead to enhancing the stability of international peace, to the protection of the rights of man, and to reducing the evils and abuses of national power."[51] According to liberalism, international law can provide incentives to cooperate and organize predictable consequences to punish states that do not cooperate. But according to realism, international law is often irrelevant to global politics. After all, the international community is anarchic; that is, there is no central authority or government. The business of government is making, applying, and enforcing laws; because the international political system has no government, it is only natural to conclude that international law either does not really exist or is not really law.

That is a common opinion for several reasons, one of which is that states (or their representatives) so often behave in violent and unethical ways. Also, there is no established way to enforce legal rules in the international system. A law in domestic systems is virtually by definition a rule that is enforced or has force behind it. If there is no enforcement in the global political system, there is no law. Add to this lack of enforcement mechanisms the lack of an authoritative legislative body to formulate laws, and the basis for law in the international system does in fact seem extremely flimsy.

Sources and Principles

Although there is no enforcer and no legislative organ for the global community, there is a centralized judicial body, the International Court of Justice, or World Court. It is the successor to the Permanent Court of International Justice, which was established in 1920. As described in the UN Charter, the World Court has fifteen members elected to nine-year terms by the General Assembly and the Security Council. Article 38 of the Statute of the International Court of Justice contains a widely accepted statement of the sources of international law. (Since there is no international legislature, international laws have to come from somewhere else.) The statute asserts that international law is based on (1) international treaties; (2) international custom; (3) the general principles of law recognized by civilized nations; (4) previous judicial decisions; and (5) the writings of recognized legal scholars or qualified publicists. The two most important sources of contemporary international law are treaties and customs. Treaties (also called agreements, protocols, conventions, charters, and pacts, among other terms) are between international actors and are binding only to those actors that sign and ratify them. The United Nations Treaty Collection, a depository of treaties, contains more than

500 major multilateral treaties, in addition to many bilateral treaties. While treaties are written products, customs are based on behavior. International customary law is based on the general practices of states or states acting as if there is an accepted law governing their behavior. "The main evidence of customary law is to be found in the actual practice of states, and a rough idea of a state's practice can be gathered from published material—from newspaper reports of actions taken by states, and from statements made by government spokesmen . . . and also from a state's laws and judicial decisions."[52] State behaviors pertaining to freedom of the high seas, the immunities of diplomats, behaviors in wartime, and territorial jurisdiction have been interpreted as evidence of international customary law. Once a custom is recognized as international law, all states are bound to it, even if they have not consented or if it is not a universally accepted custom. Treaties are becoming the more important source of international law, as states have increasingly preferred to codify existing customary practices.[53]

There is little doubt, then, that international law exists, on paper at least. But there is still room for much doubt about its effectiveness. Despite hundreds of treaties, treatises, and rulings by courts, the international legal structure is so filled with loopholes and ambiguities that the ability of international law to constrain state behavior is questionable. Perhaps the most fundamental loophole lies at the heart of international law in the form of the concept of sovereignty.

As developed originally by Jean Bodin in *De Republica* (1576), *sovereignty* refers to the supreme lawmaking and law-enforcing authority within a given territory. A state is sovereign in the sense that it is a source of, but not subject to, laws. This notion of sovereignty, which is clear enough within a certain territorial area, becomes problematic when its implications for relations between territorial units are considered: "What in law and logic could be the appropriate relationship between two sovereign states, each incorporating an authority that alleged itself to be supreme, and which recognized no superior?"[54] The answer is that all states must be considered absolutely equal in legal terms.

On this absolute legal equality is based the principle of nonintervention. No state has the right to interfere in the affairs of any other, since that would imply that the interfering state is somehow superior. Another implication of sovereignty and sovereign equality is that the only rules that are binding on states are ones to which they consent.[55] Even when states give their consent to certain rules, they are often "so vague and ambiguous and so qualified by conditions and reservations as to allow the individual nation a very great degree of freedom of action whenever they are called upon to comply with a rule of international law."[56] Typically, states can be taken into a court of international law (such as the World Court) only if they are willing.[57] And even if they have created law, in effect, by signing a treaty, states are not necessarily bound by that law. One long-standing principle of international law inserts a kind of implicit escape clause into every treaty signed by sovereign states. Referred to as *clausula rebus sic stantibus,* this principle stipulates that treaties are binding only "so long as things stand as they are."[58] In other words, if the circumstances as they stood at the time of the signing of the treaty change in some vital way, as determined by one of the signatories to that agreement, the treaty is no longer considered binding. This principle is "capable of being used, and . . . often has been used, merely to excuse the breach of a treaty obligation that a state finds inconvenient to fulfill."[59]

The Impact of International Law

International law, devoid of any centralized enforcement authority and formulated by states in such a way as to preserve their freedom of action, is often cleverly avoided, openly flouted, or simply ignored. When Iranians seized American hostages at the U.S. embassy in Tehran in 1979, the United States took its case to the International Court of Justice. The World Court ruled against the Iranian government but had no effective means to enforce its judgment. The hostages remained trapped in the embassy for 444 days. The Nicaraguan government repeatedly charged the Reagan administration with violations of international law. The World Court ruled in June 1986 that those complaints were valid. But the United States simply rejected that ruling (and other similar ones), and the court had no apparent effect on the Reagan administration's campaign to depose the Sandinistas in the Nicaraguan government.

Kellogg-Briand Pact   Treaty that attempted to outlaw war.

Perhaps the most famous, or infamous, example of the impotence of international law is the **Kellogg-Briand Pact** of 1928, officially the Treaty Providing for the Renunciation of War as an Instrument of National Policy, or the Pact of Paris. This treaty was an attempt to outlaw international war. In retrospect, with the Second World War and many other wars having been fought since then, the attempt looks idealistic to a foolish extreme. Indeed, "the shape of the international system during the Cold War reinforced this realist perspective. International institutions and judicial bodies such as the United Nations and the International Court of Justice . . . were hobbled by both the bipolar split in world politics and its aggravation of tensions between the developed and developing worlds."[60]

Despite the obvious validity of a claim that the international legal system has serious flaws, the case against international law is usually overstated. International laws are often broken, but so are domestic laws, as the homicide rate in most major U.S. cities demonstrates. The fact that murders occur in every society does not commonly lead to the conclusion that laws against murder have no effect or are not really laws. Granted, domestic laws have force behind them. Some murderers are arrested and punished. But the idea that "law works because it is a command backed up by force [is] essentially false."[61] The U.S. government routinely obeys rulings by the U.S. Supreme Court, even though the Court commands no troops or other means to enforce those rulings.

In short, laws, including international ones, are sometimes obeyed even if the fear of punishment is absent. President Truman obeyed the Supreme Court out of respect for the system and with a sense that the system was worth preserving even if it meant losing on the issue at hand. Most people, most of the time, perhaps obey laws not merely because they fear punishment but, because they believe the laws are just or beneficial in principle. Similarly, in global politics, "nations have a common interest in keeping the society running and keeping international relations orderly. They observe laws they do not care about to maintain others which they value, and to keep the system' intact."[62] Furthermore, upholding international law has become a test of sorts of a state's credibility. "Every nation's foreign policy depends substantially on its 'credit'—on maintaining the expectation that it will live up to international mores and obligations. Considerations of 'honor,' 'prestige,' 'leadership,' 'influence,' 'reputation,' which figure prominently in governmental decisions, often weigh in favor of observing law."[63] Leaders may also uphold international law to get "credit" from their domestic constituents who often have internalized and support principles of international law.[64]

Furthermore, most people obey the majority of laws much of the time, because cooperation pays. That is, the benefits from cooperative, law-abiding behavior outweigh the costs, at least in the long run. Take the simple example of the law in most countries requiring motorists to stop at red traffic lights. Even if all the police in a city were to go on strike, reducing to zero the probability that violators would be arrested, chances are that most people would continue to obey this law. To do otherwise would risk injury or death in a traffic accident. That law, to an important extent, is self-enforcing.

Roughly analogous situations obtain in the realm of international law. For example, there are laws against the mistreatment of personnel representing foreign countries. In fact, diplomatic personnel are in some respects above the law, being granted **diplomatic immunity.** Any government that mistreats diplomats from other countries could expect its own diplomats to be targets of retaliation. That is clearly one reason the laws regarding the treatment of diplomats have rarely been violated. When the Iranian government held U.S. diplomatic personnel as hostages in 1979 and 1980, its behavior was virtually without precedent.

diplomatic immunity Freedom from arrest or prosecution granted to foreign representatives.

There are also many consistently observed laws having to do with routine international interactions in the areas of trade, communications, and immigration. These areas are sometimes referred to as private international law to distinguish them from public international law, which governs relations between governments and other international actors such as international organizations and nongovernmental organizations. Disputes in these areas are almost always successfully dealt with through legal channels.

International law is not entirely lacking in enforcement either:

> The traditional toolbox to secure compliance with the law of nations consists of negotiations, mediation, countermeasures (reciprocal action against the violator) or, in rare cases, recourse to supranational judicial bodies such as the International Court of Justice. . . . For many years, these tools have been supplemented by the work of international institutions, whose reports and resolutions often help "mobilize shame" against its violators. But today, states, NGOs, and private entities, aided by their lawyers, have striven for sanctions with more teeth. They have galvanized the UN Security Council to issue economic sanctions against Iraq, Haiti, Libya, Serbia, Sudan, and other nations refusing to comply with UN resolutions.[65]

In sum, "international law provides the framework for establishing rules and norms, outlines the parameters of interaction, and provides the procedures for resolving disputes among those taking part in these interactions. . . . [International law also acts] . . . as a normative system [and] provides direction for international relations by identifying the substantive values and goals to be pursued."[66] While violations of international law may appear blatant, "the reality as demonstrated through their behavior is that states do accept international law and, even more significant, in the vast majority of instances they obey it."[67]

International law in the twenty-first century is addressing more global concerns, such as the environment and economic cooperation. It is also addressing ethics, particularly human rights. While contemporary international law is still organized around the principles of sovereignty and nonintervention, there have been significant challenges to these notions in the post–Cold War era. "We have seen some erosion of the concept of state sovereignty and of some of its earlier implications, such as state sovereign immunity. The international system has accepted a fundamental permutation of state societies as a result of the International Human Rights Movement: . . . How a state treats its own inhabitants is now of international concern and a staple of international politics and law."[68]

Ethics, Morality, and International Politics

ethics Standards for evaluating right and wrong.

The current developments in international law concerning human rights are attempts to codify certain values and **ethics** and apply them to global politics. What is ethical and what is legal can be dealt with separately even in discussions of domestic politics. Not all legal behavior is ethical, and illegal behavior (civil disobedience of unjust laws, for example) is not necessarily unethical for individuals within the context of domestic political systems. But legality and morality are even more tenuously related for states in the global community than they are for individuals in domestic politics. Most domestic political systems have regular, accepted procedures for translating ethical values into legal, enforceable rules. Murder is considered unethical in virtually every society, and it is also illegal, meaning that rules against it are enforced, with violators punished according to established procedures. Like other communities, the international one is based in part on shared ethical standards intended to induce more orderly and predictable behavior among states as they interact. Yet in the international community, there is typically more diversity of opinion about what is ethical or moral.

According to a commonly held view, moral principles have nothing to do with international politics, even though they are discussed regularly. If defenders of national policies are to be believed, the policies of every state in the world conform rigorously to the highest ethical standards and are motivated primarily by the purest altruistic motives.[69] But in the standard skeptical view, morality in the context of international politics is like the weather: Everybody talks about it, but nobody does anything about it.

Opinions such as these are not often totally without foundation, and skepticism about the role of moral principles in international politics is supported by considerable evidence and logic. First, historically as well as in modern times, many important actors in international politics have behaved in blatantly immoral ways, apparently free from the influence of ethical considerations. Also, the peoples of the world have very disparate ideas about what constitutes moral behavior. Then, too, because the international political system is anarchic, there is no central authority, no government, nobody responsible for enforcing laws designed to enforce morality. "The moral requirements of a state which has somehow to survive in a context of states each of which is potentially a violent criminal and above which there is no political superior with a monopoly of authority to enforce law and order, must be different from that of an individual in an orderly civil society."[70]

This fairly typical statement that the moral requirements of states are different from those of individuals seems suspiciously like a euphemistic way of saying that they do not have any moral requirements at all, except to do whatever they must to protect themselves. And this idea, this skepticism about the role of morality in politics, attracts support from widely divergent points on the ideological and theoretical spectrum. Realism rejects ethics as a guide for foreign policy, arguing that states are driven instead by interests and power.[71] Similarly, Marxist writers believe that ethical justifications for political actions are "superstructure" and tools in class warfare.[72] Leon Trotsky spoke for many of his Marxist peers when he argued that "the appeal to abstract norms is not a disinterested philosophical mistake but a necessary element in the mechanism of class deception."[73]

Still, a case can be made for the proposition that moral principles should and do play an important role in international politics. Idealism makes this case, arguing that morals and values, not state interests, should and do shape individual and state behavior. Although violence is common in the international system, and there is no centralized authority to enforce moral standards, states do not continuously behave in a disorderly and immoral fashion. In other words, even though there is a constant threat that world politics will degenerate into a war of "all against all," actual warfare is not typical. "The international community possesses a variety of devices for promoting compliance with established norms. These range from such mild sanctions as community disapproval and censure by international organizations to coordinated national policies of economic embargoes of offending states."[74] Most publicity about these sanctions and embargoes focuses on the limitations of their effectiveness. But ethical principles, like laws, are also violated repeatedly by individuals within domestic political systems, and unless disorder reaches extraordinarily high levels, these numerous violations do not often provoke or justify the conclusion that ethical considerations have no effect on the behavior of individuals within those societies.

Even well-known moral skeptics concede that ethical principles do have an impact on international politics. According to one realist, for example, even "the most cynical realist cannot afford even in the interest of realism to ignore political ideals. . . . For man is at heart a moral being."[75] Similar sentiments can be found in Marxist writing. Trotsky noted that Lenin's "'amoralism' . . . his rejection of supra-class morals, did not hinder him from remaining faithful to one and the same idea throughout his whole life; from devoting his whole being to the cause of the oppressed."[76]

moral skepticism Denial that morality does or should influence actors' behaviors.

Moral skepticism, then, in the analysis of domestic as well as international politics, can be and often is taken too far. Nations do pursue values, such as economic justice, protection of human rights, and the spread of democratic political arrangements. Some of the rhetoric by national political leaders who strive for those goals is, to be sure, hypocritical. But "it is only a prejudice that these [goals] are mere masks for self-interest; neither citizens nor governments see such goals that way."[77]

moral relativism Belief that moral judgments have no objective basis.

Even if we grant that international political actors are genuinely influenced by moral standards, it may still be a waste of time to discuss seriously those standards and their application to moral problems. Individuals adhering to **moral relativism** insist that "moral judgments are just mere opinion, concerning which there is no point in arguing, as there is no point in arguing about any matters of taste or personal predilection."[78] Others reject extreme moral relativism partly out of reluctance to accept the conclusion implied by such relativism that all foreign policies and international political acts must logically be categorized as amoral, or equally immoral; that, for example, it is impossible to distinguish, morally speaking, between Hitler's attack on Belgium in 1940 and the decision by Belgium's leaders to resist that attack. Many feminists agree with idealism's criticism of realism and embrace moral issues as important in global politics. Some feminists, however, believe that morality is relative and dependent on, or constructed by, cultural contexts. In other words, they recognize the importance of morality but emphasize its variability across cultures. Other feminists see some morals and values, such as women's rights, as universal. Still others reject the idea that the debate over human rights should revolve around the extremes of cultural relativism and universalism, arguing that

> universalism and relativism are not mutually exclusive categories but rather different ends of a continuum. . . . In defining and promoting international human rights, the challenge is to assert and defend the universality of basic rights while recognizing that the formulation and application of rights claims will depend in part on the social and cultural context in which rights claims are asserted.[79]

The Ethics of War and Nuclear Deterrence

Geneva Conventions International humanitarian laws dealing with treatment of wounded or captured soldiers and civilians under enemy control.

War may seem like the breakdown of international law and moral standards in global politics, but there are legal standards applied to the purpose and conduct of war, and many times these standards are obeyed. Indeed, the laws of war are the oldest and most developed. Under the **Geneva Conventions** (1949), for example, soldiers have the right to surrender and become prisoners of war (POWs). As POWs, they are expected to be treated humanely, and the International Red Cross/Red Crescent has the right to provide food and medical supplies and to keep track of POWs and refugees during wartime. The conventions also establish rules for the protection of civilians in areas covered by war and in occupied territories. As of 2009, more than 190 states have ratified the conventions. Today, there is considerable debate over how these agreements relate to suspects of terrorism. The Policy Choices box summarizes some of the issues involved in U.S. treatment of detainees in anti-terrorist operations.[80]

Genocide Convention Treaty declaring illegal any acts intended to destroy a national, ethnic, racial, or religious group.

Additional protocols to the Geneva Conventions have declared that the right of actors in international and noninternational conflicts to choose methods of warfare is not limited. The protocols prohibit the use of weapons that cause superfluous injury or unnecessary suffering. Indeed, some acts of war are not acceptable, according to the international community. In 1948, the United Nations adopted the **Genocide Convention,** which declares that any acts intended to destroy, in whole or in part, a national, ethnic, racial, or religious group as such are crimes punishable under international law. Most states have signed the Genocide Convention.

war crimes Violations of international law governing conduct of warfare and treatment of soldiers and civilians during conflict.

After World War II, the victorious allies tried German and Japanese leaders and military officers for **war crimes** through international tribunals. More recently, Yugoslavian, Rwandan, and Liberian leaders and officials have been indicted by UN war crime tribunals. The former leader of Yugoslavia, Slobodan Milosevic, was imprisoned in 2001 and put to trial for crimes against humanity:

POLICY CHOICES

Should Traditional Laws of War Apply to Enemy Combatants in the "War on Terror"?

ISSUE: The treatment of prisoners in the U.S.-led "war on terror" has been subject to intense debate, both internationally and within the United States. Article 3 of the Geneva Conventions prohibits humiliating and degrading treatment of prisoners and grants them all judicial guarantees seen as indispensable by civilized societies. The administration of George W. Bush asserted that the Geneva Convention does not pertain to detainees suspected of terrorism and of having connections to Al Qaeda and the Taliban in Afghanistan. The terrorist suspects, held for indefinite periods and without standard legal safeguards, were confined at U.S. military bases in Guantánamo Bay, Cuba (GITMO), in Afghanistan, and in CIA detention centers in undisclosed locations. The United States also extended GITMO procedures to U.S.-controlled prisons in Iraq and rendered (handed over) suspects to be held in prisons in other countries, some known for human rights violations. These practices generated widespread condemnation, especially by European and Middle Eastern countries and human rights NGOs. In the United States, the Supreme Court and Congress challenged Bush administration policies on treatment of terror suspects. Upon assuming office, President Obama ordered the closing of the Guantánamo Bay detention center and other secret prisons and released memos detailing the interrogation techniques that were used by the Central Intelligence Agency on terrorist suspects.

Option #1: Traditional laws of war are inadequate to effectively deal with terrorism and the treatment of suspected terrorists.

Arguments: (a) International law was constructed for conventional warfare and does not apply to this new, stateless enemy. It is vague on what defines torture and "humiliating and degrading treatment," as expressed in the Geneva Convention. What is humiliating or degrading to one culture or individual may not be to another. (b) Aggressive interrogation may reveal critical information about pending attacks, such as those of 9/11. (c) The threat of harsh treatment may deter individuals from joining terrorist causes, or prevent some terrorists from engaging in more aggressive and dangerous acts.

Counterarguments: (a) International law protects all agents in wars; even illegal and irregular combatants have minimal rights under widely agreed-upon conventions. International law is clear on what constitutes humans rights violations, and U.S. efforts to define torture as only involving "organ failure" are unacceptable. (b) Information derived from torture is notoriously untrustworthy, because people will say anything to end their suffering. U.S. military manuals have long viewed prisoner abuse as ineffective for gathering quality intelligence. (c) Engaging in torture simply reinforces the negative attitude many hold of the United States, thus resulting in more recruiting and intensified resolve of potential enemies.

Option #2: The United States must embrace international law and respect the fundamental rights of detainees.

Arguments: (a) International laws, such as those against torture, are the pinnacle of humanitarianism, and abiding by them shows the United States to be a leader

(continued)

of international morality and ethics. U.S. commitments to democracy based on civil and political rights are undermined and seen as hypocritical when repressive techniques are employed. (b) Undermining the Geneva Conventions is not in the U.S. interests, because it puts its own military personnel at risk of torture if captured in future conflicts. Abiding by international law continues the norm of reciprocity; ignoring it weakens centuries-old customs that regulate the conduct of war. (c) Violating international law tarnishes the U.S. image in the world and generates condemnation from important allies. The United States loses the battle for hearts and minds when human rights violations are associated with U.S. practice, such as with the photos of abuse in the Iraqi Abu Ghraib prison.

Counterarguments: (a) International law loses the moral high ground when it protects immoral actors and tactics, such as those associated with terrorism. Furthermore, state rhetoric never matches reality, particularly in times of crisis; other states have pursued similar policies in asymmetrical conflicts in which enemy combatants do not follow conventional tactics of warfare. (b) Harsh interrogations of members of terrorist groups does not put our troops in jeopardy, because these enemies typically do not take prisoners and, in any event, are unlikely to abide by international law themselves. (c) National interests should drive U.S. policies, not international norms that infringe on state sovereignty and hinder efforts to protect a state from threats to its people.

The creation of the UN war crimes tribunals for the former Yugoslavia in 1993 and Rwanda in 1994 stemmed from the worldwide revulsion over the documented evidence of widespread killings of civilians and other human rights violations in those two conflicts. The tribunals were the first courts ever created by the United Nations to try individuals for war crimes: the victorious Allies had conducted the trials of German and Japanese officials after World War II.[81]

International Criminal Court (ICC) Permanent tribunal that tries individuals accused of genocide, crimes against humanity, and war crimes.

In 1998, 120 states took the prosecution of war crimes a step further when they voted to create an **International Criminal Court (ICC)**, a permanent tribunal with powers to try acts of genocide, crimes against humanity, and war crimes. The court is composed of eighteen judges from different countries and a prosecutor with the power to initiate cases and is located in The Hague, the Netherlands, also home to many UN war crimes tribunals and the UN's International Court of Justice. The International Court of Justice handles disputes only between states; the ICC hears cases against individuals. The ICC is not part of the UN organizational structure. It receives its funding through contributions from states, international and nongovernmental organizations, corporations, and individuals. The court has jurisdiction only over crimes committed after July 1, 2002, when it came into force. National courts have priority to try their citizens of crimes, but the court has jurisdiction when states

POLICY CHOICES

Should States Support the International Criminal Court?

ISSUE: At the Rome conference where the ICC was created, seven states voted against it: China, Iraq, Israel, Libya, Qatar, Yemen, and the United States. The United States would eventually sign the treaty on December 31, 2000, the last possible date for signature, but later it formally withdrew its support (in May 2002). The new Obama administration signaled that it is supportive of the ICC, but Russia and China remain opposed to the court. By late 2009, 108 states were parties to the ICC.

Option #1: States should sign, ratify, and support the International Criminal Court.

Arguments: (a) The ICC will have a positive influence on international society, because it will uphold the commitment to the protection of human rights and provide a means of accountability to international norms. (b) The ICC will act as a potential deterrent to future transgressors—from heads of state and commanding officers to militia recruits—and, through deterrence, lower the need for costly interventions. (c) The ICC is needed, because states are often unwilling or unable to prosecute their own citizens or leaders who commit heinous crimes.

Counterarguments: (a) The ICC is unlikely to fare any better than the World Court and UN Human Rights Commission in the extension of international law, especially because it lacks connection to established international organizations. (b) There is no evidence that the ICC will exert a deterrent effect. Individuals most likely to commit flagrant human rights violations are probably the least likely to feel the effect of international norms or moral convictions. (c) States, with established policy and judicial systems, are the best place to pursue credible justice and should not abdicate that responsibility to an international body.

Option #2: States should not support the ICC and instead should support the prosecution of war crimes, genocide, and crimes against humanity through existing, alternative mechanisms.

Arguments: (a) States will be the target of politically minded prosecutions of their leaders and military personnel; ICC safeguards against abuse of the prosecutorial system are inadequate and vague. (b) When domestic will is lacking, the international community can respond to international crimes through the UN Security Council, consistent with the UN Charter, or through ad hoc international mechanisms such as the international tribunals for the former Yugoslavia and Rwanda. (c) Any such permanent body is likely to be more inefficient than tribunals specific to the violations. The ICC is inflexible and unable to incorporate novel solutions.

Counterarguments: (a) The court has an extremely narrow jurisdiction, and judges and prosecutors must abide by strict guidelines, thereby making prosecutions based on political agendas highly unlikely; not signing means no input into the management of the ICC. (b) Ad hoc tribunals can serve only "selective justice." Why were tribunals established for the former Yugoslavia and Rwanda but not for Cambodia, for example? A permanent court administers justice more consistently. (c) Ad hoc efforts at international justice do not facilitate enduring cooperation.

(continued)

By not signing, states send a clear message to the international community that narrow self-interest is more important than global values and cooperation. Establishing a pattern of international commitment will undoubtedly promote better solutions to problems that transcend state boundaries.

are unwilling or unable to do so. The ICC came into existence in 2002, when the necessary sixty states ratified it. While some hail the creation of the ICC as "the biggest legal milestone since Hitler's henchmen were tried at Nuremberg,"[82] there has been strong opposition to the court, particularly from some of the major states (see the Policy Choices box). There is considerable doubt about its effectiveness and legitimacy given this opposition.[83] In 2009, the ICC, for the first time, issued a warrant for the arrest of a sitting head of state, President al-Bashir of Sudan. The court charged the leader with crimes against humanity and war crimes in Darfur, but the Sudanese government vowed to resist the court and immediately expelled Western aid groups in retaliation.[84]

just war Set of principles for judging conditions for when states can resort to war (*jus ad bellum*) and for the conduct of war (*jus in bello*).

Most of the laws concerning war are consistent with the **just war** tradition, based on writings of Saint Augustine of Hippo in the fifth century and Saint Thomas Aquinas in the thirteenth century:

> Just War is the name for a diverse literature on the morality of war and warfare that offers criteria for judging whether a war is just and whether it is fought by just means. This tradition, thus, debates our moral obligations in relation to violence and the use of lethal force. The thrust of the tradition is not to argue against war as such, but to surround both the resort to war and its conduct with moral constraints and conditions.[85]

Hugo Grotius, a scholar in the seventeenth century and often considered the "founder of international law," helped codify just war ideas into modern international convention. Just war principles are divided into the categories of *jus ad bellum* (laws on the use of force) and *jus in bello* (laws in war). The most important principles are listed in Table 9.2.

Just war principles are certainly violated by states, but they do serve as the foundation for moral judgments and are often applied to contemporary conflict. For example, in the case of the U.S.-led intervention in Iraq in 2003, former President Jimmy Carter, in an editorial in *The New York Times* in March 2003, cited just war principles He argued that the war was not just for the following reasons: all nonviolent options were not exhausted; aerial bombardment inevitably cannot discriminate between combatants and noncombatants; there was no evidence that tied the September 11 terrorist attacks to Iraq, which might justify violence proportional to that injury; there was no legitimate authority sanctioning the effort to change the regime; and the outcome of the war would not likely

TABLE 9.2

Just War Principles

Principle	Definition
Jus ad Bellum	
Right authority	Only a legitimate authority has the right to declare war.
Just cause	We are not only permitted but may be required to use lethal force if we have a just cause.
Right intention	In war, not only the cause and goals must be just, but also our motive for responding to the cause and taking up the goals.
Last resort	We may resort to war only if it is the last viable alternative.
Proportionality	We must be confident that resorting to war will do more good than harm.
Reasonable hope	We must have reasonable grounds for believing the cause can be achieved.
Relative justice	No state can act as if it possesses absolute justice.
Open declaration	An explicit formal statement is required before resorting to force.
Jus in Bello	
Discrimination	Noncombatants must be given immunity and protection.
Proportionality	Military actions must do more good than harm.

Source: Adapted from Mona Fixdal and Dan Smith, "Humanitarian Intervention and Just War," *Mershon International Studies Review* 42 (1998): p. 286.

be a clear improvement over what existed. Others disagreed, although the main disagreement was whether the war met these principles, not over whether just war principles should be applied to the conflict.[86]

Just war principles have been applied more broadly to the "war on terror." According to one scholar, in order to use the Just War tradition to evaluate counter-terror operations, "First of all we need to ask whether all terrorism is unjust and to understand why. Then we need to evaluate the legitimacy of the war on terror itself."[87] While some have concluded that many aspects of the anti-terror strategies of the United States have been unjust because they are disproportionate, others believe that the end goal of combating terrorism justifies certain means.[88]

The weighing of costs and benefits in the Just War tradition may seem a natural way of resolving moral dilemmas, but there is an important philosophical tradition that rejects such an approach. Deontological theories insist that the morality of an act may be independent of the consequences of that act—that certain acts (or actions based on rules) are inherently good or bad, regardless of their consequences. In this view, actions either conform to valid moral rules—for example, "We ought always to tell the truth," in which case they are moral—or they do not, and so are immoral. These rules are valid independent of whether they promote the good.[89]

In other words, according to the deontological point of view, an act is moral if it is based on valid moral principles; it is the rule on which the act is based, rather than the consequences of the act, to which one must look in order to evaluate its morality.

This stance might seem on the surface a stereotypical "head in the clouds" position that only a philosopher could love. But philosophy is full of surprises. Imagine that a police station is surrounded by a mob of people who are convinced, wrongly, that a man inside the station is responsible for the rape and murder of their friend's wife. They send a message into the station stating that if the man is not turned over to them, so that he may be dealt with in some traditionally agonizing manner appropriate to the occasion, they will set fire to the station, killing everyone inside. What is the moral decision for the commander of the station? If the man in question is surrendered, one innocent person will die. If the request to turn him over is denied, many innocent people inside the station seem destined for certain death. Would it be morally right to sacrifice the life of an innocent man to save the lives of many equally innocent people?

Perhaps not. So maybe it is *not* so self-evident that, as utilitarians argue, "our actions . . . are to be decided upon by determining which of them produces or may be expected to produce the greatest general balance of good over evil."[90] In the case of nuclear deterrence, deontologists argue that the waters are even muddier than in the example because the consequences of deterrence are so difficult to discern.

There is little doubt that nuclear weapons and the doctrine of nuclear deterrence create what is probably the most profound moral dilemma that has ever faced the human species; they also bring into focus with special clarity the more general ethical issues surrounding the use of military force. No matter what the goal to be achieved or the principle defended, the use of nuclear weapons in pursuit of that goal or in defense of that principle entails the possibility that the world will be destroyed. "If it can be shown that a nuclear war is likely to destroy the end(s) for which it is waged, it can have neither political nor moral justification."[91] If no cause can justify the risk of ending life on the planet, then it is important to ask whether it is possible to defend, on moral grounds, a policy of nuclear deterrence that is by definition based on the threat to launch a nuclear attack, which in turn could lead to the demise of the human race.

The Ethics of Intervention: Human Rights versus States' Rights

One moral issue that has come to the forefront of global politics and international law is human rights. All members of the United Nations have signed the **Universal Declaration of Human Rights,** first adopted by the General Assembly in 1948. "Underlying the evolution of human rights principles was a clear link between good governance and the maintenance of international peace and security. It was believed that the aggressive foreign policies of the Axis powers [in World War II] were caused by the militaristic nature of their political systems" which abused human rights.[92] The UN Universal Declaration commits states to promote respect for human rights and freedoms, including the right to life, liberty, freedom from torture and arbitrary detention, equality before the law without any discrimination, freedom of movement across countries, individual property rights, freedom of opinion and expression, and the right to work, education, and an adequate standard of living. Yet when the declaration was adopted,

> virtually all governments said the standards were not legally binding upon them. At that time, no specific human rights violations, apart from slavery, genocide, and gross abuses of the rights of aliens, were effectively proscribed. Virtually all states shielded themselves happily behind Article 2(7) of the UN Charter arguing that human rights was strictly an internal affair for the state concerned. While a UN Commission on Human Rights was set up, governments entirely dominated its work. . . . When the drafting of the two International Human Rights Covenants was finally completed, in 1966, it took another decade before a mere thirty-five states ratified them and brought them into operation. Thus, the UN's initial foray into the human rights area was far from promising."[93]

Numerous governments violate the human rights of their citizens. Some governments stay in power without elections, against the apparent wishes of the majority of people in the country. Other governments simply follow unwise policies, economic or otherwise, that perpetuate needless suffering among their citizens. In a just world, governments that do such things should be subject to the corrective and beneficial influence of people outside the borders of the country being victimized. In principle, a lot of problems and abuses of human rights in many countries could be solved by outside intervention.

But interference in the internal affairs of sovereign states is, for moral purposes or otherwise, against one of the most important principles of international law. The *principle of nonintervention* "is the most important embodiment of the modern idea that states should be treated as autonomous entities; it is also the main structural principle of a conception

Universal Declaration of Human Rights UN agreement that commits states to promote respect for human rights and freedoms.

of the world, dominant since the mid-seventeenth century."[94] According to most interpretations of international law, states should be left alone. Interference in their internal affairs is not permissible, even for their own good. Outsiders are permitted to intervene only to protect a government against outside interference.

Some philosophically oriented analysts of international politics find this right of states to be free of outside interference an intolerable limitation on the range of moral concern. One argument asserts, for example, that only "legitimate states should be free of interference from outsiders."[95] Another posits, in a similar way, that "unjust institutions do not enjoy the same *prima facie* protection against external interference as do just institutions."[96] And on the surface, there seems no good reason that government leaders should be able to perpetrate all manner of crimes against people under their rule and hide behind the international legal principle of nonintervention.

The idea that states can use sovereignty as justification for human rights violations has lost much of its credibility. Indeed, "the view that human rights violations are essentially domestic matters, while still put forward in an almost ritual manner from time to time, receives very little credence from the international community."[97] In the contemporary era, several analysts have noted that one reason interventions have become more acceptable (especially after the Cold War) "is the increasing acceptance of the protection of individual rights as an international norm."[98] Many of the UN peacekeeping missions, discussed earlier in this chapter,

> have had explicit human rights responsibilities. UN operations in Haiti and Rwanda even had primarily human rights mandates. Operations in Somalia and northern Iraq also included a human rights dimension. The tasks of these peacekeeping forces have included monitoring the activities of the police and security forces, verifying the discharge of human rights undertakings in agreements ending civil wars, supervising elections, encouraging authorities to adopt international human rights instruments and comply with their international human rights obligations, and providing human rights education.[99]

humanitarian interventions Threats of use of force against a state accused of perpetrating or allowing human rights violations.

Indeed, after the Cold War, there have been numerous humanitarian interventions, within and outside of the UN framework. **Humanitarian interventions** involve "the threat or use of force across state borders by a state (or group of states) aimed at preventing or ending widespread and grave violations of the fundamental human rights of individuals other than its own citizens, without the permission of the state within whose territory force is applied."[100] But despite the changing views that intervention for the protection of human rights may be appropriate, there exist many dilemmas over the use of humanitarian interventions. Legally and politically, the right of states to violate sovereignty remains controversial, even if state sovereignty is no longer seen as absolute.[101] Despite the UN Security Council's call for action to end the humanitarian crisis in Darfur, for example, the Sudanese government has successfully resisted UN peacekeeping forces for a long time with the argument that this would violate its sovereignty. Ethically, some utilitarians question whether the consequences of any military intervention are worth human rights abuses short of genocide.[102]

The difficulties of resolving internal conflicts through outside intervention and state-building efforts (discussed earlier in this chapter and in Chapter 7) raise questions about the effectiveness of humanitarian interventions. Even if the international community has the resolve and resources to deploy forces quickly enough to prevent an escalation of humanitarian abuses and to stay long enough to resolve underlying conflicts, humanitarian interventions may not be that useful and may have unintended consequences.[103] One analyst of the Rwandan genocide argues, for example, that the prospect of outside intervention may create

> perverse incentives for weaker parties in such conflicts to escalate the fighting and thereby exacerbate the suffering of their own people, because they expect or hope to attract foreign intervention. Thus a policy of intervening to relieve humanitarian emergencies that stem from internal conflicts may unintentionally increase the number and extent of such emergencies—a classic instance of moral hazard.[104]

Part of a limited humanitarian intervention, a soldier from the African Union Force stands in front of Sudanese children in Darfur.

(Beatrice Mategwa/© Reuters/Corbis)

This analyst concludes that prevention of severe human rights crises is a much more effective strategy than is humanitarian intervention.

Part of the change in how the international community views human rights has been due to the attention to this issue brought by transnational networks of nongovernmental organizations such as Amnesty International and Human Rights Watch (discussed in more detail in Chapter 4).[105] The United Nations has also become more focused on human rights. Although its Human Rights Commission was created in 1946, "the United Nations continued to build its human rights machinery through the 1990s—in particular, with the creation of the high commissioner post in 1993. In addition, the UN broadened the human rights agenda by creating two special war crimes tribunals and moving to incorporate human rights initiatives in peacekeeping operations."[106]

Women's Rights

Almost certainly the most pervasive human rights abuses in the world involve women, who constitute half of the world's population and are subjected to discriminatory policies and violent acts in virtually all countries. Women are "beaten in their homes by intimate partners; raped and otherwise sexually assaulted by law enforcement personnel while in their custody; raped in refugee camps by other refugees, local police or the military; and targeted for sexual violence based on their low social status."[107] According to the World Health Organization, women between the ages of 15 and 44 are more likely to die or be disabled as a result of violence than from cancer, malaria, or traffic accidents.

Another human rights issue involves discrimination against women, even before birth. In China, the government's population policy limits families to one or two children. "That makes parents fearful of wasting' their quota on a girl."[108] Ultrasound scanners make it possible to detect the gender of a child before birth. It is estimated that some 1.7 million unborn girls are identified in this way each year in China and subsequently aborted. In other words, as a result of government policy, approximately 12 percent of female fetuses are aborted or otherwise unaccounted for in China every year. Similar patterns can be found in other Asian countries, such as South Korea and India.[109] Economist Amartya Sen estimates that 100 million women are "missing" in **female deficit** countries, that is, countries whose female populations are smaller than they would be under "normal" circumstances; 44 million and 37 million of these missing women are in China and India, respectively. "The phenomenon of missing women reflects a history of higher mortality for females and a staunch anti-female bias in health care and nutrition in these countries."[110]

In the post–Cold War era, the international community has witnessed rape as a tool of war in the Balkans and in Africa, trafficking of girls and women in Asia, and the establishment of the Taliban in Afghanistan.

female deficit Situation in countries with female populations smaller than they would normally be.

Under Taliban rule in Afghanistan, the most extreme case of female subjugation under Islamic law,

> women must don a 'burqa,' a dark robe with only a small, heavy mesh opening to see through, before venturing out of the house. . . . The many Afghan women whose fathers, husbands or brothers have died in the country's ongoing civil war live under virtual house arrest. They are even denied a view of the outdoors, as the windows of houses where women must live must be painted over to prevent them from being seen from the street.[111]

The Taliban defended these policies as consistent with their culture and religion. The debate over respect for differences in culture versus the universality of women's rights has been an important one on the global agenda, as well as within the feminist perspective.

Consider, for example, the millions of African girls, and some girls in Asia and the Middle East, who are subjected to female circumcision, as it is called by its proponents, or female genital mutilation, as it is called by its opponents:

> Genital mutilation has been inflicted on 80 to 100 million girls and young women. In countries where it is practiced, mostly African, about two million youngsters a year can expect the knife or the razor or a glass shard, to cut their clitoris or remove it altogether, to have part or all of the labia minora cut off, and part of the labia majora, and the sides of the vulva sewn together with catgut or thorns.[112]

From one point of view, this might be considered a private matter, a culturally based custom of no legitimate interest to outsiders. Alternatively, one might argue that it may not be accepted even in cultures where it is practiced, since "a small number of African and foreign women devote their lives to fighting genital mutilation. But unless they get major help and attention, their struggle may take more generations."[113]

What should be done about widespread mistreatment and abuse of half the world's population? The United Nations is moving toward action in this realm of human rights abuses. The World Health Organization, a functional organization of the United Nations, has announced its intention to put an end to female circumcision. The United Nations also adopted in 1979 a **Convention on the Elimination of All Forms of Discrimination Against Women (CEDAW),** which had been ratified by 185 countries by early 2009. The United States is one prominent state that has refused to ratify the convention, although newly elected President Obama has indicated that he supports CEDAW. Often described as an international bill of rights for women, the convention defines discrimination as "any distinction, exclusion or restriction made on the basis of sex which has the effect or purpose of impairing or nullifying the recognition, enjoyment or exercise by women, irrespective of their marital status, on

Convention on the Elimination of All Forms of Discrimination Against Women (CEDAW) Agreement by which states commit to the principle of legal gender equality and to end various forms of discrimination against women.

a basis of equality of men and women, of human rights and fundamental freedoms in the political, economic, social, cultural, civil or any other field." States that accept the convention agree to a number of policies to eliminate discrimination against women in a variety of forms.

The post–Cold War years have seen a number of important international forums and agreements on women's human rights:

> At the World Conference on Human Rights [in Vienna in 1993], the international community recognized that women's rights are human rights, affirming that the human rights of women are universal, inalienable, and indivisible. Further, for the first time in UN history, the Vienna Programme of Action stated clearly that violence against women, whether in public or private, constitutes a violation of human rights. A year later, at the International Conference on Population and Development (Cairo, 1994) the protection of women's human rights was extended to include women's rights to reproductive and sexual decision making. The World Summit for Social Development (Copenhagen, 1995) affirmed that equality between women and men is critical to achieving social development, and that this cannot happen in the absence of human rights—including women's human rights. The culmination of these efforts came with the Fourth World Conference on Women (Beijing, 1995), the largest world conference in the history of the UN, where a strong commitment to women's rights as human rights formed the very foundation of the Beijing Platform for Action.[114]

In addition, in 1998 the International Criminal Tribunal for Rwanda designated rape as a war crime for the first time in history.

Ellen Goodman, an American syndicated columnist, argues that these collective efforts suggest that "global mistreatment of women is no longer a cultural issue."[115] That conclusion is probably premature. Two African women employed in the United States as a lawyer and a college professor, respectively, "take great exception to the recent Western focus on female genital mutilation in Africa." They go on to note that the U.S. State Department has required African governments to report on the incidence of genital mutilation and that influential lawmakers have called for discontinuation of financial aid to governments that do "not address this issue in the manner dictated by the West." "We do not believe," these African women conclude, "that force changes traditional habits and practices. Superior Western attitudes do not enhance dialogue or equal exchange of ideas."[116] The headline for their *The New York Times* article is, "The West Just Doesn't Get It." In a similar vein, the director of the East Asian and Pacific Bureau of the Ministry of Foreign Affairs of Singapore has argued that "the diversity of cultural traditions, political structures, and levels of development will make it difficult, if not impossible, to define a single distinctive and coherent human rights regime that can encompass the vast region from Japan to Burma, with its Confucianist, Buddhist, Islamic, and Hindu traditions." "Asians," he continues, "do not wish to be considered good Westerners," and he concludes that "the self-congratulatory, simplistic, and sanctimonious tone of much Western commentary at the end of the Cold War and the current triumphalism of Western values grate on East and Southeast Asians."[117]

It can certainly be argued with some legitimacy that the main concern of this spokesperson from the Ministry of Foreign Affairs in Singapore is to "delegitimize international efforts to address the abuses that particularly characterize his own government and its regional allies: detention without trial and denial of press freedoms."[118] But Americans too are capable of arguing that international standards of morality are inapplicable to special problems they face. "The U.S., no less than [other] countries . . . claims the right to pick and choose which rights to defend and international laws to uphold."[119] President Clinton, for example, when faced with refugees from Haiti trying to reach Florida, claimed that international law governing treatment of political refugees does not apply to the United States. The U.S. policy of forcing Haitians to return to Haiti without a hearing to determine their eligibility for political asylum violates an international legal requirement that they be given such a hearing. Furthermore, "although most nations have banned the death penalty, [Americans] refuse to acknowledge international law on this issue claiming, in effect, our culture gives us the right to go our own way."[120]

So persistent claims in favor of the right of states to be free of interference from outsiders, buttressed by cultural differences regarding what is moral or ethical, make it difficult to enforce the rights of women in countries where they are obviously and harshly discriminated against. Canada adopted an interesting approach to dealing with this problem. It accepted as a political refugee a woman from Saudi Arabia who argued that her opposition to discrimination against women in her homeland put her at risk.[121] One advantage of that approach is that it does not involve direct intervention in the affairs of another sovereign state, certainly not with military force. And it is conceivable that if additional countries adopted Canada's policy, thus increasing the right of exit for women from countries whose female citizens want to leave, this could increase their bargaining power in domestic political processes focusing on women's rights. In distinct contrast, when Fauziya Kasinga left her native Togo in 1994 and immigrated (illegally) to the United States rather than submit to genital mutilation, she awaited hearings for more than a year during which "she endured body searches, shackles, and poor sanitation at a federal detention center."[122]

Women's rights can also be enhanced if those rights, and violence against women, continue to be treated as development issues (discussed in Chapter 11). And the status of women can be further improved if they are specifically given increased support by the policies of governments and international agencies such as the International Monetary

Fund and the World Bank. Finally, international campaigns in the United Nations and affiliated organizations, complemented by the efforts of transnational organizations such as Amnesty International, to make women's rights a high-priority human rights issue may in the long run improve the political, legal, and economic conditions for the world's female population.

An Emerging Legal Right to Democracy

It is clear that human rights is a controversial concept on which to base decisions about which governments are legitimate targets of outside intervention. Would democracy perhaps better serve that purpose? Governments elected by their own peoples in fair, competitive elections could be assumed to be legitimate and entitled to run their internal affairs as they see fit. Undemocratic governments could justifiably be subjected to outside intervention. "From the point of view of persons nonvoluntarily subject to a regime, and unable effectively to express or withhold their consent to it, [there is] little moral difference whether the regime is imposed by other members of their own community or by foreign governments."[123]

There does in fact seem to be an emerging international legal right to democratic governance. "Democracy," according to an analysis in the *American Journal of International Law*, "is on the way to becoming a global entitlement, one that increasingly will be promoted and protected by collective international processes." According to this argument, objections to antidemocratic coups in Russia and Haiti in 1991 by leaders from other governments officially registered in such international organizations as the United Nations and the Organization of American States reflect a "new global climate" that has resulted in a "transformation of the democratic entitlement from moral prescription to international legal obligation."[124] This new legal norm has the obvious potential to be abused by more powerful countries for their own selfish purposes against weaker countries. Indeed, there has been significant unease regarding the United States' promotion of democracy and its recent association with regime change and military intervention.[125] Thus, while there does seem to be a clear trend in the international system toward equating democratic government with legitimate government, "there is no well-settled body of norms about acceptable forms of involvement in democratization across borders.[126] (See the Policy Choices box "Should States Intervene to Promote Democratization?" in Chapter 6.)

International Cooperation: Norms and Regimes

International cooperation in global politics can revolve around ideas that develop about what is right and acceptable, such as the emerging right to democracy, the growing belief that internal conditions are a legitimate arena for international concern, and the idea that the use of force is not legitimate unless for self-defense or to punish an aggressor. These ideas become reinforced through the behavior of states. States may obey laws and adhere to less explicit ethical principles despite the possibility that disobedience would bring immediate and obvious advantages. As the highly nationalistic German historian Heinrich von Trietschke, a fervent advocate of power politics, argued, "Honest and legal policies are also, ordinarily, the most effective and profitable. They inspire the confidence of other states."[127]

tit-for-tat strategy
To evoke cooperation by matching another actor's gestures.

In other words, under some circumstances, cooperation is beneficial, partly because states will reward cooperation with further cooperation. In situations structured like the prisoner's dilemma game discussed in Chapter 8, cooperation pays for both players unless one player defects. Such defections can best be avoided if participants pursue a **tit-for-tat strategy.** That is, players can most reliably evoke cooperation if they cooperate on the first move and then do whatever the other player does on subsequent moves. In time, apparently, both players may realize that every defection is met by defection and every cooperative move is reciprocated.[128]

Such consistent cooperation can be the result of merely strategic calculations, but cooperative tendencies among players can be strengthened if they are based on norms, rules, or principles. If such norms, rules, and principles become clearly established and recognized by a sufficiently large number of important states in the international system, then a **regime** may emerge. "Regimes are sets of implicit or explicit principles, norms, rules, and decision-making procedures around which actors' expectations converge in a given area of international relations."[129] Regimes "may or may not be accompanied by explicit organizational arrangements."[130] In short, regimes, capable of evoking actors' expectations that foster orderly behavior, can be based on ethical principles, international law, or international organizations.

regime Set of principles, norms, rules, and procedures in a given area of international relations.

So, for example, there is a regime in the international system regarding the issue of nuclear nonproliferation that is based in part on an explicit treaty, the Nuclear Nonproliferation Treaty (discussed in Chapter 8). This treaty in effect makes proliferation illegal for its signatories, who also cooperate in the effort to prevent the spread of nuclear weapons in ways specifically stated within the treaty. The nonproliferation regime also has an organizational basis in the form of the International Atomic Energy Agency, which implements procedures designed to detect the diversion of nuclear materials produced by nuclear power plants for the production of nuclear weapons.

But the norms or principles on which regimes are based are often less explicit, their content rather emerging and becoming clear as a result of states' actual practices and behavior. There is, arguably, a regime in the current international system regarding intervention for human rights and protection of democracy.

Realists see regimes as simply a reflection of state preferences, with little or no influence independent of states:

> The realist argument that national actions are governed entirely by calculation of interests . . . is essentially a denial of the operation of normative obligation [that is, obligation inspired by norms rather than enforced by coercion] in international affairs. This position has held the field for some time in mainstream international relations. But it is increasingly being challenged by a growing body of empirical study and academic analysis.[131]

Many point out that norms can be a powerful source of political behavior.[132] Even if individuals usually behave in essentially egocentric, self-interested ways, there are intriguing, anomalous exceptions. For example, why people bother to vote represents a long-standing puzzle for analysts of voting behavior, because a single individual's vote usually will not make a difference in a national election. It is also difficult to understand why Americans, for example, make contributions to the United Way Fund or public radio and television stations, why they risk their lives in time of war, and why they "do not always cheat when no one is looking."[133] One of the best-known advocates of social analysis based on the assumption that human beings are rational acknowledges, "I have come to believe that social norms provide an important kind of motivation for action that is irreducible to rationality or indeed to any other form of optimizing mechanism."[134]

If individuals are capable of sacrificing even their lives for ethical reasons, it does not seem so far-fetched to imagine that individual leaders may at least on occasion promote ethical considerations ahead of, though not necessarily against, the state's national interest when making government decisions.[135] Essentially, international norms "entail a collective evaluation of behavior by members of the state system in terms of what ought to be, as well as a collective expectation as to what behavior will be."[136] Constructivists (as discussed in Chapter 1) point out that what is right, wrong, appropriate, and even what is in a state's interest is the product of the collective social context of global politics. Because norms are not objective, they change over time as state behavior and collective evaluation change.[137]

The norm against slavery is a good example. "Probably the purest'— most moral, least self-interested—foreign policy action ever taken on behalf of human rights' was the British navy's suppression of the slave trade in the nineteenth century."[138] Slavery was for thousands of years considered an immutable aspect of human nature. But because of the opposition of the British, ultimately joined by many others, norms against slavery became so strong that it virtually disappeared altogether. The traditional, quite prevalent counterargument is that slavery disappeared only when and because it became unprofitable.[139] In this view, slavery's disappearance had nothing to do with moral progress and is therefore no indication that ethical principles influence the behavior of governments as well as individuals. Morality, according to one modern student of philosophy, requires "people to act in ways that do not promote their individual self-interest. . . . Living wholly by the principle of enlightened self-love just is not a kind of *morality*."[140] If regimes are based on an entirely self-interested adherence to norms, their existence (disputable as even that turns out to be) does not constitute very good evidence of the potential impact of ethical principles.

But if slavery's (and the slave trade's) disappearance was a result of truly ethical behavior, then it is at least one important example of altruistic government behavior analogous to that found among individuals, such as voting, contributing to charities, and risking death for the sake of their country. And if moral progress or cultural change is capable of eliminating a social practice of such long standing as slavery, perhaps such progress also can eliminate another seemingly indestructible custom in the global political system: international war.

Norms against War

Norms against war as an acceptable tool for states may also be evolving. "The major powers have not fought each other since 1945. Such a lengthy period of peace among the most powerful states is unprecedented."[141] As discussed in Chapter 6, democratic states have been unlikely to fight international wars against each other. The use of military force to collect international debts or establish colonies, so prevalent in the nineteenth and early twentieth centuries, has virtually disappeared, arguably because such uses of military force are no longer ethically acceptable.[142] Even in "a total war, states struggling for survival altered or transcended the expected use of particular forms of military power [such as chemical warfare, during the Second World War], in part because of intentionally constructed international prohibitions on those types of warfare."[143] One recent study of war concludes that after 5,000 years, cultural and material changes may be combining to inhibit international war. "War," according to one prominent military historian, "seems to me, after a lifetime of reading about the subject, mingling with men of war, visiting the sites of war and observing its effects, may well be ceasing to commend itself to human beings as a desirable or productive, let alone rational, means of reconciling their discontents."[144]

Perhaps, in short, the world wars of the twentieth century, combined with the historical tendency of states to ignore international law, ethical principles, and norms, have led theorists of international politics to discount too heavily the impact of norms and ethics on foreign policies and international politics. In 1989, while Soviet troops were still in Afghanistan, President Mikhail Gorbachev declared that the Soviet intervention in that country was a "sin."[145] This may have been the first time a major political leader has ever so categorized a military operation of his or her own government, especially while it was still in progress. It may be a straw in the wind along with more important indications, such as the recent absence of war between major powers or between democratic states, and the end of formal colonialism showing that we are entering an era in which the importance of ethical and legal prohibitions against the use of military force for settling disputes and resolving conflicts among nations will become increasingly apparent. "Despite confusion and uncertainty, it seems just possible to glimpse the emerging outline of a world without war."[146]

Norms versus Power

How many states does it take to accept a norm for us to say that an international norm, or regime, has truly emerged? That is a difficult question with no clear answer, and one that undergirds many international debates in contemporary global politics. What if just one state, or a small group of states, is in violation of an international norm or refuses to sign a treaty that almost everyone else has signed and ratified? Generally, we would agree that norms do not have to be universally accepted to be significant in international relations, but what if that state is (or the group of states includes) one of the most powerful in the world? What if that state is the United States in the twenty-first century?

The United States has refused to sign or ratify important international treaties (see Table 9.3). "Even as the United States seeks to strengthen the enforcement of international law for its own ends, it has often recoiled at the prospect that these norms might be enforced against it."[147] In doing so, it is asserting its sovereign right but may be undermining the legitimacy of these specific efforts at multilateral cooperation, international law generally, and the international institutions that support these efforts. Just as the U.S. refusal to join the League of Nations after World War I may not have been the sole reason leading to the failure of collective security and the onset of World War II, U.S. isolation in these particular areas may not be the only obstacle to solving the problems they attempt to address. But it is clear that the pattern of violation of these international norms exhibited by the United States, given its hegemonic position in global politics, is of great concern to the rest of the world. In the international debate over the intervention in Iraq in 2003, many states saw the U.S. conviction to pursue the invasion unilaterally in the context of its previous policies to "go it alone." Part of the opposition to U.S. foreign policy toward Iraq, then, may have been a breakdown in the tit-for-tat reciprocal cooperation that underlies the development and maintenance of international norms. This may not be in any state's long-term interests. "As the world's sole superpower, the United States can defy international standards with little fear of immediate sanction; but other states will begin to question its motives in trying to strengthen important legal regimes such as those covering nuclear and chemical nonproliferation."[148] Although

TABLE 9.3
Major Multilateral Treaties That the United States Has Not Signed or Ratified
Convention on the Elimination of All Forms of Discrimination Against Women (1979)
Convention on the Rights of the Child (1989)
Convention on Biological Diversity (1992)
Comprehensive Nuclear Test-Ban Treaty (1996)
Convention on the Prohibition of the Use, Stockpiling, Production and Transfer of Anti-Personnel Mines and Their Destruction (1997)
Kyoto Protocol to the Framework Convention on Climate Change (1997)
Rome Statute of the International Criminal Court (1998)

Note: Major multilateral treaties are those with more than 120 state parties.

the Obama administration signaled that it supports some of the treaties in Table 9.3 and the norms they embody, there has been no formal adoption of these conventions (at the time of this writing).

SUMMARY

- Modern international organizations trace their origins to the nineteenth century, when the Concert of Europe was established by the Congress of Vienna and several international functional organizations were launched. After the First World War, the League of Nations was established in the hope that it would prevent such wars from recurring. The League failed to prevent the Second World War, but its temporary existence taught U.S. policymakers that the war happened because of failure to support the League, not necessarily because organizations like the League, or the United Nations, are inherently ineffective.

- A major purpose of the United Nations is to establish a system of collective security guaranteeing that any victim of aggression in the international system will receive support from the collective weight of the entire international community. There are several logical or theoretical grounds for expecting it to be difficult to create an effective collective security system. "Aggression" is not easy to define, and even if a definition can be agreed on, its application to concrete cases can be controversial. Precommitments by some nations to other nations in the form of alliances are, strictly speaking, inconsistent with a system of collective security, since the world community must be ready to resist aggression by any state in the world. In addition, all states have a powerful incentive to let other states carry the burden of resisting aggression in any given case. The Cold War also hamstrung the efforts of the United Nations at collective security since both sides possessed the power to veto the enforcement of Chapter VII by the Security Council.

- For all these reasons, over the years the United Nations has invested a lot of time and energy in peacekeeping, as opposed to collective security. Peacekeeping involves intervening militarily in trouble spots of the world to separate antagonistic factions for long enough to allow stable relationships to be restored. Peacekeeping and peacemaking ventures have proliferated in the post–Cold War world, sometimes, with controversial effects, as in Rwanda and Somalia. Peacekeeping activities reached a peak in 1993 and 1994. After these experiences, the United Nations seemed set on scaling back peacekeeping operations, but recent missions, such as in East Timor, are quite ambitious.

- The United Nations attempts to promote peace in other ways beyond peacekeeping and collective security. These include mediating between disputes and addressing the underlying social and economic factors that contribute to conflict. The future of the United Nations will include debates about its budget and its structure.

- Continual violations of international law commonly lead to the conclusion that it is so weak and ineffectual that it does not really exist. But high crime rates within states do not lead to the conclusion that domestic law does not exist. In fact, most states obey most international laws most of the time. In part, this occurs because cooperation pays; that is, states can benefit from a reputation for being trustworthy and law abiding.

- It is commonly asserted that ethics and moral principles are irrelevant to international politics. But even realists and other moral skeptics do not adhere to such a categorical position. Even when cooperation breaks down and war ensues, international law and moral standards are applied, largely based on ideas from the just war tradition.

- Nuclear weapons create profound moral dilemmas because their use in defense of ethical principles or other values could destroy the world, or at least kill millions of people instantly. Deontological analysis of such dilemmas insists that ethical choices must be based on sound moral principles rather than on calculations regarding the empirical impact of those choices. In defense of this position, it must be admitted that it is, at best, very difficult to estimate the impact of, for example, nuclear deterrence policies or a decision to resist the Iraqi annexation of Kuwait.

- According to basic principles of international law, states should be free of interference in their internal affairs. However, the corrupt and oppressive policies of some governments against their own citizens create continuing temptations for the international community to ignore or circumvent legal prohibitions against intervening in the domestic affairs of other sovereign states. Indeed, the post–Cold War system has seen a shift away from states' rights and toward human rights, including those that are codified in the UN Declaration of Human Rights, signed by most states.

● The most pervasive human rights issue in the world at present involves discrimination against the female population. Recent years have seen a number of developments in which women's equality is seen as a part of human rights. Some argue that an emerging norm countenances international intervention on behalf of democracy when dictatorships threaten to emerge, or when existing dictatorships suppress democratic aspirations.

● Cooperative tendencies on the part of states can be enhanced if cooperation is based on established norms and recognized principles. If those norms and principles become sufficiently well established, they provide the basis for regimes. The impact of regimes is at least potentially substantial. An antislavery regime in the nineteenth century, for example, eliminated a practice long thought to be indestructible. There are some signs, such as the absence of war among democratic states, the absence of war between major powers since the Second World War, and the demise of formal colonialism, that norms against the use of violence in international politics are becoming more effective.

KEY TERMS

collective security   304
UN Charter   308
Security Council   308
General Assembly   308
Secretariat   308
International Court
  of Justice (World Court)   308
peacekeeping   312
peacemaking   314
state-building   318
positive peace   318
Economic and Social
  Council (ECOSOC)   319
international law   324
Kellogg-Briand Pact   326
diplomatic immunity   327
ethics   328
moral skepticism   330

moral relativism   330
Geneva Conventions   331
Genocide Convention   331
war crimes   331
International Criminal
  Court (ICC)   333
just war   335
Universal Declaration
  of Human Rights   338
humanitarian
  interventions   339
female deficit   341
Convention on the Elimination
  of All Forms of Discrimination
  Against Women (CEDAW)   342
tit-for-tat strategy   346
regime   346

PART IV

Interactions of Actors: Economic Relations

CHAPTER 10

Interdependence Among Rich States: International Political Economy in the North

Having examined the security relationships between states, we now begin to look at economic interactions in global politics. The study of the **international political economy** concerns the relationships between political units and political relationships, on the one hand, and economics and economic relationships, on the other. This relationship between politics and economics is important for understanding global politics.

Economics, simply put, deals with the exchange of goods and services. An economic market is composed of producers and consumers of these goods and services. Economists tell us that a market functions on the supply of goods and services produced by the sellers and the demand for goods and services consumed by the buyers. Without any restrictions on this exchange, the price of a good or service on an economic market will be determined by the relative supply and demand. But there are restrictions on the exchange of goods and services in the international economic system (just as there are in all domestic economic systems). In other words, there is no such thing as a "free" economic market. The restrictions come from politics—from values and goals of states. States may impose restrictions on economic exchange for the sake of security or for moral considerations, for example. This tension between economic forces of production and consumption and other political forces is the center of the international political economy. Economics cannot be divorced from politics (even the choice to pursue a "freer" market is a political choice), but the exact nature of what the relationship between economics and politics should be is a source of disagreement among major economic philosophies, as we will see in the discussion of economic liberalism, mercantilism, and neo-Marxism in this and the next two chapters.

Just as economics cannot be divorced from politics, politics is fundamentally shaped by economics. Politicians around the world are continually concerned about the economic impact that their policy decisions will have on their own citizens. Failing to manage such politically and socially volatile issues as unemployment and inflation, for example, can leave a political system weak and vulnerable and may result in the removal of leaders from office. Indeed, a large part of what government officials do is attempt to provide economic resources—such as jobs, tax cuts, and government subsidies—to their constituents or supporters. This is true in democracies and nondemocracies alike: All types of governments rely to some extent on the support of key groups within society, such as workers and businesses. Moreover, economic interdependence has increasingly connected the fortunes of citizens around the world, and a decision by one state to alter its trading practices, devalue its currency, or increase its minimum wage, for example, can have dramatic consequences on the economies of other states. Today, trade accounts for high percentages of the gross domestic product (GDP) of industrialized states (see Table 10.1), and financial flows between countries exceed trade flows by thirty to one.[1] Because of this interdependence, as we have seen time and again, an economic downturn in one part of the world results in hard political

international political economy Area of study focusing on the relationships between international political and economic relationships.

TABLE 10.1

An Indicator of Interdependence: Trade as a Percentage of Gross Domestic Product, 2007

Germany	72%
China	68%
France	45%
United Kingdom	38%
United States	38%
Japan	30%
Average for high-income states	49%

Source: World Bank, *World Development Indicators Database,* June 2009. © 2009 World Bank. Reproduced by permission.

choices elsewhere as jobs are lost, investment dollars dry up, and the economic landscape becomes filled with uncertainty. The recent global economic downturn demonstrates how interdependent financial sectors are and how governments are forced to respond. Just as there can be no markets free of politics, politics cannot free itself from economics.

developed countries Wealthier, more industrialized countries.

This chapter analyzes relationships among the wealthier, more industrialized, or **developed countries,** sometimes referred to as the North, because most are located in the Northern Hemisphere (although countries such as Australia are included in this category). Chapter 11 focuses on the economic relationships between the industrialized states and the poorer, **developing countries,** mostly in the Southern Hemisphere and therefore often referred to as the South (although again, states such as Vietnam are an exception). Chapter 12 looks at efforts at regional free trade and economic integration, particularly the European Union.

developing countries Poorer, less industrialized countries.

Until the 1970s, most people considered the topics discussed in this chapter to be too technical and apolitical to be of much interest to students of international political relations. The rules by which the rich industrialized states conducted international commerce with each other were devised in the four or five years after the Second World War, and several factors worked to make those rules uncontroversial, as well as apparently uninteresting. One of these factors was a steady, positive rate of economic growth in almost all the industrialized countries. Another important factor was the unquestioned U.S. domination of the world's economic transactions. As long as these factors persisted and the United States supported the structure of the economic system in the noncommunist world, economic relationships among rich countries seemed rather divorced from politics, which centered on meeting the Communist threat. But when the system ran into serious problems and American economic preeminence began to fade, those technical problems suddenly seemed very political. They had always been political, of course; what had been missing was overt political conflict over economic arrangements in the noncommunist world. This chapter examines the structure of economic relationships among the rich industrialized countries of the world and the process by which those relationships have become an increasingly prominent political issue.

The Era of U.S. Economic Predominance and the Liberal International Economic Order

The contemporary international economic system has its roots in the economic problems of the 1930s (see Chapter 2) and how the leading states after World War II attempted to build institutions and international norms to prevent a recurrence of a global economic depression. The architects of the post–World War II economic system were not solely interested in making economics work better and thus making more profit from economic exchanges. They also believed that economic prosperity and certain types of relationships between states and other economic actors were the keys to security. Many blamed the economic troubles of the 1920s and 1930s for the war. Recall from Chapter 6 that one explanation for World War II points to the poor economic conditions in Germany, which played a key role in Hitler's rise to power. This explanation also blames the protectionist policies that states adopted to try to isolate themselves from the effects of the worldwide depression. These policies did not always achieve prosperity for states, and they served to disconnect states from each other, making the choice for war a less costly one. This, of course, is liberalism's explanation of World War II, and thus the plans for the new international economic system rested on the liberal philosophy about the relationship between economics and politics. The architects of the new system attempted to build a **Liberal International Economic Order**.

Liberal International Economic Order Post–World War II attempt to construct international economic relations based on economic liberalism.

Economic Liberalism versus Mercantilism

As we saw in Chapter 1, liberalism is a perspective on global politics that focuses on interdependence, nonstate actors, and incentives for cooperation among states. It includes, but is not limited to, a recognition that economic actors such as multinational corporations have become more important in world politics and that economic interests of states and nonstate actors can constrain states, pushing them away from war and toward cooperation.

Liberalism is a general perspective and is related to a narrower philosophy of **economic liberalism.** Economic liberalism is narrower in the sense that it focuses on only economics and the relationships among individuals, firms, markets, and governments in the economic sphere. The two terms, however, share the word *liberalism* and thus share a focus on individuals, self-interests, and rights. Liberalism recognizes that

economic liberalism Economic philosophy advocating free trade to increase efficiency and wealth.

individuals following their interests will diverge from the interests of the state and thus constrain states. In an open economic system and in an open, democratic political system, individuals have the most freedom to pursue their interests and constrain the state. This is why liberalism expects democracies to be more peaceful than nondemocracies. Liberalism is founded on ideas of eighteenth- and nineteenth-century liberal philosophers such as Montesquieu, Immanuel Kant, John Stuart Mill, and Jeremy Bentham.

Economic liberalism, the narrower philosophy, also borrows ideas of individual self-interest from liberal philosophers, applying them to the realm of economics. The writings of Adam Smith are particularly important. Smith, considered to be the father of modern economics, wrote in his book, *The Wealth of Nations,* in 1776 about the importance of free markets and individual economic interests.[2] He argued that the way to greater wealth for all was through complex divisions of labor, determined by individual interests, and that production and efficiency were best achieved through market mechanisms, allowing what Smith referred to as the "hidden hand" of the market, rather than the government, to direct economic relations. According to Smith, individuals and business firms pursue their individual interests, and these are coordinated by the market system to produce what is in the society's interest: greater wealth for all. Smith wrote that "every individual is continually exerting himself to find out the most advantageous employment for whatever capital he can command. It is his own advantage, indeed, and not that of society, which he has in view. But the study of his own advantage naturally, or rather necessarily, leads him to prefer that employment which is most advantageous to society."[3] In this quotation lie two very important assumptions behind economic liberalism: that individuals do in fact act in their self-interests and that this produces a social good.

For economic liberals, it is the free market system that best coordinates economic activity, making it more efficient and producing greater wealth for all. Although Smith was primarily applying these ideas to a domestic economy, others have applied economic liberalism to the international economy. The economic liberal view on international economic relationships also stresses the free market, particularly in the form of **free trade,** or exchange across borders unrestricted by penalties, such as tariffs that place a tax on incoming goods, imposed by governments. A free trade system is Smith's ideas of individual interests coordinated by a market system, on a grander scale. Economic liberals such as David Ricardo, an early nineteenth-century economist and politician in England, argued that each country should pursue its self-interests by allowing firms to specialize in what they most efficiently produce and trade freely with one another to distribute goods to consumers, free of government intervention.[4] For Ricardo and other economic liberals, it did not make sense for governments to protect their country's jobs or profits at the expense of other countries, because the market mechanism would distribute

free trade International commerce unrestricted by state-imposed penalties such as tariffs.

comparative advantage Goods that a certain country is relatively more efficient at producing.

the jobs and profits in the most efficient way, regardless of nationality, and in a way that would provide more wealth for all in the long run. Instead, countries should allow firms to specialize in the production of goods that are in their **comparative advantage**—goods that they are relatively more efficient at producing than other countries—and selling those goods abroad. For goods that are not a country's comparative advantage, countries should import these goods from abroad, not wasting capital and labor on their production. In a free trade system, a division of labor along countries' comparative advantage will enhance global efficiency and create greater wealth for all, according to economic liberalism.

Most economic liberals believe that governments should play some role in domestic and international economies. "The role of the state is to perform the limited number of tasks that individuals cannot perform by themselves, such as establishing a basic legal system, assure national defense, and coin money."[5] Basically, the role of government in economics is to provide for **collective goods**—goods such as security, law, and education—to all. Collective goods are indivisible, so that once they are supplied to one member of a group, all members benefit, and recipients cannot be singled out and excluded from receiving the collective good. A government's role in providing for collective goods, according to economic liberals, makes sense, because it would be inefficient for firms to provide for them themselves. Imagine if McDonald's or IBM had to educate its own work force, build and maintain its own roadway, and provide for its own defense from external threats! It is more efficient for businesses to pay taxes and allow the government to coordinate efforts to provide for collective goods. Overall, however, economic liberalism sees a relatively narrow role for governments. Most important, economic liberals put economics first, above politics, and see the two as separate spheres of activity.

collective goods Goods that, once provided, are available to all group members, regardless of their individual contributions.

mercantilism Economic philosophy that asserts the primacy of the state and protection of the state's economic power.

David Ricardo and other economic liberals of the nineteenth century were reacting to another prominent philosophy of economic exchange and the relationship between economics and politics. **Mercantilism** is the philosophy that economics and politics are related, that politics should come first, and that economic activity should serve the interests of the state. Mercantilism has its roots in the fifteenth through eighteenth centuries, when states were established and the great powers began engaging in international economic relations. The rulers of the time viewed economic relations with other states as a way of amassing wealth for their own states in order to maximize power. Wealth was a tool of influence rather than an end in itself; it was used to purchase guns, territories, and mercenaries. What is important about economics, according to mercantilism, is that it serves the interest of the state in the competition for more power and influence. As long as international economic transactions benefit the state, such as when the state is selling more to others than it is buying, then all is well. When economic relations threaten the power and autonomy of a state, such as when a state is buying more than it is selling or when it becomes dependent on others for something it needs, then all is not well.

Thus, for mercantilists, economic relations with other states need to maximize profit as a means toward more power relative to other states and minimize economic loss and dependence. It is the role of the state to structure its foreign economic relations to this end. States should, for example, grant **subsidies** to their own industries so that they better compete with the industries of others. States should also protect their own industries with restrictions on imports such as **tariffs,** which are taxes on imports that make them more expensive and thus less attractive to consumers, so that profits stay at home and the country does not grow too dependent on foreign sources. There are a variety of methods of **protectionist policies** in addition to subsidies and tariffs. States can, for example, impose **import quotas** on goods (limiting the number of goods that can be imported into a country), place health and safety regulations on imported goods (making it difficult for imported goods to meet these standards), and engage in **dumping** (selling goods abroad for less than they are sold at home).

The bottom line for mercantilism is a positive **balance of trade:** more exports to other countries and fewer imports from other countries. This is important not for reasons of simple profit but for what profit buys: political power. The focus on power and state autonomy links mercantilism, an economic philosophy, with realism, a more general perspective on global politics (as described in Chapter 1). Economic liberals disagree with the protectionist policies of mercantilism and argue that politics should not drive or limit economics. The fundamental difference between mercantilism and economic liberalism is that the former sees competition with other states as the *raison d'être* of states, while the latter sees cooperation with other states as the key to economic prosperity for all. For economic liberals, it does not matter that one state may be benefiting more economically, with, for example, a positive balance of trade, than another state. What is important is that they are both benefiting more from a division of labor and free market system than if restrictions are imposed on economic activity. Put another way, mercantilism focuses on the relative gains of states (how states are faring in relation to each other) in a zero-sum competition, and economic liberalism focuses on the absolute gains of states (how states are faring generally, regardless of the gains for other states) in non-zero-sum relationships.

Mercantilists and economic liberals also disagree about the value of multinational corporations (MNCs). As discussed in Chapter 4, the number and importance of MNCs in the global economy accelerated in the second half of the twentieth century. Economic liberals see foreign direct investment (FDI) by MNCs as positive in that it facilitates free trade based on comparative advantage; MNCs can be the architects of a world-wide division of labor that is efficient, without political interference by states. Mercantilists, on the other hand, are suspicious of MNCs, because they fear that they put profits over state interests, and because they take

subsidies Financial aid from governments to domestic industries.

tariffs Import tax on foreign products.

protectionist policies Policies directed to protect domestic economy from foreign competition.

import quotas Limits on the number of goods that can be imported into the country.

dumping Selling products abroad at below-cost prices.

balance of trade Value of a state's exports minus its imports.

export platforms Countries that use incentives to attract foreign direct investment and production by MNCs.

away from the national economy by relocating jobs to other countries. Similarly, American labor unions are particularly concerned about the contribution of MNCs to U.S. unemployment. As many critics of the North American Free Trade Agreement (NAFTA) (discussed in Chapter 12) point out, MNCs repeatedly shut down factories in the United States and set up new ones in **export platforms,** where labor is cheaper—for example, in Mexico. According to labor union leaders in many industrialized countries, domestic jobs are lost directly to the laborers in the export platforms, and even more jobs are then lost indirectly, because the foreign subsidiaries monopolize export markets that otherwise could be served by national factories with domestic workers. In this view, by exporting jobs, investing money overseas, and having subsidiaries overseas that make it impossible for products made in the home country to be exported, MNCs exacerbate balance-of-trade and balance-of-payments problems for industrialized countries. In addition, goods made by domestic companies are made by overseas subsidiaries, and these products must be imported into the home country, adding further to its balance-of-trade and balance-of-payments deficits.

It can also be argued that MNCs are exacerbating the unequal distribution of wealth in industrialized societies such as the United States by moving a variety of productive jobs out of the country, leaving nothing but highly specialized occupations for which only their wealthy and highly educated citizens can qualify. A study of nine industries in the United States reveals that "multinationals create . . . jobs but that many of the jobs created [are] in the white-collar and managerial areas whereas the jobs lost [come] from the blue-collar ranks."[6]

MNCs and their defenders, including economic liberals, do not take these criticisms lightly, and in some cases, their counterarguments are convincing. The contribution of foreign investment activity by MNCs to unemployment is direct and visible, but foreign investment also makes substantial, less direct, and less visible contributions to the number of jobs in industrialized countries. The wages MNCs pay to workers overseas, for example, create increased demands for domestic-made products in the countries where they operate. And these subsidiaries need parts and capital equipment from the home country, adding again to the number of jobs in the domestic economy. The fact that DVD players can be made more cheaply in China than in the United States saves American consumers thousands (or millions) of dollars a year, and because those machines are available to them at the lower prices, they can spend the money they save on additional American products. It is also important not to overlook the fact that imports create jobs. When the United States imports automobiles from Japan, for example, *people* must transport them to dealerships, advertise them, sell them, and service them, and most of these people are Americans.

Defenders of MNCs argue that if they were somehow prohibited from setting up subsidiaries in export platforms, it would not mean more jobs for workers at home. MNCs from other countries would simply use such platforms to full advantage instead. Production facilities in the home states would not be economically viable, because they could not compete with those foreign MNC subsidiaries in places with lower costs. Of course, the governments could forbid home-based corporations from investing overseas (or tax such activity so heavily that it would not be feasible) *and* prevent the import of products made by foreign MNCs taking advantage of conditions elsewhere. But this, economic liberals argue, would be the beginning of an escalatory process involving tariffs and countertariffs, quotas and counterquotas, that would be disastrous for the entire world.

The extent to which MNCs are inclined to export jobs to states with lower wages may also be somewhat exaggerated in the minds of their critics. Low wages are obviously only one consideration these corporations take into account when they decide where to set up a subsidiary, and the available evidence suggests that it is far from the most important consideration. Developing countries have attracted an increasing share of FDI today, but it is still true that most FDI comes from and is received by developed countries. Indeed, the United States and the United Kingdom are typically the largest recipients of FDI in the world.[7] Most of this investment comes from Great Britain, Japan, the Netherlands, Canada, Germany, and Switzerland; that is, like most FDI, it originates in a rich industrialized country and is transferred to another rich industrialized country. For economic liberals, this transfer of wealth across borders is important for an efficient and prosperous global economy.

The Bretton Woods System

After World War II, most of the leaders of the major states, as well as their economic advisers, embraced the philosophy of economic liberalism as the basis for a postwar international economic system—the Liberal International Economic Order. Mercantilist policies that states adopted in the 1920s and 1930s were blamed for the economic devastation and for World War I. In particular, the protectionist trade policies adopted by states that limited imports (such as the Smoot-Hawley Act, which raised U.S. tariff rates) were blamed for spreading and deepening the economic depression around the world. States' monetary policies were a concern as well. **Monetary policies** have to do with states' decisions on printing and circulating their currency and other financial decisions that affect the flow and value of money. One tool that states have to increase the cost of imports to their country and decrease the costs of exports from their country is devaluing their currency—making their currencies worth less in relation to other currencies. If Britain, for example, whose base unit of currency is the British pound sterling, devalues its currency by printing more pound notes, then British goods are cheaper in other countries and foreign goods are more expensive in

monetary policies State decisions on printing, circulating, and otherwise affecting the value of their currency.

Britain. The effect is that foreigners will buy more British goods, and Britons will buy fewer foreign goods, thus influencing the balance of trade in a positive direction, which is exactly what mercantilists want. The problem, according to economic liberals, is that the value of the currency and goods then becomes artificial and does not reflect market mechanisms. The other problem is that when the values of currencies change so rapidly, as they did in the 1930s, business is inefficient. Businesses simply cannot plan if they cannot predict how much goods will cost them and how much profit they will make when **exchange rates** (the values of currencies in relation to each other) are unstable. Thus, the architects of the Liberal International Economic Order were primarily focused on establishing a system of free trade and providing a stable monetary system.

exchange rates Values of currencies in relation to each other.

One dilemma that economic liberalism has when applied to the international system concerns the anarchical nature of global politics. As discussed, while economic liberals prefer a minimal role for the government in economics, the government does provide a very useful function of coordinating and supplying collective goods, such as a legal system, and ensuring a sound banking system in a domestic economy. In the international system, there is no overarching government that can provide for collective goods that enhance the efficiency and safety of economic exchanges.

Economic liberalism, however, does suggest solutions to this dilemma. First, collective goods, like the rules for a free trade system, can be provided by an overwhelmingly powerful state, or hegemon, that can act like an overarching government, absorbing the costs of providing a collective good and enforcing the rules of the system. (The stable effects of a hegemon were discussed in the security realm in Chapter 6.) In the economic realm, "the liberal theory of hegemonic stability asserts that when a hegemon arises, the world economy tends to grow and prosper, as the benefits of free trade, peace and security, sound money, and so forth, stimulate markets everywhere. When the hegemon fails . . . these public goods disappear and the world economy stagnates or declines."[8] Even if a hegemon's power declines, however, a collective good can be maintained if it has been institutionalized in international organizations. These institutions serve to coordinate states and their individual contributions to collective goods. They can also serve as arbitrators and enforcers of the rules of the economic system. Recall from Chapter 9 that international norms about what is desirable behavior, such as the practice of free trade, can themselves shape state choices, particularly if they are supported by international organizations that reinforce norms. Fortunately, for the adherents to the economic liberal philosophy after World War II, there was a single state with a preponderance of economic muscle, the United States, that was in a position to serve as the hegemon and put its strength behind the construction of international institutions in the Liberal International Economic Order.[9]

Figure 10.1   The Bretton Woods System

Founded in 1944, the Bretton Woods system strove to manage the international money system, rebuild wartorn countries, and regulate international trade.

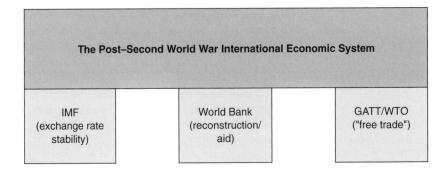

Bretton Woods system   Set of post–World War II agreements and organizations for managing the international economy.

In the five years after the Second World War, the United States led the way in an international effort to create what became known as the **Bretton Woods system.** The name comes from a meeting that was held at Bretton Woods, New Hampshire, in 1944 and attended by forty-four countries, all of them anxious to devise some economic rules and regulations that would help the world avoid the kinds of international economic catastrophes of the 1930s that had seemed to play such a key role in the process culminating in the Second World War. At that meeting in Bretton Woods and at a meeting in Geneva, Switzerland, three years later, the rules of the international economic game in the noncommunist world were hammered out. Those rules, and the system, rested on three main pillars, as shown in Figure 10.1.

The International Monetary Fund

International Monetary Fund (IMF)   Organization for promoting international monetary stability and cooperation.

The first of the three pillars of the Bretton Woods system concerned international monetary management, and the organization created to help states cope with problems in this area was the **International Monetary Fund (IMF).** By 1947, the United States and the IMF had set up an exchange rate system based on the U.S. dollar, backed by gold in order to provide a stable monetary environment for economic relations. The United States thus played a hegemonic role in international monetary relations, having a strong currency and economic wealth to back it up.[10] The price of gold was set at U.S. $35 per ounce, and that was the standard by which other currencies were to be measured. In other words, the official value of the Japanese yen, for example, would be stated in terms of its relationship to a dollar or 1 ounce of gold. The countries that joined the IMF system agreed to keep their exchange rates (the value of their currencies) in relation to dollars and gold fixed within a narrow range. The IMF monitored those exchange rates and stood ready to help any country whose currency threatened to fall lower in real value than its official exchange rate indicated.

Such a threat might originate, for example, from a consistently uneven balance of trade. Let us imagine that Italy went through a period of years when it imported much more from the United States than it exported to the United States. At the end of every year, Italy, in effect, had to settle accounts with the United States to make up the difference in the value of what it imported and exported. According to the rules of the system set up by the IMF and the United States after the Second World War, Italy had to pay up in either U.S. dollars or gold, the two being interchangeable (until 1971), because the United States had promised to support its dollars with gold. If, in order to do this, the Italian government almost entirely depleted its supply of dollars or gold (its so-called reserve currencies), international confidence in the Italian lira (Italy's currency) would have deteriorated. The official value of a lira (plural *lire*) would not have been the same as its real value. The real value (determined by what people would give up in exchange for lire) would have been lower than the official value, and everyone involved in economic transactions based on lire would have started to demand more of them in exchange for U.S. dollars (or anything else of value) than the official exchange rate stipulated. It is crises such as these that the IMF was designed to meet.

In this scenario, to prevent the real value of the lira from falling significantly lower than the official value, the Italian government would have had to support it. That means the government would have had to buy lire at the official price. As long as the Italian government was willing and able to buy lire at the official price, the real value and the official value would have stayed reasonably close. Everyone involved in transactions based on the lira would have realized that the real value and the official value were essentially identical, because the Italian government, at least, would pay the official price for its own currency. Therefore, everyone would have paid the official price for lire, secure in the knowledge that they could sell those lire to the Italian government at that price. In time, having built up confidence in the value of the lira, the government would not have to buy such great quantities. The crisis would have been over. Until the crisis passed, the Italian government would have had to obtain dollars or gold with which it could buy lire. As a member of the IMF, Italy can borrow dollars or gold from the fund to support its currency, thus keeping the official value and the real value in line and adhering to a fixed exchange rate.

From 1947 to 1971, this type of arrangement helped the rich industrialized countries to avoid most serious monetary crises, like those of the 1930s, and to keep the different national currencies at **fixed exchange rates.** From the viewpoint of economic liberalism, this stability was significant for confidence in the monetary system and international business. When the values of currencies were threatened, the member states would borrow from the IMF to support them, and the fixed official exchange rates would be maintained. People engaged in international commerce could be confident of the relative value of different currencies, and international trade and commerce were thus simplified and encouraged. The confidence engendered by fixed exchange rates was one factor

fixed exchange rates Values of currencies "pegged" to either another currency or to certain commodities, such as gold.

that contributed to the growth in trade and in the economies of the industrialized countries after the Second World War.

The World Bank

World Bank
International organization for economic assistance, first for countries recovering from World War II, then for developing countries.

The second pillar of the post–Second World War economic system was the International Bank for Reconstruction and Development (IBRD), or the **World Bank.** This organization was originally designed (as the "Reconstruction" in its name suggests) to provide capital for rebuilding countries devastated by the war. It was also supposed to aid economic development for poorer countries in the South, and at Bretton Woods, these states tried to ensure that developmental aid for them would have at least as high a priority as economic assistance to those countries devastated by the war. Those efforts were unsuccessful. The United States felt that postwar reconstruction deserved a higher priority and that economic development should be spurred primarily by domestic efforts. Outside assistance might be necessary, but the capital should come from private rather than government sources. In theory, the documents on which the World Bank was founded gave equal weight to reconstruction and development. But those documents also urged a special regard for the problems of those countries devastated by World War II; "the developed countries that dominated the World Bank unanimously agreed that European postwar reconstruction would be the first priority for the Bank."[11]

The emphasis in World Bank activities began to change as early as the 1950s. By that time, the countries devastated by the Second World War had been reconstructed. Then an increasing number of former colonies achieved independence, entered the United Nations, and began to lobby effectively for economic aid from the developed countries. Also, although under Stalin the Soviets had tended to ignore the poor countries of the world, by 1956 under the leadership of Nikita Khrushchev, the Soviets began to support development efforts and wars of national liberation in the developing world, thus making the South one of the primary theaters of the Cold War. The attitude of the United States and other developed countries about public aid to developing countries changed in response to these developments, and those changes were reflected in the activities of the World Bank. In 1956, the World Bank created the International Finance Corporation (IFC) to encourage private investment in underdeveloped countries. And in 1960, the United States took the lead in creating the International Development Association (IDA) "as a separate institution closely integrated with the World Bank."[12] The IDA makes loans at low interest rates to developing countries, to be used for development projects. In short, although the World Bank originally was concerned with relationships among the more industrialized countries of the world, over the years it has become primarily an aid-giving institution focusing on developing countries. It has come to serve as a forum for discussion among the richer countries about treatment of less developed countries rather than an organization that is directly involved in relationships among the developed countries.

The General Agreement on Tariffs and Trade

General Agreement on Tariffs and Trade (GATT) Post–World War II multilateral regime for promoting free trade.

The third pillar of the Bretton Woods system was the **General Agreement on Tariffs and Trade (GATT),** with twenty-three original countries as signatories by the time it came into force in 1948. The original plan after the war called for the creation of an institution to be known as the International Trade Organization (ITO), but opposition in the U.S. Congress killed that idea. In the beginning, the GATT was merely a trading agreement among twenty-three nations, meant to be in force only until the ITO came into being. "When the ITO failed to materialize, the GATT was transformed from a temporary agreement into a[n] . . . institutional framework in which governments pursued multilateral regulations and discussed trade policy."[13]

most-favored-nation principle Granting the same low-tariff trade status as enjoyed by a state's most-favored trading partner.

The primary function of the GATT was to encourage an increase in international trade and reduce barriers to that trade, whether in the form of tariffs, quotas, or other impediments such as regulations regarding labor standards or environmental protection (see Figure 10.2). One important means of fulfilling its main function was to encourage nations to abide by the **most-favored-nation principle.** This principle involves a commitment not to discriminate. If State A decides to give a break to State B (say, to lower its tariffs on shoes coming from State B), it must,

Figure 10.2   Changes in Tariff Rates in the Era of GATT (World Trade Organization)

Source: Data from the Centre for International Economics, office of the U.S. Trade Representative.

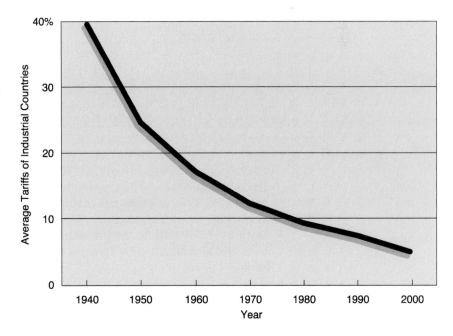

according to the GATT, give the same break to all the other GATT member states from which it imports shoes. In other words, State A is obliged to offer the same favorable terms on shoes to all states that it offers to the most favored nation among its trading partners.[14] The GATT encouraged countries to abide by the most-favored-nation principle in order to remove barriers to trade (especially tariffs). The principles on which the GATT was based come directly from economic liberalism. States should not interfere with the free trade of goods and services determined by states' comparative advantage; they should not favor one state over another for political reasons by granting them preferential trading relations. These are the principles to which states pledged when they joined the GATT.

In fact, the GATT allowed many exceptions to the most-favored-nation principle and has not come close to creating a system where free trade reigns supreme. Still, it almost certainly helped reduce barriers to international trade and thus encouraged its growth. One recent analysis found that trade among GATT members was considerably higher than we would expect without the agreement.[15] GATT negotiations occur in what are referred to as "rounds." The Kennedy Round of negotiations, for example, began in 1962 and was concluded in 1967 with agreements to reduce tariffs and expand world trade. The Tokyo Round (1973–1978) focused on lowering nontariff barriers, such as government subsidies and regulations. The Uruguay Round (1986–1993) tackled more difficult and more recently developed issues hindering free trade, such as agricultural subsidies, protection of service industries, and intellectual property rights. The most recent negotiations, the Doha Round, focused on economic development and will be discussed in Chapter 11. With this history of trade negotiations, "there can be little doubt that the GATT has had an important role in the evolution of postwar international trade relations."[16]

Another result of the Uruguay Round of international negotiations was the creation of a permanent organization, similar to the originally proposed International Trade Organization. On January 1, 1995, the GATT, whose membership had reached 122 states at the time, evolved into the World Trade Organization (WTO) (see Chapter 3 for definition).

> WTO is more powerful than GATT, incorporating trade in goods, services, and ideas and has more binding authority. . . . Replacing the GATT, which was never more than a provisional set of rules with a small secretariat in Geneva, the World Trade Organization (WTO) will be the umbrella organization covering the old GATT and all the new agreements reached in the Uruguay Round.[17]

The WTO and its role in the current global economy will be discussed in more detail at the end of this chapter.

How the System Worked

In economic terms, this system based on the IMF (supporting a dollar standard), the World Bank, and the GATT (fostering free trade) certainly worked well for the noncommunist industrialized countries. Although economic liberalis was the underlying philosophy of the Bretton Woods system, the United States acted as a hegemon, and international institutions were established to coordinate collective goods in the absence of an overarching government, purely economically liberal policies were rarely realized in practice. One way in which the system was not completely economically liberal was the fixed exchange rate system. In an ideal world, according to economic liberals, the market should determine the value of currencies, and state intervention that fixed these values was a political intrusion into economics. Another way the system deviated from economic liberalism was that free trade was not always the official policy. The United States allowed certain distortions in the system to operate against its own best short-run economic interests and in favor of Western Europe and Japan. For example, one exception to the most-favored-nation principle in the GATT rules allowed nations forming a customs union to discriminate against the outside world. The most important of these was the European Community, or Common Market, now known as the European Union (EU) (see Chapter 12), which was encouraged by the United States even though it adopted tariff barriers against U.S. products and did some harm to U.S. trading interests. Japan was allowed to use a variety of protectionist measures in the 1950s and 1960s, even though it became a member of the GATT in 1955. "Free trade was accepted where the United States did not have a comparative advantage and discrimination was tolerated where U.S. products did have an advantage."[18] Also, the United States purposely incurred balance-of-payments deficits in relation to Western Europe and Japan in the 1950s and early 1960s to provide a flow of dollars for the other industrialized countries.

Why was the United States so generous to the Western Europeans and Japanese in the 1950s and 1960s? It is safe to say that more than altruism was involved. Perhaps the most important reason concerned security. The United States felt threatened by the Soviet Union in the first couple of decades after World War II and also believed that economically prostrate (and politically valuable) countries in Western Europe and Japan were vulnerable to Communist subversion. The United States did what it could to foster its allies' rapid economic growth and thereby substantially decrease their vulnerability to such subversion, as well as increase their value as allies against the Soviet threat.

There were long-run economic advantages, too, in the types of policies adopted by the United States in the years immediately following the war. An impoverished Western Europe and Japan would not provide lucrative markets for U.S. exports. But U.S. generosity would create economic leverage for the United States in Western Europe and Japan, which would be advantageous to the United States once the other industrialized countries were back on their economic feet. Economic liberalism claims that the pie will grow larger for all in the long run, but those who have the largest slice (as the United States did with its overwhelmingly larger economy) will benefit the most. Leading the establishment of a Liberal International Economic Order also enhanced the agenda-setting power (discussed in Chapter 4) of the United States. Agenda-setting power, or structural power, was "the power to shape and determine the structures of the global political economy . . . the power to decide how things will be done, the power to shape frameworks within which states relate to each other."[19] To sum up, after the Second World War, the United States was by far the most important entity within the non-Communist world's economic system, and it had the most urgent need to see that the system worked well. Because it could not work well unless Western Europe and Japan recovered economically from the ravages of war, the United States provided important support for that recovery.

During the Bretton Woods system, trade policies deviated from pure economic liberalism in other ways. The United States, for example, protected some of its older industries such as shoes and textiles, and it subsidized agricultural products. These policies primarily stemmed from domestic political pressures rather than mercantilist principles. Simply put, "domestic groups seek protection or liberalization because such policies increase their incomes."[20] Not all domestic groups or economic sectors resist protection. Some, in fact, benefit from trade liberalization—such as shipping industries and other businesses that are dependent on imports and exports—and with increasing interdependence, more economic domestic groups organized to promote liberal trading policies.[21] With some groups pushing for liberalization and some groups advocating protectionist policies, political institutions are important factors in trade policy, because they affect which groups will have greater access to influence leaders. Furthermore, some institutions insulate leaders from societal pressures, and then it is the leaders' beliefs—liberal or mercantilist—that become critical factors in promoting or inhibiting free trade.[22] Politics affects trade policies in other ways as well. Trade sanctions and other restrictions against the Soviet Union, Cuba, and South Africa are examples of economics being used for political ends, which economic liberalism says states should avoid.

Overall, the Bretton Woods system was quite successful. World trade grew at a rapid rate, and by the 1960s, Western Europe and Japan staged remarkable recoveries from the devastation of the Second World War. By this time, the preponderant position of the United States in the noncommunist industrialized world was modified in important ways. By 1960, the United States had already allowed so many dollars to leave the country that for the first time, the value of dollars overseas became greater than the value of U.S. gold reserves. The flow of dollars out of the country continued throughout the 1960s and accelerated during the

Vietnam War. In 1952, the United States held 68 percent of all international monetary reserves; by 1977, that share had fallen to 6 percent. A similar deterioration occurred in the U.S. position in international trade. In 1947, the United States accounted for 32 percent of world exports. In 1974, it accounted for only 11 percent of world exports. In the meantime, the European Community had become the largest trading entity in the world. By 1971, the flow of cash out of the United States was so great, and imports into the United States so far exceeded U.S. exports in value, that a balance-of-payments crisis and a balance-of-trade crisis occurred simultaneously.

Nixon's Surprise

Under the rules of the Bretton Woods system in operation at that time, the United States could not devalue its currency, because the U.S. dollar, tied to the price of gold, constituted the standard by which all the other currencies were measured and on which their values were based. Because the dollar served as the anchor of the system, it could not be tampered with. In August 1971, President Nixon decided to change the rules of the system dramatically. He announced that the U.S. dollar would no longer be convertible to gold. Ever since the creation of the Bretton Woods system in the 1940s, the United States had promised to exchange dollars for gold at the rate of $35 an ounce whenever holders of dollars wished to make such an exchange. But by 1968, U.S. holdings of gold were so low that the United States was quite reluctant to give up gold for dollars; thus, it did its best to discourage such transactions. In 1971, President Nixon abandoned even the official promise to back up dollars with gold. He also imposed a 10 percent surcharge on imports into the United States, distancing the United States further from its official policy of economic liberalism. To maintain the gold standard and the collective good of fixed exchange rates, extreme financial responsibility by the United States was necessary, but the economic effects of responsibility would probably have not been acceptable politically at home.[23]

Two fundamental aspects of the Bretton Woods system were thus substantially altered in 1971. First, when the United States pulled the props out from underneath the international monetary standard, all the currencies of the world were deprived of a fixed standard by which their value could be ascertained. Fixed (and therefore stable) exchange rates soon came to an end because the standard according to which they were fixed was abolished. After the early 1970s, **floating exchange rates** replaced fixed exchange rates (see Figure 10.3). This shift means that the relative value of the different currencies is established by market forces, and the value of one currency in exchange for another is determined by what people (and central banks) are willing to pay on any given day.

floating exchange rates Relative values of currencies as determined by supply and demand of market forces.

Figure 10.3   Fluctuations in Exchange Rates After Bretton Woods, Six Industrialized Countries, 1970–1990

The values of national currencies in relationship to the U.S. dollar fluctuated substantially after fixed exchange rates were eliminated in 1971.

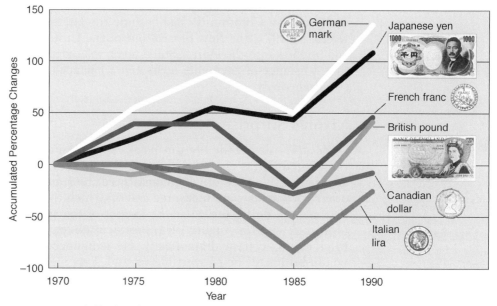

Source: Data compiled by the author from tables in the *New York Times*, circa July 1, in the selected years from 1970 to 1990.

The other aspect of the Bretton Woods system that was affected by President Nixon's announcement in August 1971 was the U.S. commitment to support the system itself. Until 1971, the United States had been willing to base its monetary and trade policies at least in part on considerations of what was good for the world economy as a whole. (Again, as noted earlier in this chapter, this does not mean that U.S. policymakers were astoundingly altruistic.) By 1971, the economic problems of the United States, both domestic and international, had become so serious that the U.S. government "demanded the right to manage its own currency in the pursuit of national objectives, just like any other country."[24]

The International Political Economy After Bretton Woods

The Economic Turmoil of the 1970s

The impact of Nixon's announcement in 1971 would have been profound under any circumstances. But the world economy was just beginning to recover and accommodate itself to that shock when it was hit in 1973 with a 400 percent increase in the price of oil. The members of the Organization of Petroleum Exporting Countries (OPEC) (see Chapter 3 for definition) set the price of oil in terms of U.S. dollars and are generally paid in dollars. With the price of oil dramatically increased, a torrent of dollars left the industrialized countries, including the United States, and went to Saudi Arabia and other leading oil producers. It can be said of any kind of money that the more of it that is around and available, the less valuable it is. When the price of oil increased, the number of dollars in circulation also increased. That is one reason that throughout most of the 1970s, the value of the dollar fell relative to gold and other foreign currencies. This fall was also probably an important factor contributing to the double-digit inflation that hit the United States and several other industrialized countries in that decade.

It was during the 1970s, too, that analysts of relationships among industrialized countries began to focus on their interdependence (as discussed in Chapter 1).[25] What were once seen as purely domestic problems in the industrialized countries came to be seen as problems with an important impact on other industrialized countries. This gave rise to protectionist pressures (that is, pressure to erect high tariff barriers or quotas to keep foreign imports out) and temptations to adopt other policies that might bring short-run benefits to individual countries. "Throughout this period international trade continued to grow, but not at the rate at which it had earlier. Under increasing pressure to stimulate economic growth, many nations reduced their tariff barriers. At the same time however, they devised new and more sophisticated ways of protecting their exports and otherwise limiting imports."[26] Indeed, in the 1970s, states began using more nontariff barriers such as government subsidies to export producers and government-imposed product standards.[27] As a result of protectionist policies, "trade among the industrialized nations quadrupled from 1963 to 1973, but increased only two and one-half times in the next decade."[28]

In the midst of the economic crises of the 1970s, the industrialized states could not develop a replacement to the Bretton Woods exchange rate system. As a substitute, they began meeting annually to try to coordinate monetary policy in the absence of a fixed system.[29] The European states also tried to build a fixed exchange rate system on a smaller scale in 1979 with the European Monetary System, a predecessor to the euro (discussed in Chapter 12). Overall, however, there was great concern that with the changes in the international economy, the stability that had been achieved under the old Bretton Woods institutions could not be duplicated. This concern was partly based on the belief that the United States, which had served as a hegemon in the system, was in serious trouble.

The Decline of American Hegemony? and New Players in the Global Economy

In the early 1980s, economic growth in most industrialized countries was slow, inflation and unemployment were high, and the price and supply of oil (and other energy resources) were uncertain. Some analysts traced those problems to the relative decline of the United States as an economic power. "Part of the world's economic problems today," explained one well-known economist,[30] "is that the United States has resigned (or has been discharged) as leader of the world economy, and there is no candidate willing and acceptable to take its place."

A widely accepted explanation for the economic problems of the United States stressed the decline in productivity (output of economic goods and services per hour of effort) in various important sectors of the American economy. And in the mid-1980s, U.S. productivity was lagging not only relative to its own past record but also in comparison with its chief competitors: Germany, Japan, France, and Britain. Persuasive historical evidence indicates that a productivity decline in a country such as the United States can have profound implications for that nation's role in the global political system. In fact, one prominent analyst of the history of the world's economic and political system argues that a relative decline in productivity is one of the first signs that a predominant state in the world system is losing its grip.[31]

Others agreed that the United States was losing its hegemonic position and were quite pessimistic about the stability of the economy in a "posthegemonic" system. The most publicized example of this speculation was historian Paul Kennedy's book, *The Rise and Fall of the Great Powers*, published in 1987.[32] Kennedy suggested that the United States was on the verge or in the process of suffering a fate similar to that of many other great powers since 1500. According to Kennedy, Spain in the 1600s, Britain in the 1900s, and Hitler's Germany in the 1940s all had a similar problem: They became overcommitted militarily. Keeping their commitments required military expenditures so great that the economies of their states, and so their political power bases, became fatally undermined. In Kennedy's view, "The United States runs the risk, so familiar to historians of the rise and fall of previous Great Powers, of what might roughly be called **imperial overstretch'**: that is to say, decision-makers in Washington must face the awkward and enduring fact that the sum total of the United States' global interests and obligations is nowadays far larger than the country's power to defend them simultaneously."

imperial overstretch
The idea that hegemonic powers overcommit resources, thus undermining their power.

Kennedy's arguments reinforced skepticism about the capitalist world system and its leader, the United States. Several writers then proclaimed the end of U.S. hegemony and explained the economic problems of the industrialized world as a result of that decline.[33] The reasoning, consistent with hegemonic stability theory, was based on an analogy with the Great Depression, during which national economies allegedly continued to contract because no leading nation had the economic strength and willingness to direct and enforce global economic cooperation.[34]

Yet the U.S. economy proved to be more resilient at the end of the twentieth century than many expected. By 1995, the value of U.S. exports as a proportion of the nation's gross national product (GNP) was higher than Japan's.[35] In addition, foreign investment in the United States and U.S. investment both increased by over 30 percent in the 1990s.[36] On many measures, the U.S. economy has done very well over the last decade compared to both Europe and Japan. Thus, the rapid decline of the economic hegemon that many had predicted in the 1970s and 1980s did not materialize.

Today, the U.S. economy remains the largest economy in the world and the major player in world economic processes, but it certainly does not dominate the world economy as it did just after World War II.[37] Now, the U.S. share of the international economy is declining relative to "emerging markets"—economies that have had rapid economic growth over the past twenty years. Leading the emerging markets is the group of countries referred to as the BRICS—Brazil, Russia, India, and China—which met formally for the first time in mid-2009. These countries, along with countries in Europe, have experienced a growth in their proportion of the world economy, while that of the United States and Japan has declined in recent years (see Figure 10.4). The U.S. share of world economic growth has also fallen. From 2002 to 2005, the U.S. share of world economic growth was 35 to 40 percent, but by 2006, the BRIC's share was greater than the U.S. share for the first time.[38] The dollar has also seen its share of the world economy fall. ". . . [B]y 2005 the euro had emerged as a clear regional and plausible global alternative to the dollar. . . . By some estimates, the euro share will rise to 30–40 percent of the global total by 2010."[39]

The rise of new players in the international economy is reflected in the development of the **Group of 20 (G-20)**—a forum for international

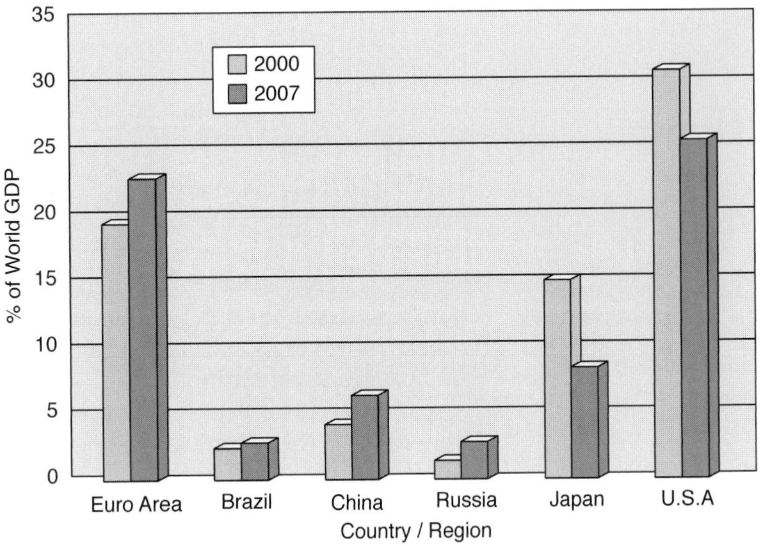

Group of 20 (G20) A forum for economic cooperation of the major economies: Argentina, Australia, Brazil, Britain, Canada, China, France, Germany, India, Indonesia, Italy, Japan, Mexico, Russia, Saudi Arabia, South Africa, South Korea, Turkey, the United States and the European Union.

Figure 10.4 "Key States' Share of World Economy"

Source: The World Bank Group, *Key Development Data and Statistics*, 2009. © 2009 World Bank. Reproduced by permission.

economic cooperation among the nineteen strongest economies plus the European Union. The G-20 represents 90 percent of the global GDP and two-thirds of the world population. The G-20 was established in response to the Asian financial crisis of the 1990s and is recognition of the growing power of states outside the Western industrialized economies. Before the G-20, the G-7 began meeting annually in the 1970s to coordinate economic policies. The group was expanded in the late 1990s to include Russia and was known as the G-8. In 2008, it was the G-20 that met to deal with the global economic crisis (discussed following). To many, this was ". . . recognition that global leadership can no longer resemble an exclusive private club. . . . The problem is not merely that US indebtedness and Western finance triggered the present crisis. It is also that, although the United States still ranks as the world's largest economy, the rise of China and other developing markets has undercut US supremacy."[40]

At the forefront of the emerging markets and the challenge to American economic hegemony is China. China's GDP is likely to exceed the United States' in the next thirty years.[41] China's economic growth has been phenomenal:

> According to official statistics, China's annual real GDP growth averaged 9.7 percent between 1989 and 2000. In aggregate terms, real urban incomes more than doubled over the same period. For many Chinese families, the increased prosperity of the 1990s can be measured by the new range of goods that they can now afford. The prizes of the 1980s included basic items such as refrigerators and television sets. Today, many Chinese families find computers, designer clothes, mobile phones, and home-entertainment centers within their reach as well. The growing prosperity is the result of the Chinese government's commitment to structural economic reforms. . . . Today, more than 40 percent of industrial output comes from private companies, and more than 30 percent of nonagricultural employees work for private or mixed-ownership firms. (In contrast, virtually no privately owned industrial firms existed in 1979 when . . . economic reform began.)[42]

Although Chinese economic growth has slowed in the recent global economic downturn, it is in comparatively better shape, as it is relatively more insulated from the international financial sector and it has massive foreign exchange reserves.[43] Indeed, it was China, along with Middle East countries, that helped delay the onset of the financial crisis in 2007 when it used its sovereign wealth funds to support already-failing American and European institutions.[44]

China's rise as a major economic player has not been without costs. Even though the Chinese transformation from a planned economy to a market-based economy has been fairly smooth, "as economic reform continues, millions of Chinese workers are being laid off each year with little hope of reemployment or adequate social welfare support. In some cities, unemployed workers are now joining together in large-scale protests, involving as many as 20,000 people at a time."[45] In the "special economic zones"—the cities that have gone the furthest toward liberalization—there is growing inequality and income disparity as well.[46] Some estimates put the inequality in China between urban and rural residents at near the highest in the world, and rural unrest has significantly increased over the last decade.[47]

In many ways, the Russian transition from classical socialism to more free market capitalism was much more tumultuous than the Chinese experience. There are many possible reasons for this, including the fact that Russia was a socialist system for a much longer time than China and that Russia simultaneously experienced the breakup of its empire, the Soviet Union.[48] The difficulties that Russia faced can also be explained by Russia's attempt to change its political system, making it more democratic, at the same time it liberalized its economy. Although this was initially met with high hopes and applauded by the Western countries that had opposed the Soviet Union during the Cold War, it has turned out to be extremely difficult and created a great deal of human suffering. Russian GDP declined almost 50 percent between 1989 and 1999; its unemployment rate (as percentage of economically active population) climbed from .08 to 1.6 percent from 1991 to 2001; the percentage of people living in poverty went from 1.5 to between 39 and 49 from 1988 to 1993; Russian life expectancy for males declined from 64.9 to 58.7 years from 1987 to 2003; and annual alcohol consumption increased from 5.3 to almost 9 liters of pure ethanol per person from 1989 to 2003.[49] Despite major aid packages from the IMF, the Russian economy remained in dire straits, and in 1998, the government was forced to devalue the Russian currency, the ruble, and default on $40 billion in domestic debt. Some argue that liberalization during the transition was not the cause of the decline in standards of living and economic growth; rather, the difficulty is Russia's unwillingness to engage seriously in liberalization.[50]

The Russian economy did, however, rebound quite well after the ruble devaluation. Since 1999, the poverty rate fell and Russia had economic growth rates of 10 percent in 2000 and 8 percent in 2007. Russia became an economically stable, emerging market and foreign investment flowed into the economy. Russia also became the third largest holder of foreign currency reserves, after China and Japan. Russia's turnaround came from many sources, including sound monetary policies and liberalization policies that were previously put in place. But Russian economic growth can also be attributed to the state's intervention in the economy, its control over the oil and gas sector, and high energy prices. This growth in Russia's economy is not even, however, as the gap between the very rich and the poor has widened.[51] And with the decline in energy demand and the fall of oil and gas prices, Russia's economy, like most in the world, fell ill by

2008, with rises in unemployment, inflation, and the poverty rate, a budget deficit, and a tightening of credit markets.[52]

centrally planned economies Economic systems in which the state determines production, consumption, and pricing of commodities.

The transitions from socialist, **centrally planned economies** in China, Russia, Eastern Europe, and Vietnam in the last two decades certainly altered the global economic system. Before these transformations, the Communist countries were outside the liberal international economic system established by the Bretton Woods conference. This means that these countries did not engage in any significant international trade with Bretton Woods countries, did not have currencies that were readily convertible into U.S. dollars (and thus did not receive assistance from the IMF), and did not receive loans for development and reconstruction from the World Bank. In effect, the Communist countries' economies developed quite independently from the economies of the rest of the world.

The economies developed independently, because they were fundamentally incompatible with the Bretton Woods system, which was premised on economic liberalism. In classical socialist economies, there is very little room for the hidden hand of the free market. Indeed, individual self-interest is seen to be detrimental to the collective interests of society, and thus a free market where individuals pursue their own interests is fundamentally at odds with the good of society as a whole. According to Karl Marx, the founder of Communist ideology, when individuals (private citizens) own factories and other means of production, wealth tends to accumulate in the hands of those individuals instead of in the hands of society at large. Moreover, such practices will result in the emergence of different social classes (the owners and the workers), and this will create further tensions in society. Because a free market will tend to create winners and losers, Communist ideological commitment to social equality and a classless society requires the virtual elimination of a market system. Thus, in most Communist countries, private property (that is, private ownership of economically valuable resources) was officially forbidden or extremely limited (although citizens could own their own household items and personal effects, and an underground economy, or black market, existed in almost every Communist economy). Without an official free market, where producers produce what they think

Rapid economic growth often comes with growing income inequality and poverty side by side with wealth, as in Hong Kong (pictured here).

(© Brian Brake/Photo Researchers, Inc.)

they can sell and buyers buy what they want and can afford, something else must regulate production, consumption, and prices. For Communist countries, that is the state. Indeed, in Communist countries such as the former Soviet Union, the state determined what was produced, how much was produced, what the price of goods would be, and how much money (wages) workers earned.

Thus, the fact that China, Russia, and other countries that until fairly recent were centrally planned economies are major players in the global capitalist system—even if they still criticize many economically liberal policies—is quite a transformation. After years of negotiation, China joined the WTO in 2001; Russia has observer status. Many of the Communist countries in central and eastern Europe are now members of the European Union, itself based on economic liberalism and free trade (see chapter 12). Within a relatively short time, the Bretton Woods system and its economic liberal principles became global, at the same time economic power was shifting and new economic realities challenged efforts at economic cooperation.

Turbulence in World Finance and the Global Economic Crisis

After the Bretton Woods system, and particularly after the end of fixed exchange rates, there have been a number of financial crises in the international economy. In 1997, for example, "Thailand's currency depreciation triggered a sudden collapse in other Asian exchange rates, causing a rash of bankruptcies among corporations and financial institutions. . . . In turn, the devaluations contributed to a slide in world commodity prices, leading currencies of other commodity producers such as Australia, Canada, New Zealand, Chile, and Mexico to plummet as well."[53] Since the end of fixed exchange rates, countries have been struggling with ways to keep currencies stable. To encourage investment, Thailand had fixed its exchange rate to keep the baht at a set price per U.S. dollar, but this value could not be sustained, particularly when Japan, a major trading partner of Thailand, saw a decline in the yen.[54] Argentina followed a similar path, pegging its currency to the dollar and eventually spiraling into economic crisis in 2001.[55]

The frequency and severity of recent financial problems are of great concern to the international community.

> Financial crises once made most people's eyes glaze over; they were the subjects of intense interest to only a limited clientele, many of whom wore green eyeshades. Not any longer. The topic has unfortunately acquired a mass audience in the second half of the 1990s. Stunning currency collapses in Mexico (1995), southeast Asia (1997), Russia (1998), and Brazil (1999) have pushed the subject to the front page. Financial conflagrations have become too frequent, too devastating, and too contagious to be ignored.[56]

At the Frankfurt Stock Exchange in Germany, a graph shows the massive downswing in international financial markets in September 2008.
(Boris Roessler/Corbis)

Although these financial crises had far-reaching implications, they were more contained than the world-wide economic downturn that began in 2007. A report to the U.S. Congress described the primary causes and spread of this crisis:

> The plunge downward into the global financial crisis did not take long. It was triggered by the bursting of the housing bubble and the ensuing subprime mortgage crisis in the United States, but other conditions have contributed to the severity of the situation. Banks, investment houses, and consumers carried large amounts of leveraged debt. Certain countries incurred large deficits in international trade and current accounts (particularly the United States), while other countries accumulated large reserves of foreign exchange by running surpluses in those accounts. Investors deployed "hot money" in world markets seeking higher rates of return. . . . [G]lobalization . . . allowed for rapid communication, instant transfers of funds, and information networks that fed a herd instinct.[57]

Stock market values across the world lost nearly half of their values in 2008.[58] The crisis threatened the banking sector in some of the wealthiest countries, such as the United States, the United Kingdom, France, and Switzerland.[59] Global financial institutions suffered heavy losses and credit dried up. According to one analyst, "This credit freeze has brought the global financial system to the brink of collapse."[60]

Many are concerned that states will respond by protecting their national economies, just as they did in response to the stock market crash of 1929 and the Great Depression of the 1930s. If this occurs, "trade liberalization efforts would languish; protectionism and mercantilism would swell."[61] Protectionist measures have already been taken in Europe, the United States, Latin America, China, and elsewhere in East Asia.[62] "There is already a push by several countries in different regions to raise tariffs to the maximum levels permitted under the Uruguay Round of the General Agreement on Tariffs and Trade."[63]

Perhaps even more troubling than protectionist policies, at least to economic liberals, is the impact the crisis is having on the support for economic liberalism itself. Indeed, the financial crisis "discredited the U.S. brand of free market capitalism. The lords of Wall Street atrociously gamed the system while supervisors slept."[64] The Policy Choices box summarizes some of the current debate about the future of liberalism and capitalism. The undermining of the credibility of economic liberalism may be a major turning point in international politics: ". . . for decades much of the United States' influence and soft power reflected the intellectual strength of the Anglo-Saxon brand of market-based capitalism. But now, the model that helped push back socialism and promoted deregulation over regulation . . . is under a cloud."[65] French President Nicolas Sarkozy has reportedly claimed *laissez-faire, c'est fini* and called for "the return of politics" to economics. The German finance minister cited Marx's analysis of the crisis-prone nature of capitalism. And, referring to the United States and other promoters of economic liberalism, the Chinese vice premier claimed: "The teachers now have some problems."[66]

Economic liberal policies of little government intervention have been challenged even in countries where free-market philosophies held almost a sacred place. "Now, searching for stability, the U.S. government and some European governments have nationalized their financial sectors to a degree that contradicts the tenets of modern capitalism. Much of the world is turning a historic corner and heading into a period in which the role of the state will be larger and that of the private sector will be smaller."[67] This trend is indeed worldwide and may be long lasting. A recent report by the U.S. government predicted that, by 2025, many of the major economies of the world will be in the form of **state capitalism**, "a system in which the state functions as the leading economic actor and uses markets primarily for political gain."[68]

Forms of state capitalism can already be seen in authoritarian countries such as China and particularly Russia.[69] And in oil-producing countries, it is the state, not private corporations, that own the large oil companies of the world, such as Saudi Arabia's Saudi Aramco, Brazil's

state capitalism
Economic system in which the government is the leading economic actor and uses markets for political purposes.

POLICY CHOICES

Should Economic Liberalism Be Abandoned as the Basis for the Global Economy?

ISSUE: The liberal international economic order depends on coordination and cooperation from states, which often takes the form of regulations and through international organizations such as the WTO. What can be agreed to in such organizations, however, might not be sufficient to protect the global economic system from certain perils. When the recent economic crisis hit, it was truly a global event. Although we might be tempted to view such economic crises as cyclical, a necessary evil, or simply part of the risks associated with development and growth, some observers disagree. They point to the inequalities that continue to plague the global economy, the injustices in how economic hardships are distributed, and the inability of individual citizens to exert control over their own destinies. Indeed, they question the philosophy of economic liberalism as the basis for the global economy.

Option #1: The global liberal economic system, albeit imperfect, should be supported by states as the best means to global growth.

Arguments: (a) Liberalism is not about greed. It simply recognizes that international trade and finance can be mutually beneficial to states, and thus represents an effective means to growth. (b) When international financial collapse occurs, it reminds states that they are fundamentally connected to each other. Far from blaming liberal economics for the challenges facing states today, we should instead celebrate the fact that states are increasingly likely to recognize their interdependence and spend their summits discussing trade instead of war. (c) We have only experienced a few decades exploring the positive impact of global free trade and global financial interaction. Had the abysmal failures of early rocketry been the guiding standard of judgment, we would never have landed on the moon. Trying times do not always implicate the times themselves.

Counterarguments: (a) When I offer to you my goods and services in exchange for your money, we are doing well by each other. When a global economy can nearly be brought to a halt because of collapsing housing market bubbles, mega-bank investment policies, and the greed of a handful of merchants on Wall Street, we are not doing well be each other. (b) Liberals are fond of noting how "a rising tide lifts all boats," but they are considerably more hesitant to admit that economic interdependence can lead to contagion and mutual economic peril. As U.S. President F. D. Roosevelt once chided, "I think we consider too much the good luck of the early bird and not enough the bad luck of the early worm." (c) Although we often tend to believe that economic progress must inevitably entail setbacks, sometimes the system is so fundamentally flawed that the pain of an "economic adjustment" can be confused with the need for a fundamental revolution.

Option #2: States should seek ways of curbing the influence of global capitalism and begin enforcing regulations that focus on people over profits.

(continued)

Arguments: (a) Even the former chairmen of the U.S. Federal Reserve, Alan Greenspan, admitted that unregulated, self-interested rational behavior produced the economic crisis, not a greater good.[1] This calls into question the guiding principles of free market capitalism. (b) There is no reason to believe that free market capitalism is the ultimate solution. States such as China and Russia have realized that growth comes from a heavy hand in the economy, not the invisible hand of the market. (c) For roughly the past three and a half centuries, the state has been the most important force in global relations. However, the greater the economic interdependence of the world, the less the state matters, and the less the state matters, the less chance people's interests are represented. The great democratic experiment where the people rule has come to this question: Are the people citizens, or employees?

Counterarguments: (a) There is nothing wrong with the basic ideas of liberalism, but they clearly do not include a "free license" for investors, which has caused so much recent economic turmoil. A free market is not one free of regulation, but rather one in which those who rise and fall on its successes and failures get to determine its rules. (b) Knocks against the expansion of trade and commerce are nothing new. At each step, advances have been highlighted by setbacks. The key is to not throw the baby out with the bathwater and instead take setbacks as simply a part of the growth process. (c) The state, however important in the development of economic systems, is far less efficient than the private marketplace. Regulating global markets squeezes out the rational economic interests of the buyers and sellers, replacing it with the cumbersome political interests of governments.

[1] Edmond L. Andrews, "Greenspan Concedes Error on Regulation," *The New York Times*, October 24, 2008.

Petrobras, and Russia's Gazprom. In addition, 'Sovereign wealth funds,' a recently coined term for state-owned investment portfolios, account for one-eighth of global investment, and that figure is rising. These trends are reshaping international politics and the global economy by transferring increasingly large levers of economic power and influence to the central authority of the state. They are fueling the large and complex phenomenon of state capitalism."[70]

Protectionism and the promotion of nationalist interests, however, have not been the only response to the economic crisis. States have also engaged in multilateral cooperation to collectively address economic problems. It is in states' interests to cooperate on financial regulation. If there is no coordination, financial institutions might flee to countries with the least stringent regulations.[71] And despite the discrediting of economic liberalism and laissez-faire capitalism, states are reluctant to abandon the free trade regime that has brought economic growth and a rise in living standards to so many countries in the past.

In November 2008, the G-20 held an emergency meeting in Washington, DC to coordinate changes in policy, regulations, oversight, and enforcement in their financial sectors.[72] The G-20 met again in London in early 2009. At this meeting,

> The Group of 20 did agree on new global rules to govern the pay and bonuses of bankers. The leaders also agreed to "name and shame" countries that erected trade barriers, intended to resist growing protectionist sentiment. But a European push for sweeping global regulation of the financial markets was blunted, to a large degree, by the United States. While the leaders agreed to create a new Financial Stability Board to monitor the financial system for signs of risks, they stopped well short of giving regulators cross-border authority. . . .[73]

A similar meeting took place in London, in 1933. Then, countries that tried to cooperate to avert or at least lessen the effects of the Great Depression failed. According to historian Walter Mead,

> Economic cooperation didn't collapse in 1929. In fact, from 1929 through most of the first four years of the Depression, there were a lot of efforts which ended up not being successful. There were strong efforts to try to put together some kind of a united front on economic issues. Unfortunately, in some ways, protectionism on trade undermined everything else. And when Franklin Roosevelt came in [in 1933], he torpedoed the London Economic Conference, which was portrayed as the last grand effort to get some kind of currency agreement, because he wanted the freedom to try to raise U.S. prices without regard for other countries. So, what happened really was that economic cooperation was the first thing that people looked to as the Depression began to break out, because it was obviously an international crisis in many respects. But the long, grinding pressure of the downturn drove countries more and more inward.[74]

Some have used the term "Bretton Woods II" to describe the attempts to address this most recent economic crisis. The idea is to use the crisis as an opportunity to rewrite and update the rules of cooperation that were set up after World War II. As one analyst writes: "A worldwide web of economic interdependence spreads risks as well as rewards, and global governance needs to evolve along with the interactions. International financial institutions, for example, are still largely structured for an era of American-dominated globalization, when businesses expanded mainly from developed to emerging economies."[75]

International Economic Institutions Today

Although the fixed exchange rate came to an end in the 1970s, the institutions created with the Bretton Woods system still function today. They are not, however, without criticism. The IMF, for example, is often criticized for the conditions it attaches to its loans. Often called "austerity packages," these typically require governments to privatize their holdings, cut government spending, and increase interest rates. The IMF attaches these strings to its loans in order to ensure that the money is spent in these ways and so that future loans will be unnecessary. Many, however, argue that IMF conditions are too liberal and force more privatization on economies than exists in most of the leading economies. Furthermore, critics charge, the IMF focuses blindly on the economic bottom line, ignoring the political causes of the economic situation in countries and the political consequences of its austerity packages. Finally, critics say that the IMF often gives bad economic advice and makes the economic situation even worse. In the IMF's handling of the Asian financial crisis, for example, leading economists "suggested that the austerity measures required by the IMF—including the imposition of high interest rates—helped spread the Asian crisis even to well-managed economies."[76] The IMF was a player in the Russian financial problems, too. With the Russian economic crisis looming, the IMF offered a $22 billion package in July 1998 to help save it from devaluation. This ounce of prevention, however, failed and the IMF was criticized by some for not doing enough and for not doing something earlier. Others say that Russia itself is to blame because it has not passed essential policies for reform.[77]

More generally,

> the seemingly relentless spread of the financial crisis from Asia to Russia and possibly to Latin America . . . has left many observers wondering whether the IMF is still able to do its job. Computerized trading has made it increasingly easy for international investors to buy and sell stocks, bonds and other securities 24 hours a day, and liberalized markets have greatly expanded their access to countries around the world. While all this facilitates the free flow of capital by making it easier for investors to quickly move their money from one country to another, it makes it harder for the IMF to keep an eye on things and avert crises before it's too late.[78]

Others defend the institution as the only hope for global efforts to stabilize trouble spots.

> The IMF, mistakes notwithstanding, was and remains crucial to economic stabilization and recovery. Despite all the controversy surrounding the IMF's policies and the withering criticism of several highly respected economists, the overwhelming weight of opinion on Wall Street and in Washington favors strengthening the fund. Not everyone agrees on the exact nature of its role, but all believe that some global institution needs to be in the center of the storm and that it is wiser to use the IMF as the starting point than to craft something altogether new.[79]

Some see the recent global downturn as a prompt for IMF reform. "The financial crisis has created an opportunity for the IMF to reinvigorate itself and possibly play a constructive role in resolving, or at the least mitigating, the effects of the global downturn."[80] Potential reforms of the IMF also include making it more flexible, increasing its lending capacity, and changing its management to reflect the weight of the new economic powers, such as China and India.[81]

The World Bank has also come under criticism recently, for trying to do too much. Through the years, the World Bank "has added new tasks to its mandate. In recent years, it has been called on for emergency lending in the wake of the Asian financial crisis, for economic management as part of Middle East peacekeeping efforts, for postwar Balkan reconstruction, and for loans to combat the AIDS tragedy in Africa. By now, its mission has become so complex that it strains credulity to portray the bank as a manageable organization. The bank takes on challenges that lie far beyond any institution's capabilities."[82]

Of all the components of the Bretton Woods Liberal International Economic Order, it is the GATT arrangement that has undergone the most transformation, particularly recently. With the establishment of the WTO in 1995, the framework of agreements that made up GATT became an international institution that provides regular monitoring of the trade policies of member countries. The WTO is more powerful than GATT and covers broader areas of international trade (such as services, intellectual properties, and trade-related investment measures). By creating an overarching body to monitor trade practices, the member countries hoped to avoid protectionist policies that tended to surface between GATT negotiations and various loopholes to free trade exploited by governments. Proponents of the WTO cited the economic benefits to a permanent institution, but many felt that the WTO might threaten national sovereignty. In the United States, such fears put the ratification of the WTO Treaty in doubt for some time.

Dispute Settlement Mechanism
WTO Procedures to deal with disputes between member-states over free trade agreements.

Concerns about threats to sovereignty are primarily associated with the WTO's **Dispute Settlement Mechanism,** which has the authority to impose sanctions on member states that violate free trade agreements. Other countries can bring complaints before the WTO if they believe a state is in violation. By 2009, more than 390 cases had been brought to the Dispute Settlement Mechanism. These included rulings against the United States on disputes brought by Venezuela and Brazil on U.S. gasoline standards and by many Latin American countries on U.S. prohibition of imports of tuna that did not use dolphin-safe fishing techniques. The United States obtained a WTO ruling against the European Union for its preferences for importing bananas from its former colonies.

According to the WTO itself, it is a myth that the Dispute Settlement Mechanism gives it power to tell other countries what to do:

The only occasion when a WTO body can have a direct impact on a government's policies is when a dispute is brought to the

WTO and if that leads to a ruling by the Dispute Settlement Body (which consists of all members). Normally the Dispute Settlement Body makes a ruling by adopting the findings of a panel of experts or an appeal report. Even then, the scope of the ruling is narrow: it is simply a judgment or interpretation of whether a government has broken one of the WTO's agreements— agreements that the infringing government had itself accepted. If a government has broken a commitment it has to conform. In all other respects, the WTO does not dictate to governments to adopt or drop certain policies.[83]

Yet it is clear that the WTO procedures are changing states' behaviors, even if they are not forced to do so. "So far, it seems that nations have been willing to abide by the dispute panel decisions rather than withdraw from the WTO when such decisions go against them. Because so much appears to be at stake for each nation by way of expected economic gain that would result from further liberalizing trade, states have felt compelled to participate in the rule-making exercise rather than being left out of it."[84]

What the WTO does do is highlight the tensions between politics and economics. The political decisions by the United States to save dolphins and decrease pollution from gasoline have come in conflict with the economic philosophy of free trade. For now, the economic side seems to have triumphed in most cases, leading several groups to protest at WTO meetings (these protests will be discussed in Chapter 14), but the tension between politics and economics continues to be at the heart of the international political economy.

SUMMARY

- The study of the international political economy concerns the relationships and tension between political units and values and economics and market relations. Alternative economic philosophies, such as economic liberalism and mercantilism, offer different perspectives on the nature of these relationships.

- The international economic system set up in the noncommunist industrialized world after the Second World War was based on the economic liberal perspective, which stresses the free market system as a coordinator of greater wealth for all and free trade. The role of governments, according to this perspective, is best limited to provider of collective goods. Economic liberals disagree with mercantilists, who put the national interests of the state before economic wealth and favor protectionist politics when national interests are at stake and to maintain a positive balance of trade.

- The international economic system after World War II was centered on three principal organizations: the IMF, the World Bank, and the GATT.

That system, based to an important extent on fixed exchange rates and free trade, worked well for the industrialized countries until the 1970s. In 1971, the United States put an end to the system in which gold and dollars were perfectly convertible at the rate of U.S. $35 per ounce of gold. The first OPEC increase in the price of oil in 1973 was another shock to the international system and helped produce a combination of high inflation and slow growth throughout the rest of the 1970s. When OPEC increased the price of oil again in 1979, the second oil shock helped throw the industrialized world into a recession. In 1982, it brought the United States the deepest recession it had experienced since World War II, and many predicted the decline of the United States as an economic hegemon. Economic growth in the 1990s, coupled with economic crises in countries like Japan, means that the United States remained the leading economy by many measures.

• The end of the twentieth and beginning of the twenty-first centuries witnessed a rapidly changing and largely unstable international economy. New players, most notably China, emerged as important economic powers and international financial crises created turbulence in the increasingly global economy. The problems that began in the U.S. financial sector in 2007 quickly spread with potentially significant long-term consequences, including the weakening of support for economic liberalism. The Bretton Woods institutions—the World Bank, the IMF, and now the WTO—remain the primary global efforts to coordinate economics across state borders, although their structure and effectiveness are often debated.

KEY TERMS

international political
  economy   355
developed countries   356
developing countries   356
Liberal International Economic
  Order   357
economic liberalism   357
free trade   358
comparative advantage   359
collective goods   359
mercantilism   359
subsidies   360
Tariffs   360
protectionist policies   360
import quotas   360
dumping   360
balance of trade   360
export platforms   361

monetary policies   362
exchange rates   363
Bretton Woods system   364
International Monetary Fund
  (IMF)   364
fixed exchange rates   365
World Bank   366
General Agreement on Tariffs and
  Trade (GATT)   367
most-favored-nation
  principle   367
floating exchange rates   371
imperial overstretch   374
Group of 20 (G-20)   375
centrally planned economies   378
state capitalism   381
Dispute Settlement
  Mechanism   386

CHAPTER 11

The Developing States in the International Political Economy

less developed countries The poorer states of the South.

This chapter discusses the economic state of countries in the South and the economic and political relations between the wealthier industrialized, or developed, states of the North and the poorer states of the South—the **less developed countries (LDCs).** On many measures, the gap between the economic prosperity in the North and the poverty in the South is growing, although there are positive trends on some dimensions and in some countries.

Various explanations have been offered as to why this gap exists and why it has been growing, at least on some criteria and in some countries. Neo-Marxist approaches (introduced in Chapter 1) posit that those relationships tend to have a deleterious impact on the poor states. These perspectives have proved to be popular for explaining problems that developing countries have faced in their quests for economic well-being and political independence. However, in recent years, the *prescriptions* or solutions offered by at least some versions of neo-Marxism have become less influential, even if some of their *descriptions* of the problems that poor countries face retain much of their credibility. Explanations based on economic liberalism focus on the internal policies of states as the cause of underdevelopment, and prescriptions for liberalizing the economies of developing states were accepted and followed by many in the immediate post–Cold War years. Liberalization policies, however, have experienced a backlash as many developed states, even those thought to be most successful, are facing continued economic problems, especially given the recent global economic downturn.

After reviewing the alternative explanations of the North-South gap and the various development strategies associated with them, this chapter concludes with a consideration of the apparently emerging consensus about the important role of women in the process of economic and political development in the poorer countries of the world and of the role of diseases such as HIV/AIDS in underdevelopment. Whatever strategies for development are chosen, the implications for addressing the North-South gap are broad because the economic relations between the rich and the poor in the world have ethical, security, and economic consequences.

The Economic Gap between the North and the South

Poverty, starvation, and glaring inequality in the distribution of the world's wealth constitute a serious problem in many respects. Millions suffer grievously from poverty, and they probably will continue to do so for a long time to come. According to a recent UN report on human development, "In the midst of an increasingly prosperous global economy, 10.7 million children every year do not live to see their fifth birthday, and more than 1 billion people survive in abject poverty on less than $1 a day."[1] Seventeen percent of the population in the developing world in recent years has not had enough to eat.[2]

According to economist Jeffrey Sachs, "the greatest tragedy of our time is that one sixth of humanity is . . . caught in a poverty trap. . . . They are trapped by disease, physical isolation, climate stress, environmental degradation and by extreme poverty itself."[3] Such statistics would be marginally more tolerable, though still distressing, if the situation were improving rapidly. But what makes poverty in the developing world, and the gap between rich and poor countries, politically explosive and ethically even more pressing are the indications that the inequalities are growing.

In 1960, the average per capita gross national product (GNP) of countries in the developed world (that is, the United States, Canada, most of Europe, Oceania, Israel, and Japan) was $6,520 (U.S. dollars); in the developing world, the figure was $361, or $6,159 less. By 1988, the average per capita GNP had increased to $13,995 in the world's rich countries and $717 in the poor countries, resulting in a gap of $13,278, an increase of $7,119 over that twenty-eight-year period (as measured in constant 1987 U.S. dollars).[4] Another source reveals that "the gap in per capita income between the industrial and developing worlds tripled, from $5,700 in 1960 to $15,400 in 1993."[5] In addition, "Thirty years ago, the income of the richest fifth of the world's population combined was 30 times greater than that of the poorest fifth. Today, the income gap is more than 60 times greater."[6] In 1993, the poorest 10 percent of people globally retained 0.8 percent of global income. The richest top 10 percent retained 50 percent of global income. In 2000, the trends changed only slightly, with the poorest 10 percent of people globally retaining 0.7 percent of global income whereas the richest top 10 percent retained 50.9 percent of global income.[7]

Some economists object to economic comparisons that simply convert income figures from various countries into dollar equivalents. Until recently, for example, the International Monetary Fund (IMF) used currency exchange rates to do this. Now its economists base their calculations on **purchasing power parities** that take into account what money actually buys in the various countries around the world. Using this measure, the picture of the North-South gap does not look much better. In 2005, the gap between the developing countries (with $2,531 per capita) and the developed countries (with $33,082) was more than $30,000.[8]

There is little prospect that this disparity will decrease in the foreseeable future. Assume that per capita GNP grows at 2 percent per year in the developed world and at 5 percent per year in the developing world over a ten-year period. This assumption is rather optimistic, implying that growth rates in the developing world will be two and a half times greater than those in industrialized countries. Even if that rather utopian dream were to come true, the gap between per capita GNPs would still increase by $2,613. Furthermore, "to halve the share of people living on $1 a day, optimistic estimates suggest that 3.7% annual growth in per capita incomes is needed in developing countries. But over the past

purchasing power parity A measure of the relative purchasing power of currencies to buy the same goods in different countries.

10 years only 24 countries have grown this fast. . . . Indeed, many have suffered negative growth in recent years, and the share of their people in poverty has almost certainly increased."[9]

The recent downturn in the global economy certainly will not help the situation. "According to the IMF, The International Monetary Fund estimates that the crisis will cost developing countries $1 trillion in lost growth. The World Bank warned that it would add more than 50 million people to those living on less than $2 a day across the globe" ("The Crisis at Home and Abroad," *The New York Times* editorial, March 5, 2009). Per capita income data, however, capture only one aspect of reality, and these data can be misleading.[10]

They are averages that do not take into account the distribution of wealth being produced. The economy of a developing country may grow very rapidly in terms of per capita GNP as a result of wealth increasingly concentrated in the hands of a select few, while most people remain worse off. In contrast, decreases in the GNP can mask improvement in living conditions for many people in poor countries. Young people make up the majority of the population of most developing countries. Before recent improvements in health care, many of them died of disease or malnutrition. "An increase in the survival rate of the poorest groups usually

Map 11.1 Low-Income Countries

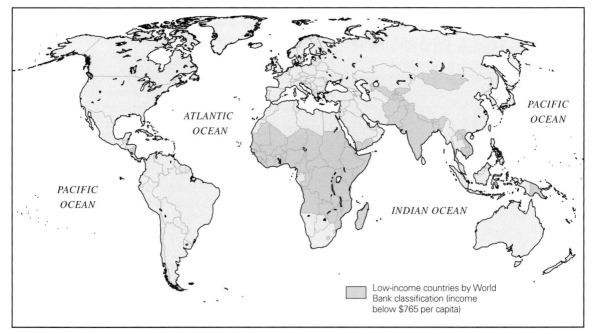

Source: "Maps," copyright © 2005 by Jeffrey D. Sachs. Data from World Bank (2004), from *The End of Poverty* by Jeffrey D. Sachs. Used by permission of The Penguin Press, a division of Penguin Group (USA) Inc.

promotes . . . a fall in per capita income. . . . The average income in the country can fall even if everybody is materially better off."[11] In short, the survival of the young, who typically have no income at all, can depress a country's per capita income, but the decrease does not necessarily indicate a worsening of living conditions as a whole.

Even in terms of income or GNP data, though, the economic picture in the developing world is not uniformly bleak. From 1970 to 1981, if "we look at annual average growth rates of per capita GNP . . . the top fifteen countries in the world were all developing [countries], far outpacing the figures for industrial countries."[12] From 1990 to 2005, the economies of the rich countries grew at about 1.8 percent a year, while those of the developing countries grew at an average rate of about 2.9 percent a year.[13]

Furthermore, a calculation of the distribution of wealth between rich and poor countries using purchasing power parities reveals that by the early 1990s, "the share of the world output produced by the rich industrial economies [dropped] to 54% from 73%."[14] Overall, much of humanity is experiencing significant economic progress.[15] Figure 11.1 shows the trends in GNI per capita in major regions and economic categories of the world.

Figure 11.1   Global Disparities in Income: Are Regions Closing the Gap?

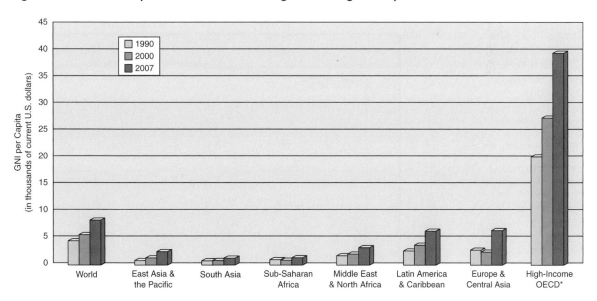

*High-Income OECD includes most EU countries, Australia, Canada, Iceland, Japan, South Korea, New Zealand, Norway, Switzerland, and the United States.

Source: World Bank, "Key Development Data and Statistics," *Millennium Development Goals,* 2009. © 2009 World Bank. Reproduced by permission.

And if we analyze quality-of-life indicators, such as life expectancy (arguably the most comprehensive statistic available), it is no longer so clear that the developing world is falling farther behind the industrialized countries with each passing year. Data on life expectancy are particularly important in this context, "since life expectancy statistics are calculated by looking at how long *all* the people in a given country live.... Although a small number of rich people can have enough money to raise the average income in a country far above what the average person has, nobody can live long enough to raise the average length of life very much."[16] In 1950, "citizens of low-income countries had a life expectancy of only 35.2 years,"[17] at a time when the average life expectancy in rich countries was about 65. By the early 1970s, life expectancy in the developing world was about 55, while it had reached 71 in rich countries.[18] Currently, the gap between life expectancy in poor countries and rich countries has diminished to about thirteen years.[19]

Human Development Index Composite index of achievements in basic human capabilities, including life expectancy, education, and income.

The improvements in life expectancy data indicate at a minimum that more people are receiving better medical care. The United Nations Development Programme has created the **Human Development Index,** which "is a composite index of achievements in basic human capabilities, a long and healthy life, knowledge, and a decent standard of living. Three variables have been chosen to represent those three dimensions: life expectancy, educational attainment and income."[20] Figure 11.2 compares the performance of the industrialized world with that of the developing

Figure 11.2   The Human Development Gap, Rich Versus Poor Countries, 1970–2005

Source: Based on United Nations Development Programme, *Human Development Report* (New York: Oxford University Press, 1996 and 2005) United Nations, *Human Development Report* (New York: Palgrave, Macmillan, 2007/2008) p. 232.

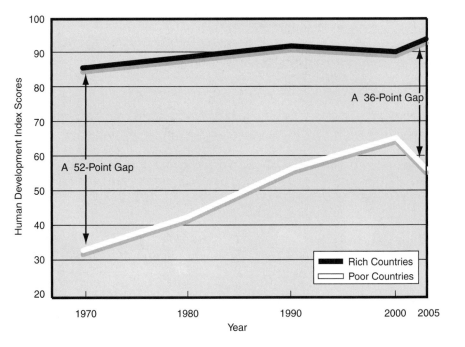

world in terms of this index over the past several decades. It shows a definite trend toward closing the gap between rich countries and poor countries on the composite, reasonably comprehensive indicator of the quality of life. In short, although it is possible that people in general, and those in poor countries in particular, are more miserable than their counterparts two, three, and four decades ago, despite being healthier, better fed, better educated, and better off, it is not likely. Why are some quality-of-life indicators showing a decline in the gap, while economic indicators are showing an increase in the gap between the North and South? There are several possible explanations, but probably the most important is that many measures in the human development index have a ceiling value. People in the North can become only so literate; there is no improving on 100 percent literacy. Thus, any advance in literacy in the poorer states will close the gap. Economic measures, on the other hand, such as GNP and GNP per capita, have no upper level. Improvements on these measures in the South can occur at the same time improvement occurs in the North, allowing for the gap to increase. Also important is the role of international organizations and nongovernmental organizations that have focused on increasingly available health care and education over the past several decades. These groups have made progress in reducing infant mortality and increasing literacy rates in the South. In contrast, there have not been comparable global efforts to increase economic well-being, partly because of the debates over effective ways to do this.

Comparisons between the standards of living in rich countries and poor countries over time, provide an important basis for evaluating pessimistic assertions about catastrophic trends in the world's distribution of wealth. But most of the data showing recent improvement in living standards in poor countries focus on averages, which can mask large discrepancies between countries in various regions. Much of the improvement in life expectancy in developing countries, for example, is the result of rather dramatic increases in the index of living standards in China and other Asian countries.[21] "The general picture of the developing world in the latter half of the twentieth century . . . is one of tremendous progress in improving health and raising incomes; child mortality has been cut in half and incomes have more than doubled. . . . These statistics, however, have been skewed by the tremendous health gains and economic growth of China"[22] and other newly industrialized states in Asia (Chinese economic growth is discussed in Chapter 10; other, newly industrialized Asian states are discussed later in this chapter).

While the dramatic improvements in China in particular and many other Asian countries in general should not be overlooked (those countries do contain a significant proportion of the developing world's population), it is also true that some countries have seen their human development scores decline in recent years.[23] Many of these countries are in sub-Saharan Africa. GDP per capita increased at an average annual rate of 5.8 percent in China from 1965 to 1990, but it decreased over the same period in Tanzania, Ethiopia, Somalia, Chad, Zaire, Uganda, Madagascar, Niger, Ghana, Togo, and Zambia. Furthermore, African states make up the vast majority of the states that rank at the bottom of the UN Human Development Index ranking.[24]

Available calorie supplies increased by more than 700 calories a day in China from 1965 to 1989, but in Ethiopia, Somalia, Chad, Malawi, Burundi, Zaire, Uganda, Madagascar, Sierra Leone, Kenya, and Togo, calorie supplies were lower in 1989 than they were in 1965.[25] Food production in sub-Saharan Africa was 20 percent lower in the 1990s than it was in 1970, when the population was half its current size. The average life expectancy for males in sub-Saharan Africa is fifty years, six years lower than the average for the developing world and only slightly better than people living in England in the 1840s.[26]

The gap between life expectancy for sub-Saharan Africa and the rest of the world has widened in recent years and "HIV/AIDS is at the heart of the reversal. In 2004, an estimated 3 million people died from the virus, and another 5 million became infected. Almost all of these deaths were in the developing world, with 70% of them in Africa."[27]

In general, living standards have probably improved in developing countries since the Second World War, perhaps even more rapidly in some respects than they have in rich countries. But there are tragic exceptions involving millions of desperate people.

The International Debt Problem

One of the reasons that the gap between the North and the South has been growing (at least according to many economic indicators) concerns the large amounts of debt many of these countries owe. Any economic progress that is made by a country with large debts is quickly eaten up by debt payments. Many countries spend huge amounts servicing their debt—paying only interest—without diminishing the principal of the original loans. Debt in the developing world takes away resources that could be spent on economic restructuring, research and development, and addressing poverty.

One root of the international debt problem involved the action of the Organization of Petroleum Producing Countries (OPEC) in 1973 of quadrupling the price of oil. The importance of oil to each domestic economy in the world and to international economic intercourse is difficult to overstate. The dramatic change in oil prices set in motion flows of capital and economic changes whose ramifications (almost all negative, including those felt by most of the oil exporters that initiated the price increase) are still felt today. First, naturally enough, the price increase brought billions of dollars to OPEC countries and other oil exporters. They deposited much of that money in large banks in the United States and Europe. Despite the entirely understandable joy created in much of the Third World by OPEC's success, the change in the price of oil put many of those countries in dire economic straits. That problem was dealt with in large measure by transforming a large portion of OPEC profits into Third World debt. "London and New York bankers voluntarily [and for a profit] became risk-bearing intermediaries for transferring the oil money from one group of developing countries—the oil exporters—to another— the non oil-producing, capital starved, less developed countries . . . of the Third World."[28]

In order to understand the tragic nature of what was to follow, it is important to realize first how wise all this seemed in the 1970s. The OPEC price increase had brought the member countries billions of dollars, which they deposited in several of the largest banking institutions in the world. That increase created a crisis for developing countries that needed to pay for their oil imports. What could have been more logical for those countries than to obtain loans from the banks that had recently received huge deposits from the oil exporters? "This recycling of oil wealth was welcomed wholeheartedly by the LDCs that wanted credit for their . . . import needs. It also served the needs of other interested parties. Industrial governments and aid donors also welcomed an easy way to finance poorer countries' import bills. Moreover, the recycling process compensated Western economies for the deflating effect of higher oil payments."[29] In other words, the fact that banks in industrialized countries could use the deposits from oil-exporting countries to provide loans for which they could charge interest to some extent offset the pain inflicted on Western economies by the higher oil prices.

The recycling process worked rather well in the 1970s. The prices of exports from developing countries rose at an average annual rate of 14.7 percent from 1973 to 1980, and the volume of their exports rose 4 percent a year during that time.[30] Real per capita gross domestic product (GDP) in developing countries grew at an annual rate of 3.2 percent from 1973 to 1980. This rate was not terrific, but considering that the growth rate in industrialized countries was only 2.1 percent in those years, it did not indicate a terrible crisis.[31]

That terrible crisis was soon to come, though, triggered by the second OPEC price increase in 1979. "With the second oil price increase, the [industrialized countries] by and large adopted anti-inflationary macro-economic policy stances. The result was a severe worldwide recession, sharply falling commodity prices, and the highest real interest rates in the postwar era."[32] In other words, when the price of oil increased dramatically for the second time in a decade, the governments of industrialized countries took several painful steps to protect themselves, mostly to avoid uncontrollable inflation. They raised interest rates; their economic growth slowed. By 1982, the U.S. economy had gone into the deepest recession since the Second World War. Recessions in most other developed countries followed.

The economic slowdown in the rich countries soon led to depression-type conditions in many LDCs. First, world trade slowed to a crawl, and developing countries found it impossible to export their commodities to the industrialized countries. The year 1981 "had the dubious distinction of being the first . . . since 1958 to experience an actual decrease in world trade in current dollar terms, a shrinkage of 1 percent."[33] The value of world trade continued to fall for the next two years. Along with the volume of exports from LDCs, the value of those exports fell as well. Food commodity prices dropped 15 percent from 1981 to 1985. The prices of minerals and metals fell 6 percent during that time. The terms of trade for developing countries, that is, the relationship between the prices of the goods they export and the goods they import, turned against them violently in 1986. They had to export 30 percent more that year to receive the same volume of imports as the previous year; the result was a loss of $94 billion to the developing world. Somewhat ironically, one of the commodities whose prices dropped most precipitously was oil. This meant that developing countries such as Mexico and Nigeria, which had benefited spectacularly from oil price increases in the 1970s, found themselves in the 1980s suffering in a way that was virtually indistinguishable from their oil-starved peers.

Many of the states in the developing world have yet to escape the debt problem of the 1980s. Developing countries had debt service payments, on average, of 4.6 percent of their GDP in 2005, up from 3.5 percent in 1990.[34] In 1999, debt service ate up over 20 percent of the value of revenue in countries such as Senegal, Zambia, and Bolivia.[35] The developing world faced severe economic problems in the late 1990s, and many of these problems continue today, particularly after the global economic downturn in 2008. "Overall, borrowing needs for developing countries are expected to exceed net capital inflows by between $350 billion and $635 billion."[36]

Explanations of the North–South Gap

Why does the economic gap between the North and the South exist and, at least on some measures, continue to grow? So far, theories purporting to answer these questions have been much more numerous than examples of success in attaining these goals. The experience of LDCs in the decades since the Second World War discredited one plan after another concerning the most effective ways to speed development.

The Historical Explanation: Imperialism

Most would agree that the roots of the North-South gap lay in the historical relationship between the colonial powers and the areas that they conquered from the sixteenth to early twentieth centuries. As discussed in Chapter 1, neo-Marxist perspectives take a historical view of global politics and how the development of capitalism and imperialism divided the world economy into a core of "haves," in which the most advanced economic activities and wealth were located, and a periphery of "have-nots," in which less advanced economic activities occurred and wealth was scarce. Colonialism was in many ways economically detrimental to the colonies. Minerals were exported, with profit going to the colonial powers, economic expertise was often limited to the colonists, and economies were developed in narrow ways to serve the interests of the colonial power. Luxury crops such as coffee were planted to serve the needs of the home populations of the colonial powers. The economic gap between the North and the South was thus established during this historical period. The North industrialized, with the help of the resources it extracted from the South, established modern infrastructure, and accumulated capital to continue its economic growth. The South, on the other hand, was forced to remain agrarian, its economic and political structures were dominated and molded to serve the interests of the colonial states, and it lagged more and more behind the development in the North. While most agree that the colonial relationship primarily benefited the North at the expense of the South, some argue that this is not the complete picture. The gap between the areas was in some ways already in place before imperialism began, and it is not clear that the growth in the North was directly due to the imperial relationship. According to one analyst,

> commerce between core and periphery for three centuries after 1350 proceeded on a small scale, was not a uniquely profitable field of enterprise, and . . . could in no way be classified as decisive for economic growth in Western Europe. . . . The commerce between Western Europe and regions at the periphery of the international economy forms an insignificant part of the explanation for the accelerated rate of economic growth experienced by the core after 1750. . . . For economic growth of the core, the periphery was peripheral.[37]

Furthermore, it is not clear that the North became rich at the expense of the poor since all regions grew economically during and immediately after the colonial period. "The key fact of modern times is not the *transfer* of income from one region to another, by force or otherwise, but rather the overall *increase* in world income, but at a different rate in different regions."[38]

Also, in this view, far from harming most countries in Latin America, Africa, and Asia, contact with colonial imperialists actually brought some degree of economic progress to those areas. Those few places that were not taken over by Europeans do not seem, on average, to have benefited greatly by that "good luck." For example, "the African states not subject to Western imperialism—Liberia and Ethiopia—are today more backward than those neighbors which [were] colonized."[39] Japan is often cited as a shining example of the good things that might have happened to areas had they not been colonized, because Japan was never formally subjected to colonial status. It is certainly an economic success story. But "Britain and other Western powers imposed treaties upon the Japanese that required something approaching free trade with the rest of the world. In particular, a treaty of 1866 restricted the Japanese to a revenue tariff of not more than 5 percent, which lasted until 1899. . . . Trade immediately expanded, and economic growth apparently picked up speed, particularly in the 1880s and 1890s."[40] It would seem difficult to trace Japan's economic success to lack of contact with the Western industrialized world.

Despite these criticisms of the historical explanation, many after World War II believed that overall, imperialism had been economically devastating to the South. It was widely believed that when the colonial relationship was severed, the states in the South would catch up economically to the North. According to **modernization theory,** the South was simply in an earlier economic stage than the North.[41] From this perspective, Britain, the United States, and the other Western industrialized countries would serve as a historical model that the new countries would try to emulate in their efforts to develop politically and economically. This meant that the new countries should adopt free enterprise systems based on individual initiative and democratic political systems. In general, modernization and development theories, popular in the 1950s, stressed that internal changes in the new states were crucial to their economic development. The people would have to be educated and socialized to give up their "old-fashioned ideas." Urbanization was considered desirable for its impact on the education and socialization processes, and industrialization, with its attendant concentration of people in cities and capital-intensive activities, was presumed to be the primary goal of developing countries. All of these processes would be accelerated by a maximum amount of contact between rich countries and poor countries in the form of international trade, foreign investment, and foreign aid.

Based on these assumptions in modernization theory, there was great optimism that the South would quickly escape poverty conditions. After all, many of these states possessed vast natural resources that were now under their control, free from colonial oppression. These optimistic hopes were largely dashed. Overall, the South did not catch up to the North, and, as we have seen, the gap between the rich and the poor in the world accelerated, particularly after the 1960s.

modernization theory Perspective that emphasizes stages of development and expects poor countries to develop as they move from traditional to modern societies and economies.

Dependency and Neo-Imperialism Explanations

Many leaders in the South, as well as many analysts in the North, have proposed one explanation to the continued and growing gap between the North and the South: The exploitative structure of the colonial period was extended with neocolonial structures, even after states gained their independence, and this neo-imperial relationship continued to disadvantage the South in the international political economy. According to neo-Marxist approaches, particularly dependency theory (introduced in

Chapter 1), the states in the South will not catch up with the states in the North until the international structure of the global economy changes.[42]

Neo-Marxists argue that after gaining independence, developing states were subjected to international power structures when they began the development process. LDCs had to compete in a system dominated economically, politically, and militarily by states that were already relatively rich and powerful. This situation, according to neo-Marxists, calls for strategies quite different from those used in earlier days by states such as Great Britain and the United States. Neo-Marxists believe that adopting a strategy similar to that relied on by the currently rich countries would perpetuate a process that many economists and historians in the North tend to overlook when they analyze the historical experience of wealthy industrialized states. That process transfers wealth from poorer regions and countries to wealthier countries. Such a redistribution of wealth, in the view of most neo-Marxists, is a more or less natural consequence of capitalism. While economists and historians in the developed states acknowledge that colonialism and imperialism existed, neo-Marxists believe they understate the extent to which economic progress in the rich northern countries was based on exploitation of the currently underdeveloped regions. In short, rich countries got rich, to an important extent, by making poor countries poor. And here again, of course, is a factor pointing in the direction of development strategies quite different from those used in earlier epochs. Current LDCs have no relatively defenseless, untouched areas available for exploitation—the key to success for capitalist states.

Neo-Marxists view the structure of the international system as the reason that they cannot escape the poverty originating in the colonial period. In particular, the structure of international trade, aid, and investment by multinational corporations works against the interests of the South. These economic structures are backed by powerful military and political structures, primarily through the foreign policies of the United States, to maintain the neo-imperialist economic domination over the South.

Why, according to the neo-Marxist perspective, does international trade tend to have a deleterious impact on poor countries? The main argument is that many poor countries depend heavily on the export of one or two raw materials or commodities; that is, they suffer from commodity concentration. They developed this reliance in the historical process of becoming integrated into the capitalist world system. As long as they depend on international trade (as most LDCs do for a very large proportion of their GNP), and especially if they are also heavily dependent on one key trading partner (often their former colonial power), they will never break out of this role to which they have been relegated in the world's division of labor. The problem is exacerbated by the rich countries' refusal to abide by the free trade doctrine when it does not suit their purposes. They erect high tariff barriers or adopt quotas to protect their own domestic economic interests against competition from cheap labor or cheap commodities in the poor countries. Indeed, the GATT trading regime seems to have worked against the South as the North has negotiated free trade for what it exports (manufactured goods) and kept protectionist barriers for goods for which the South has a comparative advantage (primary products).

terms of trade Prices of exported goods relative to imported goods.

Neo-Marxists also argue that the **terms of trade** involving the primary products on which developing countries depend have deteriorated steadily. That is, the amount of a given raw material they must export to get a manufactured product in return keeps growing. For example, the amount of rice that Myanmar must export to obtain a refrigerator from some industrialized country keeps getting larger as the years go by. Also, the prices of raw materials and commodities fluctuate in a notorious fashion. Occasionally, the prices of exports from developing countries, such as copper, coffee, or sugar, have been very high, and the producers have experienced temporary windfalls. But in the next year, the prices of those same products have dropped precipitously, and the developing countries that export them have suffered grievous balance-of-trade deficits and other painful dislocations in their highly vulnerable economies.[43]

Thus, because the South primarily earns its living by exporting primary products and because the prices of primary products are unstable, these countries are disadvantaged compared to the North and its exports of manufactured goods with stable prices.

overseas development assistance Foreign aid, aimed at economic development.

From the neo-Marxists' viewpoint, foreign aid (or **overseas development assistance**) also serves the interests of the North, because aid often supports elites in dependent countries whose interests are tied more closely to the elites of the richer capitalist countries than to their own countries. The elites often use that aid to suppress people who would like to achieve a degree of national autonomy. Furthermore, aid builds up debts that poor countries have a great deal of difficulty repaying. They must structure their economies in such a way as to earn foreign exchange rather than to feed the people in their own country. Foreign aid, neo-Marxists also point out, is usually "tied." That is, it can be spent only on products or services provided by the donor country. In this way, it serves primarily as a crudely disguised subsidy to the corporations and firms that provide these products and services to the countries receiving foreign aid.

In recent years, when foreign aid levels have dropped, private banks have to some extent stepped in where governments have backed out. Now many developing countries (Mexico and Brazil, for example) have crushing debts to private banks, and those debts have the same deleterious effects as debts to governments for foreign aid. Also, particularly now that poor countries have built up international debts, to qualify for more aid or loans they must follow recommendations for restructuring their economies laid down by international organizations such as the International Monetary Fund (IMF) or the International Bank for Reconstruction and Development (IBRD). The reform efforts advocated by the IMF in particular (and based on economic liberalism) call for the governments of developing countries to abolish import controls, devalue their exchange rates, curb government expenditures (often on social services or food subsidies for the poor), control wage increases, and welcome foreign investment:[44]

> The IMF and IBRD impose stringent conditions on their borrowers; conditions . . . [according to neo-Marxists] that open the door for their penetration by the trade and investment of rich states. . . . Less developed countries not willing to conform to IMF and IBRD suggestions find themselves denied not only loans from these institutions but also credit through private channels or bilateral aid programs.[45]

Thus, from the point of view of neo-Marxists, foreign aid is a form of neocolonial political control only slightly more subtle than old-fashioned colonialism. Foreign aid is, in short, a form of imperialism.[46]

Furthermore, neo-Marxists point out that the international power structure supports the dominance of the North over the South in the international economic structures. Specifically, foreign policies of the United States are argued to work to the advantage of U.S. business interests. Especially during the Cold War, the United States consistently and energetically supported the status quo in many developing countries. In Iran, Guatemala, and Chile, to name only a few of the better-known cases, the U.S. Central Intelligence Agency (CIA) helped subvert governments that were not deemed sufficiently friendly to the U.S. government or American economic interests. Elsewhere, reactionary governments have been sustained by foreign aid, military aid, and private sources of financial support. According to some neo-Marxist critics of U.S. foreign policy, the pattern of support for the status quo throughout the developing world is motivated primarily by a desire to make the world safe for capitalism.

The Role of MNCs in Economic Dependency

Neo-Marxists also argue that economic powers in the world work to support MNC activities in the developing world, to the detriment of developing economies. MNCs attract criticism, in part, because they are so large. In fact, many of them, by some measures, are larger economic units than are developing countries themselves (see Table 4.3 in Chapter 4).

According to neo-Marxism, foreign investment in developing countries by MNCs does much more economic harm than good. For example, MNCs take more money out of countries in the form of **repatriated profits** than they put into them. During the 1960s, for example, when approximately $1 billion of capital was transferred to U.S.-controlled subsidiaries in developing countries, about $2.5 billion was being withdrawn annually from those same subsidiaries.[47] In addition, critics of MNCs point out that these companies do not bring much money into developing countries. "Over the 1966 to 1976 period, 49 percent of all net new investment funds of U.S. transnational corporations in the less developed countries

repatriated profits Money from investment that leaves a country and is returned to the investor's home country.

were reinvested earnings, 50 percent were funds acquired locally, *and only 1 percent were funds newly transferred from the United States.*"[48] In short, "the financing of foreign investment is done largely with host-country, not foreign, capital."[49]

And when MNCs engage in outsourcing—producing goods overseas primarily for export back home—there may be little investment in the local economy:

> The U.S.-Mexican border, with its two thousand or so maquila-doras ["assembly plants"], is perhaps the best-known example of such a zone. This zone provides U.S. MNCs with comparatively cheap, nonunion labor, in sites close to the large U.S. market. Taxes and tariffs are virtually eliminated, and environmental and labor laws are weakly enforced. U.S. MNCs in the garment, electronic, and auto industries have flocked to the zone, import-ing parts from the United States for assembly in Mexico and then shipping the finished products back to the United States. . . . The problem for some host countries [such as Mexico] is that such MNCs sink few deep roots into the economy, transferring little research and development and developing few linkages with local firms.[50]

Multinational corporations are now present in almost every developing country around the globe. These workers are some of Nike's 50,000 employees in Vietnam. Nike is one of Vietnam's largest private employers.
(© Steve Raymer/Corbis)

If MNCs have such bad economic effects, one might reasonably wonder why so many developing countries welcome them with open arms. In fact, there are few, if any, countries in the world today that do not actively seek foreign investment. The answer, according to neo-Marxism, is that MNCs co-opt the leadership and elites of poor countries, bribing them, in effect, to accept foreign investment that benefits those leaders and a small elite but is detrimental to the country as a whole.

Others contend that MNCs are not as bad as critics claim. Some defenders of MNCs argue that they do supply much-needed capital to developing economies and that in addition to the investment money they bring in, they also serve to improve the balance of payments of those poor countries by adding to their exports and by manufacturing products locally that would otherwise have to be imported.

Defenders of MNCs claim that most of the criticisms of MNCs are based on misunderstandings or misinformation, or both. Consider the comparison of inflow of investments by MNCs and outflows of repatriated profits for a given period of time. It is true, MNC defenders concede, that these comparisons typically show that the global companies take more money out of a country than they put into it. But such comparisons are irrelevant or misleading. The fact that corporations took more money out of a country in a given year—for example, 2005 than they put into that country in the same year does not prove that the country is being decapitalized, or otherwise impoverished, by the activities of the MNCs, because what comes out of a country in the form of repatriated profits in a particular year is not a function of the direct investments that went into that country during that time. Rather, the profits of 2005 were the result of corporate investments over several previous years. Such comparisons also ignore the fact that once capital is invested in a country, it forms the basis of a capital stock that can grow and produce more with each passing year.

In addition, the comparison of inflows and outflows of capital ignores the multiplier effect of the original investments. Each dollar invested expands the economy by some factor greater than one. A dollar paid in wages is used by the worker who earns it to buy groceries; the grocery store owner buys a pair of shoes; the shoe-store owner invests the dollar in some new furniture; and so on.

Corporate spokespersons argue that their companies transfer technology and management techniques necessary for economic development to developing countries. Critics respond that, on the contrary, the technology introduced by MNCs is capital intensive and thus inappropriate for the economies of developing countries for two basic reasons. First, although these states have an abundance of labor, the technologically sophisticated equipment MNCs use limits the need for a large labor force.[51] Second, "in countries where the overall key legal institution governing economic relations is the private ownership of productive resources . . . it follows that the larger the proportion of total output due to capital-technology resources, the greater the amount of income going to the owners of those resources."[52] Thus, in addition to creating unemployment, this capital-intensive technology can exacerbate the already unequal distribution of wealth in developing countries.

Many researchers have tried to determine the overall economic impact of MNCs on developing economies by statistically analyzing the relationship between foreign investment and economic performance, but with no clear conclusions.[53] Some have found that foreign investment in less developed countries (LDCs) retards economic growth and human development; additional recent analyses reveal that foreign investment is not associated with increased inequality in the distribution of wealth.[54] An increasingly common opinion about the impact of MNC investment in developing countries is that the nature of the impact depends on how the government of a given country deals with it (and how it is dealt with is not inevitably determined by the presence of the investment). In other words, MNC investments can have negative effects, but if they are handled properly, they can bring substantial benefits. As one noted scholar of international political economy concludes, MNCs are "neither as positive nor as negative in their impact on development as liberals or their critics suggest. Foreign direct investment can help or hinder, but the major determinants of economic development lie within LDCs themselves."[55] More recently, analysts have concluded that "FDI flows have a more strongly positive effect on economic growth in countries that have made significant investments in education and worker training than in countries that have not done this."[56]

Beyond the economic impact of MNCs on the developing world, critics of MNCs also argue that they have adverse affects on state sovereignty and other political values. According to neo-Marxists, for example, any developing country that attempts meaningful political reforms may find such efforts stifled by the formidable opposition of MNCs. The spectacular example supporting this argument involves the activities of International Telephone and Telegraph (ITT) in Chile when Salvador Allende was in power in the early 1970s. It has been established that ITT offered the CIA funds to carry out subversive activities in Chile and that the CIA later did engage in such activities (although it has never been definitively established that the CIA accepted ITT financial support for those ventures). Allende's overthrow by the Chilean military on September 1, 1973, is just an extreme example, MNC opponents contend, of the preference of MNCs for right-wing regimes that can ensure "stability" through political oppression and their willingness to take active measures to install or maintain such regimes in power.

Others charge MNCs with violation of labor rights and unethical treatment of workers. Nike, for example, has been accused of a wide variety of abuses, especially in such countries as China, Vietnam, and Indonesia, including "wretchedly low wages, enforced overtime, harsh and sometimes brutal discipline, and corporal punishment."[57] Another

ISSUE: MNC investments in developing countries can provide potential benefits but at the cost of depending on corporations whose home bases are elsewhere and whose long-term interests are more congruent with those of rich, industrialized countries.

Option #1: Discourage foreign direct investment and provide political and economic protection for corporations owned and operated by local interests.

Arguments: (a) Local talent may take a while to develop a viable corporation, but in the long run, local firms will serve the economy of the country better than subsidiaries of foreign corporations will. (b) Foreign subsidiaries are more difficult to control than are local firms, because they can always threaten to shut down the local subsidiary and move production to countries with more pliant governments. (c) Reliance on foreign investment makes a poor country more vulnerable to the negative impact of economic setbacks in rich countries.

Counterarguments: (a) Local firms will produce more expensive goods for local consumers, who will have to pay higher prices for many years until the domestic firms become as efficient as giant MNCs. (b) Local firms face severe disadvantages in their attempts to export their products. MNCs already have vast international networks of contacts and familiarity with numerous markets in different regions of the world. (c) Few countries have achieved economic success using the politics of autonomy or self-reliance. Many countries that have tried such policies so far, such as North Korea, have instead brought on economic disaster.

Option #2: Foreign direct investment can be actively encouraged; for example, by providing tax breaks to MNCs that establish subsidiaries.

Arguments: (a) Competition between foreign and domestic firms, as well as the typical higher levels of efficiency achieved by MNCs, will result in lower prices for consumer goods in countries that encourage foreign investment. (b) Subsidiaries of foreign firms will achieve greater success than local firms would by exploiting export markets around the world. (c) Foreign firms will bring with them technological and administrative know-how that will yield benefits in the countries where they establish subsidiaries.

Counterarguments: (a) Reliance on foreign subsidiaries will make the country vulnerable to decisions made by corporations with foreign headquarters. (b) Increased integration with recent globalizing forces in the worldwide economy often seems to exacerbate economic inequality. (c) Foreign subsidiaries may engage in practices harmful to the environment of the country in which they are established; any attempt to curb those practices will be met with threats to close down that subsidiary.

similar report points out that "a worker making Nike running shoes in Jakarta, Indonesia, for example, makes $2.28 a day. . . . The wage paid in Indonesia is not sufficient to live on. The Indonesian government admits that an individual needs no less than $4 a day to pay for basic human needs in an urban area such as Jakarta."[58] At first, the company responded by denying knowledge of poor working conditions, but later, in response to boycotts and protests, it announced several changes in policies, including raising its minimum working age in its factories.[59] Other MNCs have been accused of a range of human rights abuses. One U.S.-based oil company settled a case that alleged its use of slave labor to build a pipeline in Burma. Oil giants Shell and Chevron have been accused of complicity with the Nigerian government in the deaths of activists protesting environmental abuses of the companies.[60]

These are, of course, only a few examples. It has been reported that "in the world of Asian laborers, which makes goods that line the shelves of American, European, and Japanese stores, workers get fired for leaving their machines to go to the bathroom. Bosses punish tardy workers by making them stand in the sun for hours."[61] The use of child labor by MNCs in Asia and elsewhere has been widely documented.[62] Because of consumer awareness and pressure by nongovernmental advocacy groups, however, there is a growing acceptance by MNCs that they must abide by a certain **corporate social responsibility** in their business practices.[63]

corporate social responsibility Idea that corporations are accountable for the social, economic, and environmental impact of their decisions and operations.

Fairly recently, for example, Oxfam International has led a push for the jewelry industry to limit itself to selling responsibly mined gold. "These changes are partly coming about . . . because gold mining's environmental and social impacts have become impossible to ignore, especially in developing countries where [violent conflicts], political protests, corruption, and displacement of indigenous peoples have often accompanied mining."[64]

MNCs may adopt internal policies designed to show that they are treating their workers and the environment according to international norms. They also may agree to sectorwide standards, such as the Apparel Industry Partnership, designed to improve working conditions in garment factories. Finally, they may abide by the UN Global Compact, which draws on nine principles from UN human rights, labor, and environmental treaties.[65] All of these mechanisms for corporate responsibility are voluntary and

> there are vigorous debates over which codes, standards, and reporting techniques are more effective in raising corporate behavior and improving labor, human rights, and environmental practices. Many are too new to be able to fully assess; MNCs are still in the adoption and implementation phase. . . . [But] the explosion of CSR [Corporate Social Responsibility] codes and implementation techniques shows a rising acknowledgement of the power of private governance and the power of corporations to implement social and economic change.[66]

Despite the continued controversies over the economic, political, social, and environmental consequences of MNCs to developing countries, it is quite clear that "most governments seem reconciled to the prospect that, even if the costs seem high, they cannot cut themselves off from their access to global technologies and global markets, and from institutions such as multinational enterprises that contribute to that access."[67] Some of the issues involved in the debate about MNCs are outlined in the Policy Choices box.

The Economic Liberal Explanation of Underdevelopment

Proponents of economic liberalism (see Chapter 10) disagree with the neo-Marxist perspective. They argue that the international economic structure, if based on economic liberal ideas, will benefit all, both rich and poor. International trade based on the principle of comparative advantage and investment by multinational corporations is the key to all economic growth. Economic interdependence is good for the South: It allows these countries to acquire markets, capital, and technology for development.[68]

The fundamental source of disagreement between economic liberals, on the one hand, and neo-Marxists, on the other hand, is the starkly different estimates of the relative impact of external and internal factors on the process of development. Economic liberals believe that the changes necessary to bring economic progress to LDCs are largely *internal* to those countries. In short, internal domestic political and economic changes that involve liberalizing the country to remove political and social obstacles to the function of the free market are the key to economic progress. Neo-Marxists do not deny that internal changes are necessary (indeed they see the elites within poor countries as a critical problem), but from their point of view, economic liberals seriously underestimate the extent to which the problems of LDCs are caused by factors *external* to those countries, such as the structure of the international economic and political environment. Some neo-Marxists also point out the historical structure of the relationship between imperial powers and the colonized areas as the primary cause for the North-South gap. For these reasons, some neo-Marxists theories are structural, whereas economic liberalism is not.

The liberal criticism of the structural theories often points to the successful economic development story of several countries in East Asia. The argument is that these states prove that poor states can experience economic growth despite, or because of, the current international economic structure.

The "Economic Miracle" of East Asia

newly industrialized countries Countries that have experienced fairly recent economic development, such as the "Asian Tigers": Singapore, South Korea, Taiwan, and Hong Kong.

Even before China's miraculous economic growth, there were development success stories in East Asia. Singapore, South Korea, Taiwan, and Hong Kong, referred to as the "Asian Tigers," were seen as remarkable achievements in economic development (see Map 11.2). And these states, part of a group known as the **newly industrialized countries (NICs)**, have not just achieved a rapid rate of growth in the aggregate size of their respective economies. Even large increases in the GNP can leave much of the population no better off, or even relatively worse off than before, compared with only a few beneficiaries of such increases. But the Asian Tigers "have apparently been able to overcome strong cross-national patterns suggesting that good things do not tend to happen together.' . . . The East Asians' record of growth with equity' sharply distinguishes them from other developing countries that have also undergone rapid growth."[69]

This economic success was troublesome for neo-Marxist approaches, because the Asian Tigers followed development policies that were quite different from those advocated by structural theories. All four became closely integrated into the world's economic system and achieved success by stressing a high volume of exports to the industrialized states. Neo-Marxists approaches ". . . had not predicted and could not explain this record of economic growth and industrial diversification."[70] For these reasons, "by the end of the 1970s the World Bank had singled out the four Asian NICs as models to be studied by the second rung of developing countries."[71]

Map 11.2   The Asian Tigers

(© Cengage Learning)

The Asian Tigers took the lead in transforming the relationship between LDCs and the industrialized countries in the area of international trade, something that neo-Marxism suggests LDCs cannot do, because they are trapped in a role in the international trading system in which they export mostly primary products and commodities. But in fact, "while manufactures amounted to merely 5 percent of all Southern exports to the North in 1955 and only 15.2 percent in 1980, they had jumped to 53.5 percent by 1989."[72] And this trend was not wholly due to the Asian Tigers. In fact, nations accounting for about two-thirds of the population of the developing world have successfully severed dependence on their single largest traditional primary export. Diversification of exports for developing countries has progressed to the point at which "manufactures are rapidly claiming an ever larger share of exports in most developing countries, and already have a share in exports almost equal to primary products in countries representing the majority of population in the developing world."[73] Manufactured goods now account for 71 percent of the value of exports from developing countries. and one-fourth of all manufactured exports in the world.[74] In short, the four Asian Tigers have demonstrated convincingly that it is not true that the international economic and political structures permanently relegate developing countries to the role of exporting only primary products. Their success in escaping that kind of role has been duplicated elsewhere well enough to argue that it is quite relevant to the rest of the developing world.

In fact, several additional East and Southeast Asian nations went a long way toward duplicating the success of the original Tigers in the 1980s. Most East Asian countries following an outward-looking, export-oriented development strategy during the 1980s enjoyed "per capita income growth of more than 7% . . . a record exceeding anything experienced."[75]

The economies of Malaysia, Indonesia, and Thailand, for example, experienced poverty reduction, high employment, and increased life expectancy from their growth in exports of manufactured goods.[76]

As discussed in Chapter 10, China became very export oriented and open to foreign investment. By 1991, it was the second-largest recipient of foreign investment in the world.[77] During this era of increased openness and export orientation, "some 150–200 million people, equivalent to half the population of Western Europe, have worked their way out of poverty . . . a revolution in wealth-creation on a scale unparalleled in modern history."[78] More recently, "during the 1990s, India liberalized foreign trade and investment with good results. . . . It too has pursued a broad agenda of reform and has moved away from a highly regulated, planned system."[79]

Generally speaking, if you divide developing countries into two categories—those who have opened up their economies and those who have not—the former group has experienced more economic growth. Moreover, inequality within those countries has not necessarily followed.[80] Yet many states have not been able to duplicate this type of export-led success. While developing states as a whole now account for a significant portion of manufactured goods, "much of the developing world has little more than a toehold in manufacturing export markets" and "after more than two decades of rapid trade growth, high-income countries representing 15% of the world's population still account for two-thirds of world exports."[81]

Although the early success of the Asian Tigers and some other developing states is used by economic liberals to support their arguments about the causes and solutions for development, several dimensions of the experiences of many rapidly developing Asian states support neo-Marxists and other critics of economic liberalism. Taiwan has demonstrated, for example, the importance of "the eradication of colonial institutions, effective land reform, government-directed structural transformation, national management, and regulation of foreign multinationals."[82] Furthermore, "the socio-economic structure and the patterns of income distribution in South Korea and Taiwan were relatively egalitarian even before the transition to export-led growth, in large part because of the extensive business/commercial restructuring and comprehensive agrarian reforms that had been undertaken in these countries in the 1940s and 1950s."[83] Some neo-Marxist approaches advocate protective tariffs as a means of isolating developing countries from some of the harmful effects of the international economic environment and "all of the East Asian [countries], with the exception of Hong Kong, used protection to develop infant industries, even after the shift to an export-oriented strategy."[84]

And quite contrary to the principles of economic liberalism, "the authoritarian regime of South Korea . . . achieved spectacular growth rates by practicing command economics. . . . Government incentives, subsidies, and coercion fueled the drive for heavy industry in such areas as iron and steel that market forces would have rendered uncompetitive in the early stages."[85] In general, scholars analyzing the success of the East Asian states have often "emphasized the pattern of extensive state intervention in the market,"[86] consistent with more with state capitalism (see Chapter 10) then liberal capitalist economies. One prominent analyst of the success of East Asian economies concludes that "*most* Anglo-American development economists have a mistaken understanding of Korea and Taiwan as 'low-intervention' countries, especially with reference to trade, and they rely on this mistaken understanding to validate a low-intervention prescription elsewhere."[87] The rapidly developing states of East Asia (and the United States and Western Europe, for that matter), then, have neither adhered zealously to principles of free trade and the free market nor entirely avoided some of the policies that neo-Marxists might suggest. And the use of the rapid progress of East Asia as a model for economic development elsewhere became even more questionable since the economic crises hit these countries in the late 1990s, as discussed in Chapter 10. But the economic growth that they did experience does call into question fundamental tenets of structural theories regarding self-reliance and breaking away from the world capitalist system.

Development Strategies for the South

Various strategies have been offered as ways for the poorer states to develop and close the North-South gap. Development strategies are related to the explanations of underdevelopment just reviewed. In other words, neo-Marxists who believe that the cause of economic underdevelopment is the international structure will support very different development strategies than will economic liberals, who believe that the cause of economic underdevelopment lies in internal political and economic conditions. Although various theories have been more or less popular at different times, there has yet to be a complete consensus on which strategy represents the best chance for economic development.

Strategies Associated with Neo–Marxism

If, as many neo-Marxists believe, the international political and economic structures continue to work to the advantage of the North and simply exploit the South in a neo-imperialist fashion, then the solution to this condition of dependence is more independence. This is the goal of a developmental policy known as the **import substitution strategy,** which was particularly popular in the 1960s in Latin America and was advocated by some of the original neo-Marxist dependency theorists, who were from that region. "The import substitution path taken by countries like Brazil and Mexico can best be described as a series of stages during which these countries moved from being exporters of primary commodities to developing an indigenous industrial base."[88] States following this

import substitution strategy Policy to develop and protect industries to produce goods that a country has been importing.

strategy protected infant industries with tariff and nontariff barriers, curtailed imports, and tried to create a niche in manufacturing goods that could benefit from better terms of trade. Thus, rather than being dependent on the North for these higher-priced goods, they would become more self-sufficient. For some countries, like Brazil and Mexico, this worked for a while. "Through this strategy . . . Brazil, Mexico, and others were able to generate sustained economic growth. Brazil had a 9 percent annual average growth in GDP between 1965 and 1980. Mexico and Venezuela lagged behind but still averaged a growth rate of 6.5 and 3.7 respectively."[89] These growth rates did not compare to the Asian Tigers, did not distribute growth equally within the countries, and did not last into the 1980s. The debt crisis that afflicted Latin American countries in the 1980s and the slowdown in growth rates severely discredited the import substitution strategy.

In addition to advocating import substitution strategy as economic development policy for individual countries, there have been collective efforts on the part of the South to address the global gap between rich and poor. Regardless of policies that LDCs might adopt, many economic and political analysts are convinced that the gap cannot be closed unless the globe's entire economic system is transformed. In the 1970s, this basic idea culminated in the call for a **New International Economic Order (NIEO).** Neo-Marxism was influential in developing ideas that served as the basis for the NIEO and inspiring unity among the disparate group of countries referred to as the Third World. The origins of this quest can be traced to the early 1960s, when LDCs united behind the idea of a worldwide conference on this problem, resulting in the first UN Conference on Trade and Development (UNCTAD) in 1962. At about the same time, a coalition of developing southern states became known as the **Group of 77,** a name it retains even though it is now much larger. "The G-77 sought to make UNCTAD a mechanism for dialogue and negotiation between the LDCs and the developed countries on trade, finance, and other issues."[90]

With its call for a NIEO, the Group of 77 wanted more foreign aid, especially multilateral aid through both the World Bank and the IMF, rather than bilateral country-to-country aid. This aid, they argued, should not be given on the condition that they use it to buy goods from particular countries or support particular countries' policies. Foreign aid, or overseas development assistance, is a controversial tool for economic development. As mentioned, some neo-Marxists have blamed aid for underdevelopment, arguing that it often serves as a bribe to elites to gain support for further dependence on the North. Furthermore, neo-Marxists argue, aid is rarely given without conditions attached and is usually in the form of loans with which states fall further into debt. Yet the NIEO included calls for more foreign aid, without strings attached, as a kind of reparation for the imperialist policies of the North and as the only hope that many countries have for investment in future development.

New International Economic Order (NIEO) Name used to describe the developing states' goal of a reformed, more equitable international economy.

Group of 77 A coalition of developing states, now numbering over 100, that seeks to address the economic gap between the North and the South.

The criticisms of foreign aid are many (see the Policy Choices box). For economic liberals, aid is a political intrusion into the market. Many, including developing countries that are recipients of aid, recognize that other than aid for the relief of disasters, development assistance programs rarely meet their goals. There are a few success stories, but in general, the impact of foreign aid in poor countries has been disappointing. Poverty remains in these countries partly, because wealth is not easily transferable on an aggregate basis. If John Doe, an individual, inherits $10 million from his rich uncle, chances are that unless John is incredibly foolish, he will be set for life in economic terms. But wealth for millions of people in a poor country must be based at least in part on economic growth and productivity, not gifts. In short, because foreign aid cannot be sustained in sufficiently large amounts to improve the lives of people in poor countries, it can produce lasting benefits only if it is used to create self-sustaining economic growth and to increase the productivity of poor people in developing countries.

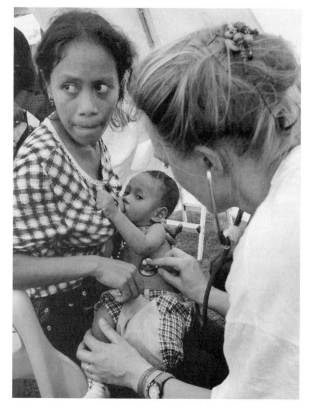

A Dutch doctor, working for Médecins Sans Frontières (Doctors Without Borders), attends to a baby boy with measles in West Timor. Many children in developing countries lack basic immunization programs for potentially deadly diseases such as measles.
(AFP/Getty Images)

The effects of foreign aid, however, are not always and everywhere bad. Although billions of dollars of aid have been dispensed in recent decades and poverty still prevails in the developing world, some data show that "aid contributes powerfully to both economic growth and human development."[91] According to economist Jeffrey Sachs, aid is a necessary tool to alleviate extreme poverty and the costs are within reason: "The truth is that the cost now is likely to be small compared to any relevant measure—income, taxes, the costs of further delay, and the benefits from acting. . . . All of the incessant debate about development assistance, and whether the rich are doing enough to help the poor, actually concerns less than 1 percent of rich-world income."[92] Sachs argues that this aid should be based on country-specific assessments of needs and carefully implemented and monitored for successful results.[93] Others argue that there is no historical basis for assuming that foreign aid will do anything to improve economic conditions.

With the NIEO, the South also argued for a new international currency to replace the U.S. dollar, freer access to markets in rich countries, and commodity agreements to stabilize the prices of raw materials and

ISSUE: The question of whether states in the North should provide more foreign assistance to the South is a controversial one in debates on economic development. Most states in the North do provide some foreign assistance to the South. In absolute terms, the United States is the number one supplier of foreign aid to the South (giving over $27 million in 2005), followed by Japan (with over $13 million in 2005). The amount of aid relative to a country's gross national income (GNI), referred to as its **aid burden**, varies across countries in the North, with the United States coming in at or near the bottom of rich countries (giving 0.22 percent of its GNI) and Scandinavian countries coming in at the top (Norway's aid burden, for example, was 0.94 percent in 2005). Overall, government foreign aid to the South first diminished immediately after the end of the Cold War but has recently increased, and in 2005, a group of wealthy states agreed to double their foreign aid to Africa and provide $40 billion in debt relief, but not all have delivered on this promise. Governments are not the only suppliers of development assistance to the South. International organizations, such as the United Nations, and nongovernmental humanitarian agencies, such as Save the Children and Oxfam, also provide some aid and assistance to the developing world.

aid burden Percentage of a country's GNI that goes to foreign assistance.

Option #1: The developed countries should offer more foreign aid to the poorer countries.

Arguments: (a) The economies are in such dire shape that only aid will jump-start any growth, as did the Marshall Plan for Western Europe following World War II. (b) The North, like all other actors with excess resources, is morally obligated to help the starving. Aid is the most direct form of humanitarian assistance that states can provide. (c) Because the North's imperialism is partly responsible for the economic conditions of the South, the North has a special obligation to make amends, much as was demanded of Germany after World War I for its imperialist ambitions.

Counterarguments: (a) Aid prolongs dependencies and inefficiencies and retards rather than stimulates growth. (b) States' first obligation is to provide for their own citizens. Poverty in the South is due to corrupt leaders, and further aid would simply stay in their pockets and not alleviate any suffering. (c) The South suffers from far more than a simple history of being dominated, and demanding reparations in the form of foreign aid diverts attention from more fundamental and immediate development problems.

Option #2: The developed countries should limit or curtail foreign aid to the South.

Arguments: (a) The countries of the developing world should focus on exporting their way out of their economic situation instead of requesting aid. (b) It is the problem of the developing world and is not for the North to solve. (c) Aid is simply a way to impose cultural values by demanding certain actions from the recipient.

Counterarguments: (a) Because of historical inequities as well as the structure of trade between the North and the South and biases against goods from their countries, developing economies cannot compete and simply export their way to growth. (b) Addressing the North-South gap is in the long-term economic and political interests of the North. (c) The mission of foreign aid became distorted by the Cold War competition for client states and could instead be refocused on alleviating human suffering without expectations from donors.

primary products on which they depend. A change in the decision-making process of key international economic organizations, such as the IMF and the World Bank, was also proposed to give more control to the South (something the IMF did only recently, in 2006, when it gave more voting power to states such as China and Mexico).[94] Finally, the South pushed for international controls over foreign investment and international management of projects to develop the wealth on the world's seabeds.

Nevertheless, "by the close of the 1970s the South's strategy based on unity, commodity power, and the NIEO had reached a dead end."[95] The North, experiencing severe economic crises of its own, was not inclined to address the demands of the South. The South could not maintain a unified voice, and the oil crisis served to create a new gap within the South between the oil-producing rich states and the oil-importing poor ones. Finally, the success of some developing countries, such as the Asian Tigers, within the old system and the new willingness of the most populous Communist country in the world, the People's Republic of China, to open up and become more closely integrated with the world's economic system as currently constituted all combined to take some of the steam out of the campaign on behalf of the NIEO.

Part of the optimism that the South could succeed in a collective effort like the NIEO came from the success of OPEC in redistributing wealth from the North to at least some of the countries in the South. Throughout the 1970s, OPEC countries cooperated to control the price of oil by agreeing on production limits and succeeded in changing the structure of the international economy that had previously served the North's interests. Before OPEC,

> Western oil companies dominated the petroleum industry from exploration to marketing and had historically provided cheap and abundant access to the energy needs of the industrialized world. The cartel's pricing actions helped dampen economic growth and spurred an inflationary trend in the developed countries. From the standpoint of relations between the developed and less developed nations, the latter were to gain considerable leverage for the time being. The developed countries—being highly dependent on oil-exporting countries for their energy— could no longer ignore the considerable impact oil-producing countries from the South had on the economic well-being of the industrialized world.[96]

economic cartel
Association of states aiming to control production and pricing of a commodity.

Thus, an **economic cartel** that seeks to control production over an important commodity such as oil was seen as another potential strategy for economic development.

Efforts to duplicate OPEC's strategy have largely been unsuccessful. And just as OPEC's success in the 1970s helped garner the NIEO a lot of attention, OPEC's disarray in the 1980s contributed to the virtual disappearance of the NIEO from that decade's agenda. By the 1980s, attempts by producers of other raw materials to duplicate OPEC's success were thoroughly frustrated, as recession depressed prices for most commodities. Today, OPEC members still cooperate to cut or raise oil production to affect the price of oil and their profits, but the organization is much less militant and more pragmatic. OPEC, as an organization, no longer attempts to use oil for political purposes, as it did in the 1970s, although some of its member states, such as Venezuela, have attempted to translate their recent rise in their profits from oil into international political clout.[97]

Liberalization Strategies

Economic liberalism proposes that the key to greater wealth for all, both developed and developing countries alike, is liberalization or little political interference in economic markets. This means that economic liberals advocate free trade practices so that states avoid protecting domestic industries. Liberals also urge privatization of internal economic practices so that states allow the hidden hand of the market to determine which sectors of the economy will be competitive and serve as the country's comparative advantage in trade with others.

export-oriented strategy Economically liberal strategy involving exports that fill and profit from a niche in the international political economy.

The policy known as **export-oriented strategy** is associated with the liberal economic philosophy. Made popular by the success of the Asian Tigers, this strategy involves finding a niche in the international economy and exporting goods to fill, and profit from, that niche.

A second major component of this export-led growth strategy—one that is also seen by advocates of the liberal model as a crucial ingredient for development—involved promoting a high level of savings and investment (including intense efforts in research and development). The liberal perspective suggests that without the necessary capital, basic investments in infrastructure, resource development, and equipment growth would be quite impossible. Hence, capital formation is central to development.[98]

The practice of the export-led strategy by the Asian Tigers did not completely match the economic liberal model. Instead of the market's determining comparative advantage and the economic niche, for example, the governments were heavily involved in *creating* economic sectors that would be good for export. Economic liberals believe that a better strategy would include less interference by the government. In general, then, the development strategies associated with economic liberalism differ from those associated with dependency by focusing on how much poor countries could benefit from engaging, rather than abandoning or changing, the international economic structures. The obstacles to economic growth, according to economic liberals, are to be found in corrupt and inefficient governments.

Although the import-substitution policies were popular in the 1960s, the liberalization policies became the favored path to development in the 1990s. *The New York Times* reported in 1993 that

> almost 40 years after the emergence of the so-called Dependency School in Latin America, the theorists who argued that developing countries need to protect their resources from being ravaged by multinational corporations, the argument has been turned around. . . . Now . . . hopes are being pinned on the prospect of interdependence with the United States and other advanced industrial nations, through diversified and efficient economies that can compete in free trade.[99]

structural adjustment programs Conditions attached to IMF and World Bank loans requiring countries to liberalize and privatize based on the principles of economic liberalism.

Indeed, the conditions attached to IMF and World Bank loans, known as **structural adjustment programs,** were requirements that countries liberalize and privatize based on the principles of economic liberalism in order to receive aid from the organizations. In short, by the mid-1990s, market-oriented and export-oriented strategies seemed to have evoked something of a consensus among academics and policymakers in the richer industrialized countries as well as politicians in power in the poorer countries of the world. "The so-called **Washington Consensus** was the prescription for . . . ills in the developing countries. . . . The consensus in the political Washington' of Congress and the executive branch and the technocratic Washington' of the international financial institutions, the Federal Reserve Board, and think-tanks"[100] was for developing states to allow market-determined interest and exchange rates, liberalize trade and foreign direct investment, and privatize state-owned businesses, among other measures.

Washington Consensus The idea, as advocated by the United States and largely accepted in the developing world in the 1990s, that economically liberal strategies were the best path for development.

But the consensus was far from perfect, and many criticized the IMF for its strategies and the consequences of its programs. "The IMF prescription has been budgetary belt tightening for . . . [countries] much too poor to own belts. IMF-led austerity has frequently led to riots, coups, and the collapse of public services. In the past, when an IMF program has collapsed in the midst of social chaos and economic distress, the IMF has simply chalked it up to the weak fortitude and ineptitude of the government."[101]

In Latin America in particular, there was growing impatience with the market-oriented reforms that swept through the region in the 1990s "Latin America is swerving left, and distinct backlashes are under way against the predominant [free-market] trends of the last 15 years. . . . [T]he economic, social, and political reforms implemented in Latin America starting in the mid-1980s had not delivered on their promises. With the exception of Chile . . . the region has had singularly unimpressive economic growth rates."[102]

The disillusionment with liberal economic policies resulted in a recent political makeover of Latin America, with leftist and populist leaders coming to power in, for example, Venezuela, Brazil, Bolivia, Argentina, and Uruguay. In Venezuela, President Hugo Chavez transformed the hostility over Washington-supported economic programs in the developing world to a more general anti-U.S. orientation, making alliances with Iran, Cuba, and others opposed to U.S. policies.[103]

The backlash against economic liberalism in Latin America can be seen more widely around the world after the global economic downturn of 2008. As discussed in Chapter 10, many blamed unregulated capitalism for the problems in the financial sector in the United States and other Western economies and the spread of recession. In the developing world too, political leaders are rejecting economic liberal strategies and embracing state capitalism. State intervention, and outright ownership, of key economic sectors seem to have worked economically for emerging markets, such China and Russia, and state-run oil companies brought high profits to oil exporting countries in recent years.[104]

In addition to the largely unfulfilled promises of economic liberalization policies, critics of market and export-oriented strategies can point to such places as Kerala, a state in India with 30 million people (making it about as populous as Canada), for potentially valuable lessons about the development process. In 1957, voters in Kerala elected the first Communist majority to the state legislature. Since then, Kerala's voters have elected solidly leftist governments, which have included the Communist Party of India-Marxist and the Communist Party of India.[105] Kerala is one of India's poorest states, and yet its population has achieved the highest life expectancy and literacy rate in India, as well as the lowest infant mortality rate and birthrate.[106]

It might also be relevant to point out in this context that life expectancy in the People's Republic of China is 70 years. In some respects, health care in China is better than in the United States. For example, life expectancy at birth in Shanghai, China's largest city, reached 75.5 years, just as life expectancy in New York City, the largest city in the United States, was 73 years for whites and 70 years for nonwhites. And while China has adopted many market-oriented policies in recent years, its health care system is a government-based system established in the Maoist era.[107] Cuba is another example of a Communist state that has achieved relatively high human development indicators, including life expectancy (77 years), despite a fairly weak and noncapitalist economy.

In short, problems in many states that adopted economically liberal policies, as well as some successes in places such as Kerala in India, Cuba, and the People's Republic of China, seem to point to the conclusion that socialist policies might have been prematurely buried under a kind of public relations onslaught by the forces in favor of market-oriented capitalism and export-led development in the late 1980s and on into the 1990s. But the point of this discussion is that the terms *socialism* and *capitalism* are not free of ambiguities. In their purest forms, those terms denote extreme ends of a continuum, and most countries fall somewhere in the middle of that continuum. It is important to recognize that "the concept of market' is . . . broader than that of 'capitalism.'"[108] The essence of a market is the central role of prices arrived at in bargaining between buyers and sellers, while the essence of capitalism is the private ownership of the means of production and the existence of free labor. Theoretically, at least, socialist states could establish market systems. The most populous country in the world, China, seems to be trying to put this theory into practice.

Because virtually all the countries of the world have mixed economies, with the government playing an active role in the economy even if market forces also play an important role, some students of political economy have concluded that "capitalism is too ambiguous a label to be used as an analytical category."[109] But while it is important to acknowledge that it is difficult to establish precisely the point at which capitalism ends and socialism begins (or vice versa), the distinction between capitalism and socialism is not necessarily meaningless. The problems leading to the demise of the former Soviet Union may well suggest with some force that it is a mistake for governments to expropriate virtually all the means of production; that is, it is possible to go too far in the socialist direction. And as we have seen, the experiences of the past economic successes of countries in East Asia do not indicate that governments in developing countries should give private entrepreneurs or market forces an entirely free rein. Rather, they seem to demonstrate that governments might be well advised to take an active role in the economy, but in a manner that is compatible with and supportive of at least some market forces.

Today, most developing countries neither shun participation in the international political economy, as some neo-Marxists suggest, nor do they accept economic liberal prescriptions without question. Rather, developing countries seek to change economic relationships to further development. In international trade, for example, developing countries continue to stress the disadvantages to them in current trading practices. "The world's highest trade barriers are erected against some of its poorest countries: on average the trade barriers faced by developing countries exporting to rich countries are three to four times higher than those faced by rich countries when they trade with each other."[110] In the WTO's **Doha Round** of trade negotiations (begun in 2001), the developing countries have tried to lower tariffs on goods and services originating in the South and to address the agricultural subsidies that developing states provide. These subsidies, including U.S. subsidies to cotton producers and the European Union's subsidies for sugar, make it difficult for developing states to compete. But the Doha talks have yet to make progress on these issues and talks collapsed in the summer of 2008. "The nominal cause of the collapse was a technical issue relating to agricultural trade. But that was a proxy for deep and longstanding differences between developed and developing countries over the role of trade in development and how to define a fair deal."[111] Some have criticized the

Doha Round WTO negotiations, begun in 2001, involving a number of issues related to free trade, many of which are significant to economic development in the South.

Doha Round for being too narrow and have called on the WTO to negotiate broader changes to address the shift in global economic power toward emerging markets.[112]

Addressing Gender Inequality and Disease

Analyses of the challenges confronting developing countries highlight the role that women can play in economic development and the role that diseases play in underdevelopment.

It appears that economic conditions in most developing countries can benefit from efforts to address gender inequalities and improve economic conditions for women. Recall from Chapter 1 that part of the feminist perspective on global politics stresses the need to consider the impact of international relations on women and the role that women play in the world. As discussed in more detail in Chapter 9, women are subjected to various forms of economic and political discrimination by the men who dominate the economic and political systems of virtually every country of the world. In the poorer countries, gender bias is arguably a more serious problem. In other words, "gender bias is a worldwide phenomenon, but it is especially pernicious in the Third World, where most of women's activity takes place in the non-wage economy for the purpose of household consumption."[113] Citing these patterns of work, some feminists criticize liberal development policies if they involve cutbacks in government spending on health care, child care, or education, which "can dramatically increase the burden on the unpaid female-dominated sector of the economy. Because neoliberal economic analysis measures only the paid sector of the economy, it does not recognize this impact and thus suffers from a key gender bias."[114] Because women make up about half the population of every country in the world, this problem has come to be seen by many specialists in economic development as a major obstacle to economic progress in poor countries. "Gender bias is . . . a primary cause of poverty, because in its various forms it prevents hundreds of millions of women from obtaining the education, training, health services, child care, and legal status needed to *escape* from poverty."[115]

One dramatic example of the importance of bringing women into the economic mainstream of a country pertains to one of the poorest countries of the world, Bangladesh.[116] In 1983, the **Grameen Bank** ("village" bank) was founded by Muhammad Yunus, a professor of economics. Yunus' original idea was to provide very small loans (**microfinancing**) to people in general, but his ideas were not originally received with enthusiasm by economists or bankers. "'Where is the collateral?'" the bankers asked. "'These people can't even read.'"[117] Yunus ultimately had to take out the first loans himself. Those loans were put to good use and repaid, but still local bankers would not provide the capital to fund more such loans on a continuing basis. Yunus had to get the support of the government to enable poor people to obtain these loans so that they could become,

Grameen Bank
Founded by Muhammad Yunus to provide very small loans to poor individuals, particularly women.

microfinancing
Financial services, such as small loans, that are often provided to individuals or groups with low economic status.

in effect, entrepreneurs. Today, the Grameen Bank grants loans to more than 7 million people and has branches in more than 84,000 Bangladeshi villages. More than 97 percent of its loans are repaid.[118]

Originally, loans from the Grameen Bank were divided about equally between men and women. But Yunus soon discovered that "in the families in which the women received the loans, the children were better cared for, the houses were better maintained." He also found that while women spent the money on their families, men often squandered it on luxuries or drugs. Women also repaid the loans more dependably.[119] The result is that today, nearly all the borrowers are women. "When a bank focuses on women, according to Yunus, the impact on society is greater. Men are more likely to use additional income to make their own lives more comfortable. . . . Poor women who have a little extra income use it to bring back their children who have been living with and working with other families. When the children come back, their mothers see that they receive an education."[120] One study found that women who receive Grameen loans have better-nourished and better-educated children, particularly their daughters. These women are also more likely to

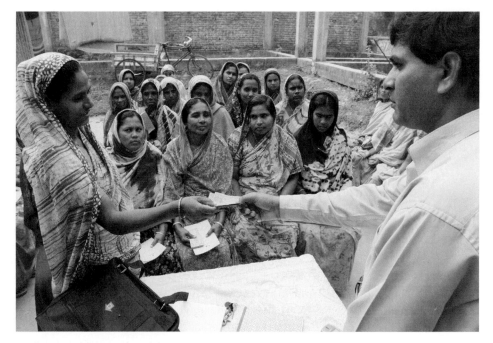

Women receive small loans to start businesses from the Grameen Bank. Muhammad Yunus, founder of the Grameen Bank in Bangladesh, was awarded the Noble Peace Prize in 2006 for his efforts to address poverty, seen by the Nobel Committee as key to achieving lasting peace.

(© Philippe Lissac/Godong/Corbis)

use contraception more consistently, as are other women in their village, even if they did not receive any loans themselves.[121] And approximately 65 percent of those who get loans averaging about $100 have achieved significant economic improvements in their lives. About half have risen above the poverty line.[122]

What is most important about the Grameen Bank is the generally applicable nature of its lessons and successes. Indeed, the Grameen model has been replicated in more than forty countries, with significant results.[123] In 2006, Muhammad Yunus received the Nobel Peace Prize, recognizing him as a pioneer in microfinancing for the advancement of development and human rights.[124] The importance of focusing development efforts on women, as done in the Grameen Bank, has also become commonly accepted wisdom. "Several studies suggest that income is more likely to be spent on human development when women control the cash."[125]

In particular, these studies find that increases in women's income improve the nutritional status of families seven times as much as do equivalent increases in the incomes of men. "In Cote d'Ivoire, it has been calculated that if women had as much control over cash income as men, the share of food in the household would go up by 9%, while that of cigarettes would fall by 55% and that of alcohol by 99%."[126] Reducing gender equality can greatly influence the lives of children in terms of child mortality and malnutrition.[127] In short, evidence is rapidly accumulating in support of the proposition that political efforts to allow women to benefit from market forces are key to alleviating poverty in the developing world.

A second aspect of life in the developing world concerns the economic impact of diseases such as HIV/AIDS and malaria. Malaria, a disease transmitted by a specific type of mosquito, is treatable, yet still kills approximately 1 million people annually, mostly children in sub-Saharan Africa.[128]

As mentioned previously, Africa is also suffering from the majority of AIDS-related deaths, although the problem is not isolated there, as India, Ukraine, and Russia are experiencing significant infection rates as well.[129] The number of AIDS deaths has accumulated to over 35 million (see Figure 11.3).

The relationship between economic conditions and disease is not one-way. Poverty creates conditions for disease, and disease, in turn, contributes to poverty. In the case of malaria, for example, the poor cannot afford insecticides, screens for windows and doors, and bed nets, which are highly effective for reducing transmission of the disease. Once a region is infected, malaria impedes economic growth. "It is worth remembering how malaria and yellow fever delayed the construction of the Panama Canal for more than thirty years. . . . Only after the United States invested heavily in a mosquito-control effort . . . was the canal constructed. Malaria to this day can stop a good investment project in its tracks, whether

Figure 11.3 Estimates of Cumulative AIDS Deaths Worldwide, 1980–2005

Source: From *Vital Signs 2006/2007: The Trends That Are Shaping Our Future* from Worldwatch Institute, p. 77. © 2006 Worldwatch Institute. www.worldwatch.org.

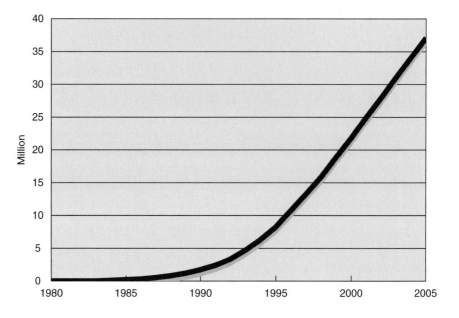

a new mine, farm region, or tourist site."[130] At the household level, the AIDS disease can be economically debilitating, because individuals are too sick to work, and medicine and treatment can use more than one-third of household income.

> Beyond the household, HIV/AIDS is eroding the social and economic infrastructure. Health systems are suffering from a lethal interaction of two effects: attrition among workers and rising demand. . . . HIV/AIDS is eroding human capacity on a broad front. Zambia now loses two-thirds of its trained teachers to HIV/AIDS, and in 2000 two in three agricultural extension workers in the country reported having lost a co-worker in the past year.[131]

The World Health Organization Commission on Macroeconomics and Health, determined that the main causes for the gap in life expectancy between Africa and the rest of the world included AIDS, malaria, tuberculosis, vaccine-preventable disease, acute respiratory infection, and nutritional deficiencies.[132]

Most believe that the international community's response to these diseases has been too little and too late. The World Bank sponsored one project on AIDS before 1993 and only spent $15 million a year on AIDS in Africa from 1988 to 1999.[133]

> In 2004 the world spent an estimated $6 billion combating the [HIV/AIDS] virus through the Global Fund to Fight AIDS, Tuberculosis, and Malaria. Had resources been on this scale

20 years ago, the epidemic could have been reversed. Today, that amount is insufficient to contain the crisis. . . . The international community's response to a global public health threat has been plainly inadequate.[134]

The Global Fund to Fight AIDS, Tuberculosis, and Malaria was announced at a UN summit on AIDS in 2001. This fund and the $15 billion pledged in 2003 by the United States are indicators that these diseases have finally arrived on the agenda of the international community. However, like other forms of foreign assistance, financial packages for the HIV/AIDS problem have their critics. According to economist William Easterly, "If money spent on treatment went instead to effective prevention, between three and seventy-five new HIV infections could be averted for every extra year of life given to an AIDS patient. Spending AIDS money on treatment rather than on prevention makes the AIDS crisis *worse*, not better."[135]

The Role of the International Organizations in Economic Development

Although the United Nations began primarily as an international organization concerned with security issues (as discussed in Chapter 9), it is a major player in economic development as well. Indeed, more than 80 percent of UN personnel work on topics of human welfare.[136]

> The United Nations has devoted much effort to the elaboration of operation programs for economic development. Loans apart, the UN system mounts more than 10,000 development projects per year . . . To this emphasis more recently was added the control and treatment of AIDS, malaria and tuberculosis. Together, they involve commitments of money, people's work, and hope on a scale never before reached by international agencies. [137]

The United Nations plays a role in economic development through its agencies, such as the UN Development Program (UNDP), the UN Children's Fund (UNICEF), the World Health Organization (WHO), and the UN Population Fund (UNFPA). These agencies collect information, administer development assistance, make recommendations regarding development issues to member-states, and organize conferences to publicize economic-related problems.

Recently, the United Nations has attempted to coordinate development efforts by focusing on specific development goals for this millennium, spelled out in the United Nations Millennium Declaration, which was signed by all UN member states in 2002. The **Millennium Development Goals (MDGs),** listed in Table 11.1, attempt to cut poverty in half by 2015. Supporters argue that these goals are "bold but achievable, even if dozens of countries are not yet on track to achieve them."[138] According to critics, however,

Millennium Development Goals (MDGs) UN targets for achieving significant progress on issues such as poverty, education, gender equality, health, and the environment in developing countries.

TABLE 11.1

UN Millennium Development Goals for 2015

Eradicate extreme poverty and hunger.
Achieve universal primary education.
Promote gender equality and empower women.
Reduce child mortality.
Combat HIV/AIDS, malaria, and other diseases.
Ensure environmental sustainability.
Develop a global partnership for development.

> The MDGs are already losing traction because governments have limited power to directly affect these outcomes. Most of the world is closer to meeting the MDGs now than it was a decade ago, but that is largely because human welfare has generally been improving. . . . The MDGs . . . do not constitute a strategy that informs the actions of governments, companies, and NGOs. Most of what the MDGs envision is beyond the power of any enterprise to deliver.[139]

According to the UN MDG report in 2008, there has been some progress, and some goals are on track for 2015. For example, enrollment in primary education is up in most parts of the world, and the number of deaths from measles and AIDs is down. But carbon dioxide emissions continue to increase, and malnourishment, poverty levels, and deaths in childbirth remain at high levels.[140]

Moral, Economic, and Security Implications of the North–South Gap

The ethical implications of trends in poverty and economic inequality in the world are clear enough, even though they are not often spelled out explicitly. If poverty is being alleviated as fast as can reasonably be expected, then there is not such a pressing need logically, politically, or morally for greater sacrifices on the part of the people and countries in the industrialized world. Yet if millions are suffering (a fact not much in dispute) and the situation is rapidly getting worse in at least some regions, drastic steps, including even painful sacrifices by the rich, might seem clearly called for on pressing moral grounds. Although, as indicated by the statistics quoted at the beginning of the chapter, there is some good news about the prospects for growth in the developing world, it is wrong to conclude that the lot of people in developing countries is improving so fast that no actions or sacrifices by people in richer countries are necessary.

If the current desperate economic conditions in many developing countries were caused by the policies and actions of industrialized countries in the past, then the case for drastic action is that much stronger. Although it is difficult to conclude with confidence that current economic problems in developing countries are primarily the fault of imperialism and colonialism in previous centuries, there arguably remains a strong moral obligation on the part of people in rich countries to assist those starving in poor countries, even if the poverty creating that suffering is not entirely their fault. One can argue that mere coexistence on the same planet creates a moral obligation among human beings to aid each other in times of stress and that coexistence obliges rich countries to help poor countries regardless of the origins of their economic problems. According to one international ethicist, ". . . the global poor have a compelling moral claim to some of our affluence and that we, by denying them what they are morally entitled to and urgently need, are actively contributing to their deprivations."[141]

Beyond morality, there are economic consequences for the rest of the world if the South remains poor. From a purely economic standpoint, poverty is not good for business. The North cannot make money from an impoverished state that cannot buy its exports. Furthermore, interdependence in the global economy means that poverty may be localized, but it cannot be isolated. When instability and economic crises occur in the South, the result is financial losses for northern businesses. In general, poverty and lack of adequate resources present tremendous obstacles for individual economic productivity, not to mention creative expression, such as in the arts and sciences.

In the view of many, the North-South gap is not simply a problem of the lack of wealth in the South but of the excess of wealth in the North. Indeed, from this vantage point, the luxurious lifestyles of the wealthy result in unnecessary waste and environmental destruction (as will be discussed in Chapter 13). Making the distribution of wealth around the world more equitable might reduce the excesses of the North as much as alleviate the suffering of the South.

There are also consequences for world security. Recall from Chapter 6 that poor economic conditions can prompt leaders to blame (justly or unjustly) these conditions on external foes and even initiate war in an attempt to divert the public's attention to an outside enemy. Poor economic conditions can also breed ethnic conflict as groups compete for scarce resources. Economically devastating conditions can foster terrorist groups to form and facilitate their continued recruitment from populations that find their situation hopeless. From the North's perspective, economic development may help prevent conflicts to which the North will often have to respond in order to prevent the spread of war and other forms of violence.

Economic development may also be important for democratic values. The relationship between economics and democracy is controversial. Which must come first: democratization or economic development? The fact that the countries with the highest per capita GNPs and life expectancies are democratic convinces a lot of people that democracy is a necessary condition for economic success.[142] And there is an impressive theoretical as well as empirical case to be made for the argument that political democracy provides a promising basis for economic development. Some argue, for example, that "the conditions that are needed to have individual rights needed for maximum economic development are the same conditions that are needed to have a *lasting* democracy."[143] That is why only stable democracies have reached the highest levels of economic development and have maintained those levels across generations. In contrast, "though experience shows that relatively poor countries can grow extraordinarily rapidly when they have a strong dictator who happens to have unusually good economic policies, such growth lasts only for the ruling span of one or two dictators."[144]

One recent analysis of the relationship between democracy and economic growth, as well as broader indexes of the physical quality of life in developing countries in the 1980s, concludes that democracy and economic performance mutually reinforce each other. "Improvements in economic well-being will facilitate the transition to democracy and full provision of political rights will enable nations to promote economic prosperity."[145] Other analysts report that the correlation between democracy and economic growth is more a result of the impact of growth on democracy than of democracy on growth.[146] Still another research report argues that "the level of economic development does not affect the probability of transitions to democracy but . . . affluence does make democratic regimes more stable."[147] In addition, it is clear that "the growing number of affluent authoritarian states suggests that greater wealth alone does not automatically lead to greater political freedom. Authoritarian regimes around the world are showing that they can reap the benefits of economic development while evading any pressure to relax their political control."[148] The connections between economic development and democratization and the implications of the North-South gap in general illustrate the complex relationships between politics and economics that are at the heart of the global economy.

SUMMARY

- On many economic measures, there exists a considerable chasm between the rich countries in the developed world and the poor developing countries. The gap in the average GNP per capita between the North and the South is increasing. In terms of such indicators as life expectancy and the UN Human Development Index, the difference is almost certainly decreasing, at least for most parts of the developing world. Still, millions of people in poor countries are suffering, and in many countries their plight worsens each year. The economic conditions in some developing countries are more difficult to address because of debt obligations.

- Poverty in developing countries and the North-South gap have been explained by a variety of theoretical perspectives. Most agree that the roots of the gap can be traced back to the colonization of the South by the North and the economic consequences of imperialism for the colonized areas. Many, however, expected the countries in the South to develop just as those in the North did once they were independent. When they did not, neo-Marxists pointed to the domination of the global economic system by rich, powerful capitalist states, which, it claims, makes it necessary for LDCs to adhere to policies of economic development radically different from those based on democracy and capitalism historically followed by most of the currently rich countries. The terms of trade, aid, and investment by multinational corporations, according to neo-Marxist approaches, put the South at a structural disadvantage.

- Economic liberals point to the benefits of economic interdependence that the South can receive if it reforms internally. Liberals note the early success of East Asian states, which adopted strategies emphasizing exports and market forces, but critics point to the heavy hand that governments played in these economies.

- In Latin America in the 1960s, neo-Marxists approaches were popular and associated with the strategy of protecting industries to produce substitutes for imported goods. Although this worked for a while for some states, such as Mexico and Brazil, it is largely discredited as a development strategy today. In the 1970s, states in the South attempted to band together in the NIEO, which called for reform of many of the international economic structures and practices and more unconditional aid. With economic crises in many countries in the North and with the diminished effectiveness of OPEC as a cartel, the NIEO lost its significance as a rallying cry from the developing world.

- Liberalization strategies, such as export-oriented growth, became more accepted by developing states in the 1990s, and liberal reform packages are usually the requirements for IMF aid. However, worsening conditions in many states that followed liberal policies and examples of successful human development programs in some nonliberal states have prompted many recent criticisms of this approach to economic development.

- Government policies to modify market forces in favor of women show signs of producing important economic benefits. Development strategies, including microfinancing, focused specifically on giving women more control of economic resources have produced quite a bit of evidence to support their effectiveness. Recently, the role of diseases such as malaria and HIV/AIDs in underdevelopment has received more attention, because poverty contributes to high infection rates and diseased populations can further impede economic development.

● The question of economic development is of concern for both the North and the South, as well as for the international community as a whole. For the North, the moral implications of the poverty in parts of the developing world compared to the excessive wealth in the developed states are important to consider, regardless of the cause of the North-South gap. Economically and politically, one can argue that economic development in the South is in the interests of the North.

KEY TERMS

less developed countries
 (LDCs)   390
purchasing power parity   391
Human Development Index   394
modernization theory   400
terms of trade   402
overseas development
 assistance   402
repatriated profits   403
corporate social
 responsibility   403
newly industrialized countries
 (NICs)   409
import substitution strategy   412

New International Economic
 Order (NIEO)   413
Group of 77   413
aid burden   415
economic cartel   416
export-oriented strategy   417
structural adjustment
 programs   418
Washington Consensus   418
Doha Round   420
Grameen Bank   421
microfinancing   421
Millennium Development Goals
 (MDGs)   425

CHAPTER 12

Regional Economic Integration in the Global Political Economy

With an increasingly interdependent global economy, the purpose and future of state boundaries in the international system come into question. Indeed, economic liberalism, one of the dominant economic philosophies (as discussed in the previous two chapters), would see the withering away of the political interference that "artificial" state boundaries can have on efficient economic exchanges as a positive trend. Many contemporary states recognize the potential economic benefits of **economic integration**—the replacement of national economies with larger (in most cases, regional) ones. "One of the most striking facts about the modern global political economy is that it is organized strongly on a regional basis. For all the talk of globalization, many indicators of globalization (for example, trade, foreign direct investment, international institutions) are directed toward regional partners."[1] Today, more than 400 regional trading arrangements have been reported to the World Trade Organization. Attempts at regional economic integration have increased in recent times, partly because the end of the Cold War means that states have more freedom to cooperate economically and partly because the end of the Bretton Woods system and American economic hegemony (as discussed in Chapter 10) have led states to search for alternative paths to economic stability.

economic integration
The replacement of national economies with larger—in most cases regional—ones.

Yet, as with most other economic choices, efforts at integrating economies often conflict with other political values, such as state sovereignty. This tension has been apparent throughout the history of the most successful effort at regional economic integration: the European Union (EU) in Western Europe. This chapter introduces the EU and examines the debates about how to integrate its political institutions, the history of integration, and some of the most pressing issues reflecting the relationship between politics and economics in the EU's future. The chapter then examines other, less ambitious efforts at regional economic cooperation in the developing world and across the North-South divide.

Economic and Political Integration in Western Europe

Shortly after the Second World War, the threat of Soviet domination led Winston Churchill to call for a United States of Europe. In the succeeding years, there were several attempts to bring European countries closer together. The impetus toward international organization in Europe received two important boosts in 1948. First, the Soviets backed a successful coup in Czechoslovakia. Second, they blockaded West Berlin, cutting it off from all supplies from the West. The United States responded by supplying the city from the air. One immediate response to the perceived Soviet threat was the creation of the North Atlantic Treaty Organization (NATO). Another was more serious consideration of politically and economically integrating Western Europe.

It is important to recognize that the motivations behind the current EU, the most successful effort at integration by sovereign states, were both political and economic in nature. Politically, leaders of the time, including the leadership in the new superpower, the United States, were convinced of the general liberal perspective on the causes of World War II. Recall that the liberal explanation of the war focused on how states attempted to compete economically through mercantilist policies rather than cooperate. According to this perspective, states that are more interdependent with one another will be less likely to fight one another because war brings too many economic costs. The explanation also blamed the autocratic nature of regimes, such as Germany's under Hitler's dictatorship, which did not allow for the public to constrain its leaders from going to war. Furthermore, the poor economic conditions in the 1930s made states vulnerable to leaders like Hitler who promised prosperity in exchange for power. So one motivation behind post–World War II efforts at European integration was to build a community of states that were economically connected (with special importance of connecting Germany to the rest of Western Europe), had open political and economic systems, and were prosperous for the purpose of addressing internal and external threats to security in the newly emerging Cold War. The postwar aid package provided by the United States, the Marshall Plan, required that recipient states coordinate their economic recovery efforts and was thus an important effort to encourage integration for political goals.

Economically, the states wanted to integrate their economies to achieve greater growth. European countries after World War II were economically devastated. Economic liberalism proposes that the best road to wealth is to eliminate political barriers to economic exchange. So the states, as well as American and European businesses, wanted to eliminate tariffs and other trade barriers and eventually create a single market to make business easier and more profitable. Given these motivations behind European integration, the question remained as to how the states should go about it. Integration theory offers two distinct alternatives: federalism and functionalism. Both alternatives were considered by west European leaders, although a hybrid of the two, neofunctionalism, best describes the actual process of integration.

Federalism versus Functionalism

federalism Approach to integration involving central political institutions to impose political and economic union.

The heart of **federalism,** as a theory of integration, is summarized neatly in the slogan, "The worst way to cross a chasm is in little steps." In other words, any attempt to unify several states into a federal union must be comprehensive, not incremental. There must be at the start a central government, even though the lower-level political units would retain some powers, and the incipient federal government must be given substantial political power from the beginning. An overarching political system, like the federal government in the United States, is needed to impose integration, according to this perspective. Along these lines, Ren Pleven, French premier in 1950, suggested the creation of an all-European army.

The United States originally opposed this plan but was persuaded to support it by the summer of 1951.[2] This was a federalist idea par excellence, going to the heart of the sovereignty of the separate European states—the control of their armies. Leaders in the United States hoped that this plan would allow the Europeans to thwart any aggressive designs the Soviets might have and to rearm the Germans without giving them control of weapons or troops. Five out of the six states involved in the plan to create the integrated European army (the European Defense Community) approved it. But, in 1954, the French parliament voted to postpone further discussion of the idea, and it faded away, as did many of the grander federalist plans.

Functionalism provides an alternative way of integrating and was more attractive to the leaders of many states who were worried about giving up their sovereignty to a **supranational** (authority above the state level) federal institution. Whereas federalism is a top-down approach, starting with overarching political institutions, functionalism is a bottom-up approach, starting with cooperation among private and some public actors in uncontroversial technical areas, such as uniform standards for road signs across countries and projects to build roads that cross borders. So-called functional organizations had made significant advances in the nineteenth century. Various river commissions were created for the purpose of regulating international commerce and transport, and organizations such as the International Telecommunications Organization (1875), the Universal Postal Union (1874), and the International Office of Weights and Measures (1875) were established.

These institutions are not directly related to preventing conflict, but according to a form of functionalist theory, they may ultimately serve that end. If the tasks that these organizations undertake proliferate, they may eventually control such a significant portion of international intercourse that they could serve as a basis for some type of world government. A world of states that had become so closely intertwined in a mesh of functional activities and appreciative of the benefits brought by functional organizations would be unlikely, according to this functionalist theory, to degenerate into international warfare.[3] Functionalism assumes that integration will occur gradually as states create small-scale administrative institutions to coordinate these activities and as they find it to their advantage to allow these institutions to take over, fulfilling some functions of the state. Eventually, these connections will become denser between states, and states will find it useful to cooperate in less technical, more controversial areas until, like the peeling away of layers of an onion, sovereignty will be transferred to a supranational entity that performs all the functions of the original states.

Although wary of the all-at-once approach of federalism, most west European leaders were not comfortable with allowing integration to proceed as gradually as in functionalism and felt that more direction was needed for the integration process. This compromise position is known as

functionalism
Bottom-up approach to integration involving cooperation among states and private actors, beginning in technical areas.

supranational
Authority of an organization above the state level.

neofunctionalism
Approach to integration involving development of some central political institutions and cooperation to create spillover effects for further integration.

neofunctionalism. Neofunctionalists, led by Jean Monnet of France, often referred to as the founder of the modern European integration, stressed the development of some central political institutions, with the power to oversee and direct integration, whereas functionalists were satisfied with more loosely knit organizations, and federalists wanted supranational organizations. Neofunctionalists also stressed that states should seek out activities that are specifically defined but also politically important. In other words, economic cooperation should not be limited to just technical areas at first, as functionalists argue. According to neofunctionalists, the strength of an integration organization that selects its initial activities wisely will grow with time. Monnet, for example, used the goal of integrating the coal and steel markets as a rationale for promoting the integration of social security and transportation policies. He argued that this was the only way to counteract distortions in coal and steel prices.[4] As the member states saw the economic benefits resulting from the activities of the central organization, neofunctionalists believed, they would be willing to give that organization broader authority. One technical task would create **spillover effects** in other tasks until the integrating forces were virtually overwhelming. The neofunctionalist organization would end up running everything; at this stage, the process of giving it political power would be little more than a formality, to which the formerly independent member states would have no objections.[5]

spillover effects
Integration generated by cooperation in technical areas that leads to cooperation in other areas.

These ideas were put into practice by way of the Schuman Plan (named for Robert Schuman, the French foreign minister), proposed in 1950. Devised by Jean Monnet, the plan called for the creation of a common market in Europe for the coal and steel industries. In 1951, the six states of France, West Germany, Italy, Belgium, the Netherlands, and Luxembourg signed the Treaty of Paris, launching the **European Coal and Steel Community (ECSC).** These six states agreed to reduce trade barriers to coal and steel and to coordinate policies (such as taxes and production) in this economic area. Cooperation in coal and steel was an important first step. Coal and steel were key to Europe's industrial growth and recovery from the war. This agreement also tightly linked together Europe's eternal rivals, France and Germany. France and Germany had long fought over territories important for coal and steel, such as Alsace-Lorraine (now part of France in the northeast corner, bordering Germany). Free trade of coal and steel made it irrelevant, at least economically, who actually owned this land.

European Coal and Steel Community (ECSC) 1951 agreement among six European states to integrate their coal and steel economic sectors.

By almost any standard, the ECSC was an immediate success. The benefits its members derived were sufficiently obvious that by 1955, negotiations were under way for a more comprehensive approach to European integration. These negotiations culminated in the **Treaty of Rome,** signed by the same six states in 1957, which created two new organizations, the European Economic Community (EEC) and the European Atomic Energy Community (Euratom). These two organizations, together with the ECSC, formed the nucleus of what became known starting in 1967

Treaty of Rome 1957 agreement by France, West Germany, Italy, Belgium, the Netherlands, and Luxembourg to economically integrate and establish the institutions that now constitute the European Union.

as the European Community (EC). When the Treaty of Maastricht (discussed later in the chapter) came into effect in late 1993, the organization officially adopted its current name, the European Union.

The Institutions of the European Union

The Treaty of Rome outlined the structure of institutions for the EEC (and now the EU), much like the constitution of a country, and by signing the Treaty of Rome, states agreed to eventually integrate economically and politically. The EU has, in effect, executive, legislative, and judicial institutions.

European Court of Justice Judicial EU institution that primarily settles disputes concerning the provisions of EU treaties and law.

The **European Court of Justice,** for example, fulfills a role that is somewhat like that of the U.S. Supreme Court. The court consists of one judge from each member state. The primary function of the court is to settle disputes concerning the provisions of the treaties that established the organization, as well as laws passed with respect to the treaties. Although the court is one of the more obscure institutions in the EU, it has acquired supranational powers of some significance.[6] Historically, in courts of international law, only states can be heard. Individuals are not allowed to take legal complaints to such courts, and states traditionally have insisted that this custom be adhered to rigorously. But individuals in the EU can be heard before the European Court of Justice, and there have been cases in which the supreme court of a member state has deferred to the judgment of this court. The European Court of Justice also can hear cases brought by member states, other institutions of the EU, and corporations affected by treaty provisions. The court hears a number of such cases every year and appears to be developing the potential to become a supranational judicial institution. "Its rulings are binding for all Courts of the Member States, which have to set aside national law if it does conflict with European law."[7] If states do not comply with the court's ruling, it can impose fines on them.

European Commission Represents EU interests as a whole and proposes and implements policies.

Council of the European Union Composed of representatives of each member state, this is the primary policymaking body of the EU.

European Parliament EU legislative body, whose representatives have been directly elected since 1979.

The executive functions of the EU are shared by the **European Commission** and the **Council of the European Union** (formerly the Council of Ministers).[8] The Commission is the supranational part of this executive "branch" within the institutional structure. It is made up of commissioners appointed by each of the national governments, but they are to act in the interests of the EU as a whole, independent of their home states. There is currently one commissioner from each member state. The commissioners prepare the first draft of the council's budget every year and propose policies to the Council. The Commission also guides legislation through the **European Parliament.** The European Commission is headed by a president, who is chosen by the member states and endorsed by the European Parliament. Some Commission presidents, such as Jacques Delors (president from 1985 to 1994), have been very important in guiding the entire institutional framework.

The Council of the European Union reviews and approves decisions made by the European Commission, and each minister is accountable to the state he or she represents.

The Council consists of ministers from the national governments of all the EU countries. Meetings are attended by whichever ministers are responsible for the items to be discussed: foreign ministers, ministers of the economy and finance, ministers for agriculture and so on, as appropriate. Each country has a number of votes in the Council broadly reflecting the size of their population, but weighted in favour of smaller countries. Most decisions are taken by majority vote, although sensitive issues in areas like taxation, asylum and immigration, or foreign and security policy, require unanimity.[9]

Over the years, major decisions have been passed on to the heads of all state governments. The heads of the separate governments, like the other ministers in the Council, represent the individual interests of the member states, and it is clear that the members' leaders must approve measures of substantial importance. If the EU ever becomes truly supranational, one of the most obvious institutional changes that will be required would involve giving the Commission greater independence from the Council and heads of the state governments.

The European Parliament is in formal terms the legislative body of the EU, although at this stage in the development of the EU, most of the legislative functions are still carried out by the executive bodies of the Commission and the Council of Ministers. The European Parliament is probably the least powerful of the major institutions making up the EU, but it is also one of the most intriguing. It took an important step forward in 1979, when its members began to be directly elected to the body. (Previously, they had been selected by the parliaments of the member nations.) Parliamentary elections are held every five years. The European Parliament currently has 732 members, and they organize themselves along ideological rather than national lines. Normally, for example, the Christian Democratic delegates from the various member states sit, caucus, and vote together, as do the delegates from various Green parties, rather than acting in concert with the other delegates from their respective countries.

Representatives to the European Parliament voted in 2004 to open EU membership talks with Turkey.
(Vincent Kessler/Corbis)

Until 1987, the Parliament's role was restricted to minor budget issues.[10] Since then, the European Parliament has gained control over about one-third of the budget—the part that does not involve the Common Agricultural Policy (a very large part of the budget, as we shall see) or foreign aid. Also since 1987, "the Parliament has had the right to amend or reject legislation approved by the Council, which can overrule the Parliament only by a unanimous vote."[11] And the Maastricht Treaty gives the Parliament the right to veto decisions made by the Council.[12] That treaty also makes it possible for the Parliament to approve the president of the Commission as well as the Commission as a whole, and to make the Commission as a whole resign if a two-thirds majority so votes. As the only directly elected body within the EU, the Parliament perhaps can be expected to play an increasingly important role in the organization's future.

The Process of Integration

How well have the institutions of the EU worked? Answering that question involves first discussing the question, "What exactly are they trying to accomplish?" The ultimate goals of the community are both political and economic, but the intermediate steps are almost completely economic in nature. The beginning of the economic integration process is the creation of a **free trade area** in which tariffs among the member states are eliminated. The member states achieved free trade in many areas by the late 1950s. A free trade area is supposed to increase trade among member states, but free trade areas can be easily infiltrated. A state outside the organization could simply export goods into the member state with the lowest tariffs. Once that was done, the goods could be exported from the infiltrated member state to the other members of the organization and escape the tariffs of the other states as if they had come from within the free trade area. An obvious solution to this problem involves the adoption of a common tariff by the states in the organization, to be applied to all imports coming from the outside. If this is accomplished, the organization reaches the status of a **customs union,** as the European Community did by 1969. With this step, the organization began to bargain as a single unit in trade talks, such as General Agreement on Tariffs and Trade (GATT) negotiations, with outside states.

The next step up the ladder of economic integration is to establish a **common market.** In addition to abolishing intraorganization tariffs and creating a common external tariff, a common market allows the components of production—that is, capital and labor—to move freely across national boundaries. Entrepreneurs from one member state can invest without restriction in any other member state, and workers can freely migrate to any state in the organization to find work. If the member states cooperate to the extent that they jointly plan monetary, fiscal, and social policies, they form an **economic union.** If they turn the planning of these policies over to a unified, supranational body such as the European Commission, total economic integration is accomplished. According to

free trade area
Geographical area where tariffs and other trade restrictions among member states are eliminated.

customs union
Agreement by a group of states to apply common tariffs on imports from all other states.

common market Area that allows member states to freely move components of production such as capital and labor across borders.

economic union
Cooperation of member states to jointly plan monetary, fiscal, and social policies.

neofunctionalist ideas, once economic integration reaches this advanced stage, the central integrating organization will be running virtually everything anyway, so there will be no strong objection to advances toward political integration and the emergence of a new state-like entity.[13]

The process of integration, however, has not been so smooth. While much progress was made in the first decade of the community, further integration came to a virtual standstill in the 1970s. This was partly due to the economic turmoil of the 1970s (as discussed in Chapter 10). European states, heavily dependent on foreign energy supplies, suffered greatly with the oil shocks of that decade. Furthermore, aging populations made expansive welfare programs much more expensive and without a strong revenue base to pay for them. Facing these economic crises, many European states were reluctant to undergo short-term costs (like further lowering tariffs) for the long-term benefits of economic integration. Indeed, the 1970s and early 1980s were the height of "Europessimism," with dire predictions about the future of the community. Instead of deeper political or economic integration, the organization turned to broader integration, doubling its membership in the 1970s and early 1980s. Table 12.1 shows the expansion of the European Union.

TABLE 12.1

The Expansion of the European Union

Original members: 1957	**Fourth enlargement: 1995**
Belgium	Austria
Germany (plus East Germany in 1991)	Finland
France	Sweden
Italy	
Luxembourg	**Fifth enlargement: 2004**
Netherlands	Cyprus
	Czech Republic
First enlargement: 1973	Estonia
Denmark	Hungary
Ireland	Latvia
United Kingdom	Lithuania
	Malta
	Poland
Second enlargement: 1981	Slovakia
Greece	Slovenia
Third enlargement: 1986	**Sixth enlargement: 2007**
Portugal	Bulgaria
Spain	Romania

Single European Act
1985 agreement calling for the establishment of a single European market.

Efforts at deeper integration finally surfaced again in 1985 when the European Commission drafted a white paper titled "Implementing the Internal Market." It called for 300 measures to remove physical, technical, and fiscal barriers to true economic integration. By December 1985, the heads of the member governments had approved the **Single European Act** (based on the white paper), calling for the establishment of a single European market by 1992. "The year 1992 promised the creation of a larger, more dynamic market, with the wealth and political power that would flow therefrom. To achieve this big goal, however, required each nation to sacrifice its interests on hundreds of smaller issues, many of which had important domestic political impacts."[14] On January 1, 1993, the European Single Market went into effect, thus officially creating the economic union toward which the organization had been striving since 1957. The Single European Act also called for important changes in voting procedures in the European Council. By 1987, European Community decision-making procedures provided for majority voting rather than unanimous voting on certain issues. Previously, every state had, in effect, veto power over any proposal, because a unanimous vote was required to pass it. The Single European Act also strengthened the power of the European Parliament, as discussed earlier.

Maastricht Treaty
1991 EU agreement to work toward common currency, common foreign and security policy, and common justice and internal policy.

Optimistic about the Single European Act and the end of the Cold War, the European foreign ministers in 1991 signed the **Maastricht Treaty,** an ambitious document that, among other things, changed the name of the organization to the European Union. Maastricht established three pillars: a common currency, a common foreign and security policy, and a common justice and internal policy. If all three of these goals are accomplished, the EU will become something much closer to a state-like entity.

euro Common currency of the European Monetary Union, first used by citizens in 2002.

Only one of these goals, a common currency, has been achieved by most EU members. In January 1999, banks began trading in the new currency, the **euro** (€), and in January 2002, citizens in twelve European states began purchasing goods in euros. Within a few months, the national currencies, such as the Italian lira, the German mark, and the French franc, became illegal currency, and the European Monetary Union (EMU) was in place across the twelve participating countries. The European Central Bank is an institution roughly analogous to the U.S. Federal Reserve, with authority over the new European currency.[15]

Establishing a common currency certainly simplifies commercial transactions within the EU, and perhaps in the long run it will be an economic boon to most member countries:

> Monetary union offers a number of potential benefits to member countries. Adoption of a single currency is designed to help stabilize prices, the main object of the EMU and the European Central Bank's foremost obligation under its charter. A single currency will eliminate trading against swings in currency values, reducing a major cost of trade both within Europe and with non-European importers and exporters. A single currency

also will make it harder for companies to charge more for their products in one country than another, thus making it easier for consumers to pay fair prices.[16]

In short, the euro is what economic liberalism wants: economic exchange without political barriers that create artificial obstacles like national currencies.

The establishment of the EMU was not an easy political or economic decision for the EU, and at several points after the adoption of the Maastricht Treaty, there were significant doubts that the euro would ever happen. It was partly over objection to the EMU that a majority of Danish voters refused to ratify the Maastricht Treaty in a referendum in 1992. Later, Denmark passed a weaker version of the treaty, opting out of many controversial provisions, as did Great Britain. When the euro came into existence, three key states—Britain, Denmark, and Sweden—chose not to participate. As of this writing, they are still not members of the "eurozone." Most of the newest states in central, eastern, and southern Europe, who joined the EU in 2004 and 2007, cannot use the euro until they meet certain economic standards. Since 2007, Slovenia, Cyprus, Malta, and Slovakia have adopted the euro, bringing the total of eurozone countries to sixteen.

Part of the pessimism surrounding the euro had to do with the extremely difficult process of coordinating national economies before they could integrate monetarily. Stringent criteria, such as low interest rates, low inflation rates, and low national debt, were required to be eligible to participate in the EMU. For many west European states, their economies already in trouble (in 1998, for example, Spain's unemployment rate was 18.8 percent, and Greece's inflation rate was 4.5 percent),[17] meeting these criteria by cutting government spending meant facing serious political opposition. A common currency also means a loss of sovereignty. Devaluing one's own national currency is a popular way to deal with economic problems. With the establishment of the euro, the members gave up this option, and their economic fate largely rests in the hands of the overarching institutional framework of the EU.

The Future of the European Union

The euro has fared well since its introduction, emerging as a strong alternative to the U.S. dollar, despite early predictions that it would fail. Yet how EU member states manage their differences over economics associated with the euro is still an open question. Although the Central European Bank is in charge of the value of the euro, the EU still exists as separate national political and economic systems in many ways. States in the eurozone must coordinate their economies (levels of deficits, inflation rates, and so forth) for the euro to work. Soon after the euro was established, Germany risked exceeding the deficit limit that states have to maintain. This crisis threatened "the credibility of the financial architecture that underpins the . . . euro."[18] Part of the problem is that states are still in control of revenue generation (taxes) and spending, and they may have very different priorities and philosophies from each other and from the Central European Bank. Currently, there are no set procedures for coordinating these other aspects of economic policy with monetary policy. The strain that this creates is most evident during economic crises. In the economic downturn that was in place in Europe by 2008, states were constrained in their response. Because they must follow the lead of the European Central Bank, they cannot unilaterally stimulate their economies. And noneuro countries have seen their currency values fall in relation to the euro, thereby increasing their debt to European banks. By 2009, a rift between older and newer EU members developed over stimulus packages and "bailouts" to the economies in the worse shape. According to the foreign editor of a major German newspaper:

> The European Union will now have to prove whether it is just a fair-weather union or has a real joint political destiny. We always said you can't really have a currency union without a political union, and we don't have one. There is no joint fiscal policy, no joint tax policy, no joint policy on which industries to subsidize or not. And none of the leaders is strong enough to pull the others out of the mud."[19]

Beyond the euro, the two fundamental political goals established in the Maastricht Treaty remain on the EU's agenda. "The Maastricht Treaty . . . created . . . a specific intergovernmental pillar for the Common Foreign and Security Policy (CFSP). It created concepts of action joint and common which member states would undertake. It provided for a CFSP budget. . . . The CFSP was born in optimism."[20] This optimism was quickly shattered in the early 1990s when the EU could not find a common voice or strategy in its approach to the breakup of Yugoslavia and the resulting wars in the Balkans. The division over intervention in Iraq in 2003 reinforced skepticism over a unified foreign policy. In foreign and security policy, Europe still seemed to be in the shadow of the United States and NATO. Indeed, the goal of creating a common foreign policy for the EU highlights the organization's relationship to NATO. If the EU is to have a common foreign and security policy, it will need some authority over the deployment of its members' military forces. One of the many complications facing the coordination of activities between NATO and the EU is that the memberships do not overlap entirely. The United States is not in the EU, of course, but neither are NATO members Canada, Iceland, Norway, and Turkey. And with the recent enlargements of the EU, some of the newest EU members—Austria, Cyprus, Finland, and Sweden—are not a part of NATO.

Perhaps the most dramatic implication of the third pillar of Maastricht—the common justice and internal policy—would involve doing away entirely with border controls among the member states.

Already most of the members have introduced common border controls and allow freedom of movement for all individuals who are nationals of the other states. The Maastricht Treaty and the subsequent Amsterdam Treaty (1997) also introduced the idea of "European citizenship," whereby Europeans could work, own property, vote, and even run for some offices in any EU country in which they were residing. In many ways, these notions challenge state sovereignty the most, and because of the backlash, with many states opting out of the most controversial provisions of Maastricht, these questions of deeper integration have taken a backseat to questions of broader integration.

On the immediate agenda of the EU is the question of implications of enlargement. The largest enlargement took place in 2004, adding ten new countries—Cyprus, the Czech Republic, Estonia, Hungary, Latvia, Lithuania, Malta, Poland, Slovakia, and Slovenia. Romania and Bulgaria joined in January 2007. Many other countries in Europe see the economic and political benefits of EU membership and are knocking at the EU's doors to get in. Turkey, Croatia, and Macedonia are candidate countries, in membership negotiations with the EU. In order to join the EU, states need to fulfill certain economic and political conditions. They must "be a stable democracy, respecting human rights, the rule of law, and the protection of minorities; have a functioning market economy; [and] adopt

The Maastricht Treaty was passed over strong objections by citizens in several member states in the European Union, such as the French farmers pictured here. Farmers worried that the Treaty's further economic integration would jeopardize agricultural subsidies they received from the French government.
(Jack Dabaghian/Corbis)

the common rules, standards and policies that make up the body of EU law."[21] When the membership expanded in 2007 to twenty-seven countries, the EU became much larger in population size and geographical scope and looked much different than it had previously. If all of the states that want to join are admitted and if Norway and Switzerland change their minds, the EU would grow to thirty-one states. The Policy Choices box summarizes some of the debate over joining the EU.

There are economic as well as political challenges that accompany expansion of the EU. As diverse as the previous fifteen member states were, they all had fairly prosperous economies compared to the states that joined the EU in 2004 and 2007. Many in the EU worry that admission of these new states will require costly investments in the infrastructures, technology, and education systems of the poorer countries. Furthermore, most of the recent members from east-central Europe have a substantial agricultural sector. Agricultural subsidies, allocated through the EU's

Common Agricultural Policy Designed to provide food at affordable prices, this policy gives substantial subsidies to European farmers

Common Agricultural Policy, were already a significant part of the EU budget and increased drastically with the addition of the new east-central European countries. If subsidies to farmers are cut, then cheaper products from eastern Europe will overwhelm the western European agricultural sector, something that many politically powerful farmer interest groups oppose.

Turkey's potential membership in the EU is complicated by many factors. The EU ". . . sees liabilities in Turkey's size, its uneven economic development, its less advanced democratic development, its borders with dangerous countries, and its Islamic proclivities. There is consequently strong resistance to a political, economic, and cultural marriage with Turkey."[22] Many in Turkey have lost confidence that the EU is negotiating membership in good faith and believe Europeans are highly prejudiced against Muslims.[23] Even if these problems can be overcome, any enlargement of the EU will make it even more difficult to govern, not to mention hammer out something like a common foreign policy for the entire organization.

Indeed, there is concern that the entire organizational structure of the EU would be overwhelmed with more ministers in the Council, more commissioners in the Commission, and more representatives in the Parliament, not to mention more languages for EU business. Most important, more national interests that would have to be coordinated in the EU might mean that serious steps toward integration would be difficult at best. For this reason, many are considering a two-tier system in the EU, with one tier composed of a subset of states that are economically capable and politically willing to commit to further economic and political integration and another tier composed of states with lower levels of integration among them. The EU recently launched a major review of its structure and a "constitutional convention" to consider ways to make the organization more accountable, democratic, and streamlined.

ISSUE: Although the economic benefits to regional integration in the European Union are attractive, the decision to join and fully participate in deeper integration can be a controversial one for many states. Two governments, Norway and Switzerland, have failed in national votes to get a majority of their citizens to approve membership. Other states that are members of the EU, such as Great Britain, Sweden, and Denmark, have opted out of key agreements, refusing, at least at first, to join the common currency. While many other states in central, eastern, and southern Europe, such as Hungary and Poland, recently joined the EU with great enthusiasm, there was some political opposition to this within these countries. Given the economic prospects, why would anyone object to joining the EU?

Option #1: States should wholeheartedly join the EU's integrative efforts.

Arguments: (a) The EU will promote economic efficiency for member states by reducing tariffs and facilitating international trade. (b) The EU will promote political stability and reduce the chances of war between states by more closely connecting states' interests. (c) The EU will generate a greater ability to act together, thus avoiding situations in which single states can become obstacles to collective actions that can solve problems.

Counterarguments: (a) Economic benefits will not be evenly distributed to all states. (b) Forcing unwilling actors to work together can often result in greater friction and animosity rather than greater harmony. (c) As the EU grows in size, decision making will become more and more difficult, resulting in collective inaction as opposed to collective action.

Option #2: States should stay out of the European Union or opt out of key agreements like the common currency.

Arguments: (a) Giving up sovereignty jeopardizes states' ability to provide for their own citizens and make decisions that will benefit those who elected their leaders. (b) Greater economic integration, such as with a common currency, means that efficient economies will be adversely affected by economic downturns in places outside their control. (c) The EU will attempt to impose western European culture and values on central, eastern, and southern European states should they decide to join.

Counterarguments: (a) Citizens will retain the right to elect their own leaders and determine important issues in their own communities. (b) A common currency will reduce economic fluctuations, thus minimizing the severity of all states' economic difficulties. (c) The democratic nature of the EU will ensure that each state has a voice in determining policies, thereby preventing "cultural imperialism."

The discussion about the future of the community took the EU back to the early years with federalism and functionalism as two proposed pathways toward the future.

The most fundamental divide . . . is whether the union will move toward a more federalist model. Among those pushing for that is Germany, which would probably increase its power under a more democratic system. In the complex voting system now in place, it is underrepresented, given the size of its population. But former President Jacques Chirac of France and former Prime Minister Tony Blair of Britain argued vehemently that the union must remain an organization of states united, 'not a united states.' Early drafts of the declaration calling for the convention were rejected for sounding too much in favor of a federalist system.[24]

By 2005, however, the leaders of the EU agreed on a Constitutional Treaty, which reiterated many earlier agreements, increased further the power of the European Parliament, proposed a new way to weight the votes of member states, and attempted to strengthen EU external relations.[25] The Constitutional Treaty required unanimous approval to be ratified. It was defeated when a majority of voters in France and the Netherlands rejected it in referenda, signaling deep opposition to further integration. "The constitution's rejection by founding members of the EU does not in itself spell the end of the union, but it both reflects and deepens a profound crisis in the process of European unification—one that has no obvious solution."[26] Most analysts believe that the "no" votes were not rejections of the treaty's specific provisions, but instead reflected concerns over economic problems, opposition to ruling parties, immigration fears, and skepticism about recent and future enlargement.[27] In the summer of 2007, the EU reached a new constitutional agreement, the **Lisbon Treaty,** which attempts to streamline and democratize its institutions and to enhance the power of the EU President and a foreign policy chief. All EU members ratified the Lisbon Treaty, except Ireland. In a referendum in 2008, Irish voters rejected the treaty, concerned that it would infringe on Irish sovereignty in areas such as taxation, military neutrality, and abortion. In 2009, the EU formally guaranteed Ireland that the treaty would not affect these areas in an attempt to get Ireland to hold a second referendum.[28] Although Ireland did support the Lisbon Treaty in a second vote, there remain serious doubts about whether the EU can satisfy all members in its attempts to reform itself and achieve any of the extremely ambitious goals it has set for itself.[29] But the organization does have a rather impressive track record of disproving the predictions of skeptics and pessimists.

Lisbon Treaty 2007
EU agreement that streamlines decision making and strengthens the positions of the EU president and foreign policy chief

Economic Integration among Developing States

The thrust toward international integration has a different emphasis among less developed countries (LDCs). In Western Europe, the primary motive, at least in the beginning, was probably the avoidance of war. In the developing world, the primary motive for integration is quite clearly economic. The hope is that by integrating the markets of several countries, their collective economic systems will benefit from economies of scale. In many cases, each developing country cannot by itself provide a market big enough to justify setting up expensive factories that produce heavy machinery. But if the markets of several small countries are combined, a firm with access to the enlarged market may be able to survive and help the members develop economically. Furthermore, political leaders in LDCs also hope that economic integration will allow them to deal better with what they see as unfair competition from industrialized countries.

Many of the regional cooperation efforts in the developing world are only functional in nature, in that they typically involve "collective state action within defined confines controlled by participating governments. Collective state action in this respect is not meant to usurp national authority or to displace sovereignty. Functional cooperation by member states entails minimal regional bureaucracy at best, and national governments are the gatekeepers between the national and regional levels, and, thus, can slow down or completely halt the construction of a regional political order."[30] Other efforts have varying degrees of regional integration, which involves "a process of creating a larger political entity, whose institutions possess or demand jurisdiction over preexisting national ones. Regional integration can be intentional by governmental agents to forge 'the rules of the game,' thus implying the eradication of, usually, economic barriers."[31]

Obstacles to Integration among LDCs

In theory, the argument for economic integration sounds convincing. In practice, the results of integration efforts among LDCs have been mixed at best, with no organization in the developing world even approaching the level of institutional development of the EU. One reason may be that neofunctionalism does not work as well in less industrialized countries. The economies are less complex, making spillover from one technical economic task to another less likely to occur. Even when spillover does occur, the typical integrating organization in the developing world lacks the necessary administrative and bureaucratic infrastructures to take advantage of the situation. In contrast, bureaucrats have been in abundant supply to take advantage of any opportunity to expand the role of the EU.

These factors are important impediments to the integration of LDCs, but there is little doubt that the most serious obstacle arises from the creation of problems inside the integrating organization similar to those in the outside world that the LDCs in such organizations are trying to escape. One important motive for integration in the developing world is the hope that free trade areas or customs unions will give industries in these countries a chance to survive in competition with corporations in developed countries. But when developing countries get together in an integrating organization, they create the same kind of market pressures and advantages for relatively developed states inside these organizations that exist in the outside world. For example, industries attracted by the commercial opportunities inside a new customs union tend to gravitate toward the most economically advanced state in the organization, because that state will probably have a larger supply of workers used to the rigors of industrial labor. In addition, the infrastructure (roads, ports, and so on) will be better equipped to handle the demands of modern business, and the consumers in that country will have more money to buy goods produced by the new firm. This does not necessarily mean that inside a free trade area, where free trade and a free market prevail, the rich get richer and the poor get poorer. But it probably does mean that the rich will experience a disproportionate share of some benefits brought about by the integration process.[32] In turn, even if every state in the regional organization is better off than it was before integration, the gap between the richer and poorer states may grow. And the growing gap has produced tensions inside economic communities that threaten almost constantly to tear them apart.

Moreover, regional economic cooperation in the developing world is often affected by the North-South dependent relationship and individual states' efforts to address that relationship. In Africa, for example,

> all African states are in one North-South dialogue or another with the EU. . . . Whereas these North-South arrangements are meant to provide concessions to and facilitate the development of African countries, there is always the possibility that these accords could be competing with Africa's regional groupings for loyalty. Indeed, there is evidence that North-South arrangements . . . or extra-African aid linkages have hindered South-South trade and cooperation and also undermined the goals and cohesion of Africa's regional groups.[33]

In addition, civil wars and regional military rivalries, much more common in the developing world than in contemporary Western Europe, hinder regional cooperation in these areas. In general, neofunctionalist theory argues that integration is most likely to occur when the region's members have democratic institutions with strong societal interest groups, have few class and ethnic conflicts, and are advanced capitalist economies. "Such countries would have much to gain from an expansion of capitalism to the regional level."[34] These conditions are rarely met in regions of the developing world.

There have been differences in the histories of the different organizations in the developed world, of course. But organizations such as the East African Community (Kenya, Uganda, and Tanzania); the Latin American Free Trade Area (consisting of most South American states plus Mexico, disbanded in 1980); the Andean Common Market (Bolivia, Chile, Colombia, Ecuador, Peru, and Venezuela); the Economic Community of West African States (ECOWAS); and the Association of Southeast Asian

Nations (ASEAN) have all experienced difficulties and tensions created by a perceived unequal distribution of the benefits of integration.[35]

Consider, for example, one of the most ambitious efforts at regional integration in the developing world: the **East African Community** (EAC) of Kenya, Uganda, and Tanzania. "For a decade after the EAC's inception in 1967, the three countries shared common currency and banking systems, common postal services, shared railways and airline, and a common university system."[36] In many ways, the EAC's chances for integration were strong: The member nations shared a common colonial (British) heritage that left them with common, overlapping administrative structures and a common language at the time of independence. Yet differences over economic strategies (Kenya was more capitalist oriented and Tanzania more socialist oriented), differences over political regimes (Tanzania was quite critical of the dictatorship of Idi Amin in Uganda), and the strong growth of the Kenyan economy relative to its neighbors led to the collapse of the EAC after a decade.[37] The EAC was revived in the 1990s, reestablished a customs union in 2004, and expanded to include Burundi and Rwanda.

No other regional cooperative effort in Africa, or anywhere else in the developing world, has come close to the earlier EAC, or to the EU, although there are over 200 regional economic arrangements in Africa alone.[38] The **Economic Community of West African States (ECOWAS)** has attempted to learn from the lessons of past failed attempts at regional integration (see Map 12.1). "To assure an equitable distribution of the benefits that accrue from the undertaking, the Fund for Cooperation, Compensation, and Development was set up."[39] The purpose of this fund is to distribute money from the wealthiest economies within the region (such as Nigeria) to the poorest. This effort is similar to the EU's Structural Funds and the Cohesion Fund, by which the wealthier states such as Germany helped develop poorer regions, such as southern Italy and northern England and the whole of Ireland. The difference, however, between this type of fund in the EU and in ECOWAS is that the wealthiest state in a region in the developing world is still relatively poor and cannot, or will not, adequately subsidize the development of other states. Yet, ECOWAS "has proven its resiliency, despite coming close to disintegration several times. Moreover, the community recently called for the creation of a single currency. Admittedly, the group may not be close to adopting a single currency any time soon, but the mere fact that its members agreed to do so at this time, calculated posturing or not, must not be easily dismissed."[40]

East African Community
Economic organization that included Kenya, Uganda, and Tanzania and was highly integrated during the late 1960s and early 1970s.

Economic Community of West African States (ECOWAS) Regional group founded in 1975 with the objective of integrating economies of several West African countries.

Map 12.1   Members of the Economic Community of West African States (ECOWAS)

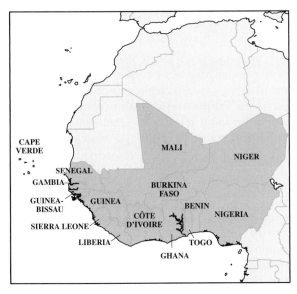

(© Cengage Learning)

In terms of scale, perhaps the most ambitious effort at regional cooperation in Africa is the pan-African Economic Community (AEC), established in 1991. The AEC is realistic in the sense that it calls for integration to occur over a forty-year process (similar to the EU). In other ways too, the AEC is patterned after the EU. "The pan-African integration process was intended to be implemented in six phases, culminating in the functioning of, among other entities, a pan-African economic and monetary union, an African central bank, a single African currency, and a pan-African parliament."[41] If ever achieved, the continent-wide community would be impressive, but efforts are likely to be complicated for all the reasons discussed previously.

Economic integration is a hot topic in Central and South America as well. There have been many regional agreements since 1990 to liberalize trade within Latin America and the Caribbean. Six Central American presidents signed an accord in 1993 aimed at creating a trade bloc involving Guatemala, Nicaragua, Honduras, El Salvador, Costa Rica, and Panama. In 1991, Argentina, Brazil, Paraguay, and Uruguay formed the Common Market of the South, known as **Mercosur.** From 1991 to 1994, Mercosur's members cut their tariffs sharply, to the point that most goods traded among its members are now tariff free. The clearest single measure of Mercosur's progress is the growth in trade that it has prompted. From $4 billion in 1990, trade among its four members tripled to $14.5 billion by 1995.[42] In 2006, Venezuela became the fifth member of Mercosur (pending ratification by the other members), expanding the regional agreement to include 250 million people and over a trillion dollars of gross domestic product.[43] Bolivia, Chile, Colombia, Ecuador, and Peru are associate members. "The MERCOSUR aims at completing a customs union . . . , and its ultimate goal is a common market."[44] Although Mercosur has provisions for third-party binding arbitration of disputes between its members, there is no enforcement, and conflicts have thus far been settled through state-to-state negotiations.[45] Mercosur, like the African Economic Community, has expressed intentions to evolve into an EU. Already with common external tariffs, it aims for a common market and political institutions similar to the European Commission and the European Parliament. "Considering the insufficiency of conditions favorable to political institutionalization (for example, economic interdependence, dedicated regional leadership, and stable security arrangement), however, it is unlikely that MERCOSUR will establish a workable supranational governance system in the near future."[46]

Other regional economic efforts in the developing world have been less willing to discuss neofunctionalist structures, such as third-party arbitration. For example, the ten-member ASEAN organization, which was created in the 1960s to maintain regional order in Southeast Asia, has been "extremely reluctant to create a supranational body with a binding authority."[47] The importance of ASEAN, however, has grown with Chinese economic growth and with China's decision to help ASEAN states out

Mercosur A South American free trade zone created in 1991 by Argentina, Brazil, Paraguay, and Uruguay, joined by Venezuela in 2006.

of their financial crises in the 1990s. China also recently concluded a free trade agreement with ASEAN which will be one of the largest free trade zones in terms of its combined economic wealth and the number of people within it.[48]

Economic integration as part of a development strategy is an idea that clearly persists in Africa, Latin America, and Asia. Yet as was the case with integration in Western Europe in the 1970s, economic hard times can put the brakes on integrative efforts. The economic crises in Asia and Latin America and the global economic downturn have made many states in these regions wary of the short-term costs of integration, even if they recognize the potential for long-term gains.

Economic Integration across the North–South Divide

Recently, regional integration efforts have seen more diverse memberships. "The early integration initiatives in the 1950s and 1960s were either among the advanced countries (North-North integration) or among the developing countries of the South (South-South integration). In the mid-1980s, a new breed of integration emerged among countries with different levels of economic development (North-South integration)."[49] Like the economic cooperation attempts within the South, these efforts have not achieved anything close to the levels of integration in the EU.

North American Free Trade Agreement (NAFTA) Free trade zone created in 1994 by the United States, Mexico, and Canada.

The 1994 launching of the **North American Free Trade Agreement (NAFTA)** between Canada, Mexico, and the United States constituted an especially interesting experiment from the point of view of international integration theories, because the disparity in average income between Mexico and the United States was greater than that between any other pair of bordering states in the world. In 1991, the gross domestic product per capita in Mexico was about $7,010, whereas in the United States, it was about $24,680.[50] According to both critics and supporters of free trade and economic integration, this disparity should make the impact of both free trade and economic integration particularly pronounced and beneficial (or disastrous) depending on one's point of view.

The major point of NAFTA was to eliminate within ten years all restrictions on trade in manufactured products and cross-national investment and to remove all tariffs and quotas on agricultural goods within fifteen years:

> The NAFTA is a preferential trade arrangement, and thus its scope of activity remains largely limited to trade and investment, although it has been used as a forum for discussing and implementing standards for labor and the environment. NAFTA has an institutional basis for dispute settlement . . . in which the third party's ruling is non-binding and without proper enforcement authority. In addition, . . . [the agreement] establishes a separate dispute settlement mechanism regarding anti-dumping

and countervailing duties. Panel decisions are binding and have "direct effect" in domestic laws, creating a binding obligation under national law.[51]

According to its supporters, the agreement would bring benefits to all three economies involved. Consistent with economic liberalism, Mexico, the United States, and Canada would allocate their productive energies to those activities at which they are most efficient. More would be produced, and better-paying jobs would ultimately be created in all three countries. But according to its critics, especially in the United States, hundreds of thousands of U.S. jobs would be lost as industries relocated to Mexico to take advantage of the low wages there. Mexican critics, on the other hand, worried about having Americans dominate their economy. Others worried that increased integration with Canada and the United States would worsen economic inequalities in Mexico and that increased economic clout in the hands of the Mexican rich would slow or eliminate political reform in Mexico.[52]

On the very day that NAFTA officially went into effect (January 1, 1994), the Mexican government was faced with an armed rebellion in the southern state of Chiapas. And the rebels in the Zapatista National Liberation Army in Chiapas were motivated at least in part by opposition to NAFTA. One of their leaders denounced NAFTA as a "death sentence" for Mexico's Indians.[53] What was defended in some important U.S. circles as a step crucial to the survival of a friendly government in Mexico had apparently provoked a rebellion, creating serious doubts about its stability.

After more than fifteen years of NAFTA, there is still no consensus on its effects. Some point to the fact that, "on aggregate, the NAFTA has been a tremendous boost to Mexican trade and investment. . . . In dollars, Mexico's exports to the United States have more than doubled since the entry into force of the NAFTA, while exports to Canada have more than tripled."[54] In 1999, Mexico replaced Japan as the United States' second-largest trading partner, after Canada. Canadian and U.S. foreign direct investment in Mexico has also surged since NAFTA went into effect.[55] Supporters of NAFTA point out that the Mexican economy seems to be benefiting. Since the beginning of the twenty-first century, inflation and the value of the peso have been relatively stable. Overall, NAFTA supporters argue that Mexico

> successfully has decoupled its economy from the old boom-and-bust, high-inflation, debt-ridden model that characterized it and much of Latin America until the 1980s. When Mexico's old protectionist model crashed and burned in the debt crisis of 1982, it took seven years to regain its international credit rating and for U.S. exports to Mexico to regain their pre-crisis level. After the peso crisis of 1994–95, it took Mexico only seven months to regain its credit rating and 17 months for U.S. exports to Mexico to recover.[56]

Others argue that more Mexicans are now under-employed in low-paying jobs and overall income inequality in Mexico has increased:

> NAFTA has not delivered the promised benefits to workers in Mexico, and few if any of the agreement's stated goals has been attained. . . . In many ways (such as the stagnation of the manufacturing share of employment), the entire process of development has been halted, and in some cases it even may have been reversed. . . . The question that remains is whether Mexico can, under NAFTA, restart its stalled development and find a way to redistribute the benefits of the resulting growth.[57]

Mexico's growth rates for the past several years have only been around 3 percent, not enough to provide a solid base of employment. There is also a downside to the surge in exports from NAFTA. The Mexican economy is now much more vulnerable to economic downturns in the United States. As a result, the economy suffered in 2001 and 2008 when U.S. demand declined.[58] As for the effects on the United States, one report concluded that NAFTA has had minimal effects, positive or negative, on the U.S. economy.[59]

Just how influential NAFTA turns out to be in the Western Hemisphere, and possibly the rest of the developing world, will depend largely on how well the Mexican government deals with the impact of NAFTA on Mexico's economy. Despite some of the potential drawbacks, NAFTA is quite attractive to other Latin American developing states. Chile has already expressed its desire to join NAFTA, and Chile and the United States signed a bilateral free trade agreement in 2003. There are also plans for a larger, Western Hemisphere regional trade area. At the Summit of the Americas, held in 1994, thirty-four states in North, Central, and South America agreed to negotiate a Free Trade Area of the Americas (FTAA), which would eliminate barriers to trade and investment.

> When the United States proposed the Free Trade Area of the Americas (FTAA) in the 1990s, the idea was to integrate all Western Hemisphere countries (save for Cuba) . . . into a single institution that followed the practices set forth in what is now the World Trade Organization. Most hemispheric countries were initially in favor of the proposal—and many still are. Venezuela was not among them, but this was expected. Brazil's opposition was more serious, in that the FTAA without Brazil's participation would exclude the dominant country in South America and, with it, the other three countries of the Common Market of the South (Mercosur)—Argentina, Paraguay, and Uruguay. The US response was to conclude instead a number of free trade agreements—with Chile and the five countries of the Central American common market, plus the Dominican Republic. Free trade agreements were also negotiated with Panama and

Colombia, but the US Congress has yet to approve them. The status quo, as a result, is neither a unified trade grouping in the . . . region (which the FTAA would have created) nor trade integration between the separate clusters in South America. Instead the region has separate political groupings . . . and economic arrangements that partially overlap with the political divisions."[60]

Negotiations were meant to complete the FTAA by 2005, but remain stalled.

Asian Pacific Economic Cooperation (APEC) Regional economic agreement among twenty-one economies including Australia, China, Japan, Russia, and the United States.

Another attempt at regional economic cooperation across the North-South divide is the **Asian Pacific Economic Cooperation (APEC)** agreement. Established in 1989, it comprises twenty-one economies, from Australia to Southeast Asia, China, Japan, and Russia, to across the Pacific from Canada, the United States, and Mexico (see Map 12.2). APEC, however, is at a very low level of economic cooperation. Member states have pledged to decrease trade barriers, but there is no formal institution or enforcement mechanism.

Japan's nationalistic disposition, along with the importance attached to national sovereignty among the newly independent East Asian countries, has proven to be a strong impediment to institutional integration. The absence of working regional security arrangements, hot wars waged in Korea and Vietnam . . . , the fears of domination by Japan and China, and the existence of territorial disputes must have aggravated the concerns about national sovereignty and relative gains from cooperation.[61]

Regional Integration, Supranationalism, and the International Political Economy

The debate between functionalism and neofunctionalism still undergirds many efforts at regional cooperation. As we have seen, there is quite a difference in the institutionalization of these areas of economic cooperation among the major regions despite the fact that there is a fairly high level of intraregional trade and one or two leading economic powers within each region. Table 12.2 compares these institutions, as well as some of the other regional areas. As Choi and Caporaso note with respect to the EU, NAFTA, and APEC, "Working with just these three cases, it is difficult to evaluate testable hypotheses. Perhaps the variable institutional patterns have to do with the taming of sovereignty in Western Europe, as well as the waning of nationalism."[62] In particular, Germany, after World War II, decided that it would embrace multilateralism and Europeanism over German nationalism. The United States and Japan, for their part, have resisted supranational notions in NAFTA and APEC. Moreover, many of the smaller states in Western Europe concluded that institutionalization was the way to prevent a resurgence of German nationalism,

Map 12.2   Members of the Asian Pacific Economic Cooperation (APEC) Agreement

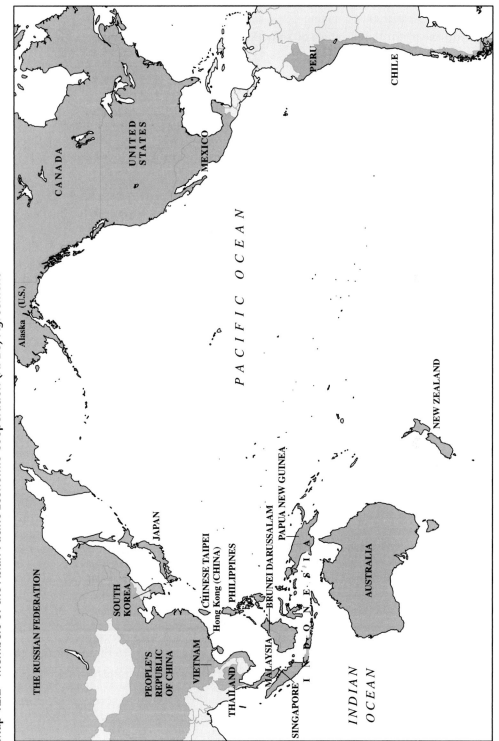

Comparing the Institutionalization of Some Regional Economic Agreements

Region	Institution	Level of Regional Trade*	Scope of Activity	Level of Institutional Authority in Dispute Settlement†
Europe	European Union (economic union)	55.2%	Comprehensive	High
Americas	NAFTA (free trade area)	51.7%	Trade and investment	Medium
	Mercosur (projected customs union)	25.1%	Trade and investment	Medium
Asia and the Pacific	AFTA (free trade area)	20.4%	Trade and investment	Low
	APEC (projected free trade area)	69.7%	Consultation on numerous issues	None

* Intraregional exports as a percentage of all exports, 1998.

† High = third-party review, binding ruling, direct effect in domestic law. Medium = third-party review, binding in some areas, direct effect in domestic law in some areas. Low = third-party review, nonbinding.

Source: From *Handbook of International Relations* ed. By Walter Carlsnaes, pp. 480, 481, 483, 484, 485, 493, 494. Reproduced by permission of SAGE Publications, London, Los Angeles, New Delhi and Singapore.

while smaller states in North America and Asia still worry that regional institutions will be dominated by the United States or Japan.

It is important to note that despite the lack of institutionalization, significant regional cooperation has been achieved, as is evident in Table 12.2. Intraregional trade among countries in the Free Trade Area of the Americas was already at 60 percent of all exports of the countries in the regions in 2001, despite lacking even a free trade agreement.[63] Indeed many, including functionalists, would argue that informal institutions and practices can be just as effective at facilitating cooperation as formal institutions. Some East Asian states, particularly Japan, seem to prefer informal business networks that "can reduce the demand for formal/legal protection by internalizing" economic cooperation.[64] Yet,

> the rejection of formal, supranational institutions or the utility of informal institutions . . . is not likely to persist. . . . The benefits of formal institutions are likely to increase with growing economic interdependence or integration. . . . In fact, East Asian countries have become more receptive to legalist resolution of trade disputes under the WTO dispute settlement procedures, and ASEAN has developed a more sophisticated institutional structure in recent years.[65]

What will be the effect of regional integration on the world economy? From the point of view of the developing world, efforts to link their economies to the richer economies in the North and break down the structural barriers that they see inhibiting growth are one hoped-for effect. From an economic liberal point of view, regional integration is good, because it enhances free trade among the participating economies; but it can be bad, because it tends to erect protectionist obstacles between the regional group and the rest of the world. According to one economic analyst,

> the spectre of global fragmentation is haunting the global trading system and with it international financial markets. The fear is that progress toward global integration over the past four decades will be reversed as the world economy splits up into three regional trading blocs, each centered on a major currency, each closed to outsiders. . . . But . . . the major regional initiatives currently under way are more likely to represent the building blocks of an integrated world economy than stumbling blocks which prevent its emergence. . . . The forces initiating these developments are the very opposite of protectionism. They represent positive, integrative responses to the pressures exerted by globalization. If accompanied by parallel progress at the GATT, regionalization could be a potent mechanism for freeing world trade and investment and harmonizing national institutional practices.[66]

In this way, the globalization of the economy (discussed in more detail in Chapter 14), which is represented by the WTO, and the regionalization of the economy, which is represented by the EU and NAFTA, may work in tandem.

Both of these processes also call into question the functioning of the state. Whether it is state-directed cooperation, the transfer of some political authority to a larger political entity with some supranational powers, or somewhere in between, states involved in these economic cooperative efforts are potentially ceding some sovereignty, as they will have less control over their national economies.[67] If economic decisions in the future rest more and more in the hands of regional organizations, global organizations, or multinational corporations that can travel freely across political boundaries, states will lose a significant degree of their sovereignty. The forces at work against the state and the ability of states to cope with global challenges and globalization are the subjects of the next part of this book.

Theoretical Perspectives on Regional Institutions

While federalism and functionalism help describe *how* states go about regional cooperation, other theoretical perspectives (introduced in Chapter 1) offer insights on why states build regional institutions, how these institutions are designed, and what effects they have on their members.[68] Realism, for example, assumes that institutions come from powerful states that use them to further state interests, and they do not to see international organizations as autonomous means of resolving conflicts. "In a world where conflict is the norm, institutions are neither necessary nor sufficient for cooperation."[69] Institutions are simply forums for powerful states to exercise their influence and disproportionately reap any benefits. Institutions have no autonomy and independence from their member states; because participation in international institutions is voluntary, states are free to abandon their membership when the particular institution no longer serves their interests. Indeed, regional institutions reflect power and power relations in the broader international environment.[70] Hegemons, for example, may use regional arrangements to dominate states within the region and to balance against another great power outside the region. Smaller states may "bandwagon" (see Chapter 8) with a stronger state to share in the benefits of the arrangement or they may join together in a regional institution to balance against an outside threat. Along these lines, realists would stress the importance of the Soviet threat to the creation of the European Community and the role of regional instability in the creation of ASEAN.

Liberalism, as a broad theoretical perspective stressing the importance of interdependence, sees a greater role for regional institutions.[71] States create these institutions in order to facilitate and manage interdependent relations and to provide collective goods, such as free trade (see Chapter 10). Liberalism argues that institutions decrease uncertainty about cooperation and lower the costs of transactions in an anarchical system, making relations more efficient. While important, however, regional organizations are simply arenas for cooperation and states remain important actors, although institutional arrangements can change state preferences over time. Analyses of regional organizations, such as NAFTA, that focus on the economic benefits of economic cooperation and the way these organizations are beneficial to the interests of all states is consistent with the liberal perspective.

Regional institutions also make sense from a constructivist perspective.[72] For constructivism, institutions and their design reflect converging norms of international behavior and identities, including regionally-based identities (such as what is "European" and what is not). Institutions act to socialize their members to common ideas and can change states' interests, by transforming their beliefs and identities. More experience with shared rules facilitates further institutionalization. Contrary to both realism and liberalism, constructivism expects institutions to act more autonomously from their member states, as they adopt their own culture and identity. Constructivists would point to the importance of an "Asian" identity to regional organizations like ASEAN and to the autonomy and separate culture that has developed in the bureaucracy of the EU.

Finally, domestic political explanations (see Chapter 5) also have something to say about regional institutions.[73] "[D]omestic-politics arguments focus on how domestic constituencies advance their interests by creating institutions" and how, in turn, regional institutions affect the distribution of power and interests within a country.[74] From a domestic political perspective, for example, we would expect internationally-oriented domestic actors, such as business groups, to advocate for higher levels of institutionalization and legalization to ensure compliance of beneficial arrangements among states. The creation of APEC, for example, has been traced to the interests of domestic political groups who benefit from globalization converging across borders.[75] Other domestic actors, however, such as the military, would resist institutionalization on the grounds that it would diminish sovereign control. The particular nature of the domestic political system would affect how these competing domestic interests are able to influence the design and working of the regional institution.

SUMMARY

- The most successful attempt at economic regional integration is the European Union, which has made significant strides toward the creation of a more unified, federal type of political entity since its founding in 1957. The drive behind a more united Europe after World War II had both political and economic motivations.

- The path of integration that west European states have followed is primarily neofunctional, involving the creation of some institutions to guide integration while avoiding an all-at-once federal unification. These institutions include the European Commission, the Council of the European Union, and the directly elected European Parliament.

- Some of the most significant steps toward deeper political and economic integration have occurred fairly recently: The Single European Act went into effect in 1987, and the Maastricht Treaty was implemented in 1993. The Single European Act officially removed many of the remaining economic barriers to integration, and the Maastricht Treaty called for all members of the EU to use a common currency and to move toward coordination of defense and foreign policies, as well as legal processes within their countries. The common currency, the euro, was established among twelve countries and circulated among their citizens beginning in 2002. Sixteen countries now use the euro.

- Movement toward a common defense and foreign policy has been slow, complicated partly by the desire to add new members from central and eastern Europe. Many are concerned that the expansion of the EU will overburden the EU's institutions, making effective choices and policy more difficult. Recently, the Lisbon Treaty was negotiated in an attempt to streamline and democratize EU institutions.

- Economic integration efforts involving developing countries have persisted since the 1960s. Those efforts have floundered repeatedly, partly because the poorer nations involved in those organizations perceive that they receive a smaller share of the benefits of integration than the richer states. Despite the obstacles, there have been a number of new regional economic integration efforts in the developing world.

- NAFTA is an example of regional economic integration that aims to integrate relatively wealthy nations (the United States and Canada) with a developing state (Mexico). Trade among NAFTA's members has increased, but the indicators of the effects on the Mexican economy have been mixed.

- Regional integration efforts such as NAFTA and APEC vary greatly in the level of institutionalization and scope of economic cooperation. Even without institutionalization, however, functional economic cooperation in the form of high levels of intraregional trade can challenge the autonomy of sovereign states and can contribute to economic globalization.

- Theoretical perspectives offer alternative explanations for why regional institutions are created, how they are designed, and what effects they have on member states. Realism focuses on the importance of power relations, both inside and outside the region, and expects institutions to have no independence or real effect. Liberalism stresses the greater efficiency that institutions provide by coordinating the similar interests of various states. Constructivism points out how institutions reflect shared identities and develop their own autonomous identities. Finally, domestic political explanations trace the origin and operation of regional institutions to domestic actors' interests.

KEY TERMS

economic integration   432
federalism   433
functionalism   434
supranational   434
neofunctionalism   435
spillover effects   435
European Coal and Steel
  Community (ECSC)   435
Treaty of Rome   435
European Court of Justice   436
European Commission   436
Council of the European
  Union   436
European Parliament   436
free trade area   438
customs union   438

common market   438
economic union   438
Single European Act   440
Maastricht Treaty   440
euro   440
Common Agricultural
  Policy   444
Lisbon Treaty   446
East African Community   449
Economic Community of West
  African States (ECOWAS)   449
Mercosur   450
North American Free Trade
  Agreement (NAFTA)   451
Asian Pacific Economic
  Cooperation (APEC)   454

PART V

Global Challenges

The Global Environment and Its Inhabitants

I t is possible to analyze global politics from a viewpoint that emphasizes the extent to which a global community, as opposed to a set of interdependent but still separate states, exists. Such a viewpoint has become increasingly relevant, partly because a set of interrelated problems highlights the extent to which people everywhere are connected by the global environmental system. Food and natural resource shortages, high levels of population growth, deterioration of the ozone layer, and significant climate change all seem to be problems that cannot be solved by individual states. They all make the common fate of people in the global community dramatically visible.

This chapter focuses on these global environmental challenges. It describes some of the most important problems facing the world community and analyzes the debates over how serious the problems will become in the next few decades. The debates often pit optimists against pessimists over the severity of the problems and involve further disagreements over workable solutions. Even when most agree on the challenge and it seems in the interest of all to cooperate to address the problem, political and economic interests complicate global efforts. This chapter discusses these interests as obstacles to cooperation on collective goods, such as clean air and biodiversity, as well as how different theoretical perspectives view global environmental politics.

Environmental Challenges

T he international environment has always been an interdependent system. The rain that falls in one part of the globe, for example, evaporated from lakes in another part of the globe. But it was not until the 1960s that the connections among states through the international environment were seriously recognized. "While individual environmental treaties date back more than a century, the environment is a relatively new field of international law,"[1] and a fairly new issue in international politics.

Atmospheric Conditions and Climate Change

Air pollution was one of the first environmental challenges to reach the international agenda. "As countries industrialized in the first half of the century, environmental pollution issues became more prevalent. . . . Perhaps the most famous international environmental dispute . . . began in the 1930s when the United States complained that sulfur dioxide emissions from a smelter located across the border in Canada damaged U.S. crops."[2] As the effects of industrialization accumulated in the second half of the twentieth century, concern for pollution within countries prompted a number of the industrialized states to pass national environmental protection laws. These countries soon realized, however, that the air around them could not be protected through national efforts alone.

"Particularly in Europe where many environmental issues such as air and water pollution inherently present transboundary issues, the emerging environmentalism moved to the international level."[3]

In 1968, Sweden, facing transboundary pollution problems in the form of acid rain, organized an international conference on the global environment.[4] Sweden also hosted the first UN conference on the environment, known as the **Stockholm Conference,** in 1972. This conference,

Stockholm Conference First UN Conference on the environment, in 1972.

> . . . marked the culmination of efforts to place the protection of the biosphere on the official agenda of internal policy and law. Specific aspects of the environment had been the objects of international negotiations and arrangements, but the concept of the collective responsibility of nations for the quality and protection of the earth as a whole did not gain political recognition until the years immediately preceding the Stockholm Conference.[5]

Today, air pollution remains an important part of the international environmental challenge. Perhaps the most notorious pollution results from the world's reliance on fossil fuels (coal, oil, and natural gas) to generate most of its industrial energy. Carbon dioxide is released into the atmosphere when these fuels are burned. In 2007, 8.2 billion tons of carbon were added to the atmosphere through fossil fuel combustion, up 2.8 percent from 2006 and 22 percent from 2000.[6] Annual emissions of carbon dioxide have increased more than 80 percent since 1970.[7] These emissions have a rather dramatic effect on the concentration of carbon dioxide in the atmosphere.

Part of the rise in concentration of carbon dioxide is due to deforestation in the world. When trees die, carbon dioxide is added to the atmosphere in two ways. As the dead trees rot, they release carbon dioxide into the air. Also, trees consume carbon dioxide in the process of photosynthesis. When they die, less photosynthesis occurs; thus, less carbon dioxide is absorbed. "Already, more than half of the forested belt around the tropics—once about 5.5 million square miles—has been lost. Pristine tropical forests in West Africa, Madagascar, the Philippines, and Brazil have been reduced to less than 10 percent of their natural areas. India has virtually no original forests remaining. Moreover, scientists estimate that at least 34 million acres of tropical forests are still being cleared yearly due to the insatiable global demand for land, timber, crops and such valuable commodities as gold and oil; millions more acres are partially logged."[8] According to satellite data, deforestation in Brazil was so extreme by 1987 that the Amazon rain forest was reduced in size by 8 million hectares, an area about the size of Austria;[9] by 1989 the deforested area was larger than the size of Japan,[10] and the pace of deforestation in the Amazon increased by 34 percent in the early 1990s.[11] In addition to the link to rising levels of carbon dioxide in the air, deforestation also creates problems with flooding, food supplies, and biodiversity (discussed later in the chapter).

Constant emissions of large amounts of carbon dioxide into the atmosphere through fossil fuel combustion and deforestation combine with the pollution of the atmosphere by volatile chemicals known as chlorofluorocarbons (CFCs) to produce the greenhouse effect and a global warming trend. CFCs prevent infrared radiation from escaping the earth's atmosphere, thus making their own contribution to the global warming effect. In addition to their possible role in the process leading to global warming, CFCs may have helped to destroy the ozone layer in the upper atmosphere over the polar regions and, recently, over the entire world. The ozone layer screens out a portion of the ultraviolet radiation from the sun. Because that layer decreased by about 2 percent worldwide between 1969 and 1986, allowing 4 percent more radiation to reach the earth, an increase in skin cancer is expected.[12]

The rise in carbon emissions, CFCs, and the concentration of carbon dioxide in the atmosphere is worrisome because it could dramatically change climate throughout the world. "Unprecedented increases in global temperatures have occurred in tandem with record levels of greenhouse gas concentrations and emissions. . . ."[13] Global warming in recent times, over the fifty-year period from 1956 to 2005, was twice the rate of warming in the 100-year period from 1906 to 2005 and eleven of the last twelve years have had the warmest global surface temperatures on record (since 1850, when recordkeeping began). The hottest year in recorded history was 2005. (see Figure 13.1).[14] Global average

Figure 13.1   Global Average Land-Ocean Temperature at Earth's Surface, 1880–2007

Source: Worldwatch Institute, *Vital Signs 2009: The Trends that Are Shaping Our Future,* p. 56. © 2009 Worldwatch Institute. www.worldwatch .org.

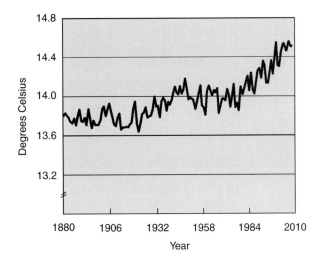

temperature is due to increase significantly by 2100. "More important than the average warming is the effect it may have on climates. Things will not just get warmer, climatologists predict, some places will, but others will get cooler, wetter, drier, or cloudier. The average warming is merely the engine that will drive the changes. The term 'global warming' is mischievous in suggesting that hot summers are what it is all about."[15]

global warming Long-term rise in world's surface temperatures and lower atmospheric temperatures caused by certain "greenhouse" gases such as carbon dioxide.

If current trends continue, global warming could have catastrophic effects all over the world, mostly because of rising global sea levels due to melting polar ice caps, as well as permanently lower levels of rainfall in once-fertile croplands.[16] Around the world, many coastal cities could be completely lost to a rising global sea level. In Bangladesh, a rising sea level might put 18 percent of the country's habitable land under water, making 17 million people environmental refugees.[17] Climate models also suggest that global warming may permanently reduce rainfall in the U.S. Midwest, reducing crop yields in an area that produces 50 percent of the world's corn and 60 percent of its soybeans.[18] Chronic water shortages already plague many countries and over 40 percent of the world's population.[19]

Other effects on public health are created as well:

> Warm weather speeds up insect metabolism: in warm years, insects often grow quicker, breed more frequently, and migrate sooner. . . . Many of the world's most dangerous insects for agriculture, forestry, and public health are tropical or subtropical in origin; almost by definition they are poised to follow the retreat of temperature barriers.[20]

There is still some debate about this trend (discussed in more detail following), but there does seem to be a growing consensus in the world's scientific community that a warming trend is in place on a global scale and that human activities are in part responsible. In a recent report, the Intergovernmental Panel on Climate change concluded "Some planned adaptation (of human activities) is occurring now; more extensive adaptation is required to reduce vulnerability to climate change. Unmitigated climate change would, in the long term, be *likely* to exceed the capacity of natural, managed and human systems to adapt."[21]

Shrinking Natural Resources

In the 1970s, the view that the world would soon run out of several important natural resources gained widespread acceptance.[22] The energy crises of that decade were the major force making that idea so popular. By the middle of the 1980s, the world had recovered from the shock of the

Figure 13.2 World Oil Consumption, 1965–2007

Source: Worldwatch Institute, *Vital Signs 2009: The Trends that Are Shaping Our Future,* p. 29. © 2009 Worldwatch Institute. www.worldwatch.org.

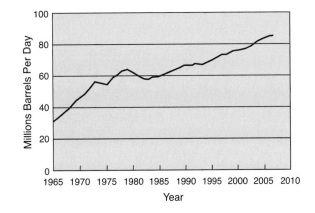

second major increase in the price of oil in 1979, and the glut of oil on the world market had driven prices down and threatened the unity of the Organization of Petroleum Exporting Countries (OPEC). Thus, the notion that supplies of natural resources were running dangerously low for the entire world fell from favor.

Nevertheless, many analysts feel that the oil glut brought about a false sense of security. Indications are that the demand for energy will increase dramatically in the coming decades, spurred in part by economic growth in China and India. World consumption of traditional fuel supplies and electricity consumption per capita climbed between 1980 and 1998 (see Figure 13.2 on world oil consumption), and fossil fuel consumption is projected to increase by 57 percent between 1997 and 2020.[23] "Energy is the master resource' [because] the extraction of all other resources depends on availability and prices of energy."[24] In other words, if increasing demand does deplete supplies of energy resources, all the other natural resources will become more difficult to obtain.

As previously mentioned, deforestation is another issue on the international environmental agenda. Not only do fewer trees relate to climate change, but deforestation also means fewer energy supplies and food supplies for many people living around forest areas. The shrinking of the rain forests also represents a threat to the earth's biodiversity. "Since rainforests are thought to harbor about half the world's species of plants and animals, researchers worry that destruction of the globe's genetic library will hamstring efforts to create new medicines and more productive crops."[25]

In addition, fresh water is a scarce commodity in many parts of the world. "More precious than oil, yet routinely wasted, water is arguably the world's most pressing resource issue. . . . Global water consumption rose sixfold between 1900 and 1995—more than double the rate of population growth—and continues to grow rapidly as agricultural, industrial, and domestic demand increases."[26] Much of the world's population experiences frequent water shortages and more than one billion people do not have access to safe drinking water.[27] According to an environmental vice president of the World Bank, "The wars of the [twenty-first century] will be over water instead of oil or politics."[28] Ocean water is at risk as well, harming another source of food supply.

> Chemicals, solids, and nutrients from agricultural runoff, oil and gas development, logging, dredging, filling, and mining are routinely dumped directly into the ocean or otherwise end up in rivers and streams and make their way to the world's oceans. Some of the effects of ocean pollution include destruction of the world's fisheries, climate and sea level change brought on by changes in ocean temperature, and the destruction of salt marshes, mangrove swamps, coral reefs, and beaches which means the loss of habitat and biological diversity.[29]

This comes at the same time that land resources, or the availability of cropland, are diminishing as well.[30]

Threats to the environmental well-being of the world's waters and cropland have serious implications for human health. Certainly one of the most dismal facts about the world today is that so many people are starving. One recent estimate suggests that more than 1 billion people in the world are chronically malnourished and that the number of hungry people in the world has been rising over the past few years.[31] Children bear the brunt of this problem. Children are seriously affected by malnourishment as it affects them daily and can impair their development. "About one quarter of all children in developing countries are considered to be underweight and are at risk of having a future blighted by the long-term effects of undernourishment."[32]

The United Nations estimates that if current trends continue, it would take more than 130 years to eradicate world hunger.[33] Equally distressing are some signs that the problem is likely to get worse. From 1950 to 1975, world food production outpaced world population growth. But growth in food production slowed in the decades after 1975 as demand increased with a growing world population, raising doubts about how long adequate food supplies can be maintained.[34] In addition to contributing to world hunger, the shrinking of natural resources relative to demand has the potential to contribute to international conflict. Conflict over fishing rights and water is common in many parts of the globe:

> The risk of violence over the allocation of shared water supplies is especially acute where fresh water is scarce, particularly where major river systems constitute the main source of water

for two or more countries. The Nile, for example, is the main source of water for Egypt and Sudan, and a significant source for several other states; the Jordan River is vital to Israel and Jordan, while the Tigris-Euphrates system is a major source for Iraq, Syria, and Turkey. Because these states have failed to agree on the manner in which the flow of these rivers is to be divided among them, discord can arise whenever one country in a system appropriates more water than what others consider its fair share. That these countries often disagree on other matters only adds to the danger that disputes over water supplies will lead to conflict.[35]

In general, the developing world is already witnessing violent conflicts related to environmental scarcities.[36] Oil is particularly associated with conflict. "Among developing countries, an oil-producing country is twice as likely to suffer internal rebellion as a non-oil-producing one. The conflicts range in magnitude from low-level secessionist struggles, such as those occurring in the Niger Delta and southern Thailand, to full-blown civil wars, such as in Algeria, Colombia, Sudan, and, of course, Iraq."[37] Conflict over scarce resources led one analyst to a very dire prediction: "Within the lifetimes of our children and grandchildren, these environmental scarcities may cause widespread social disorder and violence, including war, revolution, ethnic violence, riots and coups that topple established governments."[38]

Overpopulation

The potential for food shortages and starvation (as well as many other global problems) stems in important part from the rapid growth of the earth's population (see Figure 13.3). It took from the beginning of the human species until 1804 for the world's population to reach 1 billion. The second billion was added in a little over 120 years (in 1927), and the third billion took only a little over thirty years (1960). By 1974, the world's population reached 4 billion, the fifth billion was added in only thirteen more years (by 1987), and the sixth billion was added in just thirteen more (by 2000). The annual growth rate of the globe's total population was an average of 1.6 percent from 1975 to 1999. This declined to an average of 1.18 percent annual growth today and is expected to decline to 0.34 percent by 2050. Even with a decline in growth, the United Nations currently projects world population to reach 9.1 billion by 2050.[39] It is difficult to reverse population growth trends easily due to **population momentum.** Many years of high growth mean that more people will be entering their reproductive years in the future, giving more potential for growth.

population momentum Tendency for population to continue to grow due to high numbers of individuals at childbearing age.

What makes the situation particularly problematic is that population grows fastest in areas of the world where poverty is stark. The six

Figure 13.3 World Population, 1750–2200

Source: From *The Skeptical Environmentalist: Measuring the Real State of the World*, p. 46 by Bjorn Lomborg, © 2001. Reprinted with the permission of Cambridge University Press.

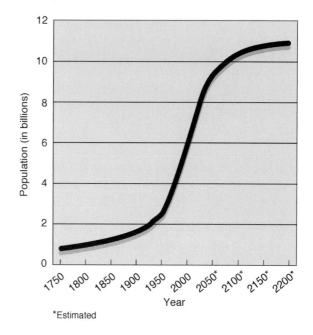

*Estimated

countries that accounted for half of the population growth in 2000 were India, China, Pakistan, Nigeria, Bangladesh, and Indonesia. Between now and 2050, population growth will be highest in many poor countries, including Ethiopia, the Democratic Republic of Congo, and the United Republic of Tanzania.[40] Population increased by 69 percent in low-income countries between 1975 and 1999, compared to a 17 percent increase in high-income countries in the same period. Population experts agree that the population explosion has been brought about by two major factors, both related to economic development. One is the success of medical science. Population growth is a function of fewer people dying, rather than more people being born.[41] In 1650, the average life expectancy was only about thirty years. In 1968, it was about fifty-three years, and by 1999, it had increased to seventy.[42]

Nevertheless, great numbers of children still die at an early age, and this too adds pressure to the upward trend in population. Large families serve as a form of social security in many developing countries. Parents want to have several children to support them in their old age. And because the infant mortality rate is so high in many developing countries, they are likely to want to play it safe, adding more children to the family in anticipation of the early loss of several of them. Also, in some rural settings especially, children can be economic assets as agricultural laborers even before the parents reach old age, providing an added incentive for large families.[43] Thus, the **fertility rate** (the average number of children born to women) differs across levels of economic development. In developing countries, the fertility rate is 2.46, while in high-income

fertility rate Average number of children born to women.

replacement level Fertility rate at which the number of children replace their mother and father.

demographic transition theory Proposition that population growth is significantly influenced by economic development effects on death rates and birthrates.

countries, the fertility rate is 1.64.[44] Note that the fertility rate in the wealthier countries is lower than the **replacement level** (two children to replace their father and mother after they die). Below-replacement-level fertility rates mean that population levels will decline (some are already declining) in the high-income countries.

The **demographic transition theory** describes the relationship between economic development and population growth. In very poor, underdeveloped countries, death rates are high for lack of medical treatment, and birthrates are high because of high infant mortality and the need for many children to help provide for the family welfare. High death rates and birthrates make for little or no population growth. This is the situation the whole world was in before medical advances in the nineteenth and twentieth centuries. When states develop enough so that medicine that prolongs life expectancy is widely affordable, death rates fall, but birthrates remain high and population grows rapidly. This is the part of the transition that most of the developing countries are currently in. Once countries become more economically advanced, medicine that increases life expectancy and decreases infant mortality is available, and children are seen as economic drains rather than assets. Because modern welfare states provide old age insurance, people do not need to have many children to take care of them as they age. In this final part of the demographic transition, which is where most developed countries are now, death rates and birthrates are low, making population growth minimal or even negative. Figure 13.4 graphically shows the demographic transition for Sweden and Sri Lanka, showing how, in both countries, death rates declined before birthrates, leading to population growth. Once birthrates decline, population growth slows, and even becomes negative when the death rate rises as the population ages. According to one economist, this transition is "one of the most fundamental of all social changes during the era of modern economic growth."[45]

The demographic transition theory does not completely capture population dynamics. Many countries have experienced a decline in birthrates prior to high economic development, and others continue to have steady birthrates despite economic development. The theory leaves out many factors beyond economics that play a role in fertility decisions, such as culture, access to and attitudes toward birth control, and government population policies.[46] What seems particularly critical to lowering birthrates is the status of women. "Education, particularly of girls, has been shown to be the factor most closely related to fertility decline, by delaying marriage and first births. Increasing equality between the sexes in legal, economic, and social affairs raises the cost of children by making roles other than childbearing more feasible and attractive to women."[47] Recognizing the importance of women's status, the World Population Conference held in Cairo in 1994 emphasized raising women's status as the key to reducing birthrates.

**Figure 13.4
Demographic Transition:
Birth and Death Rates in
Sweden (1750–2050) and
Sri Lanka (1910–2050)**

Source: From *The Skeptical
Environmentalist: Measuring the
Real State of the World,* p. 124 by
Bjorn Lomborg, © 2001. Reprinted
with the permission of Cambridge
University Press.

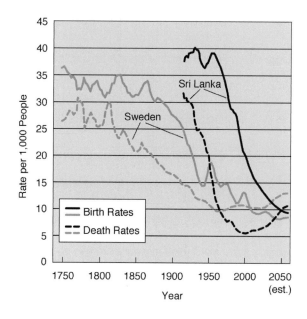

Controlling population has become a critical issue for high-growth states. Large populations place more pressure on environmental systems and make economic development more difficult. Population growth also contributes to social and political conflict within and between states. The population density of Bangladesh, for example, is more than 1,000 people per square kilometer. The state of Assam in India, just across the border, has approximately 340 people per square kilometer, resulting in a massive migration of Bengalis to Assam. Recurring attacks in India against Bengalis are in part related to this demographic pressure.[48]

Assessments of the Challenges: Optimists and Pessimists

Part of the debate on how to respond to environmental challenges such as population growth and shrinking natural resources has revolved around questions about the severity of the problems. The disparity of opinions in the various analyses of the future of the globe is disconcerting. The opinions exist on a full range of pessimism to optimism. "It appears," one informed analyst of such work concludes, "that highly intelligent individuals, who presumably read each other's work and who appear to respond to one another, are not convincing one another, and perhaps are not even communicating."[49] Predicting the future of the world over the next twenty, fifty, or one hundred years is obviously tricky. But the debate between pessimists and optimists for the world's future is not for lack of studies on the problems. With that in mind, let us turn to an evaluation of the arguments made by the optimists and the pessimists.

Food Supplies

It would be easy, considering the headlines in the recurring famine crises in Africa, to conclude that pessimistic predictions about food supplies are were accurate. Some observers, for example, predicted that land for agricultural use would be intolerably scarce by the middle of the twenty-first century. These predictions, made in the late 1970s and early 1980s, were based in part on rising grain prices, but these prices fell unexpectedly and dramatically in the 1980s.[50] Such predictions have by now a rather lengthy history among those who are pessimistic about the future with respect to these problems. Paul Ehrlich made an international reputation for himself with the 1968 publication of *The Population Bomb*, in which he predicted that "the battle to feed humanity is already lost, in the sense that we will not be able to prevent large-scale famines in the next decade."[51] He claimed that general famine was certain to strike even the United States by the 1980s, and that millions or more would have starved to death in developing countries by that time.

Optimists, on the other hand, suggest that greater efficiency in food production techniques can provide more than enough food supplies for a growing global population.[52] The well-known environmental optimist, Julian Simon, has argued that even at our current levels of agricultural efficiency, "the entire present population of the world can be supplied from a square area about 140 miles. . . ."[53] He also pointed out, less speculatively, that "the record of food production entirely contradicts the scary forecasts. The world trend in recent decades shows unmistakably an increase in food production per person."[54] Furthermore, "what the United Nations defines as chronic malnutrition' has declined 16 percent" since the 1960s.[55] In addition, the United Nations reports that the goal of reducing global poverty by half by 2015 is within reach.[56]

This does not mean, however, that chronic food shortages and famine are not a problem for many states and for the global community. As economist Amartya Sen points out, "Starvation is the characteristic of some people not *having* enough food to eat. It is not the characteristic of there *being* not enough food to eat. While the latter can be a cause of the former, it is but one of many *possible* causes."[57] If there is enough food in the environment, starvation and famine become problems of economic entitlement, ownership and access, distribution networks, and domestic and international politics.[58]

Population Growth

The history of demographic predictions is replete with errors and marked by continuing modifications. The predictions of Thomas Malthus in the nineteenth century, for example, proved to be very misleading. One recent analysis of population forecasts notes that

> *The Population Bomb* appeared twenty-five years ago. . . . Written by the biologist Paul Ehrlich . . . it was a gloomy book for

a gloomy time. A new Dark Age would [according to Ehrlich] cloud the world, and "men [would] have to kill and eat one another." A well-regarded book, *Famine 1975!* predicted that hunger would wipe out the Third World that year. . . . In 1972 a group of researchers at MIT . . . [issued] *The Limits to Growth*, which used advanced computer models to project that the world would run out of gold in 1981, oil in 1992, and arable land in 2000. Civilization itself would collapse by 2070.[59]

Despite these gloomy warnings, which relied in part on rapid population growth, the UN Population Division in 1975, for the first time in its history, revised its estimate of future population growth downward and population growth peaked in the 1960s.[60] In fact, from 1965–1970 to 1980–1985, fertility in poor countries decreased by 30 percent. "If the decrease continues, it will surely be the most astonishing demographic shift in history."[61] Figure 13.3 demonstrates the "S-curve" shape of predicted population levels, with growth leveling off around the middle of the twenty-first century.

Population estimates have often been wrong in the past, and the latest predictions may be wrong, too. But even if the population of the world grows much faster than expected, disaster, in terms of food supplies or other aspects of the quality of life, will not necessarily result.[62] It is quite commonly pointed out that "the parts of the world that have done most poorly economically are also those where projected population growth rates are the highest."[63] But it is quite possible that poverty leads to population growth, not the opposite. Indeed, some studies "have found no association between the population growth rate and per capita income growth rate" and "the empirical evidence thus indicates no negative correlation between the rate of population growth and the standard of living."[64] Julian Simon insists that population "density has a *positive* effect on the rate of economic growth" and that, more fundamentally,

> the standard of living has risen along with the size of the world's population since the beginning of recorded time. And with increases in . . . population have come less severe shortages, lower costs, and an increased availability of resources, including a cleaner environment, and greater access to natural recreational areas. And there is no convincing reason why these trends toward a better life . . . should not continue indefinitely.[65]

This does not imply that some population control program cannot contribute to economic growth. In many developing countries, such as Mexico, Egypt, and India, rapid population growth continues, and bringing it under control is almost certainly a desirable goal. At the same time, however, it is clear that the predictions made during the 1960s and 1970s about impending planet-wide disasters resulting from population growth outstripping the world's food production capabilities seem unduly alarmist.

Reserves of Natural Resources

Similarly, the dire warnings about energy resources in the 1970s confronted overwhelmingly contrary evidence in the 1980s. Consider first the most publicized warnings of the 1970s—those regarding oil. After OPEC successfully quadrupled the price of oil in the winter of 1973, those that advocated a halt to economic growth as a way of preserving natural resources used the price increase as proof that the world's supply of energy resources was running low. But in fact, the increase proved no such thing. The members of OPEC were not running out of oil; they were just charging more for it. World oil production actually increased in 1973.[66] OPEC raised the price of oil again in 1979, and shortages again developed. But in the mid-1980s, Saudi Arabia and other OPEC members, as well as non-OPEC countries, flooded the world with cheap oil in attempts to gain larger shares of the market. In addition, changes in the manufacturing processes and shifts in the large economies away from manufacturing to service industries created less of a demand. As a result, the price of a barrel of oil fell through most of the 1990s. Since 1999, the world has seen a steady increase in the price of oil, particularly since 2003 (see Figure 13.5). In 2008, oil prices were quite high, reaching more than $145 per barrel. The rise in prices from 1999 to 2008 is attributed to increased demand (particularly in China), decreased spare oil production capacity, and the political events, crises, and natural disasters that have disrupted production or threaten to disrupt future production. With the global economic downturn, demand for energy shrunk and oil prices plummeted in the second half of 2008. World wide consumption of oil fell in 2008, for the first time since 1983.

Table 13.1 shows an interesting series of predictions about the depletion of oil reserves in the United States. Although the table covers only

Figure 13.5   World Oil Prices 1965–2007

Source: Worldwatch Institute, *Vital Signs 2009: The Trends that Are Shaping Our Future,* p. 30. © 2009 Worldwatch Institute. www.worldwatch.org.

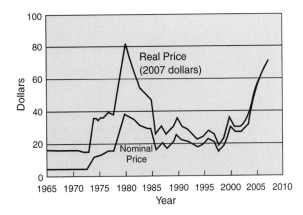

TABLE 13.1

A Short History of Predictions about U.S. Oil Supplies, 1866–1949

Date	Prediction	What Actually Happened
1866	Synthetics available if oil production should end (U.S. Revenue Commission)	In next 82 years, the United States produced 37 billion barrels with no need for synthetics
1885	Little or no chance of oil in California (U.S. Geological Survey)	8 billion barrels produced in California since that date, with important new findings in 1948
1891	Little or no chance of oil in Kansas or Texas (U.S. Geological Survey)	14 billion barrels produced in these two states since 1891
1908	Maximum future supply of 22.5 billion barrels (officials of U.S. Geological Survey)	35 billion barrels produced since 1908, with 26.8-billion-barrel reserve proven and available on January 1, 1949
1914	Total future production only 5.7 billion barrels (official of U.S. Bureau of Mines)	34 billion barrels produced since 1914, or six times this prediction
1920	U.S. needs foreign oil and synthetics: peak domestic production almost reached (director of U.S. Geological Survey)	1948 U.S. production in excess of U.S. consumption and more than four times 1920 output
1931	Must import as much foreign oil as possible to save domestic supply (secretary of the interior)	During the next 8 years, imports were discouraged, and 14 billion barrels were found in the United States
1939	U.S. oil supplies will last only 13 years (radio broadcasts by Department of the Interior)	New oil found since 1939 exceeds the 13-year supply known at that time
1947	Sufficient oil cannot be found in United States (chief of Petroleum Division, State Department)	4.3 billion barrels found in 1948, the largest volume in history and twice our consumption
1949	End of oil supply almost in sight (secretary of the interior)	Petroleum industry demonstrated ability to increase U.S. production by more than 1 million barrels daily in the next 5 years

Source: Presidential Energy Program, Hearings Before the Subcommittee on Energy and Power of the Committee on Interstate and Foreign Commerce, House of Representatives. First sessions on the implication of the President's proposals on the Energy Independence Act of 1975. Serial no. 94-20, p. 643. Washington, DC: U.S. Government Printing Office, February 17, 18, 20, 21, 1975.

the period from 1866 to 1949, it could easily be extended. For example, "in 1979 the United States Central Intelligence Agency concluded that global oil output must fall within a decade ahead' and that the world does not have years in which to make a smooth transition to alternative energy sources.' In essence, the CIA experts were arguing that the world's primary energy supply needed to be converted to a different source within months, an utter impossibility. A generation later, oil output is more than 10 percent higher than it was in 1979."[67]

One reason that pessimistic predictions of long-term shortages are often inaccurate is that they were based on estimates of known reserves. But these estimates provide a misleading basis for such predictions.[68] For example, we now know that for resource after resource, estimates of known reserves made in the 1950s proved by 1970 to be drastically low.[69] This degree of underestimation happens with regularity, in part because of the economic incentives operating on those who gather data on known reserves. Usually the original sources of such data are companies interested in the commercial exploitation of a given resource. Once a company has located reserves that are projected to last, say, thirty years, it is unlikely even to attempt to find additional reserves for at least two important reasons. First, because the company will not be able to sell those reserves for thirty years, there is little incentive to spend time and energy locating them. Second, if known reserves become too abundant, they exert a strong downward pressure on the price of that resource. Today's known reserves are at the highest level (see Figure 13.6).[70] In light

Figure 13.6   World's Known Oil Reserves and World Oil Production, 1920–2000

Source: From *The Skeptical Environmentalist: Measuring the Real State of the World*, p. 124 by Bjorn Lomborg, © 2001. Reprinted with the permission of Cambridge University Press.

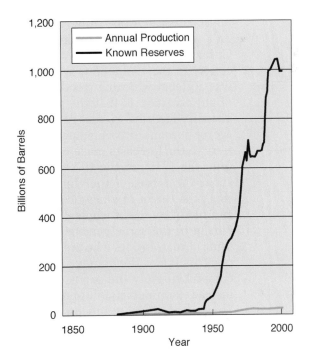

of these data, even most pessimists no longer argue that the world is in imminent danger of running short of oil. Paradoxically (but, as we have, seen, actually quite predictably), both fossil fuel consumption *and* proven reserves have steadily increased through the past fifty years or so.

In general, optimists seem on fairly firm ground when they assert that "the potential supplies of all the important minerals are sufficient for many lifetimes."[71] Still, pessimists have a valid point when they emphasize that more than 50 percent of the global oil reserves are estimated to be in the Middle East, a region currently vulnerable to political instability and conflict. It is possible that market forces will ultimately solve this problem, that the concentration of current known reserves will spark the discovery of huge reserves outside the Persian Gulf,[72] and that the world's supply of inexpensive, readily accessible oil will continue well into the twenty-first century. But it might be prudent to develop alternative sources of energy, even if the world is not about to run out of oil, given the role of fossil fuel in other environmental challenges.[73]

Pollution and Climate Change

Pessimistic predictions about the impact of various forms of pollution on the global atmosphere are difficult to ignore, even though they are based on scanty evidence. That evidence is often weak, because pollution is a relatively recent concern, and data on relevant problems rarely go back more than twenty to thirty years.

There has been considerable debate over predictions of the greenhouse effect. For one thing, it is not entirely clear that industrialization on a worldwide scale will have a warming effect on the global climate. Climatologists do not have a particularly impressive record of prognostication. In the 1930s, they were predominantly of the opinion that there was a global warming trend. Spencer Weart, a specialist in the history of physics, asserts that the greenhouse effect rhetoric of the 1930s was virtually identical to that of the 1980s and 1990s—"of irreversible damage, of humankind overstepping its bounds in horrifying fashion."[74] Contrary to the forecasts made in the 1930s, the global temperature declined from the 1940s to the 1970s. This had an apparent impact on forecasts about the future of the globe's climate: One article in 1975 suggested that "the threat of a new ice age must now stand alongside nuclear war as a likely source of wholesale death and misery for mankind."[75] In fact, "many of the same persons who [warned] about global *cooling* are the same climatologists who are now warning of global *warming*."[76]

This is not the context in which to attempt to sort out or evaluate comprehensively the opposing arguments about global warming. Let us instead examine a couple of reasons why the issue is so difficult to resolve. First, global climate processes are so complex and affected by so many countervailing factors that making predictions about their future course is risky.[77] Tropical deforestation, for example, continues at an alarming rate and may make an important contribution to global warming. Less noted is the fact that in North America and Eurasia, forests are growing larger and absorbing more carbon dioxide.[78]

Debate has also centered on the relative impact of human versus natural processes in climate change. Approximately 200 billion tons of carbon are emitted into the atmosphere by natural processes such as volcanic eruptions, plant decay, and forest fires. Almost exactly that same amount is removed from the atmosphere every year, also by natural processes "breathed in" by trees or taken from the air by ocean plankton, for example. Human activities contribute a very small percentage of the amount produced by these natural processes. Skeptics charge that this relatively insignificant amount cannot have a substantial impact on global climate. Skeptics also question the dire predictions that global warming will produce.[79]

An additional aspect of the global warming debate concerns the relationship between pollution and economic growth. Economic growth is perceived to be part of the problem by many, but it may be that growth is an important part of the solution. In the early stages of industrialization, economies are not wealthy enough to pay the costs of environmental protection.[80] As a result, although it is difficult to prove that things were worse in the previous times, because there are virtually no precise measures of pollution from the nineteenth century, pollution was a serious problem even then. Novelist Charles Dickens described one nineteenth century English town in this manner: "It was a town of machinery and tall chimneys, out of which interminable serpents of smoke trailed

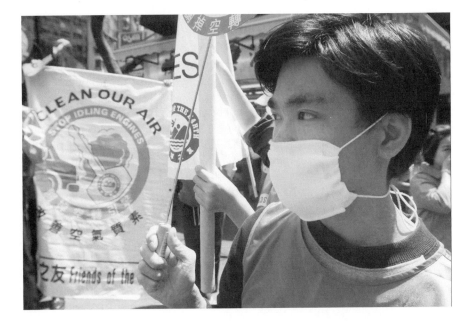

A protester from the environmental group Friends of the Earth wears a mask during a demonstration in Hong Kong's business district, urging drivers to shut off idling engines. Residents of cities such as Hong Kong, Beijing, Bangkok, and Mexico City often wear masks to protect their health from significant air pollution.

(© Bobby Yip/Corbis)

themselves for ever and ever, and never got uncoiled. It had a black canal in it, and a river that ran purple with ill-smelling dye, and vast piles of buildings full of windows, where there was a rattling and a trembling all day long."[81]

Nineteenth-century industrial centers in the United States, such as New York City and Chicago, also experienced significant pollution problems. The Chicago River was reportedly polluted with grease so thick on its surface that it looked like a liquid rainbow.[82]

A comparison of contemporary developing societies with industrialized countries provides additional support for the assertion that economic growth and environmental deterioration do not necessarily go hand in hand. For example, developing states typically have water pollution problems, brought about by poor sanitation systems, that are more serious than those of industrialized societies. The crowding in the slums of major cities in many poor countries creates additional serious pollution problems. Economic growth may exacerbate some pollution problems for poor countries in the short run, but ultimately such growth is likely to be a necessary condition for the alleviation of pollution. One study of the relationship between economic growth and pollution revealed that "some problems decline as income increases."[83] As per capita income increases, "some problems initially worsen but then improve as incomes rise."[84] Economic growth, while certainly capable of damaging the environment, also can lead to environmental improvements. And even rather stringent steps to protect the environment need not stifle economic growth. In fact, energy conservation, which can, for example, decrease the amount of carbon dioxide emitted into the atmosphere, can also increase the efficiency of an economy and even speed up growth. In 1974, in the wake of the first OPEC-induced energy crisis, one study predicted that if current trends continued, energy use in the United States would double between 1970 and 1987. It also predicted that even if the United States adopted a "zero-growth policy option," energy use would still increase about 20 percent. Instead, energy consumption decreased from 1970 to 1987, while the economy grew.

Still, the debate over global warming and the role of economic development may subside in future years as more and better evidence becomes available. In 1995, "in an important shift of scientific judgment, experts advising the world's governments on climate change are saying for the first time that human activity is a likely cause of the warming of the global atmosphere."[85] The story refers to a report published by the Intergovernmental Panel on Climate Change (IPCC), consisting of more than 2,000 scientists assembled by the United Nations to advise the world's governments on climate policy. According to an analyst from the Worldwatch Institute, "Sophisticated computer modeling and actual measurements of the atmosphere are now converging with uncanny accuracy . . . increasingly the computer answers are corroborated by direct observation. By 1995, the fit looked too close to be pure coincidence; the . . . IPCC

... concluded that human activity is warming the earth."[86] In the IPCC's most recent assessment, they conclude the increase in carbon dioxide and other greenhouse gases is due to human activities and the net effect has been one of warming in the global climate system.[87]

Complex Relationships Connecting Environmental Challenges

One of the most pessimistic perspectives on the environmental challenges facing the globe points out the difficulty of solving one problem without causing another to worsen. In the 1970s, the results of an analysis of all these problems based on a computer simulation of the world were published in a report titled *The Limits to Growth*, which provoked a torrent of both praise and criticism that continues to this day; it has sold more than 30 million copies in thirty languages since it was published in 1972.[88]

Computer simulations of social systems allow social scientists a form of experimentation that would not otherwise be possible.[89] Once a simulation is operational, it can be used to obtain answers to a multitude of questions such as what would happen if the world were this way. The answers are quite often surprising, because social systems can behave counter-intuitively. Actions designed to solve problems may have no effect or may make the problems worse.[90]

The world system, according to the designers of *The Limits to Growth* simulation, operates in just such a fashion. Measures that seem designed to alleviate problems actually make them worse or have an impact on other parts of the system that creates even worse problems. Given the rampant poverty and starvation in the global system, for example, a seemingly logical solution would involve substantially increased food production and economic development. But *The Limits to Growth* simulation shows that increased economic growth would help alleviate poverty and starvation in the short run, but in the long run it would exacerbate all the other problems. Because more food would be available, the population would grow faster. In time, increases in income would help bring the population under control, but the same economic growth would accelerate depletion of natural resources and dramatically increase levels of pollution.

Part of the problem with the economic growth solution is that it depletes the earth's natural resources. What if, through intensified exploration, the amount of available natural resources doubled? According to *The Limits to Growth*, a rise in available resources would allow industrialization to accelerate until pollution reached dangerous levels. And even if the amount of natural resources doubled, growth would be so rapid that these reserves would be used up in a few years. Even with the more optimistic assumptions that nuclear energy will permanently satisfy the world's energy needs and that recycling programs will conserve supplies of natural resources effectively, the world's population is still doomed to a sad end. Pollution again will lead the system to collapse within a hundred years. Even population control policies that achieved zero population grown would be disastrous, according to *The Limits to Growth*. Industrial growth would accelerate as capital accumulation was facilitated by the decreased pressure of the population explosion, but the eventual depletion of nonrenewable resources would bring a sudden collapse of the economic system.[91]

There is just one problem left unattacked. Surely it would seem that pollution control can have only good results. In the simulation, pollution controls would allow industrialization levels to reach heights unattainable in a world that would otherwise have choked to death. But because people would no longer die of emphysema, cancer, lead poisoning, birth defects, and other pollution-related diseases, population growth would continue. Ultimately, arable land would be depleted, and food production would not be able to keep up with the population growth.

Is there no escape? There is, according to the authors of *The Limits to Growth*, but the path entails a drastically new and comprehensive approach to the world's problems. If the world is to avoid disaster, conservation and pollution control must be combined with a halt in economic growth. There are limits to growth, and the world is on the verge of reaching those limits. *The Limits to Growth* simulation and its proposal to limit economic growth has attracted imitators and critics since its publication. Its dire predictions were based on evidence that was questioned on a number of grounds, such as those discussed earlier in the chapter. Its value, however, was to point out the difficult balancing act that the global community must undertake if it believes that these global challenges are severe enough to warrant solutions.

The scientific debate over the severity of environmental problems and the consequences of possible solutions has affected efforts by the international community to deal with these global issues:

> Science has received particular attention as a force promoting environmental cooperation. . . . Scientists certainly do influence international negotiations, not least because scientists' methods and rules of . . . legitimacy are an alternative to strictly interest-based bargaining. That said, those methods and rules do not prevent bias and partiality in the arguments and facts scientists offer and even less prevent policy-makers from selectively using or ignoring science to support interest-based positions.[92]

The Politics of Environmental Cooperation

Despite the uncertainty of the problems, the international community has been concerned enough to put many environmental issues on the global agenda. The first major international environmental meeting, the

UN Stockholm Conference in 1972, has been followed by a number of additional efforts at environmental cooperation:

> Spurred on by the success of Stockholm, the remainder of the 1970s saw a proliferation of international environmental treaties addressing mostly conventional or "first generation" environmental issues such as air or water pollution. . . . Wildlife conservation and habitat protection also took a front seat in the 1970s. . . . As the 1980s approached, the conventional issues of air pollution gave way to . . . a "second generation" of environmental issues involving more complex and global processes inextricably connected with development issues. Many of the conventions of the 1980s and 1990s required more global consensus. Examples include the Vienna Convention on the Protection of the Ozone Layer, and the related **Montreal Protocol**. . . . Also critical during the 1980s was negotiation of the **UN Convention on the Law of the Sea,** which set out a broad constitution for the oceans including critical provisions on protecting the ocean environment. . . . The **Framework Convention on Climate Change** (1992) and the **Convention on Biological Diversity** (1992) are all further examples of the complicated and global approach now occupying much of international environmental treaty-making.[93]

Montreal Protocol
1987 treaty requiring reductions in use of CFCs and, later, almost all ozone-depleting substances.

UN Convention on the Law of the Sea   Treaty adopted in 1982 with broad rules on protecting the ocean environment.

Framework Convention on Climate Change
1992 agreement among industrialized states to work toward reduction of greenhouse emissions.

Convention on Biological Diversity
Treaty requiring national strategies for conservation of a variety of species and plants, genetic variations, and ecosystems.

Kyoto Protocol   1997 treaty that calls for industrialized countries to reduce greenhouse gas emissions.

The biodiversity and climate change agreements were concluded at the same time as the United Nations Conference on Environment and Development held in Rio de Janeiro in 1992 (often referred to as the Rio Summit or the Earth Summit). This was the most significant global meeting on the environment to date, with more than 100 heads of state in attendance and more than 1,000 representatives of nongovernmental organizations. The conference resulted in a nonbinding agreement based on very broad and complex negotiations. The agreement covered every environmental issue, as well as development, and included many domestic social and economic policy changes. The Rio Summit also created norms and expectations about environmental cooperation.[94]

Following the summit in Rio, the Framework Convention on Climate Change led to intense negotiations that ultimately resulted in the 1997 **Kyoto Protocol,** which calls for industrialized countries to reduce their greenhouse gas emissions by at least 5 percent by 2012. Some countries are targeted to reduce their emissions by as much as 8 percent. One of the controversial aspects of the protocol concerns the allowance of emission credits. Some states such as Russia and the developing world were not obliged to reduce emissions and could sell their credits to countries that were obliged to reduce emissions. The fact that developing states, which will contribute to greenhouse emissions in the near future as they industrialize, were not required to curb emissions led the United States (one of the largest greenhouse gas producers) to announce in 2001 that it would refuse to ratify the Kyoto Protocol. The protocol went into effect in February 2005 when the states that account for 55 percent of the carbon emissions for the top-emitting group of states ratified the treaty.

> The future of the climate change regime still hangs in the balance. Nevertheless, what was once criticized by many to be void of any potential for success has shown the world that progress indeed remains possible. . . . Although major issues remain, the continued injection of science into the policymaking process, along with necessary financial and technical assistance to the developing countries, may help the various veto coalitions to make the necessary compromises for a strong climate change regime in the future.[95]

The United States is the only industrialized country not participating in the agreement. Although President Obama is supportive of some emission controls and a new climate control international treaty, he faces significant domestic opposition.[96] The Policy Choices box outlines some of the arguments for and against the Kyoto Protocol and other international efforts to address climate change.

The Environment as Collective Goods and Common Pools

tragedy of the commons Metaphor used to describe the difficulty of achieving cooperation on natural resources that would have long-term benefits for all, given the short-term benefits of resource exploitation to individuals.

These efforts at environmental cooperation have not been easy, and many believe that most have largely failed to address some of the most challenging global environmental issues. Why this is so is best illustrated by a metaphor known as the **tragedy of the commons.** Garrett Hardin, a human ecologist, first used the phrase *tragedy of the commons* in 1968 to describe overgrazing in nineteenth-century English villages. As Hardin explains, the tragedy of the commons develops when there is a pasture in a community open to all, and each herder must decide whether to add one more animal to his or her herd of cattle. All the gain from a decision to do so will go to that herder, but the cost of that decision, overgrazing on the pasture, is shared by all the herders. Because of this, each herder is tempted to add to his or her herd. If each herder makes that decision, which is rational on the individual level, collectively they will ruin the pasture for everybody by overgrazing.[97]

Similarly, all states would be better off if, for example, pollution-creating activities were curbed. But each state individually can manufacture a product in a manner unrestricted by expensive pollution controls and thus put the product on the international market at a low price. All the profits from the sales of that product will go to the polluting state, but the cost—the increasingly polluted atmosphere—is shared by all. Because each country can see a clear profit for itself from manufacturing a product without pollution controls, all states are tempted, rationally, to take steps that collectively will ruin the atmosphere for the entire globe. Although

POLICY CHOICES

Supporting the Kyoto Protocol

ISSUE: Signed in December 1997, the Kyoto Protocol to the Framework Convention on Climate Change called for a worldwide reduction of emissions of carbon-based gases by an average 5.2 percent below 1990 levels by 2012, although different countries adopted different targets. Although many countries have ratified the protocol, there has been much internal debate about ratification in many countries, and some countries, including countries responsible for large emissions, have not ratified the Kyoto Protocol and efforts to create a new climate change treaty face many obstacles. The debate illustrates the difficulties in environmental cooperation.

Option #1: All countries should support and ratify the Kyoto Protocol.

Arguments: (a) Emissions of carbon-based gases are contributing to global warming, with disastrous consequences for the future. (b) It is necessary for all major industrialized states to support the protocol, especially large states like the United States, because they are responsible for the majority of emissions. (c) Not supporting the agreement means becoming isolated on the environmental issue, which might jeopardize efforts to achieve cooperation on other issues.

Counterarguments: (a) The evidence linking carbon-based emissions to global warming and climate change has been mixed. (b) The industrialized states can still continue to produce large emissions under Kyoto, because the protocol allows for large-emissions-producing states to trade credits with low-emissions-producing states. (c) States must look out for their own interests and cooperate on an issue-by-issue basis.

Option #2: States should not support and ratify the Kyoto Protocol if it is not in their interests.

Arguments: (a) The developed world is not required to curb emissions, but some developing states, such as China and India, are currently contributing significantly to global emissions. (b) Meeting the Kyoto targets and paying the penalties if they are not met are too costly to business and the economy. (c) There are alternative ways, such as voluntary programs, that states can encourage to help solve the global warming problem.

Counterarguments: (a) It would be too costly for the developing states to join Kyoto now. It is assumed that the developing world will one day join the protocol; in the meantime, the European Union has pledged a fund to help them clean their emissions. (b) Investing now in emission-reducing technologies will make for more efficient, and profitable, economies in the future. (c) Voluntary programs do not work. Although enforcement is not possible, there must be agreed-on rules, incentives, and penalties to facilitate cooperation on an issue that is in the interest of all.

the parallels between Hardin's example of the nineteenth-century English commons and contemporary international environmental problems are clear, many caution against the conclusion that states are necessarily caught in a "tragedy":

> It is popularly believed that the actors involved in . . . [such] problems, whether individuals or governments, are trapped in an inexorable "tragedy of the commons" from which they cannot extract themselves. . . . Empirical and theoretical work on. . . . [these] situations, however, has shown that the "inexorable" nature of the problem results more from the assumptions used by theorists than from constraints that are universally present in all . . . situations.[98]

Yet the tragedy of the commons metaphor is useful in understanding some of the obstacles to environmental problems because it points out the difficulties of preserving something that is in the long-term collective interest of all, despite the short-term interest to undermine preservation.

Environmental conditions such as clean air, clean water, healthy supplies of natural resources, and a commons grazing area are similar to collective goods. Recall from Chapter 10 that all people benefit from collective goods regardless of their participation in maintaining the good. National defense, for example, is a collective good that everyone benefits from regardless of how much tax they pay to support the national defense system. Indeed, even citizens who cheat and do not pay taxes benefit from this collective good. International environmental problems are similar to collective goods, but are technically known as **common pool resources (CPRs)**, because, unlike true collective goods, they can be spoiled by one actor. Common pool resources "are afflicted by an additional problem that is not encountered in situations of public goods: use of the resource by one individual may have adverse consequences for others."[99] Both collective goods and common resources, however, face the problem of who is to provide for the good or resource.

common pool resources (CPRs) Goods that can be spoiled by one actor.

> In both types of situations, a key problem is how to induce contributions to provide benefits from as many beneficiaries as possible. The classic problem of public goods, which also afflicts CPRs, is under provision. When there are many beneficiaries, each of whose contribution is small relative to the cost of provision, the good will not be supplied in optimal quantity, unless institutional arrangements exist that induce incentives to provide it.[100]

In the international system, the problems of under-provision and adverse consequences by individual actors are compounded by the lack of an overarching authority to coordinate the maintenance and provision of collective goods. To solve some of the most important environmental problems requires the coordination of several states. But the temptation to follow short-term national interests over collective interests or even long-term national interests is often too high.

Because of the nature of these problems, the world's states are having a difficult time cooperating in a way that might effectively deal with the dangers of global warming, shrinking natural resources, and population growth. It is in individual states' interests to pollute, cut down forests, and exploit cheap resources. In some circumstances, it is in the individual world citizen's self-interest to have more children. Yet the collective result of these individual decisions can mean that everyone's welfare, including that of future generations, is compromised if today's environmental problems accumulate to threaten the carrying capacity of the earth, just as over-herding turned common pastures into desert in nineteenth-century villages.

Political Obstacles to Environmental Cooperation

In addition to the general problems of getting independent actors to contribute to collective goods, international environmental cooperation is affected by a number of existing political divisions. Perhaps the most important division complicating recent efforts is the North-South debate on environmental challenges.

> Inequitable economic relations between North and South have proven to be a crucial element of the political context of global environmental politics, as on other issues. The developing states' perceptions of the global economic structure as fundamentally inequitable often shape their policy responses to global environmental issues and their strategies for negotiating on issues as different as elephants and climate.[101]

The poorer developing countries point out that the blame for the environmental problems we are facing today lies with the past and current actions of the richer developed states. It was, after all, during the time of the North's industrialization that pollution and resource scarcity developed. Developed countries ". . . account for about 7 out of every 10 tonnes of CO_2 that have been emitted since the start of the industrial era."[102] Today, developed countries consume more than nine times as much electricity per capita as developing countries and emit over six times as much carbon dioxide per capita.[103] The United States alone consumes 35 percent of the world's resources but constitutes only 6 percent of the global population. The United Kingdom produces more carbon dioxide than Egypt, Nigeria, Pakistan, and Vietnam combined; Texas emits more than the total region of sub-Saharan Africa; and an air-conditioner in Florida produces more CO_2 emissions in one year than a person living in Afghanistan or Cambodia does in a lifetime.[104] "Moreover, the poorest people in the poorest countries—which consist of several hundred million adults and children, and include subsistence farmers, landless rural workers, and destitute and homeless people in expanding mega cities—still do not consume *any* commercial fuels or electricity directly."[105] The demand for paper and wood products from the rain forests of the world is primarily located within the North as well. Demand for coffee in the North has also resulted in coffee plantations' replacing rain forest land. "In Latin America, so many trees have been felled to create coffee plantations that migratory songbirds are losing vital winter habitat. As consumers of fully one-third of the world's coffee, Americans contribute to such environmental degradation."[106]

Thus, the South argues that much of the environmental damage is due to current and past abuses by the North so the North should bear the greatest burden, particularly the financial burden of solving environmental challenges. The North, for its part, points out that it is the developing world that accounts for the large and growing emissions of greenhouse gases.[107] China, for example, is highly dependent on coal-fired power plants for its electricity. With its growing economy, it is the fastest-growing source of carbon dioxide emissions in the world and has passed the United States as the country that emits the most carbon dioxide.[108] Because of the role that the industrializing South will play in future environmental degradation, the North argues that the South is the key to preventing future problems. The South, however, fears that environmental cooperation comes at the expense of development. For the South, the priority is to meet the short-term economic needs of the current generation. While developing countries may share concern about the future of the global commons, many are facing severe poverty, a deadly killer on a massive scale, right now. "Poverty is already a worse killer than any foreseeable environmental distress, according to the chief economist of the World Bank. Nobody should kid themselves that they are doing Bangladesh a favor when they worry about global warming."[109] For the South, then, sacrificing economic development, which the North already enjoys, is unacceptable.

Recognizing this dilemma, there has emerged a consensus in the international community that cooperation on environmental issues must take seriously the question of the South's economic development. The term **sustainable development** captures this idea. The consensus on sustainable development can be traced back to 1983 when the United Nations created a commission to study global environmental problems and possible solutions. Chaired by the prime minister of Norway, Gro Harlem Brundtland, the commission produced a report (known as the Brundtland report) in 1987 titled *Our Common Future*, which

sustainable development
Development that meets current economic needs without compromising future economic growth and environmental health.

> took an integrated approach to environment and development issues. Indeed economic development was as central to the report as were environmental issues. The Brundtland Commission did not invent the term sustainable development, but it did popularize the term and place it squarely in the center of

international policymaking. The Commission's definition of sustainable development remains the most famous definition of the term: "development that meets the needs of the present without compromising the ability of future generations to meet their own needs."[110]

While most of the international environmental community agrees that environmental cooperation must be pursued with economic development in mind, there is no consensus on how to do this and whether the emphasis should be placed on sustaining the environment or developing economies.[111]

The disagreements between the North and the South were certainly evident at the Rio Earth Summit in 1992:

> The issue of inequitable consumption patterns as a cause of global environmental degradation was elevated to a new status in international politics at the insistence of the developing countries. The issue was woven through several chapters of Agenda 21 as well as the Rio Declaration and the Statement of Forest Principles, making it a major theme of the entire conference. Industrialized countries were asked to accept responsibility to change their "unsustainable lifestyles."[112]

The developing countries failed, however, to get the wealthier countries to agree to policies aimed at changing consumption patterns or to certain debt-reduction programs that the South argued were important for economic development. The developed countries failed to get the poorer countries to agree on particular forest management policies.

Disagreements between the North and the South over responsibility issues also surfaced during the Kyoto Protocol negotiations. In this meeting,

> Brazil presented an analysis that compared the relative responsibility of Annex I (industrialized) countries and of non–Annex I (developing) countries for climate change, not just in terms of carbon dioxide emissions in a given year, but in terms of carbon dioxide concentrations because of historical emissions. It showed that the responsibility of non–Annex I countries for accumulated emissions would not equal that of Annex I countries until the middle of the 22nd century.[113]

Efforts at environmental cooperation have continued to be affected by the differences between the developing and developed states. For the 2002 World Summit on Sustainable Development, the developing states succeeded in preventing the word "environment" from even appearing in the name of the conference.[114] "At the climate change talks in Copenhagen in 2009, a group of developing states walked out of the meetings at one point, arguing that the developed countries were not doing enough to control carbon emissions." These differences, however, were not always obstacles to cooperation. The developing states, for example, signed the 1987 Montreal Protocol after a fund was established to help them switch to the more costly substitutes for CFC that would not contribute to ozone depletion.[115]

The North-South debate is not the only political division in the world complicating cooperation on environmental challenges. States that are in similar positions economically do not always agree on environmental issues. The European Union states, for example, were prepared to adopt specific targets and deadlines for conversion to renewable sources of energy at the 2002 World Summit, but the United States disagreed and successfully blocked their efforts to include targets and dates in the final program. And at the Rio Earth Summit in 1992, on many issues,

> countries were not united along development lines. Developing countries themselves were split over such issues as climate change (oil producing nations vs. small island states), fisheries (distant water fishing countries vs. coastal countries), and population growth (Catholic and Muslim countries vs. more secular countries). Industrialized countries disagreed on a number of issues, including ODA [overseas development assistance] levels (Nordic countries vs. the United States), fisheries (distant water fishing countries vs. coastal countries), hazardous and radioactive waste disposal, and the need to reduce excessive production.[116]

In general, most efforts at environmental cooperation produce divisions between those that are more affected by the problem and those that are not. On the issue of transboundary air pollution, for example,

> those states that had been the victims of . . . acid rain—notably Sweden, Finland, and Norway—took the initiative to negotiate for stringent and binding regulations on emissions of sulfur dioxide and nitrogen oxide. But the industrialized states that were net exporters of acid rain formed a veto coalition, in large part because of their reliance on coal-fired power stations, which accounted for two-thirds of all sulfur dioxide emissions.[117]

Just like other issues in international relations, the fact that states are not unitary actors and face domestic pressures at home can complicate efforts at environmental cooperation.[118] Business and environmental groups have been key domestic players in global environmental debates. Some states are quite susceptible to business interests opposed to environmental agreements. After ten years of negotiations on the Law of the Sea Treaty, for example, the United States rejected the treaty in 1982, citing its concern that the treaty rules for governing mineral resources in the deep seas were contrary to private enterprise principles. Business interests may represent themselves at international environmental meetings. At the Kyoto Summit on global warming, "the most powerful MNCs [multinational corporations] representing oil and car manufacturers worked to defeat stringent new environmental standards that might decrease carbon emissions (and thereby cut into the sales of existing fuels or cars)."[119]

The environment and business interests can also clash in free trade negotiations.[120]

> When the GATT [General Agreement on Tariffs and Trade], . . . was negotiated just after World War II, there was not mention of the word *environment*. At that time no one saw much connection between trade liberalization and environmental protection. In fact, for the next 40 years, trade and environmental policymakers pursued their respective agendas on parallel tracks that rarely, if ever, intersected. The wake-up call for environmentalists was the U.S. ban on tuna from Mexico and Venezuela on the ground that their fleets did not meet U.S. standards for minimizing dolphin kills in tuna fishing [as required by the 1972 **Marine Mammal Protection Act**]. In 1991 the GATT declared that the U.S. ban was illegal under the rules of international trade. U.S. environmentalists were alarmed that a national environmental law could be overturned by the GATT and began to take seriously the environmental implications of trade.[121]

Marine Mammal Protection Act U.S. law that prohibits the sale of tuna if it is not caught with "dolphin-safe" fishing methods.

Environmental values clashed with free trade principles again in the negotiation of the North American Free Trade Agreement (NAFTA) in 1992. Environmentalists worried that less strict environmental laws in Mexico combined with free trade would mean that U.S. companies would relocate to Mexico, where they could pollute without penalty, creating more environmental damage. A coalition of consumers, labor groups, and environmentalists worked to make NAFTA the first trade agreement to have supplemental agreements on environmental issues.[122] While some areas of the North American environment have seemed to improve due to NAFTA-related agreements, other areas seem to be deteriorating, and the debate between environmentalists and free traders continues as NAFTA may expand into a larger Free Trade Area of the Americas (see Chapter 12).[123]

Since its creation in 1995, the World Trade Organization (WTO) has heard a number of cases of environmentalists versus free traders. These cases included issues such as U.S. laws requiring fuel imports to meet "clean" gasoline standards and imported shrimp to be caught by vessels that do not endanger sea turtles. The United States and the European Union (EU) have also been involved in a WTO dispute over U.S. use of genetically modified organisms (GMOs) in agriculture. The EU, which views GMOs in food as unsafe, placed a moratorium on GMO imports from 1999 to 2004, but the WTO recently ruled that this ban violated WTO free trade laws. Although those who advocate more liberal trade now have to contend with environmental challenges, it is unclear which value has the advantage. It is true that the WTO treaty recognized the importance of securing "the optimal use of the world's resources in accordance with the objective of sustainable development."[124] On the other hand, the Framework Convention on Climate Change specifies that cooperative efforts on global warming should abide by GATT/WTO trade principles.[125]

Value differences have also affected global cooperation on environmental issues. Population growth is one example. Although the United States took the lead in the 1960s in funding family planning programs in the developing world, funding for international population programs has been controversial. As discussed in Chapter 9, some domestic groups succeeded in getting Congress to cut off funding for any organization involved in abortion activities. The Clinton administration reinstated the funding, amid considerable controversy, the subsequent Bush administration returned to the policy of withholding money from the United Nations Population Fund, and the Obama administration reinstated the funding once again.[126] There has also been a value clash over particular countries' population control programs. "China's one-child policy—the toughest population-control policy in the world—has been especially criticized for allegedly forcing pregnant women who already have a child to have abortions, even late in pregnancy."[127]

The relationship between population growth and the status of women has also generated value conflicts in global efforts to curb population growth. At the 1994 World Population Conference in Egypt, women's rights groups pushed for the funding of programs to educate girls and women generally and to promote women's equality, arguing that more economic and political freedom is the key to decreasing birthrates in the developing countries. Other groups, including the Catholic Church and some Islamic countries, allied to block some of these population proposals. The Policy Choices box outlines some of the issues in the debate on population policy.

Despite the numerous obstacles, cooperation on environmental challenges is possible. Because of the Montreal Protocol, for example, the total consumption of CFCs has dropped dramatically. "The Montreal Protocol is the best example so far of a regime that has been continually strengthened in response to new scientific evidence and technological innovations."[128]

Theoretical Perspectives on Environmental Cooperation

The major theoretical perspectives (see Chapter 1) for understanding global politics can shed light on international environmental cooperation, even though it is a fairly new area in world politics. In looking at the prospects for environmental cooperation, realism, would expect cooperation to be very difficult, given states' self-interested motivations to guard their power and autonomy.[129] Furthermore, environmental issues constitute "low politics" and do not demand the attention of states compared to "high politics," such as national defense.[130] When cooperation does occur, realism would expect international agreements to reflect the interests of the most powerful states strongly. On the issue of climate change, for example, realists would point out the influence of the United States. In the negotiations on the Framework Convention on Climate Change, "the United States opposed the others (particularly a number of European countries) that wanted a timetable for greenhouse gas emission reductions. Largely because of the U.S. position, the members of the international community could only agree to the provision that industrialized countries would try to ensure that their greenhouse gas emissions in the year 2000 were no higher than they were in 1990."[131]

While not denying that state interests are important, liberalism, as a theoretical perspective, would also highlight the importance of nonstate and substate actors in global environmental politics. These actors include the World Wildlife Fund, which was established in 1961 with the aim of protecting endangered species and habitats. "It is the largest private NGO devoted to conservation with a $40 million annual budget and over 5 million members in 28 different countries. The WWF has over 800 projects underway and works with 7,000 NGOs in developing countries to help preserve wildlife and educate people."[132] Perhaps the most famous nonstate environmental group is **Greenpeace.** "Greenpeace's goal is to influence national and international environmental legislation the world over even if it means practicing civil disobedience on the high seas."[133] In May

Greenpeace NGO that seeks to influence national and international environmental policy.

A Greenpeace ship blocks the entrance to a British military supply port in January 2003, to protest against the approaching war with Iraq. Greenpeace actively works against the negative effects to the environment that can result from, for example, dumping on the high seas, nuclear testing, and military interventions.

(AFP/Getty Images)

POLICY CHOICES

Addressing Population Growth

ISSUE: Given the seemingly obvious connection between more and more people on the planet and a wide variety of environmental problems—such as rain forest depletion, global warming, and hunger—it may be surprising to note that not everyone agrees that curbing population growth is a good policy. Still, despite compelling objections, most of the world's most populous countries are engaged in one or another form of population control.

Option #1: Global efforts to reduce population growth should be redoubled, and effective family planning programs should be supported.

Arguments: (a) Overpopulation is at the root of many serious environmental problems, as more and more people create greater and greater demands on the planet. (b) Economic success depends on creating sustainable growth within countries. Poor countries will remain poor as long as their populations continue to grow excessively. (c) Without education about family planning, people will naturally continue to procreate, thereby adding to the population problem.

Counterarguments: (a) Environmental destruction is related to excessive consumption associated with global capitalism, not excessive population. If wealthy countries would scale back their luxurious lifestyles, global population could safely exceed current projections. (b) Historically, population growth has frequently occurred alongside or in advance of economic progress. People should be viewed as a resource, not a burden. (c) Individuals' right to procreate should not be threatened for political convenience. People are not cattle, and implementing population control policies fundamentally degrades people who naturally pursue a most basic human desire.

Option #2: The international community should turn its attention to other serious global problems, rather than continuing to support policies aimed at reducing population growth.

Arguments: (a) Raising overpopulation fears opens the door for prejudicial reactions toward the poor and likely lessens political will to address catastrophic illnesses such as AIDS. (b) People respond to economic factors in their decisions to have children. Countries should focus on raising standards of living, and population growth will then take care of itself. (c) Population pressures are correctly considered local problems and should be dealt with only by individual states rather than the international community.

Counterarguments: (a) Programs aimed at limiting population growth often have other benefits, such as promoting the use of condoms and educating and empowering women. (b) Without government intervention, people will continue to make the decision to have more children based on cultural factors and religious beliefs. (c) Excessive populations within states all too often spill over to other states in the form of immigrants, refugees, and regional instability, thus turning a local problem into a global one.

2002, for example, a Greenpeace boat rammed into France's America's Cup yacht to protest the team's sponsor, a nuclear power company owned by the French government. This was just one incident in Greenpeace's history with France.[134] In 1985, the Greenpeace ship *Rainbow Warrior* was sunk in an assault by French special forces, apparently in order to prevent it from protesting French nuclear testing.

The large number of NGOs at the 1992 Rio Summit is further evidence that the actors emphasized in the liberal theoretical perspective are shaping environmental cooperation. On the global warming issue specifically,

> . . . [W]hile the FCCC [Framework Convention on Climate Change] is a creature of states, and the international climate regime is dominated by governments, as a formal matter, nonstate actors are encouraged and enabled to participate in its operation and evolution. In practice, NGOs are now a pervasive presence.[135]

Liberalism would also focus on the importance of international organizations as actors that facilitate and provide incentives for cooperation. On the topic of climate change, for example, international organizations have certainly been instrumental as regular multilateral meetings, requirements to publish reports, and ongoing monitoring and assessment have facilitated implementation of the FCCC.[136] Generally, international institutions can affect environmental cooperation in three key ways:

(1) They can contribute to more appropriate agendas, reflecting the convergence of political and technical consensus about the nature of environmental threats;

(2) They can contribute to more comprehensive and specific international policies, agreed upon through a political process whose core is intergovernmental bargaining; and

(3) They can contribute to national policy responses which directly control sources of environmental degradation.[137]

Beyond specific organizations, liberals point to the emergence of international regimes as focal points for environmental cooperation. As discussed in Chapter 9, international regimes are implicit or explicit rules and norms that govern actors' behaviors. Not all international regimes all equally effective. The regime to govern Antarctica, for example, has been effective at keeping the region open for scientific research and other agreed-on activities. This can be contrasted with many of the attempted international fisheries regimes, which have generally not achieved their goal of preventing overfishing.[138] It appears that regimes that, among other things, address domestic opposition forces within states are more likely to be effective at securing environmental cooperation.[139]

The neo-Marxist perspective on global environmental politics would stress the structure of economic capital, particularly energy capital, in the world and its effects on cooperation attempts.[140] On the greenhouse issue, for example, neo-Marxists would point to the structure of oil capital and the oil companies' power to thwart cooperation that would harm their interests.

> The reaction of many of the companies involved in fossil fuel production use (particularly coal and oil) has been as would be expected by a historical materialism [neo-Marxist] analysis. Consider, for example, the Global Climate Coalition—a grouping of (primarily) U.S. industry interests that has been working hard to discredit the international scientific consensus on climate change and to highlight the economic costs of reductions.[141]

Neo-Marxist perspectives, particularly dependency theory, would also highlight the many disagreements between the North and the South over environmental issues:

> Although many officials of developing countries . . . recognize the seriousness of local and global environmental degradation for their own economic future, many of them regard environmental regimes for ozone and climate, for example, as a means by which industrialized countries will maintain their control over resources and technology or even gain control over resources now located in the South. One developing-country delegate to the second meeting of the parties to the Montreal Protocol in 1990 declared that for "some countries," the protocol was a "pretext" to place new obstacles in the way of efforts by developing countries to develop their economies.[142]

ecoimperialism
Perspective that sees the North's position on environmental issues as indirect control the South.

From this perspective, the North's positions on environmental issues are simply instances of "**ecoimperialism**."[143]

Constructivist perspectives on international politics would emphasize the importance of norms and discourse that have been constructed on environmental cooperation.[144] They would also point out the differences in the understandings of environment:

> This insight helps explain much about global environmental politics. One of the consistent mishaps in international environmental affairs is the assumption that all parties concerned with climate change, biological diversity, and so forth share the same understanding of the problem. To take the most obvious example: many northern states and nongovernmental organizations (NGOs) work on behalf of wilderness preservation and biological diversity in the developing world. Yet, many in the developing world argue that one person's wilderness is another person's home, and that what is a valued endangered species to some is

dinner, a threat, or potential income to another. . . . "Nature," as such, is not a single realm with a universalized meaning, but an ideational canvas on which one project's one's sensibilities, cultural attributes, economic conditions, and social necessities.[145]

Feminist perspectives would also point out the gendered meanings of nature and the environment. Some feminists argue that women and women's views have a special connection to environmental issues. Both women and the natural environment, for example, fall prey to domination on a global level through the production and consumption patterns created and maintained by the international market. The ramifications of the international economic system for the natural environment are most readily apparent in underdeveloped regions and, by extension, in the lives of the rural people who depend on the natural world for their survival. Because the daily tasks of providing for basic needs usually fall to women in these communities, women are the most acutely aware of the results of environmental destruction. The actions these women have taken to reclaim the natural environment as their home have grown into an international **ecofeminist movement**.[146] Feminist activists have been an important part of environmental politics, particularly on issues of population and the importance of women's status in changing population dynamics.

ecofeminist movement Group with perspective that links oppression of women with environmental abuse.

SUMMARY

- The global community can be analyzed as an integrated entity rather than simply a group of interrelated but separate states. Global environmental problems lend themselves to such analyses because the hole in the ozone layer, for example, does not respect international boundaries. Since the 1970s, states have increasingly recognized the importance of environmental issues and have placed global environmental cooperation on the international political agenda.

- Important environmental challenges include pollution, damage to the ozone layer, deforestation, global warming, availability of natural resources and food supplies, and overpopulation. An integrated analysis of such global problems as the population explosion, famine, depletion of natural resources, global warming, and threats to the ozone layer in the upper atmosphere reveals that ostensible solutions to any one of those problems might unexpectedly make related problems even more serious. The role of economic development and industrialization in contributing to environmental problems has been part of the debate on the global environment.

- Analysts of environmental issues tend either to be very pessimistic about the future of the global community or optimistic that admittedly serious problems can be dealt with. Pessimistic predictions from the 1960s and the 1970s about the population explosion, food shortages, and depletion of energy resources, for example, have proved premature at best. And economic growth, which tends to be distrusted by many pessimistic analysts, can create resources to devote to the solution of global environmental problems.

● Although states, nongovernmental groups, and international organizations have become concerned about many environmental issues, cooperation on solutions to these issues has proved difficult, partly because collective action requires states to take action that is not necessarily in their short-term individual interests. Cooperation is also complicated by divisions between states in the North and states in the South over what economic development is sustainable, as well as by conflicts between environmental issues and free trade, business interests, and values related to reproduction.

● Despite these hurdles, there have been numerous efforts in recent years to deal with environmental problems. These include the Montreal Protocol on chlorofluorocarbons, the Framework Convention on Climate Change and the Kyoto Protocol, and the Convention on Biological Diversity.

● Theoretical perspectives stress different factors for understanding global environmental cooperation. Realism focuses on the importance of large states that, seeking to protect their sovereignty and other interests, can effectively block global initiatives on the environment, while liberalism stresses the significance of international and nongovernmental organizations in environmental negotiations. Neo-Marxists point to the structure of energy capital in the world and how it affects attempts at cooperation. Constructivist and feminist perspectives look at the hidden meaning in discourse and understandings about the environment.

KEY TERMS

Stockholm Conference   466
global warming   468
population momentum   471
fertility rate   472
replacement level   473
demographic transition
   theory   473
Montreal Protocol   485
UN Convention on the Law of
   the Sea   485
Framework Convention on
   Climate Change   485

Convention on Biological
   Diversity   485
Kyoto Protocol   485
tragedy of the commons   486
common pool resources
   (CPRs)   488
sustainable development   490
Marine Mammal Protection
   Act   493
Greenpeace   495
ecoimperialism   498
ecofeminist movement   499

CHAPTER 14

Globalization: Contemporary Dynamics and the Future of World Politics

What Is Globalization?
- Economic Globalization
- Political Globalization
- Cultural Globalization
- Factors behind Globalization

A Historical Perspective on Globalization: How New Is It?
- Historical Roots
- Distinctive Characteristics of Contemporary Globalization

Globalization and Its Discontents
- Unequal Globalization
- Nationalism as a Countertrend
- Other Sources of Opposition to Globalization

Globalization and the State: The Future of World Politics
- "The State Is Dead"
- "Long Live the State"
- Understanding the Future of Globalization and the State

Summary

Key Terms

This final chapter discusses a dynamic that is perhaps the central characteristic of global politics in contemporary times. Globalization arguably is the most important process affecting relations between states, as well as nonstate actors, today. Many of the previous chapters have already raised some of the topics that are critical to a discussion of globalization. The growing number and significance of multinational, nongovernmental, and terrorist organizations and the implications for the power and autonomy of states (Chapter 4); the changing role of conflict in the international system (Chapter 7); the growing significance of international organizations, law, and norms in the post–Cold War system (Chapter 9); the rise and consequences of interdependence and liberalization in the international political economy (Chapter 10); the spread of capitalism and regional integration (Chapters 11 and 12); and the global nature of and global solutions to environmental problems (Chapter 13) are all linked to the globalization process. Any discussion of globalization raises the question of how new this process really is, and if it is occurring at all. This question pushes us to assess globalization in historical and theoretical perspective (Chapters 1, 2, and 3).

This chapter brings together these themes related to globalization by first defining it, examining the evidence for economic, political, and cultural globalization, and reviewing the factors, such as technology, behind it. The chapter then assesses the novelty and scope of globalization and its political opponents and contrary trends. We end with a look at the effects of globalization on states and the consequences for future ways in which global politics might operate and be understood.

What Is Globalization?

Globalization is one of the most used, and perhaps overused, terms to describe world politics today:

> Indeed, globalization is in danger of becoming, if it has not already become, the cliché of our times. . . . Clichés, nevertheless, often capture elements of the lived experience of an epoch. In this respect, globalization reflects a widespread perception that the world is rapidly being molded into a shared social space by economic and technological forces and that developments in one region of the world can have profound consequences for . . . individuals or communities on the other side of the globe.[1]

Globalization is similar to *interdependence*, and the two terms are often used interchangeably. Recall from Chapter 1 that according to the theoretical perspective of liberalism, *interdependence* means that what happens inside one state can have significant effects on what happens inside another state and that there has been a rise in the significance of nonstate and substate actors, which connect states in a network of relations.

While the fortunes of states may have always been connected, or interdependent, liberalism proposes that the interdependence between states and other actors reached an unprecedented level by the 1970s. This is one reason, as we will discuss following, that some say the current globalization is not really new, that it is merely a continuation of the trends apparent in the 1970s.

Although the concepts of globalization and interdependence are similar, globalization places more emphasis on the growing similarity of people, places, and things in a "borderless world."[2] Economies, for example, are not simply more connected; the distinctions between them are becoming less meaningful. Definitions of globalization typically stress the "increase in interconnections, or interdependence, a rise in transnational flows [like the preceding definition of interdependence], *and* an intensification of processes such that the world is in some respects, becoming a single place."[3] Globalization is then the process of reaching that single place, a global village. There is evidence for this global homogenization process, which makes people, places, and things around the world more similar in many interrelated areas. The most important arenas for globalization are economic, political, and cultural.

Economic Globalization

It is in the economic sphere that we most think of and refer to globalization. In a globalized economy, borders and distance do not hinder economic transactions.[4] In many ways, a global marketplace has developed. If **economic globalization** trends continue, the world will presumably approach a single economy.

economic globalization
Economic integration approaching a single world economy.

With respect to world trade, for example, "today all countries trade internationally and, with the odd exception like North Korea, they trade significant proportions of their national income."[5] Indeed, the percentage of the world's GDP that is traded increased from 42 percent in 1980 to 62 percent by 2007.[6] One component of the rise in world trade is trade in services, as compared to trade in goods. "Today, a global marketplace is developing for retail sales as well as manufacturing. Law, advertising, business consulting, and financial and other services are also marketed internationally."[7] As a result, it is difficult to find anything—goods or services—to buy that did not originate somewhere else. Starbucks coffee shops are everywhere, as are McDonald's restaurants. Indeed, Western products, including Kinko's, Gerber, Coca-Cola, Starbucks, Kentucky Fried Chicken, Haagen-Dazs, and Dunkin' Donuts, are readily available in China. McDonald's has more than 900 restaurants, with 60,000 employees in China, and in a recent survey, almost half of Chinese children believed that McDonald's was a Chinese company.[8]

As seen here in India, mixture of traditional dress and high technology is a common sight in today's globalized world.

(Jami Tarris/Getty Images)

Another major aspect of economic globalization concerns international financial flows:

> Globalization often implies abandoning national ties and embracing supranational alliances. In international finance, this is more than a buzzword; it is a reality. . . . Nationality simply means less than it did even a year ago. Global financial products are accessible in national markets and national investors can operate in global markets. Investment banks used to split up their analyst teams by country to cover a national market; now they tend to do it by industrial sector across all major countries.[9]

The international banking market rose to 48 percent of world output in 2006, as compared to 10 percent in 1980.[10] As noted in Chapter 4, foreign direct investment has reached unprecedented levels. World foreign exchange levels have skyrocketed as well.[11] Indeed,

> there are few more pervasive images of globalization than men and women at their trading desks in the City of London or Wall Street frantically buying and selling currencies and assets from around the globe at the push of a button. Although heavily concentrated in the three main centres of London, Tokyo, and New York, world foreign exchange trading averages a staggering $1,490 billion every working day. In addition billions of dollars of financial assets are traded daily across the globe. . . . The development of new financial instruments, the deregulation of national financial markets

and the growth of international banks and other financial institutions have created a functioning global financial system.[12]

The recent world financial crises (as discussed in Chapter 10) showed the consequences of financial globalization. Economies are more vulnerable than ever before as foreign exchanges of currencies, which can now be executed on a twenty-four-hour basis, cause the value of many currencies to plummet overnight and the internationalization of banking and financial assets mean that problems in one economy undermine confidence in the entire system.

The primary actors facilitating economic globalization are multinational corporations (MNCs), increasingly referred to as global corporations. McDonald's, for example, has restaurants in more than 119 countries.[13] As discussed in Chapter 4, these businesses are more global, more numerous, and bigger than ever before. Accounting for most of world trade, particularly in technology and private research and development,

> the operations of MNCs are central to processes of economic globalization. They play a significant role in the globalization of trade, finance, technology and (through output and media ownership) culture, as well as in the diffusion of military technology. But MNCs are implicated most centrally in the internationalization of production and services activity; they can be conceived as stretching business across regions and continents.[14]

Alongside the legitimate global marketplace, an illegal global market has been growing as well, contributing to economic globalization.[15] "The forces shaping the legitimate global economy are also nourishing globally integrated crime.... Huge increases in the volume of goods and people crossing borders and competitive pressures to speed the flow of trade by easing inspections and reducing paperwork make it easier to hide contraband."[16] Although estimates of international crime are not completely reliable, many believe that international crime is a $1 trillion a year business, an amount equal to about 4 percent of the total international economy. Half of this is thought to be in narcotics trade.[17]

Economic interdependence, in terms of trade and finance, has certainly been present among the wealthy countries of the North, integrated together after World War II in the Bretton Woods system (as discussed in Chapter 10). What makes current economic dynamics global is the spread of these practices to most of the rest of the world. The fall of the Communist bloc and the change in leadership and economic policies in China led to linkages between these countries and the West and their incorporation into the global trading and financial systems.

Linkages between the North and South are growing as well. One economist argues that "the most notable features of the new world economy are the increasing links between the high- and low-income countries.... The great novelty of the current era is the extent to which the poorer nations of the world have been incorporated in the global system of trade, finance, and production as partners and market participants rather than colonial dependencies."[18] In terms of trade, most countries by 1990 had a trading relationship with most of the other countries in the world.[19] While trade between the developed and developing states still dominants the developing states' economies, trade between developing economies has risen over the last several decades.[20]

International financial flows are more global today as well, incorporating the transition economies of the former Communist bloc and the developing countries. By the 1990s, international investors were increasingly interested in emerging markets (see Chapter 10). As a result, investment companies' portfolio allocations became increasingly global in coverage.[21] Net private capital flows to developing countries jumped from $208 billion in 2003 to $961 billion in 2007.[22]

Multinational corporations are also found in new locations:

> All regions of the globe, to a greater or lesser extent, are both the home of and host to MNCs or their foreign affiliates. But what is striking is the scale of MNC activity within, and from the developing countries. . . . In the late 1980s developing countries were home to some 3,800 indigenous MNCs; by the mid-1990s . . . this had more than doubled. This is an indication of the expanding reach of global production and distribution systems.[23]

Incorporation of the developing and transition economies into the world economic system occurred with these countries' liberalization (diminishing government restrictions) of their own economies (see Chapters 10 and 11). Since the end of the Cold War, most countries liberalized their foreign investment regulations and actively encouraged inward investment. Indeed, from 1992 to 2001, 95 percent of adjustments that states made to their trade policies were in the direction of liberalization.[24] In this way, the world has witnessed a homogenization of economies. Rather than the mix of market economies, planned economies, and hybrid economies that characterized the Cold War period, most economies moved in the direction of liberal market economies, more similar to the economies of the wealthy North. This homogenization in terms of liberalization was institutionalized on a global scale. The institutions of the Bretton Woods system, such as the World Bank and the International Monetary Fund (IMF), now incorporate more countries around the world. Most important, the formalization of the General Agreement on Tariffs and Trade (GATT) principles into the World Trade Organization (WTO) and the expansion of WTO (discussed in Chapter 10) to include most of the countries of the world (153 of the approximately 193 countries by mid-2009) have institutionalized a global trading regime. And as discussed in Chapter 12, even the increasing regionalization of the world economy may work in tandem with the globalization of economic relations.

Political Globalization

political globalization
Extension of political power and activity across state boundaries.

International institutions such as the WTO and the IMF are contributing to another form of globalization: **political globalization**—"the stretching of political relations across space and time; the extension of political power and political activity across the boundaries of the modern nationstate."[25] It is characterized by the rise in number and significance of international and regional organizations and nonstate transnational actors.[26] The transnational networks of international organizations and nongovernmental organizations that play political roles arguably compose a new system of **global governance**.[27]

global governance
Multiple, interconnecting spheres of political authority beyond sovereign states.

As discussed in Chapter 9, the United Nations has become more active since the end of the Cold War and has taken on more roles, such as peacemaking and humanitarian intervention, without the consent of sovereign states. Although far from a world government, the United Nations is clearly acting as a global governing system: providing a forum for debate, codifying developing norms, and at times enforcing norms through its executive body, the Security Council. More recently, the United Nations helped to create the International Criminal Court (ICC) to deal with cases of genocide, crimes against humanity, and war crimes (see Chapter 9). The ICC began functioning on a permanent basis in July 2002 and represents the trend toward political globalization. The number of recent multilateral international agreements, often negotiated in the UN framework, to deal with global challenges such as environmental threats (see Chapter 13) is also contributing to the globalization of issues as states recognize that certain problems are transnational and require cooperation across state boundaries. Yet global governance is

> not only the formal institutions and organizations through which the rules and norms governing world order are (or are not) made and sustained—the institutions of state, intergovernmental cooperation and so on—but also all those organizations and pressure groups—from MNCs, transnational social movements to the plethora of non-governmental organizations—which pursue goals and objectives which have a bearing on transnational rule and authority systems. . . . Clearly, the United Nations system, the World Trade Organization, and the array of activities of national governments are among the central components of global governance, but they are by no means the only components.[28]

As seen in Chapter 4, the growth of NGOs and their capacity to influence world politics are striking characteristics of today's global system. Not only do they serve as pressure groups, but they also are performing a variety of political functions that states have failed to provide or have handed over to NGOs. As such, they are increasingly important participants in global governance.

Along with the United Nations, NGOs influence the norms and regimes that are becoming increasingly global. As discussed in Chapter 9, norms regarding women's rights and human rights, for example, can have powerful effects on states' behavior, and a number of norms have reached almost global acceptance and are becoming codified in international law. Indeed,

> changes in international law have placed individuals, governments and non-governmental organizations under new systems of legal regulation. . . . One significant area in this regard is human rights law and human rights regimes. "The defence of human dignity knows no boundaries," observes Emilio Mignone, an Argentinean human rights campaigner. . . . This statement captures important elements of the international human rights regime as a global political and legal framework for promoting rights.[29]

Another emerging global norm is democracy. As we saw in Chapter 9, there is greater acceptance today that democratic governance is a legal right. The growing democratization of the world is an additional form of political globalization. Countries are becoming more similar as democracy as a form of government has spread to more parts of the globe (see Chapter 3). This homogenization of politics has meant that by the 1990s, most of the people in the world lived in systems that could be characterized as "free" or "partly free."[30] This development has been referred to as the "globalization of democracy."[31]

Cultural Globalization

cultural globalization
Worldwide spread of similar norms, values, and practices.

The spread of democracy as a political system is associated with the spread of democratic values that is part of **cultural globalization.** Culture involves values, norms, traditions, and practices, and many see a homogenization of what people do, think, and value around the world. People are buying the same products, listening to the same music, playing the same video games, eating the same food, and watching the same television programs.

> Few expressions of globalization are so visible, widespread and pervasive as the worldwide proliferation of internationally traded consumer brands [such as Coca-Cola], the global ascendancy of popular cultural icons [such as Madonna] and artifacts [such as Harry Potter books], and the simultaneous communication of events by satellite broadcasts [for example, by CNN] to hundreds of millions of people at a time on all continents.[32]

Cultural globalization means that norms, practices, symbols, and values from one culture have spread globally. Cees Hamelink, in his book,

Cultural Autonomy in Global Communications, records these "experiences of the international scene":

> In a Mexican village the traditional ritual dance precedes a soccer match, but the performance features a gigantic Coca-Cola bottle.
>
> In Singapore, a band dressed in traditional Malay costume offers a heart-breaking imitation of Fats Domino.
>
> In Saudi Arabia, the television station performs only one cultural function—the call for the Moslem prayer. Five times a day, North American cops and robbers yield to the traditional muezzin.
>
> In its gigantic advertising campaign, IBM assures Navajo Indians that their cultural identity can be effectively protected if they use IBM typewriters equipped with the Navajo alphabet.[33]

The spread of Western culture to Asia, particularly China, has been rapid. "Until the late 1970s and early 1980s," for example, "most people paid little attention to their calendar birth date if they remembered it at all. McDonald's and its rivals now promote the birthday party—complete with cake, candles, and silly hats—in television advertising aimed directly at kids," and by all indications, it is working.[34] Similarly, most Chinese people never drank coffee until Starbucks opened in China. Now there are approximately 700 Starbucks stores in China.

Popular culture is perhaps the most pervasive aspect of cultural globalization. "The globalization of the music industry," for example,

> has . . . taken a number of forms. First it has involved the creation of transnational corporations producing and marketing records. Second, it has involved the import and export of musical products and the penetration of national markets by foreign artists and music. Third, it has in part been based on a broader transfer of styles and images that are largely rooted in American youth culture and black cultures.[35]

The film industry has experienced globalization as well, with U.S., Indian, French, Italian, and British films attracting audiences all over the world. The share of box office receipts that come from imported films (usually from the United States) was high by 1990 in many countries—over 60 percent in France and Japan, 80 percent in Italy, and over 90 percent in the United Kingdom and Sweden.[36] The story for television is similar. *Sesame Street* is broadcast in more than 100 countries, and 84 million people worldwide watch *CSI: Miami* each week. CNN is another example of the homogenization of television programming. CNN is broadcast in more than 200 countries and has become an important news source for a significant number of people, including leaders.

Cultural globalization also has its linguistic form.

We can apply the idea of globalization to language in a number of ways. The first and most obvious is the diffusion of any one individual language across the globe. The second sense in which languages or language capacities have been globalized is through the diffusion of bilingualism or multilingualism, easing the transmission of cultural products and ideas. Although there are over 5,000 languages in the contemporary world and many more dialects and regional variations, . . . ten to twelve languages [such as Japanese, German, Arabic, Russian, French, and Chinese] now account for the first language of over 60 percent of the world's population. . . . But it is English that stands at the very centre of the global language system. It has become the lingua franca par excellence. . . . It has become the central language of international communication in business, politics, administration, science and academia as well as being the dominate language of globalized advertising and popular culture.[37]

English is the language used for international computing and international safety procedures as well.

migration
Movement of people across countries.

Cultural globalization is occurring at the personal level too, as more and more people have moved to other countries. **Migration** patterns have become global, with almost every state in the world exporting emigrants or importing immigrants. Immigration from the former Soviet Union and Eastern Europe, sealed off during the Cold War, became part of the global migratory flow once again by the 1990s.[38] In addition to migration, cultures come into contact with one another when **refugees** cross borders. A refugee is a person who is outside his or her country of nationality and cannot return owing to a well-founded fear of persecution because of race, religion, nationality, political opinion or membership of a particular social group.[39]

refugees
Persons who have left their home countries to flee political persecution or conflict conditions.

People fleeing war conditions are also considered refugees. There were more than 11 million refugees in 2009, a population bigger than some states, and up from 8.4 million in 1980.[40]

As a result, many states have a large "foreign" population as a result of heavy levels of migration and refugee flows, and once-distinct cultures are arguably giving way to a more shared global experience. Worldwide tourism, "which generates jobs, offers foreign exchange, and shapes mental images of peoples and places,"[41] is also affecting cultural globalization and is on the rise. In the past two decades, for example, the number of people who traveled internationally more than doubled, from 287 million a year to 595 million a year.[42]

One aspect of globalization is the extent to which it is dominated by the United States. How much, in other words, is globalization a process of mutual homogenization, and how much is it simply Americanization? The Americanization of the world can be seen in economic globalization, because U.S.-based MNCs and products dominate the global marketplace, and in political globalization, because the United States is a major player in international institutions and the development of global norms. But it is in the cultural globalization area that charges of Americanization, and even **cultural imperialism,** are most debated. Clearly, the United States dominates cultural globalization in all aspects, from the global music industry (Madonna and Michael Jackson) to food (McDonald's and Kentucky Fried Chicken) to films (Disney) and television (CNN) and the global predominance of the English language. Yet are Americans and American culture untouched by cultural globalization? Arguably they are not. "Foreign" food—sushi, Thai, Ethiopian—is more popular than ever before in the United States, and not just in major cities. And "according to the Italian culinary magazine *Gambero Rosso*, there are about twice as many reasonably authentic Italian restaurants *outside of Italy* as there are McDonald's restaurants *in all of the world*, including the United States."[43] WorldBeat music is quite popular in the United States, and two recent crazes in American youth culture were also imports: Harry Potter from Great Britain and Pokémon from Japan. Moreover, recent trends in television watching around the globe show a decline in the popularity of U.S. shows in favor of local ones. "A recent survey by Nielsen Media Research found that 71% of the top 10 programs in 60 countries were locally produced."[44] In sports, Michael Veseth points out that although basketball is arguably an "American" game that is going global, many players in the U.S. National Basketball Association are from other countries. He also notes that the United States does not dominate—in fact, hardly even participates in—soccer, which is more of a global sport, followed by fans in most parts of the world."[45] According to Joseph Nye, "The idea that globalization equals Americanization is common but simplistic."[46]

Factors behind Globalization

One of the primary factors behind contemporary globalization—economic, political, and cultural—is the revolution in technology, particularly as it pertains to communication and the information revolution.[47] **Distance-shrinking technologies** allow different parts of the world to be connected. People can talk with one another more easily and cheaply than ever before, they can travel to various parts of the globe more quickly, and they can share information across borders instantaneously.

For example, the number of main telephone lines in the world almost doubled between 1991 and 2001, and the number of mobile cellular phone owners increased from 16 million in 1991 to over 4 billion in 2008. In the same time frame, the number of international telephone traffic minutes more than tripled. The changes in computer technology have made a tremendous impact on communication and information processing. In 1980, there were probably fewer than 2 million computers in the entire world, and most of them were mainframes, or very large computers. By 1991, there were about 130 million computers, and most of those were personal, or desktop, computers (PCs). From 1991 to 2005, the number of PCs grew by more than 600 percent, to over 800 million. During that same time, the Internet

cultural imperialism
Dominance of one country's culture over others.

distance-shrinking technologies
Communication and information tools that allow different parts of the world to be easily connected.

became usable for most people with PCs, and the number of Internet users skyrocketed from 4.4 million in 1991 to over 1 billion by 2006.[48]

New information technology, particularly computers and the Internet, has the ability to transform the way the people around the world communicate and interact. These technologies are an important part of economic, political, and cultural globalization. In terms of economics, new technologies have decreased transport costs and contributed to the growth of trade to unprecedented levels.[49] Furthermore, advances in communications have drastically increased the velocity of international financial transactions by allowing trading to occur on a twenty-four-hour basis around the world.[50] Technological advances have contributed to the illegal global market as well. "The largely unregulated multi-trillion-dollar pool of money in supranational cyberspace, accessible by computer 24 hours a day, eases the drug trade's toughest problem: transforming huge sums of hot cash into investments in legitimate business."[51]

Technology is no doubt having an impact on politics and political globalization. "The most powerful engine of change in the relative decline of states and the rise of nonstate actors is the computer and telecommunications revolutions."[52] In authoritarian Yugoslavia, for example, the Serbian opposition at Radio B92 used the Internet to get their message out when President Milosevic had shut the radio station down. After the cyber-broadcast, international pressure led to the reopening of the station.[53] Human rights groups have also used the Internet to get international attention:[54]

> Within hours of the first gunshots of the Chiapas rebellion in southern Mexico in January 1994 . . . the Internet swarmed with messages from human rights activists. The worldwide media attention they and their groups focused on Chiapas, along with the influx of rights activists to the area, sharply limited the Mexican government's response. What in other times would have been a bloody insurgency turned out to be a largely nonviolent conflict. "The shots lasted ten days," José Angel Gurria, Mexico's foreign minister, later remarked, "and ever since, the war has been . . . a war on the Internet.[55]

Technology is changing the political relationships between states as well. Capturing territory, for example, is not what it used to be. After the Iraqi invasion of Kuwait, Iraq discovered that the Kuwaiti government and banks had already electronically transferred all of the money from the accounts and could use this money to help fund the ouster of the Iraqi army from Kuwait.[56] Technological developments, particularly the Internet, may be changing the very nature of security threats:

> Increasingly, security is defined not by the numbers of weapons in place or the number of troops that can be deployed at a

moment's notice but by the ability to gain or deny access to critical information. . . . Just as the concept of security is changing, so is the definition of threats. Because the Network puts extraordinary power in the hands of individuals and small groups, its existence inevitably heightens concerns about terrorism. . . . As more and more business activity takes place on the Web, the specter of economic terrorism will also rise. For example, the existence of the Network makes it possible for malicious hackers to crash the New York Stock Exchange, to siphon billions of dollars of "digital cash" from banks, or to seize control of computers that manage electric powergrids.[57]

Communication revolutions are also a factor in cultural globalization. New, less costly, more efficient, and better-quality ways of storing and transmitting music, for example, mean that music can be shared more easily around the globe. Similarly, music, programs, and news can be better shared on television with the development and spread of satellites and cable television. "Both of these technologies allow television corporations to circumvent the regulatory capacity of nation-states to some degree, and to break from the national limits of terrestrial broadcasting structures."[58] Social networking applications, such as Facebook, also operate globally.

In general, the information revolution technologies facilitate cultural globalization. "By drastically reducing the importance of proximity, the new technologies change people's perceptions of community. Fax machines, satellite hookups, and the Internet connect people across borders with exponentially growing ease while separating them from natural and historical associations within nations."[59] And although language differences are an obstacle to globalization, programs on the Internet can translate webpages or search the Internet across languages. Some argue that this "will further loosen culture from its geographic moorings, thereby contributing to the creation of a free-floating cosmopolitan class that is not restricted by national identity."[60]

Despite the undeniable importance of technological developments in contemporary globalization, the technological factor cannot be divorced from politics. "If historical experience demonstrates anything, it is that integration is not technologically determined. If it were, integration would have gone smoothly forward over the past two centuries. On the contrary, despite continued falls in the costs of transport and communications in the first half of the twentieth century, integration actually reversed course."[61] Certain states, groups, and interests stand to gain from globalization and have actively pushed for globalizing technologies and policies:

> While technological openings may in some sense have "driven" the process of opening markets and societies, technological advances do not occur in an economic or political vacuum.

Sustained political and investment decisions drive technological advances. Scientists did not happen upon the discovery of powerful supercomputers, tiny microchips, and fiberoptic telecommunications links by accident. These advances came about through sustained investment, political, and social policy that harnessed resources in pursuit of technological progress, and pursued technological innovation as a tool to advance economic and political goals.[62]

Certain states benefit more from globalization than others and have pursued decidedly pro-globalization policies. In other words, "globalization is not destined, it is chosen."[63] The economically liberal policies and capitalist practices of the United States (see Chapter 10), for example, mean that globalization, at least in its economic form, "is largely an American creation, rooted in the period after World War II and based on U.S. economic might."[64] Historical and political factors associated with the end of the Cold War—the spread of capitalism and a largely unchallenged unipolar international system—have also facilitated globalization. Globalization, however, was probably not inevitable and is likely not irreversible. States have made other choices and still can serve as anti-globalization forces (to be discussed following). Even though, for example, the United States has done much to further economic and cultural globalization, it does not always support newly emerging international norms and agreements, as discussed in Chapter 9.

A Historical Perspective on Globalization: How New Is It?

hyperglobalizers
Individuals who believe contemporary globalization has produced a new and unique era.

globalization skeptics
Individuals who believe globalization has long, historical roots.

This summary of the evidence for economic, political, and cultural globalization and the technological developments related to it may impart the sense that we have indeed entered a completely new era of global politics. This is one school of thought on globalization, which David Held and his colleagues refer to as the *hyperglobalist thesis*. "For the **hyperglobalizers** . . . contemporary globalization defines a new era in which peoples everywhere are increasingly subject to the disciplines of the global marketplace. . . . Economic globalization is constructing new forms of social organization that are supplanting, or will eventually supplant, traditional nation-states as the primary economic and political units of world society."[65] The **globalization skeptics,** for their part, point to long historical trends in arguing that globalization is not new at all.[66] Indeed, some say that globalization is as old as history itself. If globalization is the increase in contact of people across geographical space, then "when groups of people first came into contact with one another through conquest, trade, and migration, the globe began to shrink."[67]

Historical Roots

Many skeptics point out that recent technological developments connected to globalization are simply part of long-term trends, dating back centuries from sail power to steam power, from the telegraph to the telephone, and from commercial air travel to e-mail.[68] And although trade and financial relations across political borders can be traced back to antiquity, early international economic relations were fairly limited.[69] Some skeptics would suggest that the sixteenth century, with the development of capitalist modes of production, is the real starting point of economic globalization.[70] Others use indicators from early in the twentieth century to show that connections between economies are not that different from those of today. For example, a comparison of the leading economies' dependence on world trade (exports and imports as a percentage of GDP) in 1910 and near the end of the twentieth century shows that the proportion of world production in global markets is not incredibly higher for most countries, contrary to what one might expect (see Table 14.1). The United States is the only leading economy to see a doubling of its ratio of trade to gross domestic product (GDP) during the century.

From 1870 to 1914, world trade expanded greatly, and for some commodities, such as rice and wheat, truly global markets were formalized.[71] During this time, Great Britain provided financial stability by supplying a gold standard to give confidence in its currency. "Indeed, for the skeptics, the classical Gold Standard era prior to the First World War is taken as a benchmark for financial globalization, in so far as they argue that the scale of net flows was greater than at any time since and that adherence to the rules of the Gold Standard meant that countries had to subordinate their domestic economic policy to a rigid set of international rules."[72] Of course, it was in the period after World War II that world trade levels grew at a remarkable rate, with the establishment of the Bretton Woods fixed exchange rate system and the General Agreement on Tariffs and

---

TABLE 14.1

Leading Economies' Dependence on World Trade (Exports and Imports as Percentage of GDP)

	1910	1995
United Kingdom	44%	57%
Germany	38	46
France	35	43
United States	11	24

Source: Martin Wolf, "Will the Nation-State Survive Globalization?" Foreign Affairs, pp. 178–191. Reprinted by permission of Foreign Affairs, January/February 2001. © 2001 by the Council on Foreign Relations, Inc. www.ForeignAffairs.com.

Trade (as discussed in Chapter 10). Thus, many date the beginning of economic globalization to the immediate postwar period and view today's global economy as nothing more than the continuation of these historical trends.

In the realm of political globalization, there is also historical precedent. After all, in the age of empires—from Roman to British—large areas came under the control of imperial states (see Chapter 2), making these areas more integrated in some ways than the sovereign state system of approximately 193 countries today:

> Undoubtedly, the rapidly developing empires of Britain and of other European states were the most powerful agents of globalization in the late nineteenth century. . . . At issue was not simply an intensification of European expansion along a continuum that ran back through earlier centuries, but a new order of relations of domination and subordination among the major regions of the world, aided by new communications and transport infrastructures which facilitated new mechanisms of political control.[73]

The development of global governance is also not new. Even the beginning of the twentieth century witnessed the growth of organizations and regulatory regimes, such as the International Telegraph Union established in 1865, so that "by 1914 . . . significant aspects of global affairs were already subject to international regulation by world organizations . . . [which] gradually extended beyond the boundaries of Europe to embrace a global jurisdiction."[74] Others would argue that political globalization really began in the 1970s with the rise of nonstate actors including the Organization of Petroleum Exporting Countries (OPEC), Amnesty International, and Greenpeace, although these too had historical precedents, the International Red Cross among them.

Current cultural globalization is a long-established trend and nothing new, say some skeptics. Empires, in addition to providing political uniformity, also homogenized cultures in various ways. Latin and Greek served as official languages, and Rome-built theaters and amphitheaters spread drama and poetry across the Roman Empire. The British Empire globalized culture as well:

> At its height the British Empire was the most global of any formal empire . . . [and] there was a strong cultural . . . dimension to both the execution of British dominance and the maintenance of complex links between centre and periphery. . . . This took a multiplicity of forms, but two of the most important were the conduct of imperial educational policy and the establishment of an imperial communications infrastructure, both of which offer clear examples of the globalization of culture and communications.[75]

In education, for example, the English language and English ideas and cultural practice were the basis of the curriculum in the English model of education established for elites throughout the British colonies.[76]

Historically, religion, such as Islam and Christianity, has also served as a powerful force of cultural integration. World religions "are systems of belief and ritual that have had the capacity at crucial historical moments to reach out from their place of origin and embrace, convert and conquer other cultures and other religions. . . . World religions unquestionably constitute one of the most powerful and significant forms of the globalization of culture in the pre-modern era, indeed of all time."[77] In the nineteenth and twentieth centuries, diverse cultures were shaped by secular globalizing ideological forces and belief systems such as socialism, liberalism, and the scientific mode of thinking that influenced peoples throughout the world.[78]

If immigration, in addition to technology, is a conduit of cultural globalization, then there is another reason to doubt the novelty of today's global village, because high immigration is also not without precedent. Mass migration peaked in 1815 when approximately 60 million Europeans emigrated. In the 1890s, immigration to the United States soared, increasing the population by 9 percent during that single decade. In the 1990s, the United States had one of the highest immigration rates in the world, but the increase in the population was only 4 percent over the decade.[79] "The current era of globalization has not even approached the cosmopolitanism and openness to migration that characterized the pre-1914 phase."[80]

Distinctive Characteristics of Contemporary Globalization

While it is clear that current economic, political, and cultural dynamics have historical roots and are not completely novel, most agree that there are quantitative and qualitative differences between the past and the present.[81]

In between the hyperglobalists and the skeptics on the debate on globalization are the **transformationalists**:

transformationalists
Individuals who view globalization as both historically rooted and unprecedented.

> Transformationalists make no claims about the future trajectory of globalization; nor do they seek to evaluate the present in relation to some single, fixed ideal-type "globalized world," whether a global market or a global civilization. Rather, transformationalist accounts emphasize globalization as a long-term historical process. . . . Such caution about the exact future of globalization is matched, nonetheless, by the conviction that contemporary patterns of global economic, military, technological, ecological, migratory, political and cultural flows are historically unprecedented.[82]

The distinctiveness of contemporary global politics concerns the scope and velocity of recent technological developments and economic, political, and cultural globalization. In terms of scope of globalization, more parts of the world are connected through technology than ever before. Although television, for example, has been around for a long time, it is only with recent developments in satellites and cable that more people have access to television and to programs and news from different countries. Moreover, while economic integration and liberalization increased throughout the twentieth century, it was primarily limited to the advanced economies. Overall, "today the world trading system is defined both by an intensive network of trading relations embracing virtually all economies and by evolving global markets for many goods and some services."[83]

The velocity of globalization is also distinct. "Many communications improvements have been taking place over the last century, but the contemporary speed of change, the enlargement of capacity for information (and capital) transmission and the proliferation of communications media have not been experienced before."[84] And although the degree of financial interdependence may not be drastically different from some past eras, the speed at which the transmission of financial exchange can take place is remarkably faster.[85] Efficiency has increased along with velocity, so that

> there is no denying quantum changes. . . . Along with major technological breakthroughs in production systems, communications, and transportation . . . the reduction of barriers has markedly accelerated the movement of goods, services, capital, labor, and knowledge. Not only is there a major rise in the velocity of transactions, but the cost of various types of transport, telephone calls, and computers has plummeted. For example, owing to satellite technology, the price of a three-minute call from New York to London dropped from $244.65 in 1930 to $31.58 in 1970, and to $3.32 in 1990.[86]

The degree of institutionalization of integration and coordination in political globalization may also be unique. "The nineteenth century was a world of unilateral and discretionary policy. The late twentieth century, by comparison, was a world of multilateral and institutionalized policy."[87]

Thus, transformationalists argue that while it is important to keep in mind the historical roots of today's global politics, it is also wise to recognize the changes that are taking place.

Globalization and Its Discontents

While some argue that globalization is not new, others insist that it is not really happening at all.[88] The "globalization" processes outlined previously, some say, are not truly global, but rather limited to specific parts of the world. Furthermore, the unevenness of globalization is causing devastation among those who are becoming more marginalized from the "globalizers" of the world. National and subnational cultures are under pressure, and because of this, some see a resurgence in local cultures rather than movement toward a global culture. Finally, globalization faces considerable political opposition from those who see it as a threat to their values and interests.[89]

Unequal Globalization

As discussed in Chapter 11, the economic gap between the North and the South, as measured by many indicators, is worsening despite any trends in economic globalization and, some argue, because of globalization.[90] This is due in part, according to the skeptics' argument on economic globalization, to the fact that the world economy is not globalized but is in fact concentrated in Europe, Japan, and North America:

> For most skeptics, if the current evidence demonstrates anything it is that economic activity is undergoing a significant "regionalization" as the world economy evolves in the direction of three major financial and trading blocs, that is Europe, Asia-Pacific and North America. . . . In comparison with the classical Gold Standard era, the world economy is therefore significantly less integrated than it once was.[91]

Furthermore, skeptics point to the marginalization of the developing world: "the creation of a global market has resulted in a growing divide between rich and poor, with new pockets of affluence arising in areas of widespread poverty and stagnation. Rapidly changing class dynamics are often a source of friction and become especially explosive when new class disparities correspond to long-standing ethnic and religious divisions. Thus, while globalization has improved living conditions in some countries, it has also increased the risk of conflict in others"[92] and between the North and the South.

Part of the inequality stems from the vast differences that the North and the South have in terms of their access to the revolutions in technology.[93] North America, Europe, and Japan, for example, account for 75 percent of all international telephone calls. On average, individuals in the richest countries currently use 36.6 minutes of international telephone traffic per person per year, while individuals in sub-Saharan Africa average 1 minute per person per year.[94] Similarly, in 1992, there were 498 TV sets per 1,000 people in the developed countries, compared to 61 sets per 1,000 people in the developing world.[95] Access to mobile phones, computers the Internet is also very uneven across the globe (see Table 14.2). Within regions, there are significant differences as well. In Asia, 10 percent of individuals in Bhutan have used the Internet, compared to 68 percent in Japan. In the Americas, 68 percent of individuals in the United States have used the Internet, compared to 7 percent in Ecuador.[96]

TABLE 14.2

Global Use of Information and Computer Technology

	Mobile Cell Phone Subscribers per 100 inhabitants	Internet Users per 100 inhabitants	Estimated PCs per 100 inhabitants
Developed Economies	92	24	62
Transition Economies	77	3	10
Developing Economies	33	4	5
Least Developed Economies	10	0.2	0.7

Source: From *The Global Information Society: A Statistical View*, 2008. Copyright © 2008, United Nations. Reproduced with permission.

This inequality in access to technological developments contributes to the growing economic inequalities between the North and the South. It also means that much of the world is simply not part of the "global" culture that is supposedly developing.

Political globalization is arguably not truly global either. Indeed, "international civil society remains embryonic. Many nongovernmental organizations reflect only a tiny segment of the populations of their members' states. They largely represent only modernized countries."[97] Furthermore (as discussed in Chapters 9 and 11), international organizations such as the United Nations and the International Monetary Fund are often criticized by the South for being dominated by the North and their interests rather than truly global governing organizations.

Nationalism as a Countertrend

Another argument against the development of a globalized world, particularly a global culture, concerns the presence and persistence of local and national loyalties and identities:

> Globalization has not profoundly challenged the enduring national nature of citizenship. Economic life takes place on a global scale, but human identity remains national—hence the strong resistance to cultural homogenization. Over the centuries, increasingly centralized states have expanded their functions and tried to forge a sense of common identity for their subjects. But no central power in the world can do the same thing today, even in the European Union. There, a single currency and advanced economic coordination have not yet . . . resulted in a sense of postnational citizenship. . . . A world very partially

unified by technology still has not collective consciousness or collective solidarity.[98]

Perhaps ironically, revolutions in global communication, such as the Internet, may drive people apart rather than bring them together: "The ability the Net gives us to endlessly filter and personalize information means that, more than ever before, we can also build virtual gated communities where we never have to interact with people who are different from ourselves."[99]

Even in countries where access to global technologies and information is the highest, such as in the United States, global culture is not necessarily taking root. "Compared with their counterparts in other nations, citizens born in the United States know fewer foreign languages, understand less about foreign cultures, and live abroad reluctantly, if at all."[100]

Access to international news has not resulted in a more globally informed population. Indeed, most newspapers and news broadcasts around the globe are dominated by local stories.[101] This domination of news sources by local stories has probably always existed, but curiously it seems to have become more pervasive following the end of the Cold War. At the same time that new communication technologies have made it far easier to link events and people separated by large geographic distances, people in many countries seem to have become less interested in that available information.

Not only are subglobal identities persisting despite trends in globalization, they may be stronger. Indigenous peoples, such as those in Chiapas, Mexico, are uniting to fight against what they see as a threat to their local culture. As discussed in Chapter 12, the timing of the Zapatista-led revolution in Chiapas, to coincide with the day the North American Free Trade Association (NAFTA) went into effect, was a shot across the globalization divide. Others oppose the Americanization or Westernization of globalization. The French and the Canadians, for example, have passed recent laws to provide for minimum quotas for domestic films shown in cinemas and domestic musicians broadcast over radio airwaves. Many adherents to fundamental versions of religions oppose the dominance of Western values; some are opposing this with terrorist acts (see Chapter 7).[102] And (also discussed in Chapter 7) ethnic conflicts became particularly pervasive, severe, and consequential immediately following the Cold War. Ethnic strife continues to threaten the integrity and even the existence of a set of countries that girdles the globe.

Many globalization skeptics believe that advances in fundamentalism and nationalism mean that "rather than the emergence of a global civilization, . . . the world is fragmenting into civilizational blocs and cultural and ethnic enclaves."[103] Samuel Huntington, in his influential 1996 article, "**The Clash of Civilizations?**" argued that in the future, global conflict will revolve around differences in "civilizations," such as Western, Confucian, Japanese, Islamic, Hindu, Slavic-Orthodox, and

"The Clash of Civilizations?"
Title of article by Samuel Huntington asserting that future global conflict will revolve around cultural differences.

Latin American. According to Huntington, "The interactions between peoples of different civilizations are increasing; these increasing interactions intensify civilization consciousness and awareness of differences between civilizations and commonalities within civilization."[104]

In another influential work, *Jihad vs. McWorld*, Benjamin Barber characterized the fragmentation of the world along conflicting identities. He wrote that there is a

> grim prospect of a retribalization of large swaths of humankind by war and bloodshed: a threatened balkanization of nation-states in which culture is pitted against culture, people against people, tribe against tribe, a Jihad in the name of a hundred narrowly conceived faiths against every kind of interdependence, every kind of artificial social cooperation and mutuality: against technology, against pop culture, and against integrated markets.[105]

Yet he also acknowledged the forces of globalization, stating that there was also prospect for a "future in shimmering pastels, a busy portrait of onrushing economic, technological, and ecological forces that demand integration and uniformity and that mesmerize peoples everywhere with fast music, fast computers, and fast food—MTV, Macintosh, and McDonald's—pressing nations into one homogeneous global theme park, one McWorld tied together by communications, information, entertainment, and commerce."[106] Barber's primary thesis was that what is unique about current global politics is that these forces of disintegration and integration were occurring simultaneously and at very high levels: "caught between Babel and Disneyland, the planet is falling precipitously apart and coming together at the very same moment."[107]

Even if globalization is not actively opposed by nationalist, local, or civilization identities, these alternatives provide a check on homogenization.[108] As one group of globalization analysts argue,

> we agree that some things become more similar around the world as globalization proceeds. . . . But we do not think this leads to a homogeneous world, for three reasons. First, general rules and models must be interpreted in light of local circumstances. Thus regions respond to similar economic constraints in different ways; . . . the same television program means different things to different audiences; McDonald's adapts its menu and marketing to local tastes. Second, growing similarity provokes reactions. Advocates from many cultures seek to protect their heritage or assert their identity—witness the efforts of fundamentalists to reinstate what they consider orthodoxy, the actions of indigenous peoples to claim their right to cultural survival, and the attempt of Asian leaders to put forth a distinctive

Asian model of human rights. Third, cultural and political differences have themselves become globally valid. The notion that people and countries are entitled to their particularity or distinctiveness is itself part of global culture.[109]

Other Sources of Opposition to Globalization

The developing world and national and ethnic identities are not the only factors working in opposition to globalization. As discussed in Chapter 10, labor groups are often critical of multinational corporations, the flag-bearers of economic globalization, charging that in the process of globalizing production, MNCs create high unemployment in areas they leave and exploit workers in areas where they relocate. Local producers also criticize MNCs and economic globalization, warning that local "mom-and-pop" grocery stores, cafés, and cinemas are being crowded out by chain stores with a global reach. Other criticisms come from environmentalists. While political globalization includes new and more extensive international agreements to protect the environment, economic globalization is often seen as the cause of environmental problems:

> Although contemporary environmental abuses have their antecedents in earlier periods of history, globalization coincides with new environmental problems such as global warming, depletion of the ozone layer, acute loss of biodiversity, and forms of transborder pollution (e.g., acid rain). . . . Moreover, some ecological problems are clearly the result of global cross-border flows, as with certain kinds of groundwater contamination, leaching, and long-term threats traceable to importing hazardous wastes.[110]

Environmentalists also contend that economic globalization involves "the spread of a global consumer culture that . . . embodies a world view unconcerned with the ecological consequences of human economic activity."[111]

On many issues, the labor and environmental movements have not agreed. But along with other groups that oppose globalization, they have found common ground. The first sign of this new coalition against globalization came in 1999 in Seattle at a meeting of the World Trade Organization. Known as the Battle for Seattle, the protests involved an estimated 10,000 representatives from labor unions, environmentalists, farmers, consumer activists, religious people, women's activists, student groups, and anarchists. The protests blocked WTO representatives from attending negotiation meetings and, in the end, the WTO was forced to close the meeting without even a final formal declaration, partly due to the protests. "It was a surprise ending to a week of stunning developments, in which the opponents of WTO-facilitated corporate globalization exerted more influence over the negotiating process than any could have expected."[112] Anti-globalization protests have continued at key economic international meetings, such as the G-20 meeting in London in 2009 in which thousands participated in a protest titled "March for Jobs, Justice, and Climate." One activist, Tony Juniper of Friends of the Earth UK, explains the evolution of the "antiglobalization" coalition from the environmentalists' perspective:

> For the past 10 years we've been locating ourselves more in the bigger economic debate and less in the "save the whales" type of debate. Talking about rainforests led us into talking about Third World debt. Talking about climate change led us to talk about transnational corporations. The more you talk about these things, the more you realize the subject isn't the environment any more, it's the economy and the pressures on countries to do things that undercut any efforts they make to deal with environmental issues. By the time we got to Seattle, we were all campaigning on the same basic trend that was undermining everybody's efforts to achieve any progressive goals. That trend is the free market and privileges for big corporations and rich people at the expense of everything else.[113]

Opposition to globalization became more intense as many blame globalization and economic liberalism for the global economic downturn that began in the United States in 2007 (see Chapter 10). According to the magazine, the *Economist*: "The integration of the world economy is in retreat on almost every front. The economic meltdown has popularised a new term: deglobalisation."[114] Foreign direct investment is declining, as is world trade, and European and U.S. public opinion is increasingly suspicious of globalization and trading relationships.[115] In addition, "The institutional foundations of globalization—such as the rules that oblige governments to keep their markets open and the domestic and international politics that allow policymakers to liberalize their economies—have weakened

Anti-globalization protest prior to the G-20 summit in London in 2009.

(Andy Rain/Corbis)

considerably in the past few years. Politicians and their constituents in the United States, Europe, and China have grown increasingly nervous about letting capital, goods, and people move freely across their borders. And energy—the most globalized of products—has once more become the object of intense resource nationalism, as governments in resource-rich countries assert greater control and ownership over those assets."[116] The backlash following the recent economic crisis may be more on focused on economic globalization and economic liberalism in particular. Globalization, as we have discussed, occurs in many forms. One analyst, for example, argues that globalization is not limited to trade and investment; globalization means much more:

> Jihadists in Indonesia, after all, can still share their operational plans with like-minded extremists in the Middle East, while Vietnamese artists can now more easily sell their wares in European markets, and Spanish magistrates can team up with their peers in Latin America to bring torturers to justice. . . . Around the world, all kinds of groups are still connecting, and the economic crisis will not slow their international activities. In some cases, it might even bolster them.[117]

Yet any opposition to globalization is important, because it will likely shape the future of globalization. It is not necessarily the case that globalization proceeds in a linear fashion and cannot be reversed: "Over the past decades, many have recited a reassuring mantra that globalization . . . is irreversible. This view is historical unsustainable."[118] Indeed, despite the presence of more and more globalizing technologies throughout much of the twentieth century, parts of the world at times become more economically isolated (as in the 1930s) or more politically isolated (as during the Cold War). This is because groups favoring integration engaged with groups against integration in political battles, and the anti-integration interests often won. Similarly, the debate over contemporary globalization will be characterized by advances by both pro- and anti-globalization forces. The Policy Choices box summarizes some of the arguments in this debate.

Globalization and the State: The Future of World Politics

Another potential source of opposition to globalization is sovereign states. After all, if globalization continues on the path that many predict, state borders will become meaningless, states will lose their power to nonstate actors, and sovereignty will no longer be the dominant principle of world politics, as it has been since the Treaty of Westphalia was signed in 1648. Many say this has already occurred (recall the discussions on multinational corporations and other nonstate actors in Chapter 4). Others argue that the state is still strong, able to resist and even benefit from globalization.

POLICY CHOICES

Is Globalization Desirable?

ISSUE: States face choices with respect to how much their policies promote or limit globalization. Many face substantial opposition to globalization-promoting policies from environmentalists, human rights groups, and labor unions, for example. Many states are also concerned about the effects of globalization on their own sovereign authority.

Option #1: States should pursue policies that promote globalization.

Arguments: (a) Globalization is good business. State economies will profit if political restrictions on trade and financial flows are reduced, and consumers will have more choice at less cost for products from around the world. (b) If states embrace globalization, the capacity of state leaders to needlessly and heartlessly coerce their citizens will be diminished. Citizens will become central, respecting human rights will become the norm, and individual liberty will flourish at the expense of dictators and despots. (c) Globalization allows solutions to the growing list of humankind's interconnected problems. International organizations, and NGOs are in a better position than states to help solve global challenges such as environmental degradation.

Counterarguments: (a) Removing barriers to legitimate economic activities has unacceptable costs. Terrorism, drug trafficking, international crime, and the nearly free flow of nuclear materials will increasingly flourish as globalization expands. (b) Globalization affords new opportunities for those attempting to suppress individual liberties. Technology is ultimately under the control of the state, which can use it to suppress human rights. (c) Nonstate actors such as the United Nations and various NGOs do not have a good track record for solving problems and are not accountable to any constituency.

Option #2: States should limit or reverse policies that contribute to globalization.

Arguments: (a) Limiting or reducing the global perspective in state policies would refocus attention where political decisions rightly belong: on the domestic front, where states have the most insight and ability to improve the lives of their citizens. (b) States exist on the basis of sovereignty and are almost by definition dedicated to its preservation. Although individual citizens may wish to transcend their state boundaries, states themselves would be well served to limit losses to their sovereignty due to globalization, lest they find themselves unable to carry out necessary functions of good government. (c) Increasing globalization is simply another means by which rich and powerful states can further advance their already enviable positions. States that now find themselves at a disadvantage in the system should struggle relentlessly to prevent further disparities, not to encourage them.

Counterarguments: (a) Globalization should not be seen as a competitor to domestic politics, but rather as a resource by which citizens can improve their lives and their futures. (b) The fact of globalization has already reduced the sphere of effective policymaking for states, favoring markets, nonstate organizations, and individuals. States thus have less and less control over a global phenomenon such

(continued)

as globalization. Any state that individually seeks to limit globalization is not likely to have an appreciable impact. (c) Globalization is in large part a consequence of an increasingly competitive global market. If states limit or reverse globalization policies, especially economic ones, they will find themselves at a disadvantage, and their citizens will suffer the economic consequences.

"The State Is Dead"

According to the "hyperglobalists," globalization dynamics, particularly those associated with economic globalization, signal the eventual end to the sovereign state.[119]

> Hyperglobalizers argue that economic globalization is bringing about a "denationalization" of economies through the establishment of transnational networks of production, trade and finance. In this "borderless" economy, national governments are relegated to little more than transmission belts for global capital, or ultimately, simple intermediate institutions sandwiched between increasingly powerful local, regional and global mechanisms of governance.[120]

There are numerous ways in which the state is challenged by economic globalization. First, the rapid exchange of goods, services, and capital on the global market might undermine the abilities of governments to control inflation and unemployment through national policy. Second, the mobility of labor, production, and capital might undermine states' effectiveness at establishing employment, safety, and environmental standards. Third, greater interdependence means that national economies, on whose fate governments rest, are more vulnerable to shocks and crises from abroad, with greater consequences at home.[121] Finally, the rise of global governance in the international political economy challenges state authority. "The global regulation of trade, by bodies such as the WTO, implies a significant renegotiation of the Westphalian notion of state sovereignty."[122]

The growing illegal marketplace and the associated growth of globalized organized crime is also a challenge to state authority. Early in 1990, Italy's parliamentary Anti-Mafia Commission sent a message to the UN General Assembly to the effect that organized crime was "taking on the characteristics of an extremely dangerous world calamity":[123]

> Modern criminal power has surpassed the ability of governments to contain it. International organized crime is too big; nobody knows how to deal with it. Perhaps it cannot be dealt with as long as the world is divided into nearly two hundred sovereign states. While the big crime syndicates simply

go where the money is, sovereign states cannot do anything simply. . . .[124]

In addition to international economic organizations such as the WTO that represent a challenge to states, there are other forms of global governance that arguably threaten state sovereignty:

Until recently, international organizations were institutions of, by, and for nation-states. Now they are building constituencies of their own and, through NGOs, establishing direct connections to the peoples of the world. The shift is infusing them with new life and influence, but it is also creating tensions. States feel they need more capable international organizations to deal with a lengthening list of transnational challenges, but at the same time fear competitors. Thus they vote for new forms of international intervention while reasserting sovereignty's first principle: no interference in the domestic affairs of states. . . . At the same time, governments . . . have driven some gaping holes in the wall that has separated the two. . . . International accords . . . drew explicit links between democracy, human rights, and international security, establishing new legal bases for international interventions. In 1991 the U.N. General Assembly declared itself in favor of humanitarian intervention without the request or consent of the state involved. A year later the Security Council took the unprecedented step of authorizing the use of force "on behalf of civilian populations" in Somalia. Suddenly an interest in citizens began to compete with, and occasionally override, the formerly unquestioned primacy of state interests.[125]

Contemporary migration is another challenge to states. If they are unable to stop it, illegal immigration demonstrates the inability of states to maintain their own borders, the territorial expression of sovereignty.[126]

States are being challenged by cultural globalization as well. Governments that want to control the political culture of their citizens by, for example, limiting their access to liberal values and Western media, are having more difficulty doing so with new technological developments. It is not, however, cultural globalization that threatens states as much as the backlash to a global culture. As national and local identities resist homogenization of culture, "regions as far-flung as Catalonia, Northern Italy, Quebec, and Scotland, . . . provinces in China, and [regional] states in India, have taken globalization as their cue to pursue greater autonomy within the nation-state."[127]

"Long Live the State"

The globalization skeptics caution against exaggerating the impact of current economic, political, and cultural trends on the sovereign state. "Far from considering national governments as becoming immobilized by international imperatives, they point to their growing centrality in the regulation and active promotion of cross-border economic activity. Governments are not the passive victims of internationalization but, on the contrary, its primary architects."[128]

The state, for example, continues to control economic policy areas.

> In . . . various ways globalization' does inhibit governments' freedom of maneuver in economic policy but it does not eliminate it. Governments can do much to make their economies more or less attractive to investors: by supporting infrastructure development, education and training; increasing the efficiency and lowering the cost of services through competition or regulatory change; and improving the workings of labour markets.[129]

Furthermore, states often have a choice, and their choice is not necessarily determined by globalization forces. "There is a tendency to exaggerate the impact of globalization. Many of the constraints on national freedom of action are self-imposed."[130] Joining the single currency or pegging one's currency to the dollar is a choice some governments make, and some do not (see Chapter 12).

It is the states themselves that have been the architects of international agreements that constrain them. "Global governance will come not at the expense of the state but rather as an expression of the interests that the state embodies. As the source of order and basis of governance, the state will remain in the future as effective, and will be as essential, as it has ever been."[131] And as discussed in Chapter 4, state interests and the interests of MNCs and NGOs are not necessarily in conflict, but when there is a conflict of interests, states can still prevail.

The technological revolutions associated with globalization are not inherently a challenge to state authority. "Ironically, the technology that is supposed to make globalization inevitable also makes increased surveillance by the state, particularly over people, easier than it would have been a century ago."[132] States can use technology to enhance their power. A recent study found that at least twenty-six states filter a wide range of Internet material, include information on politics, human rights, sexuality, and religion.[133]

Many governments, including China, Indonesia, Thailand, Turkey, and Tunisia have recently blocked access to popular sites such as YouTube. Beginning in 2009, China required all new computers to include software that censors "unhealthy information."[134] Government filters are not always effective, but some states impose strict penalties for individuals using the Internet and fax machines for "subversive" purposes. States also have the power to undermine technologies that NGOs use:

> Encryption, for example—the technology that allows communications to be scrambled and kept private—is a vital tool of human rights work; it allows fieldworkers to collect, transmit,

and store communications in a way that does not compromise the safety of victims and witnesses. If governments outlaw or restrict strong encryption, human rights workers and their clients will be deprived of an important digital asset that would help them to take on corrupt powers.[135]

Overall, despite historical technological change and integration, states have not become weaker political units. "On the contrary, in the countries with the most advanced and internationally integrated economies, governments' ability to tax and redistribute incomes, regulate the economy, and monitor the activity of their citizens has increased beyond all recognition. This has been especially true over the past century."[136] Sate capitalism (as discussed in Chapter 10), may be the primary economic model in the future and involves a strong role for governments in their economies.

Understanding the Future of Globalization and the State

The transformationalist viewpoint lies in between the predictions that the state will wither away and the contentions that the state is strong, or even stronger today than ever before:

> At the core of the transformationalist case is a belief that contemporary globalization is reconstituting . . . the power, functions and authority of national governments. . . . Rather than globalization bringing about the "end of the state," it has encouraged a spectrum of adjustment strategies and, in certain respects, a more activist state. Accordingly, the power of national governments is not necessarily diminished by globalization but on the contrary is being reconstituted and restructured in response to the growing complexity of processes of governance in a more interconnected world.[137]

So what kind of world will this restructuring produce? Admittedly, "after three and a half centuries, it requires a mental leap to think of world politics in any terms other than occasionally cooperating but generally competing states, each defined by its territory and representing all the people therein. Nor is it easy to imagine political entities that could compete with the emotional attachment of a shared landscape, national history, language, flag, and currency."[138] To take this mental leap, we return to the theoretical perspectives introduced in Chapter 1. Globalization is in many ways a challenge to these perspectives, because most of them were conceived before the shape of current global politics could be seen. Accordingly, most of these perspectives do not have a clear answer on what the future of the world will be. What these perspectives can do for us, however, is provide a list of factors that will likely be important in the restructuring of world politics and the debate over globalization. In Chapters 2 and 3, we used these perspectives to look at the history of international relations through different lenses. Each perspective focused on different time periods and the meaning and importance of historical events. Similarly, in this chapter, each of the theoretical perspectives can comment on the future of globalization. Each perspective stresses different dynamics that are significant to the future of the world political system. Table 14.3 summarizes the aspects of globalization that each perspective emphasizes.

Realism would agree with the skeptical argument on the state, as outlined previously. For realists, the state will, and should, jealously guard its sovereign power and seek to increase it when it can. States are expected to oppose any efforts or processes that are a threat to their autonomy. Recent U.S. opposition to the International Criminal Court is consistent with the realist perspective. Realists would also argue that there is more historical continuity than change in global politics. "The 'realist' orthodoxy insists that nothing has changed international relations since Thucydides and Machiavelli: a state's military and economic power determines its fate; interdependence and international institutions are secondary and fragile phenomena."[139] While realists would not deny the growing number of MNCs and NGOs on the world scene, they would maintain that the primary actors remain states and the dominant factor that underlies international politics remains the competition for power among states. When the interests of nonstate and state actors collide, realists would argue that states maintain the capability and

TABLE 14.3

Theoretical Perspectives on Globalization

Theory	Emphasized Aspects of Globalization
Realism	States can and will protect sovereignty; power remains the currency of global politics
Liberalism	Global politics continues to be transformed by interdependence; individuals will challenge traditional authority structures
Idealism	Human rights and other liberal values will spread; debates over values underlie globalization
Neo-Marxism	Globalization rooted in historical spread of capitalism; unevenness of globalization fuels class divisions
Constructivism	Construction of international norms underlies globalization; some values and ideas are privileged over others in defining globalization
Feminist perspectives	Globalization has gendered economic consequences; globalization spreads ideas of gender equality

the will to prevail. Thus, the dominant theme of the future for realists is the continual reassertion of sovereignty as the defining characteristic of states.

Liberalism, as a theoretical perspective, is better equipped to deal with current and future globalization processes. Whereas realism stresses continuity, contemporary liberalism sees great change and emphasizes the transformation of global politics that has arisen from the development of complex interdependence in the second half of the twentieth century. Liberalism would expect that as the degree and scope of interdependence continue to increase; states will have to coordinate their activities further;[140] nonstate and substate actors will become increasingly important; traditional matters of security will become less important on the international agenda (replaced by transnational issues such as environmental problems); military force will become even less frequent and less effective; and institutions of global governance will take on more functions once reserved by states. Globalization is, however, more than interdependence, as discussed at the beginning of this chapter. What, then, does the liberal theoretical perspective contribute to our understanding of globalization, beyond the observations it made about interdependence in the 1970s? To answer this question, liberals return to their roots of classical liberal philosophy and stress the importance of individual interests and rights.[141] Liberalism would expect that values of freedom, for example, will continue to spread and elevate the status of the individual in world politics through democratization, freedom of movement, and human rights above state rights.

> The long-standing pattern whereby compliance with authority tends to be unquestioning and automatic is conceived to have been replaced by a more elaborate set of norms that make the successful exercise of authority much more problematic. . . . By virtue of their newly acquired skills, people are more able and ready to question authority, and in turn the new authority relationships have facilitated the development of new, more decentralized global structure.[142]

In this regard, the dominant theme of the future for liberalism is the transformation of the political system through new authority relationships.

Sharing some of liberalism's philosophical roots, idealism would also expect more emphasis on human rights and values of freedom. Idealism, with its focus on values over interests, would expect the debate over globalization and the future path that globalization takes, to be heavily determined by values. Debates over cultural imperialism, the ethics of humanitarian intervention, and the value of local cultures and indigenous peoples will drive the political struggles over economic, political, and cultural globalization in the future, according to the idealist perspective.

The neo-Marxist perspective has something to say about globalization as well. Indeed, globalization has renewed interest in neo-Marxist theory.[143] According to some neo-Marxists, globalization is not necessarily new but is instead rooted in the development of capitalism in the sixteenth century. From that time, states have not been the most important actors in global politics. Instead, class divisions between the core in the North and the periphery in the South were the dominant feature of the world economic and political system. Contemporary globalization then is simply the intensification of this historical pattern—further spreading the capitalist mode of production—and the global class conflict between the developed and developing world will be the dominant theme of the future. The unevenness of globalization will continue and will be the source of this conflict. Furthermore, neo-Marxists view globalization as a tool to

> . . . deny developing countries the possibility of building their national economies. Thus, the internationalization and globalization of macro-economic policies transforms poor countries into open economies and "reserves" of cheap labor and natural resources. . . . In addition, multinational corporations, as carriers of technology, capital, and skilled labor between states, have reinforced the negative effects of foreign capital penetration by creating enclave economies within the host countries, which are characterized by small pockets of economically developed regions, in contrast to the larger peripheral areas that exhibit extreme poverty and little progress, thus enlarging the gap between the rich and the poor. . . . In this sense, globalization is producing a new kind of hegemony that fuses power and wealth in a kind of "corporcracy" of financial markets and corporations that rule the world. . . .[144]

From the constructivist perspective, globalization is what states, and nonstate actors, make of it. In other words, it is not the actual reality of economic, political, and cultural globalization that is important; it is how these processes are being socially constructed, or understood, in the world society. Thus, the important thing to know about globalization and its future is how it is being interpreted and shaped by actors and the social context. Constructivists would want to know: Who is defining what globalization means? How are some cultural values and norms, such as those promoted by Disney and McDonald's, becoming privileged to be part of the global culture while others are not? How are new international norms such as human rights becoming internalized by states and defining their interests and identities? The future of globalization and the future of the state are not determined by actors' interests but rather by how global politics is constructed along the way.

Feminist perspectives are also interested in how the features and concepts of globalization are constructed and have hidden assumptions about gender and gender relations. Some feminists worry, for example, that economic globalization, because it involves the spread of economic liberal ideas of individual interests rather than community interests, is a process that reflects masculine understanding more than feminine understanding and relations. Other feminists concentrate on the consequences of globalization for women. Because women make up a disproportionate number of the poor, particularly in the developing world, feminists often oppose globalization that contributes to widening the gap between the North and the South.[145] On the other hand, if globalization means diminished power for states, which are largely controlled by men, and the diffusion of norms that promote gender equality, feminists would see positive signs for women in globalization. In a systematic analysis of the effects of globalization on women, one study concluded that "global norms and institutions make a difference for the quality of life and status of women. . . . [W]hen domestic cultures are more open to international influences, outcomes for women improve, as measured by health, literacy, and participation in the economy and government.[146] Overall, the feminist perspective would stress the relations between men and women and the gendered understandings of those relations as an important part of the evolution of the future of global politics.

SUMMARY

- Globalization is arguably the most important process affecting relations between states and nonstate actors today. It refers to the high degree of interdependence between people and other actors and the homogenization of economic, political, and cultural life across the globe.

- Economic globalization involves moving toward a global marketplace. Evidence for economic globalization includes unprecedented levels of trade, including trade in services, high levels of international financial flows, including worldwide foreign exchange, the growing importance and presence of multinational corporations, and a growth in globally integrated crime. Economic relations are more global today than before the end of the Cold War, as developing countries, former Communist countries, and current Communist countries (like China) are participating in trade and financial flows to a greater extent.

- Political globalization involves new political actors and transnational political activities in a new system of global governance. The United Nations and other international organizations are part of this system and are engaging in policies that increasingly challenge state sovereignty. NGOs are also more influential and provide representation and services across borders. International and nongovernmental organizations are helping to create, and at times enforce, global norms, such as human and democratic rights.

- Cultural practices are becoming globalized as people are listening to the same music and watching the same television programs and films. The English language is facilitating the spread of cultural values and practices, as are high levels of migration, refugees, and worldwide tourism. While the majority of instances of cultural globalization are of American products, values, and practices becoming part of non-American cultures, Americans too are being exposed to other cultures.

- Technological developments, particularly revolutions in communication such as satellites, computers, and the Internet, are an important engine behind globalization, because they make it easier for economics, politics, and cultures to cross borders.

- While hyperglobalists argue that globalization is without precedent, skeptics point to the historical roots in economic, political, and cultural relations. International finance and trade at the turn of the century, for example, in some ways integrated states to a greater degree than they do today, and empires, particularly the British empire, globalized politics and culture in previous times. Transformationalists recognize these historical roots but argue that there is something quantitatively and qualitatively distinct about current globalizing dynamics that are transforming world political relations. Many point to the scope and velocity of these current dynamics as distinct features of globalization today.

- Skeptics point out that the scope of globalization is not really that global, given the vast differences in economics, politics, culture, and access to technology between the North and the South. Many argue that globalization is in fact further marginalizing the developing world, and many opponents to globalization can be found in the South. Others oppose globalization because they see it as a threat to local and national loyalties, and the persistence and growth of nationalism in recent years is an important countertrend to cultural globalization. Other sources of opposition to globalization are labor and environmental groups.

- The debate over globalization involves the relationship between global forces and the sovereign state. Some see current trends culminating in the eventual end to the state in a borderless world. Others argue that states are able to counter some losses to their power and are even the engines behind globalization. The various theoretical perspectives on world politics point to different aspects of the state-global relationship in the future. Realists, for example, bet on the state to survive, and control, globalization. Liberals focus more on nonstate actors, particularly individuals and their new ability to challenge the authority of states.

KEY TERMS

economic globalization 503
political globalization 507
global governance 507
cultural globalization 508
migration 510
refugees 510
cultural imperialism 511

distance-shrinking
  technologies 511
hyperglobalizers 514
globalization skeptics 514
transformationalists 517
"The Clash of
  Civilizations?" 521

References

Chapter 1 (pages 1–23)

1. Thucydides, *History of the Peloponnesian War*, trans. Rex Warner, ed. M. K. Finley (London: Penguin, 1972).

2. Hans J. Morgenthau, *Politics Among Nations: The Struggle for Power and Peace*, 3rd ed. (New York: Alfred A. Knopf, 1965). Other important works on realism include Edward Hallett Carr, *The Twenty Years' Crisis, 1919–1939: An Introduction to the Study of International Relations* (London: Macmillan Press, 1974 [1939]); Reinhold Niebuhr, *Moral Man and Immoral Society* (1960 [1936]); John Herz, "Idealist Internationalism and the Security Dilemma," *World Politics*, Vol. 2(2) (January 1950): pp. 157–180; and Raymond Aron, *Peace and War: A Theory of International Relations*, trans. R. Howard and A. B. Fox (New York: Doubleday, 1966). Kenneth N. Waltz, *Realism and International Politics* (New York: Routledge, 2008). For recent discussions of realism, see John J. Mearsheimer, *The Tragedy of Great Power Politics* (New York: W. W. Norton, 2001), and Jack Donnelly, *Realism and International Relations* (Cambridge: Cambridge University Press, 2000).

3. Realists disagree whether states try to simply maximize their security or maximize their power over others. See John J. Mearsheimer, *The Tragedy of Great Power Politics* (New York: W. W. Norton, 2001); and Stephen G. Brooks, "Dueling Realisms," *International Organization* 51(3) (Summer 1997): pp. 445–477.

4. The emphasis on anarchy and the distribution of power in the international system, as opposed to power-hungry human nature, is most pronounced in the version of realism known as *neorealism*. See Waltz, *Theory of International Politics* and Mearsheimer, *The Tragedy of Great Power Politics* (New York: W. W. Norton, 2001).

5. Thomas Hobbes, *Leviathan*, ed. Michael Oakeshott (New York: Macmillan, 1962), p. 100.

6. Robert O. Keohane and Joseph S. Nye, *Power and Interdependence: World Politics in Transition* (Boston: Little, Brown, 1997). Keohane and Nye's discussion of contemporary liberalism serves as the primary source for the discussion of complex interdependence in this book. For other works on liberalism, see David A. Baldwin (ed.), *Neorealism and Neoliberalism: The Contemporary Debate* (New York: Columbia University Press, 1993); Michael W. Doyle, *The Ways of War and Peace* (New York: Norton, 1997); and Andrew Moravcsik, "Taking Preferences Seriously: A Liberal Theory of International Politics," *International Organization* 51 (Autumn 1997).

7. For a review of the role of international organizations in international security, see Lisa L. Martin and Beth A. Simmons, "Theories and Empirical Studies of International Organizations," *International Organization* 52(4) (1998). The emphasis on international institutions is especially important in the "neoliberal" or "neoliberal institutionalist" version of liberalism. See, for example, Robert Keohane, *After Hegemony* (Princeton, N.J.: Princeton University Press, 1984), and Kenneth A. Oye (ed.), *Cooperation Under Anarchy* (Princeton, N.J.: Princeton University Press, 1986).

8. John Mearsheimer, "The False Promise of International Institutions," *International Security* (1995): 19.

9. See Montesquieu, *De L'Esprit des Lois*, trans. Nugent, Thomas, rev. J. V. Prichard (Chicago: Encyclopedia Britannica: 1955), and Immanuel Kant, *Perpetual Peace*, ed. Lewis White Beck (New York: Macmillan, 1957).

10. See John Stuart Mill, "On Liberty," in *Essential Works of John Stuart Mill*, ed. Max Lerner (New York: Bantam, 1961).

11. See Michael J. Mazaar, "George W. Bush, Idealist," *International Affairs* 79 (May 2003): pp. 503–522; Michael C. Desch, "America's Liberal Illiberalism: The Ideological Origins of Overreaction in U.S. Foreign Policy," *International Security* 32 (Winter2007/2008): pp. 7–43.

12. There are a variety of theories and approaches that fall under the neo-Marxist umbrella. These include world economic systems analysis, dependency theory, radical political economy, and neo-Gramscian and anti-globalization ideas. See, for example, Immanuel Wallerstein, *World-Systems Analysis: An Introduction* (Durham, N.C.: Duke University Press, 2004); Fernando Henrique Cardoso and Enzo Faletto, *Dependency and Development in Latin America* (Berkeley: University of California Press, 1979); and Robert A. Packenham, *The Dependency Movement: Scholarship and Politics in Development Studies* (Cambridge, Mass.: Harvard University Press, 1992); Robert W. Cox, *Political Economy of a Plural World* (London: Routledge, 2002); Malcolm C. Sawyer, *The Challenge of Radical Political Economy* (New York: Harvester Wheatsheaf, 1990); Stephen Gill, *Power and Resistance in the New World Order* (New York: Palgrave Macmillan, 2003).

13. William R. Thompson, "Introduction: World System Analysis with and Without the Hyphen," in William R. Thompson (ed.), *Contending Approaches to World System Analysis* (Thousand Oaks, Calif.: Sage, 1983), p. 12.

14. Immanuel Wallerstein, "Patterns and Perspectives of the Capitalist World-Economy," in Paul Viotti and Mark V. Kauppi (eds.), *International Relations Theory* (Boston: Allyn and Bacon, 1999), p. 370.

15. For one of the classic theories of imperialism, see John A. Hobson, *Imperialism: A Study* (Ann Arbor: University of Michigan Press, 1965). More recently, Immanuel Wallerstein, *World-Systems Analysis: An Introduction* (Durham, N.C.: Duke University Press, 2004).

16. See, for example, Fernando Henrique Cardoso and Enzo Faletto, *Dependency and Development in Latin America* (Berkeley: University of California Press, 1979) and Robert A. Packenham, *The Dependency Movement: Scholarship and Politics in Development Studies* (Cambridge, Mass.: Harvard University Press, 1992).

17. Friedrich Kratochwil, *Rules, Norms, and Decisions* (Cambridge: Cambridge University Press, 1989); Nicholas G. Onuf, *World of Our Making: Rules and Rule in Social Theory and International Relations* (Columbia: University of South Carolina Press, 1989); and Alexander Wendt, *Social Theory of International Politics* (Cambridge: Cambridge University Press, 1999). James Fearon and Alexander Wendt, "Rationalism versus Constructivism: A Skeptical View," in Walter Carlsnaes, Thomas Risse, and Beth Simmons (eds.), *Handbook of International Relations* (New York: Sage Publications, 2002): pp. 52–72; Timothy Dunne, "The Social Construction of International Society," *European Journal of International Relations* 1(3) (September 1995): pp. 367–390. On different types of constructivism, see Ted Hopf, "The Promise of Constructivism in International Relations Theory," *International Security* 23(1) (Summer 1998): pp. 171–200; Audie Klotz and Cecelia Lynch, *Strategies for Research in Constructivist International Relations* (2007).

18. Alexander Wendt, "Anarchy Is What States Make of It: The Social Construction of Power Politics," *International Organization* 17 (1991): pp. 383–392.

19. Martha Finnemore and Kathryn Sikkink, "International Norm Dynamics and Political Change," *International Organization* 52, no. 4 (Autumn 1998): pp. 887–917.

20. Mary Caprioli, "Feminist IR Theory and Quantitative Methodology: A Critical Analysis," *International Studies Review* 6, no. 2 (June 2004): pp. 253–269. J. Ann Tickner, "Feminist Perspectives on International Relations," Chapter 14 in W. Carlsnaes, T. Risse and B. Simmons (eds.), *Handbook of International Relations* (New York: Sage Publications, 2002); V. Spike Peterson, "Transgressing Boundaries: Theories of Knowledge, Gender, and International Relations," *Millennium: Journal of International Studies* 21, 2 (Summer 1992): pp. 183–206.

21. J. Ann Tickner, "You Just Don't Understand: Troubled Engagements Between Feminists and IR Theorists," *International Studies Quarterly* 42 (1997): p. 624.

22. Jim George, *Discourses of Global Politics: A Critical (Re)Introduction to International Relations* (Boulder, Colo.: Lynne Rienner, 1994), p. 26.

23. The World Bank Group. "Quick Query: Millenium Development Goals," http://ddp-ext.worldbank.org/ext/DDPQQ/showReport.do?method=showReport (accessed May 26, 2009).

24. Francis Fukuyama, "Women and the Evolution of World Politics," *Foreign Affairs* vol. 77, no. 5 (September–October 1998): 33. See Caprioli, "Feminist IR Theory and Quantitative Methodology" for a review of empirical studies on this issue. See also Swanee Hunt, "Let Women Rule," *Foreign Affairs* 86(3) (May/June 2007): pp. 109–110.

25. Tickner, "You Just Don't Understand."

26. Mary Caprioli, "The Myth of Women's Pacifism," in John T. Rourke (ed.), *Taking Sides: Clashing Views on Controversial Issues in World Politics*, 9th ed. (Guilford, Conn.: Dushkin/McGraw-Hill, 2000), p. 267.

27. Cynthia Enloe, *Bananas, Beaches, and Bases: Making Feminist Sense of International Politics* (Berkeley: University of California Press, 1989).

28. Tickner, "You Just Don't Understand," p. 625.

29. United Nations Development Program, *Taking Gender Equality Seriously: Making Progress, Meeting New Challenges* (New York UNDP, 2006).

30. United Nations Population Fund, 2002, "State of World Population 2002: Women and Gender Inequality," http://www.unfpa.org/swp/2002/english/ch4/page3.htm (accessed May 26, 2009).

31. Christine Sylvester, *Feminist International Relations: An Unfinished Journey* (Cambridge: Cambridge University Press, 2002).

Chapter 2 (pages 24–52)

1. Much of this section is drawn from Adam Watson, *The Evolution of International Society: A Comparative Historical Analysis* (London: Routledge, 1992).

2. Thucydides, *History of the Peloponnesian War*, trans. Rex Warner, ed. M. K. Finley (London: Penguin, 1972).

3. Samuel Edward Dawson, *The Lines of Demarcation of Pope Alexander VI and the Treaty of Tordesillas* (Ottawa: J. Hope & Sons, 1899).

4. Watson, *Evolution of International Society*, pp. 146–147.

5. Carlton J. H. Hayes, *A Political and Social History of Modern Europe* (New York: Macmillan, 1921), p. 231.

6. James L. Brierly, *The Law of Nations*, 2nd ed. (New York: Oxford University Press, 1963), p. 11.

7. Edward Morse, *Modernization in the Transformation of International Relations* (New York: Free Press, 1976), pp. 330–334.

8. John Herz, *International Politics in the Atomic Age* (New York: Columbia University Press, 1959), pp. 50–51.

9. Hendrik Spruyt, "Institutional Selection in International Relations: State Anarchy as Order," *International Organization* 48 (Autumn 1994): pp. 527–536.

10. Richard Bean, "War and the Birth of States," *Journal of Economic History* 33 (March 1973): p. 208.

11. Spruyt, "Institutional Selection," p. 550.

12. Karen Rasler and William Thompson, "War Making and State Making: Governmental Expenditures, Tax Revenue, and Global War," *American Political Science Review* 79 (June 1985): pp. 491–507.

13. Frederick L. Schuman, *International Politics: An Introduction to the Western State System*, 6th ed. (New York: McGraw-Hill, 1958), pp. 70–71.

14. Richard Rosecrance, *Action and Reaction in World Politics* (Boston: Little, Brown, 1963), p. 20.

15. Ibid., p. 34.

16. Samuel J. Barkin and Bruce Cronin, "The State and the Nation: Changing Norms and the Rules of Sovereignty in International Relations," *International Organization* 48 (Winter 1994): pp. 107–130.

17. "So long as Great Britain as an industrial nation had no equal, it was the most powerful nation on earth, the only one that deserved to be called a world power." Hans J. Morgenthau and Kenneth W. Thompson, *Politics Among Nations*, 6th ed. (New York: Knopf, 1958), p. 138.

18. William R. Keylor, *The Twentieth Century World* (Oxford: Oxford University Press, 1992), p. 34.

19. Benjamin J. Cohen, "A Brief History of International Monetary Relations," and Charles P. Kindleberger, "The Rise of Free Trade in Europe," in Jeffrey A. Frieden and David A. Lake (eds.), *International Political Economy: Perspectives on Global Power and Wealth* (New York: St. Martin's Press, 1995).

20. Erich Weede, *Economic Development, Social Order, and World Politics* (Boulder, Colo.: Lynne Rienner, 1996), p. 51.

21. Keylor, *Twentieth Century World*, p. 206.

22. Immanuel Wallerstein, *The Modern World-System* (New York: Academic Press, 1974, 1980).

23. Joan Robinson, *Economic Philosophy* (Chicago: Aldine, 1962), p. 45.

24. Watson, *Evolution of International Society*, pp. 273–274.

25. Anthony Haigh, *Congress of Vienna to Common Market* (London: Harrap, 1973), p. 67.

26. Watson, *Evolution of International Society*, p. 249.

27. See Kier Lieber for the argument that the Germans expected a protracted war. Keir A. Lieber, "The New History of World War I and What It Means for International Relations Theory," *International Security*, Vol. 32, No. 2 (Fall 2007), pp. 155–191.

28. Richard Pipes, *The Russian Revolution* (New York: Vintage Books, 1990).

29. Arthur Sweetser, *The League of Nations at Work* (New York: Macmillan,1920), p. 5, as cited in Inis L. Claude, *Swords into Plowshares*, 3rd ed. (New York: Random House, 1964), p. 40.

30. William L. Shirer, *The Collapse of the Third Republic* (New York: Simon & Schuster, 1969), p. 114.

31. Ibid., pp. 57–58.

32. He became eligible for parole in six months and was released after only nine months in prison.

33. Alexander de Conde, *A History of American Foreign Policy* (New York: Scribner's, 1963), pp. 559–560.

34. Paul Johnson, *Modern Times* (New York: Harper & Row, 1983), p. 246. This is a predominant opinion, but for an alternative interpretation, see Susan Strange, "Protectionism and World Politics," *International Organization* 39 (Spring 1985): pp. 239–240.

35. John Kenneth Galbraith, *Money: Whence It Came, Where It Went* (New York: Bantam Books, 1975), p. 274.

36. De Conde, *History of American Foreign Policy*, p. 526.

37. James Dugan and Laurence Lafore, *Days of Emperor and Clown* (Garden City, N.Y.: Doubleday, 1973), p. 80.

38. William L. Shirer, *The Nightmare Years: 1930–1940* (Boston: Little, Brown, 1984), p. 242.

39. Cited in William L. Shirer, *The Rise and Fall of the Third Reich* (New York: Simon & Schuster, 1960), p. 796.

40. V. Spike Peterson, "Security and Sovereign States: What Is at Stake in Taking Feminism Seriously?" in V. Spike Peterson (ed.), *Gendered States: Feminist (Re)Visions of International Relations Theory* (Boulder, Colo.: Lynne Rienner Publishers, 1992), p. 43.

Chapter 3 (pages 53–94)

1. Peter Calvocoressi, *World Politics Since 1945*, 6th ed. (New York: Longman, 1991), p. 231.

2. Gabriel Kolko and Joyce Kolko, *The Limits of Power* (New York: Harper & Row, 1972); David Horowitz, *The Free World Colossus* (New York: Wang & Hill, 1965); Gar Alperowitz, *Atomic Diplomacy* (New York: Random House, 1965).

3. Louis W. Koenig (ed.), *The Truman Administration: Its Principles and Practice* (New York: New York University Press, 1956), pp. 296–301.

4. This version of the event is accepted by most Western sources, although the North Koreans claimed that they were responding to an attack by the South, and one well-known Western journalist argues that the United States was at least partially responsible for the onset of the Korean War. I. F. Stone, *The Hidden History of the Korean War* (New York: Monthly Review Press, 1952).

5. Richard J. Barnet, *The Roots of War* (Baltimore: Penguin Books, 1971), p. 274.

6. The majority of troops opposing North Korea, though, were South Korean.

7. "Review of UN and U.S. Action to Restore Peace," *Department of State Bulletin*, 1950, p. 46.

8. Allen S. Whiting, *China Crosses the Yalu* (New York: Macmillan, 1960), pp. 108–109.

9. Geoffrey Stern, "Soviet Foreign Policy in Theory and Practice," in F. S. Northedge (ed.), *The Foreign Policies of the Powers* (New York: Free Press, 1974), p. 134.

10. John G. Stoessinger, *Why Nations Go to War*, 6th ed. (New York: St. Martin's Press, 1993), p. 81.

11. This section is drawn from accounts in Stephen E. Ambrose, *Rise to Globalism: American Foreign Policy Since 1938* (New York: Penguin Books, 1988); William R. Keylor, *The Twentieth Century World: An International History* (Oxford: Oxford University Press, 1992); and Wayne C. McWilliams and Harry Piotrowski, *The World Since 1945: A History of International Relations* (Boulder, Colo.: Lynne Rienner, 1993).

12. Keylor, *Twentieth Century World*, p. 359.

13. Lloyd S. Etheredge, *Can Governments Learn?* (New York: Pergamon Press, 1985), p. 20.

14. Bruce J. Allyn, James G. Blight, and David A. Welch, "Essence of Revision: Moscow, Havana, and the Cuban Missile Crisis," *International Security* 14 (Winter 1989–1990): p. 139.

15. Ibid., p. 165. These missiles were obsolete and had already been slated for removal before the missile crisis began.

16. James G. Blight, Joseph S. Nye, Jr., and David A. Welch, "The Cuban Missile Crisis Revisited," *Foreign Affairs* 66 (Fall 1987): p. 176.

17. Ibid., pp. 397–398.

18. Henry A. Kissinger, *White House Years* (Boston: Little, Brown, 1979), pp. 693–746.

19. Louis Kriesberg and Ross Klein, "Changes in Public Support for U.S. Military Spending," *Journal of Conflict Resolution* 24 (March 1980): pp. 79–111.

20. Michael Howard, "The Springtime of Nations," *Foreign Affairs* 69 (1989–1990): p. 17.

21. *Los Angeles Times*, December 17, 1989, p. 1.

22. "Since 1979, the politics of Latin America have been transformed by the longest and deepest wave of democratization in the region's history." Karen Remmer, "Democracy and Economic Crisis: The Latin American Experience," *World Politics* 42 (April 1990): p. 315.

23. Makau wa Mutua, "African Renaissance," *New York Times*, May 11, 1991, 1:13.

24. Freedom House, *Freedom in the World*, edition, 2008, http://www.freedomhouse.org/uploads/Chart116File163.pdf (accessed May 20, 2009).

25. United Nations, *Human Development Report 2002* (New York: Oxford University Press, 2002), p. 1.

26. Ibid. See also United Nations, *Human Development Report 2002* (New York: Oxford University Press, 2002), pp. 20–21.

27. Larry Diamond, "The Democratic Rollback: The Resurgence of the Predatory State," *Foreign Affairs* 87(2) (March/April 2008): pp. 36–48; see also Arthur A. Goldsmith, "Making the World Safe for Partial Democracy? Questioning the Premises of Democracy Promotion," *International Security*, Vol. 33, no.2 (Fall 2008): pp. 120–147.

28. Hassan M. Fattah, "Democracy in the Arab World, a U.S. Goal, Falters," *New York Times* (April 10, 2006). See also Mahmood Monshipouri, "The Bush Doctrine and Democracy

Promotion in the Middle East" in David P. Forsythe, Patrice C. McMahon, and Andrew Wedeman, *American Foreign Policy in a Globalized World* (New York: Routledge, 2006), pp. 313–334. See also Tamara Cofman Wittes, Freedoms Unsteady March: Americas Role in Building Arab Democracy (Brookings Institution Press, 2008) and Marina Ottaway and Julia Choucair-Vizoso (Eds.) Beyond the Façade: Political Reform in the Arab World (Carnegie Endowment for International Peace, 2008.)

29. Thomas Carothers, "The Backlash Against Democracy Promotion," *Foreign Affairs* 85(2) (March/April, 2006).

30. Ted Robert Gurr, *Peoples Versus States: Minorities at Risk in the New Century* (Washington, D.C.: United States Institute of Peace Press, 2000) and Monty G. Marshall and Ted Robert Gurr, *Peace and Conflict 2005: A Global Survey of Armed Conflicts, Self-Determination Movements, and Democracy* (College Park, Md.: Center for International Development and Conflict Management, 2005).

31. See Ahmed S. Hashim, "Iraq's Civil War," *Current History* (January 2007), pp. 3–10. See also Judith S. Yaphe, "Iraq: Are We There Yet?" *Current History* (December 2008): 403-409.

32. See Gérard Prunier, "The Politics of Death in Darfur," *Current History* (May 2006): pp. 195–202. John Predergrast and Colin Thomas-Jensen, "Sudan: A State on the Brink? *Current History* 108(718).

33. Robert I. Rothberg (ed.), *When States Fail: Causes and Consequences* (Princeton, NJ: Princeton University Press, 2004).

34. On Iraq, see Judith S. Yaphe, "Iraq: Are We There Yet?" *Current History* (December 2008): pp. 403–409; on Afghanistan, see Thomas Barfield, "The Roots of Failure in Afghanistan," *Current History* (December 2008): pp. 410–417.

35. Robert I. Rotberg, "Failed States in a World of Terror," *Foreign Affairs* 81 (4) (July/August 2002): pp. 127–40. Also see Stewart Patrick, "'Failed' States and Global Security: Empirical Questions and Policy Dilemmas," *International Studies Review*, 2007 Vol. 9(4): 644-62. On Afghanistan, see Barnett R. Rubin and Ahmed Rashind, "From Great Game to Grand Bargain," *Foreign Affairs*, Nov/Dec 2008, Vol. 87 Issue 6, pp. 30–44.

36. Lucien Crowder, "We Are All Nation Builders Now," *Current History* (January 2009): pp. 9–13.

37. Bruce Hoffman, *Inside Terrorism* (New York: Columbia University Press, 2006), p. 294.

38. Bruce Ridel, "Pakistan: The Critical Battlefield," *Current History* (November 2008): pp. 355–361.

39. Charles Krauthammer, "The Unipolar Moment," *Foreign Affairs* 70 (Winter 1990/91): pp. 23–33 and Josef Joffe, *Überpower: The Imperial Temptation of America* (New York: W. W. Norton and Company, 2006). Also see Joseph S. Nye, Jr., *The Paradox of American Power: Why the World's Only Superpower Can't Go It Alone* (Oxford: Oxford University Press, 2002). Also see Stewart Patrick, "'Failed' States and Global Security: Empirical Questions and Policy Dilemmas," *International Studies Review*, 2007 Vol. 9(4): pp. 644–662. On Afghanistan, see Barnett R. Rubin and Ahmed Rashind, "From Great Game to Grand Bargain," *Foreign Affairs*, Vol. 87(6) (Nov/Dec 2008): pp. 30–44.

40. Ivo H. Daalder and James M. Lindsay, *America Unbound: The Bush Revolution in Foreign Policy* (Washington, D.C.: Brookings Institution Press, 2003).

41. The Bush Doctrine is best described in the report issued by President Bush to the U.S. Congress in September 2002. See *The National Security Strategy of the United States of America* http://www.whitehouse.gov/nsc/nss.html (accessed December 21, 2006).

42. Daalder and Lindsay, *America Unbound: The Bush Revolution in Foreign Policy.*

43. Pew Global Attitudes Project, "America's Image Slips, But Allies Share U.S. Concerns Over Iran, Hamas," Pew Research Center, report released June 13, 2006, available at http://pewglobal.org/reports/display.php?ReportID=252 (accessed December 26, 2006).

44. Ibid. For more on the Latin American reaction to the United States, see Michael Shifter, "The U.S. and Latin America Through the Lens of Empire," *Current History* (February 2004): pp. 61–67.

45. Peter Warren Singer, "America, Islam, and the 9–11 War," *Current History* (December 2006): pp. 415–422. See also Byman, D. 2007. "Al Qaeda," *Foreign Policy* 159 (March/April): 42-3.

46. Zbigniew Brzezinski, "Hegemonic Quicksand," *The National Interest* (Winter 2003/2004): pp. 5–16. See also Dalia Mogahed, 2006. "Muslims and Americans: The Way Forward." http://www.muslimwestfacts.com/mwf/File/109480/Muslims_and_Americans.pdf (May 19, 2009).

47. Daalder and Lindsay, *America Unbound: The Bush Revolution in Foreign Policy*, p. 195.

48. Pew Global Attitudes Project, "Some Positive Signs for U.S. Image: Global Economic Gloom–China and India Notable Exceptions." Pew Research Center, report released June 12, 2008, available at http://pewglobal.org/reports/pdf/260.pdf; Pew Global Attitudes Project, "Global Public Opinion in the Bush Years (2001–2008) America's Image; Muslims and Westerners; Global Economy; Rise of China" Pew Research Center, report released December 18, 2008, available at http://pewglobal.org/reports/display.php?ReportID=263; Ethan Bronner, "The Promise: For Many Abroad, an Ideal Renewed," *The New York Times* (November 5, 2008).

49. United Nations Development Programme, *Human Development Report 2005* (New York: Oxford University Press, 2005), p. 116. Reprinted by permission of Oxford University Press.

50. Alan Sorensen, "A Panic Made in America," *Current History* (January 2009), 3–9, p. 6; Roger C. Altman, "The Great Crash, 2008: A Geopolitical Setback for the West," *Foreign Affairs*, Vol. 88(1) (Jan/Feb2009); Ian Bremmer, "State Capitalism Comes of Age," *Foreign Affairs*, May/Jun2009, Vol. 88(3).

51. Harold James, "The Late, Great Globalization," *Current History* (January 2009), 20–25, pp. 20–21.

52. Alan Sorensen, "A Panic Made in America," *Current History* (January 2009), 3–9, p. 6; Moisés Naím, "Think Again: Globalization." *Foreign Policy* 171 (March/April 2009): pp. 28–34.

53. Alan Sorensen, "A Panic Made in America," *Current History* (January 2009), 3–9, p. 7.

54. See, for example, Harold James, "The Late, Great Globalization," *Current History* (January 2009): pp. 20–25; Christopher Layne, "China's Challenge to US Hegemony," *Current History* (January 2008): pp. 13–18; Kishore Mahbubani, "America's Place in the Asian Century," *Current History* (May 2008): pp. 195–200; Roger C. Altman, "The Great Crash, 2008: A Geopolitical Setback for the West," *Foreign Affairs* (Jan/Feb2009), Vol. 88(1).

55. Daniel W. Drezner, "The New New World Order," *Foreign Affairs* 86(2):34–46, p. 34.

56. For a good discussion of theoretical perspectives on the end of the Cold War and the post-September 11 era, see

Barry Buzan, "Implications for the Study of International Relations," in Mary Buckley and Rick Fawn (eds.), *Global Responses to Terrorism: 9/11, Afghanistan and Beyond* (London: Routledge, 2003): pp. 296–309.

57. For a summary of this perspective on globalization, see Arie M. Kacowicz, "Globalization, Poverty, and the North-South Divide," *International Studies Review* (2007), Vol. 9: pp. 565–580.

58. Jutta Weldes and Diana Saco, "Making State Action Possible: The United States and the Discursive Construction of 'The Cuban Problem,' 1960–1994," *Millennium: Journal of International Studies* 25 (1996): p. 363.

59. Christian Reus-Smit, "Constructivism," in Scott Burchill, Andrew Linklater, Richard Devetak, Jack Donnelly, Matthew Patterson, Christian Reus-Smit, and Jacqui True, *Theories of International Relations*, 3rd ed. (New York: Palgrave Macmillan, 2005): pp. 188–212.

60. Cynthia Enloe, *The Morning After: Sexual Politics at the End of the Cold War* (Berkeley: University of California Press, 1993), p. 5.

61. Ibid., p. 23.

62. Ibid., p. 243.

Chapter 4 (pages 95–139)

1. Anthony D. Smith, *National Identity* (Reno: University of Nevada Press, 1991), p. 14.

2. Charles O. Lerche, Jr., and Abdul A. Said, *Concepts of International Politics in Global Perspective*, 3rd ed. (Englewood Cliffs, N.J.: Prentice Hall, 1979), p. 120.

3. In fact, it can be argued that "the concept of power is perhaps the most fundamental in the whole of political science." Harold D. Lasswell and Abraham Kaplan, *Power and Society* (New Haven, Conn.: Yale University Press, 1950), p. 75.

4. Hans J. Morgenthau, *Politics Among Nations*, 4th ed. (New York: Knopf, 1967), p. 26.

5. "Power is the means by which international actors deal with one another. It implies possession." Walter S. Jones and Steven J. Rosen, *The Logic of International Relations*, 4th ed. (Boston: Little, Brown, 1982), p. 229.

6. David Baldwin, "Power Analysis and World Politics," *World Politics* 31 (January 1979): pp. 161–194.

7. The following discussion is based in large part on James Lee Ray and Ayse Vural, "Power Disparities and Paradoxical Conflict Outcomes," *International Interactions* 12 (1986): pp. 315–342.

8. Cynthia A. Cannizzo, "The Costs of Combat: Death, Duration, and Defeat," in J. David Singer (ed.), *The Correlates of War II: Testing Some Realpolitik Models* (New York: Free Press, 1980).

9. Kevin Wang and James Lee Ray, "Beginners and Winners: The Fate of Initiators of Interstate Wars Involving Great Powers Since 1495," *International Studies Quarterly* 38 (March 1994): pp. 139–154.

10. Zeev Maoz, "Resolve, Capabilities, and the Outcomes of Interstate Disputes, 1816–1976," *Journal of Conflict Resolution* 27 (June 1983): p. 220.

11. Patricia L. Sullivan, "War Aims and War Outcomes: Why Powerful States Lose Limited Wars," *Journal of Conflict Resolution* 2007; 51; 498.

12. For an overview of asymmetric warfare and its importance in current U.S. security policy, see Donald M. Snow, *National Security for a New Era: Globalization and*

Geopolitics, 2nd ed. (New York: Pearson Longman, 2007), Chapter 9.

13. Gil Merom, *How Democracies Lose Small Wars* (Cambridge: Cambridge University Press, 2003).

14. Peter Schweizer, in *Victory: The Reagan Administration's Secret Strategy That Hastened the Collapse of the Soviet Union* (New York: Grove/Atlantic, 1996).

15. Karen Rasler and Kenneth W. Thompson, "Predatory Initiators and Changing Landscapes for Warfare," *Journal of Conflict Resolution* 43 (August 1999): 411–433.

16. For a discussion of the motivation explanation, including the Vietnam example, see Merom, *How Democracies Lose Small Wars*, pp. 11–14.

17. Andrew Mack, "Why Big Nations Lose Small Wars: The Politics of Asymmetric Conflict," *World Politics* 27(January 1975): p. 197.

18. Steven Rosen, "War Power and the Willingness to Suffer," in Bruce M. Russett (ed.), *Peace, War, and Numbers* (Beverly Hills, Calif.: Sage, 1972).

19. J. David Singer, "Peace in the Global System: Displacement, Interregnum, or Transformation," in Charles W. Kegley, Jr. (ed.), *The Long Postwar Peace* (New York: HarperCollins, 1991), p. 73.

20. For those reasons, A. F. K. Organski and Jacek Kugler, *The War Ledger* (Chicago: University of Chicago Press, 1980), pp. 33–34, for example, use the gross national product (GNP), discussed below, as their basic measure of power.

21. Joseph S. Nye, Jr., *Understanding International Conflicts* (New York: Longman, 2000), p. 57. See also Joseph S. Nye, Jr., *The Paradox of American Power* (New York: Oxford University Press, 2002). Joseph S. Nye, Jr., Soft Power: The Means to Success in World Politics. 2005 New York: Public Affairs.

22. Joseph S. Nye, Jr., *Bound to Lead: The Changing Nature of American Power* (New York: Basic Books, 1990), and Nye, *The Paradox of American Power*.

23. Michael Barnett and Raymond Duvall, "Power in International Politics," *International Organization* 59 (Winter 2005): pp. 39–75

24. Andrew F. Krepinevich, Jr., "How to Win in Iraq," *Foreign Affairs* 84(5) (September/October 2005): pp. 87–104. See also Rob de Wijk, "The Limits of Military Power," in Alexander T. J. Lennon (ed.), *The Battle for Hearts and Minds: Using Soft Power to Undermine Terrorist Networks* (Cambridge, Mass.: MIT Press, 2003), pp. 3–28.

25. Stevano Guzzini, "The Concept of Power: A Constructivist Analysis," *Millenium: Journal of International Studies* 33(3) (2005): pp. 495–521. Martha Finnemore, "Legitimacy, Hypocrisy, and the Social Structure of Unipolarity: Why Being a Unipole Isn't All It's Cracked up to Be," *World Politics* 61, no. 1 (January 2009), 58–85.

26. Barnett and Duvall, "Power in International Politics," p. 56.

27. J. Ann Tickner, "Hans Morgenthau's Principles of Political Realism: A Feminist Reformulation," *Millennium* 17 (1988): p. 434.

28. Baldwin, "Power Analysis and World Politics," p. 166.

29. David Baldwin, "Interdependence and Power: A Conceptual Analysis," *International Organization* 34 (Autumn 1980): p. 497.

30. James F. Dougherty and Robert L. Pfaltzgraff, Jr., *Contending Theories of International Relations*, 3rd. ed. (New York: Harper & Row, 1990), pp. 61–64.

31. Nicholas J. Spykman, *The Geography of Peace* (New York: Harcourt, Brace, 1944), p. 43.

32. For a recent geopolitical analysis on the importance of the Indian Ocean, see Robert D. Kaplan, "Center Stage for the Twenty-First Century, *Foreign Affairs*, March/April 2009, Vol. 88 Issue 2, p16-32.

33. The 1999 figures are from the World Development Indicators database, World Bank, August 2, 2000 (http://www.worldbank.org/data/).

34. John Allen, *Student Atlas of World Politics* (New York: Dushkin/McGraw-Hill, 2000), pp. 108–110.

35. A related measure is gross domestic product (GDP). Whereas GDP includes only the goods and services produced within a country by all people residing there, both citizens and noncitizens, GNP includes the total product of a country's nationals (citizens), whether or not they reside in that country. These differences tend to be offsetting to some extent for most countries; therefore, the figures are quite similar for most countries.

36. International Monetary Fund. World Economic Outlook Database: April 2009 Edition, http://www.imf.org/external/pubs/ft/weo/2009/01/weodata/index.aspx Accessed 28 May 2009.

37. United Nations Development Programme. 2007/2008. 2007/2008 *Human Development Report*. http://hdrstats.undp.org/en/indicators (accessed May 20, 2009).

38. see, for example, Harold James, "The Late, Great Globalization," Current History, January 2009: 20-25; Christopher Layne, "China's Challenge to US Hegemony," Current History, January 2008: 13-18; Kishore Mahbubani, "America's Place in the Asian Century," Current History, May 2008: 195-200; Roger C. Altman, "The Great Crash, 2008: A Geopolitical Setback for the West," Foreign Affairs, Jan/Feb2009, Vol. 88, Issue 1; Daniel W. Drezner, "The New New World Order," Foreign Affairs 86(2):34-46.

39. Minxin Pei, "The Dark Side of China's Rise," *Foreign Policy*, no. 153 (March/April 2006): 32-40.

40. Steve Chan, "Is There a Power Transition between the U.S. and China? The Different Faces of National Power," *Asian Survey* 45(5) (September-October, 2005):687-701.

41. Thomas Risse-Kappen, "Bringing Transnational Relations Back In: Introduction," in Thomas Risse-Kappen (ed.), *Bringing Transnational Relations Back In* (Cambridge: Cambridge University Press, 1995), p. 3.

42. Joan Edelman Spero and Jeffrey A. Hart, *The Politics of International Economic Relations*, 7th ed. 2010 Belmont, CA: Thomson Wadsworth, p. 129.

43. Union of International Associations, *Yearbook of International Organizations: Guide to global and Civil Society Networks* Edition 44 2007/2008, Vol. 2: Geographic Volume International Organization Participation: Country Directory of Secretariats and Membership (Munich, Germany: KG Saur, 2007), pp. 1716-1719.

44. Matthew Lynn, "Can Mercenaries Defeat the Somali Pirates?" The Spectator, April 25, 2009, p. 28, http://www.lexisnexis.com.www2.lib.ku.edu:2048/us/lnacademic/auth/checkbrowser.do?ipcounter=1&cookieState=0&rand=0.6543800247699174&bhcp=1.

45. Thomas Risse, "Transnational Actors and World Politics," in Walter Carlsnaes, Thomas Risse, and Beth A. Simmons (eds.), *Handbook of International Relations* (Thousand Oaks, Calif.: Sage, 2002), pp. 257–258. See also Daphné Josselin and William Wallace, "Non-state Actors in World Politics: A Framework," in Daphné Josselin and William Wallace (eds.), *Non-State Actors in World Politics* (New York: Palgrave Macmillan, 2001), pp. 1–20.

46. Risse-Kappen, "Bringing Transnational Relations Back In," p. 4.

47. Risse, "Transnational Actors and World Politics," p. 258; Josselin and Wallace, "Nonstate Actors in World Politics."

48. W. Clausen, "The Internationalized Corporation: An Executive's View," *Annals* 403 (September 1972): p. 21.

49. Robert S. Walters and David H. Blake, *The Politics of Global Economic Relations*, 4th ed. (Englewood Cliffs, N.J.: Prentice-Hall, 1992), p. 104.

50. William Manchester, *The Arms of Krupp* (Boston: Little, Brown, 1968).

51. David Turner and Pete Richardson "The Global Business." The OECD Observer no. 234 (October 2002): 27-8, http://www.oecdobserver.org/news/fullstory.php/aid/850/The_global_business_.html

52. Joan Edelman Spero and Jeffrey A. Hart, *The Politics of International Economic Relations*, 7th ed. 2010 Belmont, CA: Thomson Wadsworth, p. 135-136.

53. Ibid, p. 129.

54. United Nations Conference on Trade & Development. 2008. World Investment Report 2008: Transnational Corporations and the Infrastructure Challenge. New York: United Nations Publications.

55. "Fortune's Global 500: The World's Largest Corporations," *Fortune*, August 7, 1995, p. F-1.

56. United Nations Conference on Trade & Development. 2008. *World Investment Report 2008: Transnational Corporations and the Infrastructure Challenge*. New York: United Nations Publications, http://www.unctad.org/en/docs/wir2008p1_en.pdf, p.7.

57. OECD Investment Committee. 2008. "OECD FDI Outflows and Inflows Reach Record Highs in 2007 and Look Set to Fall in 2008." *OECD Investment News*, Iss. 7 (June): 1-3, http://www.oecd.org/dataoecd/18/28/40887916.pdf (May 21, 2009).

58. Robert B. Reich, "Who Is Us?" *Harvard Business Review* 90 (January–February 1990): p. 59; see also Robert Reich, *The Work of Nations: Preparing Ourselves for 21st Century Capitalism* (New York: Knopf, 1991).

59. Gross national product is closely related to GDP. Whereas GDP includes only the goods and services produced within a country by all people residing there, both citizens and noncitizens, GNP includes the total product of a country's nationals, whether or not they reside in that country. These differences tend to be offsetting and the figures are quite similar for most countries.

60. Robert A. Pastor, "The Future of North America: Replacing a Bad Neighbor Policy." *Foreign Affairs* 87 (July/August 2008): 84-98, p.90.

61. Ethan B. Kapstein, "The Myth of the Multinational," *National Interest* 26 (Winter 1991–1992): p. 56.

62. Louis W. Pauly and Simon Reich, "National Structures and Multinational Corporate Behavior: Enduring Differences in the Age of Globalization," *International Organization* 51 (Winter 1997): p. 22.

63. Not all analysts of the relationship between states and MNCs agree, of course. One analysis, for example, asserts that "nowadays governments have only the appearance of free choice when they set out to make rules." Jessica T. Mathews, "Power Shift," *Foreign Affairs* 76 (January–February 1997): p. 57. Reprinted by permission of Foreign Affairs. Copyright © 1997 by the Council on Foreign Relations, Inc. www.ForeignAffairs.com

64. Pauly and Reich, "National Structures and Multinational Corporate Behavior," p. 25, Abstract. See also Paul N.

Doremus, William W. Keller, Louis W. Pauly, and Simon Reich, *The Myth of the Global Corporation* (Princeton, N.J.: Princeton University Press, 1998).

65. Barnett and Duvall, "Power in International Politics," p. 50.

66. Lester M. Salamon, "The Rise of the Nonprofit Sector," *Foreign Affairs* 73 (July–August 1994): p. 109.

67. Margaret E. Keck and Kathryn Sikkink, *Activists Beyond Borders* (Ithaca, N.Y.: Cornell University Press, 1998). Kenneth Anderson and Marlies Glasius, "Civil Society: Do NGOs Wield Too Much Power?" In *Controversies in Globalization: Contending Approaches to International Relations*, eds. Peter M. Haas, John A. Hird, and Beth McBratney. 2010 Washington, DC: CQ Press, 359–382.

68. P. J. Simmons, "Learning to Live with NGOs," *Foreign Policy* 112 (Fall 1998): p. 83. For an analysis of the causes of NGO growth, see Kim D. Reimann, "A View from the Top: International Politics, Norms and the Worldwide Growth of NGOs," *International Studies Quarterly* 50(1) (March 2006): pp. 45–67.

69. United Nations Department of Economic and Social Affairs. "Consultative Status with ECOSOC," http://esango.un.org/paperless/Web?page=static&content=intro (accessed May 21, 2009).

70. Risse, "Transnational Actors and World Politics"; Ann Marie Clark, Elisabeth J. Friedman, and Kathryn Hochstetler, "The Sovereign Limits of Global Society: A Comparison of NGO Participation in UN World Conferences on the Environment, Human Rights, and Women," *World Politics* 51 (1998): pp. 1–35; Martha Fennemore and Kathryn Sikkink, "International Norm Dynamics and Political Change," *International Organization* 52 (1998): pp. 887–917.

71. See, for example, Thomas Rochon, *Mobilizing for Peace: The Antinuclear Movements in Western Europe* (Princeton, N.J.: Princeton University Press, 1988).

72. Kendall W. Stiles, *Case Histories in International Politics* (New York: Longman, 2001), p. 387.

73. Paul Wapner, "Politics Beyond the State: Environmental Activism and World Civic Politics," *World Politics* 47 (April 1995): pp. 311–340.

74. On the role of NGOS in human rights, see Daniel A. Bell and Joseph H. Carens, "The Ethical Dilemmas of International Human Rights and Humanitarian NGOs: Reflections on a Dialogue between Practitioners and Theorists." *Human Rights Quarterly* 26 (May 2004): 300–329.

75. International Committee of the Red Cross, *History of the International Committee of the Red Cross*, www .icrc.org (accessed December 8, 2003).

76. David Forsythe, *Human Rights and World Politics*, 2nd ed. (Lincoln: University of Nebraska Press, 1989).

77. *Amnesty International Report* (London: Amnesty International, 1993), p. 327.

78. Tracy LaQuey with Jeanne C. Ryer, *Internet Companion: A Beginner's Guide to Global Networking* (Reading, Mass.: Addison-Wesley, 1993), p. 12.

79. Risse, "Transnational Actors and World Politics," p. 260.

80. Maryann K. Cusimano, Mark Hensman, and Leslie Rodrigues, "Private-Sector Transovereign Actors—MNCs and NGOs," in Maryann K. Cusimano (ed.), *Beyond Sovereignty* (Boston: Bedford/St. Martin's, 2000), p. 276.

81. Ibid., p. 262.

82. Simmons, "Learning to Live with NGOs," p. 88.

83. Robert O. Keohane, "Global Governance and Democratic Accountability," In *Taming Globalization: Frontiers of Governance*, eds. David Held and Mathias Koenig-Archibugi. 2003. Cambridge: Polity Press, 130-159.

84. Ibid. Also see *The Economist*, "NGOs: Sins of the Secular Missionaries," January 29, 2000.

85. Mathews, "Power Shift," pp. 52, 65.

86. Josselin and Wallace, "Non-state Actors In World Politics."

87. Stephen D. Krasner, "Power Politics, Institutions, and Transnational Relations," in Risse-Kappen, *Bringing Transnational Relations Back In*, pp. 277–278.

88. For a constructivist discussion of the power of discourse of NGOs, see Anna Holzscheiter, "Discourse as Capability: Non-State Actors' Capital in Global Governance," *Millennium: Journal of International Studies* 33(3) (2005): pp. 723–746.

89. Barnett and Duvall, "Power in International Politics," p. 50.

90. Keck and Sikkink, *Activists Beyond Borders*.

91. Thomas Risse and Stephen C. Ropp, "International Human Rights Norms and Domestic Change: Conclusions," in Thomas Risse, Stephen C. Ropp, and Kathryn Sikkink, *The Power of Human Rights: International Norms and Domestic Change* (Cambridge: Cambridge University Press, 1999): pp. 234–278.

92. Ibid.; on the Moroccan case, also see Sieglinde Granzer, "Changing Discourse: Transnational Advocacy Networks in Tunisia and Morocco," in Risse, Ropp, and Sikkink, *The Power of Human Rights*, pp. 109–133. On the conditions under which shaming is effective, see James C. Franklin, "Shame on You: The Impact of Human Rights Criticism on Political Repression in Latin America," *International Studies Quarterly* (2008) 52, 187–211.

93. Kal Raustiala, "States, NGOs, and International Environmental Institutions," *International Studies Quarterly* 41 (1997): p. 720.

94. Risse, "Transnational Actors and World Politics," p. 260.

95. Keck and Sikkink, *Activists Beyond Borders*, Chap. 5. However, Don Hinrichsen argues that some NGOs work specifically against women's rights issues; see Worldwatch Institute, "Ladies, You Have No Choice," *World Watch Magazine* 17(2) (2004), www.worldwatch.org.

96. Walter Enders and Todd Sandler, "Patterns of Transnational Terrorism, 1970–1999: Alternative Time-Series Estimates," *International Studies Quarterly* 46 (2002): p. 146.

97. David E. Long, "Countering Terrorism Beyond Sovereignty," in Maryann K. Cusimano (ed.), *Beyond Sovereignty* (Boston: Bedford/St. Martin's, 2000), p. 105.

98. Examples compiled and presented in Cindy C. Combs, *Terrorism in the Twenty-First Century* (Upper Saddle River, N.J.: Prentice Hall, 2000), pp. 3–4.

99. Enders and Sandler, "Patterns of Transnational Terrorism," p. 146.

100. Walter Enders and Todd Sandler, "Distribution of Transnational Terrorism Among Countries by Income Class and Geography After 9/11" *International Studies Quarterly* 50 (June 2006): pp. 367–393.

101. Walter Enders and Todd Sandler, "Is Transnational Terrorism Becoming More Threatening?" *Journal of Conflict Resolution* 44 (June 2000): p. 309.

102. Combs, *Terrorism in the Twenty-First Century*, p. 88.

103. Ibid., p. 89.

104. Ibid., p. 91.

105. Martha Crenshaw, "Why America? The Globalization of Civil War," *Current History* (December 2001): p. 431.

106. Michael T. Klare, "Waging Postindustrial Warfare on the Global Battlefield," *Current History* (December 2001): p. 435.

107. Long, "Countering Terrorism Beyond Sovereignty," pp. 104–105.

108. Audrey Kurth Cronin, "Rethinking Sovereignty: American Strategy in the Age of Terrorism," *Survival* 44 (2002): pp. 119–120. See also Barak Mendelsohn "Sovereignty Under Attack: The International Society Meets the Al Qaeda Network," *Review of International Studies* 2005. 31: 45–68.

109. Stanley Hoffman, "Clash of Globalizations," *Foreign Affairs* 81 (July–August 2002): p. 107.

110. Bruce Hoffman, *Inside Terrorism* (New York: Columbia University Press, 2006), pp. 3–20.

111. de Wijk, "The Limits of Military Power," p. 20.

112. Mark Juergensmeyer, "Terror in the Name of God," *Current History* (November 2001): p. 361.

113. Martha Crenshaw and Cusimano Love, "Networked Terror," in Cusimano Love, *Beyond Sovereignty*, pp. 125–129.

114. S. Hoffman, "Clash of Globalizations," p. 112.

115. Long, "Countering Terrorism Beyond Sovereignty," p. 96.

116. Cronin, "Rethinking Sovereignty," p. 134. See also Jusuf Wanandi, "A Global Coalition Against International Terrorism," *International Security* 26 (Spring 2002).

117. S. Hoffman, "Clash of Globalizations," p. 107. For an alternative view, see Kenneth N. Waltz, "The Continuity of International Politics," in Ken Booth and Tim Dunne (Eds.) *Worlds in Collision: Terror and the Future of Global Order* (New York: Palgrave Macmillan, 2002): pp. 348–353, and Colin Gray, "World Politics as Usual after September 11: Realism Vindicated," in Ken Booth and Tim Dunne (eds.) *Worlds in Collision: Terror and the Future of Global Order* (New York: Palgrave Macmillan, 2002): pp. 226–234.

118. See, for example, Risse, "Transnational Actors and World Politics"; Josselin and Wallace, "Non-state Actors in World Politics"; and Maryann Cusimano Love, "Nongovernmental Organizations: Politics Beyond Sovereignty," in Maryann Cusimano Love (ed.), *Beyond Sovereignty*, 2nd ed. (Belmont, Calif.: Thomson Wadsworth, 2003), for a discussion of the relationship between and among these trends.

119. Cusimano, Hensman, and Rodrigues, "Private-Sector Transovereign Actors—MNCs and NGOs." in Cusimano, *Beyond Sovereignty*, p. 255. See also Cusimano Love, "Nongovernmental Organizations."

120. Mathews, "Power Shift," p. 50.

121. See Risse, "Transnational Actors and World Politics."

122. Wapner, "Politics Beyond the State: Environmental Activism and World Civic Politics," pp. 311–340.

123. James N. Rosenau, *Turbulence in World Politics: A Theory of Change and Continuity* (Princeton, N.J.: Princeton University Press, 1990).

Chapter 5 (pages 140–180)

1. Charles F. Hermann, "Policy Classification: A Key to the Study of Foreign Policy," in James N. Rosenau, Vincent Davis, and Maurice East (eds.), *The Analysis of International Politics* (New York: Free Press, 1972), p. 72.

2. Steven Philip Kramer, "French Foreign Policy: The Wager on Europe," in Ryan K. Beasley, Juliet Kaarbo, Jeffrey S. Lantis, and Michael T. Snarr (eds.), *Foreign Policy in Comparative Perspective: Domestic and International Influences on State Behavior* (Washington, D.C.: CQ Press, 2002).

3. Martin Sampson III, "Exploiting the Seams: External Structure and Libyan Foreign Policy Changes," in J. Rosati, J. Hagan, and M. Sampson (eds.), *How Governments Respond to Global Change* (Columbia: University of South Carolina Press, 1994).

4. Thomas D. Risse, Daniela Engelmann-Martin, Hans-Joachim Knopf, and Klaus Roscher, "To Euro or Not to Euro? The EMU and Identity Politics in the European Union," *European Journal of International Relations* 5 (1999): pp. 147–187.

5. Yale H. Ferguson and Richard W. Mansbach, *The Elusive Quest Continues: Theory and Global Politics* (Upper Saddle River, N.J.: Prentice Hall, 2003), p. 122.

6. Gabriel Almond, *The American People and Foreign Policy* (New York: Harcourt Brace Jovanovich, 1950).

7. Miroslav Nincic, *Democracy and Foreign Policy* (New York: Columbia University Press, 1992), p. 27.

8. Bruce M. Russett, *Controlling the Sword* (Cambridge, Mass.: Harvard University Press, 1990), p. 89.

9. Nincic, *Democracy and Foreign Policy*, p. 28.

10. Joan Beck, "Americans Are Saps at Maps and Not Too Hot at Anything Else," *Tampa Tribune*, August 5, 1988, A:11.

11. National Public Radio report in July 1993.

12. Thomas Risse-Kappen, "Public Opinion, Domestic Structure, and Foreign Policy in Liberal Democracies," *World Politics* 43 (July 1991): p. 481. In support of this conclusion, Risse-Kappen cites Tom W. Smith, "The Polls: America's Most Important Problem, Part I: National and International," *Public Opinion Quarterly* 49 (1985): pp. 264–274 and Elizabeth Hann Hastings and Philip K. Hastings (eds.), *Index to International Public Opinion, 1982–1983* (Westport, Conn.: Greenwood Press, 1984) and *Index to International Public Opinion, 1983–1984* (Westport, Conn.: Greenwood Press, 1985).

13. John P. Robinson, *Public Information About World Affairs* (Ann Arbor, Mich.: Institute for Social Research, 1967), p. 1.

14. Richard Sobel, *The Impact of Public Opinion on U.S. Foreign Policy Since Vietnam* (New York: Oxford University Press, 2001), p. 13.

15. James N. Rosenau, *Turbulence in World Politics* (Princeton, N.J.: Princeton University Press, 1990), p. 373.

16. Ibid., p. 354.

17. Ibid., pp. 339, 343.

18. Almond, *The American People and Foreign Policy*; Ole R. Holsti, "Public Opinion and Foreign Policy: Challenges to the Almond-Lippmann Consensus," *International Studies Quarterly* 36 (December 1992): p. 439.

19. Robert Y. Shapiro and Benjamin I. Page, "Foreign Policy and the Rational Public," *Journal of Conflict Resolution* 32 (June 1988): pp. 243–244. See also Philip Everts and Pierangelo Isernia (eds.), *Public Opinion and the International Use of Force* (London: Routledge, 2001) and Philip Everts, *Democracy and Military Force* (New York: Palgrave, 2002).

20. Pierangelo Isernia, "Where Angels Fear to Tread: Italian Public Opinion and Foreign Policy," in Brigitte L.

Nacos, Robert Y. Shapiro, and Pierangelo Isernia (eds.), *Decisionmaking in a Glass House: Mass Media, Public Opinion, and American and European Foreign Policy in the 21st Century* (Lanham, Md.: Rowman & Littlefield, 2000), p. 281.

21. John R. Oneal, Brad Lian, and James H. Joyner, Jr., "Are the American People 'Pretty Prudent'? Public Responses to U.S. Uses of Force, 1950–1988," *International Studies Quarterly* 40 (June 1996): p. 273; see also Bruce W. Jentleson and Rebecca L. Britton, "Still Pretty Prudent: Post-Cold War American Public Opinion on the Use of Military Force," *Journal of Conflict Resolution* 42(4) (August 1998): pp. 395–417.

22. Juliet Kaarbo, Jeffrey S. Lantis, and Ryan K. Beasley, "The Analysis of Foreign Policy in Comparative Perspective," in Beasley, Kaarbo, Lantis, and Snarr, *Foreign Policy in Comparative Perspective*, p. 14.

23. Jon Hurwitz and Mark Peffley, "How Are Foreign Policy Attitudes Structured? A Hierarchical Model," *American Political Science Review* 81 (1987): pp. 1099–1119. For a discussion of foreign policy belief structure in European publics, see Everts and Isernia, *Public Opinion and the International Use of Force*.

24. Sidney Verba and Richard A. Brody, "Participation, Policy Preferences, and the War in Vietnam," *Public Opinion Quarterly* 34 (1970): pp. 325–332; cited in K. J. Holsti, *International Politics* (Englewood Cliffs, N.J.: Prentice-Hall, 1995), p. 261.

25. Jürgen Schuster and Herbert Maier, "The Rift: Explaining Europe's Divergent Iraq Policies in the Run-Up of the American-Led War on Iraq," *Foreign Policy Analysis* 2(3) (July 2006): pp. 223–244; Steve Chan and William Safran, "Public Opinion as a Constraint against War: Democracies' Responses to Operation Iraqi Freedom," *Foreign Policy Analysis* 2(2) (April 2006): pp. 137–156.

26. Richard J. Barnet, *The Roots of War* (Baltimore: Penguin Books, 1971), p. 243.

27. Risse-Kappen, "Public Opinion, Domestic Structure, and Foreign Policy in Liberal Democracies," p. 481.

28. For examples of public influence of foreign policy outside the United States, see Everts and Isernia, *Public Opinion and the International Use of Force*.

29. Natalie La Balme, "Constraint, Catalyst, or Political Tool?" in Nacos, Shapiro, and Isernia, *Decisionmaking in a Glass House*, p. 277.

30. Philip J. Powlick, "The Attitudinal Bases for Responsiveness to Public Opinion Among American Foreign Policy Officials," *Journal of Conflict Resolution* 35 (December 1991): p. 636; see also Robert Shapiro and Lawrence Jacobs, "Who Leads and Who Follows? U.S. Presidents, Public Opinion, and Foreign Policy," in Nacos, Shapiro, and Isernia, *Decisionmaking in a Glass House*; R. M. Entman, *Projections of Power: Framing News, Public Opinion, and U.S. Foreign Policy* (Chicago: University of Chicago Press, 2004).

31. Douglas C. Foyle, "Leading the Public to War? The Influence of American Public Opinion on the Bush Administration's Decision to Go to War in Iraq," *International Journal of Public Opinion Research* 16(3) (2004): pp. 269–294; see also Steven Kull, Clay Ramsay, and Evan Lewis, "Misperceptions, the Media, and the Iraq War," *Political Science Quarterly* 118(4) (2003–04): pp. 569–598.

32. John Mueller, *Retreat from Doomsday: The Obsolescence of Major War* (New York: Basic Books, 1989).

33. Richard A. Brody, *Assessing the President: The Media, Elite Opinion, and Public Support* (Stanford, Calif.: Stanford University Press, 1991), p. 77.

34. Bradley Lian and John R. Oneal, "Presidents, the Use of Military Force, and Public Opinion," *Journal of Conflict Resolution* 37 (June 1993): p. 277.

35. Philip Everts and Pierangelo Isernia, "The Polls-Trends: The War in Iraq," *Public Opinion Quarterly* 69(2) (Summer 2005): 264–323, p. 275.

36. Philip Everts, "Introduction," in Everts and Isernia, *Public Opinion and the International Use of Force*, p. 18.

37. John Mueller, "The Iraq Syndrome," *Foreign Affairs* 84(6) (November–December 2005): p. 44.

38. Everts, "Introduction," p. 19. See also Everts and Isernia, "The Polls-Trends: The War in Iraq," and Everts, *Democracy and Military Force*, especially pp. 158–181.

39. Pierangelo Isernia, "Conclusion," in Everts and Isernia, *Public Opinion and the International Use of Force*, p. 270, and Everts and Isernia, "The Polls-Trends: The War in Iraq": pp. 264–323.

40. Mueller, "The Iraq Syndrome." For more on U.S. public opinion on the Iraq war, see Christopher Gelpi, Peter D. Feaver, and Jason Reifler, "Success Matters: Casualty Sensitivity and the War in Iraq," *International Security* 30(3) (Winter 2005/06): pp. 7–46; and Ole R. Holsti, "American Public Opinion and Foreign Policy: Did the September 11 Attacks Change Everything?" in David P. Forsythe, Patrice C. McMahon, and Andrew Wedeman, *American Foreign Policy in a Globalized World* (New York: Routledge, 2006), pp. 141–171.

41. See R. Sobel, *The Impact of Public Opinion on U.S. Foreign Policy Since Vietnam, Constraining the Colossus* (New York: Oxford University Press, 2001).

42. Jeffrey S. Lantis, "The Evolution of German Foreign Policy," in Beasley, Kaarbo, Lantis, and Snarr, *Foreign Policy in Comparative Perspective*, p. 80.

43. Risse, Engelmann-Martin, Knopf, and Roscher, "To Euro or Not to Euro?"

44. Foyle, "Leading the Public to War? The Influence of American Public Opinion on the Bush Administration's Decision to Go to War in Iraq," pp. 288–289.

45. As quoted in Donald M. Snow and Eugene Brown, *United States Foreign Policy: Politics Beyond the Water's Edge* (Boston: Bedford/St. Martin's, 2000), pp. 250–251.

46. Patrick E. Tyler, "A New Power in the Streets," *New York Times*, February 17, 2003.

47. Quoted in Richard W. Stevenson, "Antiwar Protests Fail to Sway Bush on Plans for Iraq," *New York Times*, February 19, 2003.

48. Melvin Small and J. David Singer, "The War-Proneness of Democratic Regimes, 1816–1965," *Jerusalem Journal of International Relations* 1 (Summer 1976): pp. 50–69 and Steve Chan, "Mirror, Mirror on the Wall . . . Are the Freer Countries More Pacific?" *Journal of Conflict Resolution* 28 (December 1984): pp. 617–649.

49. Kaarbo, Lantis, and Beasley, "The Analysis of Foreign Policy in Comparative Perspective," p. 17.

50. T. Clifton Morgan and Kenneth H. Bickers, "Domestic Discontent and the External Use of Force," *Journal of Conflict Resolution* 36 (March 1992): pp. 25–52.

51. Edward D. Mansfield Jack Snyder, *Electing to Fight: Why Emerging Democracies Go to War* (Cambridge, Mass.: MIT Press, 2005).

52. Kurt Taylor Gaubatz, "Election Cycles and War," *Journal of Conflict Resolution* 35 (June 1991): pp. 212–244.

53. Recently, though, this assertion has at least become controversial, with several analysts reporting that by

some measures, at least, democratic states are in fact less conflict or war prone than states. For the most recent analyses, see Bruce Russett and John Oneal, *Triangulating Peace: Democracy, Interdependence, and International Organizations* (New York: W. W. Norton, 2001); Kenneth Schultz, *Democracy and Coercive Diplomacy* (Cambridge: Cambridge University Press, 2001); Paul K. Huth and Todd L. Allee, *The Democratic Peace and Territorial Conflict in the Twentieth Century* (Cambridge: Cambridge University Press, 2002); and David L. Rousseau, *Democracy and War* (Stanford, Calif: Stanford University Press, 2005).

54. Risse-Kappen, "Public Opinion, Domestic Structure, and Foreign Policy in Liberal Democracies," p. 511.

55. Ibid. See also Richard Eichenberg, *Public Opinion and National Security in Western Europe* (Ithaca, N.Y.: Cornell University Press, 1989).

56. Stephen D. Cohen, Joel R. Paul, and Robert A. Blecker, *Fundamentals of U.S. Foreign Trade Policy: Economics, Politics, Laws, and Issues* (Boulder, Colo.: Westview Press, 1996), p. 106.

57. Donald M. Snow and Eugene Brown, *United States Foreign Policy: Politics Beyond the Water's Edge* (Boston: Bedford/St. Martin's, 2000), p. 184.

58. Juliet Kaarbo, "Power and Influence in Foreign Policy Decision Making: The Role of Junior Coalition Partners in German and Israeli Foreign Policy" *International Studies Quarterly* 40 (December 1996): pp. 501–530; Joe D. Hagan, Philip P. Everts, Haruhiro Fukui, and John D. Stempel, "Foreign Policy by Coalition: Deadlock, Compromise, and Anarchy," *International Studies Review* 3 (Summer 2001): pp. 169–216.

59. Joe Hagan, *Political Opposition and Foreign Policy in Comparative Perspective* (Boulder, Colo.: Lynne Rienner, 1993), p. 47.

60. Kaarbo, Lantis, and Beasley, "The Analysis of Foreign Policy in Comparative Perspective," p. 17.

61. David Truman, *The Governmental Process* (New York: Knopf, 1951); G. David Garson, "On the Origins of Interest-Group Theory: A Critique of a Process," *American Political Science Review* 68 (December 1974): p. 1505.

62. Kaarbo, Lantis, and Beasley, "The Analysis of Foreign Policy in Comparative Perspective," p. 15; see also Stephen D. Krasner, *Defending the National Interest: Raw Materials Investments and U.S. Foreign Policy* (Princeton, N.J.: Princeton University Press, 1978); Jack Snyder, *Myths of Empire: Domestic Politics and International Ambition* (Ithaca, N.Y.: Cornell University Press, 1991); Helen Milner, "Resisting the Protectionist Temptation: Industry and the Making of Trade Policy in France and the United States During the 1970s," *International Organization* 41 (1987): pp. 639–666.

63. Stefanie Ann Lenway, *The Politics of U.S. International Trade* (Boston: Pitman, 1985), p. 34.

64. Ibid., p. 26.

65. Snow and Brown, *United States Foreign Policy*, p. 185.

66. William P. Avery, "Domestic Interests in NAFTA Bargaining," *Political Science Quarterly* 11 (Summer 1998): p. 284.

67. This powerful coalition of the armed forces, Congress, and influential groups in the private sector, particularly private industry, is often referred to as the "iron triangle." See Gordon Adams, "The Iron Triangle: Inside the Defense Policy Process," in Charles W. Kegley, Jr., and Eugene Wittkopf (eds.), *The Domestic Sources of American Foreign Policy: Insights and Evidence* (New York: St. Martin's Press,

1988) and James R. Durth, "The Military-Industrial Complex Revisited," in Joseph Kruzel (ed.) *1989–1990 American Defense Annual* (Lexington, Mass.: Lexington Books, 1989): pp. 195–215.

68. Steve Chan, "Grasping the Peace Dividend: Some Propositions on the Conversion of Swords into Plowshares," *Mershon International Studies Review* 39 (April 1995): 53–95.

69. Paul Johnson, *Modern Times* (New York: Harper & Row, 1983), p. 639.

70. John H. Cushman, "The Coming Crunch for the Military Budget," *New York Times*, November 27, 1988, 4:1.

71. Thomas Hartley and Bruce Russett, "Public Opinion and the Common Defense: Who Governs Military Spending in the United States?" *American Political Science Review* 86 (December 1992): p. 910.

72. For a recent analysis of the military-industrial complex, see James Fallows, "The Military-Industrial Complex," *Foreign Policy* 133 (November/December 2002): 46–48.

73. See, for example, Christopher M. Jones, "The V-22 Osprey: Pure Pork or Cutting-Edge Technology?" in Ralph G. Carter (ed.), *Contemporary Cases in U.S. Foreign Policy: From Terrorism to Trade* (Washington, D.C.: CQ Press, 2002), pp. 217–247; and Brad Knickerbocker, "Return of the 'Military-Industrial Complex'?" *Christian Science Monitor*, February 13, 2002: p. 2.

74. Kendall W. Stiles, "The Military-Industrial Complex: Defense Spending," *Case Histories in International Politics*, 4th ed. (New York: Pearson Longman, 2006), p. 91.

75. John G. Stoessinger, *Why Nations Go to War*, 6th ed. (New York: St. Martin's Press, 1993), p. 189.

76. J. David Singer, "Peace in the Global System: Displacement, Interregnum, or Transformation?" in Charles W. Kegley, Jr. (ed.), *The Long Postwar Peace* (New York: HarperCollins, 1991), p. 63.

77. Lawrence Freedman and Efraim Karsh, "How Kuwait Was Won: Strategy in the Gulf War," *International Security* 16 (Fall 1991): p. 10.

78. For a recent review of research on the diversionary theory, see Ahmer Tarar, "Diversionary Incentives and the Bargaining Approach to War," *International Studies Quarterly* 50(1) (March 2006): pp. 169–188.

79. See, for example, Clifton T. Morgan and Kenneth Bickers, "Domestic Discontent and the External Use of Force, *Journal of Conflict Resolution* 36 (1992): pp. 25–52; Ross Miller, "Domestic Structures and the Diversionary Use of Force," *American Journal of Political Science* 39 (1995): pp. 760–785; and Tarar, "Diversionary Incentives and the Bargaining Approach to War." H. E. Goemans, "Which Way Out? The Manner and Consequences of Losing Office," *Journal of Conflict Resolution* 52 (December 2008): 771–794.

80. Charles W. Ostrom and Brian L. Job, "The President and the Use of Force," *American Political Science Review* 80 (1986): pp. 554–566; see also B. Fordham, "The Politics of Threat Perception and the Use of Force: A Political Economy Model of U.S. Uses of Force, 1949–1994," *International Studies Quarterly* 42 (1998): pp. 567–590.

81. David J. Brulé, "Congress, Presidential Approval, and U.S. Dispute Initiation." *Foreign Policy Analysis* 4 (October 2008): 349–370.

82. Robert D. Putnam, "Diplomacy and Domestic Politics: The Logic of Two-Level Games," *International Organization* 42 (1988): pp. 427–460. The "selectorate theory" also makes some of these points and emphasizes differences across political institutions. See Bruce Bueno de Mesquita, James D. Morrow, Randolph M. Siverson, and Alastair Smith, "An Institutional Explanation of the Democratic Peace," *American Political Science Review* 93 (1999): pp. 791–807 and Bruce Bueno de Mesquita, James D. Morrow, Randolph M. Siverson, and Alastair Smith, *The Logic of Political Survival* (Cambridge, Mass.: MIT Press, 2003).

83. Avery, "Domestic Interests in NAFTA Bargaining," p. 305.

84. Graham T. Allison, *Essence of Decision* (Boston: Little, Brown, 1971); Morton H. Halperin, "Why Bureaucrats Play Games," *Foreign Policy* 2 (Spring 1971): pp. 70–90; John D. Steinbruner, *The Cybernetic Theory of Decision* (Princeton, N.J.: Princeton University Press, 1974).

85. Jiri Valenta, "The Bureaucratic Politics Paradigm and the Soviet Invasion of Czechoslovakia," *Political Science Quarterly* 94 (1979): pp. 55–76.

86. Charles F. Parker and Eric K. Stern, "Bolt from the Blue or Avoidable Failure? Revisiting September 11 and the Origins of Strategic Surprise," *Foreign Policy Analysis* 1(3) (November 2005): pp. 301–331. See The National Commission on Terrorist Attacks Upon the United States, *The 9/11 Report* (New York: St. Martin's, 2004).

87. Heather Wilson, "Missed Opportunities: Washington Politics and Nuclear Proliferation," *National Interest* (Winter 1993–1994), p. 29.

88. Ibid., p. 29.

89. George Friedman, *America's Secret War* (New York: Doubleday, 2004), p. 262.

90. Charles Lindblom, "The Science of 'Muddling Through,'" *Public Administration Review* 19 (Spring 1959): p. 81.

91. This discussion of the missile crisis relies heavily on Graham Allison's work. See Allison, *Essence of Decision*; Graham Allison and Philip Zelikow, *Essence of Decision* 2nd ed. (New York, NY: Longman, 1999).

92. Bruce J. Allyn, James G. Blight, and David A. Welch, "Essence of Revision: Moscow, Havana, and the Cuban Missile Crisis," *International Security* 14 (Winter 1989–1990): p. 153.

93. Allison, *Essence of Decision*, p. 110

94. Ibid., p. 130. The account of this episode involving the quarantine procedures can be found on pp. 127–132 in Allison, *Essence of Decision*. However, the validity of Allison's account has been challenged by, among others, Dan Caldwell, "A Research Note on the Quarantine of Cuba, October 1962," *International Studies Quarterly* 22 (December 1978): p. 628.

95. The National Commission on Terrorist Attacks Upon the United States, *The 9/11 Report*, p. LXXXIX.

96. Ibid. See also Parker and Stern, "Bolt from the Blue or Avoidable Failure? Revisiting September 11 and the Origins of Strategic Surprise," especially pp. 316–317.

97. Fred I. Greenstein, *Personality and Politics: Problems of Evidence, Inference and Conceptualization* (Chicago: Markham, 1969); Margaret G. Hermann, "When Leader Personality Will Affect Foreign Policy: Some Propositions," in James N. Rosenau (ed.), *In Search of Global Patterns* (New York: Free Press, 1976).

98. S. Freud and W. C. Buillitt, *Thomas Woodrow Wilson: A Psychological Study* (Boston: Houghton Mifflin, 1967).

99. Michael D. Young and Mark Schafer, "Is There Method in Our Madness? Ways of Assessing Cognition in International Relations," *Mershon International Studies Review* 42, supplement 2 (1998): pp. 63–96.

100. Steven Philip Kramer, "Blair's Britain After Iraq," *Foreign Affairs* 82(4) (July/August 2003): pp. 90–104 and Stephen Benedict Dyson, "Personality and Foreign Policy: Tony Blair's Iraq Decisions," *Foreign Policy Analysis* 2(3) (July 2006): p. 298.

101. Kramer, "Blair's Britain After Iraq."

102. For an analysis of George W. Bush's operational code, see Jonathan Renshon, "Stability and Change in Belief Systems: The Operational Code of George W. Bush," *Journal of Conflict Resolution* (December 2008) 52(6): 820–849.

103. Dyson, "Personality and Foreign Policy: Tony Blair's Iraq Decisions"; see also Mark Schafer and Stephen G. Walker, "Political Leadership and the Democratic Peace: The Operational Code of Prime Minister Tony Blair," in Ofer Feldman and Linda O. Valenty (eds.), *Profiling Political Leaders: Cross-Cultural Studies of Personality and Behavior* (Westport, Conn.: Praeger, 2001): pp. 21–35 and Mark Schafer and Stephen G. Walker, "Democratic Leaders and the Democratic Peace: The Operational Codes of Tony Blair and Bill Clinton," *International Studies Quarterly* 50(3) (September 2006): pp. 561–583.

104. Dyson, "Personality and Foreign Policy: Tony Blair's Iraq Decisions," p. 298.

105. Richard K. Herrmann and Michael Fischerkeller, "Beyond the Enemy Image Spiral Model: Cognitive-Strategic Research After the Cold War," *International Organization* 49 "How Kuwait Was Won," p. 16.

106. Ole Holsti, "Cognitive Dynamics and Images of the Enemy," *Journal of International Affairs* 21 (1967): p. 25.

107. Alex Roberto Hybel, *Power over Rationality* (Albany, N.Y.: State University of New York Press, 1993), pp. 8–9.

108. Freedman and Karsh, bridge: Cambridge University Press, 2005).

109. Ibid., p. 15.

110. Singer, "Peace in the Global System," p. 63.

111. Freedman and Karsh, "How Kuwait Was Won," p. 36.

112. Dyson, "Personality and Foreign Policy: Tony Blair's Iraq Decisions," p. 298.

113. Arjen Boin, Paul 't Hart, Eric Stern, and Bengt Sundelius, *The Politics of Crisis Management: Public Leadership under Pressure* (Cam (1995): pp. 415–450.

114. Juliet Kaarbo, "Prime Minister Leadership Styles in Foreign Policy Decision-Making: A Framework for Research," *Political Psychology* 18 (1997): pp. 553–581.

115. Margaret Hermann, "Leaders and Foreign Policy Decision-making," in D. Caldwell and T. McKeown (eds.), *Diplomacy, Force, and Leadership: Essays in Honor of Alexander George* (Boulder, Colo.: Westview Press, 1993), p. 82.

116. Fred I. Greenstein, "The Leadership Styoe of Brack Obama: An Early Assessment," *The Forum:* 7 Iss. 1, Article 6, (11 pages) http://www.bepress.com/forum/vol7/iss1/art6 Accessed 31 May 2009.

117. Margaret G. Hermann, Charles F. Hermann, and Joe D. Hagan, "How Decision Units Shape Foreign Policy Behavior," in C. F. Hermann, C. W. Kegley, Jr., and J. N. Rosenau (eds.), *New Directions in the Study of Foreign Policy* (Boston: Allen and Unwin, 1987), p. 314; see also Margaret G. Hermann, Thomas Preston, Baghat Korany, and Timothy M. Shaw, "Who Leads Matters: The Effects of Powerful Individuals," *International Studies Review* 3 (2001): pp. 83–131.

118. Dyson, "Personality and Foreign Policy: Tony Blair's Iraq Decisions," p. 299.

119. Ibid., especially pp. 299–303.

120. Irving L. Janis, *Victims of Groupthink* (Boston: Houghton Mifflin, 1972); Yaacov Vertzberger, "Collective Risk Taking: The Decision-Making Group," in Paul 't Hart, Eric K. Stern, and Bengt Sundelius (eds.), *Beyond Groupthink* (Ann Arbor: University of Michigan Press, 1997).

121. Paul 't Hart, Eric K. Stern, and Bengt Sundelius "Foreign Policy-making at the Top: Political Group Dynamics," in 't Hart, Stern, and Sundelius, *Beyond Groupthink*, p. 10.

122. Bob Woodward, *Bush at War* (New York: Simon & Schuster, 2002), p. 256.

123. William Branigin and Dana Priest, "Senate Report Blasts Intelligence Agencies' Flaws," *washingtonpost.com*, http://www.washingtonpost.com/wp-dyn/articles/A38459–2004Jul9.html.

124. Alexander Moens, *The Foreign Policy of George W. Bush: Values, Strategy, and Loyalty* (Aldershot, UK: Ashgate, 2004), p. 200.

125. See 't Hart, Stern, and Sundelius, *Beyond Groupthink*.

Chapter 6 (pages 181–214)

1. See Francis A. Beer, *Peace Against War* (San Francisco: Freeman, 1981), pp. 20–34, for a discussion and confirmation of this widely cited estimate on the number of years without war. For the average number of wars per decade, see Meredith Reid Sarkees, Frank Whelon Wayman, and J. David Singer, "Inter-State, Intra-State, and Extra-State Wars: A Comprehensive Look at Their Distribution over Time, 1816–1997," *International Studies Quarterly* 47 (2003): pp. 49–70.

2. William Eckhardt, *Civilizations, Empires and Wars: A Quantitative History of War* (Jefferson, N.C.: McFarland & Company, 1992), p. 174.

3. Ibid., p. 174.

4. Ibid., p. 175. For a recent discussion of why the twentieth century was so violent, see Niall Ferguson, "The Next War of the World," *Foreign Affairs* 85(5) (September/October 2006): pp. 61–74.

5. UNICEF, *Child Protection From Violence, Exploitation and Abuse*, http://www.unicef.org/protection/index_armedconflict.html, July 31, 2006. Difficulties in determining what constitutes a war-related casualty and a general lack of accurately recorded information regarding civilian casualty levels make estimation of these figures prone to inaccuracy, but, according to Klaus Jurgen Gantzel and Torsten Schwinghammer, *Warfare Since the Second World War* (New Brunswick, N.J.: Transaction Publishers, 2000), p. 138, "most likely the percentage of civilians (noncombatants) killed in relation to military personnel (combatants) has risen steadily since the industrialization of war, beginning with the U.S. Civil War (1861–1865)."

6. Lotta Harbom, Erik Melander, and Peter Wallensteen, "Dyadic Dimensions of Armed Conflict, 1946–2007," *Journal of Peace Research* 45(5) (2008): 697-710, pp. 697–8.

7. Sarkees, Wayman, and Singer, "Inter-State, Intra-State, and Extra-State Wars," pp. 60–61.

8. Harbom, Högbladh, and Wallensteen, "Armed Conflict and Peace Agreements," pp. 617–619. For a discussion of trends in major power warfare, see Jack S. Levy, Thomas C. Walker, and Martin S. Edwards, "Continuity and Change in the Evolution of War," in Zeev Maoz and Azar Gat (eds.), *War in a Changing World* (Ann Arbor: University of Michigan Press, 2001), pp. 15–48.

9. Lotta Harbom, Erik Melander, and Peter Wallensteen, "Dyadic Dimensions of Armed Conflict, 1946–2007," *Journal of Peace Research* 45(5) (2008): 697–710, pp. 698.

10. Charles King, "The Five-Day War: Managing Moscow After the Georgia Crisis," *Foreign Affairs* (November/December 2008) 87(6).

11. Richard Little, "Structuralism and Neo-Realism," in Margot Light and A. J. R. Groom (eds.), *International Relations: A Handbook of Current Theory* (London: Pinter, 1985), p. 74.

12. J. David Singer, "The Level-of-Analysis Problem in International Relations," in Klaus Knorr and Sidney Verba (eds.), *The International System* (Princeton, N.J.: Princeton University Press, 1961), p. 77.

13. Kenneth Waltz, *Man, the State, and War* (New York: Columbia University Press, 1959), p. 3. Waltz is merely describing this kind of theory here, not advocating or defending it.

14. Ibid., p. 221.

15. Kenneth N. Waltz, "The Origins of War in Neorealist Theory," *Journal of Interdisciplinary History* 18 (1988): 615–628.

16. Martin Wight, "The Balance of Power and International Order," in Alan James (ed.), *The Bases of International Order* (Oxford: Oxford University Press, 1973), p. 100.

17. Ibid., pp. 104–105, 108.

18. Edward V. Gulick, *Europe's Classical Balance of Power* (Ithaca, N.Y.: Cornell University Press, 1955), p. 76.

19. Ibid., p. 39.

20. Seyom Brown, *New Faces, Old Forces, and the Future of World Politics* (Glenview, Ill.: Scott, Foresman, 1980), p. 24.

21. Karl W. Deutsch and J. David Singer, "Multipolar Power Systems and International Stability," in James N. Rosenau (ed.), *International Politics and Foreign Policy*, 2nd ed. (New York: Free Press, 1969), pp. 317–318.

22. Kenneth Waltz, "International Structure, National Force, and the Balance of World Power," in Rosenau, *International Politics and Foreign Policy*, p. 306.

23. Ernst B. Haas and Allen S. Whiting, *Dynamics of International Relations* (New York: McGraw-Hill, 1956), p. 50.

24. J. David Singer, Stuart Bremer, and John Stuckey, "Capability Distribution, Uncertainty, and Major Power War, 1820–1965," in Bruce M. Russett (ed.), *Peace, War, and Numbers* (Thousand Oaks, Calif.: Sage, 1972).

25. To count as a war for the purposes of this study, a conflict had to have resulted in at least one thousand battle deaths. Melvin Small and J. David Singer, *Resort to Arms: International and Civil Wars, 1816–1980* (Thousand Oaks, Calif.: Sage, 1982).

26. A related analysis of the major powers that focused on the distribution of power among *blocs*, or coalitions of states, found that the concentration of power among those blocs correlated with war in the period from 1830 to 1914 but not in the period from 1919 to 1965. See Richard J. Stoll, "Bloc Concentration and Dispute Escalation Among the Major Powers, 1830–1965," *Social Science Quarterly* 65 (March 1984): pp. 48–59.

27. Gulick, *Europe's Classical Balance of Power*, pp. 19–20.

28. D. Scott Bennett and Allan C. Stam, *The Behavioral Origins of War* (Ann Arbor: University of Michigan Press, 2004), p. 147.

29. Charles Krauthammer, "The Unipolar Moment," *Foreign Affairs*, 70 (Winter 1990/91): pp. 23–33.

30. For a recent discussion of contemporary unipolarity and its consequences, see the special issue of *World Politics*, "Unipolarity, State Behavior, and Systemic Consequences," edited by G. John Ikenberry, Michael Mastanduno, and William C. Wohlforth, January 2009.

31. Robert Gilpin, *War and Change in World Politics* (Cambridge: Cambridge University Press, 1981).

32. Samuel P. Huntington, "The Lonely Superpower," *Foreign Affairs* 78(2) (March-April 1999): pp. 35–49.

33. Josef Joffe, *Überpower: The Imperial Temptation of America* (New York: W. W. Norton and Company, 2006). Also see Joseph S. Nye, Jr., *The Paradox of American Power: Why the World's Only Superpower Can't Go It Alone* (Oxford: Oxford University Press, 2002) and Ivo H. Daalder and James M. Lindsay, *America Unbound: The Bush Revolution in Foreign Policy* (Washington, D.C.: Brookings Institution Press, 2003).

34. F. K. Organski, *World Politics*, 2nd ed. (New York: Knopf, 1968). For recent research on power transition theory, see Jacek Kugler and Douglas Lemke (Eds.) *Parity and War* (Ann Arbor: University of Michigan Press, 1996) and Ronald Tammen, Jacek Kubler, Douglas Lemke, Allan Stam, Carole Alsharabati, Mark Abdollahian, Brian Efird, and A. F. K. Organski, *Power Transitions* (New York: Chatham House, 2000).

35. Greg Cashman, *What Causes War? An Introduction to Theories of International Conflict* (Lexington, Mass.: Lexington Books, 1993), p. 248.

36. William C. Wohlforth, "Unipolarity, Status Competition, and Great Power War," *World Politics* 61(1) (2008): pp. 28–57; Christopher Layne, "The Unipolar Illusion Revisisted: The Coming End of the United States' Unipolar Moment," *International Security* (Fall 2006) 31(2):7–41.

37. Douglas Lemke and Ronald L. Tammen, "Power Transition Theory and the Rise of China," *International Interactions* 29 (2003): pp. 269–271. See also G. John Ikenberry, "The Rise of China and the Future of the West: Can the Liberal System Survive?" *Foreign Affairs* 87(1) (January/February 2008):23–37; Aaron L. Friedberg, "The Future of U.S.-China Relations: Is Conflict Inevitable?" *International Security* 30(2) (2005): pp. 7–45; Thomas Christensen, "Fostering Stability or Creating a Monster? The Rise of China and U.S. Policy toward East Asia" *International Security* 31(1) (2006): pp. 81–126; and William C. Wohlforth, "Unipolarity, Status Competition, and Great Power War," *World Politics* 61(1) (2008): pp. 28–57.

38. See, for example, John R. Oneal, Bruce Russett, and Michael L. Berbaum, "Causes of Peace: Democracy, Interdependence, and International Organizations," *International Studies Quarterly* 47(3) (2003).

39. Robert O. Keohane and Joseph S. Nye, *Power and Interdependence* (New York: HarperCollins, 1989), p. 27. See also Michael W. Doyle, *Ways of War and Peace* (New York: Norton, 1997).

40. Keohane and Nye, *Power and Interdependence*, p. 29.

41. According to Kim and Rousseau, recent empirical evidence on pacifying effects of interdependence has been mixed (Hyung Min Kim and David L. Rousseau, "The Classical Liberals Were Half Right (or Half Wrong): New Tests of the 'Liberal Peace', 1960–88," *Journal of Peace Research* 42(5): pp. 523–543. See also Bennett and Stam, *The Behavioral Origins of War*, p. 141. For recent reviews of this literature, see Edward D. Mansfield and Brian M. Pollins, (eds.) *Economic Interdependence and International Conflict: New Perspectives on an Enduring Debate* (Ann Arbor: University of Michigan Press, 2003).

42. Waltz, "Origins of War in Neorealist Theory," p. 621.

43. John Lewis Gaddis, "The Long Peace: Elements of Stability in the Postwar International System," *International Security* 10 (Spring 1986): pp. 99–142.

44. See J. A. Hobson, *Imperialism: A Study* (Ann Arbor: University of Michigan Press, 1965).

45. Greg Cashman, *What Causes War?* (San Francisco: Jossey-Bass, 1993), p. 130.

46. V. I. Lenin, *Imperialism: The Highest Stage of Capitalism* (New York: International Publishers, 1939).

47. Jack Snyder, *Myths of Empire: Domestic Politics and International Ambition* (Ithaca, N.Y.: Cornell University Press, 1991).

48. See John M. Owen, "How Liberalism Produces Democratic Peace," *International Security*, vol.19, no.2 (Fall 1994): 87–125.

49. Bruce Bueno de Mesquita, James D. Morrow, Randolph M. Siverson, and Alastair Smith, "Testing Novel Implications from the Selectorate Theory of War," *World Politics* 56 (April 2004): pp. 363–88.

50. Cashman, *What Causes War?* p. 146.

51. See Chapter 5 for application to the Iraqi decision for war in 1990.

52. Michael W. Doyle, "Kant, Liberal Legacies, and Foreign Affairs," *Philosophy and Public Affairs* 12 (Summer 1983): p. 213.

53. Jack S. Levy, "Domestic Politics and War," *Journal of Interdisciplinary History* (Spring 1988): p. 661.

54. Michael W. Doyle, "Liberal Institutions and International Ethics," in Kenneth Kipnis and Diana T. Meyers (eds.), *Political Realism and International Morality* (Boulder, Colo.: Westview Press, 1987), p. 191.

55. James Lee Ray, *Democracy and International Conflict* (Columbia: University of South Carolina Press, 1995), pp. 124–125.

56. William R. Thompson, "Democracy and Peace: Putting the Cart Before the Horse?" *International Organization* 50 (Winter 1996): pp. 141–174.

57. David E. Spiro, "The Insignificance of Liberal Peace," *International Security* 19 (Fall 1994): pp. 50–86.

58. See Henry S. Farber and Joanne Gowa, "Polities and Peace," *International Security* 20 (Fall 1995): pp. 123–146.

59. John Lewis Gaddis, "The Long Peace," p. 112.

60. Katherine Barbieri, "Economic Interdependence: A Path to Peace or a Source of Interstate Conflict?" *Journal of Peace Research* 33 (February 1996): pp. 29–50.

61. James Lee Ray, "The Democratic Path to Peace," *Journal of Democracy* 8 (April 1997): pp. 49–64.

62. Dina A. Zinnes, "Constructing Political Logic: The Democratic Peace Puzzle," *Journal of Conflict Resolution* 48(3) (June 2004): pp. 430–454. Michael D. Ward, Randolph M. Siverson, and Xun Cao, "Disputes, Democracies, and Dependencies: A Reexamination of the Kantian Peace," *American Journal of Political Science* 51(3) (2007): pp. 583–601; Vesna Danilovic and Joe Clare, "The Kantian Liberal Peace (Revisited)," *American Journal of Political Science* 51(2) (2007): pp. 397–414; David Lektzian and Mark Souva, "A Comparative Theory Test of Democratic Peace Arguments, 1946—2000," *Journal of Peace Research* 46(1) (2009): pp. 17–37.

63. Zeev Maoz and Nasrin Abdolali, "Regime Types and International Conflict, 1816–1976," *Journal of Conflict Resolution* 33 (March 1989): pp. 3–36; Zeev Maoz and Bruce Russett, "Alliances, Contiguity, Wealth, and Political Instability: Is the Lack of Conflict Among Democracies a Statistical Artifact?" *International Interactions* 17, no. 3 (1992): pp. 245–268; Oneal et al., "The Liberal Peace: Interdependence, Democracy, and International Conflict"; John R. Oneal and James Lee Ray, "New Tests of Democratic Peace," *Political Research Quarterly* 50 (December 1997): pp. 751–775.

64. Spencer Weart, "The History of Peace Among Republics," *Journal of Peace Research* 31 (August 1994): pp. 299–316.

65. Carol R. Ember, Melvin Ember, and Bruce Russett, "Peace Between Participatory Polities," *World Politics* 44 (July 1992): pp. 573–599.

66. Alex Mintz and Nehemia Geva, "Why Don't Democracies Fight Each Other? An Experimental Assessment of the 'Political Incentive' Explanation," *Journal of Conflict Resolution* 37 (September 1993): pp. 484–503.

67. Bruce Russett, *Grasping the Democratic Peace* (Princeton, N.J.: Princeton University Press, 1993). Bruce Bueno de Mesquita and David Lalman, *War and Reason* (New Haven, Conn.: Yale University Press, 1992); Bruce Bueno de Mesquita, James D. Morrow, Randolph M. Siverson, and Alastair Smith, "An Institutional Explanation of the Democratic Peace," *American Political Science Review* 93 (December 1999). John M. Owen, "How Liberalism Produces Democratic Peace," *International Security*, vol.19, no.2 (Fall 1994): 87-125; Sabastian Rosato, "The Flawed Logic of Democratic Peace Theory," *American Political Science Review* 97/4 (November 2003): 595-602.

68. Bruce Russett, *Grasping the Democratic Peace* (Princeton, N.J.: Princeton University Press, 1993).

69. Bruce Bueno de Mesquita and David Lalman, *War and Reason* (New Haven, Conn.: Yale University Press, 1992); Bruce Bueno de Mesquita, James D. Morrow, Randolph M. Siverson, and Alastair Smith, "An Institutional Explanation of the Democratic Peace," *American Political Science Review* 93 (December 1999). John M. Owen, "How Liberalism Produces Democratic Peace," *International Security*, vol.19, no.2 (Fall 1994): 87-125; Sabastian Rosato, "The Flawed Logic of Democratic Peace Theory," *American Political Science Review* 97/4 (November 2003): 595-602.

70. Bueno de Mesquita and Lalman, *War and Reason*.

71. See, for example, Bueno de Mesquita, et al., "An Institutional Explanation of the Democratic Peace" and Sabastien Rosato, "The Flawed Logic of Democratic Peace Theory," *American Political Science Review* 97 (November 2003): pp. 585–602. Bruce Russett, "Democracy, War and Expansion through Historical Lenses," *European Journal of International Relations* 15(1) (2009): pp. 9–36.

72. Margaret G. Hermann and Charles W. Kegley, Jr., "Rethinking Democracy and International Peace: Perspectives from Political Psychology," *International Studies Quarterly* 39 (1995): p. 514.

73. Sabastian Rosato, "The Flawed Logic of Democratic Peace Theory," *American Political Science Review* 97/4 (November 2003): 595-602.

74. Ibid.

75. Bruce Bueno De Mesquita, James D. Morow, Randolph M. Siverson, and Alastair Smith, "An Institutional Explanation of the Democratic Peace," *American Political Science Review* 93 (1999): pp. 791–807.

76. Miriam Fendius Elman, "Finland in World War II: Alliances, Small States, and the Democratic Peace," in Miriam Fendius Elman (ed.), *Paths to Peace: Is Democracy the Answer?* (Cambridge, Mass.: MIT Press, 1997), pp. 192–193; see also David E. Spiro, "The Insignificance of the Liberal Peace," *International Security* 19 (Fall 1994): pp. 50–86, and Michael W. Doyle, "Correspondence on the Democratic Peace," *International Security* 19 (Spring 1995): pp. 164–184.

77. Elman, "Finland in World War II," pp. 192–193; see also James Lee Ray, "War Between Democracies: Rare, or Nonexistent?" *International Interactions* 18 (1993): pp. 251–276.

78. Elman, "Finland in World War II," pp. 229–232.

79. Robert Gallucci, *Neither Peace nor Honor* (Baltimore: Johns Hopkins University Press, 1975), p. 48.

80. Jack S. Levy, "Organizational Routines and the Causes of War," *International Studies Quarterly* 30 (1986): p. 218.

81. Shannon Lindsey Blanton, "Images in Conflict: The Case of Ronald Reagan and El Salvador," *International Studies Quarterly* 40 (1996): p. 24.

82. Jack S. Levy, "Misperception and the Causes of War: Theoretical Linkages and Analytical Problems," *World Politics* 36 (October 1983): pp. 76–99.

83. Janice Gross Stein, "Building Politics into Psychology: The Misperception of Threat," in N. Kressel (ed.), *Political Psychology: Classic and Contemporary Readings* (New York: Paragon House, 1993), pp. 370–371.

84. John G. Stoessinger, *Why Nations Go to War* (Boston: Bedford/St. Martin's, 2001), p. 69.

85. Robert Jervis "War and Misperception," *Journal of Interdisciplinary History* 18 (Spring 1988): pp. 675–700.

86. Stephen Van Evera, "The Cult of the Offensive and the Origins of the First World War (in The Great War and the Nuclear Age)," *International Security* 9 (Summer 1984): pp. 958–107. See Kier Lieber for recent criticism of this explanation of World War I. Keir A. Lieber, "The New History of World War I and What It Means for International Relations Theory," *International Security*, Vol. 32, No. 2 (Fall 2007), pp. 155–191.

87. Barbara Tuchman, *The Guns of August* (New York: Macmillan, 1962), pp. 74–75.

88. Jervis, "War and Misperception," pp. 681–682.

89. Ibid., p. 682.

90. Stephen E. Ambrose and Douglas G. Brinkley, *Rise to Globalism* (New York: Penguin Books, 1997), pp. 70–71.

91. Stein, "Building Politics into Psychology," p. 372.

Chapter 7 (pages 215–258)

1. Lotta Harbom and Peter Wallensteen, "Armed Conflict and Its International Dimensions, 1946–2004," *Journal of Peace Research* 42 (2005): pp. 623–635.

2. Lotta Harbom, Stina Högbladh, and Peter Wallensteen, "Armed Conflict and Peace Agreements," *Journal of Peace Research* 43 (September 2006): 617 – 631; on the relationship between civil and interstate wars, see Kristian S. Gleditsch, Idean Salehyan, and Kenneth Schultz, " Fighting at Home, Fighting Abroad: How Civil Wars Lead to International Disputes," *Journal of Conflict Resolution* (August 2008) 52(4):479-506.

3. Stockholm International Peace Research Institute, *SIPRI Yearbook 2000: Armaments, Disarmament and International Security* (Oxford: Oxford University Press, 2000), p. 16.

4. Harbom and Wallensteen, "Armed Conflict and Its International Dimensions, 1946–2004," p. 627.

5. Philip Gourevitch, *We Wish to Inform You That Tomorrow We Will Be Killed with Our Families: Stories from Rwanda*

(New York: Farrar Straus and Giroux, 1998), introduction. Copyright © 1998 by Philip Gourevitch. Reprinted by permission of Farrar, Straus and Giroux, LLC.

6. Ibid., p. 53.

7. Gérard Prunier, "The Politics of Death in Darfur," *Current History* (May 2006): pp. 195–196.

8. William Pfaff, "An Invitation to War," *Foreign Affairs* 72 (Summer 1993): p. 101.

9. Gourevitch, *We Wish to Inform You*, pp. 47–48.

10. Ibid., pp. 57–58.

11. Benedict Anderson, *Imagined Communities: Reflections on the Origin and Spread of Nationalism* (London: Verso, 1983). For an application to the Kosovo conflict, see Matthew J. Hoffmann, "Social (De)Construction: The Failure of a Multinational State," in Jennifer Sterling-Folker (ed.) *Making Sense of International Relations Theory* (Boulder, Colo.: Lynne Rienner, 2006), pp. 123–138.

12. Ted Robert Gurr, *People Versus States: Minorities at Risk in the New Century* (Washington, D.C.: United States Institute of Peace, 2000), p. 5.

13. Ibid.

14. Ted Robert Gurr, "Third World Minorities at Risk Since 1945" (background paper prepared for the Conference on Conflict Resolution in the Post Cold War World, U.S. Institute of Peace, October 3–5, 1990).

15. Abdul Aziz Said, "A Redefinition of National Interest, Ethnic Consciousness, and U.S. Foreign Policy," in Abdul Aziz Said (ed.), *Ethnicity and U.S. Foreign Policy* (New York: Praeger, 1977), p. 4.

16. Gurr, "Third World Minorities at Risk Since 1945," pp. 9–10.

17. Gurr, *People Versus States*, p. 8.

18. Ibid., p. 12.

19. Ryan, *Ethnic Conflict and International Relations*, p. xi.

20. David A. Lake and Donald Rothchild (eds.), *The International Spread of Ethnic Conflict: Fear, Diffusion, and Escalation* (Princeton, N.J.: Princeton University Press, 1988), p. 41.

21. Ted Robert Gurr, *Minorities at Risk* (Washington, D.C.: United States Institute of Peace, 1993), p. 318.

22. Gurr, "Third World Minorities at Risk Since 1945," p. 2.

23. Michael E. Brown (ed.), *Ethnic Conflict and International Security* (Princeton, N.J.: Princeton University Press, 1993), p. 3.

24. For a review of research on the internationalization of ethnic conflict, see David Carment, Patrick James, and Zeynep Taydas, "The Internationalization of Ethnic Conflict: State, Society, and Synthesis," *International Studies Review* (2009) 11:63–86.

25. Gurr, "Third World Minorities at Risk Since 1945."

26. David Carment and Patrick James, "Internal Constraints and Interstate Ethnic Conflict," *Journal of Conflict Resolution* 39 (March 1995): p. 84.

27. Stephen Van Evera, "Hypotheses on Nationalism and War," *International Security* 18 (1994): p. 6.

28. R. J. Rummel, "The Armenian Genocide," draft, Department of Political Science, University of Hawaii, 1991, p. 18. See also Richard G. Hovannissian, *Remembrance and Denial: The Case of the Armenian Genocide* (Detroit, Mich.: Wayne State University Press, 1998).

29. R. J. Rummel, *Democide: Nazi Genocide and Mass Murder* (New Brunswick, N.J.: Transaction Publishers, 1992), p. 11.

30. Gurr, *People Versus States*, p. 276. See also James D. Fearon and David D. Laitin, "Ethnicity, Insurgency, and Civil War," *American Political Science Review* 97(1) (February 2003): pp. 75–90.

31. Ibid., p. 195. Ted Robert Gurr, "Minorities, Nationalists, and Islamists: Managing Communal Conflict in the Twenty-first Century," in *Leashing the Dogs of War: Conflict Management in a Divided World*, eds. Chester A. Crocker, Fen Olster Hampson, and Pamela Aall. 2007, Washington, DC: United States Institute of Peace Press, pp. 131–160.

32. Gurr, *People Versus States*, p. 223. See also Ted Robert Gurr, "Minorities, Nationalists, and Islamists: Managing Communal Conflict in the Twenty-first Century," in *Leashing the Dogs of War: Conflict Management in a Divided World*, eds. Chester A. Crocker, Fen Olster Hampson, and Pamela Aall. 2007, Washington, DC: United States Institute of Peace Press, pp. 131–160.

33. Ryan, *Ethnic Conflict and International Relations*, p. xix.

34. Jonathan Fox, "The Rise of Religious Nationalism and Conflict: Ethnic Conflict and Revolutionary Wars, 1945–2001," *Journal of Peace Research* 41: pp. 715–731.

35. Ibid., pp. 716–717.

36. Walker Connor, "Nation-Building or Nation-Destroying?" *World Politics* 24 (April 1972): pp. 319–355, cited in Ryan, *Ethnic Conflict and International Relations*, p. xxix. On the lack of attention to religion in international relations scholarship, see Daniel Philpott, "The Challenge of September 11 to Secularism in International Relations," *World Politics* 55: pp. 66–95.

37. David Carment, "The International Dimensions of Ethnic Conflict: Concepts, Indicators, and Theory," *Journal of Peace Research* 30 (May 1993): p. 146.

38. Joane Nagel, "Ethnic Nationalism: Politics, Ideology, and the World Order," *International Journal of Comparative Sociology* 34 (1993): p. 109.

39. Ibid., p. 107.

40. Saul Newman, "Does Modernization Breed Ethnic Conflict?" *World Politics* 43 (April 1991): p. 453.

41. Ryan, *Ethnic Conflict and International Relations*, p. xix.

42. Fox, "The Rise of Religious Nationalism and Conflict," pp. 715–716.

43. Newman, "Does Modernization Breed Ethnic Conflict?" p. 454.

44. Ibid., p. 455. Jerry Z. Muller, "Us and Them," *Foreign Affairs*, March/April 2008, 87:*

45. Fox, "The Rise of Religious Nationalism and Conflict," p. 718.

46. Alvin Toffler, *Power Shift* (New York: Bantam Books, 1991); Thomas L. Friedman, *The Lexus and the Olive Tree* (New York: Farrar, Straus, and Giroux, 1999).

47. Raymond C. Taras and Rajat Ganguly, *Understanding Ethnic Conflict: The International Dimension* (New York: Longman, 2002), p. 25 (emphasis in original).

48. Stuart J. Kaufman, "An 'International' Theory of Inter-Ethnic War," *Review of International Studies* 22 (1996): p. 159.

49. Prunier, "The Politics of Death in Darfur," p. 200.

50. Taras and Ganguly, *Understanding Ethnic Conflict*, 2002, p. 29, as they recount arguments by Barry R. Posen in "The Security Dilemma and Ethnic Conflict," *Survival* 35 (1993): pp. 27–47; also see Stuart J. Kaufman, "An 'International' Theory of Inter-Ethnic War," *Review of International Studies* 22 (1996):

pp. 149–171. For an application to the conflict in Kosovo, see Karen Ruth Adams, "Structural Realism: The Consequences of Great Power Politics," in Jennifer Sterling-Folker (ed.) *Making Sense of International Relations Theory*, pp. 18–37.

51. Fearon and Laitin, "Ethnicity, Insurgency, and Civil War."

52. Taras and Ganguly, *Understanding Ethnic Conflict*, 3rd edition, 2006, pp. 232, 236.

53. Steven R. David, "Internal War: Causes and Cures," *World Politics* 49 (July 1997): p. 561.

54. Gurr, *People Versus States*, p. 106.

55. Taras and Ganguly, *Understanding Ethnic Conflict*, 2002, pp. 15–16.

56. Ibid., p. 16.

57. Henri Tajfel and John C. Turner, "The Social Identity Theory of Intergroup Behavior," in Stephen Worchel and William G. Austin (eds.), *Psychology of Intergroup Relations* (Chicago: Nelson-Hall, 1986), p. 13.

58. David L. Hamilton and Tina K. Trolier, "Stereotypes and Stereotyping: An Overview of the Cognitive Approach," in John R. Dovidio and Samuel L. Gaertner (eds.), *Prejudice, Discrimination, and Racism* (Orlando, Fla.: Academic Press, 1986).

59. Taras and Ganguly, *Understanding Ethnic Conflict*, 2002, p. 5.

60. Nelson Kasfir, "Sudan's Darfur: Is It Genocide?" *Current History* (May 2005): pp. 195–202.

61. David, "Internal War," p. 565, and Brown, *Ethnic Conflict and International Security*.

62. David, "Internal War," p. 565.

63. Charles King, "The Myth of Ethnic Warfare: Understanding Conflict in the Post–Cold War World," *Foreign Affairs* (November–December 2001): p. 166.

64. Kaufman, "An 'International' Theory of Inter-Ethnic War," p. 157.

65. Rita Jalali and Seymour Martin Lipset, "Racial and Ethnic Conflict: A Global Perspective," in Demetrios Caraley and Cerentha Harris (eds.), *New World Politics: Power, Ethnicity and Democracy* (New York: Academy of Political Science, 1993), p. 60.

66. William Drozdiak, "50 Years On, Expulsion Rankles for Sudeten Germans," *International Herald Tribune*, December 6, 1996, p. 1. See also Jerry Z. Muller, "Us and Them," *Foreign Affairs*, *full cite.

67. Jalali and Lipset, "Racial and Ethnic Conflict," p. 60, using figures from Jaroslav Krejic and Vitezslav Velimsky, *Ethnic and Political Nations in Europe* (New York: St. Martin's Press, 1981). See also Jerry Z. Muller, "Us and Them," *Foreign Affairs*, *full cite.

68. Joseph Nye, "Conflicts After the Cold War," *Washington Quarterly* 19 (Winter 1996): p. 19.

69. Richard Rosecrance, "Separatism's Final Country," *Foreign Affairs* July/August 2008, 87:141–145.

70. Charles King, "The Five-Day War: Managing Moscow After the Georgia Crisis," *Foreign Affairs* (November/December 2008) 87(6).

71. Gurr, *Minorities at Risk*, p. 38.

72. Nicholas Wood, "For Albanians in Kosovo, Hope for Independence from Serbia," *The New York Times*, June 13, 2006.

73. Gurr, *Minorities at Risk*, pp. 323–324. See also Barbara F. Walter, "Does Conflict Beget Conflict? Explaining Recurrent Civil War," *Journal of Peace Research* 41: pp. 371–388. See also Ted Robert Gurr, "Minorities, Nationalists, and Islamists: Managing Communal Conflict in the Twenty-first Century," in *Leashing the Dogs of War: Conflict Management in a Divided World*, eds. Chester A. Crocker, Fen Olster Hampson, and Pamela Aall. 2007, Washington, DC: United States Institute of Peace Press, Pp. 131–160.

74. Gurr, *People Versus States*, pp. 278–279.

75. Gurr, *Minorities at Risk*, p. 139. See also Van Evera, "Hypotheses on Nationalism and War," pp. 36–37.

76. R. J. Rummel, *Understanding Conflict and War: The Conflict Helix*, Vol. 2. (Thousand Oaks, Calif.: Sage, 1976), p. 370. See also James Habyarimana, Macartan Humphreys, Daniel Posner, and Jeremy Weinstein, " Better Institutions, Not Partition," *Foreign Affairs*, July/August 2008, 87: 138-141.

77. Carment and James, "Internal Constraints and Interstate Ethnic Conflict," p. 104.

78. Larry Diamond, "Building Democracy After Conflict: Lessons from Iraq," *Journal of Democracy* 16: pp. 9–23. © 2005 National Endowment for Democracy and The Johns Hopkins University Press. Reprinted with permission of The Johns Hopkins University Press.

79. Ahmed S. Hashim, "Iraq's Civil War," *Current History* (January 2007): pp. 3–10.

80. Larry Diamond, "Building Democracy After Conflict: Lessons from Iraq," p. 18. For more on the challenges to democratization in the Middle East, see Tamara Cofman Wittes, *Freedoms Unsteady March: Americas Role in Building Arab Democracy* (Brookings Institution Press, 2008); Marina Ottaway and Julia Choucair-Vizoso (Eds.) *Beyond the Façade: Political Reform in the Arab World* (Carnegie Endowment for International Peace, 2008.), and Arthur A. Goldsmith, "Making the World Safe for Partial Democracy? Questioning the Premises of Democracy Promotion," *International Security*, 33(s) (Fall 2008), pp. 120–147.

81. Philip Gourevitch, "Zaire's Killer Camps," *New York Times*, October 28, 1996, p. A:13.

82. William Easterly, *The White Man's Burden: Why the West's Efforts to Aid the Rest Have Done So Much Ill and So Little Good* (New York: Penguin Press, 2006), p. 335. See also Alan J. Kuperman, "The Moral Hazard of Humanitarian Intervention: Lessons from the Balkans," *International Studies Quarterly*, (2008) 52, 49–80.

83. Schmid, for example, provides more than 100 definitions. Alex Schmid, *Political Terrorism* (New Brunswick, N.J.: Transaction Books, 1983), pp. 119–152. For a discussion of the changing meaning of terrorism across time, see Bruce Hoffman, *Inside Terrorism* (New York: Columbia University Press, 2006), pp. 3–20.

84. Grenville Byford, "The Wrong War," *Foreign Affairs* 81 (July–August 2002): pp. 40–41.

85. Paul Johnson, "The Seven Deadly Sins of Terrorism," in Henry Hyunwook Han (ed.), *Terrorism, Political Violence, and World Order* (1984), p. 50.

86. Long, "Countering Terrorism Beyond Sovereignty," in Maryann K. Cusimano (ed.), *Beyond Sovereignty* (Boston: Bedford/St. Martin's, 2000), p. 98.

87. Ibid, p. 98.

88. Chien-peng Chung, "China's 'War on Terror,'" *Foreign Affairs* 81 (July–August 2002): p. 8.

89. Thomas C. Schelling, "Thinking About Nuclear Terrorism," *International Security* 6 (Spring 1982): p. 66.

90. As quoted in Peter C. Sederberg, *Terrorist Myths: Illusion, Rhetoric, and Reality* (Upper Saddle River, N.J.: Prentice-Hall, 1989), p. 27.

91. Cindy C. Combs, *Terrorism in the Twenty-First Century* (Upper Saddle River, N.J.: Prentice Hall, 2000), p. 36.

92. Sederberg, *Terrorist Myths*, p. 33.

93. Ibid.

94. Philip C. Wilcox, Jr., *Patterns of Global Terrorism* (Washington, D.C.: U.S. Department of State, 1997).

95. R. J. Rummel, *Death by Government*, www.hawaii.edu/powerkills, July 21, 2006.

96. Long, "Countering Terrorism Beyond Sovereignty," p. 99.

97. Walter Enders and Todd Sandler, "Patterns of Transnational Terrorism, 1970–1999: Alternative Time-Series Estimates," *International Studies Quarterly* 46 (2002): p. 146.

98. Ibid, p. 146.

99. David C. Rapoport, "Fear and Trembling: Terrorism in Three Religious Traditions," *American Political Science Review* 78 (September 1984): pp. 659, 672, 673, 675.

100. Combs, *Terrorism in the Twenty-First Century*, p. 22.

101. David C. Rapoport, "The Fourth Wave: September 11 in the History of Terrorism," *Current History* (December 2001): pp. 419–424.

102. For a concise history of terrorism in the second half of the twentieth century, see Martha Crenshaw, "Why America? The Globalization of Civil War," *Current History* (December 2001).

103. Ibid., p. 427.

104. Ibid., pp. 426–427.

105. Christopher Dobson and Ronald Payne, *The Terrorists: Their Weapons, Leaders and Tactics* (New York: Facts on File, 1979), p. 71.

106. Combs, *Terrorism in the Twenty-First Century*, p. 79.

107. Ibid., pp. 80–81.

108. Ray S. Cline and Yonah Alexander, *Terrorism: The Soviet Connection* (New York: Crane Russak, 1984), p. 49.

109. Dobson and Payne, *The Terrorists*, p. 115.

110. Cline and Alexander, *Terrorism*, p. 51.

111. Laurie Mylroie, "The World Trade Center Bomb," *National Interest* 42 (Winter 1995–1996): pp. 3–15.

112. Hoffman, *Inside Terrorism*, pp. 272–275.

113. Laqueur, "Postmodern Terrorism," p. 29; Hoffman, *Inside Terrorism*, p. 276.

114. Steven A. Holmes, "U.S. Says Terrorist Attacks Dropped Sharply in 1992," *New York Times*, May 1, 1993, p. 4.

115. Walter Enders and Todd Sandler, "Is Transnational Terrorism Becoming More Threatening?" *Journal of Conflict Resolution* 44 (June 2000): p. 310.

116. Ibid., p. 308.

117. Crenshaw, "Why America?" p. 432.

118. Audrey Kurth Cronin, "Rethinking Sovereignty: American Strategy in the Age of Terrorism," *Survival* 44 (2002): p. 124.

119. Enders and Sandler, "Is Transnational Terrorism Becoming More Threatening?" p. 311.

120. Crenshaw, "Why America?" pp. 428–429.

121. Ahmed Rashid, "The Taliban: Exporting Extremism," *Foreign Affairs* 78 (November–December 1999): p. 31.

122. Ann M. Lesch, "Osama bin Laden's 'Business' in Sudan," *Current History* (May 2002): pp. 203–209.

123. Rashid, "The Taliban."

124. Bernard Lewis, "License to Kill," *Foreign Affairs* 77 (November–December 1998): p. 15.

125. Ibid., p. 20.

126. Elaine Sciolino, "Officials Suspect Global Terror Tie in Moroccan Blasts," *New York Times*, May 18, 2003; Douglas Jehl and Eric Schmitt, "U.S. Suggests a Qaeda Cell in Iran Directed Saudi Bombings," *New York Times*, May 21, 2003.

127. Alan Cowell, "London is Solemn on Anniversary of Blasts," *The New York Times*, July 7, 2006.

128. Olivier Roy, "Europe's Response to Radical Islam," *Current History* (November 2005), pp. 360–364.

129. John Mueller, "Is There Still a Terrorist Threat?: The Myth of the Omnipresent Enemy," *Foreign Affairs* (September/October 2006).

130. MIPT Terrorism Data Base, http:www.tkb.org, accessed October 13, 2006.

131. Laqueur, "Postmodern Terrorism," p. 36.

132. Long, "Countering Terrorism Beyond Sovereignty," p. 99.

133. Andrew H. Kydd and Barbara F. Walter, "The Strategies of Terrorism," *International Security* (Summer 2006) 31(1):49–80, p.49. For criticism of this claim, see Max Abrahms, "Why Terrorism Does Not Work," *International Security* (Fall 2006), 31(2):42–78.

134. Bard E. O'Neil, "Towards a Typology of Terrorism: The Palestinian Resistance Movement," *Journal of International Affairs* 32 (Spring–Summer 1978): pp. 34–35.

135. Combs, *Terrorism in the Twenty-First Century*, pp. 37–38.

136. Enders and Sandler, "Is Transnational Terrorism Becoming More Threatening?" p. 310.

137. Jonathan Stevenson, "Pragmatic Counterterrorism," *Survival* 43 (Winter 2001): p. 35.

138. Enders and Sandler, "Is Transnational Terrorism Becoming More Threatening?" p. 310; see also Jonathan Fox, "The Rise of Religious Nationalism and Conflict: Ethnic Conflict and Revolutionary Wars, 1945–2001," *Journal of Peace Research* 41: pp. 715–731 and Hoffman, *Inside Terrorism*, p. 85.

139. Enders and Sandler, "Is Transnational Terrorism Becoming More Threatening?" p. 310.

140. Assaf Moghadam, "Motives for Martyrdom: Al-Qaida, Sala Jihad, and the Spread of Suicide Attacks," *International Security* Winter 2008/2009, 33(3): 46–78.

141. One analysis suggests that the proportion of religious to non-religious ethnic minorities remained stable from 1945 to 2000, although religious-separatist conflicts became more violent than other separatist groups after 1980. See Jonathan Fox, "The Rise of Religious Nationalism and Conflict: Ethnic Conflict and Revolutionary Wars, 1945–2001."

142. Shibley Telhami, "It's Not About Faith: A Battle for the Soul of the Middle East," *Current History* (December 2001): p. 417. See also Christopher C. Harmon, *Terrorism Today*. 2nd ed. 2008, New York: Routledge.

143. Ibid.

144. Pape, "The Strategic Logic of Suicide Terrorism," p. 343.

145. Long, "Countering Terrorism Beyond Sovereignty," p. 102.

146. Crenshaw, "Why America?" p. 429.

147. Ibid.

148. Ibid., p. 432.

149. Bruce Riedel, "Al Qaeda Strikes Back," *Foreign Affairs*, (May/June 2007) 86(3):24-40.

150. Mark Juergensmeyer, "Terror in the Name of God," *Current History* (November 2001): p. 357.

151. On Al Qaeda, see Peter Bergen, *Holy War, Inc.* (New York: Free Press, 2001).

152. Jessica Stern, "Preparing for a War on Terrorism," *Current History* (November 2001): p. 355.

153. Rohan Gunaratna, "Al-Qaeda's Operational Ties with Allied Groups," *Janes Intelligence Review*, February 1, 2003. See also Jessica Stern, "The Protean Enemy," *Foreign Affairs* (July–August 2003): pp. 27–40. See also Bruce Riedel, "Al Qaeda Strikes Back," *Foreign Affairs*, (May/June 2007) 86(3):24–40.

154. Hoffman, *Inside Terrorism*, p. 282.

155. Brigitte L. Nacos, *Terrorism and Counterterrorism: Understanding Threats and Responses in the Post-9/11 World* (New York: Pearson Longman, 2006), pp. 55–56; Stern, "The Protean Enemy," 2003.

156. Crenshaw, "Why America?" p. 431.

157. Walter Enders and Todd Sandler, "The Effectiveness of Antiterrorism Policies: A Vector-Autoregression-Intervention Analysis," *American Political Science Review* 87 (December 1993): p. 830, emphasis added.

158. Paul Wilkinson, "State-Sponsored International Terrorism: The Problem of Response," *World Today* 40 (July 1984): p. 298.

159. Crenshaw, "Why America?" p. 428. See also Bruce W. Jentleson and Christopher A. Whytock, "Who 'Won' Libya? The Force-Diplomacy Debate and Its Implications for Theory and Policy," *International Security* 30(3) (Winter 2005/06): pp. 47–86.

160. Nacos, *Terrorism and Counterterrorism*, p. 189; "How Gadaffi Was Brought Back into the Fold," *Financial Times* January 27, 2004; "The Iraq War Did Not Force Gadaffi's Hand," *Financial Times*, March 8, 2004; and Jentleson and Whytock, "Who 'Won' Libya?"

161. Crenshaw, "Why America?" p. 428.

162. Bruce Riedel, "Al Qaeda Strikes Back," *Foreign Affairs*, (May/June 2007) 86(3):24–40.

163. Cronin, "Rethinking Sovereignty," p. 127.

164. Stern, "The Protean Enemy," 2003. Bruce Riedel, "Al Qaeda Strikes Back," *Foreign Affairs*, (May/June 2007) 86(3):24-40; Thomas Barfield, "The Roots of Failure in Afghanistan," *Current History* (December 2008): 410–417.

165. Peter Bergen and Alec Reynolds, "Blowback Revisited," *Foreign Affairs* 84 (6) (November-December 2005); Hoffman, *Inside Terrorism*, p. 293; Jon Western, "American Security, the Use of Force, and the Limits of the Bush Doctrine," in David P. Forsythe, Patrice C. McMahon, and Andrew Wedeman, *American Foreign Policy in a Globalized World* (New York: Routledge, 2006), pp. 105–121.

166. Jusuf Wanandi, "A Global Coalition Against International Terrorism," *International Security* 26 (Spring 2002): p. 187.

167. Philip Keefer and Norman Loayza, "Overview: Terrorism, Economic Development, and Political Openness," in *Terrorism, Economic Development, and Political Openness*, eds. Philip Keefer and Norman Loayza. 2008, Cambridge: Cambridge University Press, Pp. 1-16; James A. Piazza, "A Supply-Side View of Suicide Terrorism: A Cross-National Study," *The Journal of Politics* 70 (January 2008): 28–39; James A. Piazza, "Do Democracy and Free Markets Protect Us From Terrorism?" *International Politics* 45 (January 2008): 72–91.

168. James A. Piazza, "Rooted in Poverty?: Terrorism, Poor Economic Development, and Social Cleavages," *Terrorism and Political Violence* 18 (2006): pp. 159–177. For empirical support of the relationship between failed states and terrorism, see James A. Piazza, "Incubators of Terror: Do Failed and Failing States Promote Transnational Terrorism?" *International Studies Quarterly* (2008) 52:469-488.

169. Taras and Ganguly, *Understanding Ethnic Conflict*, 2006, p. 236.

170. Jessica Stern, "The Protean Enemy," p. 32.

171. Long, "Countering Terrorism Beyond Sovereignty," p. 105.

172. Combs, *Terrorism in the Twenty-First Century*, p. 82.

173. Rapoport, "The Fourth Wave," p. 424.

Chapter 8 (pages 259–301)

1. Glenn H. Snyder, *Alliance Politics* (Ithaca, N.Y.: Cornell University Press, 1997), p. 4.

2. Arnold Wolfers, "Alliances," in David Sills (ed.), *International Encyclopedia of the Social Sciences* (New York: Macmillan and Free Press, 1968), p. 269.

3. Stephen M. Walt, *The Origins of Alliances* (Ithaca, N.Y.: Cornell University Press, 1987), pp. 18–19.

4. Ibid., pp. 21–22.

5. Ibid., p. 5.

6. Ibid., pp. 21–22.

7. Christopher Layne, "The Unipolar Illusion Revisited: The Coming End of the United States' Unipolar Moment," *International Security* (Fall 2006) 31(2):7–41.

8. Ibid.

9. Randall L. Schweller, "Bandwagoning for Profit: Bringing the Revisionist State Back In," *International Security* 19 (Summer 1994): 74.

10. Ibid., p. 96.

11. Ibid.

12. Walt, *The Origins of Alliances*, p. 29.

13. William Riker, *The Theory of Political Coalition* (New Haven, Conn.: Yale University Press, 1962), pp. 32–33.

14. Bruce Bueno de Mesquita and J. David Singer, "Alliances, Capabilities, and War: A Review and Synthesis," in Cornelius Cotter (ed.) *Political Science Annual*, Vol. 4 (Indianapolis: Bobbs-Merrill, 1973), p. 266.

15. Riker, *The Theory of Political Coalition*, p. 7.

16. Glenn Palmer and J. Sky David, "Multiple Goals or Deterrence: A Test of Two Models in Nuclear and Nonnuclear Alliances," *Journal of Conflict Resolution* 43 (December 1999): p. 750.

17. On institutional and normative constraints of alliances, see, for example, John Duffield, "International Regimes and Alliance Behavior: Explaining NATO Force Levels," *International Organization* 46 (1992): pp. 819–855.

18. Jack Levy and Michael Barnett, "Alliance Formation, Domestic Political Economy, and Third World Security," *Jerusalem Journal of International Relations* 14 (December 1992): pp. 19–40.

19. Zeev Maoz, "Paradoxical Functions of International Alliances: Security and Other Dilemmas," in John Vasquez and Colin Elman (eds.) *Realism and the Balancing of Power: A New Debate* (Upper Saddle River, N.J.: Prentice Hall, 2003).

20. See Brian Lai and Dan Reiter, "Democracy, political similarity, and international alliances, 1816–1992," *Journal of Conflict Resolution* 44(2000): pp. 203–227 and Douglas M. Gibler and Scott Wolford, "Alliances, Then Democracy," *Journal of Conflict Resolution* 50(1) (February 2006): pp. 129–153; Andrew G. Long, Timothy Nordstrom, and Kyeonghi Baek, "Allying for Peace: Treaty Obligations and Conflict between Allies," *The Journal of Politics* 69 (November 2007): 1103-1117.

21. Walt, *The Origins of Alliances*, p. 35; Andrew G. Long, Timothy Nordstrom, and Kyeonghi Baek, "Allying for Peace: Treaty Obligations and Conflict between Allies," *The Journal of Politics* 69 (November 2007): 1103-1117.

22. John R. Oneal and Paul F. Diehl, "The Theory of Collective Action and NATO Defense Burdens: New Empirical Tests," *Political Science Quarterly* 47 (June 1994): p. 373; On current burden sharing problems in NATO, see Renée de Nevers, "NATO's International Security Role in the Terrorist Era," *International Security*, Vol. 31, No. 4 (Spring 2007): 34–66.

23. Mancur Olson, "An Economic Theory of Alliances," *Review of Economics and Statistics* 48 (August 1966): p. 268. There has been considerable research on the notion of alliances as a collective good. See, for example, Oneal and Diehl, "The Theory of Collective Action and NATO Defense Burdens: New Empirical Tests"; and Glenn Palmer and J. Sky David, "Multiple Goals or Deterrence: A Test of Two Models in Nuclear and Nonnuclear Alliances," *Journal of Conflict Resolution* 43 (December 1999): pp. 748–770. On current burden sharing problems in NATO, see Renée de Nevers, "NATO's International Security Role in the Terrorist Era," *International Security*, Vol. 31, No. 4 (Spring 2007): 34–66.

24. See, for example, John A. Vasquez, *The War Puzzle* (Cambridge: Cambridge University Press, 1993); and John A. Vasquez and Paul D. Senese, "Alliances, Territorial Disputes, and the Probability of War: Testing for Interactions," in Paul F. Diehl (ed.), *The Scourge of War* (Ann Arbor: University of Michigan Press, 2004), pp. 189–221. Brett Ashley Leeds, "Do Alliances Deter Aggression? The Influence of Military Alliances on the Initiation of Militarized Interstate Disputes," *American Journal of Political Science* Vol. 47, No. 3 (July 2003), pp. 427–439.

25. Bruce Bueno de Mesquita, *The War Trap* (New Haven, Conn.: Yale University Press, 1981), p. 151; Brett Ashley Leeds, "Do Alliances Deter Aggression? The Influence of Military Alliances on the Initiation of Militarized Interstate Disputes," *American Journal of Political Science* Vol. 47, No. 3 (July 2003), pp. 427-439.

26. Wallace J. Thies, "Randomness, Contagion, and Hetero-geneity in the Formation of Interstate Alliances: A Reconsideration," *International Interactions* 16 (1991): p. 348.

27. Patrick J. McGowan and Robert M. Rood, "Alliance Behavior in Balance of Power Systems: Applying a Poisson Model to Nineteenth Century Europe," *American Political Science Review* 69 (September 1975): p. 866.

28. Thomas J. Christensen and Jack Snyder, "Chain Gangs and Passed Bucks: Predicting Alliance Patterns in Multipolarity," *International Organization* 44 (Spring 1990): p. 148.

29. Thies, "Randomness, Contagion, and Heterogeneity in the Formation of Interstate Alliances," p. 349.

30. William E. Odom, "NATO's Expansion: Why the Critics Are Wrong," *National Interest* 39 (Spring 1995): p. 45.

31. Gibler and Wolford, "Alliances, Then Democracy."

32. Jerome Levinson and Juan de Onis, *The Alliance That Lost Its Way* (Chicago: Quadrangle Books, 1970), p. 77; Edward D. Mansfield and Jon C. Pevehouse, "Democratization and International Organizations," *International Organization* 60 (Winter 2006): 137-167.

33. R. W. Apple, Jr., "Europe's New Order: Making a Club, Not War," *New York Times*, May 18, 1997, 4, p. 1.

34. Edward D. Mansfield and Jon C. Pevehouse, "Democratization and International Organizations," *International Organization* 60 (Winter 2006): 137-167.

35. Milada Anna Vachudová, "The Atlantic Alliance and the Kosovo Crisis: The Impact of Expansion and the Behavior of New Allies," in Pierre Martin and Mark R. Brawley (eds.), *Alliance Politics, Kosovo, and NATO's War: Allied Force or Forced Allies?* (New York: Palgrave, 2000), p. 202.

36. Charles A. Kupchan, "NATO's Hard Choices," *The New York Times*, March 31, 2009.

37. "NATO Formally Embraces Russia as a Junior Partner," *New York Times*, May 29, 2002; John Vinocur, "Georgia Is Focal Point in U.S.-Nato-Russian Tension," *The New York Times* May 5, 2009.

38. Richard K. Betts, "The Three Faces of NATO," *The National Interest* http://www.nationalinterest.org/ Article.aspx?id=20944, accessed May 4, 2009.

39. Mark R. Brawley and Pierre Martin, "Balancing Acts: NATO's Unity and the Lessons to Learn," in Martin and Brawley, *Alliance Politics, Kosovo, and NATO's War*, p. 221.

40. Patrick E. Tyler, "Gingerly, NATO Plans Broader Role for Moscow," *New York Times*, December 7, 2001.

41. For an analysis of NATO's role in anti-terrorism, see Renée de Nevers, "NATO's International Security Role in the Terrorist Era," *International Security*, Vol. 31, No. 4 (Spring 2007): 34–66

42. Ivo Daalder and James Goldgeier, "Global NATO," *Foreign Affairs I* 85(5) (September/October 2006).

43. Richard K. Betts, "The Three Faces of NATO," *The National Interest Online*, http://www.nationalinterest.org/ Article.aspx?id=20944, accessed May 4, 2009

44. "Europe Assesses Damage to Western Relationships and Takes Steps to Rebuild," *New York Times*, April 2, 2003.

45. Richard K. Betts, "The Three Faces of NATO," *The National Interest Online*, http://www.nationalinterest.org/Article. aspx?id=20944, accessed May 4, 2009; Charles A. Kupchan, "NATO's Hard Choices," *The New York Times*, March 31, 2009.

46. For a discussion of the relationship between armaments and alliance decisions, see James D. Morrow, "Arms versus Allies: Tradeoffs in the Search for Security," *International Organization* 47 (Spring 1993): pp. 207–233.

47. Ibid.

48. Greg Cashman, *What Causes War?* (San Francisco: Jossey-Bass, 1993), pp. 175–176.

49. Sam Perlo-Freeman, Catalina Perdomo, Petter Stålenheim, and Elisabeth Sköns, "Military Expenditure," In *SIPRI Yearbook 2009 Armaments, Disarmament and International Security Summary*, 2009, pp. 10, 11. http://www.sipri.org/yearbook/2009/files/SIPRIYB09summary.pdf Accessed 9 June 2009.

50. Ibid.

51. Ibid.

52. Michael T. Klare, "The New Arms Race: Light Weapons and International Security," *Current History* 96 (April 1997): pp. 173–178. See also Small Arms Survey, *Small Arms Survey 2002: Counting the Human Cost* (Oxford: Oxford University Press, 2002) and Small Arms Survey, *Small Arms Survey 2006: Unfinished Business* (Oxford: Oxford University Press, 2006). See also Rachel Stohl and Rhea Myerscough, "Sub-Saharan Small Arms: The Damage Continues," *Current History* (May 2007) 106(700):227-233.

53. The Geneva International Centre for Humanitarian Demining, *A Guide to Mine Action and Explosive Remnants of War*. 3rd ed. 2007: Geneva: (no publishing company specified), http://www.gichd.org/fileadmin/pdf/publications/ Guide-to-MA-2007/Guide-to-Mine-Action-2007.pdf Accessed 12 June 2009

54. Hagelin et al., "International Arms Transfers," p. 380. See also Volker Krause, "Hazardous Weapons? Effects of Arms Transfers and Defense Pacts on Militarized Disputes, 1950–1995," *International Interactions* 30 (2004): pp. 349–371.

55. David Kinsella, "Nested Rivalries: Superpower Competition, Arms Transfers, and Regional Conflict, 1950–1990," *International Interactions* 21 (1995): pp. 109–125; Nils Duquet, "Arms Acquisition Patterns and the Dynamicsof Armed Conflict: Lessons from the Niger Delta," *International Studies Perspectives* 10 (May 2009): 169–185; but see William J. Durch, *Constructing Regional Security: The Role of Arms Transfers, Arms Control, and Reassurance* (New York: Palgrave, 2000).

56. Krause, "Hazardous Weapons."

57. Samuel Huntington, as quoted in Cashman, *What Causes War?* p. 172.

58. Susan Sample, "Arms Races and Dispute Escalation: Resolving the Debate?" *Journal of Peace Research* 34 (February 1997): pp. 7–22. See also John A. Vasquez, "The Probability of War, 1816–1992: Presidential Address to the International Studies Association, March 25, 2002, New Orleans," *International Studies Quarterly* 48 (March 2004): 1-28; John Sislin, and Frederic Pearson, "Arms and Escalation in Ethnic Conflicts: The Case of Sri Lanka," *International Studies Perspectives* 7 (May 2006): 137–158.

59. Cashman, *What Causes War?* p. 182. See also James D. Morrow, "A Twist of Truth: A Reexamination of the Effects of Arms Races on the Occurrence of War," *Journal of Conflict Resolution* 33 (September 1989): p. 502.

60. John Sislin and Frederic Pearson, *Arms and Ethnic Conflict* (Boulder, Colo.: Rowman & Littlefield, 2001).

61. Jack Mendelsohn, "Arms Control: The Unfinished Agenda," *Current History* 96 (April 1997): pp. 147–148.

62. Michael T. Klare and Lora Lumpe, "Fanning the Flames of War: Conventional Arms Transfers in the 1990s," in Michael T. Klare and Yogesh Chandrani (eds.), *World Security: Challenges for a New Century* (New York: St. Martin's Press, 1998), p. 161.

63. *SIPRI Yearbook 2006: Armaments, Disarmament and International Security* (Oxford: Oxford University Press, 2006), http://www.sipri.org/contents/milap/milex/mex_trends.html.

64. Klare, "The New Arms Race."

65. Kendall W. Stiles, *Case Histories in International Politics* (New York: Longman, 2002), p. 385.

66. Henry Kissinger, "Arms Control, Inspection and Surprise Attack," *Foreign Affairs* 38 (1960), cited in Stephen J. Majeski, "Technological Innovation and Cooperation in Arms Races," *International Studies Quarterly* 30 (January 1986): p. 175.

67. "Fear that the other may be about to strike in the mistaken belief that we are about to strike gives us a motive for striking, and so justifies the other's motive. . . . He thinks that he thinks we think . . . he thinks he'll attack; so he thinks we shall; so he will; so we must." Thomas Schelling, *The Strategy of Conflict* (Cambridge, Mass.: Harvard University Press, 1970), p. 207.

68. Some classic and recent sources on the game theory approach to international politics include Anatol Rapoport, *Two Person Game Theory: The Essential Ideas* (Ann Arbor.: University of Michigan Press, 1996); James D. Morrow, *Game Theory for Political Scientists* (Princeton, N.J.: Princeton University Press, 1994); David A. Lake and Robert

Powell (eds.), *Strategic Choice and International Relations* (Princeton, N.J.: Princeton University Press, 1999); Bruce Bueno de Mesquita, *Principles of International Politics: People's Power, Preferences, and Perceptions* (Washington, D.C.: Congressional Quarterly Press, 2000).

69. As quoted in John Mueller, *Quiet Cataclysm* (New York: HarperCollins, 1995), p. 323. Mueller (pp. 191–193) cites similar assertions by such well-known analysts and observers as Arnold Toynbee, Albert Einstein, Herman Kahn, C. P. Snow, and Jonathan Schell.

70. Shannon N. Kile, Vitaly Fedchenko, and Hans M. Kristensen, "World Nuclear Forces," in *SIPRI Yearbook 2009 Armaments, Disarmament and International Security Summary*, p. 16, http://www.sipri.org/yearbook/2009/files/SIPRIYB09summary.pdf Accessed 9 June 2009.

71. John W. R. Lepingwell, "START II and the Politics of Arms Control in Russia," *International Security* 20 (Fall 1995): 68. Lepingwell goes on to note, though, that "the missiles could be retargetted quickly in a crisis" (p. 68).

72. Ibid., p. 65.

73. Leonard S. Spector, Mark G. McDonough, Gregory P. Webb, and Gregory D. Koblentz, *Tracking Nuclear Proliferation*: book abstract, May 9, 1997, p. 1, http://ceip.org/pubstr96.htm.

74. Shannon N. Kile, Vitaly Fedchenko, and Hans M. Kristensen, "World Nuclear Forces," in *SIPRI Yearbook 2009 Armaments, Disarmament and International Security Summary*. p. 16, http://www.sipri.org/yearbook/2009/files/SIPRIYB09summary.pdf, Accessed 9 June 2009.

75. Ibid.

76. Ibid.

77. Reuters, "Libya Neared Nuclear Bomb, Qaddafi Says," published in *The New York Times*, July 25, 2006.

78. John. M. Deutsch, "The New Nuclear Threat," *Foreign Affairs* 71 (Fall 1992): pp. 120, 126.

79. Christopher Allan McHorney, "India and Pakistan: Newest Members of the Nuclear Club," in Ralph C. Carter (ed.), *Contemporary Cases in U.S. Foreign Policy* (Washington, D.C.: CQ Press, 2002), p. 131.

80. David J. Karl, "Proliferation Pessimism and Emerging Nuclear Powers," *International Security* 21 (Winter 1996–1997): p. 102. See also Saira Khan, "Nuclear Weapons and the Prolongation of the India-Pakistan Rivalry," in T. V. Paul (ed.) *The India-Pakistan Conflict: An Enduring Rivalry* (Cambridge: Cambridge University Press, 2005) and S. Paul Kapur, "India and Pakistan's Unstable Peace: Why Nuclear South Asia is Not Like Cold War Europe," *International Security* 30(20): pp. 127–152. See also S. Paul Kapur, "Ten Years of Instability in a Nuclear South Asia," *International Security*, Vol. 33, No. 2 (Fall 2008), pp. 71–94.

81. Scott D. Sagan, "How to Keep the Bomb From Iran," *Foreign Affairs* 85(5) (September/October 2006).

82. Sumit Ganguly, "Nuclear Stability in South Asia," *International Security*, Vol. 33, No. 2 (Fall 2008):45–70.

83. For more details, and pros and cons of the agreement, see Esther Pan and Jayshree Bajoria, "The U.S.-India Nuclear Deal," Council on Foreign Relations, http://www.cfr.org/publication/9663/, accessed May 5, 2009.

85. Kongdan Oh and Ralph C. Hassig, "North Korea's Nuclear Politics," *Current History* (September 2004): p. 277.

86. Ibid., pp. 273, 276.

87. Gawdat Bahgat, "Nuclear Proliferation: The Islamic Republic of Iran," *International Studies Perspectives* 7(2) (May 2006): pp. 124–136.

88. Ibid, p. 132; see also William J. Broad and Elaine Sciolino, "Iran's Secrecy Widens Gap in Nuclear Intelligence," *New York Times*, May 19, 2006.

89. William J. Broad and David E. Sanger, "Iran Has More Enriched Uranium Than Thought," *The New York Times*, February 19, 2009.

90. Graham Allison, *Nuclear Terrorism* (New York: Times Books, 2004).

91. David E. Sanger, "Pakistan Strife Raises U.S. Doubts on Nuclear Arms," *The New York Times*, May 3, 2009.

92. Steven J. Rosen, "A Stable System of Mutual Nuclear Deterrence in the Arab-Israeli Conflict," *American Political Science Review* 71 (December 1977): pp. 1367–1383; Shai Feldman, "A Nuclear Middle East," *Survival* 23 (May–June 1981): pp. 107–116; and Shai Feldman, "Peacemaking in the Middle East: The Next Step," *Foreign Affairs* 59 (Spring 1981): pp. 756–780.

93. Sumit Ganguly, "Nuclear Stability in South Asia," *International Security*, Vol. 33, No. 2 (Fall 2008):45–70.

94. Bruce Bueno de Mesquita and William Riker, "An Assessment of the Merits of Selective Nuclear Proliferation," *Journal of Conflict Resolution* 26 (June 1982): p. 299.

95. Kenneth N. Waltz, "The Spread of Nuclear Weapons: More May Be Better," *Adelphi Papers*, no. 171 (London: International Institute of Strategic Studies, 1982), pp. 29–30.

96. John J. Mearsheimer, "Back to the Future: Instability in Europe After the Cold War," *International Security* 15 (Summer 1990): pp. 5–56 and "The Case for a Ukrainian Nuclear Deterrent," *Foreign Affairs* 72 (Summer 1993): pp. 50–66.

97. Martin van Creveld, *Nuclear Proliferation and the Future of Conflict* (New York: Free Press, 1993), p. 124 (emphasis in the original). For more discussion on nuclear proliferation optimists and pessimists, see Dagobert L. Brito and Michael D. Intriligator, "Proliferation and the Probability of War," *Journal of Conflict Resolution* 40 (March 1996), p. 212; Sagan, "How to Keep the Bomb From Iran"; and Stephen Peter Rosen, "After Proliferation: What to Do If More States Go Nuclear," *Foreign Affairs* 85(5) (September/October 2006).

98. Michael D. Intriligator and Dagobert L. Brito, "Can Arms Races Lead to the Outbreak of War?" *Journal of Conflict Resolution* 28 (March 1984): p. 63.

99. Steve Fetter, "Ballistic Missiles and Weapons of Mass Destruction," *International Security* 16 (Summer 1991): p. 29.

100. S. Paul Kapur, "Ten Years of Instability in a Nuclear South Asia," *International Security*, Vol. 33, No. 2 (Fall 2008):71–94, p.93.

101. U.S. Department of State, "Treaty on the Non-proliferation of Nuclear Weapons," http://www.state .gov/t/isn/trty/16281.htm (accessed August 2, 2006).

102. Spector et al., *Tracking Nuclear Proliferation*, p. 2. Spector et al. go on to note, though, that before that agreement had been formalized, North Korea may have "separated enough weapon-grade material for a nuclear device."

103. James Martin Center for Nonproliferation Studies at the Monterey Institute of International Studies. "Introduction," *NTI: NWFZ Tutorial*, p. 1 (The introduction is 1 page in length). http://www.nti .org/h_learnmore/nwfztutorial/index.html Accessed 12 June 2009.

104. For a good analysis of the Senate rejection, see Christopher M. Jones, "Rejection of the Comprehensive Test Ban Treaty: The Politics of Ratification," in Carter, *Contemporary Cases in U.S. Foreign Policy.*

105. *SIPRI Yearbook 2001*, p. 455.

106. Helene Cooper, and David E. Sanger. "Citing Rising Risk, Obama Seeks Nuclear Arms Cuts: Warns of Spread of Bomb Technology in Black Market," *The New York Times*, April 6, 2009, http://query.nytimes.com/gst/fullpage.html ?res=9D00EFDE1438F935A35757C0A96F9C8B63&fta=y& scp=2&sq=obama%20comprehensive%20test%20ban%20 treaty&st=cse Accessed 15 June 2009; *The Economist.* "Barack Obama and Nuclear Weapons: Peace, Love and Understanding," April 6, 2009, http://www.economist.com/ world/europe/displaystory.cfm?story_id=13435301 Accessed 15 June 2009.

107. Ibid., p. 423.

108. For a good summary of this debate, see Shannon N. Kile, "Ballistic Missile Defence and Nuclear Arms Control," Stockholm International Peace Research Institute, *SIPRI Yearbook 2002*, pp. 2–24.

109. Fetter, "Ballistic Missiles and Weapons of Mass Destruction," p. 5.

110. Mary H. Cooper, "Chemical and Biological Weapons," *CQ Researcher*, January 31, 1997.

111. Ibid.

112. Ibid.

113. Fetter, "Ballistic Missiles and Weapons of Mass Destruction," p. 11.

114. Ibid., p. 23.

115. Cooper, "Chemical and Biological Weapons."

116. Jean Pascal Zanders, John Hart, and Frida Kuhlau, "Chemical and Biological Weapon Developments and Arms Control," in Stockholm International Peace Research Institute, *SIPRI Yearbook 2002*, p. 696.

117. John F. Sopko, "The Changing Proliferation Threat," *Foreign Policy* 105 (Winter 1996–1997): p. 8.

118. Ibid., pp. 8, 12.

119. Laurie Mylroie, "The World Trade Center Bomb," *National Interest* 42 (Winter 1995–1996): p. 3.

120. Bruce Hoffman, *Inside Terrorism* (New York: Columbia University Press, 2006), pp. 268, 278.

121. Sopko, "The Changing Proliferation Threat," p. 6.

122. Zanders, Hart, and Kuhlau, "Chemical and Biological Weapon Developments and Arms Control," pp. 701–702.

123. Hoffman, p. 272. See also Allison, *Nuclear Terrorism.*

124. Zanders, Hart, and Kuhlau, "Chemical and Biological Weapon Developments and Arms Control," p. 705.

125. Mendelsohn, "Arms Control: The Unfinished Agenda," p. 148.

126. Amitai Etzioni, "Tomorrow's Institutions Today," *Foreign Affairs* (May/June 2009) 88(3).

127. Paul K. Kerr, "CRS [Congressional Research Service] Report for Congress: Nuclear, Biological, and Chemical Weapons and Missiles: Status and Trends," February 20, 2008. http://www.dtic.mil/cgi-bin/GetTRDoc?AD=ADA47 7531&Location=U2&doc=GetTRDoc.pdf Accessed 15 June 2009.

128. Jonathan B. Tucker, "The Biological Weapons Threat," *Current History* (April 1997): p. 172.

129. Brigin Starkey, Mark A. Boyer, and Jonathan Wilkenfeld, *Negotiating a Complex World: An Introduction to International Negotiation*, 2nd ed. (Lanham, Md.: Rowman & Littlefield, 2005), pp. 3–4.

130. Ibid., p. 68.

131. Associated Press, "California and Britain Announce Agreement on Global Warming," published in the *New York Times*, August 1, 2006.

132. See Steven Poe, "Nations' Responses to Transnational Hostage Events: An Empirical Evaluation," *International Interactions* 14 (1988): pp. 27–40; Edward Mickolus, Todd Sandler, Jean Murdock, and Peter Fleming, *International Terrorism: Attributes of Terrorist Events* (Dunn Loring: Vinyard Software, 2000); and Navin A. Bapat, "State Bargaining with Transnational Terrorist Groups," *International Studies Quarterly* 50 (March 2006): pp. 213–229.

133. Alexander L. George and William E. Simons (eds.), *The Limits of Coercive Diplomacy* (Boulder, Colo.: Westview Press, 1994); Paul K. Huth, *Extended Deterrence and the Prevention of War* (New Haven, Conn.: Yale University Press, 1988); Patrick Morgan, *Deterrence: A Conceptual Analysis* (Thousand Oaks, Calif.: Sage, 1983).

134. Russell J. Leng, *Interstate Crisis Behavior, 1816–1980: Realism Versus Reciprocity* (Cambridge: Cambridge University Press, 1993), p. 191.

135. Ibid., p. 200.

136. Ibid.

137. Starkey, Boyer, and Wilkenfeld, *Negotiating a Complex World*, p. 129.

138. James Blight, Joseph S. Nye, Jr., and David A. Welch, "The Cuban Missile Crisis Revisited," *Foreign Affairs* 66 (Fall 1987): pp. 170–188.

139. Thomas C. Schelling, *The Strategy of Conflict* (Cambridge, Mass.: Harvard University Press, 1960), p. 22.

140. Robert Putnam, "Diplomacy and Domestic Politics: The Logic of Two-Level Games," *International Organization* 42 (Summer 1988): p. 34.

Chapter 9 (pages 302–352)

1. For studies on the relationship between international organizations and conflict, see Charles Boehmer, Erik Gartzke, and Timothy Nordstrom, " Do Intergovernmental Organizations Promote Peace?" *World Politics* 57 2004 (1): 1–38; Michael W. Doyle, and Nicholas Sambanis, *Making war and Building Peace: United Nations Peace Operations*, 2006 Princeton, NJ: Princeton University Press; Jon Pevehouse, and Bruce Russett, " Democratic International Governmental Organizations Promote Peace," *International Organization* 60 2006 (4): 969-1000 and the special issue of *Journal of Conflict Resolution* 52(2) (April 2008).

2. Inis L. Claude, *Swords into Plowshares*, 3rd ed. (New York: Random House, 1964).

3. These logical and theoretical requirements are taken from discussions by Claude and by John J. Mearsheimer, "The False Promise of International Institutions," *International Security* 19 (Winter 1994–1995): p. 32. Mearsheimer is particularly skeptical about the possibility of developing an effective system of collective security, and Claude, although more sympathetic, does ultimately emphasize the difficulties and barriers to implementing such a system.

4. Worldmark Press, *The United Nations* (New York: Wiley, 1977), p. 123.

5. Mearsheimer, "The False Promise of International Institutions," p. 31.

6. Ibid.

7. It is difficult to imagine the United States, for example, using military force against Israel, even if it were branded an aggressor by the international community.

8. Thomas G. Weiss, David P. Forsythe, and Roger A. Coate, *The United Nations and Changing World Politics* (Boulder, Colo.: Westview Press, 2001), p. 24.

9. Ibid., pp. 24–25.

10. Gerhart Niemeyer, "The Balance-Sheet of the League Experiment," in David A. Kay (ed.), *The United Nations Political System* (New York: Wiley, 1967), p. 49.

11. Leland M. Goodrich, *The United Nations in a Changing World* (New York: Columbia University Press, 1974), pp. 18–19.

12. Robert E. Riggs and Jack C. Plano, *The United Nations: International Organization and World Politics*, 2nd ed. (Belmont, Calif.: Wadsworth, 1994), p. 35.

13. Claude, *Swords into Plowshares*, p. 224.

14. Harold K. Jacobson, *Networks of Interdependence* (New York: Knopf, 1979), p. 194.

15. Brian E. Urquhart, "United Nations Peace-Keeping in the Middle East," *World Today* 36 (March 1980): pp. 88–89.

16. Weiss, Forsythe, and Coate, *The United Nations and Changing World Politics*, p. 55.

17. Paul F. Diehl, "The Conditions for Success in Peacekeeping Operations," in Paul F. Diehl (ed.), *The Politics of International Organizations* (Chicago: Dorsey Press, 1989), pp. 173–174.

18. Leroy Bennett, *International Organizations*, 2nd ed. (Englewood Cliffs, N.J.: Prentice-Hall, 1980), p. 157.

19. Riggs and Plano, *The United Nations*, p. 121.

20. Paul Lewis, "How the U.N. Keeps Pace As Fewer Keep Peace," *New York Times*, May 4, 1997, p. 1:7.

21. United Nations Department of Peacekeeping, "50 Years of United Nations Peacekeeping Operations," June 9, 2003, http://www.un.org/Depts/dpko/dpko/50web/1.htm.

22. Virginia Page Fortna, "Does Peacekeeping Keep Peace? International Intervention and the Duration of Peace After Civil War," *International Studies Quarterly* 48(2) (June 2004): pp. 269–292.

23. President George H. W. Bush used this phrase in numerous speeches in 1990 and 1991.

24. Renner, 1993, p. 8.

25. Weiss, Forsythe, and Coate, *The United Nations and Changing World Politics*, p. 81.

26. "In the last five years, more than 90 cases of armed conflict have broken out, practically all of them within states. . . . The UN since 1989 has been directly or indirectly involved in more than half of these cases." Ruben P. Mendez, "Paying for Peace and Development," *Foreign Policy*, no. 100 (Fall 1995): p. 22.

27. Simon Jenkins, "Leave Rwanda Alone," *London Times*, July 10, 1994, p. 1:13.

28. Ibid.

29. Philip Gourevitch, "Zaire's Killer Camps," *New York Times*, October 28, 1996, p. A:13.

30. Charles Krauthammer, "Saved by a Failure of Humanitarianism," *Tampa Tribune*, November 25, 1996, p. 13.

31. Weiss, Forsythe, and Coate, *The United Nations and Changing World Politics*, p. 89.

32. Lewis, "How the UN Keeps Pace As Fewer Keep Peace," p. 4.

33. Ibid.

34. William R. Keylor, *The Twentieth Century World: An International History* (New York: Oxford University Press, 2001), p. 511.

35. Weiss, Forsythe, and Coate, *The United Nations and Changing World Politics*, pp. 101–102.

36. Ibid., p. 62.

37. United Nations, "Basic Facts About the United Nations: Economic and Social Development," 2003, http://www.un.org/aboutun/basicfacts/ecodev.htm.

38. As quoted in Charles W. Kegley, Jr., and Eugene R. Wittkopf, *World Politics: Trend and Transformation*, 4th ed. (New York: St. Martin's Press, 1993), p. 172.

39. Jesse Helms, "Saving the UN," *Foreign Affairs* 75 (October 1996): p. 6.

40. Barbara Crossette, "U.S. Warns UN on Dues and Peacekeeping," *New York Times*, March 24, 2000.

41. John Allphin Moore, Jr. and Jerry Pubantz, *The New United Nations: International Organization in the Twenty-First Century* (Upper Saddle River, N.J.: Pearson Prentice Hall, 2006), p. 94.

42. Global Policy Forum, UN Finance, (New York), http://www.globalpolicy.org/un-finance.html, accessed June 18, 2009.

43. United Nations, "Fact Sheet: United Nations Peacekeeping," (New York), http://www.un.org/Depts/dpko/factsheet.pdf, accessed June 18, 2009.

44. Richard Falk, "Appraising the U.N. at 50: The Looming Challenge," *Journal of International Affairs* 48(Winter 1995): pp. 625–646 and Peter Wallensteen, "Representing the World: A Security Council for the 21st Century," in Paul F. Diehl (ed.), *The Politics of Global Governance: International Organizations in an Interdependent World* (Boulder, Colo.: Lynne Rienner Publishers, 1997).

45. Weiss, Forsythe, and Coate, *The United Nations and Changing World Politics*, p. 123.

46. Independent Working Group on the Future of the United Nations, "The United Nations in Its Second Half-Century," 1995, http://www.ciaonet.org/wps/yuu01.

47. Weiss, Forsythe, and Coate, *The United Nations and Changing World Politics*, pp. 123–124.

48. Moore and Pubantz, *The New United Nations: International Organization in the Twenty-First Century*, p. 73.

49. World Public Opinion: Global Public Opinion on International Affairs, "World Publics Favor New Powers for the UN," May 9, 2007, (Washington, DC), http://www.worldpublicopinion.org/pipa/articles/btunitednationsra/355.php?lb=btun&pnt=355&nid=&id=, accessed June 18, 2009.

50. Benjamin I. Page and Jason Barabas, "Foreign Policy Gaps Between Citizens and Leaders," *International Studies Quarterly* 44 (2000): pp. 358–359.

51. Steven R. Ratner, "International Law: The Trials of Global Norms," *Foreign Policy* 110 (Spring 1998): pp. 65–66.

52. Michael Akehurst, *A Modern Introduction to International Law* (London: Allen and Unwin, 1984), pp. 25–26.

53. Ratner, "International Law," p. 67.

54. Charles O. Lerche and Abdul A. Said, *Concepts of International Politics* (Englewood Cliffs, N.J.: Prentice-Hall, 1963), p. 101.

55. Abram Chayes and Antonia Handler Chayes, "On Compliance," *International Organization* 47 (Spring 1993): p. 179.

56. Hans Morgenthau and Kenneth W. Thompson, *Politics Among Nations*, 6th ed. (New York: Knopf, 1985), p. 329.

57. Ibid., p. 329.

58. J. L. Brierly, *The Law of Nations*, 6th ed. (New York: Oxford University Press, 1963), p. 335.

59. Ibid.

60. Ibid.

61. Roger Fisher, "Law and Legal Institutions May Help," in Frederick H. Hartmann (ed.), *World in Crisis*, 4th ed. (New York: Macmillan, 1973), pp. 140–141.

62. Louis Henkin, *How Nations Behave: Law and Foreign Policy* (New York: Columbia University Press, 1979), p. 51.

63. Ibid., p. 52.

64. Ibid., pp. 60–68.

65. Ratner, "International Law."

66. Charlotte Ku and Paul F. Diehl, "International Law as Operating and Normative Systems," in Charlotte Ku and Paul F. Diehl (eds.), *International Law: Classic and Contemporary Readings* (Boulder, Colo.: Lynne Rienner Publishers, 1998), pp. 6–7. For a review of theories of compliance to international law, see Kal Raustiala and Anne-Marie Slaughter, "International Law, International Relations and Compliance," in Walter Carlsnaes, Thomas Risse, and Beth A. Simmons (eds.), *Handbook of International Relations* (Thousand Oaks, Calif.: Sage, 2002), pp. 538–558.

67. Christopher C. Joyner, "The Reality and Relevance of International Law in the 21st Century," in Charles W. Kegley, Jr., and Eugene R. Wittkopf (eds.), *The Global Agenda: Issues and Perspectives* (New York: McGraw-Hill, 1998), p. 253.

68. Louis Henkin, *International Law: Politics and Values* (The Hague: Martinus Nijhoff Publishers, 1995), p. 280.

69. William Nelson, "Introduction: Moral Principles and Moral Theory," in Kenneth Kipnis and Diana T. Meyers (eds.), *Political Realism and International Morality* (Boulder, Colo.: Westview Press, 1987), p. 4.

70. Geoffrey Stern, "Morality and International Order," in Alan James (ed.), *The Bases of International Order* (New York: Oxford University Press, 1973), p. 136.

71. Morgenthau and Thompson warn against "equating the foreign policies of a statesman with his philosophic or political sympathies" and assert that "moral principles cannot be applied to the actions of states." Morgenthau and Thompson, *Politics Among Nations*, pp. 5–10.

72. Karl Marx and Friedrich Engels, "The German Ideology," in Lewis S. Feuer (ed.), *Marx and Engels* (Garden City, N.Y.: Anchor Books, 1959), p. 247.

73. Leon Trotsky, *Their Morals and Ours* (New York: Pathfinder Press, 1973), p. 27.

74. Charles R. Beitz, *Political Theory and International Relations* (Princeton, N.J.: Princeton University Press, 1979), pp. 46–47.

75. Kenneth W. Thompson, *The Moral Issue in Statecraft* (Baton Rouge: Louisiana State University Press, 1966), p. 44.

76. Trotsky, *Their Morals and Ours*, p. 45.

77. Nelson, "Introduction: Moral Principles and Moral Theory," pp. 4–5.

78. Mortimer Adler, *Ten Philosophical Mistakes* (New York: Macmillan, 1985), pp. 109–110.

79. Mark R. Amstutz, *International Ethics: Concepts, Theories, and Cases in Global Politics* (Lanham, Md.: Rowman & Littlefield, 1999), p. 76. For more on cultural relativism and universalism in theories of human rights, see the chapters by Ken Booth, Chris Brown, and Bhikhu Parekh in Tim Dunne and Nicholas J. Wheeler (eds.), *Human Rights in Global Politics* (Cambridge: Cambridge University Press, 1999).

80. For a scholarly analysis of U.S. compliance with the laws of war in Iraq, see Colin H. Kahl, "In the Crossfire or the Crosshairs? Norms, Civilian Casualties, and U.S. Conduct in Iraq," *International Security* 22(1) (Summer 2007): 7–46.

81. Kenneth Jost, "Human Rights," *CQ Researcher*, November 13, 1998; reprinted in *Global Issues: Selections from The CQ Researcher* (Washington, D.C., CQ Press, 2001), p. 218.

82. Reuters, "Judges for War Crimes Court Sworn In," *New York Times*, March 11, 2003.

83. Helena Cobban, "International Courts," *Foreign Policy* (March–April 2006): pp. 22–28.

84. Marlise Simons and Neil MacFarquhar, "Court Issues Arrest Warrant for Sudan's Leader," *The New York Times*, March 5, 2009.

85. Mona Fixdal and Dan Smith, "Humanitarian Intervention and Just War," *Mershon International Studies Review* 42 (1998): pp. 285–286.

86. Jimmy Carter, "Just War or a Just War?" *New York Times*, March 9, 2003.

87. Alex J. Bellamy, "Is the War on Terror Just?" *International Relations* Vol. 19(3) (2005): 275–296.

88. See, for example, Jean Bethke Elshtain, *Just War Against Terror: The Burdens of American Power in a Violent World* (New York: Basic Books, 2003).

89. William Frankena, *Ethics*, 2nd ed. (Englewood Cliffs, N.J.: Prentice-Hall, 1973), p. 17. Frankena (*Ethics*, p. 15) also explains that "a deontologist contends that it is possible [for] an action or rule of action to be the morally right or obligatory one even if it does not promote the greatest possible balance of good over evil for self, society, or universe." For an application of deontological pacifism to the "war on terror," see Alex J. Bellamy, "Is the War on Terror Just?" *International Relations* Vol 19(3) (2005): 275–296.

90. Frankena, *Ethics*, p. 34.

91. Robert W. Tucker, *The Nuclear Debate* (New York: Holmes & Meier, 1985), p. 132.

92. Tim Dunne and Nicholas J. Wheeler, "Introduction: Human Rights and the Fifty Years' Crisis," in Tim Dunne and Nicholas J. Wheeler (eds.), *Human Rights in Global Politics* (Cambridge: Cambridge University Press, 1999): pp. 1–28.

93. Philip Alston, "The UN's Human Rights Record," in Ku and Diehl (eds.), *International Law*, pp. 355–356.

94. Beitz, *Political Theory and International Relations*, p. 71.

95. Jefferson McMahan, "The Ethics of International Intervention," in Kenneth Kipnis and Diana T. Meyers (eds.), *Political Realism and International Morality* (Boulder, Colo.: Westview Press, 1987), p. 95.

96. Beitz, *Political Theory and International Relations*, p. 121.

97. Alston, "The UN's Human Rights Record," p. 356. See also Thomas Risse, Stephen Ropp, and Kathryn Sikkink (eds.), *The Power of Human Rights: International Norms and Domestic Change* (Cambridge: Cambridge University Press, 1999); J. Samuel Barkin, *International Organization: Theories and Institutions* (New York: Palgrave Macmillan, 2006), pp. 82–83; and Micheline R. Ishay, *The History of Human Rights: From Ancient Times to the Globalization Era* (Berkeley: University of California Press, 2004).

98. Michael Mandelbaum, "The Reluctance to Intervene," in Robert C. Art and Robert Jervis (eds.), *International Politics: Enduring Concepts and Contemporary Issues* (New York: HarperCollins, 1996), p. 533.

99. Jack Donnelly, "The Social Construction of International Human Rights," in Tim Dunne and Nicholas J. Wheeler (eds.), *Human Rights in Global Politics* (Cambridge: Cambridge University Press, 1999): pp. 71–102.

100. J. L. Holzgrefe, "The Humanitarian Intervention Debate," in J. L. Holzgrefe and Robert O. Keohane, *Humanitarian Intervention: Ethical, Legal, and Political Dilemmas* (Cambridge: Cambridge University Press, 2003), pp. 15–52.

101. Ibid., pp. 36–49 and Nicholas J. Wheeler, *Saving Strangers: Humanitarian Intervention in International Society* (Oxford: Oxford University Press, 2000).

102. Holzgrefe, pp. 18–36.

103. William Easterly, *The White Man's Burden: Why the West's Efforts to Aid the Rest Have Done So Much Ill and So Little Good* (New York: Penguin Press, 2006), pp. 311–336.

104. Alan J. Kuperman, *The Limits of Humanitarian Intervention: Genocide in Rwanda* (Washington, D.C.: Brookings Institution Press, 2001), pp. 117–118. For the exploration of this argument in the Balkan conflicts, see Alan J. Kuperman, "The Moral Hazard of Humanitarian Intervention: Lessons from the Balkans," *International Studies Quarterly*, (2008) 52, 49–80.

105. See, for example, Ann Marie Clark, *Diplomacy of Conscience: Amnesty International and Changing Human Rights Norms* (Princeton, N. J.: Princeton University Press, 2001) and Risse, Ropp, and Sikkink (eds.), *The Power of Human Rights: International Norms and Domestic Change*.

106. Jost, "Human Rights," p. 217.

107. Human Rights Watch, "World Report 1999," 2003, pp. 428–429, http://www.hrw.org/worldreport99/.

108. Nicholas D. Kristoff, "Peasants of China Discover New Way to Weed Out Girls," *New York Times*, July 21, 1993, p. A:4.

109. Ibid.

110. Amartya Sen, "The Economics of Life and Death," *Scientific American* 268 (May 1993): p. 46. See also Valerie M. Hudson and Andrea M. den Boer, *Bare Branches: Security Implications of Asia's Surplus Male Population* (Cambridge, Mass.: MIT Press, 2004).

111. Mary H. Cooper, "Women and Human Rights," *CQ Researcher*, April 30, 1999; reprinted in *Global Issues: Selections from The CQ Researcher* (Washington, D.C., CQ Press, 2001), p. 228.

112. M. Rosenthal, "Fighting Female Mutilation," *New York Times*, April 12, 1996, p. A:15.

113. A. M. Rosenthal, "A Challenge to the Clintons and the Doles," *New York Times*, May 30, 1996.

114. Charlotte Bunch and Roxanna Carrillo, "Global Violence Against Women: The Challenge to Human Rights," in Michael T. Klass and Daniel C. Thomas (eds.), *World Security*, 2nd ed. (New York: St. Martin's Press, 1994), p. 161.

115. Ellen Goodman, "Global Mistreatment of Women No Longer a Cultural Issue," *Boston Globe*; appeared in *Tallahassee Democrat*, March 5, 1993, p. A: 15.

116. Seble Dawit and Salem Mekuria, "The West Just Doesn't Get It," *New York Times*, December 7, 1993, p. A:11.

117. Bilahari Kausikan, "Asia's Different Standard," *Foreign Policy*, no. 92 (Fall 1993): p. 34.

118. Aryeh Neier, "Asia's Unacceptable Standard," *Foreign Policy*, no. 92 (Fall 1993): p. 51.

119. Beth Stephens, "Hypocrisy on Rights," *New York Times*, June 24, 1993, p. A:13.

120. Ibid.

121. "Canada Will Offer Refuge to Women," *Tampa Tribune*, March 3, 1993, Nation/World: p. 3.

122. Rosenthal, "A Challenge to the Clintons and the Doles," p. 13.

123. Beitz, *Political Theory and International Relations*, p. 179.

124. Thomas M. Franck, "The Emerging Right to Democratic Governance," *American Journal of International Law* 86 (January 1992): pp. 46–47.

125. Thomas Carothers, "The Backlash Against Democracy Promotion," *Foreign Affairs* 85(2) (March/April, 2006).

126. Ibid.

127. As quoted in Raymond Aron, *Peace and War* (New York: Praeger, 1966).

128. Robert Axelrod, *The Evolution of Cooperation* (New York: Basic Books, 1984).

129. Stephen Krasner, "Structural Causes and Regime Consequences: Regimes as Intervening Variables," *International Organization* 36 (Spring 1982): p. 186.

130. Oran Young, "International Regimes: Problems of Concept Formation," *World Politics* 32 (April 1980): pp. 332–333.

131. Chayes and Chayes, "On Compliance," pp. 185–186.

132. The following argument is largely based on James Lee Ray, "The Abolition of Slavery and the End of International War," *International Organization* 43 (Summer 1989): pp. 405–440. For a recent review of the influence of human rights norms on state behavior, see Sonia Cardenas, "Norm Collision: Explaining the Effects of International Human Rights Pressure on State Behavior," *International Studies Quarterly* 6 (June 2004): pp. 213–231.

133. Howard Margolis, *Selfishness, Altruism, and Rationality* (Cambridge: Cambridge University Press, 1982), pp. ix, 4.

134. Jon Elster, *The Cement of Society: A Study of Social Order* (Cambridge: Cambridge University Press, 1989), p. 15, cited in Chayes and Chayes, "On Compliance," p. 186. For similar arguments, see Friedrich V. Kratochwil, *Rules, Norms, and Decisions* (Cambridge: Cambridge University Press, 1989), and Frederick Schauer, *Playing by the Rules: A Philosophical Examination of Rule-Based Decision-Making in Law and in Life* (Oxford: Clarendon Press, 1991).

135. Janice E. Thomson, "State Practices, International Norms, and the Decline of Mercenarism," *International Studies Quarterly* 34 (March 1990): pp. 23–47, argues that certain norms that have developed have led to the virtual disappearance of the once common practice of recruiting foreigners to serve in national armies. Ethan A. Nadelmann, "Global Prohibition Regimes: The Evolution of Norms in International Society," *International Organization* 44 (Autumn 1990): pp. 479–526, traces the impact of moral and emotional factors on piracy, counterfeiting, drug trafficking, aircraft hijacking, and the killing of endangered species.

136. Charles W. Kegley, Jr., and Gregory A. Raymond, *When Trust Breaks Down: Alliance Norms and World Politics* (Columbia: University of South Carolina Press, 1990), p. 14. For an examination of various definitions of international norms, see Gregory A. Raymond, "Problems and Prospects in the Study of International Norms," *Mershon International Studies Review* 41 (1997): pp. 205–245.

137. Risse, Ropp, and Sikkink (eds.), *The Power of Human Rights: International Norms and Domestic Change* and Martha Finnemore, "Constructing Norms of Humanitarian Intervention," in Peter J. Kazenstein (ed.), *The Culture of National Security: Norms and Identity in World Politics* (New York: Columbia University Press, 1996).

138. Irving Kristol, "Human Rights: The Hidden Agenda," *National Interest* 6 (Winter 1986–1987): p. 10. For historical arguments supporting this view, see David Brion Davis, *Slavery and Human Progress* (New York: Oxford University Press, 1984); Seymour Drescher, *Econocide: British Slavery in the Era of Abolition* (Pittsburgh, Pa.: University of Pittsburgh Press, 1977); and David Eltis, *Economic Growth and the Ending of the Transatlantic Slave Trade* (New York: Oxford University Press, 1987).

139. Eric Williams, *Capitalism and Slavery* (Chapel Hill: University of North Carolina Press, 1944).

140. Beitz, *Political Theory and International Relations*, p. 27.

141. Robert Jervis, "The Political Effects of Nuclear Weapons," *International Security* 13 (Fall 1988): p. 80.

142. Evan Luard, *War in International Society* (London: Taurus, 1986), pp. 330–336 and Robert Axelrod, "An Evolutionary Approach to Norms," *American Political Science Review* 80 (December 1986): p. 1110.

143. Jeffrey W. Legro, "Which Norms Matter? Revisiting the 'Failure' of Internationalism," *International Organization* 51 (Winter 1997): p. 57.

144. John Keegan, *A History of Warfare* (New York: Knopf, 1993), pp. 58–59.

145. "After the Withdrawal," *World Press Review*, April 29, 1989, p. 25.

146. Keegan, *A History of Warfare*, p. 58.

147. Ratner, "International Law."

148. Ibid.

Chapter 10 (pages 353–388)

1. Joan Edelman Spero, and Jeffrey A. Hart, *The Politics of International Economic Relations*, 7th ed. (2010) Belmont, CA: Thomson Wadsworth.

2. Adam Smith, *An Inquiry into the Nature and Causes of the Wealth of Nations* (London: George Routledge and Sons, 1892), first published in 1776.

3. Ibid., p. 343.

4. David Ricardo, *The Principles of Political Economy and Taxation* (London: Dent, 1973), first published in 1817.

5. David N. Balaam and Michael Veseth, *Introduction to International Political Economy* (Upper Saddle River, N.J.: Prentice Hall, 2001), p. 49.

6. Robert S. Walters and David H. Blake, *The Politics of Global Economic Relations* (Englewood Cliffs, N.J.: Prentice Hall, 1992), p. 128.

7. United Nations Conference on Trade and Development, *World Investment Report* 2006, United Nations, New York, 2006.

8. Ibid., pp. 57–58; see also Robert Gilpen, *US Power and the Multinational Corporation* (New York: Basic Books, 1975); Robert O. Keohane, *After Hegemony: Cooperation and Discord in the World Political Economy* (Princeton, N.J.: Princeton University Press, 1984); and Charles P. Kindleberger, *The World in Depression, 1928–1939* (Berkeley and Los Angeles: University of California Press, 1973).

9. Michael Mastanduno, "System Maker and Privilege Taker: U.S. Power and the International Political Economy," *World Politics* (January 2009) 61(1):121–54, p.150.

10. See Barry Eichengreen, "Hegemonic Stability Theories of the International Monetary System," in Richard N. Cooper (ed.), *Can Nations Agree? Issues in International Economic Cooperation* (Washington, D.C.: Brookings Institution, 1989), pp. 255–298.

11. Spero and Hart, *The Politics of International Economic Relations*, p. 168

12. Ibid., p. 170.

13. Jack A. Finlayson and Mark W. Zacher, "The GATT and the Regulation of Trade Barriers: Regime Dynamics and Functions," *International Organization* 35 (Autumn 1981): p. 562.

14. The phrase "most favored nation" is clearly confusing, creating the impression that the status involves some special privilege rather than treatment equivalent to that offered to many other states. For this reason, the U.S. Congress now uses the term "normal trade relations."

15. Judith L. Goldstein, Douglas Rivers, and Michael Tomz, "Institutions in International Relations: Understanding the Effects of the GATT and the WTO on World Trade," *International Organization* (Winter 2007) 61.

16. Finlayson and Zacher, "The GATT and the Regulation of Trade Barriers," p. 602.

17. The McLeod Group, "WTO: The New Age of Trade," an advertisement appearing in the *New York Times*, April 15, 1994, p. A:14.

18. Stephen D. Krasner, "The Tokyo Round: Particularistic Interests and Prospects for Stability in the Global Trading System," *International Studies Quarterly* 23 (December 1979): pp. 496–497.

19. Susan Strange, *States and Markets*, 2nd ed. (London: Pinter, 1994), pp. 24–25.

20. Helen V. Milner, "International Trade," in Walter Carlsnaes, Thomas Risse, and Beth A. Simmons (eds.), *Handbook of International Relations* (Thousand Oaks, Calif.: Sage, 2002), p. 450.

21. Helen Milner, "Resisting the Protectionist Temptation: Industry and the Making of Trade Policy in France and the United States During the 1970s," *International Organization* 41 (1987): pp. 639–666.

22. See Milner, "International Trade," for a review of the research on political institutions and beliefs in international trade.

23. See Joanne Gowa, *Closing the Gold Window* (Ithaca, N.Y.: Cornell University Press, 1983), p. 181 and David P. Calleo, *The Imperious Economy* (Cambridge, Mass.: Harvard University Press, 1982), p. 3.

24. John Ruggie, "The Politics of Money," *Foreign Policy* 43 (Summer 1981): p. 147.

25. Robert Keohane and Joseph S. Nye, *Power and Interdependence* (Boston: Little, Brown, 1977).

26. Balaam and Veseth, *Introduction to International Political Economy*, p. 117.

27. Edward John Ray, "Changing Patterns of Protectionism: The Fall in Tariffs and the Rise in Non-Tariff Barriers," *Northwestern Journal of International Law and Business* 8 (1988): pp. 285–327.

28. Balaam and Veseth, *Introduction to International Political Economy*, p. 118.

29. The Group of Seven (often referred to as G7) consists of the United States, Britain, Canada, France, Germany, Italy, and Japan.

30. Charles F. Kindleberger, "Dominance and Leadership in the International Economy," *International Studies Quarterly* 25 (June 1981): p. 248.

31. Immanuel Wallerstein, "Friends as Foes," *Foreign Policy* 40 (Fall 1980): pp. 119–131.

32. Paul Kennedy, *The Rise and Fall of the Great Powers* (New York: Random House, 1987).

33. Keohane, *After Hegemony*.

34. Kindleberger, *The World in Depression.* Also see George Modelski, "Long Cycles, Kondratieffs, and Alternating Innovations: Implications for U.S. Foreign Policy," in Charles W. Kegley, Jr., and Pat McGowan (eds.), *The Political Economy of Foreign Policy Behavior* (Beverly Hills, Calif.: Sage, 1981).

35. Bruce Stokes, "Globalization: Workplace Winners and Losers," in Nancy Hoepli-Phalon (ed.), *Great Decisions '97* (New York: Foreign Policy Association, 1997), p. 78.

36. Ibid.

37. David H. Levey and Stuart S. Brown, "The Overstretch Myth," *Foreign Affairs* 84(2) (March/April 2005): pp. 2–7.

38. Daniel Gross, "The U.S. Is Losing Market Share. So What?" *The New York Times* January 28, 2007.

39. Michael Mastanduno, "System Maker and Privilege Taker: U.S. Power and the International Political Economy," *World Politics* (January 2009) 61(1): 121–54, p.150.

40. Alan Sorensen, "A Panic Made in America," *Current History* (January 2009), 3-9, p.7.

41. Roger C. Altman, "The Great Crash, 2008: A Geopolitical Setback for the West," *Foreign Affairs*, Jan/Feb2009, Vol. 88, Issue 1.

42. Giboy and Heginbotham, "China's Coming Transformation," p. 32.

43. Roger C. Altman, "The Great Crash, 2008: A Geopolitical Setback for the West," *Foreign Affairs*, Jan/Feb2009, Vol. 88, Issue 1.

44. Harold James, "The Late, Great Globalization," *Current History* (January 2009): 20-25, p. 25.

45. George Giboy and Eric Heginbotham, "China's Coming Transformation," *Foreign Affairs* 80 (July–August 2001): pp. 27–39.

46. Deborah S. Davis, "China's Consumer Revolution," *Current History* (September 2000): pp. 248–254.

47. Joseph Kahn, "Sharp Debate Erupts in China Over Ideology and Inequality," *New York Times*, March 12, 2006 and Lianjiang Li, "Driven to Protest: China's Rural Unrest," *Current History* 105 (September 2006): pp. 250–254.

48. For a comparison of the Russian and Chinese transitions, Sachs, *The End of Poverty: Economic Possibilities for Our Time*, pp. 162–164.

49. GDP figures from James R. Millar, "The De-development of Russia," *Current Affairs* (October 1999): p. 323; unemployment figures from Interstate Statistical Committee of the Commonwealth of Independent States, *Statistical Abstract* (Moscow, 2002), p. 293; poverty rate figures from Thomas F. Remington, *Politics in Russia* (New York: Longman, 2002), p. 15; life expectancy and alcohol consumption figures quoted in Judith Shapiro, "Health and Health Care Policy," in Stephen White, Alex Pravda, and Zvi Gitelman (eds.), *Developments in Russian Politics*, 4th ed. (Durham, N.C.: Duke University Press, 1997), pp. 177, 181, and from the World Health Organization's "WHO Europe" database, http://www.euro.who.int/hfadb, accessed November 6, 2006.

50. Anders Aslund, "Russia's Collapse" *Foreign Affairs* 78 (September–October 1999): p. 64.

51. Millar, "The De-development of Russia," p. 323.

52. Marshall I. Goldman, "Russia's Middle Class Muddle," *Current History*, 105 (October 2006): pp. 321–326 and James R. Millar, "Can Putin Jump-Start Russia's Stalled Economy?" *Current History* 99 (October 2000): pp. 329–333; Fraser Cameron, "Medvedev's First Year," *The New York Times*, May 4, 2008.

53. David D. Hale, "The IMF, Now More Than Ever," *Foreign Affairs* 77 (November–December 1998): pp. 7–8.

54. Martin Feldstein, "Refocusing the IMF," *Foreign Affairs* 77 (March–April 1998): p. 23.

55. James E. Mahon, Jr., and Javier Corrales, "Pegged for Failure? Argentina's Crisis," *Current History* (February 2002): pp. 72–75.

56. Alan S. Blinder, "Eight Steps to a New Financial Order. Back to Bretton Woods," *Foreign Affairs* 78 (September–October 1999): pp. 50–63.

57. Dick K. Nanto, Coordinator, "The U.S. Financial Crisis: The Global Dimension with Implications for U.S. Policy," Congressional Research Service, *CRS Report for Congress*, January 30, 2009, p.14.

58. Dick K. Nanto, Coordinator, "The U.S. Financial Crisis: The Global Dimension with Implications for U.S. Policy," Congressional Research Service, *CRS Report for Congress*, January 30, 2009, p.14.

59. Harold James, "The Late, Great Globalization," *Current History* (January 2009): 20–25.

60. Roger C. Altman, "The Great Crash, 2008: A Geopolitical Setback for the West," *Foreign Affairs*, Jan/Feb2009, Vol. 88, Issue 1.

61. Alan Sorensen, "A Panic Made in America," *Current History* (January 2009), 3–9, p.5.

62. Roger C. Altman, "The Great Crash, 2008: A Geopolitical Setback for the West," *Foreign Affairs*, Jan/Feb2009, Vol. 88, Issue 1; Ian Bremmer, "State Capitalism Comes of Age," *Foreign Affairs*, May/Jun2009, Vol. 88, Issue 3.

63. Ian Bremmer, "State Capitalism Comes of Age," *Foreign Affairs*, May/Jun2009, Vol. 88, Issue 3.

64. Alan Sorensen, "A Panic Made in America," *Current History* (January 2009), 3–9, p.3; see also Roger C. Altman, "The Great Crash, 2008: A Geopolitical Setback for the West," *Foreign Affairs*, Jan/Feb2009, Vol. 88, Issue 1; Dick K. Nanto, Coordinator, "The U.S. Financial Crisis: The Global Dimension with Implications for U.S. Policy," Congressional Research Service, *CRS Report for Congress*, January 30, 2009.

65. Roger C. Altman, "The Great Crash, 2008: A Geopolitical Setback for the West," *Foreign Affairs*, Jan/Feb2009, Vol. 88, Issue 1.

66. Roger C. Altman, "The Great Crash, 2008: A Geopolitical Setback for the West," *Foreign Affairs*, Jan/Feb2009, Vol. 88, Issue 1; Harold James, "The Late, Great Globalization," *Current History* (January 2009): 20–25, p. 20–21.

67. Roger C. Altman, "The Great Crash, 2008: A Geopolitical Setback for the West," *Foreign Affairs*, Jan/Feb2009, Vol. 88, Issue 1.

68. "Ian Bremmer, "State Capitalism Comes of Age," *Foreign Affairs*, May/Jun2009, Vol. 88, Issue 3; Harold James, "The Late, Great Globalization," *Current History* (January 2009): 20–25.

69. Alan Sorensen, "A Panic Made in America," *Current History* (January 2009), 3–9.

70. Ian Bremmer, "State Capitalism Comes of Age," *Foreign Affairs*, May/Jun2009, Vol. 88, Issue 3.

71. Aadita Mattoo and Arvind Subramanian, "From Doha to the Next Bretton Woods: A New Multilateral Trade Agenda," *Foreign Affairs* (January/February 2009) 88(1):15–26.

72. Dick K. Nanto, Coordinator, "The U.S. Financial Crisis: The Global Dimension with Implications for U.S. Policy," Congressional Research Service, *CRS Report for Congress*, January 30, 2009.

73. Mark Landler and David E. Sanger, "World Leaders Pledge $1.1 Trillion for Crisis," *The New York Times* April 3, 2009.

74. As interviewed by Bernard Gwertzman, "Interview: A Warning That Stimulus Plan Could Undermine U.S. Foreign Policy," published in *The New York Times*, February 3, 2009.

75. Alan Sorensen, "A Panic Made in America," *Current History* (January 2009), 3-9, p.5.

76. Mary H. Cooper, "International Monetary Fund," CQ Researcher, January 29, 1999; reprinted in *Global Issues: Selections from The CQ Researcher* (Washington, D.C., CQ Press, 2001), p. 77.

77. Hale, "The IMF, Now More Than Ever," p. 9.

78. Cooper, "International Monetary Fund," p. 81.

79. Jeffrey E. Garten, "Lessons for the Next Financial Crisis," *Foreign Affairs* 78 (March–April 1999): p. 81.

80. Dick K. Nanto, Coordinator, "The U.S. Financial Crisis: The Global Dimension with Implications for U.S. Policy," Congressional Research Service, *CRS Report for Congress*, January 30, 2009, p.60.

81. Roger C. Altman, "The Great Crash, 2008: A Geopolitical Setback for the West," *Foreign Affairs*, Jan/Feb2009, Vol. 88, Issue 1; Mark Landler and David E. Sanger, "World Leaders Pledge $1.1 Trillion for Crisis," *The New York Times* April 3, 2009.

82. Jessica Einhorn, "The World Bank's Mission Creep," *Foreign Affairs* 80 (September–October 2001): p. 22.

83. World Trade Organization, "The 10 Misunderstandings: WTO Dictates?" September1, 2006, http://www.wto.org/english/thewto_e/whatis_e/10mis_e/10m01_e.htm.

84. Balaam and Veseth, *Introduction to International Political Economy*, p. 121.See also Bernhard Zangl, "Judicialization Matters! A Comparison of Dispute Settlement Under GATT and the WTO," *International Studies Quarterly* (2008) 52:825–854.

Chapter 11 (pages 389–430)

1. United Nations Development Programme, *Human Development Report 2005* (New York: Oxford University Press, 2005), p. 3.

2. *UN Human Development Report*, 2007/2008, p. 269 http://hdr.undp.org/en/media/HDR_20072008_EN_Complete.pdf, accessed: July 9, 2009.

3. Jeffrey D. Sachs, *The End of Poverty: Economic Possibilities for Our Time* (New York: Penguin Books, 2005), p. 19.

4. Ruth Leger Sivard, *World Military and Social Expenditures 1991*, 14th ed. (Washington, D.C.: World Priorities, 1991), p. 50.

5. United Nations Development Programme, *Human Development Report 1996* (New York: Oxford University Press, 1996), p. 2.

6. Robin Broad and John Cavanaugh, "Don't Neglect the Impoverished South," *Foreign Policy* 101 (Winter 1995–1996): p. 26.

7. Duangkamon Chotikapanich, D. S. Prasada Rao, William E. Griffiths, and Vicar Valencia, "Global Inequality: Recent Evidence and Trends," *UNU-WIDER*, (January 2007). pp. 1–34 ; p. 25. http://www.wider.unu.edu/publications/working-papers/research-papers/2007/en_GB/rp2007-01/, accessed July 9, 2009. On different measures of the North-South gap, see Barry B. Hughes and Mohammod T. Irfan, "Assessing Strategies for Reducing Poverty," *International Studies Review* (2007) 9:690–710.

8. *UN Human Development Report*, 2007/2008, p. 247 http://hdr.undp.org/en/media/HDR_20072008_EN_ Complete.pdf, accessed July 13, 2009.

9. Ibid., p. 2.

10. See Charles Kenny, " Why Are We Worried About Income? Nearly Everything That Matters Is Converging," *World Development* (2005) 33(1):1–19.

11. P. T. Bauer, "The Vicious Circle of Poverty," in Mitchell A. Seligson (ed.), *The Gap Between Rich and Poor* (Boulder, Colo.: Westview Press, 1984), p. 334.

12. K. J. Holsti, "The Horsemen of the Apocalypse: At the Gate, Detoured, or Retreating?" *International Studies Quarterly* 20 (December 1986): p. 361.

13. *UN Human Development Report*, 2007/2008, pg. 295 http://hdr.undp.org/en/media/HDR_20072008_EN_ Complete.pdf, accessed July 13, 2009.

14. *Economist*, May 15, 1993, p. 15.

15. Sachs, *The End of Poverty*.

16. Max Singer, *Passage to a Human World* (Indianapolis, Ind.: Hudson Institute, 1987), p. 20.

17. Seligson, *The Gap Between Rich and Poor*, p. 401.

18. Ruth Leger Sivard, *World Military and Social Expenditures 1976* (Leesburg, Va.: WMSE Publications, 1976), p. 25.

19. *UN Human Development Report*, 2007/2008, p. 247 http://hdr.undp.org/en/media/HDR_20072008_EN_ Complete.pdf, accessed July 13, 2009.

20. Ibid., pp. 29–30.

21. Sachs, *The End of Poverty*.

22. Eugene Linden, "The Exploding Cities of the Developing World," *Foreign Affairs* 75 (January–February 1996): p. 55.

23. United Nations Development Programme, *Human Development Report 2005*, p. 24.

24. Ibid., pp. 220–222; see also Sachs, *The End of Poverty*, pp. 188–209.

25. World Bank, *World Development Report 1992* (New York: Oxford University Press, 1992), p. 218, 272.

26. United Nations Development Programme, *Human Development Report 2005*, p. 26. World Bank, *World Development Indicators* 2007, http://go.worldbank.org/ HLM7A34U90, accessed July 13, 2009.

27. Ibid, p. 26.

28. Jahangir Amuzegar, "Dealing with Debt," *Foreign Policy* 68 (Fall 1987): p. 141.

29. Ibid.

30. Anne O. Krueger, "Origins of the Developing Countries' Debt Crisis: 1970–1982," *Journal of Development Economics* 27 (October 1987): p. 168.

31. World Bank, *World Development Report 1988* (New York: Oxford University Press, 1988).

32. Krueger, "Origins of the Developing Countries' Debt Crisis," p. 169.

33. Robin Broad and John Cavanaugh, "No More NICs," *Foreign Policy* 72 (Fall 1988): p. 90.

34. *UN Human Development Report*, 2007/2008, pp. 291–292, http://hdr.undp.org/en/media/HDR_20072008_EN_ Complete.pdf, accessed July 15, 2009.

35. United Nations Development Programme, *Human Development Report 2005*, pp. 89, 283.

36. World Bank, *Global Economic Prospects 2009: Commodities at the Crossroads*, Washington, DC, 2009,

available at http://go.worldbank.org/U8Q9PXMJV0, accessed July 13, 2009.

37. Patrick O'Brien, "European Economic Development: The Contribution of the Periphery," *Economic History Review* 35 (February 1982): pp. 3, 18.

38. Sachs, *The End of Poverty*, p. 31.

39. James F. Dougherty and Robert L. Pfaltzgraff, *Contending Theories of International Relations*, 3rd ed. (New York: Harper & Row, 1990), p. 244.

40. Mancur Olson, *The Rise and Decline of Nations* (New Haven, Conn.: Yale University Press, 1982), p. 152.

41. Walt Rostow, *The Stages of Growth: An Anti-Communist Manifesto* (Cambridge: Cambridge University Press, 1960). For a review of modernization theory in the context of other research on economic development, see Sylvia Maxfield, "International Development," in Walter Carlsnaes, Thomas Risse, and Beth A. Simmons (eds.), *Handbook of International Relations* (Thousand Oaks, Calif.: Sage, 2002).

42. For a recent summary of the neo-Marxist or "radical" explanation of underdevelopment in a globalized world, see Arie M. Kacowicz, "Globalization, Poverty, and the North-South Divide," *International Studies Review* (2007) 9: 565–580.

43. On the role of trade deficits in underdevelopment, see Bruce E. Moon, "Reproducing the North-South Divide: The Role of Trade Deficits and Capital Flows," *International Studies Review* (2007) 9: 581–600.

44. Michael P. Todaro, *Economic Development in the Third World*, 3rd ed. (New York: Longman, 1985), pp. 556–557.

45. Robert S. Walters and David H. Blake, *The Politics of Global Economic Relations* (Englewood Cliffs, N.J.: Prentice Hall, 1992), p. 161.

46. Teresa Hayter, *Aid as Imperialism* (Baltimore: Penguin, 1971); Teresa Hayter, *Aid: Rhetoric and Reality* (London: Pluto Press, 1985); Cheryl Payer, *The Debt Trap: The IMF and the Third World* (New York: Monthly Review Press, 1974); and Cheryl Payer, *The World Bank: A Critical Analysis* (New York: Monthly Review Press, 1982).

47. Raymond Vernon, *Sovereignty at Bay* (New York: Basic Books, 1971), p. 172.

48. Albert Szymanski, "Comment on Bornschier," *Journal of Conflict Resolution* 28 (March 1984): p. 152, emphasis added.

49. Joan Spero and Jeffrey A. Hart, *The Politics of International Economic Relations*, 5th ed. (New York: St. Martin's Press, 1997), p. 27.

50. Leo Grunberg, "The IPE of Multinational Corporations," in David N. Balaam and Michael Veseth (eds.), *Introduction to International Political Economy* (Upper Saddle River, N.J.: Prentice Hall, 2001), p. 357.

51. Ibid., p. 276.

52. Ronald Muller, "The MNC and the Exercise of Power: Latin America," in Aziz Said Abdul and Luiz R. Simmons (eds.), *The New Sovereigns: Multinational Corporations as World Powers* (Upper Saddle River, N.J.: Prentice-Hall, 1975), pp. 61–62.

53. For a review of a large number of these analyses, see Volker Bornschier, Christopher Chase-Dunn, and Richard Rubinson, "Cross-National Evidence of the Effects of Foreign Investment and Aid on Economic Growth and Inequality," *American Journal of Sociology* 84 (November 1978): pp. 651–683.

54. Volker Bornschier and Christopher Chase-Dunn, *Transnational Corporations and Underdevelopment* (New York: Praeger, 1985); Steve Chan, "Income Inequality Among LDCs: A Comparative Analysis of Alternative Perspectives," *International Studies Quarterly*, 33 (March 1989): pp. 45–65; and Terry Boswell and William J. Dixon, "Dependency and Rebellion: A Cross-National Analysis," *American Sociological Review* 55 (August 1990): pp. 540–559. See also Stephen Kosack and Jennifer Tobin, "Funding Self-Sustaining Development: The Role of Aid, FDI and Government in Economic Success," *International Organization* 60 (Winter 2006): 205-243; Nathan M. Jensen and Guillermo Rosas, "Foreign Direct Investment and Income Inequality in Mexico, 1990-2000," *International Organization* 61 (Summer 2007): 467-487).

55. Robert Gilpin, *The Political Economy of International Relations* (Princeton, N.J.: Princeton University Press, 1987). See also Maria Carkovic and Ross Levine, "Does FDI Accelerate Economic Growth?" World Bank Conference (May 30–31, 2002), available at http://www.worldbank.org/research/conferences/financial_globalization/fdi.pdf. See also Stephen Kosack and Jennifer Tobin, "Funding Self-Sustaining Development: The Role of Aid, FDI and Government in Economic Success," *International Organization* 60 (Winter 2006): 205-243.

56. Spero and Hart, *The Politics of International Economic Relations*, p. 277; see also Cal Clark and Steve Chan, "MNCs and Developmentalism: Domestic Structure as an Explanation for East Asian Dynamism," in Thomas Risse-Kappen (ed.), *Bringing Transnational Relations Back In* (Cambridge: Cambridge University Press, 1995), pp. 112–145.

57. Bob Herbert, "Mr. Young Gets It Wrong," *New York Times*, June 27, 1996, p. A:21.

58. Bruce Stokes, "Globalization: Workplace Winners and Losers," in Hoepli-Phalon, *Great Decisions* '97, p. 80.

59. Richard A. Love and Maryann Cusimano Love, "Multinational Corporations: Power and Responsibility," in Maryann Cusimano Love (ed.), *Beyond Sovereignty*, 2nd ed. (Belmont, Calif.: Thomson Wadsworth, 2003), pp. 96–98.

60. Jad Mouawad, "Shell to Pay $15.5 Million to Settle Nigerian Case," *The New York Times*, June 8, 2009.

61. Merrill Goozner, "Asian Labor: Wages of Shame," *Chicago Tribune*, November 6, 1994, p. 1.

62. Gary Gereffi, Ronie Garcia-Johnson, and Erika Sasser, "The NGO-Industrial Complex," *Foreign Policy* 125 (July–August 2001): pp. 56–65; Love and Cusimano Love, "Multinational Corporations," p. 100.

63. See, for example, Scott Jerbi, "Business and Human Rights at the UN: What Might Happen Next?" *Human Rights Quarterly* 31(May 2009): 299-320.

64. Kirk Johnson, "With this Ethical Ring I Thee Wed," the *New York Times* (April 6, 2006) and Jane Perlez and Kirk Johnson, "Behind Gold's Glitter: Torn Lands and Pointed Questions," *New York Times* (October 24, 2005).

65. Gereffi, Garcia-Johnson, and Sasser, "The NGO-Industrial Complex"; Love and Cusimano Love, "Multinational Corporations," p. 110.

66. Love and Cusimano Love, "Multinational Corporations," pp. 111–112.

67. Raymond Vernon, *In the Hurricane's Eye: The Troubled Prospects of Multinational Enterprises* (Cambridge, Mass.: Harvard University Press, 1998), p. 61.

68. For a recent summary of the liberal explanation of underdevelopment in a globalized world, see Arie M. Kacowicz, "Globalization, Poverty, and the North-South Divide," *International Studies Review* (2007) 9: 565–580.

69. Steve Chan and Cal Clark, "Can Good Things Go Together? A Virtuous Cycle in East Asia," *International Studies Notes* 15 (Winter 1990): pp. 4–5.

70. Gary Hawes and Hong Liu, "Explaining the Dynamics of the Southeast Asian Political Economy," *World Politics* 45 (July 1993): p. 630.

71. Broad and Cavanaugh, "No More NICs," p. 81.

72. Erich Weede, *Economic Development, Social Order, and World Politics* (Boulder, Colo.: Lynne Rienner, 1996), p. 67.

73. James Riedel, "Trade as the Engine of Growth in Developing Countries, Revisited," *Economic Journal* 94 (March 1984): pp. 61–62.

74. United Nations, *Human Development Report* 2007/2008 (New York: Palgrave Macmillan, 2008, p. 288).

75. United Nations Development Programme, *Human Development Report 1996*, p. 11.

76. Ibid., p. 60. Ruth Leger Sivard, *World Military and Social Expenditures, 1987–1988* (Washington, D.C.: World Priorities, 1987), p. 49. United Nations Development Programme, *Human Development Report 1996*, p. 135.

77. Weede, *Economic Development, Social Order, and World Politics*, p. 113.

78. *Economist*, February 22, 1997, p. 20.

79. David Dollar and Aart Kraay, "Spreading the Wealth," *Foreign Affairs* 81(1), (January/February 2002), pp. 125–126; see also Sachs, *The End of Poverty*, pp. 170–187.

80. Dollar and Kraay, "Spreading the Wealth," p. 121.

81. United Nations Development Programme, *Human Development Report 2005*, p. 117.

82. Cal Clark, "The Taiwan Exception: Implications for Contending Political Economy Paradigms," *International Studies Quarterly* 3 (September 1987): p. 327.

83. Shalendra Sharma, "Neo-Classical Political Economy and the Lessons from East Asia," *International Studies Notes* 20 (Spring 1995): p. 23.

84. Stephen Haggard, "The Newly Industrializing Countries in the International System," *World Politics* 39 (January 1986): p. 351.

85. Robin Broad, John Cavanaugh, and Walden Bello, "Development: The Market Is Not Enough," *Foreign Policy* 81 (Winter 1990–1991): p. 148.

86. Hawes and Liu, "Explaining the Dynamics of the Southeast Asian Political Economy," p. 631.

87. Robert Wade, "East Asia's Economic Success," *World Politics* 44 (January 1992): p. 284.

88. David N. Balaam and Michael Veseth, *Introduction to International Political Economy* (Upper Saddle River, N.J.: Prentice Hall, 2001), p. 338.

89. Ibid., p. 339.

90. Ibid., p. 326.

91. Stephen Kosack and Jennifer Tobin, "Funding Self-Sustaining Development: The Role of Aid, FDI and Government in Economic Success," *International Organization* 60 (Winter 2006): 205-243.

92. Sachs, *The End of Poverty*, p. 288.

93. Ibid, p. 292.

94. Steven R. Weisman, "I.M.F. Votes to Enhance Power of China and Others," the *New York Times*, September 19, 2006.

95. Joan Spero and Jeffrey A. Hart, *The Politics of International Economic Relations*, 5th ed. (New York: St. Martin's Press, 1997), p. 230.

96. Balaam and Veseth, *Introduction to International Political Economy*, p. 328.

97. Jad Mouawad, "OPEC Chief Shrugs Off Oil Politics," *The New York Times*, February 4, 2006.

98. Ibid., p. 335.

99. Nathaniel C. Nash, "Chile's Engine Revs Up with Free Trade's Fuel." *New York Times*, December 26, 1993, p. 4.

100. Maxfield, "International Development," p. 469.

101. Sachs, *The End of Poverty*, p. 74.

102. Jorge G. Castañeda, "Latin America's Left Turn," *Foreign Affairs* 85(3) (May-June 2006), p.28. See also Peter Hakim, "Is Washington Losing Latin America?" *Foreign Affairs* 85(1) (January/February 2006): pp. 39–53.

103. Garcia-Navarro, "Chavez Puts Venezuela at Odds with the U.S."

104. Ian Bremmer, "State Capitalism Comes of Age," *Foreign Affairs*, May/Jun2009, Vol. 88, Issue 3.

105. Richard W. Franke and Barbara H. Chasin, "Kerala State, India: Radical Reform as Development," *Monthly Review* 42 (January 1991): pp. 4–5.

106. Broad, Cavanaugh, and Bello, "Development," p. 144; see also Amartya Sen, "The Economics of Life and Death," *Scientific American* (May 1993): pp. 4–47 and United Nations Development Programme, *Human Development Report 2005*, pp. 30–31.

107. Nicolas D. Kristoff, "Chinese Grow Healthier from Cradle to Grave," *New York Times*, April 14, 1991, pp. A:1, 6.

108. Robert Gilpin, *The Political Economy of International Relations* (Princeton, N.J.: Princeton University Press, 1987), p. 16.

109. Ibid.

110. United Nations Development Programme, *Human Development Report 2005*, p. 10.

111. Kimberly Ann Elliott, "Does the Doha Round Matter?" *Current History*, January 2009.

112. Aadita Mattoo and Arvind Subramanian, "From Doha to the Next Bretton Woods: A New Multilateral Trade Agenda," *Foreign Affairs* (January/February 2009) 88(1):15-26.

113. Jodi L. Jacobson, *Gender Bias: Roadblock to Sustainable Development* (Washington, D.C.: Worldwatch Institute, 1992), p. 6.

114. Eric Helleiner "Economic Liberalism and its Critics: The Past as Prologue?" *Review of International Political Economy* 10(4) (November 2003): p. 692.

115. Jacobson, *Gender Bias: Roadblock to Sustainable Development*, p. 7.

116. Molly Moore, "Banks Lending to Women Changes Lives of Poverty," *Tallahassee Democrat*, August 23, 1992, p. 13A.

117. Jessica Mathews, "Out of Bangladesh Emerges a Model Bank to Fight Poverty," *Tallahassee Democrat*, December 27, 1993, p. 7A.

118. Muhammad Yunus, "The Grameen Bank," *Scientific American* (November 1999): pp. 114–119 and See also The Associated Press, "Microloan Pioneer and His Bank Win Nobel Peace Prize," *New York Times*, October 13, 2006.

119. Moore, "Banks Lending to Women Changes Lives of Poverty," p. 13A.

120. Gaynelle Doll, "Unconventional Wisdom," *Vanderbilt Magazine* 79 (Winter 1997): p. 10.

121. The study was conducted by Sydney R. Schuler and reported in Yunus, "The Grameen Bank."

122. Mathews, "Out of Bangladesh Emerges a Model Bank to Fight Poverty," p. 7A.

123. Yunus, "The Grameen Bank." Oksan Bayulgen, "Muhammad Yunus, Grameen Bank and the Nobel Peace Prize: What Political Science Can Contribute to and Learn from the Study of Microcredit," *International Studies Review* (2008) 10: 525-547.

124. The Associated Press, "Microloan Pioneer and His Bank Win Nobel Peace Prize."

125. United Nations Development Programme, *Human Development Report 1996*, p. 69. L. Mayoux, "Tackling the Down Side: Social Capital, Women's Empowerment and Micro-Finance in Cameroon," *Development and Change* (2001) 32(3):435–464.

126. Ibid.

127. United Nations Development Programme, *Human Development Report 2005*, p. 62.

128. *Centers for Disease Control and Prevention*, "The Impact of Malaria, a Leading Cause of Death Worldwide." http://www.cdc.gov/malaria/impact/index.htm, accessed July 16, 2009; Malaria disproportionately affects children, especially in Africa. *World Health Organization*, "Malaria," http://www.who.int/mediacentre/factsheets/fs094/en/index.html, accessed July 16, 2009.

129. United Nations Development Programme, *Human Development Report 2052*, p. 27.

130. Sachs, *The End of Poverty*, p. 197.

131. United Nations Development Programme, *Human Development Report 2052*, p. 22.

132. Sachs, *The End of Poverty*, p. 204.

133. William Easterly, *The White Man's Burden: Why the West's Efforts to Aid the Rest Have Done So Much Ill and So Little Good* (New York: Penguin Press, 2006), p. 243

134. United Nations Development Programme, *Human Development Report 2052*, p. 27. See also Sachs, *The End of Poverty*.

135. Easterly, *The White Man's Burden*, p. 255.

136. Peter R. Baehr and Leon Bordenker, *The United Nations: Reality and Ideal* (Fourth Edition) (New York: Palgrave, 2005), p. 125.

137. Baehr and Bordenker, *The United Nations: Reality and Ideal*, p. 126.

138. Sachs, *The End of Poverty*, p. 25.

139. David Victor, "Recovering Sustainable Development," *Foreign Affairs* 85(1) (January/February 2006), p. 91.

140. United Nations, Millennium Development Goals Report 2008, available at http://www.un.org/millenniumgoals/, accessed May 21, 2009.

141. Thomas Pogge, "World Poverty and Human Rights," Ethics and International Affairs, 2005, 19; see also Peter Singer, "Famine, Affluence and Morality," *Philosophy and Public Affairs*, 1972; Ethan B. Kapstein, "Models of International Economic Justice," *Ethics and International Affairs*, 2004, vol. 18.

142. World Bank, *World Development Report 1990* (New York: Oxford University Press, 1990), p. 179.

143. Mancur Olson, "Dictatorship, Democracy, and Development," *American Political Science Review* 87 (September 1993): p. 572. See also Larry Diamond, "The

Democratic Rollback: The Resurgence of the Predatory State," *Foreign Affairs* 87(2):36-48 (March/April 2008).

144. Ibid.

145. Abbas Pougerami, "Authoritarian Versus Nonauthoritarian Approaches to Economic Development: Update and Additional Evidence," *Public Choice* 74 (1992): p. 375. See also Ronald Inglehart and Christian Welzel, "How Development Leads to Democracy," *Foreign Affairs* (March/ April 2009) 88(2):33–48.

146. Ross E. Burkhart and Michael S. Lewis-Beck, "Comparative Democracy: The Economic Development Thesis," *American Political Science Review* 88 (December 1994): pp. 903–910; John B. Londregan and Keith T. Poole, "Does High Income Promote Democracy?" *World Politics* 49 (October 1996): pp. 1–30.

147. Adam Przeworski and Fernando Limongi, "Modernization: Theories and Facts," *World Politics* 49 (January 1997): pp. 155–183; see also Adam Przeworski, Michael E. Alvarez, José Antonio Cheibub, and Fernando Limongi, *Democracy and Development: Political Institutions and Well-Being in the World, 1945–1990* (Cambridge: Cambridge University Press, 2000).

148. Bruce Bueno de Mesquita and George T. V. Downs, "Development and Democracy," *Foreign Affairs* 84(5) (September/October 2005).

Chapter 12 (pages 431–462)

1. Young Jong Choi and James A. Caporaso, "Comparative Regional Integration," in Walter Carlsnaes, Thomas Risse, and Beth A. Simmons (eds.), *Handbook of International Relations* (Thousand Oaks, Calif.: Sage, 2002), p. 480. Reproduced by permission of SAGE Publications, London, Los Angeles, New Delhi and Singapore. See also Bart Kerremans and Bob Switky (eds.), *The Political Importance of Regional Trading Blocs* (Aldershot, U.K.: Ashgate, 2000).

2. Dean Acheson, *Present at the Creation* (New York: Norton, 1969).

3. David Mitrany, *A Working Peace System* (London: Royal Institute of International Affairs, 1943).

4. Harold K. Jacobson, *Networks of Interdependence* (New York: Knopf, 1979), p. 72.

5. Ernst Haas, *The Uniting of Europe* (Stanford, Calif.: Stanford University Press), 1958.

6. Alec Stone Sweet and James A. Caporaso, "From Free Trade to Supranational Polity: The European Court and Integration," in Wayne Sandholtz and Alec Stone Sweet (eds.), *European Integration and Supranational Governance* (New York: Oxford University Press, 1998), pp. 92–133.

7. Roland Siebelink and Bart Schelfhout, "EU Basics, 1997, http://eubasics.allmansland.com.

8. Originally, the ECSC, the EEC, and Euratom had separate commissions and councils, but in 1967 they were unified into a single body.

9. "Europa: Panorama of the European Union: How is the EU Organised?" http://europa.eu/abc/panorama/howorganised/ index_en.htm, accessed September 7, 2006.

10. W. Nicoll, "EEC Budgeting Strains and Constraints," *International Affairs* 64 (Winter 1987–1988): p. 27.

11. Colleen Lutz and Diana McCaffrey (eds.), *Western European Regional Brief* (Washington, D.C.: U.S. Department of State, Bureau of Public Affairs, December 1988), p. 6.

12. Roger Kaplan, "European Union: Now What?" *Freedom Review* 25 (February 1994): p. 54.

13. Bela Balassa, *The Theory of Economic Integration* (Homewood, Ill.: Irwin, 1961), p. 2.

14. David N. Balaam and Michael Veseth, *Introduction to International Political Economy* (Upper Saddle Riddle, N.J.: Prentice Hall, 2001), p. 242.

15. See David R. Cameron, "Creating Supranational Authority in Monetary and Exchange Rate Policy: The Sources and Effects of EMU," in Sandholtz and Stone Sweet, *European Integration and Supranational Governance.*

16. Mary H. Cooper, "European Monetary Union," *The CQ Researcher*, November 27, 1998; reprinted in *Global Issues: Selections from The CQ Researcher* (Washington, D.C.: CQ Press, 2001), p. 59.

17. European Union, *Eurostat Yearbook 2003* (Europa Online).

18. John Schmid, "Berlin Looks Set to Escape Rebuke," *International Herald Tribune*, February 9–10, 2002, p. 1.

19. Stefan Kornelius, of *Süddeutsche Zeitung*, quoted in Steven Erlanger and Stephen Castle, "Growing Economic Crisis Threatens the Idea of One Europe," *The New York Times* (March 2, 2009). See also Daniel Gros, "The Dogs that Didn't Bark: The EU and the Financial Crisis," *Current History* (March 2009).

20. Geoffrey Howe, "Bearing More of the Burden: In Search of a European Foreign and Security Policy," *World Today* 52 (January 1996): p. 23.

21. "Europa: Enlargement," http://europa.eu.int/comm/ enlargement/enlargement.htm, accessed May 5, 2003.

22. Omer Taspinar, "Turkey's Fading Dream of Europe," *Current History* (March 2007).

23. Stephen Kinzer, "Turkey Finds European Union Door Slow to Open," *New York Times*, February 23, 1997, p. A:3.

24. "Europe Agrees to a Review of Changes for Its Union," *New York Times*, December 15, 2001.

25. Alberta Sbragi, "Introduction—The EU and Its 'Constitution': Public Opinion, Political Elites, and Their International Context," *PS: Political Science & Politics* 39(2) (April 2006): pp. 237–240.

26. Laurent Cohen-Tanugi, "The End of Europe?" *Foreign Affairs* 84(6) (November–December 2005): p. 55.

27. Cohen-Tanugi, "The End of Europe?"; Sbragi, "Introduction—The EU and Its 'Constitution': Public Opinion, Political Elites, and Their International Context"; and Boyka Stefanova, "The 'No' Vote in the French and Dutch Referenda on the EU Constitution: A Spillover of Consequences for the Wider Europe," *PS: Political Science & Politics* 39(2) (April 2006): pp. 251–255.

28. Stephen Castle, "Treaty to Strengthen E.U. Gets Another Chance," *The New York Times* (June 19, 2009).

29. Simon Serfaty, "No Time for a Time-out in Europe," *Current History* (March 2009).

30. Olufemi A. Babarinde, "Regionalism and African Foreign Policies," in Stephen Wright (ed.), *African Foreign Policies* (Boulder, Colo.: Westview Press, 1999), p. 217.

31. Ibid.

32. W. Andrew Axline, "Underdevelopment, Dependence, and Integration: The Politics of Regionalism in the Third World," *International Organization* 31 (Winter 1977): pp. 83–105.

33. Babarinde, "Regionalism and African Foreign Policies," p. 220.

34. Choi and Caporaso, "Comparative Regional Integration," p. 485.

35. Gert Rosenthal, "The Lessons of Economic Integration in Latin America: The Case of Central America," in Altaf Gauhar (ed.), *Regional Integration: The Latin American Experience* (London: Third World Foundation, 1985); Julius Emeka Okolo, "Integrative and Cooperative Regionalism: The Economic Community of West African States," *International Organization* 39 (Winter 1985): pp. 121–153; and Donald K. Emmerson, "ASEAN as an International Regime," *Journal of International Affairs* 41 (Summer–Fall 1987): pp. 1–16.

36. Stephen Wright, "The Foreign Policy of Africa," in Roy C. Macridis (ed.), *Foreign Policy in World Politics* (Englewood Cliffs, N.J.: Prentice Hall, 1992), p. 344.

37. Ibid.

38. Babarinde, "Regionalism and African Foreign Policies," p. 218.

39. Ibid., p. 219.

40. Ibid., p. 220.

41. Ibid., p. 222.

42. Ibid., p. 5.

43. *The Economist,* "Mercosur's Summit" (July 27, 2006).

44. Choi and Caporaso, "Comparative Regional Integration," p. 483.

45. Ibid., p. 484.

46. Ibid., p. 494.

47. Ibid., p. 484. See also David Martin Jones and Michael L. R. Smith, "Making Process, Not Progress: ASEAN and the Evolving East Asian Regional Order," *International Security* 32(1) (Summer 2007): 148–184; and Etel Solingen, "The Genesis, Design and Effects of Regional Institutions: Lessons from East Asia and the Middle East," *International Studies Quarterly* (2008) 52:261–294.

48. Kishore Mahbubani, "America's Place in the Asian Century, *Current History,* Vol. 107 (May 2008): pp. 195–200.

49. Choi and Caporaso, "Comparative Regional Integration," p. 481.

50. United Nations Development Programme, *Human Development Report 1996* (New York: Oxford University Press, 1996), p. 135.

51. Choi and Caporaso, "Comparative Regional Integration," pp. 483–484.

52. Jorge Casteñeda, "Can NAFTA Change Mexico?" *Foreign Affairs* 72 (September–October 1993): pp. 66–80.

53. *Economist,* January 8, 1994, p. 41.

54. Eric Miller, "Did Mexico Suffer Economically from the NAFTA's Environmental Provisions?" in Carolyn L. Deere and Daniel C. Esty (eds.), *Greening the Americas: NAFTA's Lessons for Hemispheric Trade* (Cambridge, Mass.: MIT Press, 2002), pp. 81–82.

55. Ibid., p. 82.

56. Daniel T. Griswold, "Has NAFTA Been a Good Deal for the Average Worker in the United States?" *Insight on the News,* February 3, 2003, p. 46.

57. Carlos Salas, "The Impact of NAFTA on Wages and Incomes in Mexico," in *NAFTA at Seven: Its Impact on Workers in All Three Nations,* Briefing Paper (Washington, D.C.: Economic Policy Institute, 2001), pp. 12, 19; see also John Audley, Sandra Polaski, Demetrios G. Papademetriou, and Scott Vaughan, *NAFTA's Promise and Reality: Lessons from Mexico for the Hemisphere* (Washington, D.C.: Carnegie Endowment for International Peace, 2003) and Luis Rubio and Jeffrey Davidow, "Mexico's

Disputed Election," *Foreign Affairs* 85(5) (September/October 2006).

58. Elisabeth Malkin, "Nafta's Promise, Unfulfilled," *The New York Times* (March 24, 2009); Sydney Weintraub, "An Economic Storm Hits Latin America," *Current History* (February 2009).

59. Audley, Polaski, Papademetriou, and Vaughan, *NAFTA's Promise and Reality.*

60. Sydney Weintraub, "An Economic Storm Hits Latin America," *Current History* (February 2009).

61. Choi and Caporaso, "Comparative Regional Integration," p. 493. See also Etel Solingen, "The Genesis, Design and Effects of Regional Institutions: Lessons from East Asia and the Middle East," *International Studies Quarterly,* Vol. 52 (2008): pp. 261–294.

62. Ibid.

63. United Nations, *UNCTAD Handbook of Statistics,* (New York: United Nations, 2002).

64. Choi and Caporaso, "Comparative Regional Integration," p. 494.

65. Ibid.

66. Robert Z. Lawrence, "Emerging Regional Arrangements: Building Blocks or Stumbling Blocks?" in Jeffrey A. Frieden and David A. Lake (eds.), *International Political Economy: Perspectives on Global Power and Wealth* (New York: St. Martin's Press, 1995), pp. 407–408. For a recent empirical analysis of this question, see Daniel Y. Kono, "When Do Trade Blocs Block Trade?," *International Studies Quarterly,* Vol. 51(2007): pp. 165–181.

67. Babarinde, "Regionalism and African Foreign Policies," p. 217.

68. This section draws from Etel Solingen, The Genesis, Design and Effects of Regional Institutions: Lessons from East Asia and the Middle East," *International Studies Quarterly* (2008) 52:261–294 and Tal Sadeh and Amy Verdun, "Explaining Europe's Monetary Union: A Survey of the Literature, *International Studies Review* 2009, 11:277–301.

69. Etel Solingen, The Genesis, Design and Effects of Regional Institutions: Lessons from East Asia and the Middle East," *International Studies Quarterly* (2008) 52:261–294.

70. See, for example, Joseph M. Grieco, "Systemic Sources of Variation in Regional Institutionalism in Western Europe, East Asia, and the Americas," *The Political Economy of Regionalism,* ed. Edward D. Mansfield, and Helen V. Milner. (1997) New York: Columbia University Press; Llyod Gruber, *Ruling the World: Power Politics and the Rise of Supranational Institutions,* (2000) Princeton, NJ: Princeton University Press.

71. See, for example, Robert Keohane, *After Hegemony: Cooperation and Discord in the World Political Economy,* (1984) Princeton, NJ: Princeton University Press; Walter W. Powell and Paul J. Di Maggio, eds. *The New Institutionalism in Organizational Analysis,* (1991) Chicago: University of Chicago Press; Barbara Koremenos, Charles Lipson, and Duncan Snidal, "The Rational Design of International Institutions," *International Organization* (2001): 55(4): 761–799.

72. See, for example, Michael Barnett and Martha Finnemore, "The Politics, Power, and Pathologies of International Organizations," *International Organization,* (1999) 53(4): 699–732; Alastair Iain Johnston, *Social States: China in International Institutions,* 1980–2000, (2008) Princeton, NJ: Princeton University Press; Ann Marie Slaughter, "International Law in a World of Liberal

States," *European Journal of International Law*, (1995) 6(4): 506–538.

73. See, for example, Stephan Haggard, "Regionalism in Asia and the Americas," *The Political Economy of Regionalism*, ed. Edward D. Mansfield, and Helen V. Milner, (1997) New York: Columbia University Press; Ellis S. Krauss, "Japan, the U.S., and the Emergence of Multilateralism in Asia,." *The Pacific Review* (2000): 13(3): 473–494; Etel Solingen, "East Asian Regional Institutions: Characteristics, Sources, Distinctiveness," *Remapping Asia: Competing Patterns of Regional Integration*, ed. T. J. Pempel, (2005): Ithaca, NY: Cornell University Press; Miles Kahler, "Rationality in International Relations," *Exploration and Contestation in the Study of World Politics*, ed. Peter J. Katzenstein, Robert O. Keohane, and Stephen D. Krasner, (1999): Cambridge, MA: MIT Press.

74. Etel Solingen, "The Genesis, Design and Effects of Regional Institutions: Lessons from East Asia and the Middle East," *International Studies Quarterly* (2008) 52:261–294.

75. John Ravenhill, "The Growth of Intergovernmental Collaboration in the Asia-Pacific Region," *Asia-Pacific in the New World Order*, ed. Anthony McGrew and Christopher Brook, (1998): London: Routledge.

Chapter 13 (pages 463–500)

1. David Hunter, James Salzman, and Durwood Zaelke, *International Environmental Law and Policy*, (New York: Foundation Press, 1998), p. 280.

2. Ibid.

3. Ibid, p. 281.

4. Ibid.

5. Lynton Keith Caldwell, *International Environmental Policy: Emergence and Dimensions*, 2nd ed. (Durham, N.C.: Duke University Press, 1990), p. 55.

6. Worldwatch Institute, *Vital Signs 2009: The Trends that Are Shaping Our Future* (Washington, DC, 2009).

7. Intergovernmental Panel on Climate Change, *Climate Change 2007: Synthesis Report* (Geneva, Switzerland, 2007), p. 30.

8. David Hosansky, "Saving the Rain Forests," *CQ Researcher*, June 11, 1999, p. 499.

9. Lester R. Brown, Christopher Flavin, and Sandra Postel, "A World at Risk," in Lester R. Brown et al. (eds.), *The State of the World 1989* (New York: Norton, 1989), p. 4.

10. Sandra Postel and Christopher Flavin, in Worldwatch Institute, *The State of the World 1991* (New York: Norton, 1991), p. 178.

11. Christopher Flavin, "The Legacy of Rio," in Linda Starke (ed.), *State of the World 1997* (New York: Norton, 1997), p. 15.

12. Cynthia Pollock Shea, "Mending the Earth's Shield," *World Watch* (January–February 1989): p. 28.

13. Worldwatch Institute, *State of the World 2002*, pp. 27–28.

14. Lauren Sorkin, "Energy and Climate Trends," *Vital Signs 2006–2007* (New York: W. W. Norton, 2006), p. 42.

15. Thomas C. Schelling, "The Cost of Combating Global Warming," *Foreign Affairs* 76 (November–December 1997), p. 9.

16. Intergovernmental Panel on Climate Change, *Climate Change 2001: Synthesis Report*, p. 6.

17. Jodi Jacobson, "Swept Away," *World Watch* (January–February 1989): pp. 2–26.

18. Wirth, "Climate Chaos," p. 25.

19. United Nations, *The Millennium Development Goals Report* 2008 (New York, 2008), p. 40.

20. Chris Bright, "Tracking the Ecology of Climate Change," in Starke, *State of the World 1997*, pp. 80, 87. See also Intergovernmental Panel on Climate Change, *Climate Change 2001: Synthesis Report*, p. 9.

21. Intergovernmental Panel on Climate Change, *Climate Change 2007: Synthesis Report* (Geneva, Switzerland, 2007), p. 73.

22. Herman Kahn, William Brown, and Leon Martel, *The Next 200 Years* (New York: Morrow, 1976), p. 84.

23. United Nations Development Program, *Human Development Report 2001* (Oxford: Oxford University Press, 2001), p. 203; Worldwatch Institute, *Vital Signs 2003*, p. 27.

24. William V. Chandler, "Increasing Energy Efficiency," in Lester R. Brown et al. (eds.), *The State of the World* 1985 (New York: Norton, 1985), pp. 147–148.

25. Hosansky, "Saving the Rain Forests," p. 500.

26. Carmen Revenga, "Will There Be Enough Water?" in *Pilot Analysis of Global Ecosystems: Freshwater Systems* (Washington, D.C.: World Resources Institute, October 2000), p. 1.

27. United Nations, The Millennium Development Goals Report 2008 (New York, 2008), pp. 40–42.

28. Robinson and Sweet, "Environmental Threats to Stability," p. 58.

29. David N. Balaam and Michael Veseth, *Introduction to International Political Economy* (Upper Saddle River, N.J.: Prentice Hall, 2001), p. 427.

30. Gary Gardner, "Preserving Global Cropland," in Starke, *State of the World 1997*, pp. 43, 54.

31. UN Food and Agriculture Organization, http://www .fao.org/news/story/en/item/20568/icode/ (accessed July 15, 2008).

32. United Nations, *The Millennium Development Goals Report 2008* (New York, 2008), p. 4.

33. Ibid., p. 21.

34. Lester R. Brown, "Reducing Hunger," in Brown et al., *The State of the World 1985*.

35. Michael T. Klare, "Resources Competition and World Politics in the Twenty-First Century," *Current History* (December 2000): p. 407.

36. Paivi Lujala, "Deadly Combat over Natural Resources: Gems, Petroleum, Drugs, and the Severity of Armed Civil Conflict," *Journal of Conflict Resolution* (February 2009): pp. 50–71.

37. Michael L. Ross, "Blood Barrels: Why Oil Wealth Fuels Conflict," *Foreign Affairs*, Vol. 87(3) (May/June 2008): pp. 2–8.

38. Thomas F. Homer-Dixon, *Environmental Scarcity and Global Security* (New York: Foreign Policy Association, 1993), p. 4.

39. United Nations, "World Population Prospects: The 2008 Revision, Highlights" (New York, 2009), available at http://www.un.org/esa/population/publications/wpp2008/wpp2008_highlights.pdf (accessed July 16, 2009).

40. United Nations, "World Population Prospects: The 2008 Revision, Highlights" (New York, 2009), available at http://www.un.org/esa/population/publications/wpp2008/wpp2008_highlights.pdf (accessed July 16, 2009).

41. Gregg Easterbrook, *A Moment on the Earth: The Coming Age of Environmental Optimism* (New York: Viking, 1995), p. 485.

42. Donnella H. Meadows, Dennis L. Meadows, Jorgen Randers, and William W. Behrens III, *The Limits to Growth: A Report for the Club of Rome*'s *Project on the Predicament of Mankind* (New York: Universe Books, 1972), p. 8; United Nations Development Programme, *Human Development Report 2000*, p. 144.

43. Barry Commoner, "How Poverty Breeds Overpopulation," in Steven C. Spiegel (ed.), *At Issue: Politics in the World Arena* (New York: St. Martin's Press, 1977).

44. United Nations, "World Population Prospects: The 2008 Revision, Highlights" (New York, 2009), available at http://www.un.org/esa/population/publications/wpp2008/wpp2008_highlights.pdf (accessed July 16, 2009).

45. Jeffrey D. Sachs, *The End of Poverty: Economic Possibilities for Our Time* (New York: Penguin Books, 2005), p. 37.

46. Dudley Kirk, "Demographic Transition Theory," *Population Studies* 50 (November 1996): pp. 361–387 and Tadeusz Kugler and Siddharth Swaminathan, "The Politics of Population," *International Studies Review* 8(4) (December 2006): pp. 581–596.

47. Kirk, "Demographic Transition Theory," p. 377.

48. Homer-Dixon, "Environmental Scarcities and Violent Conflict."

49. Barry B. Hughes, *World Futures* (Baltimore, Md.: Johns Hopkins University Press, 1985), p. 25.

50. John Tierney, "Betting the Planet," *New York Times Magazine*, December 2, 1990, p. 78.

51. Paul Ehrlich, *The Population Bomb* (New York: Ballantine, 1968).

52. Max Singer, *Passage to a Human World* (Indianapolis: Hudson Institute, 1987), p. 118; Charles C. Mann, "How Many Is Too Many?" *Atlantic Monthly* (February 1993), p. 50.

53. Julian L. Simon, *The Ultimate Resource 2* (Princeton, N.J.: Princeton University Press, 1996), p. 101.

54. Ibid., p. 87; see also Bjørn Lomborg, *The Skeptical Environmentalist: Measuring the Real State of the World* (Cambridge: Cambridge University Press, 2001), pp. 61–62, 93–102.

55. Easterbrook, *A Moment on the Earth*, p. 478.

56. United Nations, *The Millennium Development Goals Report 2008* (New York, 2008), p. 4.

57. Amartya Sen, *Poverty and Famines: An Essay on Entitlement and Deprivation* (Oxford: Clarendon Press, 1981), p. 1, emphasis in original.

58. See ibid.; Amartya Sen, "Food, Economics and Entitlements," in Jean Drèze and Amartya Sen (eds.), *The Political Economy of Hunger* (Oxford: Clarendon Press, 1990), pp. 34–52; Rehman Sobhan, "The Politics of Hunger and Entitlement," in Drèze and Sen, *The Political Economy of Hunger*, pp. 79–113; and Kirit S. Parikh, "Chronic Hunger in the World: Impact of International Policies," in Drèze and Sen, *The Political Economy of Hunger*, pp. 113–145.

59. Mann, "How Many Is Too Many?" p. 48.

60. Charles Panati and Mary Lord, "Population Implosion," *Newsweek* (December 6, 1976), p. 58; Singer, *Passage to a Human World*, p. 70.

61. Mann, "How Many Is Too Many?" p. 53.

62. Lomborg, *The Skeptical Environmentalist*, pp. 48–49.

63. Robinson and Sweet, "Environmental Threats to Stability," p. 57.

64. Mark Perlman, "The Role of Population Projections for the Year 2000," in Julian L. Simon and Herman Kahn (eds.), *The Resourceful Earth* (New York: Blackwell, 1984), p. 62.

65. Simon, *The Ultimate Resource 2*, p. 596.

66. Wilfred Beckerman, *In Defence of Economic Growth* (London: Cape, 1974), p. 250.

67. Vaclav Smil, "Energy Resources and Uses: A Global Primer for the Twenty-First Century," *Current History* (March 2002): p. 128.

68. Lomborg, *The Skeptical Environmentalist*, pp. 125–126.

69. Kahn, Brown, and Martel, *The Next 200 Years*, p. 203.

70. Lomborg, *The Skeptical Environmentalist*, p. 123; U.S. Government, Energy Information Administration, *Annual Energy Review*, http://www.eia.doe.gov/oiaf/ieo/world.html (accessed September 14, 2006).

71. Simon, *The Ultimate Resource 2*, p. 51.

72. Lomborg, *The Skeptical Environmentalist*, p. 121.

73. Michael T. Klare, "Navigating the Energy Transition," *Current History* (January 2009).

74. Easterbrook, *A Moment on the Earth*, p. 217.

75. Nigel Calder, "In the Grip of a New Ice Age," *International Wildlife* (July 1975); cited by Simon, *The Ultimate Resource 2*, p. 267.

76. Simon, *The Ultimate Resource 2*, p. 267.

77. See Lomborg, *The Skeptical Environmentalist*, pp. 263–266.

78. Easterbrook, *A Moment on the Earth*, p. 297.

79. Lomborg, *The Skeptical Environmentalist*, pp. 287–297.

80. Simon and Kahn, *The Resourceful Earth*, p. 9.

81. Quoted in T. C. Sinclair, "Environmentalism," in H. S. D. Cole, Christopher Freeman, Marie Jahoda, and K. L. R. Pavitt (eds.), *Models of Doom* (New York: Universe Books, 1973), p. 182.

82. Otto L. Bettman, *The Good Old Days They Were Terrible* (New York: Random House, 1974), pp. 5–6.

83. World Bank, *World Development Report*, p. 10; Ibid. See also Lomborg, *The Skeptical Environmentalist*, pp. 175–177.

84. Ibid. See also Lomborg, *The Skeptical Environmentalist*, pp. 175–177; Jagdish Bhagwati, "The Case for Free Trade," *Scientific American* (November 1993): p. 43.

85. William K. Stevens, "Experts Confirm Human Role in Global Warming," *New York Times*, September 10, 1995, p. 1.

86. Bright, "Tracking the Ecology of Climate Change," p. 79. The IPCC has repeated this conclusion in its more recent report, *Climate Change 2001: Synthesis Report* and in a draft of its 2007 assessment. See Andrew C. Revkin, "UN Draft Cites Humans in Current Effects of Climate Shift," *New York Times*, April 5, 2007.

87. Intergovernmental Panel on Climate Change, *Climate Change 2007: Synthesis Report* (Geneva, Switzerland), 2004.

88. Meadows et al., *The Limits to Growth*.

89. For a global simulation that explicitly takes into account political variables, see Stuart Bremer (ed.), *The Globus Model: Computer Simulation of Worldwide Political and Economic Developments* (Boulder, Colo.: Westview Press, 1987).

90. Jay Forrester, "Counterintuitive Behavior of Social Systems," in *Collected Papers of Jay W. Forrester* (Cambridge, Mass.: Wright-Allen Press, 1975), pp. 216–217.

91. Meadows et al., *The Limits to Growth*, p. 160.

92. Ronald B. Mitchell, "International Environment," in Walter Carlsnaes, Thomas Risse, and Beth A. Simmons (eds.), *Handbook of International Relations* (Thousand Oaks, Calif.: Sage, 2002), p. 505.

93. Hunter, Salzman, and Zaelke, *International Environmental Law and Policy*, pp. 289–290.

94. Gareth Porter, Janet Welsh Brown, and Pamela S. Chasek, *Global Environmental Politics* (Boulder, Colo.: Westview Press, 2000), pp. 2–27. Reprinted by permission of Westview Press, a member of Perseus Books Group.

95. Pamela S. Chasek, David L. Downie, and Janet Welsh Brown, *Global Environmental Politics Fourth Edition* (Boulder, Colo: Westview Press, 2006), pp. 127–128.

96. Garrett Hardin, "The Tragedy of the Commons," *Science,* 162 (1968): pp. 1243–1248.

97. Robert O. Keohane and Elinor Ostrom, "Introduction," in Robert O. Keohane and Elinor Ostrom (eds.), *Local Commons and Global Interdependence: Heterogeneity and Cooperation in Two Domains* (Thousand Oaks, Calif.: Sage, 1995), p. 1. See also Elinor Ostrom, *Governing the Commons: The Evolution of Institutions for Collective Action* (Cambridge: Cambridge University Press, 1990).

98. Keohane and Ostrom, "Introduction," p. 13.

99. Ibid. See also Ostrom, *Governing the Commons*.

100. Porter, Brown, and Chasek, *Global Environmental Politics*, p. 175.

101. United Nations Development Programme, *Human Development Report 2007/2008: Fighting Climate Change* (New York, 2007), p. 41.

102. United Nations Development Program, *Human Development Report 2001*, p. 203.

103. United Nations Development Programme, *Human Development Report 2007/2008: Fighting Climate Change* (New York, 2007), p. 44.

104. Smil, "Energy Resources and Uses," p. 130.

105. Hosansky, "Saving the Rain Forests," p. 508.

106. United Nations Development Programme, *Human Development Report 2007/2008: Fighting Climate Change* (New York, 2007), p. 42.

107. Elisabeth Rosenthal, "China Increases Lead as Biggest Carbon Dioxide Emitter," *The New York Times* (June 14, 2008); Neil MacFarquhar, "U.S. and China Vow Action on Climate Threat but Cite Needs," *The New York Times* (September 23, 2009).

108. Sylvia Nasar, "Cooling the Globe Would Be Nice; But Saving Lives Now May Cost Less," *New York Times*, May 31, 1992, p. 6.

109. Hunter, Salzman, and Zaelke, *International Environmental Law and Policy*, p. 290.

110. Daniel C. Esty, *Greening the GATT: Trade, Environment, and the Future* (Washington, D.C.: Institute for International Economics, 1994) and Victor, "Recovering Sustainable Development."

111. Porter, Brown, and Chasek, *Global Environmental Politics*, p. 28.

112. Ibid., p. 182.

113. Victor, "Recovering Sustainable Development."

114. Elizabeth R. DeSombre and Joanne Kauffman, "The Montreal Protocol Multilateral Fund: Partial Success Story," in Robert O. Keohane and Marc A. Levy (eds.), *Institutions for Environmental Aid: Pitfalls and Promise* (Cambridge, Mass.: MIT Press, 1996), pp. 89–126.

115. Porter, Brown, and Chasek, *Global Environmental Politics*, p. 30.

116. Ibid., pp. 83–84.

117. Mitchell, "International Environment," p. 505.

118. Maryann K. Cusimano, Mark Hensman, and Leslie Rodrigues, "Private-Sector Transovereign Actors—MNCs and NGOs," in Maryann K. Cusimano (ed.), *Beyond Sovereignty* (Boston: Bedford/St. Martin's, 2000), p. 276.

119. For a recent discussion of these issues, see Aaron Cosbey, "Reconciling Trade and Sustainable Development," *State of the World 2006* (New York: The Worldwatch Institute, 2006) pp. 134–151.

120. Porter, Brown, and Chasek, *Global Environmental Politics*, pp. 182–183; see also Esty, *Greening the GATT*.

121. Porter, Brown, and Chasek, *Global Environmental Politics*, p. 183.

122. Carolyn L. Deere and Daniel C. Esty, "Trade and Environment: Reflections on the NAFTA and Recommendations for the Americas," in Carolyn L. Deere and Daniel C. Esty (eds.), *Greening the Americas: NAFTA's Lessons for Hemispheric Trade* (Cambridge, Mass.: MIT Press, 2002), p. 334.

123. World Trade Organization, "10 Common Misunderstandings about the WTO," http://www.wto .org (accessed September 12, 2006).

124. Urs Luterbacher and Carla Norrlöf, "The Organization of World Trade and the Climate Regime," in Urs Luterbacher and Detlef F. Sprinz (eds.), *International Relations and Global Climate Change* (Cambridge, Mass.: MIT Press, 2001), pp. 279–295.

125. Todd S. Purdum, "U.S. Blocks Money for Family Clinics Promoted by U.N." *New York Times*, July 23, 2002, p. 1; and Farah Stockman, "US Again Denies Money to Population Fund," *Boston Globe*, July 17, 2004.

126. Mary H. Cooper, "Population and the Environment," *CQ Researcher* (July 1998); reprinted in *Global Issues: Selections from The CQ Researcher* (Washington, D.C.: CQ Press, 2001), p. 149.

127. Porter, Brown, and Chasek, *Global Environmental Politics*, p. 93.

128. Frank Grundig, "Patterns of International Cooperation and the Explanatory Power of Relative Gains: An Analysis of Cooperation on Global Climate Change, Ozone Depletion, and International Trade," *International Studies Quarterly*, Vol. 50 (2006): pp. 781–801.

129. Mitchell, "International Environment," p. 504.

130. Ian H. Rowlands, "Classical Theories of International Relations," in Luterbacher and Sprinz, *International Relations and Global Climate Change*, p. 46.

131. Balaam and Veseth, Introduction to *International Political Economy*, p. 418.

132. Ibid.

133. *Sunday Telegraph*, May 19, 2002, p. 12.

134. Kal Raustiala, "Nonstate Actors in the Global Climate Regime," in Luterbacher and Sprinz, *International Relations and Global Climate Change*, pp. 96–97.

135. Rowlands, "Classical Theories of International Relations," p. 58.

136. Robert O. Keohane, Peter M. Haas, and Marc A. Levy, "The Effectiveness of International Environmental Institutions," in Peter M. Haas, Robert O. Keohane, and Marc A. Levy (eds.), *Institutions for the Earth: Sources of Effective International Environmental Protection* (Cambridge, Mass.: MIT Press, 1993), p. 8.

137. Oran R. Young and Marc A. Levy, "The Effectiveness of International Environmental Regimes," in Oran R. Young (ed.), *The Effectiveness of International Environmental Regimes: Causal Connections and Behavioral Mechanisms* (Cambridge, Mass.: MIT Press, 1999), pp. 1–2.

138. Oran R. Young, "Regime Effectiveness: Taking Stock," in Young, *The Effectiveness of International Environmental Regimes*, p. 276. For more on the effectiveness of international institutions and regimes, also see Marc A. Levy, Robert O. Keohane, and Peter M. Haas, "Improving the Effectiveness of International Environmental Institutions," in Haas, Keohane, and Levy, *Institutions for the Earth*, pp. 397–426; Oran R. Young, George J. Demko, and Kilaparti Ramakrishna (eds.), *Global Environmental Change and International Governance* (Hanover, N. H.: University Press of New England, 1996); and Mitchell, "International Environment."

139. See, for example, David L. Levy and Peter J. Newell, "Business Strategy and International Environmental Governance: Toward a Neo-Gramscian Synthesis."

140. Rowlands, "Classical Theories of International Relations," pp. 51–52.

141. Porter, Brown, and Chasek, *Global Environmental Politics*, p. 179, citing a statement by H. E. Datuk Amar Stephen K.T. Yong, leader of the Malaysian delegation, at the second meeting of the parties to the Montreal Protocol, London, June 27–29, 1990.

142. For a discussion of the South's views of ecoimperialism, see Esty, *Greening the GATT*, pp. 185–188.

143. Mitchell, "International Environment."

144. Paul Wapner, "The Sovereignty of Nature? Environmental Protection in a Postmodern Age," *International Studies Quarterly* 46 (June 2002): pp. 167–187.

145. Stephanie Hallock Johnson, "An Ecofeminist Critique of the International Economic Structure," in Mary K. Meyer and Elisabeth Prügl (eds.), *Gender Politics in Global Governance* (Lanham, Md.: Rowman & Littlefield, 1999), p. 221.

Chapter 14 (pages 501–536)

1. David Held, Anthony McGrew, David Goldblatt, and Jonathan Perraton, *Global Transformations: Politics, Economics and Culture* (Stanford, Calif.: Stanford University Press, 1999), p. 1.

2. Kenichi Ohmae, *The Borderless World: Power and Strategy in the Interlinked Economy* (New York: HarperCollins, 1999).

3. James H. Mittelman, *The Globalization Syndrome* (Princeton, N.J.: Princeton University Press, 2000), p. 5, emphasis added.

4. Martin Wolf, "Will the Nation-State Survive Globalization?" *Foreign Affairs* 80 (January–February 2001): pp. 178–191.

5. Held et al., *Global Transformations*, p. 149.

6. International Monetary Fund, Issues Brief: Globalization: A Brief Overview," Washington, DC, (May 2008), Issue 02/08.

7. Jessica T. Mathews, "Power Shift," *Foreign Affairs* 76 (January–February 1997): p. 56. Reprinted by permission of Foreign Affairs. Copyright © 1997 by the Council on Foreign Relations, Inc. www.ForeignAffairs.com

8. "Buicks, Starbucks and Fried Chicken, Still China?" *New York Times*, February 25, 2002.

9. Saskia Sassen, "Global Financial Centers," *Foreign Affairs* 78 (January–February 1999): p. 81.

10. International Monetary Fund, Issues Brief: Globalization: A Brief Overview," Washington, DC, (May 2008), Issue 02/08.]

11. Mittelman, *The Globalization Syndrome*, p. 21, citing Government of Denmark, *Conditions for Social Progress*, p. 14.

12. Held et al., *Global Transformations*, p. 189.

13. Watson, "China's Big Mac Attack" and McDonald's, (http://:mcdonalds.com.hk/english/about/index.htm).

14. Held et al., *Global Transformations*, pp. 236–237.

15. Louise Shelley, John Picarelli, and Chris Corpora, "Global Crime Inc." in Maryann Cusimano Love (ed.), *Beyond Sovereignty*, 2nd ed. (Belmont, Calif.: Thomson Wadsworth, 2003.)

16. Mathews, "Power Shift," pp. 57–58.

17. Mark Galeotti, "Underworld and Upperworld: Transnational Organized Crime and Global Society," in Daphné Josselin and William Wallace (eds.), *Non-State Actors in World Politics* (New York: Palgrave, 2001), p. 213.

18. Jeffrey Sachs, "International Economics: Unlocking the Mysteries of Globalization" *Foreign Policy* 97 (Spring 1999): p. 97.

19. Held et al., *Global Transformations*, p. 167, citing T. Nierop, *Systems and Regions in Global Politics: An Empirical Study of Diplomacy, International Organization and Trade, 1950–1991* (New York: Wiley: 1994).

20. World Development Indicators (WDI), World Bank, http://web.worldbank.org/WBSITE/EXTERNAL/DATASTATISTICS/0,,contentMDK:21725423~pagePK:64133150~piPK:6413317 5~theSitePK:239419,00.html, 2009.

21. Ibid., pp. 210–211.

22 World Development Indicators (WDI) 2009, World Bank, http://web.worldbank.org/WBSITE/EXTERNAL/DATASTATISTICS/0,,contentMDK:21725423~pagePK:64133150~piPK:64133175~theSitePK:239419,00.html, 2009.

23. Ibid., pp. 244–245.

24. http://www.unctad.org/templates/Webflyer .asp?docID=5 826&intItemID=3369&lang=1)

25. Held et al., *Global Transformations*, p. 49.

26. Stanley Hoffmann, "Clash of Globalizations," *Foreign Affairs* 81 (July–August 2002): pp. 104–115.

27. Klaus Dingwerth and Philipp Pattberg, "Global Governance as a Perspective on World Politics," *Global Governance* 12(2) (April–June 2006).

28. Held et al., *Global Transformations*, p. 50.

29. Ibid., p. 65, citing A. Brysk, "From Above and Below: Social Movements, the International System, and Human Rights in Argentina," *Comparative Political Studies* 26 (1993): p. 281, for the Mignone quote.

30. R. Bruce McColm, "The Comparative Survey of Freedom: 1991," *Freedom Review* 22 (1991): p. 6.

31. Larry Diamond, "The Global State of Democracy," *Current History* (December 2000): p. 413.

32. Held et al., *Global Transformations*, p. 327.

33. Cees Hamelink, *Cultural Autonomy in Global Communications* (London: Longman, 1988), quoted in John Tomlinson, *Cultural Imperialism: A Critical Introduction* (Baltimore: Johns Hopkins University Press, 1991).

34. Watson, "China's Big Mac Attack," p. 126.

35. Held et al., *Global Transformations*, pp. 352–353.

36. Ibid., p. 356.

37. Ibid., pp. 345–346, citing A. De Swann, "Notes on the Emerging Global Language System: Regional, National and Supranational," *Media, Culture and Society* 13 (1991): pp. 309–323, and D. Crystal, *English as a Global Language* (Cambridge: Cambridge University Press, 1997).

38. Held et al., *Global Transformations*, pp. 297–299.

39. United Nations High Commissioner for Refugees, "Protecting Refugees & the Role of UNHCR," Geneva Switzerland, (March 2009), http://www.unhcr.org/basics/BASICS/4034b6a34.pdf, accessed June 5, 2009.

40. Ibid.

41. Mittelman, *The Globalization Syndrome*, p. 21.

42. Ibid., p. 21.

43. Michael Veseth, *Globaloney: Unraveling the Myths of Globalization* (Lanham, Md.: Rowman & Littlefield, 2005), p. 125.

44. "Audiences Prefer Local Flavor over U.S. Fare," *Variety*, March 24–30, 2003. See also "U.S. TV Shows Losing Potency Around World," *New York Times*, January 2, 2003.

45. Veseth, *Globaloney: Unraveling the Myths of Globalization*.

46. Joseph S. Nye, Jr., *The Paradox of American Power: Why the World's Only Superpower Can't Go It Alone* (Oxford: Oxford University Press, 2002), p. 78. See also, Moisés Naím, "Think Again: Globalization," *Foreign Policy*, 171 (March/April 2009): 28-34.

47. See ibid.

48. International Technology Union, "Key Global Telecom Indicators for the World Telecommunication Service Sector," ITU, http://www.itu.int/ITU-D/ict/statistics/ (accessed December 9, 2003). International Telecommunication Union, "Market Information and Statistics," http://www.itu.int/ITU-D/ict/statistics/at_glance/KeyTelecom99.html, accessed July 5, 2009.

49. Nye, *The Paradox of American Power*, p. 43.

50. Held et al., *Global Transformations*, pp. 213–214, italics in original.

51. Mathews, "Power Shift," p. 58.

52. Ibid., p. 51.

53. Andrew L. Shapiro, "The Internet," *Foreign Policy* 115 (Summer 1999): pp. 14–27. See also Kurt Mills, "Cybernations: Identity, Self-Determination, Democracy and the 'Internet Effect' in the Emerging Information Order," *Global Society* 6 (2002): pp. 69–87.

54. Shapiro, "The Internet."

55. Mathews, "Power Shift," p. 54; see also Mills, "Cybernations."

56. Richard Rosecrance, "The Rise of the Virtual State," *Foreign Affairs* 75 (July–August 1996): pp. 45–62.

57. Daniel F. Burton, Jr., "The Brave New Wired World," *Foreign Policy* 106 (Spring 1997), p. 34.

58. Held et al., *Global Transformations*, p. 358.

59. Mathews, "Power Shift," pp. 51–52.

60. Burton, "The Brave New Wired World," p. 36.

61. Wolf, "Will the Nation-State Survive Globalization?" p. 182.

62. Maryann K. Cusimano, "Beyond Sovereignty: The Rise of Transsovereign Problems," in Maryann K. Cusimano (ed.), *Beyond Sovereignty: Issues for a Global Agenda* (Boston: Bedford/St. Martin's, 2000), p. 22.

63. Wolf, "Will the Nation-State Survive Globalization?" p. 182.

64. Hoffmann, "Clash of Globalizations," p. 108.

65. Held et al., *Global Transformations*, pp. 2–3, and David Held and Anthony McGrew, *Globalization/Anti-Globalization* (Cambridge, UK: Polity Press, 2002).

66. Held et al., *Global Transformations*, pp. 5–7. See also P. Hirst and G. Thompson, *Globalization in Question: The International Economy and the Possibilities of Governance* (Cambridge, UK: Polity Press, 1996).

67. Mittelman, *The Globalization Syndrome*, p. 18. See also Nye, *The Paradox of American Power*, pp. 89–91, for a discussion of the limits to contemporary globalization.

68. Wolf, "Will the Nation-State Survive Globalization?" pp. 181–182.

69. Held et al., *Global Transformations*, pp. 152–154.

70. Mittelman, *The Globalization Syndrome*, p. 18.

71. Held et al., *Global Transformations*, p. 156.

72. Ibid., p. 192. Also see Harold James, *The End of Globalization: Lessons from the Great Depression* (Cambridge, Mass.: Harvard University Press, 2001).

73. Held et al., *Global Transformations*, p. 41.

74. Ibid., p. 43.

75. Ibid., p. 335.

76. Ibid.

77. Ibid., pp. 322–323.

78. Ibid., p. 339.

79. Wolf, "Will the Nation-State Survive Globalization?" p. 181.

80. Rawi Abdelal and Adam Segal, "Has Globalization Passed Its Peak?" *Foreign Affairs* (January/February 2007) 86(1):103–111.]

81. Nye, *The Paradox of American Power*, pp. 85–89. Moisés Naím, "Think Again: Globalization," *Foreign Policy* 171 (March/April 2009): 28-34.

82. Held et al., *Global Transformations*, p. 7.

83. Held et al., *Global Transformations*, p. 176.

84. Cable, *Globalization and Global Governance*, p. 15.

85. Ibid.

86. Mittelman, *The Globalization Syndrome*, p. 22, citing the International Monetary Fund, *World Economic Outlook: Globalization—Challenges and Opportunities* (Washington, D.C.: International Monetary Fund, 1997), p. 45, for the cost figures.

87. Wolf, "Will the Nation-State Survive Globalization?" p. 184.

88. There are several books with this title, including one authored by Joseph E. Stiglitz (New York: W. W. Norton, 2002) and another by Saskia Sassen (New York: New York Press, 1998).

89. Nye, *The Paradox of American Power*, pp. 100–104. See also Held and McGrew, *Globalization/Anti-Globalization*.

90. Hoffmann, "Clash of Globalizations."

91. Held et al., *Global Transformations*, 1999, pp. 5–6.

92. Michael T. Klare, "Waging Postindustrial Warfare on the Global Battlefield," *Current History* (December 2001): p. 436.

93. Nye, *The Paradox of American Power*, p. 81.

94. Held et al., *Global Transformations* p. 344, citing data from International Telecommunications Union, *Direction of Traffic: International Telephone Traffic 1994* (Geneva, Switzerland: International Telecommunications Union, 1994).

95. Ibid., p. 358, citing data from UNESCO, *Statistical Yearbook*, 1994.

96. HYPERLINK "../../Second Half/United"United Nations, *The Global Information Society: A Statistical View*, New York, 2008.]

97. Hoffmann, "Clash of Globalizations," p. 109.

98. Ibid., p. 111.

99. Shapiro, "The Internet," p. 25. See also Nye, *The Paradox of American Power*, p. 98.

100. Rosecrance, "The Rise of the Virtual State," p. 60.

101. See William C. Adams (ed.), *Television Coverage of International Affairs* (Norwood, N.J.: Ablex, 1982), and Doris Graber, *Mass Media and American Politics* (Washington, D.C.: CQ Press, 2001).

102. Nye, *The Paradox of American Power*, p. 100.

103. Held et al., *Global Transformations*, p. 6.

104. Samuel P. Huntington, "The Clash of Civilizations?" *Foreign Affairs* 72 (1993): p. 25.

105. Benjamin Barber, *Jihad vs. McWorld* (New York: Times Books, 1995), p. 4.

106. Ibid.

107. Ibid.

108. Nye, *The Paradox of American Power*, pp. 95–99.

109. Frank J. Lechner and John Boli, "General Introduction," in Frank J. Lechner and John Boli (eds.), *The Globalization Reader* (Malden, Mass.: Blackwell Publishers, 2000), pp. 2–3. See also Veseth, *Globaloney: Unraveling the Myths of Globalization.*

110. Mittelman, *The Globalization Syndrome*, p. 179.

111. Eric Helleiner, "Economic Liberalism and its Critics: The Past as Prologue?" *Review of International Political Economy* 10(4) (November 2003): pp. 685–696.

112. Robert Weissmann, "Democracy Is in the Streets," *Multinational Monitor* 20 (December 1999): p. 24.

113. Quoted in Mike Bygrave, "Where Did All the Protesters Go?" *Observer*, July 14, 2002.

114 The Economist, "Globalisation: Turning their Backs on the World," Feb 19, 2009.

115 Ibid and Moisés Naím, "Think Again: Globalization," *Foreign Policy* 171 (March/April 2009): 28–34.

116 Rawi Abdelal and Adam Segal, "Has Globalization Passed Its Peak?" *Foreign Affairs* (January/February 2007) 86(1):103–111.

117 Moisés Naím, "Think Again: Globalization," *Foreign Policy* 171 (March/April 2009): 28-34; See also Joseph S. Nye, "Which Globalization Will Survive?" *The Korea Times*, April 13, 2009.

118. But see Nye, *The Paradox of American Power*, pp. 84–85, for reasons that contemporary globalization is likely to be more long lasting than previous eras of high interdependence.

119. Ibid., especially pp. 47–50, 53–62.

120. Held et al., *Global Transformations*, p. 3. See also Sachs, "International Economics."

121. Cable, *Globalization and Global Governance*, p. 33, and Held et al., *Global Transformations*, pp. 228–234.

122. Held et al., *Global Transformations*, p. 188.

123. Claire Sterling, *Thieves' World: The Threat of the New Global Network of Organized Crime* (New York: Simon & Schuster, 1994), p. 244.

124. Ibid. See also Mathews, "Power Shift."

125. Mathews, pp. 58–59.

126. Held et al., *Global Transformations*, pp. 321–322.

127. Sachs, "International Economics," p. 109. See also Nye, *The Paradox of American Power*, p. 98.

128. Held et al., *Global Transformations*, p. 6.

129. Cable, *Globalization and Global Governance*, p. 35.

130. Ibid., pp. 33–34.

131. Wolf, "Will the Nation-State Survive Globalization?" p. 190.

132. Ibid., p. 184.

133. Doreen Carvajal, "Governments Using Filters to Censor Internet, Survey Finds," *The New York Times*, May 18, 2007.]

134. Andrew Jacobs, "China Requires Software on New PCs," *The New York Times*, June 9, 2009.

135. Ibid., p. 24.

136. Wolf, "Will the Nation-State Survive Globalization?" p. 179.

137. Held et al., *Global Transformations*, pp. 8–9.

138. Mathews, "Power Shift," p. 61.

139. Hoffmann, "Clash of Globalizations," p. 105.

140. On this thesis, see Nye, *The Paradox of American Power.*

141. Raffaele Marchetti, "Mapping Alternative Models of Global Politics," *International Studies Review* (2009) 11:133–156.

142. James N. Rosenau, *Turbulence in World Politics: A Theory of Change and Continuity* (Princeton, N.J.: Princeton University Press, 1990), p. 11.

143. Ronaldo Munck, "Globalization as the New Imperialism," *Review of Radical Political Economics* (2009) 44:380–388.

144. Arie M. Kacowiz, "Globalization, Poverty, and the North-South Divide," *International Studies Review* (2007) 9:565–580.

145. See Cynthia Enloe, *Bananas, Beaches, and Bases: Making Feminist Sense of International Politics* (Berkeley: University of California Press, 1989); Valentine Moghadam, "Gender and Globalization: Female Labor and Women's Mobilization," *Journal of World Systems Research* 5(2) (1999): pp. 367–388; Saskia Sassen, *Globalization and Its Discontents* (New York: Free Press, 1998); and Eric Helleiner, "Economic Liberalism and its Critics: The Past as Prologue?" *Review of International Political Economy* 10(4) (November 2003): pp. 685–696.

146. Mark M. Gray, Miki Caul Kittilson, and Wayne Sandholtz, "Women and Globalization: A Study of 180 Countries, 1975–2000," *International Organization* 60 (Spring 2006): p. 326.

Index

Bold page numbers indicate locations of key terms.